ASSESSING MEDIA EDUCATION

A Resource Handbook
for Educators and Administrators

LEA'S COMMUNICATION SERIES
Jennings Bryant / Dolf Zillmann, General Editors

Selected titles in media administration (William G. Christ, advisor) include:

Blanchard/Christ • *Media Education and the Liberal Arts: A Blueprint for the Profession*

Christ • *Assessing Media Education: A Resource Handbook for Educators and Administrators*

Christ • *Assessing Communication Education: A Handbook for Media, Speech, and Theatre Educators*

Christ • *Leadership in Times of Change: A Handbook for Communication and Media Administrators*

Dickson • *Mass Media Education in Transition: Preparing for the 21st Century*

For a complete list of titles in LEA's Communication Series, please contact Lawrence Erlbaum Associates, Publishers at www.erlbaum.com

ASSESSING MEDIA EDUCATION

A Resource Handbook
for Educators and Administrators

Edited by

William G. Christ
Trinity University

LEA LAWRENCE ERLBAUM ASSOCIATES, PUBLISHERS
2006 Mahwah, New Jersey   London

Lawrence Erlbaum Associates, Inc., Publishers
10 Industrial Avenue
Mahwah, New Jersey 07430
www.erlbaum.com

Cover design by Tomai Maridou

Library of Congress Cataloging-in-Publication Data

Assessing media education : a resource handbook for educators and administrators / edited by William G. Christ.
    p. cm.
Includes bibliographical references and index.
ISBN 0-8058-5225-5 (cloth : alk. paper)
ISBN 0-8058-5226-3 (pbk. : alk. paper)
1. Mass media—Study and teaching (Higher)—Evaluation—Handbooks, manuals, etc. I. Christ, William G.
P91.3.A853   2005
302.23'071'1—dc22
                                          2005051015
                                               CIP

Printed in the United States of America
10 9 8 7 6 5 4 3 2 1

*This book is dedicated to the memory
of R. Ferrell Ervin*

Contents

Preface

Assessment is an integral part of what we do as teachers, researchers, and administrators. It can be formal or informal, systematic or haphazard, harmful or rewarding. At its best, assessment can have a transforming effect on education. At its worst, it can be used as an instrument to punish people and programs.

We are living in the age of accountability. Though calls for accountability and assessment have come and gone, the current demands for proving that students are learning seem more insistent as they become codified in educational policies. The move from asking teachers what they teach to requiring programs to show that students are learning is a paradigm shift that costs blood, sweat, and tears. It requires educators to look differently at their curricula, courses, syllabuses, and measurement mechanisms.

The purpose of this book is to provide useful information to those in higher education media programs who want to create or improve their student learning assessment strategies. The book is divided into four sections. Part I describes how to develop an assessment plan with special emphasis on mission statements. Part II stresses the development of student learning outcomes. Each chapter reflects one of the eleven competencies presented in The Accrediting Council on Education in Journalism and Mass Communications requirements. Part III systematically presents both indirect and direct measures of student learning outcomes from advisory boards to examinations. Finally, Part IV provides case studies of programs at different points in their development of student outcomes.

If assessment is here to stay, then it is important for media educators to understand and use the process so that they control their own destinies. The hope is that this book will be a useful intellectual and practical resource for media educators and administrators as they grapple with the challenges of assessment.

ACKNOWLEDGMENTS

This book has been a very rewarding collaboration. I would like to publicly acknowledge the hard work of the authors involved in this project. Working with these authors has been a true pleasure. Their care and expertise will be evident to you as you read each chapter.

Second, I would like to thank the people at Lawrence Erlbaum Associates. Linda Bathgate was a major force behind the conceptualization and execution of this book. Nadine Simms has done a great job keeping the production side of the book on track. Tina Hardy did an excellent job as copy editor. The anonymous critiques of the early prospectus by conscientious reviewers made this a stronger book. I appreciate all their hard work.

From Trinity University, I would like to thank my department and the administration for their support. Trinity is an intellectually stimulating place where educational issues dealing with teaching, courses, and curricula are vigorously debated.

On a more personal note, I would like to thank those who developed the Internet and email. This project would have taken twice as long without these new communication technologies. I would also like to thank my sons Nathan and Jonathan Christ and especially my life partner, wife, and true friend, Judith Anne Christ.

Thank you one and all.

—William G. Christ
San Antonio, Texas

DEVELOPING THE ASSESSMENT PLAN

1

Introduction: Why Assessment Matters[1]

William G. Christ
Department of Communication
Trinity University

> *Accountability to my students meant: plan the course, show up in class, keep it moving, comment thoughtfully on papers, mentor when asked, submit grades, write recommendations—the usual packet of services. My obligation to my departmental colleagues: take on my share of core courses and administrative duties. To administrators and trustees: just don't make scenes, I guess; the thought rarely crossed my mind. My responsibility to society as a whole: I cheerfully held myself accountable for the wretched of the earth. . . .*
>
> —Ohmann (2000, p. 24)

If the programmatic assessment of student learning outcomes was universally acknowledged as being necessary, important, and positive, then it would not need to be defended. Yet, even those who accept the assessment of student learning outcomes in principle can find the job of planning, assessing, tabulating, and reporting so cumbersome and costly that they feel anger toward assessment efforts.

The assessment of student learning outcomes has become the acid test for media educators. It requires a paradigm shift in a faculty's thinking. Instead of focusing on traditional assessment "inputs" like faculty degrees, number of full-time faculty, research productivity, resources, facilities, equipment, diversity, and curriculum, a student learning ap-

---

[1]An earlier version of this chapter was in the Association of Schools of Journalism and Mass Communication *Insights* periodical.

proach to assessment focuses on "outputs." Instead of asking "what do faculty need to teach," the question becomes "what do we want students to learn?" "The question, 'What is basic about our discipline?' becomes 'What is basic about the discipline that students should learn and how do we know they have learned it?' " (Christ, McCall, Rakow, & Blanchard, 1997, p. 29).

Simply stated, faculty do assessment for either internal or external reasons. Yet, where we are in the assessment debates only makes sense within the broader context of off-campus forces impacting campuses. The first part of this chapter, therefore, outlines off-campus forces. Then, definitions are given and the two reasons are laid out.

OFF-CAMPUS FORCES

Jones, Jones, and Hargrove (2003) wrote that the first documented achievement tests can be linked to the mid-1800s when "the United States began an unprecedented effort to educate the masses" (p. 14). Janesick (2001, p. 89), who made a distinction between the testing movement (just after World War I) and the assessment movement, suggested that researchers should go back to the 1880s, "when Francis Galton, in London, administered tests to hundreds of persons to test sensory reactions and reaction times of volunteers," to understand the "big picture" of assessment. Both authors document the growth of public education after World War II and the transformative nature of the 1960s. Whereas Janesick argued that Howard Gardner's research on his theory of multiple intelligences almost "single-handedly starts the assessment movement" (p. 92), both researchers indicate the importance of the 1983 United States Department of Education's National Commission on Excellence in Education publication, "A Nation at Risk: The Imperative for Educational Reform" (1983), that "clearly situated public education as being in crisis and in need of major reform. The report used test scores as the indicator of success and the goal of schooling" (Jones et al., 2003, p. 15). The use of test scores as valid measures of excellence can be seen in the use of standardized tests like the Scholastic Assessment Test, American College Testing, and the Graduate Record Exam, and in the highly politicized "No Child Left Behind Act of 2001" (2002) legislation.

The Accountability Movement

Assessment is part of a larger accountability movement. Although it is clear from the previous discussion that accountability concerns are not new (see also Martin, Overholt, & Urban, 1976, pp. 33–41), Ohmann

(2000) has suggested that the current accountability movement grew out of three main forces in the late 1960s and early 1970s. The first "was an intense fiscal crisis of the state, brought on partly by war spending, but expressed chiefly as disillusionment with Great Society programs" (p. 28). Educational costs and expenditures had increased during the 1960s and there was concern that, as then deputy commissioner in the Office of Education Terrel H. Bell reported, "Money alone could not buy good education . . ." (p. 28).

Second, Ohmann (2000) argued that the accountability movement "was partly a counterthrust against liberatory ideas and experiments in 'open education,' that is, against the critique of schooling mounted by sixties visionaries and radicals" (p. 28). If the 1960s stood for student power, a democratization of higher education, and challenges to the educational status quo, then the rise of accountability in education could be seen as a direct challenge to these forces, suggesting to some that "traditional notions about the value of democracy and the value of the individual are ultimately at stake" (Martin et al., 1976, p. 6).

Finally, the third main force driving the accountability movement in education was a reaction against the "turmoil and disruption on the campuses; political action by students and faculty members . . . ; and mounting distrust of higher education by the public . . ." (Ohmann, 2000, p. 28). This led to "the increasing demand for colleges and universities to justify what they are doing and to disclose the effectiveness and efficiency of their operations" (McConnell, 1972, p. 200). Seen in this light, "one explanation for the failure of accountability advocates to heed objections by educators is that accountability is not primarily a pedagogical movement. It is an administrative system, and as such it is impervious to arguments which are based on educational concerns" (Martin et al., 1976, p. 32).

As the modern day accountability movement was building steam in the mid-1970s, there were a number of educators who wrote scathing critiques. Martin et al. (1976), in their critique of accountability in higher education, identified three major defects: "First, it lacks an adequate theoretical base" (p. 6). Accountability is a complex construct that is not always fully investigated and explicated by those who would use it (see Sarlos, 1973, pp. 65–81). Accountability tends to concentrate on behaviors and thus is informed by behavioral theory. Martin et al. argued that behavioral analysis limits education when they wrote, "because we believe that education has something to do with rational and critical thinking, introspection, and creativity, we believe that any view which confines itself exclusively to observable phenomena leaves out something essential both to the practice of science and to the process of education" (p. 6).

Besides the concern of a lack of an adequate theoretical base, basic questions dealing with accountability are not always answered. "For example, to contend that an individual or an institution ought to be accountable immediately brings to mind the questions: accountable to whom, for what, in what manner and under what circumstances?" (Wagner, 1989, p. 1). Other questions would include the following: Who should be held accountable (e.g., teachers, parents, school systems, school administrators, school teachers)? What does it mean to be accountable? When should accountability take place (e.g., grade level, proficiency level, every year)? What should be measured (e.g., knowledge, behavior, attitudes, values; see Part II)? How should accountability be measured (e.g., through portfolios, exit interviews, tests; see Part III)?

The second defect identified by Martin et al. (1976) was that accountability in education "lacks reassuring historical precedents. In fact, something very akin to accountability has been tried before and found wanting" (p. 6). They argued that the current push for accountability was only the most recent. Previous attempts had limited success.

"Third, its political implications are not reassuring to those among us who value either individuality or democracy" (Martin et al., 1976, p. 6). As stated previously, there are those who have argued that accountability, coming out of a business-training model, is not the best model for education. Bowers (1972) went so far as to argue that "teacher accountability is incompatible with academic freedom . . ." (p. 25).

> [A]ccountability proponents could argue that despite various and sometimes conflicting interpretations of accountability there is at least general agreement about the following: (1) The quality of schools can no longer be determined simply by looking at input factors such as plant facilities, the number of volumes in the library, pupil/teacher ratios or printed curricula; rather, school performance and the quality of school programs are best understood in terms of results and output, what children do or do not learn over a given period; (2) learning can be measured against costs for a specified interval as an indication of cost-effectiveness; (3) taxpayers, parents and supportive government agencies have a "right" to know about these results and the cost/benefits associated with their schools; and (4) accountability can provide this information and act as a stimulus to better school performance. (Wagner, 1989, p. 2)

Whatever the historical roots of or problems with the current accountability and assessment movements, accountability and assessment appear here to stay. (For an overview of the assessment in higher education, see Rosenbaum, 1994.)

Forces Impacting Media Education

In the late 1980s and early 1990s, as the assessment movement continued to pick up steam (see Ervin, 1988; Ewell, Hutchings, & Marchese, 1991), at least three other challenges faced media education: calls for the reinvention of undergraduate education, the convergence of communication technologies, and the philosophical and theoretical ferment in the communication field (Blanchard & Christ, 1993; Dickson, 1995; Duncan, Caywood, & Newsom, 1993; "Planning for Curricular Change," 1984, 1987; Wartella, 1994).

It was argued that the reinvention of undergraduate education called for a "New Liberal Arts" that combined elements from both traditional and newer fields and disciplines (Blanchard & Christ, 1993). There were calls for a renewed commitment from media programs to the non-major, general student; a call for the centrality of media studies in the common curriculum of all students. As people debated what should be the outcome of an undergraduate education (see Association of American Colleges, 1985; Boyer, 1987; "Strengthening the Ties," 1988), media educators were faced with the following questions: What does my program have to offer the general university student? If one of the outcomes of a university education is to be media literate, then what should we teach and what should students learn? (see Christ & Potter, 1998).

The convergence of communication technologies and the philosophical and theoretical ferment in the communication field suggested there needed to be a new way of looking at the major. Some went so far as to demand a "New Professionalism" that educated students to become broad-based communication practitioners (Blanchard & Christ, 1993; see "Planning for Curricular Change," 1984, 1987). The calls for a broad approach to communication and media education has been both supported and attacked (see Dickson, 1995, 2000; Duncan et al., 1993; Medsger, 1996). The point is that the convergence of technologies and the philosophical and theoretical ferment in the field required media educators to reevaluate their programs to determine if what they offered made sense philosophically, pedagogically, and practically.

Overlaid on these three challenges was the assessment movement. As stated earlier, assessment, as part of the accountability movement, has been part of higher education for over 35 years. What is different now is the intensity of the current debate, where accrediting agencies seem to be taking the student learning assessment part of their charge very seriously and where legislators are willing to link funding to results. Assessment continues to be both a promise and a plague for programs as educators grapple with high expectations and limited resources (see Christ & Blanchard, 1994).

Student Learning

A report by the Kellogg Commission on the Future of State and Land-Grant Universities (1997) demonstrates how assessment dovetails with current calls for college and university reforms. The Kellogg Commission (1997) wanted to turn schools into learning institutions. They suggested "three broad ideals":

> (1) Our institutions must become *genuine learning communities*, supporting and inspiring faculty, staff, and learners of all kinds. (2) Our learning communities should be *student centered*, committed to excellence in teaching and to meeting the legitimate needs of learners, wherever they are, whatever they need, whenever they need it. (3) Our learning communities should emphasize the importance of *a healthy learning environment* that provides students, faculty, and staff with the facilities, support, and resources they need to make this vision a reality. (pp. v–vi, italics in original)

The move from universities being conceptualized as *teaching* institutions to *learning* institutions has profound implications for higher education (cf. Christ, 1994, 1997). As universities become more focused on student learning than on teaching, more concerned with the outcomes of education than the inputs into education, then at least two things become evident. First, outcomes assessment of learning becomes a "logical" important "next step" in the process, and second, the classroom is seen as only one part, and sometimes one small part, of the total learning environment.

The shift from teaching to learning communities, from teacher-centered to student-centered approaches to education, changes the role of the classroom teacher. If, as the Kellogg Commission (1997) suggested, learning communities should be committed "to meeting the legitimate needs of learners, wherever they are, whatever they need, whenever they need it" (pp. v–vi), then it is clear that teaching and learning can no longer be confined to the classroom. And, as the costs of higher education have escalated, as more people lose access to traditional higher education opportunities (Council for Aid to Education, 1997), the idea of a 4-year residential university or college, where lectures are delivered in huge classrooms, may become an anachronism. Within all of these challenges, educators are asked to assess their programs and student learning.

DEFINITIONS

So what is assessment? Krendl, Warren, and Reid (1997) made an interesting distinction between assessment and evaluation in their discussion about distant learning:

> Assessment refers to any process that measures what students have learned from teaching strategies, including course-specific methods (e.g., assignments, class activities, and tests) and programmatic strategies (e.g., exit interviews or honors theses) designed to test specific content knowledge. This primary focus on academic content is a defining characteristic of student assessment. Evaluation, on the other hand, looks beyond this to examine the entire educational experience. The mesh between students' needs and their experiences during a course or program is the primary criterion in evaluation. Beyond teaching strategies, then, evaluation examines classroom interaction, the effectiveness of course/program administration, the quality of student support services, access to and quality of technical equipment, and cost-benefit analyses of distance-education programs. In short, every aspect of a distance course or program can be evaluated, whereas only students' mastery of course content is assessed (Rowntree, 1992). (p. 103)

The distinction between assessment and evaluation is useful in that it directs our attention to different levels or types of accountability. Haley and Jackson (1995) suggested a hierarchy of programmatic assessment that included four levels, where

> each level may be seen as a broader examination of the program. The four levels are: Level One—Evaluation of individual program components <peer teaching review and course evaluations>; Level Two—Perceptions and performance of graduating students <survey of seniors; senior essays; university comprehensives; departmental comprehensives; campaigns courses>; Level Three—Evaluations of key internal and external constituencies <faculty surveys; employer surveys; university alumni surveys; department graduate surveys>; and Level Four—Comprehensive program evaluation <program review; accreditation>. (p. 27)

Student learning outcomes assessment is normally positioned as a level-four programmatic evaluation. Of course, to do assessment is not easy. Morse and Santiago (2000) wrote that, "to evaluate student learning adequately, faculty must set programmatic goals, understand the profiles of students, define the desired outcomes for students and programs, develop instruments to measure those outcomes, and establish a feedback loop in which the information gained is used to effective positive change" (p. 33).

WHY ASSESSMENT?

There are two fundamental reasons for assessment. The first is external and the second is internal.

External

As mentioned earlier, demand for assessment grew out of calls for accountability. "House (1993) proposed three different types of accountability that institutions of higher education face: state- or public-controlled accountability, professional control (by professors and administrators), and consumer control" (Krendl et al., 1997, p. 109). These three types of accountability are external to the media unit and are often seen by the unit as being harmful, coercive, or irrelevant. Under these conditions, assessment, at its best, might be seen as an antidote to calls for accountability. For example, "Lombardi (1993) posits, 'To counter-attack against criticism from the public, we need to explain and teach the public what the universities do, how they do it, and why it costs so much . . . The key weapon here is accounting' " (Haley & Jackson, 1995, p. 33). In other words, assessment is seen as a weapon to be used by the beleaguered unit to answer criticisms.

The first reason for doing assessment is that certain states, regional accrediting agencies, local administrators, professional accrediting groups, parents, and students have called for or mandated assessment. If state legislatures have developed carrots and sticks based on assessment and results, then that is an excellent reason why a unit would want to do assessment. If a unit wants to be either regionally or professionally accredited and it needs to evaluate its program and student learning outcome as part of the process, then this is an excellent reason for doing assessment. If an administration says to develop an assessment plan, then this, too, is an excellent reason for doing assessment. Ideally, a unit will be able to turn the often-odious chore of assessment into a well-articulated persuasive argument about needs and expectations. Hopefully, a unit will be able to transform all its hard work into a plan for how to improve what it does. And hopefully, a unit will be given the resources to help improve its program.

Internal

The second reason to do assessment is that it has the potential to make teachers, programs, and ultimately, students, better. Assessment can help a unit be self-reflective about what is done and why it is done. It can mean discovering the strengths and weaknesses of programs and the teaching and learning process. "Assessment is an integral part of what we do as teachers, researchers, and administrators. It can be formal or informal, systematic or haphazard, harmful or rewarding. At its best, assessment can have a transforming effect on education. At its worst, it can be used as an instrument to punish people and programs" (Christ, 1994, p. x).

SUMMARY

This handbook is broken into four parts. In Part I, chapters 2 and 3 discuss how to develop an assessment plan and the importance of usable, descriptive mission statements. They argue that an assessment plan should link a university's mission statement with the program's mission that should confirm the program's core values, competencies, and knowledge. These core values, competencies, and knowledge should be linked to student learning outcomes which are clearly present in programs' curricula and courses and even exercises and experiences within courses. Once the student learning outcomes are articulated (Part II), then both indirect and direct methods can be developed to continually assess the outcomes (Part III). Finally, the results from the assessment should be fed back into the system (Part IV).

Part II discusses the challenges of developing student learning outcomes in key areas taught in many media education programs. These chapters parallel the core professional values articulated by the Accrediting Council on Education in Journalism and Mass Communications (ACEJMC, 2004), including the following:

The ACEJMC (2004) suggested that

> irrespective of their particular specialization, all graduates should be aware of certain core values and competencies and be able to:
>
> 1. understand and apply the principles and laws of freedom of speech and press, including the right to dissent, to monitor and criticize power, and to assemble and petition for redress of grievances [chapter 4, Law and Policy];
> 2. demonstrate an understanding of the history and role of professionals and institutions in shaping communications [chapter 5, History];
> 3. demonstrate an understanding of the diversity of groups in a global society in relationship to communications [chapter 6, Diversity];
> 4. understand concepts and apply theories in the use and presentation of images and information [chapter 7, Production and Graphics];
> 5. demonstrate an understanding of professional ethical principles and work ethically in pursuit of truth, accuracy, fairness and diversity [chapter 8, Ethics];

6. think critically, creatively and independently [chapter 9, Critical Thinking];

7. conduct research and evaluate information by methods appropriate to the communications professions in which they work [chapter 10, Research and Information Gathering];

8. write correctly and clearly in forms and styles appropriate for the communications professions, audiences and purposes they serve [chapter 11, Media Writing];

9. critically evaluate their own work and that of others for accuracy and fairness, clarity, appropriate style and grammatical correctness [chapter 12, Reporting and Editing];

10. apply basic numerical and statistical concepts [chapter 13, Numbers and Statistics];

11. apply tools and technologies appropriate for the communications professions in which they work [chapter 14, Public Relations, and chapter 15, Advertising].

Part III investigates different strategies for measuring student learning outcomes. Chapters 16 and 17 discuss a number of indirect measures for assessment, including ways of using institutional data, surveys, interviews, advisory boards, internships, competitions, and career data. Chapters 18 to 21 identify the pros and cons of using tests, embedded "authentic" assessment, portfolios, and capstone classes.

Part IV presents four case studies of schools in different phases of developing assessment plans and using those plans to improve their programs. Finally, chapter 26 shows how media education assessment and professional accreditation are linked and provides a warning about current accreditation arrangements.

CONCLUSION

Ultimately, there is good assessment and bad assessment. Bad assessment is when, through lack of time, resources, or will, tests or measures are thrown together to appease some outside agency or administrator. Good assessment is assessment that helps teachers and programs improve what they do so that teachers can teach and students can learn better. The American Association for Higher Education (AAHE Assessment Forum, 1997) suggested nine key

principles of good practice for assessing student learning:

1. The assessment of student learning begins with educational values; 2. Assessment is most effective when it reflects an understanding of learning

as multidimensional, integrated, and revealed in performance over time; 3. Assessment works best when the programs it seeks to improve have clear, explicitly stated purposes; 4. Assessment requires attention to outcomes but also and equally to the experiences that lead to those outcomes; 5. Assessment works best when it is ongoing, not episodic; 6. Assessment fosters wider improvement when representatives from across the educational community are involved; 7. Assessment makes a difference when it begins with issues of use and illuminates questions that people really care about; 8. Assessment is most likely to lead to improvement when it is part of a larger set of conditions that promote change; 9. Through assessment, educators meet responsibilities to students and to the public. (pp. 11–12)

After evaluating a trial batch of student learning assessment plans from a number of journalism and mass communication programs that were coming up for accreditation, the AEJMC Teaching Standards Committee (K. Hansen, personal communication, March 11, 2004) suggested the following:

1. Assessment plans should include the unit's mission statement.
2. Assessment plans should include the "professional values and competencies" all students must master, and plans should be revised to insure they conform to the final, approved language for the "professional values and competencies" as stated in ACEJMC's . . . Accreditation Standards.
3. Assessment plans should address the means by which students will be made aware of the "professional values and competencies" as they move through the program and the major.
4. Assessment plans should reflect the concept of different levels of student learning (awareness, understanding and application). The methods used to assess student learning should indicate the level at which students are expected to perform. For example, if a direct measure is being used to evaluate student mastery of the competency of writing correctly and clearly, the measurement method should reflect the level of performance expected (most likely "application" for that competency).
5. Assessment plans should clearly identify which methods are deemed to be direct and which are deemed to be indirect measures of student learning.
6. Assessment plans should clearly link the method for measuring student learning with the appropriate "professional values and competencies" that are expected to be measured through that method.
7. Assessment plans should address the "indicators" that are articulated in Standard 9 of the new Accrediting Standards to ensure that appropriate evidence is provided for site team visitors.

8. Assessment plans should specifically articulate how the assessment effort will be staffed and maintained so that assessment is ongoing.
9. Assessment plans should specifically detail how the data collected from the direct and indirect measures will be used to improve curriculum and instruction over time.

Assessment did not just happen. It has developed within a complex of powerful forces that have continued to impact higher education. Why assessment matters is a function of both external constituencies and internal needs. The bottom line is that it is useful for media educators to address the following questions: What do we want to be able to say about our students when they graduate from our program? Why do we teach what we teach? And, for assessment purposes, how do we know our students are learning what we are teaching? Hopefully, this volume will help generate a discussion that will assist us in answering these questions.

REFERENCES

Accrediting Council on Education in Journalism and Mass Communications. (2004). *New accrediting standards.* Retrieved July 24, 2004, from http://www.ukans.edu/~acejmc/BREAKING/New_standards_9-03.pdf

American Association for Higher Education Assessment Forum. (1997). *9 principles of good practice for assessing student learning.* Retrieved March 25, 2005, from http://www.aahe.org/assessment/principl.htm

Association of American Colleges. (1985). *Integrity in the college curriculum: A report to the academic community.* Washington, DC: Author.

Blanchard, R. O., & Christ, W. G. (1993). *Media education and the liberal arts: A blueprint for the new professionalism.* Hillsdale, NJ: Lawrence Erlbaum Associates, Inc.

Bowers, C. A. (1972). Accountability from a humanist point of view. In F. J. Sciara & R. K. Jantz (Eds.), *Accountability in American education* (pp. 25–33). Boston: Allyn & Bacon.

Boyer, E. L. (1987). *College: The undergraduate experience in America.* New York: The Carnegie Foundation for the Advancement of Teaching, Harper & Row.

Christ, W. G. (Ed.). (1994). *Assessing communication education.* Hillsdale, NJ: Lawrence Erlbaum Associates, Inc.

Christ, W. G. (Ed.). (1997). *Media education assessment handbook.* Mahwah, NJ: Lawrence Erlbaum Associates, Inc.

Christ, W. G., & Blanchard, R. O. (1994). Mission statements, outcomes and the new liberal arts. In W. G. Christ (Ed.), *Assessing communication education* (pp. 31–55). Hillsdale, NJ: Lawrence Erlbaum Associates, Inc.

Christ, W. G., McCall, J. M., Rakow, L., & Blanchard, R. O. (1997). Integrated communication programs. In W. G. Christ (Ed.), *Media education assessment handbook* (pp. 23–53). Mahwah, NJ: Lawrence Erlbaum Associates, Inc.

Christ, W. G., & Potter, W. J. (1998). Media literacy, media education, and the academy. *Journal of Communication, 48*(1), 5–15.

Council for Aid to Education. (1997). *Breaking the social contract. The fiscal crisis in higher education.* Retrieved March 25, 2005, from http://www.rand.org/publications/CAE/CAE100/index.html

Dickson, T. (1995, August). *Meeting the challenges and opportunities facing media education: A report on the findings of the AEJMC Curriculum Task Force.* Paper presented at the annual convention of the Association for Education in Journalism and Mass Communication, Washington, DC.

Dickson, T. (2000). *Mass media education in transition.* Mahwah, NJ: Lawrence Erlbaum Associates, Inc.

Duncan, T., Caywood, C., & Newsom, D. (1993, December). *Preparing advertising and public relations students for the communications industry in the 21st century.* A report of the Task Force on Integrated Curriculum.

Ervin, R. F. (1988). Outcomes assessment: The rationale and the implementation. In R. L. Hoskins (Ed.), *Insights* (pp. 19–23). Columbia, SC: Association of Schools of Journalism and Mass Communication.

Ewell, P. T., Hutchings, P., & Marchese, T. (1991). *Reprise 1991: Reprints of two papers treating assessment's history and implementation.* Washington, DC: American Association for Higher Education, Assessment Forum.

Haley, E., & Jackson, D. (1995). A conceptualization of assessment for mass communication programs. *Journalism and Mass Communication Educator, 51,* 26–34.

Hansen, K. (2004). *Accreditation guidelines for evaluating assessment of student learning plans* (Memorandum sent by the Committee on Teaching Standards chair to the chair of the Accrediting Council on Education in Journalism and Mass Communication accrediting committee).

House, E. (1993). *Professional evaluation.* Newbury Park, CA: Sage.

Janesick, V. J. (2001). *The assessment debate.* Santa Barbara, CA: AGC-CLIO, Inc.

Jones, M. G., Jones, B. D., & Hargrove, T. Y. (2003). *The unintended consequences of high-stakes testing.* Lanham, MD: Rowman & Littlefield Publishers, Inc.

Kellogg Commission on the Future of State and Land-Grant Universities. (1997). *Returning to our roots: The student experience.* Retrieved March 25, 2005, from http://www.nasulgc.org/publications/Kellogg/Kellogg2000_StudentExp.pdf

Krendl, K. A., Warren, R., & Reid, K. A. (1997). Distance learning. In W. G. Christ (Ed.), *Assessing communication education* (pp. 99–119). Mahwah, NJ: Lawrence Erlbaum Associates, Inc.

Lombardi, V. (1993). With their accounts in order, colleges can win back their critics. *The Chronicle of Higher Education, 39,* A40.

Martin, D. T., Overholt, G. E., & Urban, W. J. (1976). *Accountability in American education: A critique.* Princeton, NJ: Princeton Book Company.

McConnell, T. R. (1972). Accountability and autonomy. In F. J. Sciara & R. K. Jantz (Eds.), *Accountability in American education* (pp. 200–214). Boston: Allyn & Bacon.

Medsger, B. (1996). *Winds of change: Challenges confronting journalism education.* Arlington, VA: The Freedom Forum.

Morse, J. A., & Santiago, G., Jr. (2000). Accreditation and faculty. *Academe, 86*(1), 30–34.

National Commission on Excellence in Education. (1983). *A nation at risk: The imperative for educational reform.* Retrieved March 25, 2005, from http://www.ed.gov/pubs/NatAtRisk/index.html

No Child Left Behind Act of 2001. (2002). Public law 107-110. January 8, 2002. Retrieved March 25, 2005, from http://www.ed.gov/policy/elsec/leg/esea02/index.html

Ohmann, R. (2000). Historical reflections on accountability. *Academe, X,* 24–29.

Planning for curricular change in journalism education. (1984). *The Oregon Report* (Project on the Future of Journalism and Mass Communication Education). Eugene: University of Oregon, School of Journalism.

Planning for curricular change in journalism education (2nd ed.). (1987). The Oregon Report. (Project of the Future of Journalism and Mass Communication Education). Eugene: University of Oregon, School of Journalism.

Rosenbaum, J. (1994). Assessment: An overview. In W. G. Christ (Ed.), *Assessing communication education: A handbook for media, speech, and theatre educators* (pp. 3–29). Hillsdale, NJ: Lawrence Erlbaum Associates, Inc.

Rowntree, D. (1992). *Exploring open and distance learning.* London: Kogan Page.

Sarlos, B. (1973). The complexity of the concept 'accountability' in the context of American education. In R. L. Leight (Ed.), *Philosophers speak on accountability in education* (pp. 65–81). Danville, IL: Interstate.

Strengthening the ties that bind: Integrating undergraduate liberal and professional study (Report of the Professional Preparation Network). (1988). Ann Arbor: The Regents of the University of Michigan.

Wagner, R. B. (1989). *Accountability in education: A philosophical inquiry.* New York: Routledge.

Wartella, E. (1994). Foreword. In *State of the field: Academic leaders in journalism, mass communication and speech communication look to the future at the University of Texas* (p. 1). Austin: The University of Texas at Austin, College of Communication.

2

Developing the Assessment Plan

Michael L. James
Harding University

R. Ferrell Ervin
Department of Communication
Southeast Missouri State University

The American university has changed dramatically since the establishment of the colleges in the 17th century. The colonial college's White male population is now religiously, ethnically, and racially diverse. The organizational structure has changed, the curriculum has been enhanced, and the methods of academic delivery have been redefined (Pace, 1979, p. 133).

As the academic institutions have continually reinvented themselves, they have generally been treated with a "hands-off" attitude by most of their sponsors. Sometimes the goal of academic freedom clashed with "results" goals of elected officials. Regardless of the reason, public officials generally only dealt with political issues like location of campuses and sizes of capital budgets (Zumeta, 2001, p. 155).

PUSH FOR ACCOUNTABILITY

Beginning in the 1980s, state governments announced intentions to carefully review the fiscal operation of the university and to require the university to intensify reporting of student academic achievement. This reaction was due to concerns that graduates were not readily employable after graduation. Recommendations included mission clarification, reemphasis on undergraduate instruction, rewarding of improved learning, assessment of programs, and collection of data showing performance (Ervin, 1988, pp. 19–23).

Because the institutions had used a "resource-and-reputation" model of excellence (Astin, 1985), quality depended on the quantity of campus resources, the quality of admitted students, and the reputation of faculty research. This model measured resource inputs but not the quality or quantity of outputs. Astin (1985) urged institutions to replace the model with a value-added concept that looked at the cognitive development of students from admission to graduation.

Some states initiated three performance-based initiatives to encourage or force improvement on the campuses: performance reporting, performance budgeting, and performance funding. Predictably, these mandates required publishing collective results, using results to determine budget allocations, and receiving rewards for achieving targeted results (Burke & Minassians, 2002, p. 15). Acceptable indicators usually fall into four types: inputs, processes, outputs, and outcomes.

Inputs include human, financial, and physical resources received to support programs. Processes involve the means used to deliver programs (i.e., methods of assessment, use of technology, teacher training). Outputs relate to the quantity of products produced (i.e., degrees awarded, retention or graduation rates, sponsored research funding). Outcomes are usually tied to the quality of the program, that is, test scores, job placements, satisfaction surveys, and alumni (Burke & Minassians, 2002, p. 36).

ENVIRONMENT FOR CHANGE

Although some successes were tied to these indicators, the call for greater scrutiny in higher education continued into the 1990s as financial pressures grew in states where corporations downsized because of expanding technology and globalization. As these corporations began to examine their practices, business leaders applied pressure on those associated with higher education to "streamline their production processes" just as the businesses had done. Business leaders stressed that the educational institutions should study customer satisfaction, examine quality control methods that were currently in place, and be able to prove the "outcomes" of their work. Birnbaum (2000) pointed out that although academics developed many management theories and considered them absolutely appropriate for business and government, those same academics believed that performance-based management clashed with academic culture (Birnbaum, 2000).

Accreditation bodies also saw the need for improved assessment. The Accrediting Council on Education in Journalism and Mass Communications (ACEJMC Accreditation, 2004) has adopted a new set of standards to require stiffer reviews starting in the 2005–2006 academic year.

CAMPUS RESISTANCE

Sarason (1998) has suggested that most in the academe did not readily embrace assessment requests. On the surface, assessment spread across the country, but most faculties considered assessment only an added burden and window dressing. Faculty chose to turn their collective backs, perhaps because of an aversion to the connotation of quantification and measurement (Ewell & Lisensky, 1988, p. 14), until most professional and regional accreditation agencies became involved.

Faculty also reject assessment because it could be viewed as interfering with autonomy and academic freedom (AAUP, 1995). These two conjoined, deep-seated professional beliefs suggest that worthwhile intellectual activity cannot survive in an atmosphere in which outside demands exercise a dominating influence over a professor's choice and action (Becher & Kogan, 1992, p. 101).

Another reason faculty avoid assessment is because they misunderstand its real purpose. Faculty may note that a typical student will complete 30 to 45 different courses, depending on the program. They point out that during the course of this undergraduate career, a student's performance would have been measured 30 to 45 separate times and by as many as 20 to 30 professors (Pace, 1979). Erroneously, they are looking at student achievement, not measurement of programs.

ENACTING A STRATEGY FOR MEASUREMENT

Graves (2002) suggested that as the impetus for assessment has grown, many institutions have reacted with a superficial approach, adopting quickly conceived approaches without thought of the individual character of the campus and have created assessment activities that don't produce meaningful data.

All planning should be centered on an understanding of the institution and its values and should strongly incorporate the faculty. Faculty satisfaction with institutional planning is a complex concept based on collegiality, workload, and autonomy (Pollicino, 1996). Participation, which has always been deemed as essential, is not always a sufficient condition for satisfaction with the results of the strategic planning process.

Sternberg and Grigorenko (2002) suggested that the theory of successful intelligence suggests that a student's failure to achieve at a level that matches his or her potential often is a direct result of teaching and assessment practices that are narrow in conceptualization and rigid in implementation. Ewell (1988) asserted that institutional assessment programs should be organized around (a) cognitive outcomes, (b) skills outcomes, (c) attitude and value outcomes, and (d) relationships.

Strategic planning, a planning model first developed in the corporate world and now widely used by universities, is based on a mission statement, goals, and objectives used to identify appropriate responses to internal and external conditions. Often viewed as a four-step program of research, goal setting, strategy determination, and evaluation, strategic planning is a deliberate model anchored by formative research of the environment in which the institution is located, environment within the organization, and the stakeholders of the institution. This research may be casual, secondary, or primary.

Casual research is information that is already known by stakeholders, persons who have experiences with the university (faculty, students, staff, administrators, alumni, citizens in the university's service region, and other helpful individuals).

Secondary research is information that is available from external or internal sources by turning to published reports, Internet listings, and previous self-studies that may have been prepared for regional and professional accrediting agencies.

Primary research is information that may not yet be publicly articulated by using a variety of research techniques like surveys and focus groups with the stakeholders.

The Institutional Mission Statement

Based on a careful examination of the findings obtained through the three described levels of research, an organization now has a grasp of the perceived history, development, and expectations that stakeholders hold. These are key elements concerning the impact of the university and they serve as a base on which to establish relevant goals and objectives. Those visionary goals may be broadly stated at the institutional level but become increasingly more specific as they are written for an institution's academic units. For example, the institution may list the following as a goal: (a) Offer a top-quality curriculum with a solid liberal education as a foundation for preparing graduates for leadership positions in society, or (b) provide a quality education that will lead to an understanding and philosophy of life consistent with Christian ideals.

Obviously, administrators will consider different approaches to prescribing their overall mission. Some will consider research a prime goal; others will include service to community or to religious beliefs. In all cases, administrators should involve elements of the faculty and staff at each decision step.

Expanded Statement of Institutional Purpose

Although the mission statement of the university is the foundation, it must be dissected, then expanded into several statements that incorporate the purpose of the university. These may include, but are not limited to, educational, social, physical, ethical, and cultural impact areas of the institution.

There is no definitive number of goals that should be written, and the goals will vary across the varied spectra of institutions. As an example of one set of goals, Harding University (2004, p. 5) developed six concise goal statements, each derived from the overall mission statement of the university. These statements include the following:

1. The integration of faith, learning, and living.
2. The development of Christian scholarship.
3. The promotion of Christian ethics.
4. The development of lasting relationships.
5. The promotion of wellness.
6. The promotion of citizenship within a global perspective.

Each of these statements is broadened with increasing definition, and each must be met by some working division or program within the institution (Table 2.1). An example of a fleshed-out "Expanded Statement of Institutional Purpose" (Nichols, 1995), coming from the goal statements, discussed earlier, might be as follows: "The University provides programs that enable students to acquire essential knowledge, skills, and dispositions in their academic disciplines for successful careers, advanced studies, and servant leadership" (p. 24).

Identification of Program Goals

Armed with the direction goals from the institution that have been expanded, the program directors and faculty choose the statement that will be assessed and derive plans for an acceptable match. In effect, the program goal will narrow the direction for assessment.

TABLE 2.1
Steps for Developing an Assessment Plan

Steps	Action	Example
1. Mission statement of institution	Administrators determine overall direction of institution	Provide a superb curriculum with an emphasis on core values that provides a foundation for preparing graduates for leadership positions in society
2. Expanded Statement of Institutional Purpose (ESIP)	Separate institutional mission into statements for each operation area	The university provides programs that enable students to acquire essential knowledge, skills, and dispositions in their academic areas for successful careers and advanced studies
3. Identify program goals	Identify working ESIP and refine program to match requisites	Students receiving a bachelor's degree in public relations will acquire the requisite academic tools needed to develop a successful career as a PR practitioner
4. Match goal statements to desired program outcomes	Prepare goals to determine if program is actually "doing" what it purports	Program graduates will be able to prepare a successful print and broadcast advertising campaign
5. Ascertain means of assessment and criteria for success	Develop direct and indirect measures that will allow a measure of outcomes of interest	In the Senior Seminar course, students will present a resume tape or disk media project. Eighty-five percent will be judged as Excellent or Superior (A or B) by the judgment of a three-member faculty panel
6. Collection of data	Use measurement tools to return quantitative and qualitative data	Based on results of a rubric from a three-member faculty panel, 90% of students were judged as excellent on a resume tape
7. Analysis and use of results	Use results of assessment to change or maintain program quality	As a result of low ratings on a public relations campaign assessment, the capstone course was revised to include new campaign components
8. Maintain a "culture" of assessment	Encourage faculty to value use of assessment	Faculty attitude changes from resistance to adoption; use of assessment is valued

The faculty for the program area should become involved with assessment at this stage. The faculty for each program area should see different niches for the preparation of individual goal statements. This goal statement will likely remain static for a long period. A goal statement for public relations might be as follows: "Students receiving a bachelor's degree in public relations will acquire the requisite academic tools needed to develop a successful career as a public relations practitioner."

The ACEJMC (ACEJMC Mission and Practices, 2004) suggested adopting a statement similar to the following for adoption by member schools:

> Professional programs should prepare students with a body of knowledge and a system of inquiry, scholarship and training for careers in which they are accountable to: the public interest for their knowledge, ethics, competence and service; citizens, clients or consumers for their competencies and the quality of their work; and employers for their performance. (p. 2)

Matching Goal Statements to Program Outcomes

This statement of goal mission becomes the "marching order" and the challenge for each academic unit. Each program must then decide on a strategy for reaching the goal. The educational unit now must choose several statements of intended outcomes that will be present if the institutional goal is to be met. These goals can and should be cognitive, behavioral, or attitudinal. Simply speaking, the outcome to be measured seeks to find out if we are "doing" what we purport to be doing. Are we fulfilling our goal? These intended educational outcomes are about our "product" (in this case, graduates of a program) and their ability to think (attitudes), know (cognitive), and do (behavioral). For example, the unit may list the following as one of its corresponding goals: "The School of Communication will provide a curriculum that encourages and enables students to think critically and creatively while incorporating the highest ethical and professional standards." Or, the unit might write the following: "Program graduates will feel confident about having problem-solving and industry software tools that will enable them to excel in all kinds of Web development environments." Or, it could write the following: "Program graduates will be able to prepare a professional public relations campaign."

Each of these statements of intended outcomes is appropriate for academic units, but they are very different in tone. The first requires a cognitive goal measurement, the second necessitates an attitudinal goal, and the third seeks a measurement of a behavioral goal.

Another academic unit wrote the following goals:

- Students will be able to recall important details in the brief history of the profession and to generalize about its future.
- Students will be able to relate the structures and practices of advertising to the functioning of agencies/corporations/not-for-profits.
- Students will be able to identify key legal aspects of the profession and relate significant causes to current professional practices.
- Students will be able to distinguish between various forms of syndicated audience data and primary research and derive information appropriate for an advertising campaign.

Of course, there are many intended outcomes for graduates of a successful program. The new ACEJMC standards (ACEJMC Mission and Practices, 2004, pp. 2–3) list 11 specific items desirable for a fully accredited program (see chapter 1).

Certainly not all of these ACEJMC competencies, or any other competencies, need to be evaluated in any single assessment cycle. Choices must be made to define areas that are essential to the unit, those where changes are expected, and ones that have shown concern as a result of unproven data or accusations. For example, if anecdotal data indicate that students are not prepared for the job market, an outcome that should be assessed might be employer satisfaction with graduates of the program.

How many statements of intended outcomes should be enacted? Three to five outcomes should be identified for each academic program (major) each year (Nichols & Nichols, 2000, p. 19). Obviously this is a starting point, and a few programs may require slightly more or less outcome statements.

For many reasons, the faculty should be the standard-bearer for writing these statements, not the program administrator. Concerns and fears of censorship of academic freedom will be alleviated if the faculty is at the helm of assessment goal statements. But more importantly, the faculty is closest to the content of an academic area and has a greater stake in the success and mission completion of the unit.

Although many possible statements for outcomes can be written, following are strategic choices that may be appropriate for consideration:

- The department will insure that all coursework is grounded in a historical, philosophical, legal, ethical, and cultural context.
- The department will establish a program for ongoing review of the existing curriculum.
- The department will establish a plan for ongoing review of other mass communication programs at benchmark institutions to determine trends in curricular design.

- The department will monitor changes in required competencies for entry-level positions in advertising, journalism, radio, public relations, and television, as well as current hiring trends.
- The department will establish and regularly seek input from a professional advisory panel about skills deemed necessary to function effectively in the increasingly technology-rich mass media professions.

These strategies were seen as clearly appropriate for an academic unit by one group of faculty members at their institution. However, they are not directly transferable to another institution without basing them on findings from the necessary casual, secondary, or primary research of the institutional stakeholders.

Because strategies can differ significantly, an assortment of methods or tactics must be developed for reaching those goals. After the faculty of an academic unit is satisfied with a proposed outcome that can be adequately measured, based on previously announced expectations, the academic organization evaluates or assesses the achievement of the stated objectives.

Means of Assessment and Criteria for Success

Planning the actual measurement of an outcome is integral with devising the intended outcome statements. If there is not a way to measure an outcome, obviously it should not be chosen. Among academe, hotly contested bitterness sometimes erupts when we try to ascertain results through "measurement" of students. Nichols and Nichols (2000) suggested that the difficulty arises because of a lack of clear understanding regarding the use of the term *measurable,* which faculty often consider defined as the following: (a) characterized by a microscope and six-decimal-place accuracy, (b) entirely quantified and precludes qualitative judgments, and (c) is perceived primarily as standardized cognitive examinations.

Nichols (1995) suggested that if the definition of "measurable" includes a general understanding of students' abilities to know, think, and do, agreement among faculty eases.

Statements of objectives should be quite prescriptive, and should answer affirmatively to the following questions suggested by Pratt (1995, p. 149):

1. Is the outcome consistent with the institution's Expanded Statement of Institutional Purpose?
2. Does the outcome describe a reasonable or achievable outcome?
3. Is the outcome clear and measurable?

4. Is the outcome written at a reasonable level of specificity?
5. Does the outcome specify the time frame in which it will be accomplished?

The National Laboratory for Higher Education (1974) indicated that an objective should be a single statement with the following parts:

1. Responsibility—What unit is responsible for performing the objective?
2. Outcome—What is expected to occur?
3. Time—When will the goal be completed?
4. Measurement—What tools will be used to measure the accomplishment of the objective?
5. Standards of Performance—What are the required attainment levels?
6. Conditions—What conditions must be met before the objectives can be accomplished?

An example of an objective to determine students' attitudes of their academic program is shown by the following proposed assessment:

On the senior exit survey for 2004–5 graduates, 80% of electronic media graduates will agree or strongly agree that they are prepared for entry-level positions in the field, and no more than 10% will disagree or strongly disagree.

In the Senior Seminar capstone electronic media course (Fall, 2004), students will present a resume tape or disk media project. 85% will be judged as Excellent or Superior (A or B) by the judgment of a five-member faculty panel.

Collection of Data

Although not covered in detail here, the measurements should be evaluated with the following points (Rogers, 1995, p. 165):

1. Content validity—Is there a correspondence between the test content and the departmental objectives?
2. Reliability—Are the scores consistent over time and across alternate forms?
3. Is the instrument appropriate for the target population?
4. Is the data normative to allow appropriate interpretation?

Analysis and Use of Results

All of the planning, scheduling, timing, and testing is worthless unless the final analysis is complete: How can these data be used to improve or assist the program? The end result is that a program is improved. The results should not be used to fix responsibility, especially for shortcomings, on an individual faculty member (Nichols & Nichols, 2000, p. 42). Assessment results, therefore, should not be used in personnel evaluation.

Rather, the end result should be program improvement. After the results of the assessment are tabulated, they should be spread across the faculty in the program and each member should become acquainted with them. Further, the results should indicate one of three courses of action, according to Nichols and Nichols (2000, p. 51):

1. The means of assessment should be changed and re-measured.
2. The findings may indicate that no changes should be made to the curriculum.
3. The assessment data should be used to change and improve the performance of the program and, therefore, the students.

Developing and Maintaining a "Culture" of Assessment

It sounds simple. The faculty knows what the academic organization is attempting. Each faculty member knows what material is going to be presented, what activities are considered to be most important, and how and why they and their colleagues will assess the accomplishment of the goal even before the plan begins. Faculty armed with a plan and students with a course syllabus have a target at which to aim. If it is so simple, then why do administrators and faculty frequently avoid implementing the strategic planning method? The answer frequently relates to the culture of the campus, the time required to formulate the plan, and the need to continually review and revise it.

This strategic planning process, rather than being static, is a method of continuous quality improvement. It goes beyond quality control or the desire to fix defects. It goes beyond quality assurance or the desire to design "high quality" into an academic program or a class in that program. It is an ongoing process to become "forever better" (Knight & Trowler, 2000). However, researchers caution that continuous quality improvement (CQI) is only possible when the ground rules include the following: (a) the idea that improvements can always be made, (b) the faculty is empowered to use their best judgment in creating the design, and (c) the faculty is committed to working with colleagues.

As can be predicted from the previous "prescription" for assessment success, a variety of techniques can be employed. An Internet search will provide many examples of methods that can be used, assuming the mission is the same.

The web master for the University of Nevada–Reno has compiled a "links page" that views assessment plans and examples of several institutions (Assessment Plan Examples, 2004). The connections reveal a variety of assessment plans for consideration.

Strategic planning and assessment help an institution or academic unit to focus its energy to systematically gather data useful in meeting a variety of campus and accrediting assessment demands. More importantly, strategic planning is a technique where faculty jointly set standards to be achieved in the presentation of course materials and standards of mastery for individual students.

When used as a continuous quality improvement tool, data gathered in the process can be formative or diagnostic to help faculty improve a program and enable the product, students, with better preparation to continue in their academic or professional careers.

REFERENCES

AAUP. (2005). *Academic freedom and tenure*. Retrieved August 9, 2005, from http://www.aaup.org/com-a/index.htm

ACEJMC Accrediting Standards. (2004). *ACEJMC Information Center*. Retrieved from http://www.ukans.edu/~acejmc/PROGRAM/STANDARDS.SHTML

ACEJMC Mission and Practices. (2004). *ACEJMC Information Center*. Retrieved from http://www.ukans.edu/~acejmc/BREAKING/newprins.shtml

Assessment Plan Examples. (2004). Retrieved from http://www.unr.edu/assess/PlanResources/ResourcesPages/OtherInstitutionLinks.asp

Astin, A. (1985). *Achieving academic excellence*. San Francisco: Jossey-Bass.

Becher, T., & Kogan, M. (1992). *Process and structure in higher education* (2nd ed.). New York: Routledge.

Birnbaum, R. (2000). *Management fads in higher education: Where they come from, what they do, why they fail*. San Francisco: Jossey-Bass.

Burke, J., & Minassians, H. (2002). *Reporting higher education results: Missing links in the performance chain*. San Francisco: Jossey-Bass.

Ervin, R. (1988). Outcomes assessment: The rationale and the implementation. In R. L. Hoskins (Ed.), *Insights* (pp. 19–23). Columbia, SC: ASJMC.

Ewell, P. (1984). *The self-regarding institution: Information for excellence*. Boulder, CO: NCHEMS.

Ewell, P., & Lisensky, R. (1988). *Assessing institutional effectiveness: Redirecting the self-study process*. Boulder, CO: The Consortium for the Advancement of Private Higher Education.

Graves, D. (2002). *Testing is not teaching: What should count in education*. Portsmouth, NH: Heinemann.

Harding University Catalog. (2004). *General Catalog*. Searcy, AR: The Harding Press.

Knight, P. T., & Trowler, P. R. (2000). Academic work and quality. *Quality in Higher Education, 6*(2), 109–114.

National Laboratory for Higher Education. (1974). *Developing measurable objectives.* Durham, NC: Author.

Nichols, J. (1995). *A practitioner's handbook for institutional effectiveness and student outcomes assessment implementation.* New York: Agathon Press.

Nichols, J., & Nichols, K. (2000). *The departmental guide and record book for student outcomes assessment and institutional effectiveness* (3rd ed.). New York: Agathon Press.

Pace, C. (1979). *Measuring outcomes of college: Fifty years of findings and recommendations for the future.* San Francisco: Jossey-Bass.

Pollicino, E. B. (1996). *Faculty satisfaction with institutional support as a complex concept: Collegiality, workload, autonomy.* Paper presented at the annual meeting of the American Educational Research Association, New York.

Pratt, L. (1995). Statements of outcomes/objectives and assessment at the department level. In J. Nichols (Ed.), *A practitioner's handbook for institutional effectiveness and student outcomes assessment implementation* (pp. 146–156). New York: Agathon Press.

Rogers, B. (1995). Setting and evaluating intended educational (instructional) outcomes. In J. Nichols (Ed.), *A practitioner's handbook for institutional effectiveness and student outcomes assessment implementation* (pp. 157–171). New York: Agathon Press.

Sarason, S. B. (1998). *Political leadership and educational failure.* San Francisco: Jossey-Bass.

Sternberg, R., & Grigorenko, E. (2002). The theory of successful intelligence as a basis for instruction and assessment in higher education. In D. Halapren (Ed.), *Applying the science of learning to university teaching and beyond* (pp. 45–53). San Francisco: Jossey-Bass.

Zumeta, W. (2001). Public policy and accountability in higher education: Lessons from the past and present for the new millennium. In D. E. Heller (Ed.), *The states and public higher education policy: Affordability, access, and accountability.* Baltimore: The Johns Hopkins University Press.

Mission Statements[1]

William G. Christ
Department of Communication
Trinity University

Terry Hynes
College of Journalism and Communications
University of Florida

All media education programs have missions. Some missions are explicit, visionary, and useful; some are implicit, unclear, and fractured. Mission statements are "political" documents that can be used to clarify or obfuscate a unit's reality (Christ & Blanchard, 1994). They can accurately mirror a vision or simply reflect a pipe dream.

Departments might argue that they have implicit mission statements or that no matter what the mission statement says it is the faculty, courses, and facilities that define a program. Although there is merit in this argument, Blanchard and Christ (1993) argued that "explicit mission statements should be at the center of curricular discussion" (p. 82).

In a 1990 survey distributed to 258 member schools of the Broadcast Education Association, less than 56% of the large schools' departments and less than 50% of the medium and small schools' departments were identified as having mission statements (Warner & Liu, 1990). Given the growing adoption of strategic planning processes by universities in the 1980s, this was a surprisingly small number. For those seeking accreditation from the Accrediting Council on Education in Journalism and Mass Communications (ACEJMC), mission statements are an expected part of the accreditation process.

---

[1]Some of the arguments and earlier versions of this chapter can be found in Blanchard and Christ (1993), Christ and Blanchard (1994), and Christ and Hynes (1997).

In the mid-1990s, two task forces of the Association for Education in Journalism and Mass Communication (AEJMC) attempted to develop mission statements for the field. The AEJMC Vision 2000 Task Force (AEJMC, 1994a, 1994b) articulated the mission for Journalism and Mass Communication (JMC) education when it wrote:

> Since we are all consumers and to some extent producers, communication skills—in terms of both producing and interpreting messages—should be part of the basic education in a democratic society. The goal of journalism and mass communication programs is to provide students *and* the larger society with a deeper understanding of mass communication processes and to improve the practices and performance of mass media professionals. Their goal is to produce socially responsible, informed, skilled citizens who understand how various media technologies and communication processes emerge within particular social, economic, and political contexts, and thereby affect both individual identity and societal processes on a global level. Journalism and mass communication have become vital to the maintenance of an informed society. Knowledge of how we speak, how we write and think, how we inform, interpret and persuade—as well as how we are spoken to, how we are addressed, how we are envisioned, informed and persuaded—are now critical for educated people. (p. 6, italics in the original)

In 1995, after a review of numerous studies of journalism and mass communication education completed between 1982 and 1995, the AEJMC Curriculum Task Force concluded "The purpose of media education is to produce well-rounded graduates who have critical thinking skills as well as practical skills, and who have an understanding of the philosophy of the media and a dedication to the public service role that the media have in our society" (AEJMC, 1996, p. 106).

Mission statements are required for those wishing to be ACEJMC accredited. Standard 1, "Mission, Governance and Administration," of the AECJMC accreditation guidelines states that, "The policies and practices of the unit ensure that it has an effectively and fairly administered working and learning environment" (ACEJMC, 2004, p. 42). The first of the five required indicators for this standard focuses precisely on the importance of the mission statement: "The unit has a mission statement and engages in strategic or long-range planning that provides vision and direction for its future, identifies needs and resources for its mission and goals and is supported by university administration outside the unit" (ACEJMC, 2004, p. 42).

As part of its "Principles of Accreditation," ACEJMC states the mission of journalism and mass communications education as:

> Professional programs should prepare students with a body of knowledge and a system of inquiry, scholarship and training for careers in which they

are accountable to: the public interest for their knowledge, ethics, competence and service; citizens, clients or consumers for their competencies and the quality of their work; and employers for their performance. (ACEJMC, 2004, p. 13)

It presents the mission of the profession: "The mission of journalism and mass communications professions in a democratic society is to inform, to enlighten and to champion freedoms of speech and press. These professions seek to enable people to fulfill their responsibilities as citizens who mean to govern themselves" (ACEJMC, 2004, p. 13).

Apparently, there are still schools that do not think explicit mission statements are needed. Although trying to articulate mission statements is not easy, especially if there are disparate positions that are held by the tenured faculty, the debate that ensues when trying to develop statements can be very useful and important. If a program does not have a mission statement, the faculty can be asked to look at themselves, the facilities, and the courses and curricula and ask the following questions: What would an external review group say was the mission of this media program? What is it doing? Although coming across as a hypothetical exercise, in reality, the answer to the question, "What is your mission?" is very important to deans, vice presidents of academic affairs, and presidents. Programs need to be able to justify their existence to a wide range of people or else risk losing the support of administrators or legislatures. As Galvin (1992, p. 24) suggested, developing goals and mission statements can produce at least four benefits: (a) clarifying organizational purpose, (b) forcing consensus on what is important, (c) creating a framework against which to evaluate resource allocation, and (d) reinforcing a commitment to student learning.

WHAT SHOULD MISSION STATEMENTS LOOK LIKE?

Although there is not a cookbook answer to the question, "What should mission statements look like?" there have been recommendations about what a mission statement could contain. For example, Ackoff (1986), in a book dealing with writing mission statements for businesses, wrote that a mission statement should have five characteristics. First, "*it should contain a formulation of the firm's objectives that enables progress toward them to be measured. To state objectives that cannot be used to evaluate performance is hypocrisy*" (p. 39, italics in original). It is important that the objectives of a mission statement are not simply a string of "operationally meaningless superlatives such as *biggest, best, optimum, and maximum*" (Ackoff, 1986, p. 38, italics in original). This first characteristic is especially important in an age of accountability. Viable assessment strategies need to tap not only what is taught but what is learned. Mission statements and objectives should be linked so that measurable assessment strategies can be developed.

Ackoff's (1986) second characteristic is that "*a company's mission statement should differentiate it from other companies*. It should establish the individuality, if not the uniqueness of the firm" (p. 39, italics in original). The question for media programs is as follows: What is the unique, intellectual, academic contribution of the media program to the university? Programs that are too similar to other programs within the same university may open themselves up to being merged or eliminated.

Ackoff's (1986) third point is "*a mission statement should define the business that the company wants to be in, not necessarily is in*" (p. 40, italics in original). From technical schools to liberal arts and sciences colleges to research universities, from teaching programs to research institutes, the "business" of education is diverse. This point underscores that mission statements should be powerful statements of vision. "Not only should they clarify a unit's objectives and distinctiveness, but they should illuminate a unit's potential" (Blanchard & Christ, 1993, p. 83).

Ackoff's (1986) fourth suggestion is that "*a mission statement should be relevant to all the firm's stakeholders. . . .* The mission should state how the company intends to serve each of them" (p. 41, italics in original). Programs in higher education serve a number of stakeholders including students, alumni, faculty, staff, administrators, parents, legislators, and so forth. A mistake a unit can make is to "forget" that one of its largest stakeholders is the university or college as a whole. Linking the unit's mission statement to the university's mission statement is critical. If a unit does not firmly position its mission within the mission of the university as a whole, it becomes easier for administrators to see the unit as a "loose cannon" that needs to be controlled.

The last characteristic of a mission statement, according to Ackoff (1986), is that "*a mission statement should be exciting and inspiring*. It should motivate all those whose participation in its pursuit is sought. . . . It does *not* have to appear to be feasible; it only has to be *desirable . . .*" (p. 41, italics in original). In the current era of accountability, Ackoff's comment that a mission does not have to appear to be feasible may not serve a unit well. Outcomes should be linked to mission statements, and therefore, the mission statements need to be in a language that is exciting, inspiring, and feasible.

To Ackoff's (1986) list should be added the following: "The mission statement should accurately reflect the educational philosophy of your program" and "should reflect the mission statement of the university/college in which the unit is housed" (Blanchard & Christ, 1993, p. 84).

Combining these characteristics, we might come up with a list of questions that include: Who are we? What needs do we address and how do we analyze or respond to those needs? How do we respond to key constituents? What is our philosophy or core values? What makes us unique or distinctive? How do we know when we are true to our mission or when we veer off course? How do we create ways to readdress systematically our mission and goals? (Blanchard & Christ, 1993, adapted from Bryson, 1988, p. 105; Galvin, 1992, p. 23; see also Appendix A for another series of questions about mission statements).

STATEMENTS OF MISSION AND PURPOSE

Although media education programs have much in common, they also differ, based variously on the nature of the missions of their institutions (e.g., whether teaching or research is the main focus), university or program size, university or program service areas (e.g., local–regional focus or national–international focus), disciplines included within the media unit or the disciplinary unit in which a media program is housed (e.g., a media program which includes traditional speech and rhetoric-based curricula or media instruction housed in an English Department), and structural program configuration (e.g., a department within a larger college or an independent media college or department). Any combination of these factors can lead to different visions and missions for a media unit. Thus, it is clear that there is no one mission for media education but rather a variety of missions and purposes. (The following examples are from a Christ & Hynes (1997) Association for Education in Journalism and Mass Communication/Association of Schools of Journalism and Mass Communication Education Joint Committee report. The names of the schools have been removed because the quotes are meant to be illustrative of the ideas presented and may no longer apply to the specific programs.)

With respect to Ackoff's (1986) first characteristic, linking measurable objectives to mission statements can be used to indicate success. Whether it is ACEJMC, state, or regional accreditation, assessment has become an important part of what we are expected to do as educators. Programs need to be prepared to use their mission statements and objectives as a focal point of their assessment strategies (Christ, 1994, 1995, 1997). For example, one school stated that its mission was "to educate, train and develop students to become professional journalists, broadcasters, graphic artists/photographers, advertising and public relations practitioners and to serve as liberally educated members of the institutions, communities and societies in which they live and work"

(Christ & Hynes, 1997, p. 78). It then listed six "intended outcomes" linked to the mission: graduating people who were

> good writers and communicators; knowledgeable of the necessary equipment and technologies in journalism and communications; practically trained through internships, production work, professionally affiliated clubs, projects and related activities; skilled to enter, maintain and advance in their chosen media or related professional careers and goals; counseled by teachers, program advisers and others to understand the role and impact of the media and practitioners; creative, adaptable and aware of the ever-changing needs of the multimedia professions and the interdependent world in which they live, work and make their contributions. (Christ & Hynes, 1997, p. 79)

The point is that these objectives, which were linked to the mission statement, provide a framework which can ultimately, after each objective is carefully "operationalized," be used to measure success (see Appendix B).

Ackoff's (1986) second characteristic encourages mission statements that identify a program's uniqueness relative to other programs. This can be approached from at least two directions. First, a media program obtains an advantage (especially in a time of reduced or limited resources) by indicating what unique or special contributions it makes to the university as a whole. The program may be similar to other programs at other universities, but it should not be similar to other programs in the same university. Second, to the extent that media programs in different universities identify similar ways in which they uniquely contribute to their institutions, the constellation of those "similarly unique" elements may be identified as a basis of shared roles for media programs across institutions.

The uniqueness of different programs tends to fall into three categories: specialized knowledge, values, skills, and objectives of the program; the special publics or stakeholders with which they are concerned; and a particular environment of which they are part or are trying to create. (These similarly unique characteristics are also discussed later, in the "Patterns" section.)

Knowledge, Values, Skills, and Objectives

Some schools emphasize their uniqueness in terms of knowledge, values, skills, or objectives. For example, a school might choose to accentuate the technology and the global aspects of its orientation by stating the following:

"The department embraces technology as a communication tool, celebrates its commitment to professionalism, and leads the campus community in the use of technology, globalization initiatives, and diversity by reaching out to other units on campus, other universities, both internationally and domestically, and to the communication industry in collaborative curricular, teaching, research, and creative opportunities." (p. 79)

Others tend to be very specific about different kinds of courses or areas of study when they indicate that they want to "introduce students to the historical, public policy, legal, and ethical issues related to the roles and effects of the mass media as important social institutions" (p. 79).

Still other programs stress an integration of particular areas, whether it be scholarly work and professional practice or "through a program that is both integrative and holistic—one which introduces students to the intellectual traditions and disciplines, to the rest of higher education, and to contemporary communications practice" (p. 79).

Some programs might list a variety of skills students are required to master, including critical thinking, information gathering, and written, oral, and visual communication skills, reporting, and production. The uniqueness of programs often is reflected in the clustering of these skills, or in the way in which the skills are associated with other elements deemed valuable in the program. For example, schools have argued that graduates of their schools "should be well grounded in the liberal arts and instilled with the skills to make critical inquiry into matters of culture, technology, ethics, and responsibilities of the media in the world," whereas others stress "critical thinking, creativity, and personal integrity, or the development of basic skills in writing, mathematics, foreign language, and computers" (p. 80).

Some programs stress professional or personal values when they include statements like the following in their missions: "to imbue students with the highest ethical and professional standards so that they understand and address competently the diversity of issues and ideas that confront them now and in the 21st century" (p. 80). Others demonstrate how values and knowledge are intertwined:

"The ability of people to govern themselves in a democratic society can be no better than the quality of news and information they receive. The Founding Fathers recognized this principle in the First Amendment, which attempts to guarantee that no government can censor the free flow of information, information which people need in order to be informed and to think critically and well. This principle is just as vital in our modern world, where the lack of timely, reliable, high-quality information leads to erroneous impressions and flawed public policy. . . . (Our program) prepares students to search for, gather, and present news in words and pictures according to the highest standards of truth, honesty, fairness, clarity, courage, independence, importance, perseverance, and service to the democratic ideals that underlie the First Amendment." (p. 80)

Programs in colleges affiliated with or sponsored by a particular religion, might include a spiritual dimension in their mission statements: "The mission . . . is to plan, organize, and implement an undergraduate and graduate journalism and mass communication teaching program that reflects commitment to the education of an effective graduate who will appreciate the interaction of spiritual, academic, societal, and professional values within the context of the university and college missions" (p. 80).

Still other programs stress their own values or commitments over student values when they write that they are "committed to free speech, freedom of the press, and open inquiry" (p. 81).

Specific Outcomes. Although some mission statements emphasize courses or areas of study, skills, and values as intrinsic components of the program, other mission statements might frame their role in terms of *outcomes*: we want to graduate students who "recognize the value of thorough reporting and understand the public has a right to accurate information reported fairly" (p. 81). Or, graduates of the undergraduate program are expected to understand the "(a) roles, structures, and functions of a free American press within a global society; (b) the roles and functions of advertising and public information within society; and (c) a professional communicator's roles, functions, process, and skills of the specialty area within the profession" (p. 81).

Whom the Faculty Were Trying to Serve

Higher education serves a variety of "publics" or stakeholders. Whether it is the students, practitioners, or the community at large, many mission statements show their uniqueness by emphasizing whom they want to attract or serve. As one might expect from professionally oriented media programs, the industries and professional practices for which programs prepare students are key stakeholders reflected in many media statements. This is most evident in the mission statement and standards developed by ACEJMC for accreditation (presented earlier in this chapter).

Christ and Hynes (1997) found that of the 176 mission and purpose statements they analyzed, 121 (68.7%) indicated that part of their mission was to prepare students for specific industries (e.g., newspapers, broadcasting, public relations, advertising) or to provide students with specific professional skills that could be used in such industries (e.g., reporting, graphics design, advertising strategies). Forty (22.7%) explicitly noted a commitment either to attract or serve a diverse faculty or student population, or, in some other way, to foster racial or cultural diversity. Language consistent with this commitment included the following: (a) "to attract and nurture a diverse student body and faculty providing students with attitudes in harmony with America's pluralistic society and consistent with the liberal education philosophies of higher education," or (b) "the school contributes to and uses state-of-the-art knowledge in the fields of print and broadcast journalism; radio, television and film; human and mass communication; communication sciences and disorders, and advertising and public relations, with particular emphases on unserved, underserved and under-represented populations" (Christ & Hynes, 1997, pp. 81–82).

Service to practitioners and the community also is talked about in the "Patterns" section later.

Unique Environment in Which the Program Is Located or Environment the Program Is Trying to Create

Some programs cite location as a special part of their mission, either because they are state-supported institutions or because they see their environment as an important educational element of what they offer. Some programs focus on the advantages, opportunities, and special commitments of their geographic location in articulating their mission, saying things like, "This setting allows students to combine academic and professional interests in a program that matches precept with example, education with experience. The setting also allows the faculty to be responsive to the needs of the communication industry and area professionals through programs of research, continuing education, and professional service" (p. 82).

Other programs describe their mission, in part, as creating a special "place" or "environment." An example is a program that said its department and faculty

"strive to provide an educational environment wherein students analyze the theories and concepts of communication, consider its history and impact, and develop a level of expertise in production and performance. The department ensures students the opportunity and educational foundation to consider societal implications and ethical considerations of communication practices, procedures and policies." (p. 82)

As noted earlier in this chapter, Ackoff's (1986) third characteristic of mission statements concerns the power of the vision they reflect or their potential to move a program to a new level of its growth and development. Some programs use the word *vision* in statements that precede their mission statements. Others incorporate a more comprehensive vision into their statements of purpose. The ACEJMC vision statement, for example, includes the following:

> Journalism and mass communication transmit and interpret culture and bind society together, making them among the most vital forces in the maintenance of any society and fundamental to democratic government and a free society. They embody the spirit of a free press and are central to the preservation and advancement of the values provided under the First Amendment.
>
> Because of their importance to society, journalism and mass communication demand the highest possible level of integrity, fairness, understanding, and skill from both practitioners of journalism and mass communications and the educators who teach the practitioners. (ACEJMC, 2004, p. 8)

A "vision" of the role and function of media programs within the broader communications field and within the traditions of the liberal arts is also stated by some:

> "The school is part of the rapidly changing field of communication, and journalism and mass communication (JMC) is an essential, founding component of that field. It is a tradition of teaching and inquiry that sees professional media education as a discourse deeply embedded in the spirit and substance of the liberal arts, modern and ancient. The skills taught in the JMC curriculum—information-gathering, writing, editing, message creation, oral presentation, interpretation, criticism and the harnessing of technology to human needs—are fundamental tools of liberal education in every age." (p. 83)

For some programs, the environment they are trying to create includes not only preparing people for careers but also elevating, improving, or challenging the current practice of the profession: "The faculty is committed to a scholarly environment in which theoretical, historical, critical, and technological methodologies help students to question, challenge, and improve all forms of communication" (p. 83).

Mission statements which are relevant to all of an organization's stakeholders is Ackoff's (1986) fourth characteristic, as noted earlier. The following illustrates how this characteristic can be included in a unit's mission statement: "In broad terms, the department's primary objective is to help students acquire knowledge, understanding and skills. . . . The department, however, also seeks to serve the university and its objectives, and to provide service to high schools and community colleges in the state, to local news media and professional associations, to its own alumni, and to the community in general" (p. 83).

Some programs state their linkages to the larger university: "The principal mission of the Communication Department derives from those of the university and the College of Arts and Sciences in which the department is housed: to provide a firm grounding in the liberal arts and sciences and strong professional preparation, to the end that students are educated for satisfying lives and successful careers" (p. 84).

As indicated earlier, mission statements should reflect the educational philosophies of their programs. However, mission and purpose statements alone are not adequate evidence on which to judge the entire educational philosophy of a program. Shades of differences between programs with similar missions also may not be clear from mission statements alone.

PATTERNS

As noted earlier, there are similarities among different media programs and their mission statements. Analyzing those similarities can lead to a deeper understanding of the core values and other elements that help create a unified field of study in journalism and mass communication.

Professional Education and the Liberal Arts

One of the most fundamental questions addressed by media education mission and purpose statements concerns the relation of the programs to the liberal arts and sciences. If one end of a continuum of media education is a trade school orientation that stresses skills to the exclusion of contextual courses like history, economics, philosophy, psychology, English, or mass media processes and effects, the other end of the continuum is an orientation that stresses studies courses to the exclusion of application to practice.

Many programs embrace the idea that media education involves preparing a liberally educated professional. Even programs which express a near-balance in combining professional preparation with a liberal arts context, however, differ in some of the nuances of that balance.

Mission Statement Language. Examples of broad mission statement language include the following: (a) to "prepare students for productive and socially responsible careers in journalism and mass communication in the context of a liberal education"; (b) to "educate students broadly in the liberal arts, enabling them to become productive and creative citizens and leaders in their profession, community, and nation"; (c) "to develop liberally educated, professionally trained communicators who are equipped intellectually and ethically to convey the issues of contemporary society" (p. 85); and (d) to provide "educational experiences that enrich and integrate the liberal arts and sciences with communication and media studies and practices. To this end, the Department of Communication seeks to educate students (a) to become communicators and media sense-makers, for themselves, their clients, and their communities; (b) to understand their obligations as citizens within global and cultural communication contexts shaped by media; and (c) to recognize their opportunities and responsibilities as ethical, self-directed practitioners within changing information, technological, and communication environments" (p. 85).

Specific Mission Statement Language. Examples of more specific mission statement language linked to specific media education areas include the following: (a) "The Communication Department strives to provide quality education to students to enable them to speak, write, and think clearly, critically, and creatively. The department is committed to a liberal education in the arts and sciences as well as to professional training in the skills of journalism, public relations, advertising, video technology, and speech communication"; (b) "to provide professional education in the areas of advertising, journalism (print and broadcast), and public relations, in the context of a strong college liberal arts curriculum . . ."; and (c) "to prepare students for careers in journalism and public relations by teaching professional skills and media research techniques; to increase the importance of a broad liberal arts basis of education so that students are educated 'for life,' not just for a living; to retain the traditional, basic strengths of a media-based curriculum—information gathering, writing, editing, media law, and ethics, while adapting the curriculum to dramatic changes in mass communication professionals" (pp. 85–86).

Teaching, Research, and Service

Another framing device for articulating a program's mission or purpose lies in the three traditional university mission areas of teaching, research (and creative activities), and service. Many schools expect faculty to teach, conduct research, and serve their schools, communities, and profession. Some schools include this expectation in their mission statements when they state that their school "recognizes three important parts to its academic and professional mission—to educate undergraduate and graduate students, to create and disseminate knowledge, and to provide service that will enhance standards of performance"; or that the college "focuses its activities on instruction in the professional disciplines of journalism and mass communications; adding to the body of knowledge in those professions through research, scholarship, and creative activity; and service to those professions and to the community at large." Other media programs stress one of the three areas (teaching, research, or service): "Teaching is the single most important responsibility of a . . . faculty member" (p. 86).

Practitioner, Citizen, and Consumer Preparation

Preparation to Be a Practitioner. Although most media programs explicitly see their mission as preparing people for careers, the discussion of career preparation differs in terms of how and where it is emphasized in mission statements. Some mission statements say that career preparation is the primary mission: (a) "The primary goal of the Division of Mass Communication is to train students to be effective and productive communicators using mass media as a tool"; or (b) "our mission is to provide students the concepts and skills necessary to enter mass communication careers in a socially responsible way, and the resources to think critically about the role and impact of mass communication in society" (p. 87).

Some mission statements suggest that preparation is part of a broader mission or context and are specific about how career preparation requires knowledge (understanding), skills, and value: the mission "is to advance the profession of journalism by educating highly skilled and broadly knowledgeable professionals with a passion for their craft.

This is accomplished in two ways. First, the faculty must encourage an understanding of the role of mass media in the contemporary socio-cultural, political, and economic environment, and an appreciation for journalistic principles and traditions. Second, the faculty must teach the skills for gathering, analyzing, and communicating information effectively" (p. 87).

Teaching communication skills is mentioned in a number of mission statements: (a) the mission is "to develop effective communication skills among our students . . . to prepare students for careers in advertising, broadcasting, journalism, and public relations . . ."; or (b) "our goal is to instill the fundamental skills necessary for a journalist—writing, reporting, and interviewing" (p. 87).

Critical or analytical thinking is another explicit theme mentioned across mission statements: the mission of our program (a) "is to teach its students to think critically and to apply that thinking to the collection, organization, and communication of information through the public media. Analytical thinking is essential to clear writing, which is at the heart of good journalism"; (b) "we teach students to gather information, to present it clearly and to think critically within a legal and ethical framework"; or (c) one of our instructional goals is "to provide intellectual preparation that emphasizes the capacity to think critically and creatively, the ability to solve problems effectively in a professional context, and the ability to cope with change in the professional world . . ." (pp. 87–88).

Some mission statements attempt to place the teaching of skills within a broad context: the department's goal "is to develop liberally educated women and men who understand the vital role of the written and spoken symbol as they adapt to and challenge their environments, and who can express themselves accurately, clearly, grammatically, creatively, and persuasively . . . while we teach our students specific skills required to perform effectively in the communications-related industries and arts, those same skills—writing, reporting, speaking, listening, thinking creatively—are broadly applicable to a wide range of careers and interests. Mastery of them assures a student a life of flexibility and enrichment, no matter what career paths and changes he or she might choose" (p. 88).

Preparation to Be a Citizen or Consumer.   Some programs explicitly state that their mission is to educate students as citizens and consumers: (a) "To educate undergraduate students so they are productive citizens in the communities in which they live . . ."; (b) "to educate consumers about the functions and importance of news media and related agencies in American life"; or (c) "to foster informed citizens and consumers of the media by offering course work for general education" (p. 88).

The Nonmajor Student

Being committed to the liberal arts for many programs means making sure that students get a liberal education from outside the unit while professional education and training is provided inside the unit. However, some programs see their mission as being to serve the liberal education needs of nonmajors and the general student, a position which programs sometimes use to argue their centrality to the total university mission: a program can argue that its mission is to (a) "contribute to the enhancement of liberal arts education in the university"; (b) "students from other disciplines, seeking to improve their communications skills and knowledge about the media and their impact on society, will find a variety of course offerings"; (c) the program "articulates the connection between communication and the purpose of the university . . . communication is central to the mission of the university"; or (d) the aim is "to provide all students with the opportunity to gain an understanding of the principles, processes, and practices of human communication through a series of foundational courses. These courses are designed to assist in the preparation for careers in law, teaching, business, and other related fields" (p. 88).

Linkage to Practitioners and the Community

Some programs specify in their mission statements their relationship to practitioners and the general community. This aspect of mission statements differs from the earlier discussion regarding programs' role in preparing a student to be a practitioner, citizen, or consumer. Rather, this aspect of the mission statements articulates linkages to practitioners or the community.

Linkage to Practitioners. In terms of practitioners, the relationship is presented in three ways. First, practitioners are seen as a resource for schools. Second, schools see themselves as offering educational opportunities to practitioners. Third, schools see the program–practitioner relationship as mutually beneficial. An example of the first is a school which states that it includes national leaders from the communications industry on an advisory board explicitly to support the unit's mission. An example of the second is a school that offers continuing education to regional professionals. The third is exemplified in statements such as the following: "Faculty members work to maintain mutually constructive relationships with professional and academic communities by sharing expertise and knowledge with appropriate local, national, and international organizations" (p. 89).

Linkages to the Community. Linkages to the community also tend to fall into three categories. First, are programs that create linkages when they refer to their students as part of the larger community: "founded on the premise that college students will graduate into a changing world. Success in that world is contingent on their ability to adapt by calling on appropriate knowledge, skills, and abilities when needed" (p. 89).

The second category suggests that the educational unit should serve the community through such things as continuing education: the school "has a major role to play in providing short-term educational opportunities to regional, national, and international communities with nondegree programs offered through corporate, nonprofit, and governmental agencies" (p. 89).

The third category of statements link media programs to the community by including statements about the important social purposes of media and the programs' function to educate students about the role of media in society: a program "provides students with a dynamic program of skills and conceptual courses devoted to the practice and social impact of journalism" (p. 89).

SUMMARY

Media education mission statements and statements of purpose are as diverse as the programs, colleges, and universities they represent. Even when many programs include the same value or components, the context of programs and the discussion may radically alter the salience of that value or component from one program to another. Even so, there are patterns or commonalities across many programs.

Though it is hard work and can take many hours of intense negotiations among faculty, developing a mission statement is an important step in the assessment process. If taken seriously, the mission statement can be a touchstone for faculty as they grapple with the difficult intellectual work of developing student learning outcomes and measurements.

REFERENCES

Accrediting Council on Education in Journalism and Mass Communication. (2004). *Journalism and mass communications accreditation, 2004–2005.* Lawrence, KS: Author.

Ackoff, R. L. (1986). *Management in small doses.* New York: Wiley.

Association for Education in Journalism and Mass Communication Curriculum Task Force. (1996). Responding to the challenge of change. *Journalism and Mass Communication Educator, 50*(4), 101–119.

Association for Education in Journalism and Mass Communication Vision 2000 Task Force. (1994a, August). *Report No. 1: The identity and structure of the AEJMC.* Report presented at the annual convention of the AEJMC, Atlanta, GA.

Association for Education in Journalism and Mass Communication Vision 2000 Task Force. (1994b, August). *Report No. 2: The viability of JMC units within universities.* Report presented at the annual convention of the AEJMC, Atlanta, GA.

Blanchard, R. O., & Christ, W. G. (1993). *Media education and the liberal arts: A blueprint for the new professionalism.* Hillsdale, NJ: Lawrence Erlbaum Associates, Inc.

Bryson, J. M. (1988). *Strategic planning for public and nonprofit organizations.* San Francisco: Jossey-Bass.

Christ, W. G. (Ed.). (1994). *Assessing communication education: A handbook for media, speech, and theatre educators.* Hillsdale, NJ: Lawrence Erlbaum Associates, Inc.

Christ, W. G. (1995). The role of journalism and mass communication education in the university of the future. Speech given during the 1993 AEJMC plenary session. *Insights* (Winter). Columbia, SC: Association of Schools of Journalism and Mass Communication.

Christ, W. G. (Ed.). (1997). *Media education assessment handbook.* Mahwah, NJ: Lawrence Erlbaum Associates, Inc.

Christ, W. G., & Blanchard, R. O. (1994). Mission statements, outcomes and the new liberal arts. In W. G. Christ (Ed.), *Assessing communication education* (pp. 31–55). Hillsdale, NJ: Lawrence Erlbaum Associates, Inc.

Christ, W. G., & Hynes, T. (1997). The missions and purposes of journalism and mass communication education. *Journalism and Mass Communication Educator, 52*, 74–98.

Erwin, P. T. (1991). *Assessing student learning and development.* San Francisco: Jossey-Bass.

Galvin, K. N. (1992). Foundation for assessment: The mission, goals and objectives. In E. A. Hay (Ed.), *Program assessment in speech communication* (pp. 21–24). Annandale, VA: Speech Communication Association.

Warner, C., & Liu, Y. (1990). Broadcast curriculum profile (a freeze-frame look at what BEA members offer students). *Feedback, 31*(3), 6–7.

Whitney, D. R. (1970). Improving essay examinations: I. Writing, essay questions. *Technical Bulletin No. 9.* Iowa City: Evaluation and Examination Service, University of Iowa.

APPENDIX A: QUESTIONS ABOUT MISSION STATEMENTS (FROM CHRIST & BLANCHARD, 1994, PP. 49–50)

1. Does our program have an explicit mission statement?

2. When was the last time we discussed our mission and/or mission statement?

3. How well does the mission of our academic program reflect and support the mission of our institution as a whole?

4. If an outside group came to our school, what would it identify as our strengths and weaknesses?

5. How committed are we to the general education of non-majors? What kinds of experiences (e.g., courses, apprenticeships, workshops, lecture series, and so forth) do we offer to the general student? What kind of commitment has our department made to the liberal education of all students?

6. Most of us would argue that our discipline is basic. But can we explain what is basic about our discipline? How has our program defined itself in terms of what is basic or fundamental to a liberal education and what is basic and fundamental to our discipline?

7. How is our academic unit perceived on campus by the faculty and by the administration? Are we considered intellectual leaders in communication and media studies and sense-makers of the communication/information age? Are we considered partners in the liberal arts? Do we consider it important to be considered campus leaders in communication, media studies and/or the liberal arts? If not, what academic units on campus are providing these functions?

8. Assuming we are always in the process of developing and fine-tuning our mission does our mission statement:

    a. contain a formulation of our goals and objectives that enables progress toward them to be measured?

    b. differentiate our program from other programs at the university and possibly other universities?

    c. define the "business" we want to be in?

    d. allow us to be establish priorities that are relevant to our stakeholders?

    e. describe how we plan to serve our stakeholders?

    f. excite and inspire, especially, faculty and students?

    g. reflect the educational philosophy of our program?

9. If we weren't preparing students for entry level jobs, would we still have a justification for existing?

10. What is the relationship we should foster with practitioners?

APPENDIX B: MISSION STATEMENTS LINKAGE
TO THE ASSESSMENT PLAN

1. Identify mission and purposes

a. Mission of school.

b. Mission of program.

c. Mission of journalism and mass communications.

d. Mission of education in journalism and mass communications.

e. Confirm core values, competencies, and knowledge.

f. Link specific values, competencies, and knowledge to outcomes.

g. Link curriculum to outcomes.

h. Link courses to curriculum to outcomes (outcome statement on each syllabus).

i. Within courses, link specific course units, exercises, and experiences to outcomes.

   1. Awareness (Knowledge): Lowest-level category, involves the remembering or recall of specifics. Key words: To define, recall, recognize. Sample test plan: Define "media censorship."

   2. Understanding (Comprehension): A low level of understanding, including acts of translating, interpreting, and extrapolation. Ideas are not related to one another. Key words: To translate, transform, state in one's own words. Sample test plan: Can properly interpret the use of three-point lighting.

   3. Application (Application): The use of abstraction to perform in a new situation. Key words: To generalize, relate, organize, classify. Sample test plan: Can use the criteria of the "Central Hudson Gas & Electric" case to support the banning of alcohol advertising.

   4. Analysis: Breaking down the elements of a situation and clarifying the rankings or relations among the elements. Key words: To distinguish, detect, discriminate, contrast. Sample test plan: Can identify differing motives of producers, advertisers, citizen groups, and audiences in the production of media texts.

   5. Synthesis: Combining elements to constitute a new pattern or structure. Key words: To produce, modify, restructure, originate, derive. Sample test plan: Can develop a 1-min news report explaining the constitutional grounds for a recent Supreme Court decision (adapted from Whitney, 1970, p. 3, and Erwin, 1991, pp. 39–40).

2. Determine best method to assess outcomes.

a. Direct methods: Entry-level testing, sectional and departmental exams, capstone courses, portfolio assessment.

b. Indirect methods: Grade distribution, student retention and graduation, probation and dismissal, internships and placement, student performance in local, regional, and national contests, student surveys and exit interviews, and alumni surveys (ACEJMC, 2004).

3. Results need to provide feedback into the system and be continuous.

DEVELOPING STUDENT LEARNING OUTCOMES

Law and Policy

Jennifer Henderson
Department of Communication
Trinity University

On December 13, 1906, the Board of Curators of the University of Missouri voted the first School of Journalism into existence. Along with courses in news writing and layout, a course in newspaper jurisprudence was one of the first required courses added to the curriculum. This course dealt primarily with libel law and federal mail regulations (Norton, 1999). Since that time, the field of journalism and mass communication has expanded exponentially, and the legal and regulatory knowledge needed to survive in a career in communication has grown along with it. For example, in 1906, the United States Supreme Court had ruled on only a handful of cases involving media-related issues. Today, the Supreme Court has ruled on almost 400 cases involving speech, press, and media ownership. To fully understand the complexities of media law and policy today, students need to acquire knowledge regarding more than 20 distinct legal issues (see Table 4.1) and at least 10 distinct skills that accompany this knowledge (see Table 4.2).

ACCREDITATION AND ASSESSMENT

The Accrediting Council on Education in Journalism and Mass Communication (ACEJMC) passed Principles of Accreditations that set forth as one of its professional values and competencies the goal that all graduates in those programs seeking Association for Education in Journalism and Mass Communication (AEJMC) accreditation should "understand and apply the principles and laws of freedom of speech and press, including the right to dissent, to monitor and criticize power, and to assemble and petition for redress of grievances" (ACEJMC, 2005). This is a very broad mandate considering the quantity and diversity of knowledge needed to "understand and apply" all legal issues as journalism and mass communication is clearly not a field with one, but rather many and varied "professional practices."

Even beyond the 104 AEJMC accredited programs in the United States, many additional journalism and mass communication departments are also struggling to meet regional and university-wide assessment plans for accreditation. For example, Towson University in Maryland explained that one of the fundamental reasons it engages in assessment is that universities "are required to do so in order to stay accredited. The U.S. Department of Education, the Middle States Commission on Higher Education, and the Maryland Higher Education Commission all require that we engage in systematic, ongoing assessment" (Suskie, 2002). As part of its assessment plan, Towson requires the establishment of "clear, measurable expected outcomes of student learning," the systematic "gathering, analyzing, and interpreting" of evidence, and the use of "resulting information to understand and improve student learning" (Towson University, 2004).

Meeting all of these accreditation requirements, from federal and state governments, universities, regional educational commissions, and academic associations, is a daunting task to most faculty members who are also juggling teaching, advising, service, and a research agenda. In fact, selecting what knowledge, skills, and assessment tools would best meet these criteria is a time-consuming and arduous task most faculty in the field have put off in lieu of other obligations. Unfortunately, as the deadlines for formal assessment plans by accrediting bodies draws nearer, it is time to begin the difficult work of assessment.

In the area of media law and policy, the task of establishing criteria for learning and tools to assess that learning most often falls to the one faculty member in a journalism and mass communication program charged with teaching law-related courses. These faculty members have multiple choices for instruction, texts, and complementary materials. The combination of these is both endless and overwhelming. For example, currently, there are almost a dozen textbooks published in the areas of mass media or First Amendment law. These textbooks either target communication students (see, e.g., Carter, Franklin, & Wright, 2001; Pember & Calvert, 2005; Teeter & Loving, 2001), providing a broad overview of the law on a large number of topics, or a law school population where Constitutional and First Amendment law is a requirement (see, e.g., Van Alstyne, 2002). In addition to textbooks for class use, there are also academic books that focus on one area of media law and policy such as libel (Amponsah, 2004; Bezanson, Cranberg, & Soloski, 1987), advertising, and public relations (Moore, Farrar, & Collins, 1998), or new media (Hiller & Cohen, 2002). Another 20 texts address telecommunication policy and media regulation (see, e.g., Black, 2001), but only a handful target college-age students in educational settings. Each of these choices emphasizes different legal and regulatory issues and offers different approaches to the teaching, learning, and assessment of media law and policy coursework. So, how do faculty members charged with this task begin to identify and combine the knowledge and resources needed to meet the requirements of accrediting organizations?

Whatever issues and text faculty select as the core of their media law and policy course, these will not be enough to meet the expectation of accreditation and assessment required by most universities or the ACEJMC. To be realistic, a single faculty member cannot possibly address all legal and regulatory issues a student needs on graduation in one semester- or quarter-long course. It will take an entire journalism and mass communication department faculty or more likely, a university faculty, to introduce students to the concepts needed to "understand and apply the principles and laws of freedom of speech and press" (ACEJMC, 2005).

GETTING STARTED

The Knowledge Matrix

One of the first steps in assessment of mass media law and policy coursework is the identification of key concepts, laws, and cases students need to know on graduation to (a) work in the "real world" as communication professionals, or (b) become engaged citizens. These factors emphasize knowledge needed by media professionals in workplace situations. They do not overlook, however, media literacy as a liberal arts component, helpful for all U.S. citizens.

The first matrix (Table 4.1) highlights the key points of knowledge that can be used to "understand ... the principles and laws of freedom of speech and press" (ACEJMC, 2005). Please keep in mind there is currently no canon of legal decisions or academic works identified by media law and policy scholars as essential to understanding the field. Both textbooks and syllabi in the field of media law and policy, however, reveal common points of understanding that can be described, identified through key concepts and laws, and tied to landmark legal decisions. Although media law and policy scholars will and should debate which key concepts and cases ought to be included in such a Knowledge Matrix, the knowledge points and accompanying concepts and cases provide a broad outline for beginning this discussion across programs in the field.

The Knowledge Matrix included in Table 4.1 separates out knowledge points that may be combined during classroom teaching. They reflect the most commonly taught media law and policy issues. This matrix is offered as a guide for the inclusion of important points, concepts, laws, and cases, not as an outline for a course syllabus. The author does not mean to imply that every concept or case relating to each of these knowledge points has been included or that the concepts and cases included are those essential to fulfilling the ACEJMC requirements. Rather, the matrices included here provide the first outline of key concepts and cases that can be used for assessment purposes. The matrices, then, are a jumping off point for future discussion of assessment in the areas of media law and policy.

The second matrix (Table 4.2) identifies skills needed to apply the "principles of freedom of speech and press," as required by ACEJMC as well as other accrediting organizations. As Christ (1997) explained, "All successful courses teach skills" (p. 4). The skill component in media law and policy courses, however, may not be the kind we immediately think of when we think of media education. For example, a skill such as video production clearly will not be addressed in media law and policy courses. Critical thinking skills and writing skills, however, are essential to teaching and assessing coursework in this area of communication.

Although these broad knowledge and skill points, and specific concepts, laws, and cases, form a foundation for a successful course in media law and policy, many may be addressed in courses outside of the mass media law and policy class. For example, material regarding the history of the First Amendment may be taught in a course on media history, American history, or American government; Federal Trade Commission regulation material may be found in advertising, marketing, and other business courses; and, libel may be addressed in newspaper, magazine, broadcast, or new media writing and management courses. Skills such as writing a legal brief may be acquired in a Constitutional Law course in the Political Science Department, composing summaries of federal regulations may be learned in a Business Law course, and critical thinking skills related to law may be taught in ethics courses in the Philosophy Department.

To best ensure that each of these knowledge points and skills competencies are being addressed over the course of a student's undergraduate career, communication departments can develop a checklist of knowledge points and skills competencies (using the two matrices in Table 4.1 and Table 4.2 as a guide). The checklist should be presented to all departmental faculty members at the end of each school year. Each faculty member would then write in the course name of any course he or she is teaching that covers one of these knowledge points or skills competencies. A complementary student checklist could be developed to present to graduating seniors during the final semester of their academic career. On this checklist, students would write in the names of courses where they believed they acquired the knowledge points or skills competencies both inside and outside journalism or mass communication departments. This kind of assessment at the departmental level highlights specific knowledge points and skills competencies that may have been missed. By combining the faculty and student checklists, the department can see gaps in the matrix and work to correct them. So, for example, if a department's faculty agree to include 20 knowledge points and 5 skill competencies on their checklist for the media law and policy course, the compilation of the two checklist surveys at the end of the school year would reveal if 15 of the 20 knowledge points were taught or all 5 of the skills competencies were learned.

ASSESSING KNOWLEDGE

Formal Assessment Tools for Knowledge Points in Media Law and Policy Courses

Exams and Quizzes. Traditional formal assessment tools generate useful information for both students and teachers as to which knowledge points students have acquired and which remain elusive. Quality exams ask students to identify and define key concepts or laws, such as "consent agreement" or the "Children's Online Privacy Protection Act," explain legal tests such as the "Commercial Speech Doctrine" or "Miller Test," and apply all of this knowledge to theoretical problems such as ones that place students in decision-making positions: for example, "You are the editor of a daily newspaper . . ."

In September of 2000, ACEJMC agreed on three criteria—awareness, understanding, and application—that should guide assessment of student learning in mass communication programs. Borrowing from Bloom's (1956) *Taxonomy of Educational Objectives,* these three criteria represent the "knowledge" (awareness), "comprehension" (understanding), and "application" (application) elements of Bloom's cognitive domain. Including all of these three elements—awareness, understanding, and application—can be difficult to achieve on one exam, but not impossible. Following are examples of how to integrate these three aspects of assessment in media law and policy courses using the Knowledge and Skills matrices in Table 4.1 and Table 4.2.

- Definitions—To assess both awareness and understanding of key concepts, exams and quizzes should contain a "definition" or "key terms" section. In this section, students would be required to provide a definition for key concepts presented by the instructor. Using the Knowledge Matrix as a guide, faculty could choose from among the key concepts to create this section of an exam or quiz. For example, when covering material about the U.S. Court System, an instructor could simply include the words *en banc, petitioner,* or *per curiam opinion.* The student would then show awareness and understanding by providing a short, one- or two-sentence description of the term.
- Short Answer Questions—Another excellent way of assessing both awareness and understanding of media law and policy concepts is the short answer question. A well thought-out short answer question often includes the phrase, "describe," rather than "what." For example, when addressing libel issues, faculty might ask the following: "In which jurisdiction may a libel plaintiff bring a court action? Describe two libel cases where jurisdiction was at issue." By including a "describe" component as well as reference to key cases, faculty can assess a student's awareness and understanding of both key concepts and key cases in one area of law or policy. When short answer questions are limited to "what" questions, such as "What are the key elements of the *Miller* Test?" a student's awareness but not understanding is tested.
- Essay Questions—Long answer questions, in the form of an essay or other written work, are often good for comparison of key concepts or cases. These kinds of questions allow faculty to assess awareness, knowledge, and application. For example, an essay question regarding commercial speech might be as follows: "Compare and contrast the Supreme Court decisions in *Valentine v. Chrestensen* (1942), *New York Times v. Sullivan* (1964), *Bigelow v. Virginia* (1975), and *Virginia State Board of Pharmacy v. Virginia Citizens Council* (1976)."
- Simulation Questions—Abridged versions of role-playing scenarios (discussed later) can be included on exams and quizzes. These types of questions, which place students in the role of a decision maker facing real-world law or policy decisions, are a strong tool for assessing the application of knowledge and skills in media law and policy courses. For example, questions such as the following can be used:

> You are an investigator at the FTC. A case has come to your attention that involves a new pasta product that claims it is, "wholly organic"

and contains "no carbs." What criteria would you employ to determine if this claim is false, deceptive, or misleading? Would you fine this product's producer? Why or why not?

• Case Problems—Described in detail later, case problems are an excellent way to combine the three elements of learning set forth by ACEJMC. For exams, case problems should be (a) limited to knowledge students were required to learn for an exam (not include additional research), (b) limited in scope (only address one aspect of a knowledge point, for example, appropriation, rather than all privacy torts), and (c) limited in number of questions (due to time constraints).

As with all assessment tools, two key components of these tools that must not be forgotten are grading and feedback. To be effective as assessment tools, Schafer (1991) concluded that results must be clear to the student as well as the professor. If students are not given the opportunity to discuss the answer or the grading of exams with faculty, Schafer (1991) explained that the assessment has not fulfilled the goals it was designed to achieve. Time must be set aside after exams are returned to answer student questions regarding unlearned or mislearned information on the tests.

Case Problems. The case problem asks students to use all of the elements of learning—awareness, understanding, and application—to address complex situations. Case problems also assess key concepts, cases, and skill acquisitions outlined in the Knowledge and Skill matrices.

The effectiveness of teaching using the case method, engaging in the text (Boehrer & Linsky, 1990) by using the "story of a problem" to explain complex ideas (Seeger, 1994, p. x), is well documented, especially in law courses (Merseth, 1991). Barnes, Christensen, and Hansen (1994) explained that the case method "puts students in an active learning mode," and "gives them first-hand appreciation of, and experience with, the application of knowledge to practice" (pp. 3–4).

Case problems are an extension of the case method, borrowing its basic tenets and applying them as assessment tools. Case problems require students to apply decisions from a series of past legal cases to a new scenario. Each case problem is made up of a fictional legal situation followed by two or three specific questions, directing a student to identify and then apply a key legal test. In effect, students in this situation are asked to act as a judge, weighing past precedent to determine the outcome of the current case.

Answers to case problems are not simple. Often students think through their reasoning on paper, and rather than presenting a coherent

argument supported by examples from past cases, they produce an of-
ten-lengthy and sometimes incoherent short essay. As Wasserman
(1994) explained, the case method, and for our purposes the case problem, is "far from linear." It "folds over upon itself, backs up," and "re-
turns to retrace steps" (p. 84). It is in this nonlinear process of sorting
through legal decisions, weighing their relative importance, and applying them to a new situation that learning—especially learning about the
difficulty of legal decision making—is taking place.

It is important to note that most students will not do well on the first
assigned case problem (and may not on the second or third), and several should be assigned over the course of a semester. Most college students have not been taught how to synthesize information in this way,
drawing from the past and predicting the outcome of the future. Of the
three elements of Bloom's (1956) *Taxonomy of Educational Objectives*,
application is clearly the most difficult for students to master.

Case problems, despite their difficulty for both students and faculty,
are an excellent assessment tool for media law and policy courses. By
reviewing student response to these scenarios, faculty can easily see
which case material was presented clearly to students and which material was confusing and needs further clarification. This, in turn, provides
an excellent opportunity to reiterate key points that may have been lost
in the rush of learning.

Two informal applications of the case method that can also be used
as assessment tools are: "Guilty or Not Guilty?" and "Is This?" scenario
problems. Rick Peltz, Associate Professor of Law at the University of Ar-
kansas, Little Rock, uses "Guilty or Not Guilty?" scenario problems to assess student learning on the issue of plagiarism. In each problem, Peltz
presents a short scenario and then the question, "Guilty or Not Guilty?"
For example, one scenario regarding missing attribution and plagiarism
reads:

> A law review note contains three major ideas taken from a non-
> identified Internet source. The student insists that the material is pub-
> lic knowledge and does not have to be attributed. Guilty or Not Guilty?

Getting the answer "right" is not the essential factor with this tool. The
"why" question following each short scenario is even more important.
The "why" tells an instructor that the student understands the concepts
relayed, rather than simply offering an educated guess as to the outcome of the problem.

Along with each brief "Guilty or Not Guilty" scenario, Peltz has also
created a complementary response guide for faculty. The guide reminds

faculty of the key issues involved in each scenario as well as offers suggestions on how to respond to the "why" portion of the scenario. This "answer key" turns assessment back into learning, and is an essential component of these kinds of scenario problems.

The "Is This?" scenario problems also borrow from traditional case method teaching. In applying this method to classroom exercises, the faculty briefly describes a real-world scenario. Then, immediately following the explanation, asks, "Is This?" For example, when discussing false and deceptive advertising situations, the faculty member would read a short scenario such as the following: "NordicTrack, Inc. claimed in an hour-long infomercial that people who used its ski exerciser could lose 'eighteen pounds in twelve weeks.'" Then the faculty member would ask the following: "Is this false or deceptive advertising? Why or why not?" This approach also works well in assessing knowledge of other key legal issues such as copyright law, with the question changed to the following: "Is this copyright infringement or fair use?" Or, the "Is This?" scenario problem could be applied to the issue of candidate access to broadcast time: "Is this station required to offer time to the candidate? Why or why not?"

Role Playing. Van Ments (1989) has described role playing as a "particular type of simulation that focuses attention on the interaction of people with one another. It emphasizes the functions performed by different people under various circumstances" (p. 186). This assessment tool is widely believed to be a way for students to become actively engaged in classroom learning (Blatner, 2002) and has been used effectively in business (Cage, 1997), science (Francis & Byrne, 1999), and social science courses (Bair, 2000). More importantly, it is an excellent match for media law and policy issues. The process of legal decision making is structured in such a way as to provide instant "roles." For example, students could serve as lawyers, defendants, or petitioners, witnesses or experts, in a libel trial. The trial could take place over the course of 2 or more days with one dedicated to a summary judgment— an essential component of real-world libel cases as such a small percentage of these cases actually make it to trial.

Role playing can also be used effectively to show how government regulation or oversight works in practice rather than theory. For example, students could role-play public hearings on the adoption of new Federal Communications Commission ownership rules, with each student or student group representing a specific interest, nonprofit organization, or corporation.

Although it is often a difficult task, faculty should develop roles for all students in a role-playing situation, or if the class is large, schedule multiple role-playing situations so every student is guaranteed participation, and subsequently, assessment of knowledge and skills.

Although faculty often use role-playing situations as a game—a welcome break from lecture—in reality, good role-playing scenarios take significant preparation on the part of faculty as well as a significant contribution by students. Role playing requires students to both understand and be able to verbally express their understanding of key legal issues or policy procedures.

Role playing is one of the most useful teaching and formative assessment tools available for faculty. Assessments of role playing can be either formal or informal, formative or summative. For example, faculty may (a) comment on or correct incorrect procedures or understandings as the scenario progresses, (b) stop the role playing at key points to ask questions or underscore important elements, or (c) grade each student following the role-playing scenario on a series of criteria such as understanding of legal principles, use of facts, or expression of ideas.

Informal Assessment Tools for Knowledge Points in Media Law and Policy Courses

The best media law and policy courses combine both formative and summative assessment. Formative assessment in media law and policy courses may come from both informal and formal measures. Angelo and Cross (1993) suggested that planned informal assessment such as "The Muddiest Point" (having students answer "what was the muddiest point in my lecture today?"), "The Minute Paper" (asking students to write for 1 min on "what was the most important" or "what questions remain" from the session's discussion), or "One Sentence Summary" (summarizing in one sentence what today's lecture was all about), is an excellent way for faculty, especially new faculty, to put their fingers on the pulse of student learning in the classroom. These tools can easily be adapted to media law and policy courses. For example, The Minute Paper could be transformed into "A Minute of Law," a summary of the cases and outcomes from the day's discussion. If the day's lecture revolved around The First Amendment and Public Education, then a "Minute of Law" could include a brief description of *Tinker v. Des Moines Independent School District* (students wore black arm bands to school protesting the war in Vietnam; the U.S. Supreme Court said it was protected speech), *Hazelwood v. Kuhlmeier* (articles on pregnancy and divorce in a high school newspaper were censored by school officials; the U.S. Supreme Court said censorship was acceptable when pedagogical or discipline involved), *Frasier v. Bethel School District* (a student gave a speech in support of a classmate and was suspended from school; the suspension was upheld by the U.S. Supreme Court), and all other cases covered by the instructor during that class period.

Similarly, the One Sentence Summary could be converted to the "Legal Test Summary," asking students to write down the applicable legal test for the subject of the day (e.g., Question: What five elements do courts consider in libel cases? Answer: Identification, Publication, Defamation, Falsity, Fault). As in the use of all assessment tools, especially informal, formative tools, faculty should leave time not just for the answering of the question, but either during that class period or the next, devote time to the clarification of points misunderstood by members of the class.

The quantity and quality of learning may also be revealed to an observant professor in the daily interactions of students. For example, discussions among students or questions from students may reveal confusion regarding topics or anxiety about upcoming exams. These are important assessment measures that would not appear in planned informal or even formal evaluations. This "observant" assessment is only useful, however, when teachers (a) document the specific concerns and confusion, and (b) engage to clear up the uncertainty or anxiety. These informal, formative assessment tools, by their nature of being unobtrusive in classroom learning, are often accurate reflections of student understanding throughout the academic term.

They can also be startling. Faculty should be prepared for confusion and misunderstandings, even when they believe they have prepared a lecture worthy of a Nobel laureate. As Gerald J. Baldasty of the University of Washington reminded teaching assistants in a TA training session, September 24, 1999, "Don't ask if you don't want to know." Of course, he was not encouraging educators to avoid informal assessment, just to be prepared for what may arise from it.

ASSESSING SKILLS

Tools for Assessing Skills in Media Law and Policy Courses

Legal Briefs and Statute Summaries. Many teaching and assessments tools employed in media law and policy courses are borrowed from law school instruction. The most commonly used cross-over assignment is the legal brief. The legal brief assignment requires students to formally summarize a case opinion. It includes such elements as the citation of the case, the primary facts of the case, the majority opinion of the court, any dissents to the majority opinion, and the reasoning behind the majority, concurring, or dissenting opinions. A traditional legal brief assignment presented in a law school classroom can easily be modified to introduce media law students to the anatomy of case law.

Similar to the legal brief, the statute summary asks students to read complex statutory law or regulations and then summarize the key points in a brief paragraph, page, or essay. Both the legal brief and statute summary exercises (a) help students understand that material discussed in classes is often a very short summary of the legal issues or regulations challenged, and (b) assess two important student skills outlined in the Skills Matrix (Table 4.2): synthesis and expression of key legal documents.

Debates. Many media law and policy faculty employ topical debates to assess student understanding and application. Debates are an excellent assessment tool to employ when faculty are attempting to explain the complexities of controversial issues. For example, a debate structured around the topics of hate speech or flag burning, or prior restraint during wartime, allows students to explore the nuances in complex legal situations.

Debates can be planned as a discussion between individuals or teams. Harwood, McKinster, Cruz, and Gabel (2002) recommended that a debate problem "be one that can be viewed from at least four different perspectives" (p. 442). Debates can be highly regulated, with time allotments set forth for each speaker, or free form, with sides rebutting points as they are made. No matter what the rules of the debate, the essential elements are the same. All students should be required to (a) conduct research supporting their position prior to the debate; (b) apply knowledge from classroom learning; (c) articulate the law, legal decision making, and their positions in front of others; (d) publicly defend their positions; and (e) refute other's positions. In essence, the role-playing tool could be designed to assess seven of the eight skill competencies: finding legal cases from citations, reading legal decisions, reading government statutes or regulations, applying past precedent to cases, articulation of key legal concepts and decisions, critical thinking, and the synthesis of information.

Both debates and role-playing exercises are forms of performance tests often used in the speech communication field. According to Stiggins and Bridgeford (1984), with performance tests, students are asked to apply knowledge they have previously learned, complete a preset task according to criteria set forth for the task, that is observable, and rated by a qualified judge (in this case, the faculty member). These kinds of performance tests are excellent indicators of skills acquisition, especially the kinds of skills needed for professionals in mass communication or law. It is important to acknowledge here that some percentage of students in media law and policy courses (varying widely by course and institution) will pursue a career in law rather than journalism or other mass communication professions. The skills described in Table 4.2 can be applied equally to any of these professions.

SUMMARY

Assessing media law and policy coursework is a new undertaking for most journalism and mass communication departments. Until this time, no systematic approach of identifying the knowledge and skills needed by students in these departments has been developed for media law and policy curricula. The knowledge points, skill competencies, and tools for assessment related to free speech and press set forth in this chapter provide a baseline for discussion among faculty for what students should know or show on graduation and how best to measure that knowledge and those skills in the academic areas of media law and policy. The decision for including or excluding knowledge points or skills competencies from the curriculum in media law and policy should not fall on the shoulders of one faculty member as does much of the teaching in this area at many universities. It is imperative that all colleagues in a department are committed to teaching "the principles and laws of freedom of speech and press, including the right to dissent, to monitor and criticize power, and to assemble and petition for redress of grievances" as set forth in the ACEJMC (2005) accreditation standards, and that those beyond the department are convinced of its importance.

Faculty and administrators at the University of Missouri in 1906 understood the importance of law in the basic education of journalism professionals. That kind of foresight is even more important in a time of dramatically increased litigation and government regulation. Knowledgeable and skilled media professionals, and more importantly, students able to contribute successfully to democratic decision making, should be the overarching goal of journalism and mass communication departments. Media law and policy coursework is an integral component of that goal that cannot be overlooked.

REFERENCES

The Accrediting Council on Education in Journalism and Mass Communication. (2005). "ACEJMC Accrediting Standards." Retrieved March 15, 2005, from http://www.ku.edu/~acejmc/PROGRAMS/STANDARDS.SHTML#std2

Amponsah, P. N. (2004). *Libel law, political criticism and defamation of public figures.* New York: LFB Scholarly Publishing.

Angelo, T., & Cross, K. P. (1993). *Classroom assessment techniques* (2nd ed.). San Francisco: Jossey-Bass.

Bair, S. (2000). Developing analytical and communication skills in a mock-trial course based on the famous Woburn, Massachusetts case. *Journal of Geoscience Education, 48,* 450–454.

Barnes, L., Christensen, C. R., & Hansen, A. (1994). *Teaching and the case method: Text, cases, and readings* (3rd ed.). Boston: Harvard Business School Press.

Bezanson, R. P., Cranberg, G., & Soloski, J. (1987). *Libel law and the press: Myth and reality.* New York: Simon & Schuster.

Black, S. K. (2001). *Telecommunication law in the internet age.* San Francisco: Morgan Kaufmann.

Blatner, A. (2002). *Role playing in education.* Retrieved June 29, 2004, from http://www.blatner.com/adam/pdntbk/rlplayedu.htm

Bloom, B. S. (Ed.). (1956). *Taxonomy of educational objectives: The classification of educational goals: Handbook I, cognitive domain.* New York: Longmans, Green.

Boehrer, J., & Linsky, M. (1990). Teaching with cases: Learning to question. In M. D. Svinicki (Ed.), *The face of college teaching. New directions for teaching and learning* (pp. 41–57). San Francisco: Jossey-Bass.

Carter, T. B., Franklin, M. A., & Wright, J. B. (2001). *The first amendment and the fourth estate: The law of mass media.* New York: Foundation Press.

Christ, W. G. (1997). Defining media education. In W. G. Christ (Ed.), *Media education assessment handbook* (pp. 3–21). Mahwah, NJ: Lawrence Erlbaum Associates, Inc.

Francis, P., & Byrne, A. (1999). The use of role-playing exercises in teaching undergraduate astronomy and science. *Publications of the Astronomical Society of Australia, 46,* 203–211.

Harwood, W., McKinster, J., Cruz, L., & Gabel, L. (2002). Acting out science: Using senate hearings to debate global climate change. *Journal of College Science Teaching, 31*(7), 442–447.

Hiller, J., & Cohen, R. (2002). *Internet law and policy.* New York: Pearson.

Merseth, K. (1991). The early history of case-based instruction: Insights for teacher education today. *Journal of Teacher Education, 42*(4), 243–249.

Moore, R., Farrar, R., & Collins, E. (1998). *Advertising and public relations law.* Mahwah, NJ: Lawrence Erlbaum Associates, Inc.

Norton, W. (1999). Journalism education has a rich heritage. *Journalism Alumni News, 9.* Retrieved June 9, 2004, from http://journalism.unl.edu/an/spring99/dean.html

Pember, D., & Calvert, C. (2005). *Mass media law* (2005/2006 ed.). New York: McGraw-Hill.

Seeger, J. A. (1994). Access: The case starts here. *Case Research Journal, 14,* x.

Schafer, W. (1991). Essential assessment skills in professional education of teachers. *Educational Measurement: Issues and Practice, 10*(1), 3–6.

Stiggins, R. J., & Bridgeford, N. (1984, April). *The nature, role and quality of performance assessment in the classroom.* Paper presented at the annual meeting of the American Educational Research Association, New Orleans, LA.

Suskie, L. (2002). *Why assess?* Retrieved April 30, 2004, from http://pages.towson.edu/assessment/why.htm

Teeter, D. L., Jr., & Loving, B. (2001). *Law of mass communications* (10th ed.). New York: Foundation Press.

Towson University. (2004). *Towson University guiding principles for the assessment of student learning.* Retrieved April 30, 2004, from http://pages.towson.edu/assessment

Van Alstyne, W. W. V. (2002). *The American First Amendment in the twenty-first century.* New York: Foundation Press.

Van Ments, M. (1989). *The effective use of role play: A handbook for teachers & trainers.* New York: Nichols.

Wasserman, S. (1994). *Introduction to case method teaching: A guide to the galaxy.* New York: Teachers College Press.

TABLE 4.1
The Knowledge Matrix

Knowledge Point	Key Concepts	Course	Assessment Tool	✓	Key Laws and Cases[a]	Course	Assessment Tool	✓
History of the First Amendment	Why we have a Bill of Rights Who supported or opposed the Bill of Rights Original Intent Clauses of the First Amendment Fourteenth Amendment Marketplace of Ideas				Gitlow v. New York (1925)			
Sources of the Law	Administrative Law Common Law Constitutional Law Equity Law Statutory Law							
The U.S. Court System	Federal Courts District Courts Appellate Courts 11 Circuit Courts DC Circuit Federal Circuit Supreme Court State Courts Trial Courts Appellate Courts							

Knowledge Point	Key Concepts	Course	Assessment Tool	✓	Key Laws and Cases[a]	Course	Assessment Tool	✓
	Appeal Process							
	Direct Appeal							
	Writ of Certiorari							
	Kinds of Lawsuits							
	Civil							
	Criminal							
	Litigants							
	Petitioner							
	Defendant							
	En Banc							
	De Novo							
	Jury							
	Demurrer							
	Verdict							
	Supreme Court Hearing							
	Legal Briefs							
	Oral Arguments							
	Amicus Curiae Brief							
	Supreme Court Opinions							
	Majority Opinion							
	Dissenting Opinion							
	Per Curiam Opinion							
	Memorandum Order							
	Quash							
	Dictum							
	Vacate							

(Continued)

TABLE 4.1
(Continued)

Knowledge Point	Key Concepts	Course	Assessment Tool	✓	Key Laws and Cases[a]	Course	Assessment Tool	✓
First Amendment Theories	Absolutist Theory Preferred Position Balancing Theory Ad Hoc Balancing Theory Meiklejohnian Theory Access Theory							
Sedition	Zinger Trial Clear and Present Danger Test				Alien and Sedition Acts (1798) Espionage (1917) and Sedition (1918) Acts Scheneck v. U.S. (1919) Debs v. U.S. (1919) Whitney v. California (1927) The Smith Act (1940) Dennis v. U.S. (1951) Yates v. U.S. (1957) Brandenberg v. Ohio (1969) The Patriot Act (2001)			
Prior Restraint	When Censorship Can Occur: National Security Legally obscene				Near v. Minnesota (1931) Organization for a Better Austin v. Keefe (1971) The Pentagon Papers (1971) U.S. v. Progressive (1979) Snepp v. U.S. (1980) Ward v. Rock Against Racism (1989)			

Knowledge Point	Key Concepts	Course	Assessment Tool	✓	Key Laws and Cases[a]	Course	Assessment Tool	✓
Press Taxation					Grosjean v. American Press Co. (1931) Minneapolis Star v. Minnesota Commissioner of Revenue (1983) Arkansas Writer's Project v. Ragland (1987) Texas Monthly v. Bullock (1989) Leathers v. Medlock (1991)			
Time, Place, and Manner	Forum Analysis: Traditional Public Forums Designated Public Forums Public Property Not a Public Forum Private Forums Zoning Laws Litter Ordinances				Lovell v. Griffin (1938) Martin v. City of Struthers (1943) Cantwell v. Connecticut Amalgamated Food Employees Local 590 v. Logan Valley Plaza (1968) Lloyd Corporation v. Tanner (1972) Hudgens v. NLRB (1976) Pruneyard Shopping Center v. Robins (1980) Lakewood v. Plain Dealer Publishing Co. (1988) Forsyth County v. The Nationalist Movement (1992) Cincinnati v. Discovery Network (1993) Watchtower Bible and Tract Society v. Stratton (2002)			

TABLE 4.1
(Continued)

Knowledge Point	Key Concepts	Course	Assessment Tool	✓	Key Laws and Cases[a]	Course	Assessment Tool	✓
First Amendment and Public Schools	The *Hazelwood* Test				*Tinker v. Des Moines* (1969) *Hazelwood v. Kuhlmeier* (1988) *Frasier v. Bethel School District* (1986) *Kincaid v. Gibson* (3rd Cir. 2001) *Hosty v. Carter* (2003)			
Symbolic Speech					*U.S. v. O'Brien* (1968) *Cohen v. California* (1971) *Texas v. Johnson* (1989)			
Hate Speech	Fighting Words Doctrine Incitement Speech v. Action				*Chaplinsky v. New Hampshire* (1942) *Village of Skokie v. National Socialist Party* (1978) *Planned Parenthood v. American Coalition of Life Activists* (9th Cir. 2001) *R.A.V. v. St. Paul* (1992) *Virginia v. Black* (2003)			
First Amendment and Elections					*Buckley v. Valeo* (1976) *Bipartisan Campaign Reform Act* (2003) *McConnell v. FEC* (2003)			

Knowledge Point	Key Concepts	Course	Assessment Tool	✓	Key Laws and Cases[a]	Course	Assessment Tool	✓
Libel	Defamation				New York Times v. Sullivan (1964)			
	Elements of Libel				Gertz v. Welch (1974)			
	Publication				Time, Inc. v. Firestone (1976)			
	Republication				Keeton v. Hustler (1984)			
	Identification				Calder v. Jones (1984)			
	Defamation				Hutchinson v. Proxmire (1979)			
	Per Se				Wolston v. Reader's Digest (1979)			
	Per Quod				Keeton v. Hustler (1984)			
	Falsity							
	Fault							
	Plaintiffs							
	Public Officials							
	All-Purpose Public Figures							
	Limited Purpose Public Figures							
	Private Persons							
	Actual Malice							
	Negligence							
	Summary Judgment							
	Statute of Limitations							
	Jurisdiction							
	Venue Shopping							
	Defenses							
	Truth							
	Privilege							
	Absolute							
	Qualified							

(Continued)

TABLE 4.1
(Continued)

Knowledge Point	Key Concepts	Course	Assessment Tool	✓	Key Laws and Cases[a]	Course	Assessment Tool	✓
	Opinion Rhetorical Hyperbole *Milkovich* Standard The *Ollman* Test Fair Comment and Criticism Consent Right of Reply Neutral Reportage Damages Actual Damages Special Damages Presumed Damages Punitive Damages Retraction Statutes Criminal Libel							
Intentional Infliction of Emotional Distress					*Hustler v. Falwell* (1988)			
Privacy	Appropriation Right of Publicity Right to Privacy Intrusion False Light Fictionalization Distortion Publication of Private Matters				*Sidis v. F-R Publishing Corp* (1940) *Barber v. Time* (1942) *Booth v. Curtis Publishing Co.* (1962) *Time v. Hill* (1967) *Cantrell v. Forest City Publishing Co.* (1974)			

Knowledge Point	Key Concepts	Course	Assessment Tool	✓	Key Laws and Cases[a]	Course	Assessment Tool	✓
	The *Booth* Rule Rape Victims and Privacy Descendibility Consent Privacy Over Time				*Cox Broadcasting v. Cohen* (1975) *Virgil v. Time* (1975) *Zacchini v. Scripps-Howard Broadcasting* (1977) *Howard v. Des Moines Register* (Iowa 1979) *Sipple v. Chronicle Publishing Co.* (1984) *Duncan v. WJLA-TV* (D.D.C., 1984) Electronic Communication Privacy Act (1986) *Middler v. Ford Motor Co.* (9th Cir. 1988) *The Florida Star v. BJF* (1989) *White v. Samsung Electronics* (9th Cir. 1992) Children's Online Privacy Protection Act (1998) The Patriot Act (2001)			
Obscenity	Bad Tendency Test The Hicklin Rule The *Roth-Memoirs* Test Variable Obscenity The *Miller* Test				Comstock Act of 1873 *Roth v. U.S.* (1957) *Memoirs of a Woman of Pleasure v. Massachusetts* (1966)			

(Continued)

TABLE 4.1
(Continued)

Knowledge Point	Key Concepts	Course	Assessment Tool	✓	Key Laws and Cases[a]	Course	Assessment Tool	✓
	Zoning Regulation Test Internet Jurisdiction Child Pornography Children's Access to Indecent Materials Scientier				Ginsberg v. New York (1968) Stanley v. Georgia (1969) Miller v. California (1973) Erznoznik v. City of Jacksonville (1975) City of Renton v. Playtime Theaters, Inc. (1986) U.S. v. Thomas (6th Cir. 1996) Reno v. ACLU (1997) Mainstream Loudoun v. Board of Trustees of the Loudoun County Library (1998)[a] Child Online Protection Act (1998) Children's Internet Protection Act (2001) U.S. v. American Library Association (2003)			
Newsgathering	Trespass Harassment Fraud Misrepresentation Failure to Obey Lawful Orders Freedom of Information Act Nine Exemptions Sunshine Laws				Dietemann v. Time, Inc. (2nd Cir. 1971) Branzburg v. Hayes (1972) Pell v. Procunier (1974) Saxbe v. Washington Post (1974) Houchins v. KQED (1978) Cassidy v. ABC (1978)[a]			

Knowledge Point	Key Concepts	Course	Assessment Tool	✓	Key Laws and Cases[a]	Course	Assessment Tool	✓
					Richmond Newspapers v. Virginia (1980) *Ayeni v. CBS, Inc.* (E.D.N.Y. 1994) *Desnick v. Capital Cities/ABC, Inc.* (3rd Cir. 1995) *Wolfson v. Lewis* (E.D.Pa 1996) *Veilleux v. NBC* (D.Me. 1998) *Food Lion v. Capital Cities/ABC, Inc.* (4th Cir. 1999) *Wilson v. Layne* (1999) *Hanlon v. Berger* (1999) *Bartniki v. Vopper* (2001)			
Protecting News Sources					*Cohen v. Cowles Media Co.* (1991)			
Free Press and Fair Trial	*Nebraska Press Association Test* The *Press-Enterprise* Test Bench-Bar-Press Guidelines Voir Dire Change of Venue Change of Veniremen Continuance Admonition to the Jury Sequestration of the Jury Restrictive Orders				*Nebraska Press Association v. Stuart* (1976) *Landmark Communications v. Virginia* (1976) *Smith v. Daily Mail Publishing Co.* (1979) *Press-Enterprise v. Riverside Superior Court* (1980) *Richmond Newspapers v. Virginia* (1980) *Chandler v. Florida* (1981) *U.S. v. CNN* (S.D.Fla. 1994)			

(Continued)

TABLE 4.1
(Continued)

Knowledge Point	Key Concepts	Course	Assessment Tool	✓	Key Laws and Cases[a]	Course	Assessment Tool	✓
Immaterial Property Law	Plagiarism Patents Trademarks							
Copyright	Six Rights of Copyright Reproduction Derivative Works Distribution Performance Display Digital Performance Fair Use Test Sweat of the Brow Doctrine Misappropriation Recording Industry Association of America Freelancing Rights All First Serial First N. American Serial Simultaneous One-Time				*AP v. INS* (1918) *Lipman v. Commonwealth* (2nd Cir. 1973) Copyright Act (1976) *Harper & Row Publishers v. Nation Enterprises* (1985) *Salinger v. Random House* (2nd Cir. 1987) *Feist v. Rural Telephone* (1991) *Basic Books v. Kinko's Graphics Corp.* (1991)[a] *Los Angeles News Service v. Tullo* (2nd Cir. 1992) *Campbell v. Acuff-Rose* (1994) *New York Times v. Tasini* (2001) Sonny Bono Copyright Extension Act (1998) Digital Millennium Copyright Act (2000) *Kane v. Comedy Partners* (S.D.N.Y. 2003)			

Knowledge Point	Key Concepts	Course	Assessment Tool	✓	Key Laws and Cases[a]	Course	Assessment Tool	✓
Commercial Speech	The Commercial Speech Doctrine Better Business Bureau National Advertising Division National Advertising Review Board (NARB)				Valentine v. Chrestensen (1942) New York Times v. Sullivan (1964) Bigelow v. Virginia (1975) Virginia State Board of Pharmacy v. Virginia Citizens Council (1976) Central Hudson v. Public Service Commission (1980) Posadas de Puerto Rico Association v. Tourism Co. (1986) Rubin v. Coors Brewing Co. (1995) Anheuser-Busch Inc. v. Schmoke (1996) 44 Liquormart, Inc. v. Rhode Island (1996) Food and Drug Administration Modernization Act of 1997 Greater New Orleans Broadcasting Association v. U.S. (1999) Lorillard Tobacco Co. v. Reilly (2001) Nike v. Kasky (2003)			

(Continued)

TABLE 4.1
(Continued)

Knowledge Point	Key Concepts	Course	Assessment Tool	✓	Key Laws and Cases[a]	Course	Assessment Tool	✓

FTC Regulations	FTC Definition of False or Deceptive Advertising
	Puffery
	FTC Approaches to Stopping False and Deceptive Advertising
	   Guides
	   Voluntary Compliance
	   Consent Agreement
	   Litigated Orders
	   Substantiation
	   Corrective Advertising
	   Injunctions
	   Trade Regulation Rules
	Kinds of Deceptive Advertising
	   Testimonials
	   Bait and Switch
					The Amended Lanham Act (1988)			

Knowledge Point	Key Concepts	Course	Assessment Tool	✓	Key Laws and Cases[a]	Course	Assessment Tool	✓
FCC Regulation	Spectrum Scarcity Licensing Multiple Ownership Rules Regulation History Fairness Doctrine Family Hour Political Access Rules Children's Programming Indecency FCC Sanctions Letter of Reprimand Cease and Desist Order Fines Short-Term Renewal Revocation of License				*FCC v. Pacifica Foundation* (1978) *Kennedy for President Committee v. FCC* (D.C. Cir. 1980) *FCC v. WNCN Listeners Guild* (1981) *League of Women Voters v. FCC* (D.C. Cir. 1984) Children's Television Act (1990) *Action for Children's Television v. FCC* (3rd Cir. 1995) Broadcast Indecency Enforcement Act of 2004			

Note. FTC = Federal Trade Commission; FCC = Federal Communications Commission.

[a]All cases listed are U.S. Supreme Court decisions unless otherwise noted.

TABLE 4.2
The Skills Matrix

Skill Competency	Course	Assessment Tool	✓
Finding Legal Cases from Citations			
Reading Legal Decisions			
Writing Legal Briefs			
Reading Government Statutes and Regulations			
Applying Past Precedent to Current Cases			
Articulation of Key Legal Concepts and Decisions			
Critical Thinking			
Synthesis of Information			

History

Penelope B. Summers
Department of Communication
Northern Kentucky University

We are in a great haste to construct a magnetic telegraph from Maine to Texas; but Maine and Texas, it may be, have nothing important to communicate.
—Henry David Thoreau, *Walden* (1954; cited in Merritt & McCombs, 2004, p. xv)

Unless bold actions are taken . . . journalism may lose its soul.
—Allen (2000, p. 1)

CHANGE AND ADAPTATION

Change and adaptation are hallmarks of American media history resulting from ongoing revisions in political, cultural, economic, behavioral, and technological environments of this country and of the world. Journalism has served both as impetus and as manifestation of change. History reflects those changes and contemporary practice drives them. To understand the profession and where it is going, one also must understand what its values have been in the past and what its values are now—what has changed and what endures.

Present values can be found by observing current practices and reviewing critiques in professional publications and documents. For example, the State of the News Media 2004 report (Project for Excellence in Journalism II, 2004) discusses current journalistic practices and criticisms from within the profession. Many of the issues mentioned in the report provide the historian with a number of points to consider in examining how the past brought the field to the present. In its overview, the report contends, ". . . journalism is in the midst of an epochal transformation, as momentous probably as the invention of the telegraph or television" (Project for Excellence in Journalism I, 2004, p. 1).

The report identifies eight major trends of concern in American media (Project for Excellence in Journalism I, 2004, pp. 2–3), but key in identifying current professional values is item number 4 on that list. "Journalistic standards now vary even inside a single news organization" (Project for Excellence in Journalism I, 2004, p. 3).

The Conclusion section of the 500-page report asserted the following: "To reverse the slide in audience and trust will probably take a major change in press behavior, one that will make the news more relevant and customizable and at the same time suggest to the public, as it did briefly after September 11, that the news industry is more concerned with the public good than Americans suspect" (Project for Excellence in Journalism I, 2004, Conclusion, p. 1).

In the throes of change, media, and journalism in particular, today are coming under inexorable fire both internally and externally. But understanding the changing role of media through history can enlighten these uncertain times. Consider, for example, the following modern concerns about professionalism in journalism.

Frank Edward Allen (2000), President and Executive Director of the Institutes for Journalism and Natural Resources, speaking at the National Press Club, said that the role of the press is in trouble because consolidation of news media ownership, tabloid habits of journalists, the shortening news deadline cycle, and an ensuing decline of news standards, are corrupting American journalism.

Media critics complain that the culture and the business of journalism have been debased and the pursuits of profit and recognition have distorted values and encouraged nonstop, ludicrous prattle. According to a supplement to the Project for Excellence report, shallowness in journalism worries journalists. "News people are not confident about the future of journalism. . . . Increasingly, journalists worry that the economics of journalism are eroding quality" (Kovach, Rosenstiel, & Mitchell, 2004, paragraphs 1–2). The authors further claimed that journalists believe a cherished principle of journalism is being violated—the independence of the newsroom about editorial decision making.

Couple these laments with recent practices such as the media mea culpa for using unreliable sources, local television news presentations of a public relations campaign piece as news, and the alleged deception of Walter Cronkite which lured him into doing a promotional piece as news. Mix in Jayson Blair and Jack Kelley, and the Federal Communications Commission's sometimes illusory and equivocal indecency standards following the Bono, Jackson, and Stern episodes. Add a dash of jingoism and bottom-line sensationalized pandering, and one has a recipe for loss of credibility.

What are the professional values among those who have practiced American journalism? The profession more clearly needs to delineate journalistic values to the public, especially in this time of change. That means educators, too, must delineate those principles in an historic context and ensure that students transfer such knowledge when they practice journalism.

Writing in the American Society of Newspaper Editors' (ASNE) *The American Editor* magazine, John Irby (Irby, 2000) pondered whether inferior journalism education contributes to the newspaper industry's deteriorating credibility, and whether universities and educators are preparing students to practice the craft of journalism.

Journalism educators, many of whom come from the profession, are as concerned as the public and current practitioners with deteriorating standards. However, journalism historians, in particular, know that much of the criticism is not new but is simply in the context of today's urgency. Journalism critics and professional journals when Hearst's *Journal* practiced "the journalism of action" were filled with similar angst and circumspect gnashing of teeth (Campbell, 2004).

The issue of defining current standards for the study of history is brought up because, to assure that students understand the importance of these values in current and past practices, educators must first define them as curricular goals in the history class. Historians understand that "an awareness of the future is best insured by preserving a record of the past" (Hoffmann, 1999, p. 1). Furthermore, students in upper division journalism classes like the history course should be aware of what current critics of and in the profession are saying. The latter becomes pedagogically important, because relevance to prior knowledge is considered of utmost importance in the literature on learning theories. Today's events and admonitions are precursors to making the study of history relevant, and students live in today.

ACEJMC (2003) has provided a working set of competencies which encompasses both methods (e.g., research, critical examination, and evaluation) and practices (e.g., independent thinking, global considerations, creativity, and applications). Historically, the profession has provided those competencies and values through dynamic practices that are discussed, refined, and adapted in the context of the times.

And, despite the difficulty in nailing down standards even within a single newsroom (cited earlier, Project for Excellence in Journalism II,

2004), there are some enduring journalism standards and practices. Reflection on the following yields broad principles that students should understand on entering journalism and media professions.

PUBLIC SERVICE AND EDUCATION

Legal scholars and historians consider a free press, the only enterprise specifically mentioned in the U.S. Constitution, essential to successful self-governance. Within the confines of U.S. jurisprudence and 20th-century interpretation, the media are given great content latitude to operate.

However, the global view of the role of media as educator can be seen in different press systems as well (Altschull, 1995): "Like a Wagnerian opera, a leitmotiv runs through the structures and the ideologies of the news media of the world. The unifying element is agreement on the role of the media as educator" (Altschull, 1984/1995, p. 279). For example, the educational role of the media in the U.S. market system is to provide divergent information and let the consumer choose from the marketplaces of ideas and goods. In a Marxist system, the role is to provide the received view, and in a developing system, the role of education is to provide information that promotes change.

Habermas (1996), in line with Gurevitch and Blumler's 1990 outline of mass media functions, said the following:

> The mass media ought to understand themselves as the mandatory of an enlightened public whose willingness to learn and capacity for criticism they at once presuppose, demand and reinforce; ... they ought to preserve their independence from political and social pressure.... (p. 378)

A related point of agreement among international journalists is an obligation to represent dissenting voices and to serve the public. The perceptions of public service vary depending on the political, social, and economic system in which the press operates, and the practices among international journalists on this value differ depending on the security of the operant government. Nevertheless, the resolve in this value seems to transcend governments.

Although the public service value of media is clear, just how that is accomplished is an issue of current as well as historical concern. For example, Merritt and McCombs (2004) hailed public journalism as the true purpose of the press in a self-governing society. On the other hand, Straumanis (2002) described public journalism (when practiced as a democracy that focuses on community, harmony, and the positive in society) as detrimental to press freedom, and as destructive of the libertarian and individualistic values of press freedom American-style.

INDEPENDENCE

Closely related to public service and press freedom is the value of independent thought, practice, and power found in professional guidelines and practices. This value resonates in the ability of the media to serve as watchdogs on social, political, and economic powers, and to serve as the fourth estate of government. John Peter Zenger's trial in 1735 provides a good example of the formative times of the press and its perceived independence from the laws of sedition. Likewise, Olasky (1989/1990) suggested that the independence value grew from the Protestant Reformation and from a belief that reporting earthly events merely reflected God's intent quite independently of what the king wished to see in print. The Penny Press papers and yellow press also extolled their independence from dominant power, and claimed to be reporting for the common good.

Support of independence and public service standards are also found in avowed independence from advertising. The *Boston Daily Times* on October 11, 1837, stated the following: "To the advertising public we are impartial" (cited in Schudson, 1978, p. 19). The *Printers Ink* statement of advertising standards is another example of independence, and *New York Times v. Sullivan* (1964) discussed the necessity of independence of the news-editorial department from the advertising department at the newspaper.

The value on integrity is closely related to independence and egalitarian public service. Even in times of the partisan press, the Penny Press, and the excesses of yellow journalism, professionals placed value on the integrity of "doing the right thing." Joseph Pulitzer's efforts to shame officials into action through his reporting as the people's champion come immediately to mind. His claim to integrity centered on the principle that he was devoted to the public welfare, was independent, and was never afraid to attack wrongdoing. Pulitzer justified the sensational, gossipy excesses in which his *New York World* indulged as an economic necessity to win readers and entice them into the important public affairs issues his paper reported (Emery & Emery, 1988).

Hearst's *Journal* proudly proclaimed when "things are going wrong (the *Journal*) should set them right, if possible" (cited in Campbell, 2004, p. 17). *The New York Sun* was largely indifferent to politics and claimed to "shine for all" in its presentation of the news of the day (Schudson, 1978).

TRUTH

Independence may imply that one is free from influence, but objectivity, a common value in the profession, may not be attainable. Objectivity obviously was not valued in the partisan press, so how did it become important to journalists today? Was it an economically driven value to increase wire service markets? Did the increasing diversity of educated voices require it? How does it serve self-governance? Although especially applicable for this value, such questions can be used throughout the history course for each of the identified values.

Schudson (1978) claims that objectivity means statements can be trusted if they are subjected to established rules legitimized by the profession. "Facts here are not aspects of the world, but consensually validated statements about it," he said (p. 7). In other words, if everyone agrees that the emperor has beautiful clothes, then he must not be naked.

In addition, such a consensual nature of facts leads to the declaration by a few about which groups should be acknowledged as acceptable sources, and that practice, in turn, contributes to media parroting information that may not be accurate. Examples of this very problem are evident in reporters' falsifications, in reliance on a questionable single source, and in sole reliance on official sources.

The shared value of "truth" confounds the objectivity factor, especially in current times when the dominant paradigm proclaims that truth is subjective. The question becomes, "Whose truth?" and "What is the basis?" Students are skeptical of anyone who claims to know the "truth" through their experience with relative "truths" that have emerged from public policymakers regarding everything from sex to weapons of mass destruction. John Stuart Mill in his 1835 *Essay on Liberty* (as cited in Jensen, 1998) described truth as process-driven and made no pretense that anyone would ever get there. The best to hope for may be a continuing process that eliminates what is not true. Truth also may be the process Emmanuel Kant described when he talked about the categorical imperative of always telling the truth with the caveat that truth is based on what knowledge one has at a particular time (as cited in Bok, 1978).

Perhaps students best can learn these vaguely defined values through the historical practices of those professionals who have espoused them as purposes of the press—the practices of striving for accuracy and fairness. When compared with the notions of objectivity and truth, the goals of accuracy and fairness appear more attainable. Attempts to maintain fairness and accuracy are represented most obviously in newsgathering and reporting practices of seeking myriad sources and seeking the context in which issues emerge, at least as up to date as possible. Such practices have emerged through historic practices of the press. Like objectivity, accuracy and fairness may not have been of major concern to those in the early American press who vied for lucrative government printing contracts in contrast to journalists today who worry about inaccuracy and shallowness in gathering and reporting the news. The contrast is especially striking because such divergent practices are connected by their contemporary economic and survival pressures of the times.

Identifying values that endure comes through looking at how practices have reflected them over the years. Professional organizations, ombudsmen, and even specially appointed commissions have examined the role of the press in America, from the Alien and Sedition Act and the Hutchins Commission to the present. Most recently, the Project for Excellence in Journalism (I, 2004) asserted the following: "The central purpose of journalism is to provide citizens with accurate and reliable information they need to function in a free society . . ." (Project for Excellence in Journalism I, p. 1).

Based on the project's nine professional standards, four resonating values (change, independence, public service, and truth) are outlined in Appendix A. They are by no means exhaustive, and they are by no means mutually exclusive.

JOURNALISM HISTORY SCHOLARSHIP

Novelist James Michener has been variously credited with saying, "Journalism is history in a hurry" (Allen, 2000, paragraph 4, p. 1). His statement, often quoted by professionals but rarely attributed, provides a comfortable nexus between history and journalism. The methods of journalism are similar in some ways to the methods of the general field of history, and this similarity also serves as a logical connection between teaching the competencies and values of journalism through the lens of history.

Cloud (2000), on the occasion of the 26th anniversary of *Journalism History*, analyzed the path of journalism history scholarship over the period since the journal's debut. She reported that the most striking difference was the dramatic decrease in the number of historiography articles, including those on the role of journalism history in the curriculum. Only 2% of articles published between 1990 and 2000 dealt with historiography, and 15% of the articles in the first 16 years dealt with the subject. Cloud said that the percentage of historical biography publications decreased in the journal between 1990 and 2000. Overall, most of the articles published in the journal focused on the journalist, on the medium, or on the message. Cloud, calling for historians to examine the feedback loop in the mass communication process, suggested that media and messages change as a result of contemporaneous feedback, and journalism historians should include this element in their analyses.

Mindich (2000) suggested that the synthesis between journalism and mainstream historical methods can bring the complex context of the day into better focus. He suggested an interpretive approach in the study of journalism history that puts cases and events into broader contexts. Examining the central issue of news and minority voices can provide insight, for example, into why Frederick Douglass went into the newspaper business.

Blanchard and Kenan (1999) also urged journalism historians to branch out and explore broader methodological approaches, perhaps melding social and behavioral science methods with historical methods. Instead of only continuing in the tradition-bound research approach strictly adhering to the method of the history discipline, journalism historians and educators should also use methodologies of the communications discipline, she submitted.

What Cloud (2000), Mindich (2000), and Blanchard and Kenan (1999) are suggesting is reevaluation and reinvigoration of the history course. Analyzing history course syllabi, Voss and Beasley (2003) reported that journalism history courses predominantly focus on biographies (heroes and heroines), eras (partisan press to journalism 2004), technological developments (printing press to Internet), creation of a mass audience, general media (newspapers, magazines, electronic media, advertising, and public relations, etc.), or political and economic frameworks (First Amendment press freedom and society). Furthermore, they found that most courses use lecture, book reviews, papers, and exams as the primary methods employed for content delivery, activities, and assessments.

Covering hundreds of years of developments and contexts in a single term is daunting to say the least. Organizing the presentation and activities of such a course around strengths of the professor and around how students learn can be both more fruitful for students, more rewarding for professors, and more efficient for assessing student growth and learning.

RELEVANT LEARNING THEORIES

A brief discussion of several prominent learning theories can shed light on how to build assessment into the syllabus of the history course.

A key element in most learning theories is that of relevance to the learner. Even quite gifted teachers and students fail when the information holds no meaning for the learner. Media historians should understand the value that relevance of subject matter has to learning, especially given their field of study which is not concerned with discrete variables that occur in a vacuum but with interrelated issues in the context of the times.

Jean Piaget's (Sutherland, 1999) model of cognitive development described two mechanisms for learning: assimilation and accommodation. The former relates to the modification of new material to fit with existing knowledge and experience and subsequent storage in memory. Accommodation is the process by which the information in memory is transformed into new material as new observations occur. Both are necessary for learning, and learners seek equilibrium between the two. If a student assimilates but does not accommodate, there is detachment from the information, in other words, he or she sees no real-world connections. If the converse occurs, imitation is often the result and he or she simply practices rote learning (Sutherland, 1999). A balance of assimilation and accommodation must be the goal for long-term learning to occur.

If what students have stored in memory is inconsistent with new information, not necessarily a bad thing, the assimilation requires attention to rectify that new information with the old. That is where accommodation comes into play. The student, in adjusting the new information with what he or she knows, seeks real-world examples that create a different understanding than either his or her existing knowledge or the new information alone can provide. This sounds very similar to some communication systems theories and with some information processing theories regarding central processing, attention, and memory.

Sutherland (1999) argued convincingly that Piaget's work with developmental learning (based on biology and age) can also be applicable to adults (those 18 and older), because the stages of learning are more accurately defined qualitatively rather than quantitatively. Anecdotal evidence is abundant in the commiseration among college educators that many students function at the concrete operational level of thinking rather than at Piaget's highest level (formal operational, the ability to think and reason abstractly).

Recall and redundancy are also recognized among theorists for effectively promoting learning. According to Halpern and Hakel (2003), practicing the retrieval of information with minimal cues, across applications, and over time, is the most important variable in long-term retention and transfer. Recall creates a path for retrieval and practice turns the path into a well-traveled superhighway with easy access.

Transfer of knowledge is currently being discussed in educational circles as the ability of learners to apply knowledge across content and
context. Essentially, transfer allows learners to apply learned concepts
to new situations and problems. The concept is especially pertinent in
light of Accrediting Council for Education in Journalism and Mass Communication (ACEJMC) values and competencies because it requires
critical, analytic, original thinking, and provides for applications well beyond the classroom and certainly in the profession.

Benjamin Bloom (1956) provided a set of stages of learning based as
well on cognitive psychology. His six progressive stages (knowledge,
comprehension, application, analysis, synthesis, and evaluation) that
learners go through are assessable at each stage.

Eisner (2000) characterized Bloom's approach to education as one
that discourages comparing students to each other. Such comparisons
put learners in competition with each other rather than with the material they are to master. If the driving force for education, retention, and
lifelong learning is to attain the goal of master learning, educators must
cease assessing who is quickest.

Perry's (1970, 1981) developmental model has gained wide adoption
among those in the higher education community, based on research
with college-age learners about how they make meaning of the world
and how they view learning. Like Bloom's (1956) *Taxonomy of Educational Objectives,* it identifies stages through which a learner passes as
he or she moves from novice to expert. Perry outlined nine positions on
the path. The first four are epistemological and intellectual in nature and
the last five are moral and ethical in nature. Subsequent researchers
(Katung, Johnstone, & Downie, 1999; Moore, 2001) have regrouped
them into three categories for assessing where students are in their
learning process. At the dualistic stage, students see the world in terms
of good and bad, right and wrong. At the multiplistic level, students recognize qualitative, contextual, and relativistic reasoning, but reliance on
authority continues. At the relativistic stage, students realize knowledge
and values operate contextually, but a right–wrong value system can still
operate.

Hesketh and Laidlaw (2002) provided a brief synopsis of three methods to learning that draws heavily from the aforementioned models.
The behavioral method is an active learning method where students
learn through application. Frequent practice and redundancy in varied
contexts (transfer) is essential, and reinforcement, such as praise and
positive feedback, works to increase motivation. The cognitive method
relies on learner understanding relative to prior knowledge, and mandates organizing materials so learners actively can discern links. Pro-

viding timely feedback based on performance factors serves as the primary motivation.

The third method they offered is the humanistic method emphasizing relevance to the learner in terms of what he or she needs to function in life. Student choice in terms of methods and materials, according to the humanistic approach, provides for significant learning because it places the responsibility squarely on the learner's shoulders. Motivators under this method include self-identified learner goals and needs and the provision of a noncompetitive, collaborative, and relaxed environment for students.

Social constructivist theorists also advocate collaborative settings for effective learning. From this perspective, learning is a based on human relationships rather than on relationships between a person and things (Bruffee, 1994). Three tenets of this type of learning model are as follows: (a) judgment regarding content can be learned better in groups; (b) people tend to let go of biases not held by the group, thus, freeing them from personal agendas; and (c) individual learning of judgment is enhanced with the interpretation of the group.

Elwood and Klenowski (2002) suggested that assessment itself should be used in a shared community through collaboration requiring learners to assess their own work and the work of their peers, to assess the materials and activities of the course, and to assess the instructor's performance. This formative and inclusive assessment practice by a shared community, the authors contended, serves to improve both teaching and learning.

One problem of collaborative learning in the classroom (Bruffee, 1994) relates to the relative nonautonomous nature of assigned groups. Because the communities are not voluntary, and are overseen by the professor, they are subject to some "authority" other than those who naturally emerge as group leaders or are designated as such by the group.

Critical learning theorists might agree. Welten (2001) argued that bureaucratic and administration intervention with voluntary communities erodes the structure of communication in a just learning society. Without autonomy from authority, civil society of which Habermas (1996) spoke (like collaborative learning communities) may serve to defeat the very thing it is reputed to promote, learning and participation.

This is not by any means a complete list of learning theories, and the brief descriptions are not meant to fully explain or to diminish the many nuances and complexities of each. It is admittedly heavy on the cognitive learning theories, perhaps because a great deal has been published from that perspective over a long period of time.

The theoretical principles and their syntheses are included in Appendix B which outlines competencies and suggested assessment tools for determining student learning.

POSSIBLE ASSIGNMENTS AND ASSESSMENTS

Coupling professional competencies and values to be assessed with learning theories in light of the rich content of journalism and media history culminates in methods of practical learning, teaching, and assessing. Amidst the cacophony of voices of media critics, Henry (1998) asked if journalism education is a lost cause. "Why teach accuracy, intelligent interviewing, concise writing and critical thinking if the industry outside my classroom seems bent on discarding its own values?" (p. B-9). This question likely occurs to many journalism educators at some point, probably late in the term. Students observe practices in media and want to know why they are learning something else in class. Even worse, they see people being paid high salaries and awarded recognition and legitimacy for these practices.

Henry (1998) answered his own question: "The quick answer is that journalism education is more important today than ever, and that teachers at journalism schools do have some power to strengthen the profession by instilling appropriate professional values in our students" (p. B-9).

The history course can be done in a way that assures students are learning the traditions, competencies, and values of the profession and honing ways to transfer that learning to professional problems and practices. Teaching journalism through history and teaching history through journalism can enhance connections for students.

Journalism history educators are positioned to make use of the methods of journalism while also teaching some of the methods of history— teaching history through journalism. For example, the use of primary and secondary sources, interviewing techniques, and analyses of documents, are common to the study and practices of both fields. Even the first quantitative newspaper content analysis, conducted by former *New York World* editor John Gilmer Speed in 1894 (cited in Sumpter, 2001), provides both a sense of New York newspapers at that time and a sense of artifact examination.

Student replication could not likely be done because Speed's methods for selection were not clear (Sumpter, 2001). Perhaps that is another good lesson for students in the rigors of analysis and replication of studies in search of the "truth"—the history of media research. Speed's report demonstrates the state of New York City newspapers at the time whereas the study itself presents the structured analysis of media to demonstrate that media not only reflect but also lead society.

RELEVANT HISTORICAL ANALYSIS

Also melding history and journalism, Callahan (2004) assigned students a comparative analysis of newspapers published on their own 18th birthdays with those of a grandparent and a parent. Students chose a focus (front pages, local news, national news, financial reports, classified advertising, or even design and layout). They were also required to interview the relative as well as provide a personal narrative for their own 18th birthdays. According to Callahan, the assignment was to introduce students to connections between the past and the present and to excite them about examining old papers.

Assessment of such an assignment can be ongoing and can appraise many components of learning professional values as well as history, depending on the particular adaptation. According to Hesketh and Laidlaw (2002), assessment should come frequently, in a variety of forms (verbal public praise, constructive suggestions, and sometimes a grade), and it should be presented as feedback to allow the learner to fill in the gaps.

Assessment can be both formal and informal. It can consist of simply repeating a question throughout the semester across contexts to ascertain assimilation, accommodation, and transfer of knowledge. Or it can consist of assigning heavily weighted grades. Students sometimes complain about being left out of the process if they do not receive a grade for their work (Taras, 2002). But, although grading is an important part of validation and the learning process, assessment is much more than grading—it is about learning.

The source interview portion of the 18th birthday assignment might be assessed on the basis of structure and a written journalistic report. The interviewee can assess the media report of the interview for accuracy and fairness. An oral presentation or journal of the findings can be assessed using both presentation and content criteria. Critical thinking skills can be assessed on the basis of comparative and contrasting findings about such issues as writing styles, story placement, the content of classified advertising, the nature of personal ads, editorial stances taken, and the like among the sources used (primary and secondary over several time frames).

Students can also assess each other's progress through open discussion, perhaps even without the professor's presence. This collaborative learning situation can serve as motivators to those students who are slow in their research, provide insights into problems they may encoun-

ter, and allow them to share findings with peers in an autonomous setting.

This rich assignment is not only "relative," as the title of Callahan's
(2004) article suggests, it is also relevant because it places the student
and his or her relatives in history and the media are there to record it.

FAIRNESS, ACCURACY, AND INDEPENDENCE

With a wealth of information available, including the audio collection of
interviews available at the Library of Congress American Memory online
site, Professor Edward Gallagher (2004) of Lehigh University created
and conducted, with a team of instructors, an online course incorporating aural records as a way of conducting historical inquiry.

One assignment incorporates professional journalistic values through
practical competencies and is especially adaptable to the media history
course. The exercise requires students to write an historical narrative,
incorporating the aural records of interviews conducted the day after
the Pearl Harbor bombing, and format it for a half-hour National Public
Radio broadcast about the reactions of the (wo)man-on-the street. Students create a script or audio storyboard presenting the information in
an organized, enlightening, and listener-friendly format. They also have
to write a script introducing the piece, connecting the audio passages,
and closing the show. Students must listen to the tapes and critically
evaluate them for content and form. Because some individual interview
records are as long as 14 min, students must discriminate as to which
statements best illuminate the narrative thread of their production and
choose those passages for inclusion.

Assessment can be based most obviously on organization, creativity,
and focus, but assessments based on accuracy, fairness, and balance of
the report are also relevant, especially since all in the course have access to the records. In addition, one might assess on the basis of diversity of viewpoints and interview subjects that were chosen for inclusion
in the program. Since all scripts must be submitted to the discussion
board and all must comment, peer assessment provides additional
feedback from which the student can learn.

By using publication and production competencies learned in journalism skills classes, Gallagher's (2004) assignment requires the student
to become a journalist and an historian using balance, accuracy, and
fairness in representation, an important issue within the lessons of context, framing, agenda setting, and the economics of time and space.
Original documents and ensuing publications, such as Congressional in-
quiries, President Franklin D. Roosevelt's speech, personal memoirs, or

military reports, could also be incorporated to demonstrate how "facts" might change as other perspectives become public.

The Library of Congress has a number of aural records available online, including recordings of landmark U.S. Supreme Court oral arguments and opinions. In addition, many university libraries contain oral history collections catalogued by topic that would serve for similar assignments.

FICTION AS FACT

Although there is still a great deal of debate about the use of Hollywood films in teaching history, Sprau (2001) contended that the research increasingly points to solid pedagogical practice in their use. He suggested that films are a comfortable medium for students and can provide the impetus for students to work in both concrete and abstract manners to complete their assignment.

Students choose an historically based film to view and consult with the professor about what to look for in viewing the film, like representations of historical fact, costumes, underrepresentation or overrepresentation of ethnic or gender groups, and the use of stereotyping to tell the story. This priming and the actual viewing of the film are part of the concrete stage of learning, and they provide the impetus for second-stage learning, the reflective stage. Reflection on issues such as meaning and representation continues and is encouraged through discussion of the film experience, journal entries, or a journalistic entertainment movie review.

Students in the third stage of analyzing, interpreting and explaining their experiences, are assessed on the basis of project proposals for case studies, presentations, or papers. This stage also requires students to use primary and secondary documents including published reviews of the film, historical accounts and artifacts from the time period, and interviews with people who remember the context depicted.

The final result of the project, and the fourth stage, is assessed on the student's production and application of the abstract concepts in the form of a case study, a commentary on the historical accuracy of the film, or a critical analysis of fairness of images portrayed.

A number of films reflect historical events that are related to media, and could serve to promote such concepts as sensationalism, accuracy, the use of stereotyping in storytelling, the demeanor of the journalist, the role of the media in exposing wrongdoing, or the economics of media. One of the criticisms of using film for pedagogical purposes is that students may believe it as a more accurate representation than it is.

Hence, it is important to require students to examine the representations as a sort of feedback loop of what Hollywood perceives to be the role of media.

CONNECTING THE PAST TO THE PRESENT—RELEVANCE

Based on the suggestions of the Piagetian model, creating an atmosphere of substantial relevance to the learner can enhance the outcomes of the history course experience. Students must relate a written paraphrase of an historical statement about media today and present their analysis of that relation to the class with support from current media literature in a medium of their choosing. Examples of statements might include the following: (a) Freedom of the press belongs to those who own them, (b) Those in the cave see only the shadows on the wall and believe reality to be the same, (c) The technology (of the telegraph) enables Maine to find out what Texas is doing, but what if nobody in Maine cares? and (d) Television is a vast wasteland.

When later provided the citation and source of the statement, they must examine the context in which it was made, using both primary and secondary sources. Students create another presentation that puts the statement within the commentator's social, political, economic, and technological environment.

Students must first assimilate the historical statement with what they know of modern media, whether the statement is a decade old or a millennium old. The relevancy connection exercises critical thinking skills, one purpose of the assignment. The presentations reflect accommodation of the information by requiring them to convert the assimilated information in their memory to a different form. This process happens at each stage of the assignment reinforcing the transfer of knowledge, the study of media, and the study of history. Students reportedly have excelled in the creativity part of this assignment, performing slam poetry to convey the content, writing and performing or recording songs, writing parodies, creating editorial cartoons, and even producing audio and video pieces.

These four assignment suggestions are meant to stimulate educators to create course activities that incorporate the content of media history, the competencies and values of the profession, and an understanding of how student learning can be assessed. There are a number of other suggestions available in the AEJMC Scholastic Division's annual Great Ideas for Teachers publication that can be quite useful to the journalism historian. The AEJMC History Division offers teaching, research, and professional freedom and responsibility sessions and publishes the *CLIO* newsletter, *Journalism History,* and a web page with useful links. Media history educators are encouraged to both submit their work to these outlets and make use of them for pedagogical purposes.

CONCLUSION

Educators should welcome the process of assessment of learning that has shifted emphasis from what teachers do to what and how students learn. If students are learning clearly articulated abstract concepts and how to transfer those concepts into practice, then, educators are successful in what they do. If learning is the true purpose of higher education, then learning should be the focus of new strategies, and assessment of student learning is the key to determining strategies.

Henry's (1998) statement that journalism education is more important than ever rings especially true at this juncture of what media analysts promise to be an epochal transformation of journalism. Educators and the journalism profession are responsible for historical transmission of values and competencies that a press central to self-governance requires. Assessment is simply a tool by which we can determine if future journalists can transfer those enduring values to future problems and issues in creative and change-friendly ways.

Methods of history and journalism overlap in some ways, and the history course serves the two-fold purpose of reinforcing journalistic skills (competencies) while examining media values in an historical context that provides the foundation for what media are today.

The journalism history course is uniquely positioned to call on students to demonstrate both the competencies and the values of the profession. The study of history stimulates the intellect and hones the ability to critically analyze and evaluate, competencies imperative for practicing journalism. It requires one to listen carefully to diverse voices and to differing versions of events while recognizing that American media are part of the larger media world, also essential to the practice of journalism. It further sensitizes one to recognize his or her own interpretive frame in striving for fairness and accuracy, fundamental to being a good journalist and to being an educated citizen of the world.

REFERENCES

Accrediting Council for Education in Journalism and Mass Communication. (2003). *Accrediting standards*. Retrieved March 14, 2005, from http://www.ku.edu/~acejmc/PRO-GRAM/STANDARDS.SHTML

Allen, F. E. (2000). *The trouble with environmental journalism.* Remarks prepared for the National Resources Council of America Roundtable at the National Press Club, Washington, DC. Retrieved May 3, 2004, from http://www.naturalresourcescouncil.org/networking/pastspeakers.cfm

Altschull, H. (1995). *Agents of power: The media and public policy.* New York: Longman. (Original work published 1984)

Blanchard, M. A., & Kenan, W. R., Jr. (1999). The ossification of journalism history. *Journalism History, 25,* 107–112.

Bloom, B. S. (Ed.). (1956). *Taxonomy of educational objectives: The classification of educational goals: Handbook I, cognitive domain.* New York: Longmans, Green.

Bok, S. (1978). *Lying: Moral choice in public and private life.* New York: Random House, Pantheon.

Bruffee, K. A. (1994). Making the most of knowledgeable peers. *Change, 26*(3), 39–44. Retrieved April 1, 2005, from http://search.epnet.com/login.aspx?direct=true&db=aph&an=9407150366

Callahan, C. (2004). Far away and personal: Generating enthusiasm for history proves "relative." *Clio, 38,* 3–4.

Campbell, W. J. (2004). 1897. *Journalism History, 39*(4), 15–22.

Cloud, B. (2000). The variety of journalism history: 26 years of scholarship, *Journalism History, 26*(4), 141–146. Retrieved March 9, 2005, from http://search.epnet.com/login.aspx?direct=true&db=tth&an=4442526

Eisner, E. W. (2000). Benjamin Bloom 1913–99. *Prospects: The quarterly review of comparative education, 30*(3), 1–7. Paris: UNESCO, International Bureau of Education. Retrieved March 5, 2005, from http://www.ibe.unesco.org/International/Publications/Thinkers/thinhome.htm

Elwood, J., & Klenowski, V. (2002). Creating communities of shared practice: The challenges of assessment use in learning and teaching. *Assessment and Evaluation in Higher Education, 27*(3). Retrieved May 3, 2004, from http://search.epnet.com/login.aspx?direct=true&db=aph&an=6699593

Emery, M., & Emery, E. (1988). *The press and America: An interpretive history of the mass media* (6th ed.). Englewood Cliffs, NJ: Prentice Hall.

Gallagher, E. (2004). *Virtual Americana: Studying American culture online.* Retrieved April 1, 2004, from http://www.lehigh.edu/~ineng/VirtualAmericana/VA-title.html

Habermas, J. (1996). *Between fact and norms: Contributions to a discourse theory of law and democracy.* Cambridge, MA: MIT Press.

Halpern, D. F., & Hakel, M. D. (2003). Applying the science of learning to the university and beyond. *Change, 35*(4). Retrieved May 5, 2004, from http://search.epnet.com/login.aspx?direct=true&db=aph&an=100407046

Henry, N. (1998, September 25). Journalism education: A lost cause? *Chronicle of Higher Education, 45,* B 8–9.

Hesketh, E. A., & Laidlaw, J. M. (2002). Facilitating learning: Principles of effective teaching and learning. *Medical Teacher, 24,* 479–482.

Hoffmann, J. (1999). Megalomania or a gift to the ages? *Journalism History, 25,* 149–155.

Irby, J. (2000, September). Uniting the educational and working worlds [Electronic version]. *The American Editor.*

Katung, M., Johnstone, A. H., & Downie, J. R. (1999, January). Monitoring attitude change in students to teaching and learning in a university setting: A study using Perry's developmental model. *Teaching in Higher Education, 4*(1). Retrieved April 1, 2004, from http://search.epnet.com/login.aspx?direct=true&db=aph&an=1547331

Kovach, B., Rosenstiel, T., & Mitchell, A. (2004). Journalists' Survey: Commentary on the survey findings: What journalists are worried about. In *Project for Excellence in Journalism:*

The state of the news media 2004: An annual report on American journalism. Retrieved June 6, 2004, from http://journalism.org

Merritt, E., & McCombs, M. (2004). *The two w's of journalism.* Mahwah, NJ: Lawrence Erlbaum Associates, Inc.

Mindich, D. T. Z. (2000). Understanding Frederick Douglass. *Journalism History, 26,* 15–22.

Moore, W. S. (2001). Understanding learning in a postmodern world: Reconsidering the Perry scheme of intellectual and ethical development. In B. Hofer & P. Pintrich (Eds.), *Personal epistemology: The psychology of beliefs about knowledge and knowing* (pp. 1–3). Mahwah, NJ: Lawrence Erlbaum Associates, Inc.

New York Times v. Sullivan, 376 U.S. 967. (1964). Also available at http://www.bc.edu/bc_org/avp/cas/comm/free_speech/nytvsullivan.html

Olasky, M. (1989/1990). Whatever is, is wrong: Antinomianism and the teaching of journalism history. *Academic Questions, 3,* 40–50.

Perry, W. G. (1970). *Forms of intellectual and ethical development in the college years.* New York: Holt, Rinehart & Winston.

Perry, W. G. (1981). Cognitive and ethical growth. The making of meaning. In A. W. Chickering (Ed.), *The modern American college* (pp. 76–116). San Francisco: Jossey-Bass.

Project for Excellence in Journalism I. (2004). *Professional guidelines: A statement of shared purpose.* Retrieved June 24, 2004, from http://journalism.org/resources/guidelines/principles/purpose.asp

Project for Excellence in Journalism II. (2004). *The state of the news media 2004: An annual report on American journalism.* Retrieved May 5, 2004, from http://journalism.org

Schudson, M. (1978). *Discovering the news: A social history of American newspapers.* New York: Basic Books.

Sprau, R. (2001). I saw it in the movies: Suggestions for incorporating film and experiential learning in the college history survey course. *College Student Journal, 35,* 101–111.

Straumanis, A. (2002, Spring). Twilight of press freedom: The rise of the people's journalism. Book Review, *Journalism History, 28*(1). Retrieved April 5, 2004, from http://search.epnet.com/login.aspx?direct=true&db=aph&an=6797249

Sumpter, R. S. (2001). News about news. *Journalism History, 27*(2). Retrieved April 5, 2004, from http://search.epnet.com/login.aspx?direct=true&db=aph&an=5255085

Sutherland, P. (1999). The application of Piagetian and neo-Piagetian ideas to further and higher education. *International Journal of Lifelong Education, 18*(4). Retrieved January 5, 2004, from EBSCO database.

Taras, M. (2002). Using assessment for learning and learning from assessment. *Assessment and Evaluation in Higher Education, 27*(6). Retrieved January 5, 2004, from http://search.epnet.com/login.aspx?direct=true&db=aph&an=7584453

Voss, K. W., & Beasley, M. H. (2003). Mass communication history. In M. D. Murphy & R. L. Moore (Eds.), *Mass communication education* (pp. 425–433). Ames: Iowa State University Press.

Welton, M. (2001). Civil society and the public sphere: Habermas's recent learning theory. *Education of Adults, 33*(1), 20–35. Retrieved March 30, 2005, from http://search.epnet.com/login.aspx?direct=true&db=aph&an=4356732

APPENDIX A
Knowledge and Values Matrix

Knowledge Competency[a]	Description	Key Concepts	Examples
Change and Adaptation	The media both drive and adapt to change	Technology	Printing press, telegraph, photography, broadcast, Internet
		Economics	Partisan press and printing contracts; Penny Press—populist papers, yellow journalism competition . . . MBAs in the newsroom, convergence
		Audience	Elite audience of the educated; mass literacy, immigration, mass audience, information and entertainment seekers, demassification, diffusion of innovation
Public Service	Media serve the public interest by providing responsible reporting and discussion in the "marketplace of ideas" that enlightens public values	Media within a social and political system	Comparative media operations, media as change agents
		Forum for criticism	Continuing critical examination of social and political power structures, activist journalism, diversity of voices
		Education	Reliance on media for information about the unfamiliar, alerting to matters of public import, what the public needs to know to self-govern
		Advocacy	Diverse voices, representing the disenfranchised as well as those in power, taking a position
		Entertainment	Agenda setting and providing provocative ways to think of social issues

Independence		The media must be free from censorship both externally and internally
	Government	First Amendment philosophy, the role of media within a socio-political system, licensing
	Economic	Philosophical separation of news-editorial, entertainment and advertising divisions, checkbook journalism, conglomeration, audience acceptance
	Source issues	Consensual nature of news and pack journalism, attempted manipulation of news by sources (e.g., rise of public relations), media as watchdog or lapdog
Truth		The philosophical nature of "truth" is essential to journalistic performance
	Defining "Truth"	Libertarian, postmodern and communitarian and belief system natures of truth, versions of "truth" appear in history and in journalism
	Objectivity	Belief in science and in the ability to discern truth, journalist as "fly on the wall," reporter's ability to put aside perspective
	Accuracy and Verification	Fact as fiction (especially in entertainment media), misrepresentation by omission, agenda setting by dominant powers
	Fairness and Balance	Many sides to a story, audience is mass but is made up of individuals and groups and requiring comprehensive and representative coverage, alternative media

[a]Arranged alphabetically and drawn primarily from professional values contained in the Project for Excellence in Journalism II (2004) Report.

APPENDIX B
Skills Matrix

Skill	Outcome	Suggested Assessment Tools
Identifying sources for historical inquiry	Understand that historians use eras, biographies, and historiography to examine history [Bloom (1956) knowledge, comprehension and application; Perry (Katung, Johnstone, & Downie, 1999) dualism]	Ongoing discussion and quizzes, or in class response paragraphs covering primary text and reading material. Comparison and contrasting of positions taken by differing accounts.
Locating historical primary and secondary sources	Understand that sources of history (and media) reflect the context of the times and may be subject to interpretation of diverse sources; both seek the "truth" of the times [Bloom (1956) analyze, synthesize, and evaluate; Perry (1970), multiplism, relativism; Hesketh and Laidlaw (2002), behavioral method; Halpern and Hakel (2003) relevance; Bruffee (1994) collaborative learning; Elwood and Klenowski (2002) collaborative assessment]	Interview sources (or examine sources from the time through such means as letters to the editor). Examine media records (old newspapers, biographies, films, etc.). Examine original documents such as public policies, market indices, or institutional adoption of new technology for information. Demonstrate how an accurate and fair account of history emerges through many avenues and voices, and how media have (or have not) portrayed the times fairly and accurately through source use (e.g., Callahan's (2004) 18th birthday assignment). A critique of the newspaper content analysis by John Gilmer Speed in the 1890s might also serve as an assessment tool to determine the importance of replicable methods and interpretations of the results.
Examining primary and secondary documents related to an independent press	Understand that the notion of a free and independent press is deeply rooted in American media practices, and how media advocates have fought battles to retain that independence	Discussion, through role playing, of why press freedoms were included in the founding of the United States as articulated in such primary documents as the U.S. Constitution, the *Federalist Papers* or in U.S. Supreme

		Court decisions. (In designing the role playing, debate or chautauqua, also consider such artifacts as Thomas Jefferson and John Adams' dispute of the Alien and Sedition Acts; through letters and public exchanges; through John Milton's *Aeropagetica* or John Stuart Mill's *On Liberty*; through oral arguments on landmark free press cases, or perhaps through an examination of Peter Zenger's seditious libel trial.)
	[Bloom (1956) evaluate; Perry (Katung et al., 1999) commitment, responsibility; Hesketh and Laidlaw (2002) behavioral learning, cognitive learning, humanistic learning; Bruffee (1994) collaborative learning]	One might also use a chautauqua or a role-playing assessment tool by drawing from historical media criticisms, like the content analysis by John Gilmer Speed.
		If performance is not an option because of factors like large class sizes, students could be evaluated on a journalistic report representing these debates fairly and accurately to the public.
		The quote assignment discussed in the text of this chapter is pertinent to this skill. Explaining a statement of media criticism as it relates to today's media.*
Articulating current media practices through consideration of historical media practices	Understand that media must adapt with the times to survive; they both drive social and technological change and reflect it	Explaining the same statement of media criticism in the context of the times in which it was written.
	[Piaget (Sutherland, 1999) assimilation and accommodation; Halpern and Hakel (2003) relevance, recall and redundancy; Bloom (1956) synthesis; Perry (Katung et al., 1999) relativism]	Examine primary and secondary documents (e.g., public policy enacted following the Standard Oil monopoly series) for evidence of social change promoted by media.
		Finally, explaining the distinctions between the times in the history of media that make the statement pertinent both then and now. That is, explaining the changes and adaptations media have made in response to technology, economic and social contexts, and changes the media have promoted in society. The latter can be both positive and negative, such as the invention of miniature audio and video devices that allow media to cover more accurately, but risk invasion of privacy.

(Continued)

Skill	Outcome	Suggested Assessment Tools
		*Selecting the quote is important, and can be applicable for a variety of media and media-related fields. For example, one might wish to use, "The public be damned," for a public relations student. Activist journalism could rely on Hearst's statement of a responsibility to right any wrong.
Distinguishing between fact and fiction	Understanding the nature of truth in history and as presented by media, and the interpretative underpinnings of both [Bloom (1956) evaluation; Perry (Katung et al., 1999) relativism; Piaget (Sutherland, 1999) assimilation and accommodation; Kolb (Sprau, 2001) concrete and abstract learning; Halpern and Hakel (2003) relevance; Bruffee (1994) autonomy; Hesketh and Laidlaw (2002) humanistic learning; Halpern and Hakel (2003) relevance]	Using media with which students are familiar, such as film (e.g., Hollywood representations of history, media and media issues), books (e.g., biographies of media practitioners) or current media criticisms (e.g., the Project for Excellence in Journalism 2004 report). Students select an item, examine it and describe for others the representation of history and media in the context of a fictionalized account. They also must conduct primary and secondary research of the times and the media and explain "creative license" taken into account for the particular version of history.
Demonstrating how media have traditionally set public agendas and framed social issues	Understand that media lead in adoption of new ideas and methods through indirect ways [Hesketh and Laidlaw (2002) behavior, cognitive and humanistic learning; Kolb (Sprau, 2001) concrete and abstract learning; Piaget (Sutherland, 1999) assimilation and accommodation]	A good way to assess this concept is the Gallagher assignment discussed in the text using aural documents. Although it could be easily adapted to use of other documents such as letters, public policies and the like. Requiring students to make production decisions based on the economy of space and time teaches them firsthand how selecting materials and framing them for presentation can result in varying interpretations of the truth.

aDrawn primarily from professional values contained in the Project for Excellence in Journalism II Report (2004) and ACEJMC Accrediting Standards (2004).

Diversity

Barbara Bealor Hines
Journalism Department
Howard University
John H. Johnson School of Communication

Living in a diverse society places demands on everyone. Nowhere does it impact more than in the communications industry. Chambers (2003) reported that research at the University of Georgia's Selig Center estimates that by the year 2007, Blacks and Hispanics will control nearly $2 trillion in spending power, represent nearly 30% of the population, and control 20 cents of every dollar spent. Communicators, no matter their specialization (i.e., journalists, advertising professionals, public relations professionals, speech and hearing specialists, visual and design professionals), will work in those communities of color and diverse voices as they develop careers, establish families, and make professional, educational, personal, and political contributions to their community.

Diversity means exploring a variety of ethnic voices in reporting all types of stories, especially when it breaks a stereotype. Diversity teaches positive lessons, allowing viewers to enjoy the sight of sources of color rather than be surprised by them. Diversity challenges assumptions in research for advertising and public relations campaigns. The inclusion of Black, Asian American, Hispanic, and Native American voices—mainstreaming—is even more important in the 21st century as the population of non-Whites grows and increasingly enters the mainstream. Establishing different voices and perspectives helps diversity goals but may not increase multiculturalism.

Multiculturalism has a broader context: it evidences a respect and understanding for the social and cultural nuances of a particular segment of society. To work successfully in a multicultural environment, individuals must learn to accept differences and to honor and treat people with dignity, regardless of those differences. For professionals working in the field of communications, not taking into account the range of diverse communities can produce work that lacks a variety of voices in a variety of colors. When that happens, the results are all too typical:

- Sound bites from Black experts on civil rights.
- B-roll of a Black woman surrounded by children talking about welfare.
- Features about overachieving Asian students.
- News stories about Hispanics protesting immigration policy.
- Offensive images lacking cultural sensitivity in advertising campaigns.
- Too little or nothing at all on Native Americans.

Just because an individual's skin is a particular color does not mean that the person is an authority on all issues important to that particular race. One does not have to be Black to specialize in the history of the civil rights movement. Reviewing statistics about economic issues such as welfare confirm that more White women are on welfare than Black. As the United States continues to truly become a melting pot of cultures, it will be increasingly important for individuals to understand stereotypes and how they affect a community.

Diversity refers to the presence of differing cultures, languages, ethnicities, races, sexual orientations, religious sects, abilities, classes, ages, and national origins of people in an institution or community such as a school, workplace, or neighborhood.

Diversity improves reporting by presenting the achievements of individuals, not entire ethnic groups. August Wilson is not one of the most successful "Black" playwrights of our time, he is simply one of the most successful playwrights of our time. And although it can instill pride in a race to focus on a person's color, there is a difference. It is easy to fall into the trap of identifying people by their hue, rather than by the magnitude of their achievements. It is important that journalists and other communications professionals realize that citing diverse sources is not only professionally appealing, it makes economic sense. Diversity is not a test of political correctness; it is a test of moral and journalistic integrity (Tucker, 1999).

The U.S. Census Bureau reports that in the next 50 years, the number of Latinos and Asian Americans in the United States will triple, whereas the White non-Latino population will increase a mere 7%. The Asian

American population will experience the biggest increase in the United States, expanding from 10.7 million in 2000 to 33.4 million in 2050, an increase of 213%. The African American population will experience more modest growth of 71%, rising from 35.8 million to 61.4 million, while White non-Latinos will exhibit the most minimal increase, growing from 195.7 million to 210.3 million (Johnson, 2004).

But the changes in demographics don't just affect ethnicity. An evolving workforce also offers incredible dynamics for business. And today, there are six primary dimensions to diversity: age, ethnicity, gender, physical abilities and qualities, race, and sexual and affectional orientation. The term *diversity* encompasses much more than affirmative action. Daniels (2001) cited one company's use of the term diversity that pushed race to the fringes. In 1995, Federated Department Stores, parent of Macy's and Bloomingdale's, covered two groups—women and minorities—in their human resource guidelines and advertising and promotion. In 2001, the number had grown to 26 and included such categories as seniors, the disabled, homosexuals, atheists, the devout, marrieds, singles, introverts, extroverts, and more.

Educators are regularly challenged to address this concept, instructing students in the importance and moral imperative implicit in diversity. Increasingly, faculty address social issues that may conflict with their personal beliefs. Issues like stereotypes and prejudice, discrimination, harassment, exclusion, and isolation should be discussed in the classroom setting. Yet, depending on the campus environment, there may be limitations to the discussion that can unfold (i.e., the university's mission). For students, however, having a sense of a diverse world is critical. Technology, which is increasingly favored by the current generation of college students, can provide a useful way to help students learn about people of color, with diverse voices and lifestyles and to integrate function and learning.

ASSESSMENT CHALLENGES

As the requirement to report the results of assessment of student learning grows, faculty and administrators must develop innovative direct and indirect measures to confirm student achievement at various levels.

Ewell (2001) cited five examples that may be used to report student levels of attainment:

1. Faculty-designed comprehensive or capstone examinations and assignments.

2. Performance on external or licensing exams.
3. Authentic performances or demonstrations.
4. Portfolios of student work over time (i.e., multiple semesters).
5. Samples of representative work generated in response to typical course assignments.

In its 2003 revision of the accrediting standards, the Accrediting Council on Education in Journalism and Mass Communications (ACEJMC) included diversity in two standards: Curriculum and Instruction (#2) and Diversity and Inclusiveness (#3). These standards are effective September 2004 and will be reviewed by site teams on visits during the 2005 to 2006 academic year (Accrediting Council on Education in Journalism and Mass Communications, 2004).

Standard 2, "Curriculum and Instruction," requires curriculum and instruction "that enable students to learn the knowledge, competencies and values the Council defines for preparing students to work in a diverse global and domestic society" (ACEJMC, 2004, p. 43). That means that assessment of student learning outcomes must be developed to show that students have a broad understanding of diversity in all sequences or programs in the unit.

Standard 3, "Diversity and Inclusiveness," "fosters understanding of issues and perspectives that are inclusive in terms of gender, race, ethnicity and sexual orientation" (Accrediting Council on Education in Journalism and Mass Communications, 2004–2005, p. 46). Programmatic assessment will be required to document achievements in this area. Aarons (2004) called the wording in the revised Standard 3 a "landmark decision" because of the inclusion of sexual preference as a part of a sweeping revision of the standards. Others might disagree based on religious or philosophical beliefs.

The ninth standard, "Assessment of Learning Outcomes," requires each unit to define specific goals for learning that students must achieve based on the "Professional Values and Competencies" established by the Council. It also stipulates that units "use results to improve curriculum and instruction" (Accrediting Council on Education in Journalism and Mass Communications, 2004–2005, p. 52).

The Council developed these "professional values and competencies" because individual professions in journalism and mass communication require specialized values and levels of expertise. In addition to the specific competencies developed concerning the law, history, and theories of the discipline, understanding the diversity of groups in a global society in relation to communications is one of the values programs must use when they measure student learning.

Through individual self studies, the Council believes that schools will use three criteria in developing assessment plans: awareness, understanding, and application. Using the findings, schools or programs will then work to strengthen outcomes.

This kind of assessment is not limited to professional programs. Regional accrediting groups, including the Middle States Association of Colleges and Schools, the North Central Association of Colleges and Schools, and the Southern Association of Colleges and Schools (to name just a few), also include diversity of programs in their assessment standards.

BUILDING PLANS THAT INCLUDE ASSESSABLE STATEMENTS

Whether the school, department, or unit is developing an assessment plan for a professional or regional accreditation, or for internal purposes, it must have a well-designed strategy and implementation timetable. The unit must first start with its university mission and add blocks that will uphold the foundation. The university goals and objectives are developed from the mission and are explicit in defining what the university hopes to accomplish. Appendix A provides a model template that includes the mission statement, goals, and objectives. The mission may be broad, but the goals and objectives help to streamline how the mission will be accomplished. Once those goals are established, the unit defines its plan. In many instances, the unit goals may also reflect the "professional values and competencies" articulated by the Accrediting Council. Examples of those goals include the following:

- Provide programs that represent diverse cultures, backgrounds and viewpoints, and foster an environment that welcomes such diversity (Northwestern State University). (2003a)
- Insure that students appreciate the importance of diversity in the communications industry (Howard University). (2003c)
- Exhibit sensitivity to diversity through communication practices (California State University/Fullerton). (2003)
- Students demonstrate a critical understanding of media diversity issues as they relate to media professions and audiences (Syracuse).
- Students should know how ethnicity, race, gender and class interact with law, public policy, employment, social relations and culture in American society (Central Michigan).

With the goals articulated, programs can establish specific strategies to insure that objectives can be measured and determine how often they want to assess them. What determines success for a program? If the goal is to ensure that students appreciate the importance of diversity, there would be outcomes that help define that goal. Things like "syllabi include diverse representation of voices of color and lifestyle" and "students demonstrate ability to operate in diverse environments" would be the language to help establish a benchmark for success. The program can then quantify the number of speakers presenting diverse voices in the classroom; require a student writing, editing, or design portfolio showing examples featuring samples of diverse content the student has created that would include print or design articles reflecting comprehension of some social or cultural nuance; or require a campaign that was created for a multicultural audience.

The Department of Journalism (2003b) at California State University at Northridge has created a "Cultural Diversity Statement for Skills Courses" that requires a paragraph in all course syllabi: "Students in this course are strongly encouraged to broaden their journalistic experiences, with the instructor's help, by including in their work people and subjects such as: ethnic, racial and religious minorities; the elderly, disabled and poor; gay men and lesbians, and other similar groups" (p. 2). The intent is to ensure that student work reflects the diversity of the community.

The Cultural Diversity Statement specifies the following: "The above statement is mandated for skill courses. A stated commitment to cultural diversity in journalistic work is as relevant in a photography or graphics course as it is in a reporting class. In addition, the statement applies to the practica and their related publications/broadcasts" (California State University–Northridge Department of Journalism, 2003, p. 2).

A smaller program may select regular, repeated assessment of all courses, whereas a larger program may select to assess learning outcomes by discipline or sequence on a rotating schedule. If a school has six sequences to evaluate, it may choose to select two per academic year and develop specific student learning outcomes to be tested for those sequences. At the end of 3 years, each program will have undergone scrutiny and a comparative evaluation may be completed.

Faculty at the Walter Cronkite School of Journalism and Mass Communication at the Arizona State University selected three strategies to conduct learning outcomes assessment in its initial year of assessment (2001–2002). First, all students in the Mass Communications Law class, the highest level class in the Walter Cronkite School, would be given a set of 20 questions of basic knowledge of media law, ethics, and history.

Answers were analyzed by computer, with the assessment criteria being the percentage of correct responses for each student and the mean score for all students.

Because the primary mission of the Walter Cronkite School is to prepare students to enter positions in media fields, faculty evaluated both student internships and student projects completed in a sample (50%) from four advanced courses in each concentration to be evaluated. During the first year, the news-editorial, broadcast journalism, and public relations concentrations were assessed. The faculty asked local media professionals to help evaluate the projects using a four-category scoring hierarchy: Exemplary, Proficient, Acceptable, and Unacceptable for the world of work.

One major question provided the base for the evaluation of student learning for internships: Would the professional site supervisor hire the student if an entry-level position were available? Responses indicate whether the student was prepared at an adequate level to assume an entry-level media position.

At the S.I. Newhouse School of Public Communications (2003) at Syracuse University (with more than 1,800 students), a faculty committee developed a grid that defined unit goals, objectives, student learning outcomes, and assessment tools. The School has 12 main goals for 5 different constituencies: students, alumni, the academy, parents and prospective students, and the community.

One of the goals for students is that they will "enhance their practical career skills with knowledge essential for enlightened, ethical leadership" (ACEJMC Self Study, Assessment Plan—S.I. Newhouse School of Public Communications, 2002, p. 2). An objective of the goal is for students to demonstrate a critical understanding of media diversity issues as they relate to media professions and audiences. For the learning outcomes, students are required to seek out a diversity of perspectives and voices when developing media content. They must also respect the views and opinions of others. Students demonstrate those outcomes in their capstone courses, through the use of alumni surveys, in discussions in their critical issues courses, and through service learning projects.

In courses, students are asked to keep a journal in which they can react to class ideas and readings on diversity-related concepts (i.e., race, ethnicity, gender, privilege) and to the concept of diversity itself. They also engage in critical analyses of media texts where they identify prosocial or diverse content, as well as problematic portrayals. They also discuss the implications of the racial and gender identities of people who create media content.

Another student learning objective designed to meet that same goal requires students to demonstrate a critical understanding of globalization issues as they relate to media professions and audiences. The student learning outcome teaches them to respect the views and opinions of others and to appreciate the benefits of exposure to diverse cultural perspectives. In addition to the survey instrument, students must complete a university language requirement, critical issues courses, and service learning.

Being able to assess the student's ability to understand the diversity of groups in a global society in relation to communications requires that issues of this nature be covered in the myriad of courses offered in a program and throughout the university setting. Students need to be challenged to produce work that stretches the norm and embraces different communities from the ones in which they are most comfortable. A strong sense of cultural identity and sensitivity does not just happen; it is carefully cultivated no matter where the program is located geographically or the composition of its student body.

Diversity can be incorporated across the curriculum, although it takes time and a concerted effort. It starts by incorporating activities into the curriculum that Dunlap (2003) called "points of entry—places where you can infuse principles of diversity." Students in a reporting class might be assigned to attend a community activity where the participants represent different ethnicities. Their assignment would be to conduct interviews, take photos or b-roll, and write a news or feature story. Or they might be assigned to participate in third-place reporting or civic mapping, to help them find out the nature of a community (McQueen, 2003). Advertising students in a research class could do content analysis of ads targeted toward a specific ethnic group compared to one targeted toward the general market (Frazier, 2003).

At many universities, faculty and administrators rely on examples of class work and in-depth exit interviews to determine the student's knowledge about issues of diversity. Activities such as these help students as they prepare to enter the workforce to understand the struggle of understanding real and perceived differences. These types of curricular activities can also provide the basis for developing tools to measure a student's grasp of the concept of diversity.

MEASUREMENT

How does a program measure success? Some indicators may currently be present; others can be refined or initiated. Texas Tech University (2003) used a combination of seven factors.

Classroom and Laboratory Performance

This is used to help determine the comprehension of lecture materials and the student's abilities to demonstrate or exercise the skills introduced in a particular class. Examinations, papers, presentations, case studies, writing and photography projects are evaluated to assess comprehension and ability. These assessments are continuous and described in detail in each course syllabus.

Capstone Course Presentations

These are made by students in advertising and public relations at the completion of their final courses in campaigns and measure their planning abilities, production skills, and their ability to present complex ideas. Clients, faculty, and graduate students attend to provide comments and critiques; faculty members grade the presentations.

Student Competitions

There are a number of competitions through the Public Relations Student Society of America, Texas Public Relations Association, Texas Advertising Federation, the Hearst Foundation, the Broadcast Education Association Scriptwriting competition, and other organizations, that provide an opportunity for students to compare their skills to those in other schools. Each competition has its own system for assessment or evaluation but all are based on some program of independent judging and critique. Many of these competitions are held annually, and in some cases, quarterly.

Internships

These provide students "real-world" opportunities to apply their classroom and laboratory learning and to obtain realistic evaluations from diverse media professionals. Students are evaluated by their media sponsor, by the internal internship sponsor, and by a faculty visit to the site. Because of a university's location, internships are often completed during summer. However, opportunities exist year round. Often, faculty supervisors can encourage students during their internship to work for an organization that they might not readily choose and one that could challenge their normal level of comfort.

Course Evaluations

Student perceptions of course content, pedagogy, and teacher performance are measured. They are multiple-choice and open-ended questionnaires administered at the end of each class.

Student Exit Surveys

These provide students an opportunity to make broad observations about their learning experiences and to make comments they think are appropriate after they are assured of graduation. Exit and alumni surveys measure graduates' perceptions of their readiness for work in a diverse society.

Portfolios

Students in all specializations are given the opportunity to show that they have completed a body of work that reflects their ability to apply concepts taught in classes and laboratories. Portfolios are reviewed three times a year, prior to each graduation, and follow a template that the school recommends.

For many faculty and administrators, incorporating inclusivity into the curriculum is a primary goal for the unit. School location, student body demographics, or the university's mission can provide the impetus to develop classroom activities that will help to provide the desired results. These results may relate to the specific requirements of regional or professional accrediting bodies or internal university or college requirements.

The study of communications demands inclusion. Yet faculty and administrators sometimes tend to forget just how easy it may be to include activities in the curriculum that will help to ensure success in meeting program goals and objectives. The Council has published a volume, *Diversity: Best Practices* (Accrediting Council on Education in Journalism and Mass Communications, 2003), to help.

Media diversity courses are increasingly popular classes and attract an eclectic array of speakers to campus. Courses like Community Journalism (Texas–Austin); Race and Ethnicity in the Media (Drake); Race and Ethnicity in the New Urban America (Columbia); Women, Minorities and Media (Oregon); Critical Perspectives on News and Critical Perspectives on Electronic Media and Film (Syracuse); Economics, Persuasion and the Global Marketplace (Syracuse); Cross Cultural Journalism (Missouri); and History of Multicultural Media (Howard), can provide students with the context to understand and compete in a diverse work force. Activities can be developed in these courses that will help a unit meet its diversity efforts.

Communications Job Fairs (Howard, Penn State, Grambling), Journalism Day (Syracuse, Northwestern State, Miami), newsmakers and speaker series (American, North Carolina, Louisiana State), and alumni advisory boards (Florida, Florida A&M, Texas State), ensure that universities maintain connections with the media industries and offer opportunities to experience diverse voices.

Resources to assist schools and faculty in understanding and implementing activities that foster inclusivity are available in multiple formats: lesson plans, syllabi, directories of media professionals, and from many locations like the World Wide Web, libraries, alumni organizations, diversity organizations, foundations, and educational associations (see Appendix B).

Student internships are often cited as the capstone course for a school's curriculum. They offer a unique measurement of the student's level of achievement because they are generally offered after the student has completed a prescribed sequence of courses or core coursework. Internships are offered at sites ranging from advertising agencies to broadcast outlets, newspapers, magazines, online publications, public relations and corporate communications departments, and more.

A site supervisor is charged with working with the student on a predetermined schedule and reporting observations of the student's level of achievement to the college or university.

Faculty members can track the student's achievement through regular meetings with the student and an evaluation form that can be administered once or twice during the semester or quarter. The size of the program and cooperation by external supervisors may limit the administration of the evaluation to one time during the student's experience.

The student evaluation form can be general in nature, but may be customized to reflect the specifics of the discipline (i.e., advertising, broadcast journalism, print, visual journalism, public relations, television and radio production). It should include some measurement related to the ability to compete in a multicultural environment.

For quantification purposes, the form may include a numerical rating scale from 1 to 5 (1 = *poor,* 2 = *below average,* 3 = *average,* 4 = *above average,* and 5 = *excellent*). The numerical scale is used to rate traits like responsibility, self-confidence, creativity, initiative, personal appearance, communication skills, interpersonal relations, or professional skills.

Qualitative or open-ended questions may be included so that the supervisor has the opportunity to go beyond just numbers to reflect on the student's holistic experience. These questions may be similar to questions used by human resource personnel to measure individual achievement:

1. What has the individual (student) contributed to the company?
2. What are the individual's (student's) most significant strengths?
3. How could the individual (student) improve?
4. What is the individual's (student's) promise for success in a diverse workforce?
5. Would you hire this individual (student), given the person's background, aptitude, attitude, and ability? Why or why not?

The faculty supervisor or internship director plays an important role in documenting the success of student learning. A benchmark can be established by tabulating the results for distribution and discussion by faculty members. At this point, faculty can use the data to discuss possible changes to the unit's overall curriculum as well as individual courses.

CONCLUSION

Because of legal challenges facing colleges and universities relating to admissions and retention and overwhelming demographic changes, faculties and administrative personnel are reassessing how diversity fits into their programs. Mission statements are being revised to reflect the environment and variables that used to be titled affirmative action. Faculty and administrators are using assessment to document how inclusion can strengthen student learning.

As change happens, learning occurs. Implementing an assessment plan that includes student learning outcomes can strengthen a program and make a college or university distinct.

In establishing student learning outcomes, develop a plan that becomes a roadmap to success. Write it to complement the university's mission statement so that it becomes a cohesive plan for the future.

The numbers and performance statements that are generated from this plan may not always be good ones. The benefit of having a plan that helps to identify student learning outcomes keeps the program focused.

And because of that focus, participants can revise when necessary, and replicate where prudent. The plan will be dynamic, not static, and help to ensure the unit's success.

REFERENCES

Aarons, L. (2004). Sexual orientation added to accrediting curriculum standard. *AEJMC News, 37*(4).

Accrediting Council on Education in Journalism and Mass Communications. (2003). *Diversity: Best practices, a handbook for journalism and mass communications educators.* Lawrence, KS: Author.

Accrediting Council on Education in Journalism and Mass Communications. (2004). *Journalism and mass communications accreditation, 2004–2005.* Lawrence, KS: Author.

Chambers, J. (2003). Incorporating diversity into the advertising curriculum. *Journal of Advertising Education, 7*(2), 12.

Daniels, C. (2001). Too diverse for our own good? *Fortune Diversity Career Guide, 4.*

Department of Communications. (2003). *Assessment plan.* Fullerton: California State University, Department of Communications.

Department of Journalism. (2002). *Assessment plan.* Mt. Pleasant: Central Michigan University, Department of Journalism.

Department of Journalism. (2003a). *Assessment plan.* Natchitoches, LA: Northwestern State University, Department of Journalism.

Department of Journalism. (2003b). *Assessment plan.* Northridge: California State University, Department of Journalism.

Department of Journalism. (2003c). *Assessment plan.* Washington, DC: Howard University, Department of Journalism.

Dunlap, L. (2003). *A syllabus worth of difference. Poynteronline.* Retrieved June 30, 2004, from www.poynteronline.com

Ewell, P. (2001, September). *Accreditation and student learning outcomes: A proposed point of departure.* Occasional paper of the Council for Higher Education Accreditation, Washington, DC.

Frazier, C. (2003). The diversity puzzle: Incorporating diversity into the advertising curriculum. *Journal of Advertising Education, 7*(2), 8.

Johnson, A. (2004). *In 2050, half of U.S. will be people of color. DiversityInc.* Retrieved March 18, 2004, from http:www.diversityinc.com

McQueen, M. (2003). Diversity in sourcing teaching module. In *The rainbow sourcebook.* Indianapolis: Society of Professional Journalists. Available at www.spj.org/rainbowsourcebook

School of Mass Communication. (2003). *Assessment plan for undergraduate students in mass communication.* Lubbock: Texas Tech University, School of Mass Communication.

S.I. Newhouse School of Public Communications. (2002). *Assessment plan.* New York: Syracuse University, S.I. Newhouse School of Public Communications.

Tucker, M. (1999). Diversity workshop presented to Maryland–Delaware–District of Columbia Press Association. Ocean City, MD: MDDCPA.

Walter Cronkite School of Journalism and Mass Communication. (2001). *Assessment plan*. Tempe: Arizona State University, Walter Cronkite School of Journalism and Mass Communication.

APPENDIX A: HOWARD UNIVERSITY

Outcomes Assessment and Institutional Effectiveness: Assessment Plan Template 1

Department/School/Administrative Unit: **Department of Journalism**
Submitted by: Phillip Dixon, Chair   Academic Year 2003–2004

Expanded Statement of Institutional Purpose (In this section, please provide a statement that demonstrates how your department/unit relates to your college or schools statement of institutional purpose, and through the college/school to the Howard University mission and goals)

Mission: The Department of Journalism has a historical mission to provide academic and professional training in journalism for a culturally diverse population. Through its expertise and tradition, the program emphasizes a commitment to a free and responsible press, access to and leadership in experiential learning, growth and development of new media technology and research in those areas that impact the dissemination of information and the media's depiction of the various cultures that combined, formulate our world.

The Department is dedicated to preparing students to work in the media, who will contribute to the advancement of society through their insightful and accurate portrayal of newsworthy events and occurrences and their impact on location, national and international communities. This dedication is extended to include the messages that are communicated by the providers of various products and services in their efforts to reach various markets. In concurrence with the University's quest for solutions to human and social problems and the School's commitment to promote liberation from social injustice, the Department will be a major contender in the struggle to ensure that the media provide fair and equitable representations of all people.

Goal(s):

1. Prepare students to compete in print, broadcast and online newsrooms and the boardrooms of advertising and public relations agencies and other integrated marketing communications organizations.

2. Insure that students appreciate the importance of diversity in the communications industry.
3. Prepare students to understand the importance of the First Amendment and the law appropriate to professional practice.

Outcomes Assessment and Institutional Effectiveness: Assessment Plan Template 2

Department/School/Administrative Unit: **Department of Journalism**
Submitted by: Phillip Dixon, chair   Academic Year: 2003–2004

Goal 1: Prepare students to compete in print, broadcast and online newsrooms and the boardrooms of advertising and public relations agencies and other integrated marketing communications organizations.

Intended Educational (Student), Research or Service Outcomes, Administrative Objectives or Expected Results (In this section, clearly articulate the expected results related to each goal. Try to make the objectives results-oriented). It is best to specify the objectives for each goal—e.g., Goal 1 may have two objectives labeled as Objective 1a and Objective 1b. Duplicate and use this page as often as necessary)

Objective: Students demonstrate a working knowledge of the skills, ethics and expectations of mass media professionals and mass media institutions.

- **Performance Criteria/Indicators for Success** (What will students/customer be able to do, to be, possess or perceive when the goal is accomplished?)

Student will be able to write effectively.
Student will be able to demonstrate ability to apply basic numerical and statistical concepts.
Student will demonstrate ability to think critically, to recognize and define problems and to rank solutions practically and ethically.
Student will demonstrate a working knowledge of communications technology and understand the need to stay abreast of technology.

- **Performance Activities:** (What will be done to achieve the goals and objectives?)

Student will complete all core courses with a grade of "C" or better.

Student will complete a Supervised Internship with a grade of "C" or better.

Student will complete the capstone course of their sequence with a grade of "C" or better.

- **Methods of Assessment** (the procedures, strategies, or tools by which you will collect information to validate the outcome objective and the method of analysis to be used)

  Evaluation tools will include performance-based activities in class, external research projects, internship supervisors and clients evaluations, portfolio reviews and surveys of both alumni and employers.

- **Use of Findings:** (Statement of how data will be used for improvement) Analysis will provide benchmarks for faculty to review similar courses at other universities.

- **Feedback Channel and Assessment Timeline** (Who is going to collect the assessment data? When, how often and to whom will the results be reported?)

  Results will be presented to the Curriculum Committee for course review and revision and forwarded to Executive Committee for full departmental faculty review.

Goal 2: Ensure that students appreciate the importance of diversity in the communications industry.

Intended Educational (Student), Research or Service Outcomes, Administrative Objectives or Expected Results (In this section, clearly articulate the expected results related to each goal. Try to make the objectives results-oriented). It is best to specify the objectives for each goal— e.g., Goal 1 may have two objectives labeled as Objective 1a and Objective 1b. Duplicate and use this page as often as necessary)

Objective: To prepare students to interact and collaborate with people different from themselves in the workplace.

- **Performance Criteria/Indicators for Success** (What will students/ customer be able to do, to be, possess or perceive when the goal is accomplished?)

  Student will demonstrate ability to articulate their values and culture and to respect the values and cultures of people different from themselves.

- **Performance Activities:** (What will be done to achieve the goals and objectives?)

  Student will successfully complete required sequence courses with a grade of "C" or better.

- **Methods of Assessment** (the procedures, strategies, or tools by which you will collect information to validate the outcome objective and the method of analysis to be used)

  Evaluation tools will include performance-based activities in class, external research projects, internship supervisors and clients evaluations, portfolio reviews, surveys of alumni and surveys of employers.

- **Use of Findings:** (Statement of how data will be used for improvement)

  Analysis will enable faculty to assess social, educational and political changes in the workplace.

- **Feedback Channel and Assessment Timeline** (Who is going to collect the assessment data? When, how often and to whom will the results be reported?)

  Results will be presented to the Curriculum Committee for course review and revision and forwarded to Executive Committee for full departmental faculty review.

Goal 3: Prepare students to understand the importance of the First Amendment and the law appropriate to professional practice.

Intended Educational (Student), Research or Service Outcomes, Administrative Objectives or Expected Results (In this section, clearly articulate the expected results related to each goal. Try to make the objectives results-oriented). It is best to specify the objectives for each goal— e.g., Goal 1 may have two objectives labeled as Objective 1a and Objective 1b. Duplicate and use this page as often as necessary)

Objective: To prepare students to work legally and ethically.

- **Performance Criteria/Indicators for Success** (What will students/ customer be able to do, to be, possess or perceive when the goal is accomplished?)

Students will demonstrate understanding of the importance of the First Amendment and the law appropriate to professional practice.

Students will be able to articulate and assert their rights under the First Amendment as journalist and communicators and recognize how their work may put the rights of others in jeopardy.

Students will be able to explain First Amendment principles and are mindful of fairness and proportionality.

- **Performance Activities:** (What will be done to achieve the goals and objectives?)

Evaluation tools will include performance-based activities in class, external research projects, internship supervisors and client evaluations, portfolio reviews and surveys of employers.

- **Methods of Assessment** (the procedures, strategies, or tools by which you will collect information to validate the outcome objective and the method of analysis to be used)

Successful completion of Communications Law, Supervised Internship and capstone course.

- **Use of Findings:** (Statement of how data will be used for improvement)

Analysis will provide benchmarks for faculty to review similar courses at other universities.

- **Feedback Channel and Assessment Timeline** (Who is going to collect the assessment data? When, how often and to whom will the results be reported?)

Results will be presented to the Curriculum Committee for course review and revision and forwarded to Executive Committee for full departmental faculty review.

APPENDIX B: DIVERSITY RESOURCES

Web Sites: General

http://www.diversityinc.com
http://www.diversityweb.org
http://www.poynter.org

http://www.freedomforum.org/diversity
http://www.newseum.org
http://www.blackcollegewire.org
http://www.newswatch.sfsu.edu
http://www.multicultural.com
http://www.notrain-nogain.org/divers/div.asp
http://www.census.gov/pubinfo/www/hotlinks.html
http://www.maynardije.org

Professional Organizations

http://www.nabj.org
http://www.nahj.org
http://www.naja.org
http://www.aaja.org
http://www.nlgja.org
http://www.asne.org
http://www.awrt.org

General African American

http://www.blackenterprise.com
http://www.blackvoices.com
http://www.essence.com
http://www.founders.howard.edu
http://www.melanet.com
http://www.nbcdi.org
http://www.bcw.org
http://www.naacp.org
http://www.nul.org

General Asian American

http://www.apiahf.org
http://www.cacf.org
http://www.kimsoft.com
http://www.nikkeiheritage.org
http://www.naaapdc.org
http://www.asian-nation.org

General Hispanic

http://www.aeth.org

http://www.hispanicfund.org
http://www.hispaniclink.org
http://www.laraza.com
http://www.hispanicbusiness.com
http://www.ushcc.com

General Native American

http://www.doi.gov
http://www.cowboy.net
http://www.nativeculturelinks.com

General Disabilities

http://www.dartcenter.org
http://www.media-disability.net
http://www.ncdj.org

General Gay, Lesbian, Bisexual, Transgender

http://www.blsg.org
http://www.nglcc.org

Curriculum Guides, Texts, or Sourcebooks

Biagi, S., & Kern-Foxworth, M. (1997). *Facing difference: Race, gender and mass media.* Thousand Oaks, CA: Pine Forge Press.
Lind, R. (2004). *Race/Gender/Media: Considering diversity across audiences.* Chicago: Pearson Education Inc.
McQueen, M. (2003). Diversity in sourcing teaching module. In *The Rainbow Sourcebook.* Indianapolis: Society of Professional Journalists. Available at www.spj.org/rainbow sourcebook
Nicholson, J. (2003). Pushing for change: Educators find new ways to teach diversity and multiculturalism in journalism schools. *Quill, 91*(6), 10–13.
O'Malley, S. (2000). Covering diversity. *Communicator, 54*(8), 49–56.
University of Missouri School of Journalism. (2000). *Guide to research on race and news.* Columbia, MO: The Ford Foundation.
Wilson, C., Guitierrez, F., & Chao, L. (2003). *Racism, sexism and the media: The rise of class communication in multicultural America* (3rd ed.). Thousand Oaks, CA: Sage.
Woods, K. (2002, August 6). *Handling race and ethnicity in descriptions: A teaching module.* Retrieved February 22, 2004, from http://poynteronline.org

7

Production and Graphics

Aaron Delwiche
Beate Gersch
Suzanne Williams-Rautiola
Department of Communication
Trinity University

The field of communication is characterized by multiple theoretical perspectives and educational objectives, with departments across the nation taking many different forms. Some programs prepare students to become communication professionals, others emphasize research methods, and others strive to balance theoretical studies with practical training. In 2003 to 2004, the Accrediting Council on Education in Journalism and Mass Communications (ACEJMC) revised its nine standards for assessing student learning outcomes. The second standard defines 11 professional values and competencies that should characterize an accredited communication program. This chapter focuses on the fourth competency, which states that all graduates should be able to "understand concepts and apply theories in the use and presentation of images and information" (ACEJMC, 2004, p. 3). Although "use" and "presentation" are combined into one learning outcome, interpretation (an important component of use) and production (a vital part of presentation) are often viewed as separate and competing curricular approaches vying for faculty positions and resources.

Some programs focus on the preparation of students for jobs within the industry, giving less attention to what practitioners would regard as "ivory tower" musings, whereas other programs reject the notion of preparing students to perpetuate current commercial programming, focusing attention on the ways that students can become more active agents of change both as audience members and as practitioners. To bridge the chasm between production and interpretation, Williams and Medoff (1997) suggested that production is central to the knowledge, skills, attitudes, affect, and values that are identified by Christ and McCall (1994) as "the What" of media education. Although it is possible for anyone to pick up a camera and record images and sounds, the educated communicator must do more; he or she

> must be able to achieve intellectual distance from the production in order to assess the content, the creative process, how the production might fit into the continually expanding communication environment (both in terms of the industry and the regulatory organizations that affect it), and how the production might be received and perceived by the audience and its various subcultures. (Williams & Medoff, 1997, p. 241)

This resonates with Van Buren and Christ's (2000) observation that production courses exemplify the constructivist teaching model in which students are viewed as "active creators of their own ideas and meaning, rather than as empty vessels to be filled with knowledge by the professor" (p. 42). According to this view, "it is through actively working with material, with peers or alone, that students solidify their understanding on a deep cognitive level" (p. 42).

Conversely, some educators in professionally oriented programs may consider theory as too removed from "the real world" to be of value in their programs. However, the use of technology involves a series of complex creative, ethical, contextual, and cultural decisions (Williams & Medoff, 1997). Further, Van Buren and Christ (2000) argued that "the integration of critical and interpretive theories allows students to make deeply interwoven and immediate connections between their creative productions and artistic, industrial, and genre conventions; social/cultural/historical context; and possible audience interpretations" (p. 42). If one accepts interpretation and criticism to be integral elements of production, the challenge is to incorporate all of the important concepts of production aesthetics and interpretive theories within one course.

In this chapter, we explore three models that could be used to guide the creation of a course focused on media production and interpretation: contextual media aesthetics, cultural studies, and media literacy. Herbert Zettl's (2005) contextual media aesthetics has been a major influence in production and preproduction courses since its introduction in 1973. Unlike traditional aesthetics which focuses on beauty and the philosophy of art, Zettl's (2005) understanding of aesthetics "deals with a number of aesthetic phenomena, including light, space, time/motion, and sound, and our perceptual reactions to them" (p. 15). The role of particular media in the construction of messages is crucial to this model. As Zettl explained, "whereas traditional aesthetics is used primarily for analysis, media aesthetics can be applied to both analysis and synthesis—production" (p. 15).

Although media aesthetics begins with the established production practices of media industries, a second approach to media interpretation is cultural studies, which encourages students to recognize the role of media in sustaining or challenging dominant values, beliefs, and institutions. A third approach, media literacy, teaches students to decode, analyze, and produce media messages. After considering the strengths and weaknesses of each model, we propose an "interpretive production framework" that synthesizes elements of all three approaches.

CONTEXTUAL MEDIA AESTHETICS

In stressing the link between aesthetics, production, and interpretation, contextual media aesthetics can be traced back to discussions about film during the first part of the 20th century. In the formative years of cinema, the study of film was closely allied with its production. Filmmaker Vsevolod Pudovkin (1929) wrote extensively about the construction of the visual experience through editing designed to guide the spectator psychologically. Filmmaker Sergei Eisenstein (1945/1969, 1942/1975) discussed the harnessing of visual energy through montage—the collision of shot, movement, and light. As the industry became more established, this debate continued through film critics such as André Bazin (1957/1971), who founded the *Cahiers du Cinema* and who influenced film directors and critics such as Jean-Luc Godard and François Truffaut. With the emergence of new aesthetic elements such as deep focus or sound, debates surfaced about their use and impact on interpretation.

As film study coalesced into a discipline in the 1950s and 1960s, scholars Rudolph Arnheim (1957), Siegfried Kracauer (1960), and others debated the nature of film as art, its relation to reality, its narrative structure, and its interpretation, closely allying the new discipline to the study of literature, theater, and art. Thus, film studies were typically incorporated in these more established, liberal arts disciplines (Bordwell, 1989).

However, the study of radio and television took a more professionally oriented path. In 1929, broadcast education began modestly with the establishment of the first college course in radio (Niven, 1961). Most early radio courses were offered as part of speech and drama, or professional programs such as journalism with production as a significant part of the course offerings (Brand, 1942; Smith, 1964). Both undergraduate and graduate degrees in radio broadcasting were being offered when television first hit the airwaves, and the new medium was subsequently added to the existing broadcasting curricula. Although there was a strong professional component, Niven (1961) reported that most of the programs in the 1960s included a broad liberal arts background along with training for entry-level job skills and a broad knowledge of the industry. A liberal arts education, reported Kucera (1963), guarded against the "danger of broadcast professional people being dominated, consciously or unconsciously, by the internal problems of the industry and not being concerned with problems of the society which they are supposed to serve" (p. 132).

As radio and television stations proliferated and large corporations developed in-house audio/video departments, there was continuing student demand for professional training as part of a communication education. Among the books that addressed the concerns of the new discipline was Herbert Zettl's *Sight, Sound, Motion* (first published in 1973 and now in its fourth edition published in 2005).

Unlike many film scholars, Zettl is not interested in linking aesthetics to philosophical disputes about art and the nature of reality. For Zettl, aesthetics is tied to its Greek origins in perception. The process begins with creators who "perceive, order, clarify, intensify, and interpret a certain aspect of the human condition . . ." (Zettl, 2005, p. 4). However, he is careful to note that we do not perceive the world in terms of absolutes but rather within contextual relations. For example, the speed of a car is difficult to judge until we evaluate it in relation to other objects. As producers, we shape the audience's perception of the speed of the car through camera angle and lens choice. Because the medium acts as a structuring agent in audio and visual productions, for Zettl, the primary contextual relations are those inherent within the medium and its interaction with the real world and include light and color, 2D space, 3D space, time and motion, and sound. He examines each of these aesthetic fields in detail, noting the specific effects created by the production elements within each field, tying those effects to perceptual and psychological processes, linking their use to established perceptual traditions in art, examining the impact of new technologies on each field, and suggesting ways that these fields might interact with one another to encourage a particular audience interpretation. This approach's key words and concepts are thus tied to the language of aesthetics, production, and interpretation. Further, for Zettl, contextual media aesthetics is not only important for interpretation and critique, but can be used formatively during the production process to assess the effectiveness of the message.

Although some might argue that students do not need to understand aesthetics to critique media messages, there are several reasons for linking both interpretation and preproduction courses to this approach.

Paul Messaris (1994) noted that although familiarity with visual conventions is not a prerequisite for comprehension of the message, the positive contributions of what he referred to as "visual literacy" include its assistance in seeing through the manipulative uses and ideological implications of visual images that rely on the ability of an image to reproduce real-life perceptual cues (pp. 4, 17). However, according to Messaris, the danger is in learning the codes—"the rules of correspondence between form and meaning" (p. 18)—and then thinking that there is one interpretation that follows those codes. Messaris suggested that interpretation requires an interaction between code and contexts, which are outside this code. He noted that often it is not the aesthetic codes that lead to differences in understanding but the contexts within which the images are placed (p. 18).

Messaris's (1994) discussion of aesthetic codes is very similar to Zettl's concept of aesthetic context, but Messaris suggests that there are considerations outside of aesthetic elements and fields that must be addressed to form a more comprehensive interpretation. In a discussion of media literacy, Zettl (1998) agreed that other theoretical approaches can be important to developing a more comprehensive interpretation but argued that a study of contextual media aesthetics is foundational, not only to academic programs with a strong production component but also to media studies programs. For Zettl, the study of audio and visual communication begins with aesthetics.

Finally, as noted earlier, one of the goals of contextual media aesthetics is to provide a framework for synthesis as well as analysis. Therefore, this approach lends itself to the incorporation of hands-on projects that meet the goals of a constructivist teaching model in which students actively create their own educational experience by working with the material (Van Buren & Christ, 2000). Projects may consist of planning productions through storyboards or mock-ups or actual print, audio, or visual messages, depending on availability of equipment.

There are several possible challenges that could interfere with combining aesthetics with other interpretive traditions. First, with the amount of information that is presented to the students in an introductory criticism course, it is difficult to find the time for an extended introduction to the aesthetic fields and other important interpretive theories. In addition, making the connection between the production process, its perceptual result, and possible interpretations may be more production detail than nonproduction students can or wish to incorporate into their understanding of interpretation.

Certain learning objectives would naturally follow from a production and interpretation course based on contextual media aesthetics. After completing such a course, students should be able to

- Readily identify and define elements that make up the five aesthetic contextual fields of light and color, 2D space, 3D space, time and motion, and sound.
- Identify the technological choices that need to be made to produce each of the elements that make up the five aesthetic contextual fields.
- Identify how the elements within the five aesthetic contextual fields contribute to the clarification, intensification, or interpretation of the message.
- Utilize the elements of the five aesthetic contextual fields to plan or produce messages.

CULTURAL STUDIES

Another approach emerges from an interdisciplinary project known as cultural studies. Attempts to reduce this approach to a concrete model would strike its practitioners as difficult at best and dangerous at worst. Scholars associated with this perspective have struggled to avoid the twin perils of rigidity and institutionalization. The desire to name, to measure, and to categorize is antithetical to the relativist leanings of this theoretical project. On the one hand, this refusal to be pinned down allows cultural studies to adapt its critique to the changing political landscape. Yet, this same tendency opens it up to charges of irrelevance from social scientists, journalists, and activists.

To understand what the cultural studies perspective has to offer, we simplify a complicated body of work. For a more comprehensive discussion of the relation between cultural studies and the field of communication, readers should consult James Carey (1988), Douglas Kellner (1995), and Grossberg, Wartella, and Whitney (1998).

Cultural studies is grounded in the works of Raymond Williams, Richard Hoggart, Stuart Hall, and other theorists once housed at the Birmingham Center for Cultural Studies. These scholars formulated their research questions and refined their critical tools in the context of the political struggles of the 1960s and 1970s. Partisan journals such as *New Left Review* and *Marxism Today* provided a forum in which theories could be proposed, debated, and refined.

Cultural studies scholars have focused more attention on the dissemination of theory via academic journals and conference papers than on pedagogical issues. Grossberg (in Wright, 2000) noted that, with notable exceptions (Giroux, 1992, 1994), scholars have been more likely to analyze soap operas and music videos than to explore the role of cultural studies in the undergraduate curriculum. Although many instructors incorporate concepts from cultural studies, attempts to define a coherent curriculum have been isolated and geographically disconnected.

This hesitation to fix a curriculum stems from cultural studies' suspicion of any assertion of a universal truth. Drawing on insights derived from semiotics, feminism, and psychoanalysis, cultural studies recognizes that human identity is socially constructed. This unsettling view of human nature has invited a range of attacks. Some suggest that this leads to cultural relativism (Horowitz, 1999), whereas others charge that postmodern views of identity erode the commitment necessary for political action (McChesney, 1996). Yet, cultural studies scholars raise important questions about the relation between meaning and power. Viewing society as a site of conflict between antagonistic groups (Kellner, 1995), they seek to understand the role of culture in sustaining oppressive social relations while discovering new resources for the further democratization of society.

Perceiving culture as contested terrain, cultural studies researchers frame their questions in strategic—almost Machiavellian—terms. How does ideology sustain the power of dominant social groups? How can social movements use cultural criticism and communication technologies to transform unequal power relations? Intriguingly, although this realm of scholarship is typically associated with the political left, many conservative activists also view culture as a political battlefield (Anderson, 2003; Horowitz, 1999). Opposing camps disagree about the nature of the terrain and ideal social outcomes, but both recognize that battle has been engaged.

The underlying assumptions of cultural studies are very different than premises that have dominated American communication research for the past 50 years. First, the emphasis on social conflict is alien to mainstream perspectives that reduce political power to the act of voting. Second, cultural studies takes a critical approach to dominant institutions and uses qualitative methods to explore its research questions. By contrast, much of traditional communication research is conducted on behalf of those same institutions with the help of quantitative research methods (Hardt, 1992; Lazarsfeld, 1941). Third, although the traditional American approach sees "communication basically as a process of transmitting messages at a distance for purposes of control" (Carey, 1988, p. 42), cultural studies is more likely to view communication as "a process through which a shared culture is created, modified, and transformed" (Carey, 1988, p. 43). These different assumptions once sparked fierce debate and political struggles, but more recently our field has managed to bridge—or at least to tolerate—these different perspectives.

Although many would question the attempt to identify a "canon of cultural studies," certain works are fundamental. Antonio Gramsci's (1929/1992) *Prison Notebooks* establish the theory of hegemony and explain how subordinate classes can be encouraged to support policies that undermine their self-interest. Roland Barthes's (1957/1972) *Mythologies* demonstrates that semiotics can be extended beyond the realm of linguistics to analyze advertisements, movies, and other media texts. Michel Foucault's (1984) essays argued that what we understand as "knowledge" is inextricably linked with complex mechanisms of power. Stuart Hall's (1980) encoding–decoding model challenged traditional models of communication by suggesting that audiences negotiate media messages in ways that reinforce, undermine, or moderate their power. Finally, James Carey (1988) has established important theoretical links between cultural studies and the American tradition of communication research.

Sadly, many of these works are accessible only to advanced students who have read widely across disciplines. For this reason, the insights of cultural studies are most usefully introduced via secondary works such as Downing, Sreberny, and Mohammadi's (1995) *Questioning the Media: A Critical Introduction;* Grossberg et al.'s (1998) *MediaMaking: Mass Media in Popular Culture;* and Sturken and Cartwright's (2001) *Practices of Looking: An Introduction to Visual Culture.* Each of these books provides accessible explanations of difficult concepts such as ideology, hegemony, and representation.

Cultural studies scholars have long feared institutionalization, worrying that attempts to define the project would sap its critical potential. For this reason, it is difficult to point to an existing model of a cultural studies curriculum. Henry Giroux (1992), who has done more than anyone to articulate the pedagogical objectives of cultural studies, argued that cultural studies pedagogy is not about "transmission of a particular skill, body of knowledge or set of values" (p. 202). This claim is consistent with the project's commitment to flexibility, but it is possible to agree on foundational concepts that should be transmitted in a cultural studies curriculum.

Students should be taught to critique structures of domination rather than serve them, and they should display healthy skepticism toward all authoritarian discourses. However, cultural studies instructors should also be open about their own normative assumptions. Conservative critics fear that such critiques are necessarily linked to the left, but it is possible to imagine a cultural studies curriculum that accommodates a range of viewpoints. For example, communication instructors often introduce representation by scrutinizing stereotyped portrayals of women, minorities, or gays and lesbians. Students could also be introduced to the notion of representation by analyzing social groups that are valued by conservatives. How is religion portrayed on television? What about members of the military? When facilitated skillfully, the subsequent classroom discussions can become exemplars of how controversial issues can be discussed with passion and civility.

In applying cultural studies to concerns of the right as well as the left, its insights can be made relevant to the 21% of students who identify as political conservatives as well as to the 24% of students who identify as liberals (Toppo, 2004). Such an approach would also protect this body of work from politically motivated attacks by linking it to the American belief that all sides must be given a fair hearing.

Cultural studies has much to offer in these deeply polarized times. From Bosnia to Rwanda, some of the worst crimes in the 20th century have been committed in the name of absolute truth and fixed identity. Cultural studies draws attention to the constructed nature of all representations. It reminds us that all interpretations of history and destiny are necessarily incomplete, while stressing the ever-changing nature of human identity. In this way, cultural studies challenges dangerous certainties of both the right and the left. But this does not mean that it is apolitical. Explicitly committed to culture as a terrain of struggle, it is a healthy alternative to the naïve assumption that political action ends at the ballot box. In preparing students to engage these ideas through speech, written work, and audiovisual productions, it also prepares them to participate in the messy work of democracy.

A critical enterprise from its inception, cultural studies teaches students to make sense of the world around them. It has never been intended as a vehicle for teaching production techniques. However, as noted in the ACEJMC competencies, interpretation and production are interrelated. Media producers should go beyond understanding the perceptual impact of the five aesthetic fields to recognizing how their creative work fits into the changing communication landscape and considering how it might be received by audiences and subcultures. For this reason, we believe that the critical learning objectives of cultural studies are an essential supplement to production outcomes. After being exposed to cultural studies, students should

- Understand hegemony as the process by which ideological representations are made to seem natural.
- Recognize the role of media messages in promoting global consumer culture.
- Realize that political power extends beyond the ballot box to encompass the entire realm of culture.
- Understand that human identity is socially constructed.

- Recognize the active role of audiences in constructing meaning.
- Understand that a range of quantitative and qualitative methods can be used to answer questions about texts and audiences.

MEDIA LITERACY

Although some commentators claim that media literacy is a recent development (Kubey, 1998), Anderson (1980) argued that attempts to foster media literacy have resurfaced periodically throughout the past century. Within the United States, efforts to promote critical analysis of media messages can be traced back at least as far as the propaganda analysis movement that flourished in the 1920s (Delwiche, 1996). During the same period, the British literary critic F. R. Leavis developed a curriculum that taught students to analyze advertisements, fiction, and political journalism (Leavis & Thompson, 1933).

In the United States, the most recent emphasis on media literacy can be linked to the National Leadership Conference on Media Literacy (NLCML). Convened by the Aspen Institute in 1992, this conference laid the groundwork for a national movement that shares resources and educational materials with teachers, parents, and concerned citizens. As defined by the NLCML, media literacy is the ability to "access, analyze, evaluate and communicate messages in a variety of forms" (Aufderheide, 1993, p. xx). Consequently, a media literate person "can decode, evaluate, analyze, and produce both print and electronic media" (Aufderheide, 1997, p. 79).

During the past decade, organizations such as the New Mexico Media Literacy Project, the Action Coalition for Media Education, and the Oregon Media Literacy Project, have emerged across the country, promoting media literacy through teaching materials, scholarly resources, workshops, and grassroots activism. The efforts of such organizations have focused primarily on Kindergarten through 12th-grade (K–12) classrooms (Christ & Potter, 1998), and have tended to be highly prescriptive. They offer workshops, lesson plans, curriculum standards, and media literacy kits that are geared toward parents and adolescents.

The National Communication Association (NCA) has also advanced media literacy standards targeted toward K–12 educators. According to these guidelines, media literate students should understand how individuals use media, the complex relation between audiences and media content, the significance of social and cultural contexts, and the commercial nature of contemporary media. They should also be able to use media to communicate with different audiences. Although these standards were developed for K–12 students, Christ (2004) suggested that they may be useful to college students and media practitioners alike.

The challenges of applying this media literacy model on the college level quickly become obvious when one considers that many college students are already media savvy. Thus, today's students are much more likely to have a rudimentary understanding of commercial structures, stereotypes, and the role of audiences in constructing meaning. The broad nature of the goals set forth for K–12 students limits the application of media literacy to a "commonsense" understanding of the relation between media production and interpretation. Once students enter college, the differing missions of communication departments—journalism and public relations tracks, for example, versus a general liberal arts curriculum—challenge the conceptualization of media literacy. Will aesthetics and production be emphasized, or does the understanding of hegemonic processes in the interpretation of media messages play a larger role?

James Potter's volume *Media Literacy* (2001) is specifically designed to extend media literacy concepts to higher education classrooms. Addressing cognitive processes, media effects, political economy, and sociocultural issues, Potter incorporated various areas of communication research that are often addressed separately. Bringing them together under the framework of media literacy establishes important and necessary linkages between related aspects of the media culture our students inhabit. As Christ (2002) noted, Potter's volume usefully synthesizes issues in traditional, social scientific communication research with concerns of the cultural studies paradigm. In so doing, he brings media literacy to a level that is appropriate for the introductory college course. However, Potter does not address any of the aesthetic elements, which are an indispensable component in understanding the relation between interpretation and production. He also does not address important critical approaches such as semiotics, narrative theory, and genre theory.

From the NLCML to the NCA, media literacy activists may differ in terms of emphasis and wording, but all would surely agree that a media literate college student should

- Understand that media messages are constructed, and that media messages construct reality.
- Understand the commercial implications of media.
- Identify ideological and political implications of media messages.
- Recognize the unique relation between form and content in each medium.
- Realize that receivers negotiate the meaning of media messages.

INTERPRETIVE PRODUCTION FRAMEWORK (IPF)

Although each of the aforementioned models has unique strengths, they are also incomplete. An approach that focuses solely on media aesthetics overlooks the political and cultural context in which media producers and consumers are located. Conversely, cultural studies privileges theoretical abstractions over a grounded understanding of production techniques. The media literacy model is a step in the right direction, but is often too rudimentary for college undergraduates. Thus, we propose an interpretive production framework that synthesizes the strengths of each approach.

In light of the rapidly changing professional world of communication, we see a need for a comprehensive approach to teaching with and about media content, such as a model of media literacy suggests. However, on the level of higher education, we need to assure that we prepare students to be well-informed citizens while also training fledgling media professionals who will someday shape future media content. An IPF acknowledges that our students will benefit far more from an all-encompassing approach that addresses the complexity of the reception and production of media messages, rather than to teach about reception, production, aesthetics, ownership, and social power relations separately. It also promotes a holistic view of communication by stressing the linkages between different approaches.

Before elaborating on this model, we should acknowledge that Zettl (1998) has also attempted to synthesize interpretation and production within a media literacy framework (see Fig. 7.1). His bidirectional model depicts the encoding and decoding of media messages as a four-tiered process. Contextual media aesthetics is the basis for this hierarchical model, with Zettl suggesting that his ideas provide "the fundamental and principal element in media literacy" (p. 84). The second level elaborates the influences of aesthetic and associative context on meaning, whereas the third level depicts the perceptual influence of cognitive and emotional maps. The fourth level is a grab bag of literary, textual, semiotic, sociological, psychological, and ideological approaches. Zettl characterizes these as "content perspectives," but this is the only level of the model that he does not discuss in his article. Indeed, one gets the sense that the fourth level is a catch-all category for interpretive approaches that did not fit into the other three levels.

Our interpretive production framework is similar to Zettl's (1998) approach, but there are some crucial differences (see Fig. 7.2). We agree that contextual media aesthetics should not be ignored, but we do not believe that this approach is an "encompassing theory" that provides

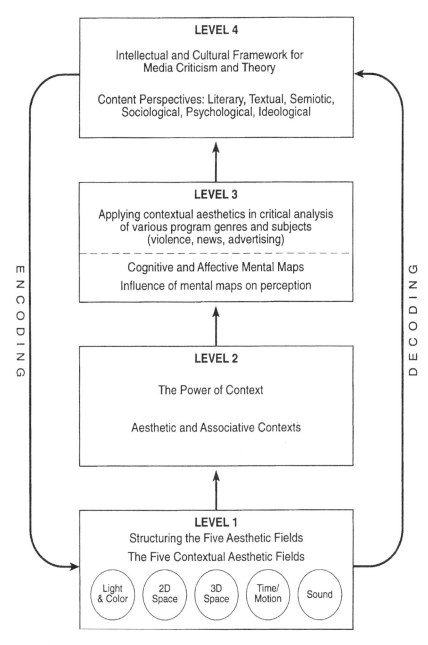

FIG. 7.1. Contextual media aesthetics as the basis for media literacy. *Note:* H. Zettl, Contextual media aesthetics as the basis for media literacy, *Journal of Communication,* 1998, v. 48, no. 1, p. 85, by permission of Oxford University Press.

Interpretive Production Framework (IPF)

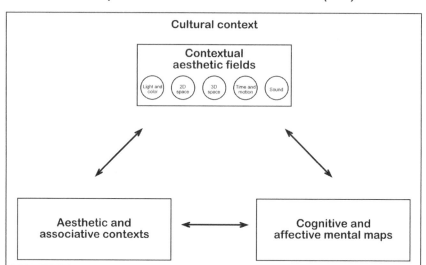

FIG. 7.2. Culture as the crucial context for interpretation and production.

the foundation for all discussions of media literacy. Consider the five aesthetic fields that constitute the first level. A substantial body of work demonstrates that culture shapes the perception of aesthetic fields such as color, space, and time (Deregowski, 1972; Eco, 1985; Mann, Siegler, & Osmond, 1968). The influence of culture on aesthetic and associative contexts (Level 2) and cognitive and aesthetic mental maps (Level 3) is even more evident. If the first three levels in Zettl's model are shaped by cultural forces, it does not make sense to relegate the "intellectual and cultural framework" to a fourth level that is dependent on the first three. Context is important, and culture is that context.

The interpretive production framework situates the discussion of contextual media aesthetics within the framework provided by cultural studies (see Table 7.1). This model is flexible enough to accommodate a range of programmatic imperatives. After all, courses focusing on the interpretation or preproduction of media messages will be shaped by the mission of the department and its place within the wider university, ranging from a purely professional or practical approach on one end of the spectrum to an exclusively theoretical approach on the other. As we envision it, the interpretive production framework is relevant to students who are working toward careers as communication professionals, students who may be interested in studying communication at a graduate

TABLE 7.1

Comparison of the Student Learning Outcomes of Three Approaches to Interpretation and Preproduction Courses and the Synthesis of These Approaches in the Interpretive Production Framework (IPF)

	Contextual Media Aesthetics	Cultural Studies	Media Literacy	IPF
Outcomes	Identify elements within five aesthetic fields	Understand hegemony as a process that naturalizes ideological representations	Understand that media messages are constructed, and that they construct reality	Draw on a range of theoretical perspectives to provide a framework to develop deeper level meanings
	Recognize technical choices that produce elements within five aesthetic fields	Recognize the role of media messages in promoting global consumer culture	Understand the commercial implications of media	Understand the role of culture in shaping the creation and interpretation of messages and the role of messages in shaping culture
	Understand how the five aesthetic fields contribute to the clarification, intensification, or interpretation of the message	Realize that political power encompasses entire realm of culture	Identify ideological and political implications of media messages	Recognize the influence of media ownership in the creation of media messages
	Use elements within the five fields to create media messages	Understand human identity is socially constructed	Recognize unique relation between form and content in each medium	Recognize the role of active audiences in using media messages to construct meaning personal identity
		Recognize the active role of audiences in constructing meaning	Realize that receivers negotiate meaning	Identify the five aesthetic contextual fields and use them to analyze or produce media messages
		Understand that range of quantitative and qualitative methods can be used to study media texts and audiences		

level, and students who have stumbled into the introductory course to fulfill a broader university requirement. This model will teach students to regard written text and images as equally important components in production and interpretation, and it will encourage them to build on foundational understandings by making connections to broader theoretical debates within the realm of social science and philosophy. This model also provides clear linkages between theory and practice.

As noted by Lewis and Jhally (1998), it is not enough to understand "the limits of . . . stereotypes," or how a text "can be read on a number of different levels" (p. 117). It is also important to understand how power relations shape messages. Although our goal is not to politicize production courses, students must understand the complex relation between the production process and the ideological structures and institutions in which these processes operate.

In summary, we believe that adopting an IPF reflects the growing need to prepare students not only to work as journalism and media professionals "in a diverse global and domestic society" (ACEJMC, 2004, p. 2), but also to enable them to understand the underlying complex structures which govern such a society. At the same time, the interpretive production framework offers us the opportunity as scholars, educators, and professionals to further bridge the gap between strictly applied and strictly theoretical approaches to our discipline and to recognize the inevitable interrelatedness between the two. This will enable all of us to "understand concepts and apply theories in the use and presentation of images and information" (ACEJMC, 2004, p. 3).

As in earlier sections of this chapter, we conclude by summarizing the learning objectives associated with the IPF. By the time students have finished a course premised on this approach, they should be able to

- Draw on a range of theoretical perspectives to provide a framework to develop the deeper level meanings of media messages, while recognizing that each theory is just one possible component of their interpretive toolkit.
- Understand the role of culture in shaping the creation and interpretation of media messages and the role of media messages in shaping culture.
- Recognize the influence of media ownership in the creation of media messages.
- Recognize the role of active audiences in using media messages to construct meaning and personal identity.
- Identify the five aesthetic contextual fields and use them to analyze or produce media messages.

REFERENCES

Accrediting Council on Education in Journalism and Mass Communications. (2004, May 1). *Standards for accreditation.* Retrieved May 26, 2004, from http://www.ukans.edu/~acejmc/BREAKING/New_standards_9-03.pdf

Anderson, B. (2003, March). Why we're not losing the culture wars anymore. *City Journal, 13*(4). Retrieved June 1, 2004, from http://www.city-journal.org/html/13_4_were_not_losing.html

Anderson, J. A. (1980). The theoretical lineage of critical viewing curriculum. *Journal of Communication, 30*(3), 64–71.

Arnheim, R. (1957). *Film as art.* Berkeley: University of California Press.

Aufderheide, P. (Ed.). (1993). *Media literacy: A report of the National Leadership Conference on Media Literacy.* Aspen, CO: Aspen Institute.

Aufderheide, P. (1997). Media literacy: From a report of the National Leadership Conference on Media Literacy. In R. Kubey (Ed.), *Media literacy in the information age* (pp. 79–86). New Brunswick, NJ: Transaction Publishers.

Barthes, R. (1972). *Mythologies* (A. Lavers, Trans.). New York: Noonday. (Original work published 1957)

Bazin, A. (1971). *What is cinema?* (Vols. 1–2; H. Gray, Trans.). Berkeley: University of California Press. (Original work published 1957)

Bordwell, D. (1989). *Making meaning: Inference and rhetoric in the interpretation of cinema.* Cambridge, MA: Harvard University Press.

Brand, R. C. (1942). The status of college and university instruction in radio training. *Quarterly Journal of Speech, 28,* 156–160.

Carey, J. (1988). Mass communication and cultural studies. In *Communication as culture: Essays on media and society* (pp. 37–68). London: Routledge.

Christ, W. (2002). Media literacy: Moving from the margins? *Journal of Broadcasting & Electronic Media, 46,* 321–327.

Christ, W. (2004). Assessment, media literacy standards, and higher education. *American Behavioral Scientist, 48*(1), 92–96.

Christ, W. G., & McCall, J. (1994). Assessing "the what" of media education. In S. Morreale & M. Brooks (Eds.), *1994 SCA summer conference proceedings and prepared remarks* (pp. 477–493). Annandale, VA: Speech Communication Association.

Christ, W. G., & Potter, W. J. (1998). Media literacy, media education, and the academy. *Journal of Communication, 48*(1), 5–15.

Delwiche, A. (1996). *Independently together: Recovering the lost art of propaganda analysis in the age of information.* Unpublished master's thesis, University of Washington, Seattle.

Deregowski, J. (1972). Pictorial perception and culture. *Scientific American, 227,* 82–88.

Downing, J. D., Sreberny, A., & Mohammadi, A. (1995). *Questioning the media: A critical introduction.* Thousand Oaks, CA: Sage.

Eco, U. (1985). How culture conditions the colors we see. In M. Blonsky (Ed.), *On signs* (pp. 157–175). Baltimore: Johns Hopkins University Press.

Eisenstein, S. (1969). *Film form* (J. Leyda, Trans.). New York: Harcourt Brace. (Original work published 1945)

Eisenstein, S. (1975). *Film sense* (J. Leyda, Trans.). New York: Harcourt Brace. (Original work published 1942)

Foucault, M. (1984). In P. Rabinow (Ed.), *The Foucault reader.* New York: Pantheon.

Giroux, H. (1992). Resisting difference: Cultural studies and the discourse of critical pedagogy. In L. Grossberg, C. Nelson, & P. Treichler (Eds.), *Cultural studies* (pp. 199–212). London: Routledge.

Giroux, H. (1994). Doing cultural studies: Youth and the challenge of pedagogy. *Harvard Educational Review, 64,* 278–308.

Gramsci, A. (1992). *Prison notebooks.* New York: Columbia University Press. (Original work published 1929)

Grossberg, L., Wartella, E., & Whitney, D. C. (1998). *MediaMaking: Mass media in popular culture.* Thousand Oaks, CA: Sage.

Hall, S. (1980). Encoding and decoding. In D. Hobson & S. Hall (Eds.), *Culture, media, and language: Working papers in cultural studies, 1972–79* (pp. 128–138). London: Hutchinson.

Hardt, H. (1992). *Critical communication studies: Communication, history and theory in America.* London: Routledge.

Horowitz, D. (1999, March 20). *Culture wars: The left's new agenda.* Paper presented at the Cardinal Mindszenty Conference, Anaheim, CA.

Kellner, D. (1995). Communication vs. cultural studies: Overcoming the divide. *Communication Theory, 5,* 162–177.

Kracauer, S. (1960). *Theory of film: The redemption of physical reality.* New York: Oxford University Press.

Kubey, R. (1998). Obstacles to the development of media education in the US. *Journal of Communication, 48*(1), 58–69.

Kucera, G. Z. (1963). Professional education for broadcasting. *Journal of Broadcasting, 7,* 123–133.

Lazarsfeld, P. (1941). Remarks on administrative and critical communication research. *Studies in Philosophy and Social Science, 9,* 2–16.

Leavis, F., & Thompson, D. (1933). *Culture and environment: The training of critical awareness.* London: Chatto & Windus.

Lewis, J., & Jhally, S. (1998). The struggle over media literacy. *Journal of Communication, 48*(1), 109–120.

Mann, H., Siegler, M., & Osmond, H. (1968). The many worlds of time. *Journal of Analytical Psychology, 13,* 33–47.

McChesney, R. (1996). Is there any hope for cultural studies? *Monthly Review, 47,* 1–18.

Messaris, P. (1994). *Visual literacy: Image, minds, and reality.* Boulder, CO: Westview.

Niven, H. (1961). The development of broadcasting education in institutions of higher education. *Journal of Broadcasting, 5,* 241–250.

Potter, W. J. (2001). *Media literacy* (2nd ed.). Thousand Oaks, CA: Sage.

Pudovkin, V. (1929). *Film technique and film acting.* London: Vision Press Ltd.

Smith, L. (1964). Education for broadcasting: 1929–1963. *Journal of Broadcasting, 8,* 383–398.

Sturken, M., & Cartwright, L. (2001). *Practices of looking: An introduction to visual culture.* New York: Oxford University Press, Inc.

Toppo, G. (2004, January 25). Survey: Freshmen more political—and more conservative. *USA Today,* p. 7D.

Van Buren, C., & Christ, W. G. (2000). Responsive essay: To why the production vs. theory dichotomy in curricular decision-making should be eliminated. *Feedback, 41*(3), 41–50.

Williams, S. H., & Medoff, N. J. (1997). Production. In W. G. Christ (Ed.), *Media education assessment handbook* (pp. 235–254). Mahwah, NJ: Lawrence Erlbaum Associates, Inc.

Wright, H. K. (2000). Pressing, promising and paradoxical: Larry Grossberg on education and cultural studies. *The Review of Education/Pedagogy/Cultural Studies, 22,* 1–25.

Zettl, H. (1998). Contextual media aesthetics as the basis for media literacy. *Journal of Communication, 48*(1), 81–95.

Zettl, H. (2005). *Sight, sound, motion: Applied media aesthetics* (4th ed.). Belmont, CA: Wadsworth.

Ethics

Margaret J. Haefner
North Park University

The best moral teaching inspires students by making them keenly aware that their own character is at stake.
—Sommers (1993, p. 18)

Those who teach media ethics have the opportunity to help students realize that they are not simply learning to "do a job." Indeed, as people preparing for careers in some of the most culturally influential professions, students must be encouraged to develop moral character based on intertwining personal and professional values. Students are required to get to the soul of the professions they are pursuing, the center at which decisions about conflicting values must be made, and from which ethical behavior emanates. Christ and McCall (1994, p. 483) suggested that not only should students understand the ethics of the profession, but they should "see if and how they are applied and [understand] and grapple with the relationship between personal and professional ethics."

This chapter draws on three trends in higher education: the move from instructor-centered teaching to learner-centered teaching (Barr & Tagg, 1995; Weimer, 2002), assessment for improvement (Astin, 1991; Mentkowski, Rogers, Doherty, Loaker, Hart, Rickards, et al., 2000; Palomba & Banta, 1999), and media ethics education (Kieran, 1999; MacDonald & Petheram, 1998). The first two are general trends that are occurring in almost any discipline of study. The third, of course, is limited to curricula in journalism and media studies that are preparing students for careers as professional communicators, as well as for graduate study. Assessment of student learning is a crucial component of learner-centered teaching, and both of them combined can enrich and enhance the effectiveness of media ethics education.

The trends in higher education in general are, in part, responses to consistent calls from politicians, parents, and practitioners for dramatic improvement in the quality of learning and preparation of students. There has been for some time a strong sentiment that higher education is turning out graduates who are ill-prepared intellectually, technically, and morally. Similarly, the performance of media professionals continues to generate skepticism among the public about whether media ethics is an oxymoron or even something that can be taught. Those who teach media ethics may have heard such comments as, "there's no such thing," or "it can be covered two paragraphs" (MacDonald & Petheram, 1998). The confluence of the emphasis on learners (rather than teachers), assessment for improvement (rather than grades), and ethical reasoning in media (rather than issues and opinions), has the potential to limit effectively the criticism of higher education in general, and media ethics education specifically.

The move toward assessment of media ethics education has been guided by such questions as the following: How do educators know that their students understand, accept, and apply professional ethics? What is reasonable to expect students to know and do as a result of ethics education? How do educators know whether their courses and curricula are effective in achieving those ends? Answers to these questions require explicating learning goals, identifying effective pedagogies, and then implementing appropriate methods of assessment. In the pages that follow, the learner-centered teaching paradigm is presented as the most appropriate for media ethics education. Learning goals and objectives are identified and several important components of media ethics education are recommended. Variables for assessment in addition to those that arise from the goals are proposed. Finally, methods for effective assessment are suggested.

Although media ethics assessment can and should take place at the program level, the focus of this chapter is on individual student and course assessment. At the program level, ethics must be integrated with the assessment of a complex array of goals and competencies for mass communication students, many of which are addressed in other chapters of this volume. Before the proper means of assessing media ethics can be addressed at the program level, effective ethics education and the means of assessing it must be defined at more "micro" levels—individuals and courses. We must know what we are looking for before we can determine where it fits in mass communication programs and assessment.

LEARNER-CENTERED TEACHING

In recent years, educators in many disciplines have chosen to shift the focus of their pedagogy from "teacher-centered" to "learner-centered." The learner-centered model of teaching, described later, is appropriate for courses in media ethics because it holds promise to enhance the effectiveness of media ethics education in terms of knowledge, moral maturity, ethical reasoning skills, and application to "real-world" media ethics quandaries.

Huba and Freed (2000) summarized some of the differences between the teacher-centered and learner-centered teaching paradigms (p. 5; see Table 8.1; see also Barr & Tagg, 1995; Weimer, 2002). Perhaps

TABLE 8.1
Comparison of Teacher-Centered and Learner-Centered Paradigms

Teacher-Centered Paradigm	*Learner-Centered Paradigm*
• Knowledge is transmitted from professor to students.	Students construct knowledge through gathering and synthesizing information and integrating it with the general skills of inquiry, communication, critical thinking, problem solving, and so on.
• Students passively receive information.	Students are actively involved.
• Emphasis is on acquisition of knowledge outside the context in which it will be used.	Emphasis is on using and communicating knowledge effectively to address enduring and emerging issues and problems in real-life contexts.
• Professor's role is to be primary information giver and primary evaluator.	Professor's role is to coach and facilitate.
• Teaching and assessment are separate.	Teaching and assessment are intertwined.
• Assessment is used to monitor learning.	Assessment is used to promote and diagnose learning.
• Emphasis is on right answers.	Emphasis is on generating better questions and learning from errors.
• Desired learning is assessed indirectly through the use of objectively scored tests.	Desired learning is assessed directly through papers, projects, performances, portfolios, and the like.
• Focus is on a single discipline.	Approach is compatible with interdisciplinary investigation.
• Culture is competitive and individualistic.	Culture is cooperative, collaborative, and supportive.
• Only students are viewed as learners.	Professor and students learn together.

the most distinguishing characteristic of learner-centered teaching is the shift in responsibility for learning from the instructor to the students. For example, in the teacher-centered paradigm, the instructor presents his or her choice of content to passive students who are evaluated for mastery of information, usually summarized in course grades. In the learner-centered paradigm, the students take "center stage" by assuming responsibility for their own learning and becoming creators of knowledge in partnership with a teacher and peers; assessment focuses on diagnosis and course improvement as a circular process. This trend is calling faculty from all disciplines to rethink what they intend as outcomes of educational experiences and the best ways to achieve them. For media ethics educators, learner-centered pedagogy encourages the kind of reflective practices, dilemma identification, cooperative learning, and learning-by-practice for practical application necessary to master the learning goals explicated earlier.

GOALS FOR MEDIA ETHICS EDUCATION

The learner-centered paradigm is appropriate for media ethics education, especially when considering the kinds of goals and outcomes that are desired for students. The Hastings Center's five goals for ethics instruction (Callahan, 1980) are presented later as a model for media ethics education because of the emphasis on critical inquiry and the potential effectiveness for a learner-centered pedagogical approach.

Stimulating the Moral Imagination

The first two goals are opposite sides of the same coin. Before anything, ethics instruction should engage the emotions and imagination of students, allowing them to feel their reactions to ethically salient issues and situations. Although the intellect is a necessary balance that should be included soon, students' affect should be awakened first. Media ethics education is more honest when it encourages students to feel their human responses that result from their value-laden humanness.

Recognizing Ethical Issues

Visceral responses should quickly be subjected to the other side of the coin, the "conscious, rational attempt to sort out those elements in emotional responses that represent appraisal and judgment" (Callahan,

1980, p. 65). Students should evaluate their immediate responses, identify unstated assumptions, and assess whether ethical analysis is called for. Although emotional responses can sometimes signal true moral messages, students must know that what they feel is right may not actually be right.

Eliciting a Sense of Moral Obligation

The major point of ethics instruction is to guide conduct. It is possible that ethical dilemmas can be recognized, discussed, and analyzed without any impact on behavior. Students should recognize an essential requirement of ethical thinking; "that it calls us to act in light of what we perceive to be right and good" (Callahan, 1980, p. 66). Furthermore, individuals are the true moral agents, and, as moral agents, we are all liable for our actions and should not blame others for our ethical shortcomings or failures.

Developing Analytical Skills

Students must cultivate the ability to use the tools of rationality in ethics. They must be put through the rigors of defining concepts, analyzing the import and effects of moral rules, and exploring the meaning and scope of ethical principles (Callahan, 1980, p. 67). Media ethics students should also define such concepts as justice, moral duty, moral rights, respect for others, dignity, and autonomy (Day, 1991; Jaksa & Pritchard, 1994), as well as traditional media concepts such as press freedom, confidentiality, and advertising puffery.

Tolerating and Reducing Disagreement and Ambiguity

Students should be able to clarify facts and layout meticulous arguments, but realize that it is not always possible to reach agreement among those with differing views. Instead of trying to prove the correct or true answers, the arguments of those with whom students disagree can be evaluated for their internal consistency and coherence, their breadth, clarity, reasoning, and so forth. Media students in particular should be good listeners and be willing to thoughtfully discuss matters with those with whom they disagree (Jaksa & Pritchard, 1994).

WHAT SHOULD BE ASSESSED IN MEDIA ETHICS EDUCATION?

The learner-centered paradigm places assessment at the center of the educational experience with the promise of enhanced learning and skillful, knowledgeable, and thoughtful application to media ethics dilemmas. Although each of the learning goals for media ethics education could be measured at the end of students' formal exposure to ethics instruction, the processes students go through to achieve the goals is perhaps the most interesting component of ethics education. Therefore, the emphasis in media ethics courses should be on formative assessment (intertwined teaching and assessment), which provides feedback to faculty and students for continual improvement throughout the course. In many people's minds, assessment is summative, which focuses on final outcomes or effects of instruction. Although summative assessment is important for clarifying changes necessary to courses and curricula on completion by students, and for documenting overall effectiveness over time, formative assessment focuses on the processes of teaching and learning, as well as on diagnosis and improvement of student learning by providing them with continual feedback about their performances as they go. Formative assessment helps faculty identify students' strengths and weaknesses, and to monitor and refine courses as they are underway. Thus, formative assessment, a central component of learner-centered teaching, is essential for media ethics education.

What comprises effective formative assessment? It is much more complex than evaluating a few assignments and assigning a final course grade. Rather, the best formative assessment accounts for a number of variables that affect student learning besides those associated with the course's content. Thus, for a professor to understand where a student is with respect to learning in a media ethics course, he or she ought to know where the student came from, what values were brought with the student to the class, and the sources of competing or conflicting values the student confronts on and off campus.

Astin's I-E-O Model

Astin's (1991) model for program assessment includes assessment of variables that certainly contribute to students' moral education, although they are not under the control of an ethics instructor. Although it is intended for program assessment, this model can easily be adapted for course assessment and media ethics, in particular. The benefit of Astin's model is that it provides a broad and well-informed context for understanding student learning, as well as guidance for assessing goals and outcomes.

Astin (1991) strongly urged accounting for a variety of variables in assessment programs. His I-E-O model presents a simple framework for considering the appropriate components of an assessment program. By measuring and evaluating inputs (I), environment (E), and outcomes (O), faculty can assess the effectiveness of courses and improvements made by students as a result of their educational experiences. The model is based on three premises: (a) the output of any course does not accurately reflect its educational impact or effectiveness in developing talent, (b) any output measure is not determined solely by a single input measure, and (c) even if good longitudinal input and output data are available, our understanding of educational processes and effects cannot be complete without accounting for students' environment while in college.

In Astin's (1991) model, inputs are those personal qualities that students bring to the educational program. Environment refers to students' experiences while in the program. Outcomes refer to the "talents" that the program is intended to develop. Astin's general questions with respect to each of the three components can be adapted for those assessing media ethics education. As input variables, media educators would ask, "Is it reasonable to suppose that an instructor should want to know something about his or her students before formal ethics instruction begins?" For instance, an instructor might want to know some general things about students such as, what are their plans and aspirations? What do they want out of college? What are their academic strengths and weaknesses? What is their socioeconomic background? What were their achievements and activities in high school? With respect to media ethics, what do they want out of a course in media ethics? What is each student's level of moral development? What are their current personal and professional values? What sources have significantly affected the values students bring to the class, sources such as family, church, youth organizations, primary and secondary education, and other ethics education in college? How aware are students of the ethical dimensions of media? How well do they think critically? How aware are they of media theory and effects? Although hardly an exhaustive list, it is evident that such an ethical profile at the start of a media ethics regimen will allow for statements of change and improvement as a result, in part, of the program.

Not only do students bring complex sets of variables with them that will affect their personal processes of goal achievement, but their environment in college during the ethics program will also influence their goal achievement. Astin (1991) suggested that it is reasonable that we should know what concurrent educational experiences students are having while in the course. Beyond the courses they are now taking, what kind of extracurricular activities do different students participate in? How are they supporting themselves? How many of them work and what kinds of jobs do they hold? What goes on in their residence halls? Are they participating in special educational programs? With respect to media ethics, are they currently working, for pay or in unpaid internships, at media outlets, either on or off campus? How active are they in other values-oriented groups, such as family, peers, church, or media organizations? How much time do they spend with the media?

Finally, Astin (1991) asked whether it is reasonable to expect that we should know something about the educational progress of each student during college and after graduation. How long is it taking them to complete their programs of study? What are students actually learning in this class and others? How do they perceive their educational experiences? How do they rate the quality of instruction they get in this course and others? Are they getting what they want out of college? What happens to students when they leave? What kinds of jobs do they hold? Do they feel we have prepared them adequately for work, for marriage, for parenthood, and so forth? For media students and alumni, how well were they prepared for ethical dilemmas they face as media professionals? How critical of media are they as citizens and consumers? (Astin, 1991).

This description of Astin's (1991) model suggests a variety of variables that could be assessed at the beginning, throughout, and at the end of media ethics education. Ethics instructors would do well to recognize at least three other variables that are particularly relevant to media ethics education: (a) students' moral and cognitive development, (b) instructors' teaching styles, and (c) students' learning styles. In Astin's I-E-O model, moral and cognitive development and learning styles could be considered both input and outcome variables, whereas instructors' teaching styles is an environmental variable. Each is important in assessing ethics education because, in many ways, the extent of individual students' achievement of the goals of stimulating the moral imagination, recognizing ethical issues, and developing analytical skills, depends on these very factors. In fact, it can be argued that students who achieve these goals have made, by some definitions, significant moral advancements, so moral development becomes an overarching goal of ethics education.

Moral and Cognitive Development

Kohlberg (1984) and others proposed that moral development, both vertical and horizontal, should be the central aim of all education (see Lickona, 1980, p. 110). Vertical development refers to achieving more complete, consonant, and integrated stages of moral reasoning, and horizontal development refers to the application of one's highest stage to wider realms of experience. Lickona (1980) pointed out that changes in moral stages are small over the course of a semester or year and that changes may be slow and not appear at all until well after instruction has occurred. These observations should not prevent moral development from becoming a goal of ethics instruction. Rather, it simply means that assessments may need to be sensitive to modest change and may need to occur over a period of time, even after graduation.

Moral Development. Kohlberg's (1984) and Gilligan's (1982) theories of moral development are two of the most dominant in ethics education. Kohlberg's model divides development into three levels with two stages each. The key variable in determining stage is how one reasons to a conclusion, not the conclusion itself. To have achieved the goals set up for instruction in media ethics is for students to have reached the third level of Kohlberg's model, called "post conventional." The two stages of moral reasoning at this level are characterized by self-reflective thinking, independence of mind in moral thought, and embracing a more comprehensive and impartial point of view (Jaksa & Pritchard, 1994, p. 97).

One problem with using Kohlberg's (1984) stage theory is its focus on the male moral voice, an "ethic of justice" that is characterized by logically derived absolute principles that equate morality with justice (Gilligan, 1982). The characteristics of the female moral voice, an "ethic of care," are not as valued. Female accentuation of relationships, compassion, and nurturance of others is considered to be only at Stage 3 in Kohlberg's model. Gilligan (1982) argued that the female voice is equally as valuable as the male voice and may be complementary to it. The male and female voices, although typically characteristic of men and women, respectively, may be found in either men or women. And, although the female moral voice may develop along a different track than the male voice, it is not less morally mature. "It is important for both women and men to know and admit that the Female System exists and is good—not necessarily better, but good" (Schaef, as cited in Johannesen, 1990, p. 131). Thus, in considering moral development as variables affecting media ethics education, instructors must be sensitive to different kinds of moral maturity and give equal value to male and female moral voices (Johannesen, 1990).

Cognitive Development. Katz and Henry (1988), McBeath (1992), and Yingling (1994) agreed that improvement in learning can only be understood when students' cognitive maturity is accounted for. One theory of cognitive development that is particularly pertinent for ethics education because it also includes ethical development is Perry's (as cited in Mc-

Beath, 1992) stages of learning. Perry identified nine growth steps, which he grouped into four major stages of intellectual and ethical development. "The Perry outline shows how students move from the need for certainties and a dependence on authority, to being able to accept ambiguity as they create meaning and order in their world . . . As in the other stage theories of development (e.g., Piaget), each stage is more complex and comprehensive than the previous one, as the student perceives increased complexities in the world and uncertainties in knowledge" (McBeath, 1992, pp. viii, x). The four major stages in Perry's model are as follows:

1. Dualism—The dualistic student sees the world in polar terms of right and wrong, good and bad, not better or worse. Right answers exist for each problem and are known by an authority, usually the teacher. The dualistic student wants directions in black and white, and will do as told by the authority without critical evaluation of the directions.

2. Multiplicity—At this stage the dualistic, authority structure is modified. Ambiguity is unwillingly acknowledged, but it is seen as a temporary thing because the final truth has yet to be determined. Everyone is seen as having a right to his or her own opinion, but the resulting uncertainty will be resolved by the authority. Students at this stage have no pattern to their thinking and the quantity of information held has more significance than the quality.

3. Relativism—Rather than accumulating quantities of information to prove right and wrong, students see all knowledge and values as contextual and relativistic. Ambiguity is accepted, and knowledge is seen as a blend of fact and opinion. Knowledge is now qualitative and some opinions are seen as important; others as not important, depending on the context.

4. Commitment—Students at the stage of commitment accept responsibility for their own ideas and actions. They hold convictions and acceptance of their own doubts; they can see their potential and their limitations. A strong sense of identity is developed as the students learn to explore and develop a sense of confidence in a relativistic world where reasonable people can disagree, where there are no pat answers and where new challenges continue to appear (McBeath, 1992, pp. viii–x).

Teaching Styles

An associated variable that seems important for assessing students' achievement of goals for media ethics education is instructor's teaching style. McBeath (1992) argued that teaching styles can have a serious effect on students' progress through Perry's stages of learning. Earlier, the learner-centered paradigm was recommended as most appropriate for media ethics education. The paradigm calls for teachers to be working at the third and fourth stages of teaching, presented later. The four stages of teaching are closely correlated to those four stages of learning. These are as follows:

1. Teacher dominated—This stage is associated with the dualistic learning stage. Its characteristics are "teaching is telling," one-way communication; questions and answers; subject matter acquisition is basic; and tests on recall.
2. Subject centered—This stage is associated with the multiplicity learning stage. Its characteristics are "teaching is telling," plus media; one way communication with some ambiguity; cites multiple authorities; students are expected to be active learners; evaluation on recall and applications.
3. Learning task oriented—This stage is associated with the relativism learning stage. Its characteristics are teaching includes group and individual work; assessment using alternative methods; different authorities and ambiguity is accepted; two-way communication for mastery; evaluation on recall, applications, implications.
4. Inquiry centered—This stage is associated with the commitment learning stage. Its characteristics are courses based on readiness level; critical inquiry encouraged; creativity supported; collaborative problem solving; evaluation based on mastery of criteria (McBeath, 1992, pp. ix–xii).

Student Learning Styles

Given differences in students' cognitive and moral development, it is not surprising that they would differ in their expectations for education, as well. These differences in expectations, or learning styles, have important implications for media ethics education because they reflect the diversity of the students in a typical classroom. And, although one might presume that all mass communication students have at least some interest in the content area, they likely have very different expectations for faculty, assignments, exams, projects, and their own work habits (Potter, 1994).

Potter (1994) identified five broad categories of learning styles from which 16 specific styles stem. The five broad style categories are as follows: (a) Dependent students want direction from instructors or texts; they want to follow the rules and get the most content out of a course for the least amount of effort; (b) Independent students take pride in setting and achieving their own goals, following their own course, and developing their own strategies for success; (c) Competitive students see the course as a game to be won; the best instructors make the game interesting and reward the best players; (d) Participant students like being part of the class because of their contact with others; the best instructors have a lot class activities that involve students; and (e) Avoidant students dislike their courses and want to be left alone by instructors; they want to have to do as little as possible to get through the course.

The discussion of Astin's (1991) I-E-O model and the emphasis on students' cognitive and moral maturity, their learning styles, and instructors' teaching styles as crucial input and environmental variables, indicate the complexity of assessing student outcomes. Their measurement is not always easy, but they ought to be considered if the goal of assessment is improved teaching and learning. In the section that follows, methods for assessing several variables that are essential to media ethics education are presented.

HOW TO ASSESS MEDIA ETHICS

This section addresses the methods available for assessing students' achievement of the five course goals laid out earlier. Throughout the literature, a debate continues as to the appropriateness of quantitative versus qualitative measures of assessment. Although quantitative measures that yield statistics about student performance and program quality are the most important means of providing information to external constituencies, many of those who advocate assessment primarily as a means of improving student learning lean toward qualitative measures. Qualitative measures provide the rich feedback that is essential to improving teaching and learning. Nevertheless, some of the additional variables mentioned already are best measured by the quantitative instruments designed specifically for them. After a very brief review of quantitative measures appropriate for moral development and values, the use of student portfolios as a comprehensive means of assessment is recommended. In addition, a variety of methods for assessing each of the five goals for a course in media ethics are suggested.

Some of the input and environment variables are appropriately measured using standardized instruments (see Table 8.2). For instance, Rest's Defining Issues Test (DIT) is a measure of moral development that is correlated with Kohlberg's (1984) stages of moral development. According to Rest, the DIT is only intended to measure moral judgment, not moral worth or likely moral conduct (as cited in Caplan, 1980, p.

TABLE 8.2
Measurement of Variables Relevant to Media Ethics Education

Variable	What Is Assessed	How to Assess
• Kohlberg's (1984) Stages of Moral Development	Level of moral judgment, moral worth, or likely moral conduct.	Rest's Defining Issues Test (see Caplan, 1980)
• Ethic of Justice versus Ethic of Care	Whether students tend to have male moral voice (justice) or female moral voice (nurturance, compassion, relationships).	Gilligan and Attanucci's Real-Life Dilemma Test (1988)
• Perry's Stages of Cognitive and Intellectual Growth	Comprehensiveness with which students perceive complexities of the world and uncertainties of knowledge.	McBeath (1992)
• Teaching styles	Extent of teacher domination versus student collaboration, one-way versus two-way communication, single versus multiple means of assessing student learning, and so forth.	McBeath (1992)
• Learning styles	Students' expectations for faculty, assignments, own work habits.	Potter and Emanuel's Student Learning Style Instrument (1990)
• Values	Several types: altruism, masculine–feminine, work-professional, instrumental versus terminal, etc.	See Grandy (1989)

142). Gilligan and Attanucci (1988) developed a Real-Life Dilemma test to measure whether students primarily hold an ethic of justice or an ethic of care. Perry's stages of cognitive and intellectual growth can be assessed by administering his instruments, as can McBeath's (1987) teaching styles measures that correlate with Perry's stages. Students' learning styles can be measured using Potter and Emanuel's (1990) Student Learning Style Instrument. Grandy (1989) listed and critiqued several instruments suitable for measuring values, including Sawyer's Altruism Scale, Bode and Page's Ethical Reasoning Inventory, Steinmann and Fox's Maferr Inventory of Masculine–Feminine Values, Super's Work Values Inventory, and Rokeach's Value Survey (all are cited in Grandy, 1989). These instruments can be useful for establishing personal values as input or environment variables, and give students a base from which to integrate professional values throughout the course.

Student Portfolios as a Comprehensive Assessment Method

In view of the complex goals for a course in ethics, student portfolios can be used as one overarching means of assessment; that is, they give students the opportunity to reflect on their own progress and evaluate their own learning (metathinking). Huba and Freed (2000) said that "student portfolios are compatible with a learner-centered approach to teaching in which students use what they know to complete important tasks" (p. 234). Fink (2003) noted that the student portfolio's "unusual power derives from the fact that it simultaneously integrates and promotes all three of the main components of instructional design: significant learning goals, active learning activities, and educative feedback and assessment" (p. 118). Portfolio assessment is the most appropriate method for formative assessment in a course because students collect work over time and portfolios are evaluated at several points throughout the semester. They lend themselves to the formative assessment of students' progress toward learning goals, assessment by both the teacher and the student. Students and professors engage in a dynamic interaction of teaching and learning that can focus students on learning rather than producing assignments that are graded once and returned, with no chance for students to reflect and improve. Student portfolios are much more than a collection of student work. "In order for a portfolio to be useful in assessment, someone must reflect and make judgments about its content" (Huba & Freed, 2000, p. 234). And, for those with a learner-centered approach, students themselves are among the most important evaluators of their own learning.

Student portfolios are ideal means of assessing student performance in a media ethics course for several reasons. First, they provide evidence of "doing" in the course through the collection of student materials, and evidence of student "learning" in the course through self-reflection on experiences in the course (Fink, 2003; Huba & Freed, 2000; Orlik, 1994; Palomba & Banta, 1999). Portfolios allow instructors to "get inside students' learning" (Romano, 1994, p. 73). They also encourage students to reflect on their own learning; in the case of media ethics, students can self-assess the extent to which they are mastering the goals throughout a semester (Diamond, 1998; Mentkowski, Rogers, Doherty, Loaker, Hart, Rickards, et al., 2000). Second, portfolios are "historical" documents in that they can show changes over time and the chronological development of students' mastery of course goals (Aitken, 1993; Arneson, 1994). Third, portfolios lend themselves well to a course format that implements formative assessment using Astin's (1991) I-E-O model by allowing students to include input information, and collect environment information that can be used to interpret final outcomes. As

Romano (1994) observed, portfolios, "measure success not simply by where learners end their journey, but also where they began, how and where they traveled, what they encountered along the way, and what they did in the face of it" (p. 73). Fourth, portfolios can help improve students' self-esteem as they compile information about their growth and accomplishments (Aitken, 1993, p. 10). Although students may be reticent at first to engage in this exercise that is, for many, the first time they've been asked about their own learning, Perry (as cited in Waluconis, 1993) found that as students progress in their studies, they look forward to the opportunity to evaluate themselves. Also, Bard (as cited in Lenning, 1988) found that students are relatively honest even when dealing with sensitive questions.

Lenning (1988) suggested two principles that should guide the use of portfolios. First, they should be just one of multiple assessment methods employed, and second, "they should include the *smallest* number of class products that provide adequate information about the goals being measured" (Lenning, 1988, p. 142). Almost anything having to do with the media ethics class can be included as an artifact in student portfolios, as long as it truly represents progress students have made. One of the beauties of portfolio assessment is their flexibility to meet the individual needs of students. Throughout the semester, students complete assignments, exams, and other measures designed to assess their progress toward the goals for the course. Rather than a portfolio becoming a "catch all," only those items that reflect progress should be included. Additionally, students' self-reflections on those artifacts and their own progress should be included (Huba & Freed, 2000).

Electronic Portfolios. The use of electronic portfolios has been increasing in recent years because, in addition to accomplishing the assessment of learning in ways similar to paper portfolios, they offer new forms of convenience for both students as they build their portfolios and for professors as they evaluate them. Canada (2002) noted that "e-folios" are convenient for students to revise and maintain, are easily navigable, and develop communication skills. For professors, paper portfolios can be tremendously time consuming to evaluate, one reason that some have never chosen to adopt portfolios despite their usefulness for assessment. "E-portfolios," especially online portfolios, are convenient and actually enhance the portfolio learning and assessment process. Two formats are used, including CD-ROM and online portfolios. CDs provide flexibility of revision and portability for students without requiring Internet access. This is an essential consideration if all students do not have access to computers and Internet service providers with enough "horsepower" to handle the transfer of large amounts of data in a timely, efficient mode. Assuming students' access to efficient Internet services, the advantages of online portfolios outweigh those of both paper and CDs (Canada, 2002, p. 71). Online portfolios (a) encourage revision, because it is easy and convenient to do; (b) always look polished despite many revisions; (c) allow for easy inclusion of nonwritten work, such as video, audio, and visual texts, and written work that is accessible on the World Wide Web; (d) are more accessible to all members of the class 24 hr a day, allowing asynchronous evaluation by students, professors, and classmates; (e) encourage peers to read and comment on each other's work, an excellent form of formative assessment during a course; and (f) allow students to easily maintain their portfolios after the course has ended.

There are some drawbacks and criticisms of portfolio assessment (Lenning, 1988; Palomba & Banta, 1999). Many practical questions can be difficult to resolve, such as what is to be collected, by whom, when, and how will the information be evaluated? Also, because there are no real prescriptions for what a portfolio should look like, instructors may take a long time to develop portfolio requirements that are useful and meaningful to students and the instructor. Even with a small number of student portfolios and even if they are online, evaluation can be very time consuming, especially if the plan requires intermittent evaluation at several points in the course or program. Evaluation of course portfolios is typically completed by the course instructor, although program-level portfolios can require sometimes difficult coordination of portfolio evaluation among several instructors. With respect to evaluation, Arneson (1994) noted that criteria for evaluation need to be clarified at the outset and be clearly linked to learning goals. Criteria may include "evidence of improvement, student effort, quality of self-evaluation, range of projects, presentation, and future goals" (Tierney, Canter, & Desai, as cited in Arneson, 1994, p. 116). Lenning (1988) also noted concern for student privacy and protection of instructors' exams and assignments for future use as considerations. One additional challenge is authenticity (Arneson, 1994; Palomba & Banta, 1999). To ensure the authenticity of student work, students should be required to demonstrate how each artifact was prepared and how it fits into the progressive growth toward course goals. Despite these challenges, however, evidence suggests that the student portfolio is an excellent overarching method of assessment, especially for reflective disciplines such as media ethics.

What Evidence Should a Portfolio Contain?

Artifacts should be selected that will allow students to reflect on their progress toward achieving the five goals for a media ethics course. Examples of artifacts that lend themselves to reflective analysis include the following: rough drafts, final copies, self-awareness journals, study skills inventories, observations, interviews, individual learning contracts, anecdotal files, videotapes, communication logs, dialogue journals, tape recordings, narrative accounts, written responses to content area textbooks, standardized tests, nonstandardized tests, peer critiques, group assessment, and cumulative folders. Students' personal reflections and analyses should accompany all artifacts. As noted earlier, these are not intended to "show and tell," but as thoughtful, reflective comments (Arneson, 1994, p. 116). Assignments and assessments must be made throughout the semester so that students can have artifacts from which to choose for inclusion in their portfolios. Following are a few suggestions about appropriate methods of assessment for each of the media ethics education goals. Any of the artifacts, then, can be selected for inclusion in the portfolio (see Table 8.3).

For the first goal, stimulating the moral imagination, instructors may consider not only having practicing media professionals speak to classes about their own experiences, but people who have been affected by the media (Christians & Covert, 1980). Films, novels, and plays can also be effective in eliciting emotions (Callahan, 1980; Christians & Covert, 1980). Students' moral imagination can be assessed through in-class observations, both by instructors and peers, role playing, students' own self-reflective written essays, or one-on-one interviews with the instructor. Lenning (1988) suggested the Behavioral Events Analysis, which is a 2½ hr, one-on-one interview that may be adapted for assessing the first goal. "Successful as well as unsuccessful students are asked to identify and describe, in concrete and generic behavioral terms, events . . . and to tell all they know about these episodes, including their own feelings before, during, and after the events" (Lenning, 1988, p. 44).

For the second goal, recognizing ethical issues, current events journals that are analyzed for ethical dimensions are useful. Students can be asked to keep media-use diaries that focus on looking for ethical components of media performance and their own relationships to media. Cases are among the most frequently used means of helping students to expand their conceptions of where and how ethical issues arise. Students should also be encouraged to look for ethical issues that arise in other classes, especially seeking out components having to do with media.

Assessing the third goal, eliciting a sense of moral obligation that results in changed behavior, is exceedingly difficult to do. Although moral behavior may be the ultimate goal of ethics teaching, observing changes in moral behavior and attributing them to a course in ethics is dubious. Even if input and environmental variables are considered as part of the behavior change, behavior is a complex phenomenon that may have no

TABLE 8.3
Assessment of Goals for Media Ethics Education

Goal	What Is Assessed	How to Assess
Stimulating the moral imagination	Students' emotional responses to ethically salient issues and situations. May be elicited by guest speakers, novels, plays, films, current media events.	1. Instructor and peer in-class or online observations. 2. Self-reflective essays. 3. Personal interviews. 4. Lenning's (1988) Behavioral Events Analysis.
Recognizing ethical issues	Students' unstated assumptions and abilities to assess whether ethical analysis is called for.	1. Current events journal. 2. Media-use diary. 3. Case analyses. 4. Reports of ethical issues that arise in other media classes.
Eliciting a sense of moral obligation	Changes in moral behavior or the will to behave ethically.	1. Written or oral self-evaluations. 2. Reports from other instructors about students' willingness to raise ethical issues outside of class (with students' permission). 3. Reports (personal or from others) about students' actions in media-related settings (jobs, internships, student newspaper, etc.).
Developing analytical skills	Students' proper use of ethical decision-making models.	1. Written or oral presentations of cases or current media events. 2. Issues brief (Warnick & Inch, 1993). 3. Games and simulations.
Tolerating and reducing disagreement and ambiguity	Students' respect for others, listening skills, and their abilities to evaluate others' arguments.	1. In-class observations of small group or class discussions, or online observations of reactions to peers' portfolios. 2. Students' essays about discussions they've had with people with whom they disagree.

relation at all to one's level of moral development or ability to reason morally. (See Lickona's [1980] discussion of social psychology in the teaching of ethics.) "With respect to behavior, however, the most important goal would be that of providing the student with those ingredients of ethical analysis and self-criticism, such that he would, if the analysis seemed to require it, both recognize the importance of changing behavior, and be prepared to change it" (Callahan, 1980, p. 70). Students' sense of the importance of changing behavior and their willingness to do so can be assessed through their own written or oral self-evaluations, instructors' observations of students in class, and students' willingness to raise issues concerning media ethics problems outside the ethics classroom in other classes (as observed by other instructors), such as "hands-on" media classes (e.g., reporting, TV, or radio production).

For the fourth goal, developing analytical skill, students' proper use of ethical decision-making models, and their proper application of moral principles, can be assessed through written or oral presentations of cases or ethical issues that arise in the course of daily life. The issues brief (Warnick & Inch, 1993) allows students to become familiar with multiple views on an issue, so as to improve their own arguments, as well as their abilities to anticipate and respond to the opinions and arguments of others. Caplan (1980) noted that games and simulations can also help to indicate students' abilities to analyze hypothetical moral problems. They can help determine the extent to which students can take sides, and articulate the reasoning underlying different points of view. They can help students put themselves in the shoes of others to see problems from something other than a personal standpoint.

For the fifth goal, assessing students' abilities to tolerate and reduce disagreement, group discussions, in which students can be observed to clarify facts and to listen carefully and nonjudgmentally, can be audiotaped or videotaped. Observations of students' performance in class can be made with attention to their willingness to discuss, challenge, and listen to classmates' and the instructor's points of view. Students can write about assigned audiotaped conversations they have with people they know will disagree with them. The instructor can listen to the tape and determine, by comparing the student's writing with the conversation, how well the student listened, clarified facts and misunderstandings, and how the student reacted to that person once the pair agreed to disagree.

CONCLUSION

The purpose of this chapter has been to articulate the goals for media ethics education and suggest means of assessing students' achievement of those goals. The Hastings Center's five goals lend themselves to the learner-centered teaching paradigm with its emphasis on student learning and formative assessment. Astin's (1991) I-E-O directs attention to a number of important variables in ethics assessment. Perhaps nowhere else in the media curriculum are moral and cognitive development and learning and teaching styles more salient than in the media ethics course, for they have the potential to affect the achievement of goals in tangible ways. The methods recommended, although far from comprehensive, are reasonable for true assessment of teaching and learning. Qualitative methods, especially student portfolios, can be time consuming and difficult, but electronic portfolios have improved the flexibility and effectiveness of portfolio assessment for both students and faculty. Portfolios yield the kinds of information that get to the heart of a media ethics class—emotions and moral imagination, analytical skills, moral will (if not behavior)—in ways that quantitative methods cannot. Courses in media ethics give instructors a unique opportunity to help students develop moral character that will carry them through personal and professional ethical dilemmas. Careful assessment can help instructors be sure that they are making the most of the opportunity, for their students' sake.

REFERENCES

Aitken, J. E. (1993, April). *Empowering students and faculty through portfolio assessment.* Paper presented at the annual meeting of the Central States Communication Association, Lexington, KY.

Arneson, P. (1994). Assessing communication competence through portfolios, scoring rubrics, and personal interviews. In S. Morreale, M. Brooks, R. Berko, & C. Cooke (Eds.), *1994 summer conference proceedings and prepared remarks* (pp. 113–123). Annandale, VA: Speech Communication Association.

Astin, A. W. (1991). *Assessment for excellence.* New York: Macmillan.

Barr, R. B., & Tagg, J. (1995, November/December). From teaching to learning: A new paradigm for undergraduate education. *Change, 27*(6), 12–25.

Callahan, D. (1980). Goals in the teaching of ethics. In D. Callahan & S. Bok (Eds.), *Ethics teaching in higher education* (pp. 61–74). New York: The Hastings Center.

Canada, M. (2002). Assessing e-folios in the on-line class. In R. S. Anderson, J. F. Bauer, & B. W. Speck (Eds.), *Assessment strategies for the on-line class: From theory to practice* (pp. 69–75). San Francisco: Jossey-Bass.

Caplan, A. L. (1980). Evaluation and the teaching of ethics. In D. Callahan & S. Bok (Eds.), *Ethics teaching in higher education* (pp. 133–150). New York: The Hastings Center.

Christ, W. G., & McCall, J. M. (1994). Assessing the "what" of media education. In S. Morreale, M. Brooks, R. Berko, & C. Cooke (Eds.), *1994 summer conference proceedings and prepared remarks* (pp. 476–493). Annandale, VA: Speech Communication Association.

Christians, C. G., & Covert, C. L. (1980). *Teaching ethics in journalism education.* New York: The Hastings Center.

Day, L. A. (1991). *Ethics in media communications: Cases and controversies.* Belmont, CA: Wadsworth.

Diamond, R. M. (1998). *Designing and assessing courses and curricula: A practical guide.* San Francisco: Jossey-Bass.

Fink, L. D. (2003). *Creating significant learning experiences: An integrated approach to designing college courses.* San Francisco: Jossey-Bass.

Gilligan, C. (1982). *In a different voice.* Cambridge, MA: Harvard University Press.

Gilligan, C., & Attanucci, J. (1988). Two moral orientations: Gender differences and similarities. *Merrill-Palmer Quarterly, 34,* 223–237.

Grandy, J. (1989). Assessing changes in student values. In C. Adelman (Ed.), *Performance and judgment: Essays on principles and practice in the assessment of college student learning* (pp. 139–161). Washington, DC: U.S. Department of Education.

Huba, M. E., & Freed, J. E. (2000). *Learner-centered assessment on college campuses.* Needham Heights, MA: Allyn & Bacon.

Jaksa, J. A., & Pritchard, M. S. (1994). *Communication ethics: Methods of analysis* (2nd ed.). Belmont, CA: Wadsworth.

Johannesen, R. L. (1990). *Ethics in human communication* (3rd ed.). Prospect Heights, IL: Waveland.

Katz, J., & Henry, M. (1988). *Turning professors into teachers.* New York: American Council on Education/Macmillan.

Kieran, M. (1999). *Media ethics: A philosophical approach.* Westport, CT: Praeger.

Kohlberg, L. (1984). *The psychology of moral development: The nature and validity of moral stages.* San Francisco: Harper & Row.

Lenning, O. T. (1988). Use of noncognitive measures in assessment. In T. W. Banta (Ed.), *Implementing outcomes assessment: Promise and perils* (pp. 41–52). San Francisco: Jossey-Bass.

Lickona, T. (1980). What does moral psychology have to say to the teacher of ethics? In D. Callahan & S. Bok (Eds.), *Ethics teaching in higher education* (pp. 103–132). New York: The Hastings Center.

MacDonald, B., & Petheram, M. (1998). *Key guide to information sources in media ethics.* London: Mansell.

McBeath, R. J. (1987). Stages in learning, teaching, and media support services. *Educational Technology, 27*(10), 50–54.

McBeath, R. J. (1992). *Instructing and evaluating in higher education: A guidebook for planning learning outcomes.* Englewood Cliffs, NJ: Education Technology Publications.

Mentkowski, M., Rogers, G., Doherty, A., Loacker, G., Hart, J. R., Rickards, W., et al. (2000). *Learning that lasts: Integrating learning, development, and performance in college and beyond.* San Francisco: Jossey-Bass.

Orlik, P. B. (1994). Student portfolios. In W. G. Christ (Ed.), *Assessing communication education: A handbook for media, speech, and theatre educators* (pp. 131–154). Hillsdale, NJ: Lawrence Erlbaum Associates, Inc.

Palomba, C. A., & Banta, T. W. (1999). *Assessment essentials: Planning, implementing, and improving assessment in higher education.* San Francisco: Jossey-Bass.

Potter, W. J. (1994). Teaching evaluation. In W. G. Christ (Ed.), *Assessing communication education: A handbook for media, speech, and theatre educators* (pp. 89–112). Hillsdale, NJ: Lawrence Erlbaum Associates, Inc.

Potter, W. J., & Emanuel, R. (1990). Students' preferences for communication styles and their relationship to achievement. *Communication Education, 39,* 234–249.

Romano, T. (1994). Removing the blindfold: Portfolios in fiction writing classes. In L. Black, D. Daiker, J. Sommers, & G. Stygall (Eds.), *New directions in portfolio assessment* (pp. 73–82). Portsmouth, NH: Boynton/Cook.

Sommers, C. H. (1993, September 12). Teaching the virtues: A blueprint for moral education. *Chicago Tribune Magazine, 255,* 14, 16, 18.

Waluconis, C. J. (1993). Student self-evaluation. In T. W. Banta (Ed.), *Making a difference: Outcomes of a decade of higher education* (pp. 244–255). San Francisco: Jossey-Bass.

Warnick, B., & Inch, E. S. (1993). *Critical thinking and communication: The use of reason in argument.* New York: Macmillan.

Weimer, M. (2002). *Learner-centered teaching.* San Francisco: Jossey-Bass.

Yingling, J. (1994). Development as a context of student assessment. In S. Morreale, M. Brooks, R. Berko, & C. Cooke (Eds.), *1994 summer conference proceedings and prepared remarks* (pp. 167–178). Annandale, VA: Speech Communication Association.

Critical Thinking

Henry Ruminski
Department of Communication
Wright State University

Educators have long acknowledged the importance of critical thinking. Congress added additional emphasis in 1990, when it passed the "Goals 2000: Educate America Act," which included this goal: "The proportion of college graduates who demonstrate an advanced ability to think critically, communicate effectively, and solve problems will increase substantially" (U.S. Department of Education, 1990, p. 6). Both before and after "Goals 2000," journalism and mass communication educators claimed critical thinking to be a major goal in media education (Accrediting Council on Education in Journalism and Mass Communication, 2003; Blanchard, 1988; Blanchard & Christ, 1993; Brown, 1991; Mullins, 1987; Shoemaker, 1993; Stark & Lowther, 1988; Steiner, 1993).

As Steiner (1993) stated

> The considerable overlap in descriptions of the liberally-educated critical thinker and the ideal journalist (one who is curious, skeptical, rational, logical, persistent, open-minded, fair, intellectually flexible) suggests that critical thinking skills are at the heart of the journalistic enterprise, yet critical thinking as such is an unstated curricular goal. (p. 98)

Steiner's (1993) view is probably generally accepted in media education. Most respondents in a survey of Association for Education in Journalism and Mass Communication (AEJMC) members agreed that teaching critical thinking is important in journalism and mass communication. However, there was little agreement as to a definition of critical thinking and most respondents questioned whether critical thinking required explicit instruction. Most respondents believed their textbooks lacked explicit instruction in how to think critically (Ruminski & Hanks, 1995), which is consistent with Shoemaker's (1987) analysis of 31 popular mass communication textbooks. A survey of National Communication Association (NCA) members produced similar results (Ruminski, Spicer, & Hanks, 2000). Yet even with these "challenges," the Accrediting Council on Education in Journalism and Mass Communication (ACEJMC) now requires that students be able to "think critically, creatively and independently" and "critically evaluate their own work and that of others for accuracy and fairness . . ." (ACEJMC, 2003, p. 3).

DEFINING CRITICAL THINKING

American education in general, at times, has not been systematic about defining and measuring critical thinking. Robert H. Ennis (1993), a major figure in the critical thinking movement in America, wrote the following: "Although critical thinking has often been urged as a goal of education throughout most of this century (for example, John Dewey's *How We Think*, 1910; and the Educational Policies Commission's *The Central Purpose Of American Education*, 1961), not a great deal has been done about it" (p. 17). And critical thinking assessment, he noted, "has been neglected even more than critical thinking instruction" (p. 179). This may be because defining and measuring critical thinking in a valid way are difficult tasks. However, several authorities on critical thinking do try to define critical thinking in a broad way that captures its complexity and is measurable (see, e.g., Ennis, 1993; Facione, 1991; Paul & Nosich, 1991).

As Christ and Blanchard (1994) correctly noted, the starting point for assessment should be "agreement about what should be assessed" (p. 479). Although most media educators probably agree that critical thinking should be assessed, there is little apparent agreement, however, among those media educators as to definition.

Surveys of both NCA and AEJMC members revealed a wide range of definitions, with respondents generally agreeing that critical thinking involves analysis (Ruminski & Hanks, 1995; Ruminski et al., 2000). These surveys also revealed a fairly widespread belief that improvement in critical thinking simply results from 4 years of college, despite significant evidence to the contrary (Keeley, Browne, & Kruetzer, 1982; King, Kitchener, Davison, Parker, & Wood, 1983; Nickerson, 1988; Perkins, 1985; Welfel, 1982). These two topics—definition and assumption of improved thinking—are related. For if critical thinking is only vaguely defined, it can be pretty much anything students do after 4 years of college and a few years in a major. But, as Cheseboro (1991) noted regarding oral communication competency, some degree of standardization is desirable so we know what we mean by competency. Therefore, the discussion which follows assumes standardization is desirable to establish some common ground.

Numerous definitions of critical thinking have been published. Sternberg (1987) pointed out that the problem with so many definitions is that "... there are many different names for the same thing ..." (p. 252). Sternberg unified the various skills and dispositions that cognitive psychologists, learning theorists, philosophers, and others have discussed as higher-order thinking under three learned functions: (a) the executive function, or metacognitive; (b) the specific thinking skills, such as inferences; and (c) the ability to acquire and organize knowledge. A definition that represents these three components of critical thinking, and one that lends itself to assessment, is found in *Critical Thinking: A Statement of Expert Consensus for Purposes of Educational Assessment and Instruction* (Facione, 1990). The definition, a product of a Delphi research project involving 46 experts in thinking, stated the following:

> We understand critical thinking to be purposeful, self-regulatory judgment which results in interpretation, analysis, evaluation, and inference, as well as explanation of the evidential, conceptual, methodological, or contextual considerations upon which that judgment is based. . . . The ideal critical thinker is habitually inquisitive, well-informed, trustful of reason, open-minded, flexible, fair-minded in evaluation, honest in facing personal biases, prudent in making judgments, willing to reconsider, clear about issues, orderly in complex matters, diligent in seeking relevant information, reasonable in the selection of criteria, focused in inquiry, and persistent in seeking results which are as precise as the subject and the circumstances of inquiry permit. Thus, educating good critical thinkers means working toward this ideal. It combines developing CT skills with nurturing those dispositions which consistently yield useful insights and which are the basis of a rational and democratic society. (Facione, 1990, p. 2)

Although this definition is wordy, complex, and expressed in typical committee language, it does seem to cover the elements included in most other definitions.

OPERATIONALIZING CRITICAL THINKING

Of all the definitions, only the Delphi consensus has been operationalized in standardized instruments measuring both thinking skills and dispositions (or attitudes). Any definition of critical thinking must address both skills and dispositions and both need to be assessed to reflect the theoretical characterizations of critical thinking (CT) commonly found and noted by Facione, Sanchez, Facione, and Gainen (1995), and including Browne and Keeley (1990), Chaffee (1992), D'Angelo (1971), Dewey (1933), Ennis (2003), Glaser (1984), Gray (1993), Kurfiss (1988), Mayfield (1991), Meyers (1986), Oxman-Michelli (1992), Paul (1990), and Wade and Tavris (1993).

The research literature on assessment of instruction in critical thinking reveals some of the strengths and weaknesses of various operational definitions of critical thinking. As Halpern (1993) reminded us, "Any assessment of student gains in the ability to think critically needs to be based upon an operational definition. . . . Although there is no absolute agreement on what constitutes critical thinking, there is sufficient overlap . . . to allow an evaluator to move beyond the definitional stage" (p. 240). Some of the definitions used in assessment studies were operationalized in commercial standardized tests such as the Watson– Glaser Critical Thinking Appraisal (WGCTA; Watson & Glaser, 1980), and others were devised by the researchers (see, e.g., Fox, Marsh, & Crandall, 1983). The WGCTA, the oldest and most used critical thinking test, contains 80 response items across five types of thinking: (a) induction, (b) deduction, (c) assumption identification, (d) interpretation of data, and (e) identification of strong versus weak arguments. There are two matching forms of the test that can be used in pretest–posttest designs. A brief description of commercial thinking tests designed for college-age students follows a brief review of research on teaching critical thinking in college and suggestions for developing critical thinking outcomes.

TEACHING CRITICAL THINKING

Relatively few empirical studies have examined the teaching of critical thinking. Fox et al. (1983) found that college students who had been directly instructed in problem-solving skills showed significantly higher gains in intellectual maturity than students who had not received such instruction. Gibbs (1985) reviewed empirical studies and found none that satisfied rigorous requirements for experimentation (namely, the use of experimental and control groups and random assignment of students to groups). However, he found that the WGCTA was the most frequently used test of critical thinking, followed by the Cornell test. He also noted that a carefully designed essay type test, such as the Ennis–Weir Essay test (Ennis, 1985), and a carefully designed essay test by Browne, Haas, and Keeley (1978), had clear-cut criteria for evaluation and interrater reliability. Gibbs concluded that "conventional curricula, not designed specifically for critical thinking instruction can produce weak positive or even negative results" (p. 147).

Halpern (1993) concluded her review by saying, "Better thinking can be learned with appropriate instruction" (p. 250). This conclusion seems to hold in studies with varying operational definitions in critical thinking tests. Bangert-Drowns and Bankert (1990) conducted a meta-analysis of 20 studies of effects of explicit instruction in critical thinking. The authors found that "results consistently favored programs that use explicit instruction methods" (p. 2). Facione (1991) developed and published a commercial multiple-choice critical thinking test to compare college students in a general education course in critical thinking to a comparable group. The group from the critical thinking course scored significantly better than the control group.

In speech communication, published research on effects of instruction on critical thinking has focused on formal debate, and the WGCTA was the instrument most often used to define critical thinking (Beckman, 1955; Brembeck, 1947; Colbert, 1987; Cross, 1971; Howell, 1943; Huseman, Ware, & Gruner, 1972). The effects of debate and any other training to improve critical thinking is easier to assess if the process is clearly defined by written outcomes that are measurable by standardized tests or other means.

DEFINING CRITICAL THINKING OUTCOMES

Identifying and writing measurable outcomes can be one of the most difficult parts of any assessment plan. Writing useful outcomes requires a clear understanding of the process to be assessed, whether that process represents an entire program or simply part of a course. The intent of the process, the nature of the instruction, the purpose of the assessment, and the intended use of any results all come into play. A variety of sources provide material useful in developing critical thinking outcomes for effective assessment (see, e.g., American Association of Higher Education Assessment Forum, 1998; Brookfield, 1997; Ennis, 2001; Issacson, 1999; Maki, 2002; McGregor, 2002; Thompson, 1996; Yancey, Harrington, Malencyzk, Peckham, & Rhodes, 2001). The following suggestions represent a synthesis of the ideas presented by those sources. Although no set of rules will apply to all outcomes, following the suggestions discussed later will help the writer develop critical thinking learning objectives that should contribute to any assessment attempt.

Critical thinking learning outcomes are statements that specify what student behavior will be at the end or some other point in the learning process. Outcomes express the knowledge, skills, and attitudes that students will acquire while proceeding through the process. Meaningful outcomes must be based on a description of what the student needs to reach some specified level. That assessment should help determine what changes in knowledge, skills, or attitudes are needed to reach the desired level. The needs assessment should determine the gap between the student's existing knowledge, skills, and attitudes, and the desired level.

The outcome statements should describe the desired condition—the knowledge, skills, or attitudes—a student needs to be successful at the desired level. Although outcomes represent the answer to the identified need and describe the product of the process, they are also helpful in planning for instruction by providing direction to the learning process. Good outcomes assist in the following: Identifying student behavior that needs to change, establishing the needed content for a course, planning the types of instruction needed to achieve the outcome, identifying what the student needs to learn, providing students with a clear description of what needs to be accomplished, providing guidelines for evaluation, and defining evidence needed for evaluation.

The writer attempting to prepare an outcome statement should have a clear understanding of several key issues before beginning. The writer will be better able to focus the outcome statements if he or she can answer these questions: Does the student have an adequate awareness level? Does the student have prior learning that must be undone? Does the student have an appropriate context for the problem or issue? Does the student have adequate motivation to join the learning process? Does the student have a clear understanding of the need for the new knowledge or skill? Does the writer have a clear understanding of the most important knowledge or skills the student needs? Does the writer have a clear understanding of potential obstacles to the learning process?

A well-written outcome must meet three essential criteria: (a) it must specify action that can be observed, (b) the specified action must be measurable, and (c) the student must perform the specified action. If the outcome is well written then the action performed by the student can be assessed. If not, the outcome probably fails to specify one of the following: who is to perform, what he or she is to perform, and what should be the result. A learning outcome should be written in the future tense using action verbs. It should identify one or more important requirements in clear language that students will be able to understand. The outcomes should clearly describe what students will be able to perform after the learning experience. Outcomes state the knowledge, skills, and attitudes that the students will gain through a course.

The following examples should help clarify the distinction between outcomes which are clearly measurable and those which present problems:

- Students will understand the need to check facts when writing a news story.
- Students will develop an appreciation for the importance of credibility for a company spokesperson.

These outcomes present problems because they cannot be easily measured. Restating them using action verbs can eliminate the problem:

- Students will list five reasons why facts should be checked when writing a news story.
- Students will explain why a company spokesperson should not lie to the media.

With the action verbs, the students have a clearer idea of what they are expected to do at the end of the class.

As these examples indicate, action verbs require behavior that is both observable and measurable, two of the requirements of a good outcome statement. Maki (2002) noted that "verbs that capture the desired student learning or development such as 'design,' 'create,' 'analyze,' 'apply,' " are more likely to define measurable outcomes (p. 9). The following are some other action verbs which can be useful in writing outcome statements: analyze, apply, choose, compare, compile, compute, create, demonstrate, describe, design, differentiate, discuss, explain, formulate, identify, list, measure, name, plan, predict, present, propose, recall, recognize, revise, select, use, and utilize.

In contrast, some verbs are unclear about what action they are specifying or are subject to different interpretations of that action. Such verbs often describe actions that are not observable or easily measured. Examples of verbs to avoid include the following: appreciate, be aware of, be familiar with, become acquainted with, gain knowledge of, learn, and understand.

Another consideration when developing outcomes is the usefulness of the outcomes. The "Nine Principles of Good Practice for Assessing Student Learning" produced for the American Association of Higher Education Assessment Forum (1998), suggested that "Assessment makes a difference when it begins with issues of use and illuminates questions that people really care about . . ." (p. 1). Outcomes that address results that others may find irrelevant receive little credibility. Many higher education institutions may have outcomes that sound full of authority but that do not survive critical examination. Careful attention to language is necessary to produce meaningful, measurable outcomes (see also Appendix A).

The final question that must be addressed in writing outcomes statements is whether to include the criteria that will be used to assess the outcome. Some choose to include the basis for determining how well a student is achieving a particular outcome. Others choose to define the evidence in the evaluation section of a syllabus or evaluation plan.

The following example of a critical thinking learning outcome should help clarify the importance of well defined outcomes. For example, if an instructor wants to determine if a media issues class is improving the critical thinking skills of his students, he might write the following outcome statement: Students completing the Mass Media Issues class will score higher on a standardized critical thinking test than they did on the pretest at the beginning of the class. This outcome specifies who is completing the action, it specifies the action to be completed, and it indicates the expected result. The use of a standardized critical thinking test makes it clear that critical thinking skills are being measured. The statement specifies a useful and meaningful outcome by measuring the level of critical thinki..g skills. By specifying a standardized critical thinking test, the writer defines how the outcome will be measured. Although a standardized test provides advantages as discussed elsewhere in this chapter, there are many outcomes for which a standardized test is not available or applicable. For those outcomes, the writer must develop a rubric, as discussed later in this chapter.

CRITICAL THINKING TESTS

There are seven standardized commercial tests of critical thinking that address various critical thinking skills (see Appendix B). However, there is only one instrument specifically designed to measure college students' critical thinking predispositions: The California Critical Thinking Dispositions Inventory (CCTDI; Facione & Facione, 1992). Another instrument, the Holistic Critical Thinking Scoring Rubric (HCTSR), lists several criteria (see Appendix C) that can be used to judge open-ended or performance-based tests (Facione & Facione, 1994). A summary of the dispositions inventory and the rubric follow later, after descriptions and commentary on college-level thinking tests (Ennis, 2003; Norris & Ennis, 1989).

As noted earlier, the WGCTA is the oldest and most widely used test, containing sections on deductive and inductive inferences, assumptions, interpretation, and evaluation of argument. The test is aimed at Grade 9 through adulthood. Norris and Ennis (1989) noted that it does not ask for judgments about the credibility of sources, semantics, or predispositions.

Overall, Norris and Ennis (1989) regarded the WGCTA as fairly well-balanced in testing for a variety of thinking skills. However, it is important to note that 16 of the 80 items on the test are deductive logic questions for which necessarily there is only one possible answer. Critics, such as McPeck (1981), understandably question the value of deductive logic in real-world reasoning. Reliability estimates for the WGCTA range from .70 to .82, and the test has a long history of testing for construct and predictive validity (Kramer & Conoley, 1992). Reports on the new form of the WGCTA offer suggestions and cautions about its use (Fawkes, Adajian, Flage, Hoeltzel, Knorpp, O'Meara, & Weber, 2002; Loo & Thorpe, 1999). In an examination of the WGCTA as a predictive tool, Gadzella, Baloglu, and Stephens (2002) noted that scores on the test accounted for little variance in student grade point averages. The Cornell Critical Thinking Test, Level X (Ennis & Millman, 1985) is aimed at junior and senior high school and college students. It has 72 items, with sections on induction, credibility, observation, deduction, and assumption. According to Norris and Ennis (1989), depending on background beliefs, students might reasonably choose different answers to some questions (pp. 61–64).

Another, somewhat different version of the Cornell Critical Thinking Test, called the Level Z test (Ennis, 1985), is aimed at Grades 7 through college, and it contains sections on prediction and experimental planning, fallacies, and definition, as well as induction and credibility. Ennis (1993) himself noted the weaknesses in both the tests he coauthored, as well as other tests. He cautioned that such tests should be used mainly for teaching purposes rather than "high-stakes" purposes such as placement or program accountability (Ennis, 1993, pp. 180–184).

Ennis (Ennis and Weir, 1985) also coauthored the only commercial essay test of critical thinking. The Ennis–Weir Critical Thinking Essay Test (1985) is aimed at Grades 7 through college, and tests for getting the point, identifying reasons and assumptions, stating a point, giving good reasons, seeing options, and reacting to equivocation, irrelevance, circularity, reversal of "if–then" relations, overgeneralization, credibility, and emotive language.

The California Critical Thinking Skills Test (CCTST; Facione & Facione, 1992) has two statistically matched forms and is described by its authors as the operationalization of the American Philosophical Association (APA) Delphi panel definition of critical thinking (Facione, 1990):

"The process of purposeful, self-regulatory judgement" (p. 2). The manual stated the following: "The CCTST is a standardized, 34-item, multiple choice test which targets those core critical thinking skills regarded to be essential elements in a college education. The items range from those requiring an analysis of meaning of a given sentence, to those requiring much more complex integration of CT skills" (Facione, 1990, p. 2).

Ennis (2003) also noted that parts of the CCTST can be useful in identifying students who are weak in critical thinking predispositions. Evaluators on a critical thinking task force examined commercially available tests and rated the CCTST as having moderately high validity and high feasibility (Cook, Johnson, Moore, Myers, Pauly, Pendarvis, Prus, & Ulmer-Sottong, 1996).

A companion instrument to the CCTST is the CCTDI (Facione & Facione, 1992). The instrument "derives its conception of the disposition toward CT from the APA Delphi Report" (Facione, Sanchez, Facione, & Gainen, 1995, p. 6). The CCTDI has 75 Likert-style items over seven dispositions, each of which is computed as a subscore. A total composite score is computed by adding the subscores. The seven scales are as follows: (a) inquisitiveness, (b) open-mindedness, (c) systematicity, (d) analyticity, (e) truth-seeking, (f) CT self-confidence, and (g) maturity (Facione & Facione, 1992).

The CCTDI and the other standardized critical thinking instruments may not adequately test students' ability to think well in specific subjects they have studied. Yet some critical thinking tests can provide valuable information about students' thinking, especially if, as Norris (1985) and Ennis (2003) suggested, students can write down or explain orally why they gave certain answers.

When assessing the effectiveness of courses or programs in improving critical thinking, some standardized instruments can help measure some aspects of critical thinking that relate to decision-making strategies in unfamiliar circumstances (Stark & Lowther, 1988). But the decision on what instrument to use depends on what thinking strategies need to be measured. Ennis (1993) offered good advice: "For comprehensive assessment, unless appropriate multiple-choice tests are developed, open-ended assessment techniques are probably needed" (p. 184).

Although the WGCTA or the Ennis–Weir Essay test can reveal certain strengths and weaknesses in students' thinking, such tests cannot tell us how a student would approach solving an unstructured problem such as developing a public relations plan. Such tests cannot tell how a student in advertising might develop an ad strategy or copy objectives.

Multiple measures should be used to measure critical thinking in media education, just as multiple measures should be used for assessment in general (Erwin, 1991). Although there are general thinking skills, there also is empirical evidence that critical thinking comprehensively defined cannot be the sum of sets of specific thinking skills. For example, experts in thinking about subjects also know a lot about those subjects. Bransford and Vye (1989) stressed the point that competent thinkers in various fields have competence in the skills and information and have practiced on problems in those fields.

CRITICAL THINKING IN MEDIA EDUCATION

Ideally, a stand-alone thinking course in critical thinking should be required of media education majors. But the outcomes established by the program for assessment purposes should be the basis of instruction for such a course. Shoemaker (1993) has described such a course designed for media majors at the University of Texas, Austin. The purpose of the course is "to enhance such skills as asking intelligent questions, supporting arguments with appropriate evidence, uncovering assumptions, and examining problems from multiple points of view" (p. 103).

Expert advice to the Association of Schools of Journalism and Mass Communication would seem to support the view that critical thinking should be assessed using measures of general thinking skills and of subject-specific skills. Ewell (1991) offered three general principles of assessment: (a) Assessment should cover knowledge and skills taught throughout the program's curriculum, (b) Assessment should provide multiple measures of student performance, and (c) Assessment procedures should provide information on multiple dimensions of student performance; that is, they should yield more than a single summative grade. At minimum, critical thinking should be taught throughout the curriculum and critical thinking should be assessed as majors complete the curriculum. Every level of thinking skills need not be taught in every course, but those skills should be taught and predispositions nurtured over the entire curriculum. Multiple measures of student performance should be taken at the completion of the student's course of study, in some senior level course such as a capstone course.

A pretest–posttest approach to assessing critical thinking within a media education program will provide evidence of change. However, such an approach can test only general thinking skills because new majors would not possess the knowledge required for subject-specific thinking tests. Also, this approach does not allow rigorous conditions with control groups and random selection. Halpern (1993) pointed out, however, that even without control groups, students can be used as their own controls, and taken together with other information, the results could provide evidence of effectiveness of critical thinking instruction.

THE ASSESSMENT PLAN

1. Give all students who enter the major a standardized critical thinking test and a dispositions inventory to establish a benchmark.
2. Interview each student and point out strengths and weaknesses identified by the standardized test. Explain the results.
3. Using the HCTSR as a guide, design media course assignments that utilize critical thinking skills. In evaluating those assignments, use the HCTSR to point out to students how their critical thinking weaknesses affect their level of achievement.
4. Give all exiting seniors the same standardized tests used initially. Compare to the benchmark to assess critical thinking development.

Selecting one of the standardized instruments already discussed to measure general critical thinking skills or dispositions is the most efficient way to proceed. A multiple-choice exam offers savings in time in administering and grading, but requires much more time in the initial construction, trials, and revisions to develop one's own valid and reliable instrument. For someone considering constructing his or her own multiple-choice exams, there are a number sources offering advice (Costa, 1985; Ennis, 2003; Jacobs & Chase, 1992; Norris & Ennis, 1989).

The initial administration of any multiple-choice instrument should be used only to refine the instrument after statistical analysis identifies problem items. If essay tests are used, intercoder reliability should be measured to ensure that coders are evaluating answers in a consistent systematic way. All the points about reliability and validity raised in earlier discussions apply to any effort to create your own test, whether general or subject specific. The most comprehensive measure of critical thinking would use a combination of a general critical thinking skills tests, essay instruments, and various performance measures.

Open-ended information-gathering techniques can take several forms, including performance-based assessment techniques. "Performance-based assessment is a type of testing that calls for demonstration of understanding and skill in applied, procedural, or open-ended settings" (Baker, O'Neil, & Linn, 1993, p. 1210).

This type of assessment, also referred to in testing literature as authentic assessment, direct assessment, and alternative assessment, is defined by these general characteristics:

1. It uses open-ended tasks.
2. It focuses on higher order or complex skills.
3. It employs context sensitive strategies.

4. It often uses complex problems requiring several types of performance and significant student time.
5. It consists of either individual or group performance.
6. It may involve a significant degree of student choice.

Performance assessment is an alternative to pencil-and-paper tasks that call for a single correct answer and it may include a variety of projects such as case studies, research reports, and portfolios. Performance assessment can measure higher order thinking, including critical thinking (Resnick & Resnick, 1992). However, higher order thinking as measured in performance assessments should be used with other measures of thinking ability to provide a check on validity. Criteria for performance evaluations should

1. Have meaning for students and teachers and motivate high performance.
2. Require the demonstration of complex cognitions, for example, problem solving, knowledge representation, and explanation, applicable to important problem areas.
3. Exemplify current standards of content or subject matter quality.
4. Minimize the effects of ancillary skills that are irrelevant to focus of assessment.
5. Possess explicit standards for rating or judgment (Baker et al., 1993, p. 1214).

Performance assessment techniques designed to fit these criteria would seem to be ideal instruments for critical thinking in media education, assuming acceptable reliability can be established. And such reliability estimates probably can be established if performance tasks are specific and raters are trained (see, e.g., Baker et al., 1993, p. 1213; Morreale, Moore, Taylor, Surges-Tatum, & Hulbert-Johnson, 1993, pp. 18–21). Scoring rubrics should match the tasks and the definition of critical thinking.

The CCTST and its companion rubric, the HCTSR, appear to be the only ones that match elements of the CT definition on which they are based, to a scoring rubric for an open-ended, or performance-based test. The rubrics also incorporate features that can measure critical thinking dispositions.

Facione and Facione (1994) illustrated how HCTSR, which is based on the APA Delphi definition of CT, can be applied to assess open-ended performance. HCTSR is in the public domain for educational purposes. It lists several broad criteria that roughly match elements of the CT definition. Numerical ratings are assigned, with 4 being the highest and 1 the lowest score, assigned to a student's presentation. The HCTSR is available for free downloading (see http://www.insightassessment.com/ HCTSR.html). The authors designed the rubric to rate classroom project presentation and assigned papers, but note that it "can be used to achieve one data point in a multi-modal plan for curriculum assessment by providing a rating of a representative sample of student work which demonstrate the students' critical thinking" (Facione & Facione, 1996, p. 132). The rubric permits the instructor to assess both critical thinking ability and some critical thinking predispositions.

The Facione and Facione (1994) model is adaptable to several areas of media education, as the following examples should help illustrate (see also Appendix D). For example, students can be asked to write an opinion piece based on assigned readings that contain opposing views. They can be informed of the purpose of the writing assignment and the critical thinking rubric by which they will be evaluated. Raters should have carefully read the information that the student uses as source material and generally agree on such things as credibility and validity of evidence, logic, interpretation of data, clarity, and so forth, related to the various sources given to the student.

Information-gathering performance assessments might include a written or oral report on a given topic, an annotated bibliography on a topic, and a list of sources and reasons why such sources might be useful for such things as radio or television news, features, commentary, or interviews. Evaluators of this kind of performance should know in advance the kind and relevance of sources to judge whether the student had considered the purpose of the information-gathering assignment, important definitions, and the relevance of various sources to the topic and purpose. Not all the critical thinking criteria presented in Facione and Facione's (1994) rubric need apply to all performance tasks; for example, an information-gathering assignment that simply requested information might not require an evaluation of evidence.

In the ethical thinking area, however, there may be a long list of criteria that would be applied to a performance assessment, such as the presentation of a position a student journalist might take on whether he or she would deceive potential sources to get information, given a case scenario. For example, would the journalist be justified in concealing his or her identity by joining a state militia suspected of domestic terrorism? Such cases call for knowledge of facts as well as ability to reason from several ethical perspectives, such as ends-to-means versus idealism.

A media management decision-making case study would be an excellent performance assessment vehicle to test real-world critical thinking. For example, Albarran (2002) presented several scenarios for management decisions. Albarran's scenarios are constructed tightly enough, and his textbook provides enough information, that raters who judge the presentations of students can consider various options, the evidence, and the arguments that could be advanced.

A student in an advanced reporting class which has covered the reporting of quantitative data could be presented with brief results of a public opinion survey and asked to evaluate its newsworthiness for a particular audience. The evaluator would judge whether the student's comments addressed the adequacy of the research method, the relevance of the sample used, and the real versus statistical significance of any findings. The evaluator also would examine the student's ability to explain why particular items would be of interest to a specific audience or challenge the conclusion based on the information presented.

A public relations assignment might involve asking the student to develop a strategy for communicating a new company policy that requires a fee on returned, nondefective merchandise. The student would be told to identify the relevant publics and the potential effects of the change, indicate how and what types of information would be gathered for planning, and suggest communication strategies and objectives that might be useful in announcing the change.

Evaluators can judge whether the student accurately identified those who would be affected by the change, both internally and externally, and whether the student clearly differentiated between the potential effects of the change on each public. The student also can be judged on the adequacy of the information on which any plan would be based. For example, evaluators could examine what kind of information is used as evidence to justify the fee and what types of arguments are used in the communication strategy. The objectives can be judged on whether they accurately reflect the problem, are achievable, and can be measured.

An advertising student could be asked to create a series of statements about a new product and explain why each statement should be considered for an advertising campaign. The instructions should be clearly constructed so that the student will know which critical thinking criteria will apply. For example, the student could be presented with a technical fact sheet and reminded that any claims about physical product qualities must be supported by factual data. The evaluator could then determine if the student has accurately assessed and interpreted the evidence.

SUMMARY

This chapter discussed the developing of critical thinking skills as a goal for media education. Several authorities on critical thinking were cited who try to define critical thinking in a broad way that captures its complexity and is measurable. Assessment of critical thinking must begin with, as Christ and Blanchard (1994) noted, "agreement about what should be assessed" (p. 479). Research suggested that although most media educators might agree that critical thinking should be assessed, there is little apparent agreement, among those educators, about how to define and measure critical thinking.

For this chapter, assessment was defined as the "process of defining, selecting, designing, collecting, analyzing, interpreting and using information to increase students' learning" (Hutchings, 1993, p. 15). The published definition of critical thinking that probably best represents these three components of critical thinking, and one that lends itself to assessment, is found in *Critical Thinking: A Statement of Expert Consensus for Purposes of Educational Assessment and Instruction* (Facione, 1990).

The need for, the nature of, and suggestions for, writing critical thinking outcomes were discussed along with methods of assessing whether those outcomes were achieved. The following instruments were discussed: The CCTDI; the WGCTA; the Cornell Critical Thinking Test, Level X and Level Z tests; the Ennis–Weir Critical Thinking Essay Test; and the CCTST.

Standardized instruments can help measure how well students acquire, evaluate, and synthesize information; however, multiple measures should be used to measure critical thinking in media education, just as multiple measures should be used for assessment in general (Erwin, 1991). Open-ended information-gathering techniques can be useful in media education and can take several forms, including performance-based assessment techniques which call for demonstration of understanding and skill.

REFERENCES

Accrediting Council on Education in Journalism and Mass Communication. (2003). *Principles of accreditation.* Lawrence, KS: Author.

Albarran, A. B. (2002). *Management of electronic media.* Belmont, CA: Wadsworth/Thompson Learning.

American Association of Higher Education Assessment Forum. (1998). *Nine principles of good practice for assessing student learning.* Washington, DC: Author.

Baker, E. L., O'Neill, H. F., & Linn, R. L. (1993). Policy and validity prospect performance-based assessment. *American Psychologist, 48,* 1210–1218.

Bangert-Drowns, R., & Bankert, E. (1990, April). *Meta-analysis of effects of explicit instruction for critical thinking.* Paper presented at the annual meeting of the American Educational Research Association, Boston, MA. (ERIC Document Reproduction Service No. ED 328 614)

Blanchard, R. O. (1988). Our emerging role in liberal and media studies. *Journalism Educator, 43*(3), 28–31.

Blanchard, R. O., & Christ, W. E. (1993). *Media education and the liberal arts: A blueprint for the new professionalism.* Hillsdale, NJ: Lawrence Erlbaum Associates, Inc.

Beckman, V. (1955). *An investigation of the contributions to critical thinking made by courses in argumentation and discussion in selected colleges.* Unpublished doctoral dissertation, University of Minnesota, Twin Cities.

Bransford, J. D., & Vye, N. J. (1989). A perspective on cognitive research and its implications for instruction. In L. B. Resnick & L. E. Klopfer (Eds.), *Toward the thinking curriculum: Current cognitive research* (pp. 173–205). Alexandria, VA: Association for Supervision and Curriculum Development.

Brembeck, W. (1947). *The effects of a course on argumentation on critical thinking ability.* Unpublished doctoral dissertation, University of Wisconsin, Madison.

Brookfield, S. D. (1997, Fall). Assessing critical thinking. *New Directions for Adult and Continuing Education, 75,* 17–29.

Brown, J. A. (1991). *Television critical viewing skills education: Major media literacy projects in the United States and selected countries.* Hillsdale, NJ: Lawrence Erlbaum Associates, Inc.

Browne, N. M., Haas, P., & Keeley, S. (1978, January). Measuring critical thinking in college. *The Educational Forum, 42,* 219–226.

Browne, N. M., & Keeley, S. M. (1990). *Asking the right questions.* Englewood Cliffs, NJ: Prentice Hall.

Chaffee, J. (1992). Teaching critical thinking across the curriculum. *Critical Thinking: Educational Imperative, 77,* 25–35.

Cheseboro, J. W. (1991). Oral communication competency and assessment. *The Carolina Speech-Communication Annual, 7,* 6–22.

Christ, W. G., & Blanchard, R. O. (1994). Mission statements, outcomes, and the new Liberal Arts. In W. E. Christ (Ed.), *Assessing communication outcomes: A handbook for media, speech and theatre educators* (pp. 31–55). Hillsdale, NJ: Lawrence Erlbaum Associates, Inc.

Colbert, K. R. (1987). The effects of CEDA and NDT training on critical thinking ability. *Journal of the American Forensic Association, 80,* 194–201.

Cook, P., Johnson, R., Moore, P., Myers, P., Pauly, S., Pendarvis, F., et al. (1996). *Critical thinking assessment: Measuring a moving target. Report & recommendations of the South Carolina Higher Education Assessment Network Critical Thinking Task Force.* Rock Hill, SC: South Carolina Educational Assessment Network. (ERIC Document Reproduction Service No. ED 413 808)

Costa, A. (Ed.). (1985). *Developing minds: A resource book for teaching thinking Part X.* Alexandria, VA: Association for Supervision and Curriculum Development.

Cross, G. (1971). *The effects of belief systems and the amount of debate experience on the acquisition of critical thinking.* Unpublished doctoral dissertation, University of Utah, Salt Lake City.

D'Angelo, E. (1971). *The teaching of critical thinking.* Amsterdam: B. R. Gruner N. V.

Dewey, J. (1933). *How we think: A restatement of the relation of reflective thinking to the educational process.* Lexington, MA: Heath.

Educational Policies Commission. (1961). *The central purpose of American education.* Washington, DC: National Education Association.

Ennis, R. H. (1985). *Cornell Critical Thinking Test, Level Z.* Pacific Grove, CA: Midwest Publications.

Ennis, R. H. (1993). Critical thinking assessment. *Theory Into Practice, 32,* 179–186.

Ennis, R. H. (2001). Goals for a critical thinking curriculum and its assessment. In A. L. Costa (Ed.), *Developing minds: A resource book for teaching thinking* (3rd ed.). Alexandria, VA: Association for Supervision and Curricular Development.

Ennis, R. H. (2003). Critical thinking assessment. In D. Fasko, Jr. (Ed.), *Critical thinking and reasoning: Current research, theory and practice* (pp. 293–313). Cresskill, NJ: Hampton.

Ennis, R. H., & Millman, J. (1985). *Cornell Critical Thinking Test, Level X.* Pacific Grove, CA: Midwest Publications.

Ennis, R. H., & Weir, E. (1985). *The Ennis–Weir Critical Thinking Essay Test.* Pacific Grove, CA: Midwest Publications.

Erwin, T. D. (1991). *Assessing student learning development.* San Francisco: Jossey-Bass.

Ewell, P. T. (1991). *Benefits and costs of assessment in higher education: A framework for choice-making.* Boulder, CO: National Center for Higher Education Management Systems.

Facione, N. C., & Facione, P. A. (1996). Externalizing the critical thinking in clinical judgment. *Nursing Outlook, 44,* 129–136.

Facione, P. A. (1990). *Critical thinking: A statement of expert consensus for purposes of educational assessment and instruction.* Newark, DE: American Philosophical Association. (ERIC Document Reproduction Service No. ED 315 423)

Facione, P. A. (1991). *Using the California Critical Thinking Skills Test in research, evaluation, and assessment.* Millbrae, CA: California Academic Press.

Facione, P. A. (1993). *The California Critical Thinking Skills Test.* Millbrae, CA: California Academic Press.

Facione, P. A., & Facione, N. C. (1992). *The California Critical Thinking Dispositions Inventory (CCTDI), and Test Manual.* Millbrae, CA: California Academic Press.

Facione, P. A., & Facione, N. C. (1994). *Holistic Critical Thinking Scoring Rubric (HCTSR).* Millbrae, CA: California Academic Press.

Facione, P. A., Sanchez, C. A., Facione, N. C., & Gainen, J. (1995). The disposition toward critical thinking. *Journal of General Education, 44,* 1–24.

Fawkes, D., Adajian, T., Flage, D., Hoeltzel, S., Knorpp, B., O'Meara, B., et al. (2002). Examining the exam: A critical look at the Watson–Glaser critical thinking appraisal exam. *Inquiry: Critical Thinking Across the Disciplines, 21,* 31–46.

Fox, L. S., Marsh, G., & Crandall, J. C. (1983, April). *The effect of college classroom experiences on formal operational thinking.* Paper presented at the annual convention of the Western Psychological Association, San Francisco.

Gadzella, B. M., Baloglu, M., & Stephens, R. (2002). Prediction of GPA with educational psychology grades and critical thinking scores. *Education, 122,* 618.

Gibbs, L. (1985). Teaching critical thinking at the university level. *Informal Logic, 7,* 137–149.

Glaser, R. (1984). Education and thinking: The role of knowledge. *American Psychologist, 39,* 93–104.

Gray, P. (1993). Engaging students' intellect: The immersion approach to critical thinking in psychology instruction. *Teaching Psychology, 20,* 68–74.

Halpern, D. F. (1993). Assessing the effectiveness for critical thinking instruction. *Journal of General Education, 42,* 238–254.

Howell, W. (1943). The effects of high school debating on critical thinking. *Speech Monographs, 10,* 99–103.

Huseman, R., Ware, G., & Gruner, C. (1972). Critical thinking, reflective thinking and the ability to organize ideas: A multivariate approach. *Journal of American Forensic Association, 9,* 261–265.

Hutchings, P. (1993). Principles of good practice for assessing student learning. *Assessment Update, 5,* 6.

Isaacson, S. (1999). Instructionally relevant writing assessment. *Reading & Writing Quarterly, 14,* 29–48.

Jacobs, L. C., & Chase, C. I. (1992). *Developing and using tests effectively: Guide for faculty.* San Francisco: Jossey-Bass.

Keeley, S., Browne, M. N., & Kruetzer, L. (1982). A comparison of freshmen and seniors on general and specific essay tests of critical thinking. *Research in Higher Education, 17,* 139–154.

King, P. M., Kitchener, K. S., Davison, M. L., Parker, C. A., & Wood, P. K. (1983). The justification of beliefs in young adults: A longitudinal study. *Human Development, 26,* 106–116.

Kramer, J. J., & Conoley, J. C. (Eds.). (1992). *The eleventh mental measurements yearbook.* Lincoln, NE: The Buros Institute of Mental Measurements.

Kurfiss, J. G. (1988). *Critical thinking: Theory, research, practice, and possibilities.* Washington, DC: Association for the Study of Higher Education.

Loo, R., & Thorpe, K. (1999). A psychometric investigation of scores on the Watson–Glaser Critical Thinking Appraisal new forms. *Educational & Psychological Measurement, 59,* 995.

Maki, P. L. (2002). Developing an assessment plan to learn about student learning. *Journal of Academic Librarianship, 28,* 8–13.

Mayfield, M. (1991). *Thinking for yourself: Developing critical thinking skills through writing.* Belmont, CA: Wadsworth.

McGregor, J. (2002). Getting to the heart of assessment: The liberal studies/professional skills program at Inver Hills Community College. *Community College Journal of Research and Practice, 26,* 723–735.

McPeck, J. E. (1981). *Critical thinking and education.* Oxford, England: Martin Robertson.

Meyers, C. (1986). *Teaching student to think critically.* San Francisco: Jossey-Bass.

Morreale, S. P., Moore, M. R., Taylor, K. P., Surges-Tatum, D., & Hulbert-Johnson, R. (1993). *The competent speaker.* Annandale, VA: Speech-Communication Association.

Mullins, E. (1987, August). *Task force report on liberal arts and sciences in journalism/mass communication.* Paper presented to the Association of Schools of Journalism and Mass Communication, New York.

Nickerson, R. S. (1988). On improving thinking skills through instruction. In E. Z. Rothkopf (Ed.), *Review of research in education* (pp. 3–57). Washington, DC: American Educational Research Association.

Norris, S. P. (1985). Synthesis of research on critical thinking. *Educational Leadership, 42*(8), 40–45.

Norris, S. P., & Ennis, R. H. (1989). *Evaluating critical thinking.* Pacific Grove, CA: Midwest Publications.

Oxman-Michelli, W. (1992). Critical thinking as critical spirit. *Resource Publication Series: Montclaire Institute for Critical Thinking, 4,* 1–13.

Paul, R. (1990). *Critical thinking: What every person needs to survive in a rapidly changing world.* Rhonert Park, CA: Sonoma State University, Center for Critical Thinking and Moral Critique.

Paul, R., & Nosich, G. M. (1991). *A proposal for the national assessment of higher-order thinking.* Washington, DC: U.S. Department of Education, Office of Educational Research and Improvement, Educational Resources Information Center.

Perkins, D. N. (1985). Postprimary education has little impact on informal reasoning. *Journal of Educational Psychology, 77,* 562–571.

Resnick, L. B., & Resnick, D. P. (1992). Assessing the thinking curriculum: New tools for educational reform. In B. R. Gifford & M. C. O'Connor (Eds.), *Changing assessments: Alternative views of aptitude, achievement, and instruction* (pp. 37–75). Boston: Kluwer.

Ruminski, H., & Hanks, W. (1995). Critical thinking lacks definition and uniform evaluation criteria. *Journalism and Mass Communication Educator, 508,* 4–11.

Ruminski, H., Spicer, K., & Hanks, W. (2000). Critical thinking in communication: A survey. *Virginia Journal of Communication, 12,* 27–47.

Shoemaker, P. (1987). Mass communication by the book: A review of 31 texts. *Journal of Communication, 37*(3), 109–131.

Shoemaker, P. (1993). Critical thinking for mass communication students. *Critical Studies In Mass Communication, 10,* 99–111.

Stark, J. S., & Lowther, M. A. (1988). *Strengthening the ties that bind: Integrating undergraduate liberal and professional study.* Ann Arbor: University of Michigan Press.

Steiner, L. (1993). Critical thinking. *Critical Studies in Mass Communication, 10,* 98.

Sternburg, R. J. (1987). Questions and answers about the nature and teaching of thinking skills. In J. B. Baron & R. J. Sternburg (Eds.), *Teaching thinking skills: Theory and practice* (pp. 250–262). New York: Freeman.

Thompson, A. (1996). *Critical thinking: A practical introduction.* New York: Routledge.

U.S. Department of Education. (1990). *National goals for education.* Washington, DC: Government Printing Office.

Wade, C., & Tavris, C. (1993). *Psychology.* New York: Harper.

Watson, G., & Glaser, E. (1980). *Watson–Glaser Critical Thinking Appraisal.* San Antonio, TX: Psychological Corporation.

Welfel, E. R. (1982). How students make judgments: Do educational level and academic major make a difference? *Journal of College of Student Personnel, 23,* 490–497.

Yancey, K. B., Harrington, S., Malencyzk, R., Peckham, I., & Rhodes, K. (2001). WPA outcomes statement for first-year composition. *College English, 63,* 321–326.

APPENDIX A

Rules for Writing Critical Thinking Outcomes

1. Write items in simple, concise language which clearly states the complete, single problem. When possible avoid negatives, such as "not" or "except," when stating the problem. If they must be used, emphasize them with a graphic device such as all caps or boldface.

2. Use either a direct question or an incomplete statement to introduce the options at the end of the item. Construct it to include words which otherwise would have to be repeated in each item.

3. State the problem so that there is only one correct or best answer. If the student is asked to select the best answer, do not offer "all of the above" or "none of the above" choices.

4. Make every option a plausible choice to force discrimination by those who do not know the correct or best answer. Present the options in a logical order, if possible.

5. Avoid unintended hints. Some examples might be a single subject in the item with plural verbs in some options or repetition or other association between key words in the item and the option.

6. Avoid any patterns such as placement or length of the correct option. Avoid options which include words such as "never" or "always" in the incorrect options.

APPENDIX B

Critical Thinking Assessment Tools

Title	Aspects Measured	Strengths and Weaknesses
Watson–Glaser Critical Thinking Appraisal Test	Induction, deduction, assumption-identification, interpretation of data, evaluation of strength of argument.	Tests variety of skills, but relies heavily on deductive logic; test is long and may fatigue examinees.
Cornell Critical Thinking Test, Level X	Induction, deduction, credibility of sources, observation, assumption-identification.	Tests variety of skills, including evaluation of source credibility, but credibility items seem too simple and answers likely depend on background beliefs.
Cornell Critical Thinking Test, Level Z	Induction, deduction, credibility, judgment, predication, experimental planning, fallacies, definitions, assumption-identification.	Relatively short test that tests some scientific method knowledge; some items unchallenging.
Ennis–Weir Critical Thinking Essay Test	Identification of strengths and weaknesses of arguments, judging relevance of arguments, evidence, analogies, accuracy of definitions.	Only standardized essay critical thinking test, requires writing, justifying judgments; but reliable only for reliable ranking and not for actual score.
The California Critical Thinking Skills Test	Inductive and deductive inferences, analysis of meaning, identification of cogent reasons, evaluations of objections to conclusion.	A short test (34 items) that tests a variety of skills, does not rely heavily on deductive logic, but contains a few convoluted word puzzles.
The California Critical Thinking Dispositions Inventory	Measure inquisitiveness, open-mindedness, systematicity, analyticity, truth-seeking, critical thinking self-confidence, intellectual maturity.	Only standardized measure of predispositions, good face validity, seems to predict actual performance; but some items may signal desirable responses.
The Holistic Critical Thinking Scoring Rubric	Provide guide for judgment of critical thinking within subject matter contexts calling for examinees to produce rather than simply respond.	Adaptability to a variety of subject-specific contexts; but reliability must be established for each task.

APPENDIX C

Holistic Critical Thinking Scoring Rubric

4. Consistently does all or almost all of the following: Accurately interprets evidence, statements, graphic, questions, etc. Identifies the salient arguments (reasons and claims) pro and con. Thoughtfully analyzes and evaluates major alternative points of view. Draws warranted, judicious, non-fallacious conclusions. Justifies key results and procedures, explains assumptions and reasons. Fair-mindedly follows where evidence and reasons lead.

3. Does most or many of the following: Accurately interprets evidence, statements, graphics, questions, etc. Identifies relevant arguments (reasons and claims) pro and con. Offers analyses and evaluations of obvious alternative points of view. Draws warranted, non-fallacious conclusions. Justifies some results or procedures, explains reasons. Fair-mindedly follows where evidence and reasons lead.

2. Does most or many of the following: Misinterprets evidence, statements, graphics, questions, etc. Fails to identify strong, relevant counter-arguments. Ignores or superficially evaluates obvious alternative points of view. Draws unwarranted or fallacious conclusions. Justifies few results or procedures, seldom explains reasons. Regardless of the evidence or reasons, maintains or defends views based on self-interest or preconceptions.

1. Consistently does all or almost all of the following: Offers biased interpretations of evidence, statements, graphics, questions information, or the points off view of others. Fails to identify or hastily dismisses strong, relevant counter-arguments. Ignores or superficially evaluates obvious alternative points of view. Argues using fallacious or irrelevant reasons, and unwarranted claims. Does not justify results or procedures, nor explain reasons. Regardless of the evidence or reasons, maintains or defends views based on self-interest or preconceptions. Exhibits close-mindedness or hostility to reason (Facione & Facione, 1995, p. 8).

APPENDIX D

Examples of Critical Thinking Tasks

Critical Thinking Elements	Problem	Student Demonstrates Critical Thinking
Definitions of terms, evaluation of source credibility, fair-minded look at opposing views, identification of assumptions.	Write editorial on controversial topic.	Write an editorial for or against banning books that contain racial slurs from school libraries.
Definitions, identification of assumptions, selection of relevant facts, documents, interpretation.	Write interpretive piece based on legal documents.	Write a feature explaining a given state's open-records law and how it affects the public.
Definitions, identification of assumptions, inductive and deductive inferences, evaluation of alternative positions vis-à-vis goals and values, reasoned justification of ethical choice.	Take a position on a question of journalism ethics.	Write a position paper for professional journalists on ethics of deceit to gain information about a religious cult by joining it for the purpose of publishing stories.
Definition (of purpose, objectives) vis-à-vis a video production, analysis of audience, resources, that is, time, budget, personnel, equipment, interpretation of objectives in visual terms.	Design a video production.	Write a preproduction plan, production schedule, and budget.
Definitions, selection of relevant facts, fair-minded consideration of alternatives, selection and analysis of data, interpretation of data.	Respond to Federal Communications Commission inquiry about minority hiring policy of station.	Write an affirmative action policy for a given television station.
Definitions, selection and evaluation of evidence, interpretation of data, identification of assumptions, evaluation of credibility of sources, synthesis of research.	Write story interpreting and evaluating a topic in scientific research.	Write an article that interprets, evaluates, and synthesizes, research on genetic basis of homosexuality, based on research, review, and evaluation of scientific opinion.
Definitions, selection of information, analysis, interpretation, evaluation.	Develop a strategy to communicate a new policy for consumer returns.	Write a public relations plan to communicate a policy of charging a restocking fee for the return of undamaged merchandise.

10

Research and Information Gathering

Rebecca B. Rubin
Alan M. Rubin
School of Communication Studies
Kent State University

Information gathering is an essential skill for all students of communication. Students need to be able to identify, locate, and use print and electronic information sources in their class, professional, and research projects. These sources are extremely valuable and are accessible in libraries and electronically. We discuss these information sources and suggest how we might assess students' skills and knowledge about using the sources. Communication students and practitioners also need to ask questions of people who have the information they need. Interviewing skills are essential for conducting some research projects. We address the use of print and electronic resources to identify and to locate people to interview. However, the actual means of conducting an interview and assessing interviewing skills is beyond our scope.

The Accrediting Council on Education in Journalism and Mass Communications has adopted new accreditation standards for colleges and universities that train mass communication and journalism students (http://www.ku.edu/~acejmc/). These standards take effect in the 2005–2006 academic year. The competency in these standards most relevant to this chapter is, "all graduates should . . . be able to . . . conduct research and evaluate information by methods appropriate to the communications professions in which they work" (Accrediting Council on Education in Journalism and Mass Communications, 2003). In this chapter, we explore the various facets of researching and evaluating information involved in information gathering.

Because there are few assessment methods in this area, we concentrate on the essential skills and recommend a body of knowledge we feel all mass media students should have. In so doing, we lay the groundwork for assessment. We also recommend some typical courses and measures through which student learning can be assessed.

SEARCHING THE LITERATURE

Communication professionals need to find information by consulting published and electronic sources, interviewing those who have the information, or conducting original investigations. When we mention research in this chapter, we are referring to an objective and systematic process of inquiry that helps us understand. Mass media students need research skills for a multitude of class assignments, ranging from script writing to media programming to audience assessments to targeting and positioning ideas and products.

Research begins when we encounter obstacles to our understanding. When that happens, we must focus our inquiry with a precise statement that identifies, develops, and narrows our search for information. To do this, we need to attend to what researchers have already learned about the area of our inquiry and to develop a plan of attack, or *"search strategy."*

In developing this plan of attack, researchers can use different strategies for searching the literature. For example, a general-to-specific strategy is beneficial when we know little about the topic or when compiling a comprehensive overview of the literature. Under these conditions, the search begins with general sources such as textbooks and handbooks. We then turn to primary sources such as journals and information compilations. We use specific finding tools, such as indexes and abstracts, to help locate these primary sources. With this strategy, we narrow our research focus as the search proceeds.

At other times, a specific-to-general strategy may be more useful. If we locate one or more key primary sources, or if the topic of inquiry is precise, the search begins with fact finding and then broadens by using finding tools such as citation indexes. We also may concentrate on specific facts if we are reporting new data, providing factual information, or seeking statistical data. The choice of the search strategy relies on what we already know and what information we still need to know.

Several sources, such as Beasley (1988), Mann (1998), Rubin, Rubin, and Piele (2005), and Ward and Hansen (1997), are useful to consult for additional information on search strategies and conducting library or documentary research.

SEARCHING THE INTERNET

As the use of technology increases, communication professionals are constantly challenged by technological shortcomings. Garrison (2000) identified some news-gathering problems when journalists try to gather information from the World Wide Web (WWW). He described several problems journalists have with the WWW—inaccurate information, bad content, outdated links, and lack of attribution—and with using Web sites—no verification, unreliable information, bad sources, questionable credibility, difficulty finding the site, and truthfulness. Similarly, Cannon (2001) argued that misinformation from Internet sources and e-mail is a severe problem facing all researchers, who need to be skeptical of both content and sources located on the WWW.

These searching difficulties highlight important Internet search functions. Using the Internet has allowed communication professionals to move beyond the telephone and personal interview to searching databases and archives for information and supporting data. The Internet allows background research, fact-checking, current events monitoring, and source identification. However, as Weinberg (1999) noted, the best investigative journalists can gather information from all three basic sources: human, document, and Internet. In this chapter, we focus on document and Internet sources.

INFORMATION-GATHERING LITERACY AND COMPETENCE

Information-literate students are independent learners and responsible users of information. They know what information they need, how to retrieve it efficiently, how to evaluate it critically, how to handle information ethically, and why the information is important in a democratic society (Colorado Educational Media Association, 2002). They have the ability to manage technology tools to access information, to solve problems confidently, to operate comfortably in confusing situations, to adapt to change, and to create quality products.

Students who are competent in information gathering act in effective and appropriate ways. They have a well-developed knowledge base and refined search skills. They know how to locate needed information for their research or problem solving, and they do it well. Information-gathering competence is a function of knowledge and skill.

Knowledge

When conducting literature searches, students first need to familiarize themselves with the organization and services of the libraries they will be using. These services include catalogs (typically electronic), document collections (such as government documents), periodicals, reference services, and electronic and online databases. Students also need to learn how to use periodical indexes, abstracts, and information collection databases. Electronic databases have become very important in information gathering.

General or secondary sources provide background about a topic of inquiry and can help researchers locate primary materials from the printed literature or electronic databases. General sources, such as encyclopedias and dictionaries, provide definitions and summarize what is known about the subject. Students also need to use finding tools, such as indexes and abstracts, to access these primary sources efficiently and to help locate needed information. Indexes and abstracts can identify relevant original research reports. In addition, if students need to find information that is not contained in published materials, directories can identify communication professionals to seek out for interviews.

Thus, information-literate students require knowledge of what types of sources exist (source knowledge), what specific sources are most useful (experiential knowledge), and how to use these sources (application knowledge). This knowledge can be taught and assessed programmatically in courses such as Communication Inquiry and Interviewing (see Table 10.1).

When researchers locate useful primary materials—such as journal articles, information compilations, research reports, books, and government documents—they need to read, understand, summarize, and synthesize materials. They need research-domain knowledge of the organizational schemes and communication terminology used in empirical research reports. For example, original empirical research reports follow a pattern of organization that begins with an introduction to the problem, and then present a review of the literature, a description of the methodology, a summary of the results, and a discussion of the implications of the results and future research directions. Research terminology and elements of research reports can be taught and learning assessed in courses such as Communication Inquiry and Research Methods.

A major goal of research methods courses is for students to increase their understanding of the original materials they read. Another important goal is for students to acquire basic knowledge of research methodology and statistics. This knowledge is needed for achieving a degree of research literacy. Learning can be assessed in research methods courses.

TABLE 10.1
Guide to Information-Gathering Competence Assessment

Knowledge	Classes	Measures
Source	Communication Inquiry, Interviewing	Tests and exams
Experiential	Communication Inquiry, Interviewing	Tests and exams Course-embedded assessment
Application	Communication Inquiry, Interviewing	Tests and exams Pretest–posttest evaluation
Research domain	Communication Inquiry, Research Methods	Tests and exams Thesis and project
Research methodology	Research Methods	Tests and exams Thesis and project

Skill	Classes	Measures
Searching	Communication Inquiry, Interviewing, Research Methods	Tests and exams Library skills test
Evaluation	Communication Inquiry, Research Methods	Thesis or project Portfolio evaluation
Note taking	Research Methods, Interviewing	Videotape of performance Portfolio evaluation
Internet	Communication Inquiry	Tests and exams Course-embedded assessment

Thus, for professional and research projects, communication students need to acquire (a) *source knowledge* of what are the research sources; (b) *experiential knowledge* of which are the most useful sources; (c) *application knowledge* of how to find, access, and use the sources and their finding tools; (d) *research domain knowledge* of how information is organized and what it means; and (e) *research methodology knowledge* of how the original studies were conducted. These five forms of knowledge directly affect the skills to use the sources.

Skill

Beyond the knowledge of information sources, students need the skills to use sources efficiently and effectively. Skill is the behavioral component of competence. When knowledge precedes skill, behavior or actions demonstrate that knowledge exists.

Besides acquiring the knowledge of communication sources and research methods, students need to develop four main types of effective information-gathering skills: (a) searching, (b) evaluation, (c) note taking, and (d) Internet use. By "effective" we mean that information gathering should be efficient, organized, and systematic.

First, students need to use effective search procedures or *searching skills*. They need to have in their behavioral repertoires the experience to use sources correctly. They need to do so to be able to draw on these skills and repeat their actions, and also to use similar research strategies when they encounter a new source for the first time.

According to Mischo and Lee (1987), library experts have identified several search skills that lead to effective online computer searching: (a) preplanning a search with a search strategy, (b) using a thesaurus to identify precise search terms, (c) typing skill and a positive attitude toward searching, (d) a good memory for database search commands, and (e) trying one's own search, no matter how difficult. In reviewing the literature on search effectiveness, Mischo and Lee found that students who conduct the most effective and successful searches started with good search strategies, understood Boolean logic and could combine terms successfully, understood print options, used the thesaurus to broaden or narrow a search, and knew how to truncate search terms. Students can demonstrate these skills in classes or through assessment measures. The Library Skills Test for Psychology Majors, for instance, assesses students' knowledge of CD-ROM systems, what is contained in PsycLIT, and the basics of searching, such as Boolean logic (Cameron & Hart, 1992). A similar test could be developed for communication students.

Reference librarians can provide instruction in the basic searching skills needed for source retrieval, and thereby, help reduce library apprehension. Bostick (1993) identified five main dimensions of library anxiety: barriers with the staff, comfort with the library, knowledge of the library, mechanical barriers, and affective barriers. Instructors should seek to structure classroom and library experiences to reinforce positive information-seeking attitudes for students. Sometimes units on library use and database searching can be integrated into classes such as Communication Inquiry or Research Methods. The relevant skills can be assessed in these classes.

Beyond searching skills, students need to be able to evaluate the information they find and to extract what is relevant from the sources they locate. Students, then, need effective *evaluation skills* to be able to assess the worth or contribution of the different sources they find, including books, chapters, and journal articles. Using sound research and writing standards, students must develop, throughout their studies, the ability to be critical of the published literature they locate, whether it is in print or electronic form.

Students also need effective *note-taking skills* and writing skills so that they can extract, outline, organize, and synthesize the information found in a search. These skills are often taught in university orientation, writing, and argumentation classes, but developed and refined throughout a student's entire course of study.

Internet skills, which we discuss more fully later in this chapter, include the basic skills of being able to log onto one's account, telnet to other systems, transfer files, send and receive mail, join LISTSERVs, use Gopher, and explore the WWW. These skills are technology focused and require knowledge of the workings of the Internet system and of basic computer protocols.

Searching Success

The attitudes and values developed throughout the course of one's education will determine future searching success. Littlejohn (1987) reported that students with training in searching were more willing to ask for help, when needed. This willingness corresponded positively with the relevance of retrieved references, one element of successful information retrieval. Su (1992) categorized over 20 measures of performance success and found three main elements: relevance (i.e., search strategy precision and recall), utility (i.e., time, effort, and cost), and user satisfaction (with search results and how they were obtained).

Su (1992), however, noted that researchers found high student satisfaction to be linked to low precision. In other words, students found searches resulting in fewer references more helpful than those resulting in more references. This confirmed Littlejohn's (1987) finding: "As long as they retrieve satisfactory results, they are not concerned that other databases or systems available at other times can provide material more pertinent to their needs" (p. 464).

User satisfaction, by itself, then, is not the best determinant of effective information gathering. Students who rely on one method of information gathering or one database will miss important data that can be uncovered more efficiently and effectively by other means. Enjoying and looking forward to exhausting all relevant information sources is at the root of good reporting, researching, and writing.

Information literacy is, perhaps, a better measure of success. A new project focused on discipline-specific standardized assessment of information literacy holds promise for future assessment in mass media sequences (information about the project is available—and current—on its Web site, http://sails.lms.kent.edu/index.php).

Information Sources

Earlier in this chapter, we outlined some basic elements of search strategies and developing competence in information gathering. In this section, we turn our attention to the types of sources students should know about and should be able to use. Much of the information in this section is synthesized and abbreviated from Rubin et al.'s (2005) *Communication Research: Strategies and Sources.* We discuss important general or secondary sources, specific or primary sources, and print and electronic finding tools for information gathering. We list important sources from each section, which can be used to assess students' knowledge and skill, in Table 10.2.

GENERAL OR SECONDARY SOURCES

General or secondary sources summarize or synthesize generally accepted findings and explanations about various topics. They help identify possible research areas when little is known about the topic. They often are the starting place when using a general-to-specific search strategy. They also help to narrow the topic to a manageable size or to choose the most relevant search terms. General or secondary sources include handbooks, textbooks, encyclopedias, dictionaries, and annual reviews and series.

Handbooks and Textbooks

Scholarly or subject handbooks help familiarize students with current topics. They provide summaries of past research, themes, and issues. Handbooks, such as Berger and Chaffee's (1987) *Handbook of Communication Science,* are often broad in their orientation. Although handbooks are soon dated, they provide important knowledge about the development of many relevant topics.

Textbooks survey a field and present easy-to-understand fundamentals and descriptions of a subject. Basic textbooks present brief summaries of existing knowledge and an author's conclusions about this information. The bibliographies at the ends of chapters are useful for locating other writings about the subject. However, bibliographies in introductory texts are often limited in scope.

Several edited handbooks, however, also serve as advanced level textbooks. Some, such as Bryant and Zillmann's (2002) *Media Effects: Advances in Theory and Research,* and Singer and Singer's (2001) *Handbook of Children and the Media,* provide broad coverage of subfields of the communication discipline. Others, such as Wells's (1996) *World Broadcasting: A Comparative View,* focus on specific aspects of media study. These advanced level texts typically provide useful summaries and syntheses of research, as well as excellent bibliographies.

TABLE 10.2
Selected Resources for Mass Media Students

Sources	Location or Publisher
General or Secondary Sources	
Media Effects: Advances in Theory and Research	Lawrence Erlbaum Associates, Inc.
International Encyclopedia of Communications	Oxford University Press
Webster's New World Dictionary of Media and Communications	Macmillan
Communication Yearbook	ICA/Lawrence Erlbaum Associates, Inc.
Specific or Primary Sources	
Communication Research	Sage
Journal of Communication	ICA/Oxford University Press
Journal of Broadcasting & Electronic Media	BEA/Lawrence Erlbaum Associates, Inc.
Critical Studies in Media Communication	NCA/Taylor & Francis
Journalism & Mass Communication Quarterly	AEJMC
Mass Communication & Society	AEJMC/Lawrence Erlbaum Associates, Inc.
Media Psychology	Lawrence Erlbaum Associates, Inc.
FACTS.com Reference Suite	http://www.facts.com/online-fdc.htm
LexisNexis Academic, Statistical, & Congressional	http://www.lexisnexis.com/academic/universe
Broadcasting & Cable Yearbook	Bowker
Finding Tools	
History of Telecommunication Technology	Scarecrow Press
Mass Media Bibliography	University of Illinois Press
Gale Directory of Publications and Broadcast Media	Gale Research/GaleNet
Mass Communications Research Resources	Lawrence Erlbaum Associates, Inc.
ComAbstracts	http://www.cios.org
Communication & Mass Media Complete	Ebsco
Sage Full-Text Collection	Sage
Social Sciences Citation Index	ISI Web of Science
NewsBank	http://infoweb.newsbank.com
Newspaper Abstracts	ProQuest Newspaper Abstracts
CIS/Index to Publications of the U.S. Congress	CIS/LexisNexis Congressional
American Statistics Index	CIS/LexisNexis Statistical
Statistical Abstract of the United States	http://www.census.gov/statab/www/
Television News Index and Abstracts	http://tvnews.vanderbilt.edu
WorldCat	OCLC's FirstSearch

Encyclopedias and Dictionaries

Encyclopedias present multifaceted information about a subject. Their essays generally have bibliographies to help locate other general and specific sources that can give background about narrower aspects of the topic. These bibliographies may be useful, depending on the scope of the essay and the publication date of the encyclopedia.

Subject encyclopedias contain overview articles that summarize what is known about a discipline. One subject encyclopedia in communication, Barnouw's (1989) *International Encyclopedia of Communications,* has over 500 essays on communication subjects and offers broad treatment of topics. More specialized encyclopedias in mass communication include Reed and Reed's (1992) *The Encyclopedia of Television, Cable, and Video,* and Bidgoli's (2003) *The Internet Encyclopedia.*

Subject dictionaries list and define terms used in a field. They also provide meanings for abbreviations, jargon, and slang. Some dictionaries, such as Diamant's (1992) *Dictionary of Broadcast Communications* and Weiner's (1996) *Webster's New World Dictionary of Media and Communications,* are particularly relevant to mass media. Subject dictionaries sometimes resemble encyclopedias by giving descriptions of and bibliographic references for terms. An example of one such source in communication is Stempel's (1999) *Historical Dictionary of Political Communication in the United States.*

Annual Reviews and Series

Two other types of useful general sources are annual reviews and series. Annual reviews provide yearly summaries of current research activities. Some are similar to edited collections of essays that are found in handbooks. One such annual review, *Communication Yearbook,* has been produced by the International Communication Association since 1977. This annual source publishes literature reviews and essays of bodies of research in many areas of communication.

Series also appear regularly. They are publications on specific themes or similar topics within a discipline. Several such series have appeared in communication since the 1970s. Two series of interest to mass media students are Sage's (1997–) *New Media Cultures* and Praeger's (1987–) *Media and Society.* Annual reviews and series are useful for selecting and refining research topics, for locating sources, and for updating bibliographies. One source that students should examine, *Books in Series* (1989–), identifies series in all disciplines.

These general sources, then, provide a general understanding of interests, concerns, and methods of communication researchers. They help identify a specific research area within communication for class assignments or research projects. General sources in other fields also are important for professional projects such as news stories or magazine essays. In many instances, handbooks, yearbooks, and annual reviews also can serve as vehicles for widening a search strategy and locating other recent sources about a chosen communication topic.

SPECIFIC OR PRIMARY SOURCES

Specific or primary sources contain original information and precise data. They help refine research questions and provide important data to develop research projects. Such sources are often the starting place when using a specific-to-general search strategy. They also may be the product of a narrowed search that seeks precise information. Specific or primary sources include scholarly journals, professional magazines, collections and archives, statistical sources, government documents, yearbooks and directories, and manuals and guides.

Journals and Magazines

Scholarly journals contain the original research in a discipline. This research typically focuses on questions that are current and significant to the discipline. Consequently, journals are important primary sources of information for communication students. Students' abilities to be effective consumers of the scholarly research, however, need to be cultivated in several classes, including those in communication inquiry and research methods. These investigations include jargon that is specific to a field, standardized stylistic and organizational structures, and scientific or humanistic methods that may be peculiar to the investigator or research topic.

Editors of the most respected journals select the research for inclusion in their journals after a careful process of refereed review. Some of the more respected journals that publish mostly research in mass media include *Communication Research, Critical Studies in Media Communication, Journal of Broadcasting & Electronic Media, Journal of Communication, Journalism & Mass Communication Quarterly, Mass Communication & Society,* and *Media Psychology.* Many of these journals are published by professional communication associations such as the Association for Education in Journalism and Mass Communication (AEJMC), Broadcast Education Association (BEA), International Communication Association (ICA), and National Communication Association (NCA).

Professional or trade magazines usually do not publish original research, although they may report about the results of research studies. They do print stories about current issues, professional trends, practical applications, and industry personnel. Awareness of the contents of some trade magazines is important to mass media students so that they keep abreast of developments in the profession. Some notable professional magazines pertinent to areas of mass media study include *Advertising Age, Broadcasting & Cable, Columbia Journalism Review,* and *Public Relations Journal.*

Collections and Archives

Original information, whether it be a fact, speech, or document, is useful for many class projects ranging from news stories to legal briefs. Students may need to locate speeches, media transcripts, historical or policy documents, or statistical data. Such information is not always easy to find, but is often accessible in collections and archives.

Published collections allow students to examine primary documents. Ash and Miller's (1993) *Subject Collections* can help locate various older collections and archives. Of particular relevance are speech, media, statistical, and legal collections.

Speech collections, such as *Vital Speeches of the Day* (1934–), provide access to original speeches by society and industry leaders. Such collections of speeches and other documents make it easier to locate and to consult the original text of these documents. In addition, speeches of the President of the United States are published in the *Weekly Compilation of Presidential Documents* (1965–). Presidential speeches also are available online at addresses such as the White House homepage (http://www.whitehouse.gov). Past presidential speeches and artifacts, which may need to be consulted when conducting historical research or for media projects such as a script or news story, can be found on-site at presidential libraries (one new archive of interviews and speeches—*The National Gallery of the Spoken Word*—is available online at http://www.ngsw.org, as is *Douglass: Archives of American Public Address,* at http://douglassarchives.org).

The content of newspapers is often compiled in one type of media collection. Newspaper collections are useful when students want to learn what journalists have said about a topic. *Editorials on File* (1970–), for example, collects newspaper editorials from over 100 newspapers (it is available online through *FACTS.com Reference Suite*). *Viewpoint*

(1976–; also available from *FACTS.com*) contains the work of newspaper and radio columnists and political cartoonists.

Typically, electronic media program collections are available on-site in a few archives, such as the Museum of Television and Radio in New York City and the Museum of Broadcast Communications in Chicago. Full-text news transcripts are available from 1990 to the present on *LexisNexis Academic*. The Vanderbilt (University) Television News Archive and the Public Affairs Video Archives at Purdue University rent audiotapes and videotapes. Vanderbilt's collection is indexed and searchable in the *Television News Index and Abstracts* (1968–; http://tvnews.vanderbilt.edu). In addition, C-SPAN programs are archived and searchable (http://www.c-spanarchives.org), and the Political Commercial Archive at the University of Oklahoma can be searched as well (http://www.ou.edu/pccenter/catalogue.htm).

Two other types of collections are useful for communication students. Measurement collections, such as Rubin, Palmgreen, and Sypher's (1994) *Communication Research Measures: A Sourcebook,* compile original research measures of communication attitudes and behavior. Such collections typically include discussions of the utility, validity, and reliability of the research measures, and are useful for those who want to conduct original research investigations or to learn about the measures used in research studies they read. Legal collections, such as *Pike & Fischer Radio Regulation* (1946–) and *Media Law Reporter* (1977–), are particularly useful for students of media policy and freedom of expression. These legal collections compile and make accessible legislative and administrative acts and court decisions. A new Web site, *Findlaw Constitutional Law Center* (http://supreme.findlaw.com), contains U.S. Constitution and Supreme Court documents.

Statistical Sources

Many government agencies and industries collect statistical data. Because these data provide useful profiles about the society and its media for many research and professional writing projects, students need to know how to search for information in them. The *American Statistics Index* (1973–) indexes statistical publications of the U.S. government, including the Federal Communications Commission (FCC) and the Census Bureau. The *American Statistics Index* also is available on CD-ROM as part of *Statistical Masterfile* and online as part of *LexisNexis Statistical.* The U.S. Department of Commerce's (1879–) *Statistical Abstract of the United States* is an annual summary of social, economic, and political statistics. It also is available on CD-ROM. Online statistics include the U.S. Census Bureau (http://www.census.gov) and American Factfinder (http://factfinder.census.gov). A gateway to federal online statistics also is available (http://www.fedstats.gov).

Trade and professional associations, as well as ratings and polling organizations, such as Arbitron, A.C. Nielsen, Standard Rate and Data, Gallup, Harris, and Roper, also have produced statistical data that are useful for mass media students.

Government Documents

Publications of the U.S. government inform media students and professionals about what is happening in Congress, the Supreme Court, and federal agencies such as the FCC. The U.S. government publishes an overwhelming number of federal statutes and regulations, congressional and agency reports, census documents, periodicals, directories, handbooks, and bibliographies.

For example, the laws of the United States are found in the U.S. Congress's (U.S. Congress, House of Representatives, 1994) *United States Code*. The U.S. General Services Administration's (U.S. General Services Administration, Office of the Federal Register, 1936–) *Federal Register* publishes executive and federal agency regulations and legal notices, which are codified or indexed in its *Code of Federal Regulations* (U.S. General Services Administration, Office of the Federal Register, 1938–) and *Code of Federal Regulations: CFR Index and Finding Aids* (U.S. General Services Administration, Office of the Federal Register, 1963–). The FCC publishes a weekly *Federal Communications Commission Reports* (Federal Communications Commission, 1934/1935–) and a yearly *Annual Report of the Federal Communications Commission* (1935–) (available from http://www.fcc.gov/). *CIS/Index to Publications of the United States Congress* (1970–) indexes and abstracts Congressional publications, legislation, and committee hearings. Most of these documents are available through *GPO Access* (http://www.gpoaccess.gov/) and *Lexis-Nexis Congressional*.

Yearbooks and Directories

Yearbooks provide current information about a field's structure and development. They also contain statistical data and other relevant information about professional services and personnel in the industry. Two useful media-related yearbooks are *Broadcasting & Cable Yearbook* (1935–) and *Editor & Publisher International Year Book* (1959–).

Directories, such as the *Gale Directory of Publications and Broadcast Media* (1869–), identify names, addresses, and factual information about media organizations such as newspapers and periodicals. Similar to yearbooks, they provide facts about the industry, and can lead students to professionals and trade organizations which may be able to provide current information not contained in other information sources. The *Gale Directory* is available online as the *Gale Database of Publications and Broadcast Media.* Other directories, such as Brooks and Marsh's (2003) *The Complete Directory to Prime Time Network and Cable TV Shows 1946–Present,* contain information about specific entities that would be useful for media history, programming, and research projects.

FINDING TOOLS

Some sources are intended to help locate primary and secondary materials that are pertinent to research topics. Indexes and abstracts, for example, help to narrow a general research topic to more specific research questions. They classify or categorize databases by authors, subjects, or titles. This sometimes helps to identify subtopics. Indexes and abstracts list both older and more contemporary writings in these areas. Bibliographies and guides to the literature also can be used for this purpose. Findings tools are the most central and important of all resources for students.

Bibliographies and Guides

Many student projects require a list of references about a topic. Sometimes such topical bibliographies appear in book or periodical form, such as Sterling and Shiers' (2000) *History of Telecommunications Technology.* More often, selective topical bibliographies are appended to journal articles, books, or chapters. Occasionally, bibliographies, such as Blum and Wilhoit's (1990) *Mass Media Bibliography,* are annotated, that is, they provide summaries of the sources. Bibliographies, then, identify useful primary and secondary sources. Inspecting and using these sources can expand a student's information search for a variety of class projects.

Guides to the literature are broad bibliographies that identify and organize periodicals, reference works, and other information sources in a field. They also specify search strategies and information for accessing and using these sources. One useful guide to research sources about the electronic media is Sterling, Bracken, and Hill's (1998) *Mass Communications Research Resources: An Annotated Guide.*

Students who are interested in communication policy and history, in particular, often need to consult the legal literature. Legal decisions affect public policy, freedom of expression, and the conduct of industry. Courses in media law or policy should inform students about primary (e.g., statutes, court decisions, agency rules) and secondary (e.g., encyclopedias, commentaries, textbooks) legal sources and how to access them with appropriate finding tools such as citators (i.e., citation indexes for legal cases), computerized search services such as LEXIS, and legal research guides. Legal guides to the literature also serve as manuals for conducting legal research. They provide access to primary sources, describe legal research procedures, and identify legal citation forms and abbreviations. Students should learn how to use at least one handy legal research guide, such as *Fundamentals of Legal Research* (Mersky, Dunn, & Jacobstein, 2002).

Indexes

Researchers use periodical indexes to find scholarly journal or magazine articles. The articles are arranged by subject heading, sometimes also by author, and occasionally, by publication. Most students are familiar with the *Readers' Guide to Periodical Literature* (1901–). Listed by their subject, this index identifies articles found in popular magazines such as *Newsweek*. This may be a useful index for investigating current events topics, and for giving historical perspective to a topic.

Specialized indexes are published within academic fields. They are more useful than periodical indexes for locating original research. These indexes, such as *Communication & Mass Media Complete* (2004–), list the articles published in the scholarly journals in the discipline. *Communication & Mass Media Complete* has combined two former indexes, *CommSearch*, a CD-ROM index produced by the National Communication Association, and *Mass Media Articles Index*. *ComAbstracts* (1997–) is available to members of the Communication Institute for Online Scholarship, and *Sage Full-Text Collection* contains PDF format articles for downloading. These sources will be used most often for locating original information contained in communication periodicals. Several indexes that are published for journal articles in other fields, such as *Business Periodicals Index* (1958–), also are useful for communication students.

Another valuable but different format is the citation index, which lists references to selected journals and books by the cited author. The index creates lists of works that have been cited in journal articles by an author. When researchers need to know the name of an author, article, or book on a specific topic, they can use a citation index to find more recently published writings in the area. Citation indexes, then, help locate other relevant sources and update bibliographies. *Social Sciences*

Citation Index (1972–) and *Arts and Humanities Citation Index* (1976–) index much of the scholarly communication literature. Both indexes are available through the *ISI Web of Science.*

Another type of index is the media index, which helps find original media writings and programs. Media indexes include indexes of newspaper articles and editorials, videotaped television programs, and films and their reviews. Media indexes are very specialized and focus on newspaper, video, or film sources.

A newspaper index helps locate news stories, editorials, and media reviews, which can be useful for preparing news programs or documentaries, studying news content, or similar projects. In printed format, these indexes usually reference only one newspaper (e.g., the *New York Times Index,* 1851–). However, electronic newspaper archives often are easily searched. *NewsDirectory.com* provides links to hundreds of online newspapers. *National Newspaper Index* (1977–), *NewsBank* (http://infoweb.newsbank.com), and *Factiva* (http://www.factiva.com) provide full-text access to many newspapers. Small newspapers can be accessed through NewsBank's *America's Newspapers* (1981–) or located using the *Gale Directory of Publications and Broadcast Media* (1869–), available through *Galenet.*

Another type of media index lists television programs, especially public affairs programming. For example, the *CBS News Index* (1975–1991) identifies on microfiche the text of CBS News productions through 1991. There are similar services for ABC News and public television. The *Transcript/Video Index* (1991–) accesses over 60 television news and public affairs programs, dating back to 1968. These programs include *CNN News,* but exclude NBC programs and *The MacNeil/Lehrer NewsHour.* Another useful source for television news programming is Vanderbilt University Archive's *Television News Index and Abstracts* (1968–). These indexes provide perspective on current events for many class projects. They also are useful for conducting content analyses of news programs.

A third type of media index references book reviews. Such reviews summarize the content and assess the value of books. Students can locate general interest or popular book reviews by using indexes such as *Book Review Digest* (1905–), as well as CD-ROM indexes such as *General Periodicals Ondisc* and *General Periodicals Index.* Many university libraries have printed guides to book reviews at the reference desk.

Abstracts

Abstracts are collections of brief summaries of primary sources and provide an idea of what the book chapter or journal article is about. *Communication Abstracts* (1978–) is the most widely used abstracting source in communication. It is available through FirstSearch and through Cambridge Scientific Abstracts. This source selectively surveys over 200 periodicals. It summarizes the major communication journals, periodicals of allied fields, and books. Another useful source for locating theses and dissertations in mass communication is *Journalism & Mass Communication Abstracts* (1963–), now available online (http://www.aejmc.org/ abstracts/). Many periodical indexes and abstracts are now available on CD-ROMs for users to retrieve via computer. The database may be available locally on CD-ROM in a library, or may be stored elsewhere in the state or region and accessed by computer protocols from a distance. Many of these databases are useful for communication students. Table 10.3 identifies some useful media databases.

In addition, computerized databases are easy to search, although they may frighten the novice. Most include online tutorials and help screens. Libraries often distribute summary sheets to help the user search the database effectively.

Effective searching involves precise, efficient, and utility search skills (Su, 1992). Students need to use exact search terms, language based on the research subject, and the online thesauruses that make searching more precise and relevant. Search strategies need to be efficient, beginning with controlled vocabulary and then broadening or narrowing the search, depending on the outcome. Having a good search plan and using Boolean logic (i.e., "and," "or," and "not") save search time. "Utility" refers to the overall worth of a search. Worth can be determined by several criteria: dollars spent (on systems where intermediaries do the

TABLE 10.3
Selected Computerized Databases

Database	Vendor	Content
ABI/Inform Global	ProQuest	Business journals
CMMC	Ebsco	Communication journals
ComIndex	CIOS	Communication journals
ERIC	ERIC	Resources in education
Government Periodicals Universe	LexisNexis/CIS	U.S. government publications
InfoTrac LegalTrac	Gale Group	Legal resources
ISI Web of Science	ISI	Social sciences and arts and humanities
LEXIS	LexisNexis	Court decisions, statutes, regulations
NEXIS	LexisNexis	News articles, government publications, and periodicals
PAIS International	OCLC	Public Affairs Information Service
Wilson Omnifile Full Text	H. W. Wilson	Readers' Guide, Wilson Social Mega Edition Science, Humanities, and General Science Abstracts

searching for you), time expended, physical and mental effort expended, and the value of the search results. Students can keep records of their search procedures and efforts for skill evaluation. They also can be tested on the relevance, efficiency, and utility of their search by having students search the same term. Students can print their search screens and produce the downloaded results for evaluation.

INFORMATION IN CYBERSPACE

The Internet

The Internet connects computer networks. It allows users to communicate with others and to locate and retrieve information from remote databases. It enables access to professional and scholarly associations, electronic periodicals, electronic indexes and abstracts, government data and publications, electronic archives of political speeches and documents, and LISTSERVs and hot lines in different areas of communication. It also is a vehicle to be researched and studied. Students need to acquire basic Internet skills to correspond with others, to log-in or telnet to remote computer sites, to use search engines efficiently, and to transfer files to their computers from a remote computer via file transfer protocol (FTP).

Journalism Web sites that identify online-searching and information-gathering tools tend to group these tools into six categories (http://bailiwick.lib.uiowa.edu/journalism/searching.html). *How-to Guides* focus on how to locate government documents, legal and news materials (Lexis/Nexis), and businesses and organizations; how to search web directories, archives, and indexes was described earlier. *Website Evaluation Tools* focus on critical thinking, assessing quality of information and the site, Boolean searching, and critical selection and analysis of information. Also, knowledge of web review services is useful in helping to evaluate web-based information. *Major Search Engines* includes several search engines useful in gathering information, such as Alta Vista, Excite, Google, HotBot, Lycos, Magellan, WebCrawler, and Yahoo! *Specialized Search Engines* include those used for searching lists and newsgroups (such as Liszt and the Directory of Scholarly and Professional E-Conferences), people (phone books), images (Alta Vista Photo Finder, Lycos Image Gallery), and software (e.g., http://www.Download.com, http://www.Shareware.com). *Meta-search Engines* (e.g., DogPile, go2net, Profusion) allow the searching of multiple search engines, all at one time. *Directories and Portals* provide information gatherers with sites devoted to customized news, web search engines, and information (e.g., e-Blast, Excite, HotBot, Lycos, Netscape Net Center). Many commercial, government, and business organizations have Internet sites and provide useful information resources.

RECOMMENDATIONS

The knowledge and skill required for information-gathering competence can best be assessed within courses, workshops, short courses, or self-tutorials. Because these elements of competence are so basic, we recommend they occur during the first 2 years of college. In particular, three specific courses should help increase students' knowledge base, develop and refine skills, and enhance students' attitudes and motivation to seek information systematically. Course descriptions are as follows:

• Communication Inquiry is an introduction to print and electronic sources of information for communication research. The emphasis is on (a) building knowledge of primary, secondary, and finding-tool sources in communication; (b) enhancing effective search strategies; and (c) developing basic Internet skills. Students learn how to use the sources and identify which are useful for specific purposes. The course helps improve source, experiential, application, and research-domain knowledge. It helps decrease library and Internet anxiety, increase appreciation of and motivation to seek appropriate information sources, and improve searching, evaluation, and note-taking skills. Assessment of information literacy can take place in this class.

• Research Methods is an introduction to the conduct of communication research. The focus is on research literacy and skill. Students learn research terminology, methodology, and applications. They read and evaluate research studies, learn how to conduct their own studies, and appreciate the systematic efforts that underlie knowledge of the field. The course helps improve research domain and research methodology knowledge. It helps decrease research and statistics anxiety, increase appreciation of and motivation to conduct original research, and improve evaluation and analytic skills.

• Interviewing focuses on the means of gathering information from other than published sources. Students learn how to ask the right questions, take field notes, and write accounts of what they are told. Information on identifying and scheduling those to interview prepares students for information gathering from knowledgeable people. The course helps improve source, experiential, and application knowledge. It helps reduce the anxiety interviewers may experience, increase appreciation of gathering information from personal sources, and improve abilities to formulate questions, evaluate sources, and synthesize information.

Knowledge Assessment

Knowledge is best assessed within structured classes, such as the three courses just described. An integral part of any communication student's course of study should be a Communication Inquiry class in information gathering, which contains knowledge about search strategies, sources, and the Internet. This class should be complemented by courses in Research Methods and in Interviewing. Together, these courses should increase students' knowledge of

- What sources exist (source knowledge).
- Which sources are most useful (experiential knowledge).
- How to use these sources (application knowledge).
- What terms mean and how research reports are organized (research domain knowledge).
- How to conduct research studies (research methodology knowledge).

Traditional examinations are useful for assessing knowledge. Recall, essay, and recognition exams can identify understanding of basic concepts, principles, and sources. In addition, information gathering, interview, and research applications and exercises can help assess basic knowledge and understanding. A thesis or project provides a comprehensive test of accumulated knowledge.

Skill Assessment

We have identified four main skills: searching, evaluation, note-taking, and Internet skills. The Communication Inquiry course can hone searching, note-taking, evaluation, and Internet skills. The Research Methods course can improve evaluation skills. The Interviewing course can help sharpen note-taking skills. All three courses assist proficiency in analyzing and synthesizing information. Precision, utility, efficiency, and effectiveness are important criteria for assessing skills. Besides performance tests, videotapes of performance and portfolios can provide information about skill development, especially changes over time.

SUMMARY

Knowledge and skill are essential components of information-gathering competence. In this chapter, we identified (a) the knowledge and skills that can help assure the research success of mass media students, and (b) the classes that can enhance competence.

First, students need to know what pertinent reference sources exist. They also need to understand which sources are most useful for different purposes, and how to choose the right source for the purpose at hand. Knowledge of how to use the print and electronic sources, including the Internet, is essential in today's online world. A Communication Inquiry class provides this type of information and helps increase students' positive regard for the process.

Second, students need to be able to read the research literature. They need to know about the language and structure of research reports, and how research is conducted. Therefore, a Research Methods class is important in the curriculum. Class exercises and experiences help students appreciate the research process and motivate them to seek comprehensive answers.

Third, when the published sources have not yet answered their questions, students need to know how to seek answers. A Research Methods class helps students formulate their own investigation to seek these answers. In addition, an Interviewing class hones students' questioning and listening skills so that they can seek answers from others.

These classes should reduce apprehension for doing research and for asking knowledgeable others for the information they need. The knowledge and reinforcement students receive in their communication courses will help them develop the information-seeking competence to assure success in their academic and professional careers.

REFERENCES

Accrediting Council on Education in Journalism and Mass Communications. (2003). *Standards for accreditation.* Retrieved July 12, 2005, from www.ku.edu/~acejmc

American Statistics Index: A Comprehensive Guide and Index to the Statistical Publications of the U.S. Government. (1973–). Bethesda, MD: Congressional Information Service.

America's Newspapers. (1981–). Naples, FL: Newsbank.

Arts and Humanities Citation Index. (1976–). Philadelphia: Institute for Scientific Information.

Ash, L., & Miller, W. G. (Comps.). (1993). *Subject collections* (7th ed., rev. & enl., 2 vols.). New Providence, NJ: Bowker.

Barnouw, E. (Ed.). (1989). *International encyclopedia of communications* (4 vols.). New York: Oxford University Press.

Beasley, D. (1988). *How to use a research library.* New York: Oxford University Press.

Berger, C. R., & Chaffee, S. H. (Eds.). (1987). *Handbook of communication science.* Newbury Park, CA: Sage.

Bidgoli, H. (Ed.). (2003). *The Internet encyclopedia* (3 vols.). Hoboken, NJ: Wiley.

Blum, E., & Wilhoit, F. (1990). *Mass media bibliography: An annotated, selected list of books and journals for reference and research* (3rd ed.). Urbana: University of Illinois Press.

Book Review Digest. (1905–). New York: H. W. Wilson.

Books in series (5th ed.). (1989). New York: Bowker.

Bostick, S. L. (1993). The development and validation of the library anxiety scale. In M. E. Murfin & J. B. Whitlatch (Eds.), *American Library Association, RASD occasional papers, No. 16: Research in reference effectiveness* (pp. 1–7). Chicago: American Library Association, Reference and Adult Services Division.

Broadcasting & Cable Yearbook (2 vols.). (1935–). New Providence, NJ: Bowker.

Brooks, T., & Marsh, E. (2003). *The complete directory to prime time network and cable TV shows 1946–present* (8th ed.). New York: Ballantine.

Bryant, J., & Zillmann, D. (Eds.). (2002). *Media effects: Advances in theory and research* (2nd ed.). Mahwah, NJ: Lawrence Erlbaum Associates, Inc.

Business Periodicals Index. (1958–). New York: Wilson.

Cameron, L., & Hart, J. (1992). Assessment of PsycLIT competence, attitudes, and instructional methods. *Teaching of Psychology, 19,* 239–242.

Cannon, C. M. (2001). Real computer virus: The Internet is an invaluable information-gathering tool for journalists. *American Journalism Review, 23,* 28–35.

CBS News Index. (1975–1991). Ann Arbor, MI: University Microfilms International.

CIS/Index to Publications of the United States Congress. (1970–). Washington, DC: Congressional Information Service.

Colorado Educational Media Association. (2002). *Colorado information literacy standards.* Retrieved March 30, 2004, from http://www.cde.state.co.us/litstandards/

ComAbstracts. (1997–). Albany, NY: Communication Institute for Online Scholarship.

Communication Abstracts. (1978–). Thousand Oaks, CA: Sage.

Communication & Mass Media Complete. (2004–). Ipswich, MA: Ebsco.

Diamant, L. (Ed.). (1992). *Dictionary of broadcast communications* (3rd rev. ed.). Lincolnwood, IL: National Textbook.

Editor & Publisher International Year Book. (1959–). New York: Editor & Publisher.

Editorials on file. (1970–). New York: Facts on File.

Federal Communications Commission. (1934/1935–). *Federal Communications Commission Reports.* Washington, DC: U.S. Government Printing Office.

Federal Communications Commission. (1935–). *Annual Report of the Federal Communications Commission.* Washington, DC: U.S. Government Printing Office.

Gale Directory of Publications and Broadcast Media (4 vols.). (1869–). Detroit, MI: Gale Research.

Garrison, B. (2000). Journalists' perceptions of online information-gathering problems. *Journalism & Mass Communication Quarterly, 77,* 500–514.

Journalism & Mass Communication Abstracts: M.A., M.S., Ph.D. Theses in Journalism and Mass Communication. (1963–). Columbia, SC: Association for Education in Journalism and Mass Communication.

Littlejohn, A. C. (1987). End-user searching in an academic library: The student view. *RQ, 26,* 460–466.

Mann, T. (1998). *A guide to library research methods* (2nd ed.). New York: Oxford University Press.

Media and Society. (1987–). Westport, CT: Praeger.

Media Law Reporter. (1977–). Washington, DC: Bureau of National Affairs.

Mersky, R. M., Dunn, D. J., & Jacobstein, J. M. (2002). *Fundamentals of legal research* (7th ed.). Westbury, NY: Foundation Press.

Mischo, W. H., & Lee, J. (1987). End-user searching of bibliographic databases. *Annual Review of Information Science and Technology, 22,* 227–263.

National Newspaper Index. (1977–). Farmington Hills, MI: Gale Group/InfoTrac.

New Media Cultures. (1997–). Thousand Oaks, CA: Sage.

New York Times Index. (1851–). New York: New York Times.

Pike & Fischer Radio Regulation. (1946–). Bethesda, MD: Pike & Fischer.

Psychological Abstracts. (1927–). Arlington, VA: American Psychological Association.

Readers' Guide to Periodical Literature. (1901–). Minneapolis, MN: H. W. Wilson.

Reed, R. M., & Reed, M. K. (1992). *The encyclopedia of television, cable, and video.* New York: Van Nostrand Reinhold.

Rubin, R. B., Palmgreen, P., & Sypher, H. E. (1994). *Communication research measures: A sourcebook.* New York: Guilford.

Rubin, R. B., Rubin, A. M., & Piele, L. J. (2005). *Communication research: Strategies and sources* (6th ed.). Belmont, CA: Wadsworth.

Singer, D. G., & Singer, J. L. (Eds.). (2001). *Handbook of children and the media.* Thousand Oaks, CA: Sage.

Social Sciences Citation Index. (1972–). Philadelphia: Institute for Scientific Information.

Stempel, G. H. (Ed.). (1999). *Historical dictionary of political communication in the United States.* Westport, CT: Greenwood.

Sterling, C. H., Bracken, J. K., & Hill, S. M. (1998). *Mass communications research resources: An annotated guide.* Mahwah, NJ: Lawrence Erlbaum Associates, Inc.

Sterling, C. H., & Shiers, G. (2000). *History of telecommunication technology: An annotated bibliography.* Lanham, MD: Scarecrow.

Su, L. T. (1992). Evaluation measures for interactive information retrieval. *Information Processing & Management, 28,* 503–516.

Television News Index and Abstracts: Annual Index. (1968–). Nashville, TN: Vanderbilt Television News Archive.

Transcript/Video Index: A Comprehensive Guide to Television News and Public Affairs Programming. (1991–). New York: Journal Graphics.

U.S. Congress, House of Representatives. (1994). *United States Code* (1988 ed.). Washington, DC: U.S. Government Printing Office.

U.S. Department of Commerce, Bureau of the Census. (1879–). *Statistical Abstract of the United States.* Washington, DC: U. S. Government Printing Office.

U.S. General Services Administration, Office of the Federal Register. (1936–). *Federal Register.* Washington, DC: U.S. Government Printing Office.

U.S. General Services Administration, Office of the Federal Register. (1938–). *Code of Federal Regulations.* Washington, DC: U.S. Government Printing Office.

U.S. General Services Administration, Office of the Federal Register. (1963–). *Code of Federal Regulations: CFR Index and Finding Aids.* Washington, DC: U.S. Government Printing Office.

Viewpoint. (1976–). Glen Rock, NJ: Microfilming Corporation of America.

Vital Speeches of the Day. (1934–). New York: City News.

Ward, J., & Hansen, K. A. (1997). *Search strategies in mass communication* (3rd ed.). New York: Longman.

Weekly Compilation of Presidential Documents. (1965–). Washington, DC: U.S. Government Printing Office.

Weinberg, S. (1999). CAR step-by-step techniques made workable. *IRE Journal, 22,* 4–5.

Weiner, R. (1996). *Webster's new world dictionary of media and communications* (rev. ed.). New York: Macmillan.

Wells, A. (1996). *World broadcasting: A comparative view.* Norwood, NJ: Ablex.

11

Media Writing

Seth Finn
David Majka
Robert Morris University

Assessment in media writing courses is both simple and complex. It is simple because the end result of all media writing assignments is an explicit real-world product—the script. It is complex because the writer is a student, not a professional. Nothing is as effortless to grade as a script that meets standards of professional quality. Nothing is as disheartening as dealing with a script that has totally missed the mark. In the real world, anything less than an "A" can be discarded. In the academic world, anything less than an "A" implicitly demands a diagnostic assessment. One purpose of this chapter is to explain how this academic ideal might be realistically pursued to the benefit of students, instructors, and academic institutions. A second, and no less challenging purpose, is to describe how systematic procedures for assessing the success of a media writing course might be implemented to serve the same constituencies in the long term.

PREPARING STUDENTS FOR ASSESSMENT

In the language of educational testing, assigning a real-life task, such as writing a newspaper article or broadcast script, and evaluating it to determine a student's mastery of the skills involved, falls within the domain of performance assessment. There are three major points to performance assessment. First, the assigned task should challenge the students to apply what they have previously learned to solving a novel problem. Second, the problem should simulate a real-life situation or task. Third, a judge familiar with the situation or the demands of the task in a real-life situation should evaluate the student's observable response (Gipps, 1994). When one contrasts the concept of performance assessment with the traditional practices used to assess learning in a liberal arts environment, objective tests and essay writing, for example, then it is immediately evident that most students have had little experience with performance assessment when they enroll in their first media writing class. Up to this point, students are much more likely to have developed competence in taking exams that tested their knowledge, comprehension, and analytical abilities than the application of their acquired knowledge to a real-life or simulated exercise.

Even students who have demonstrated their competence in writing essays and research papers now have to come to terms with a new set of circumstances, including an invisible audience and a new role for the instructor. The conventional admonition in composition texts to "know your audience" takes on a new meaning when that audience is an abstract construct rather than an instructor or classmates. For the most part, students have been conditioned to write essays and term papers for their teachers and professors, who are specialists and experts. They have been rewarded for revealing every relevant item they have uncovered in their research or can recall from their studies. Often the presentation of ideas can be incomplete or unclear, but instructors, whose primary goal is to assess their students' success at acquiring knowledge about a subject, may rely on their expert knowledge to provide missing context and give a sympathetic reading to their students' writing.

Mass media writing courses, however, force a new set of circumstances on students and instructors. The audience for a script is an imaginary public. Most members of the audience know much less about the information to be communicated than the writer. Suddenly students must function as experts, writing to an audience that cannot be relied on to use specialized knowledge to decode the intended message. If the writer is hazy about the ideas to be communicated, audience members are likely to become confused or impatient. Certainly they cannot be expected to bring into focus the foggy notions of a poorly encoded message.

This predicament of writing to an inexpert and invisible audience—typical of a mass media environment—is novel in an academic setting. Suddenly the instructor, who traditionally plays the role of motivator and sympathetic reader of student writing, moves to the sideline to render a professional judgment. The result is a rigorous evaluation based on experience. Does the script generate a meaningful message for the imagined audience? Would an experienced editor or producer accept it? The fundamental assessment of the message is based not on what the student knows about the topic, not even what the instructor can infer, but on what it communicates to an unknowing public. The student writer as expert, the instructor as judge of an invisible audience's sensibilities; this new assessment procedure must be made explicit to the media writing student.

A second major adjustment for the media writing student is the adoption of a series of peremptory writing conventions. Writing for the media requires changes in structure, strategy, and style. Print journalists have long insisted that traditional techniques of composition taught in high school and college were worse than useless. Edwin L. Shuman's 1903 text, *Practical Journalism*, set the tone for dozens of textbooks to follow with a list of exaggerated imperatives: "Put the point of your whole story into the first sentence, and the shorter the sentence the better. Whether the story be two columns or two inches long, cram the marrow of it into the first paragraph. Banish the school-essay idea that there must be an introduction or preliminary explanation of any kind" (Shuman, 1903, cited in Adams, 1993, p. 107).

In recent years, the notions underlying college composition courses have been under scrupulous review, often leading to revolutionary new approaches (Faigley, Cherry, Jolliffe, & Skinner, 1985). Nevertheless, the differences between academic writing and media writing are not always obvious to inexperienced students. When asked to write nonfiction scripts, such as radio public service announcements (PSAs), feature interviews, or minidocumentaries, students may—unless carefully coached—employ expository writing styles that have afforded them success in other writing classes (Fry, 1988; Wiist, 1997). Worse yet, they may become mired in complexity, abstraction, and inflated vocabulary, because they have been encouraged, beginning with their high school English teachers, to believe that those devices provide convincing evidence of their intellectual growth (Hake & Williams, 1981).

MAKING A SYLLABUS ASSESSMENT-FRIENDLY

Investing time in the development of a comprehensive syllabus is one especially effective way to improve the validity of student assessment in media writing courses (Tucker, 1994). First and foremost, students need an explicit description of each writing assignment if assessments of their writing are to be valid. For example, instructors often assume that students can use sample scripts in their texts as examples of correct format.

Yet many times when textbook authors collect copies of real-world scripts to exhibit differences in content, they inadvertently introduce an excessive amount of variance in formats. Novice students, trying to interpolate rules from many examples, may needlessly devote large blocks of time to resolving such issues as proper margins and headings when they should be concentrating on formulating their message and revising it.

To forestall this misplaced effort, the syllabus, as well as other written materials distributed throughout the semester, should spell out the nature of each written assignment in a way that relieves the student from the burden of working out routine procedures. That way the student's effort and the instructor's assessment jointly focus on the essential skills to be acquired and demonstrated. One of the major differences between novices and experts in undertaking a task is that the experts can isolate the vital elements of the task from the menial ones and focus their attention where needed. In explicitly describing the writing assignments—in essence giving away the answers to the simple questions—students will remain focused on essential components rather than trivial ones.

Another way a syllabus can facilitate assessment is in the careful structuring of assignments in terms of their complexity. The proper order for acquiring skills in media writing is not always as clear cut as it is in arithmetic where, for instance, multiplication precedes division. And yet it is clearly useful for instructors to consciously build one assignment on another, so that lessons learned—or not learned—in one exercise can be tested in the next. Such continuity, building on previous experience, promotes deep learning (Harlen & James, 1997). Media writing students who begin the semester by creating a 30-second live PSA based on facts gathered from a Web site should be reminded 10 weeks later, as they embark on a 30-minute screenplay based on a favorite short story, that once again they are adapting published material to a nonprint medium. This time, however, they exploit both a visual and an audio channel, using varied shots, voices, and sounds as well as elements of dramatic structure in a manner that is consistent with the techniques they have learned in their intervening assignments. Thus, the last assignment in the course explicitly functions as a capstone exercise.

COMMUNICATION THEORY AND CRITERIA
FOR WRITING ASSESSMENT

The major safeguard against teaching rote skills in a media writing course is the instructor's explicit concern with communication theory. There are, of course, elemental rules of language that a good writer must observe just as a good driver must be cognizant of traffic laws. In both cases, however, a finite list of rules cannot account for every contingency. Eventually the rules must give way to a conceptual model of a complex system that can be used to guide behavior. As scholars and researchers, communication faculty are dedicated to devising and refining communication models. In general, understanding a system serves to expand the repertoire of effective behaviors, provides rationales for what previously may have been perceived as arbitrary rules, and gives the individual confidence in assessing the effectiveness of his or her own behavior, even to the point of breaking fundamental rules in instances when they prove counterproductive. In short, a model of communication should facilitate the student's transition from novice learner to competent professional, with the additional benefit of identifying criteria for assessing effective media writing.

Different writing instructors may find different models of communication particularly suitable to their teaching approach, but even a model as commonplace as Shannon's (1949) schematic of a general communication system can be effectively employed to delineate media writing principles and practices (Finn, 1991). What makes Shannon's linear model especially appropriate (see Fig. 11.1) is its focus on the encoding and decoding of messages as the essential element of a communication system. The order of events—devising a message (at the source), encoding the message in representative symbols (at the transmitter), receiving the symbols that stand for the message (at the receiver), and inferring the message by decoding the symbols (at the destination)—denotes in precise terms the semiotic nature of all communication; in short, that the explicit meaning of a message never travels through a channel, but must be constructed at the destination based in part on knowledge the audience already possesses. By specifying the require-

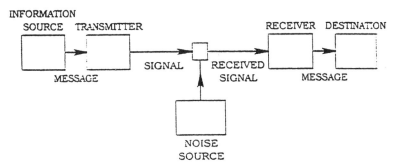

FIG. 11.1. Schematic diagram of a general communication system. *Note.* Figure from Shannon, 1949. Copyright © 1949 by the Board of Trustees of the University of Illinois Press. Used with permission of the University of Illinois Press.

ments for effective communication, Shannon's model (like many others) specifies the contingencies that a media writer must consider to communicate effectively. It is only a short step from that set of contingencies to a set of criteria for assessing media writing on which both instructors and students should be able to agree. Implicit in any communication model is the existence of a sender with a purpose, an intended audience, and a message comprised of coded symbols. It is these elements of communication, as we shall see, that constitute the components of most writing assessment systems.

THE NEW MECHANICS OF WRITING ASSESSMENT

Over the past 2 decades, dissatisfaction with the writing skills of secondary school students and freshmen entering college has generated intense support for improved methods of assessing writing instruction. Whereas none of these programs has been focused on media writing, communication faculty can exploit the wealth of experience derived from writing assessment trials to devise improved methods for assessing media writing. Writing assessment methods fall into two major categories: indirect and direct. Grammar and spelling tests that are commonly used to screen registration for journalism or media writing courses are a good example of indirect assessments of writing skill. The examiner infers a student's current writing ability from his or her skill in responding to objective questions that are believed to be empirically correlated with success in writing courses. Most writing instructors believe indirect methods provide only a crude approximation of the mental capabilities necessary for good writing. They put their trust in direct assessments of writing ability, that is, the evaluation of actual pieces of writing that a student has been assigned to complete.

Direct assessments fall into three categories, distinguished by the scoring method employed: primary-trait, analytical, and holistic scoring. Primary-trait scoring presumes that writing is successful if it appears to achieve one or more desired effects on its intended audience. Analytical scoring is the most detailed procedure. It is based on the assumption that there are four to six basic traits that underlie all types of written composition and intensive attention to these traits not only affords a rigorous evaluation of student writing but also an opportunity for the instructor to diagnose the student's weaknesses and strengths. Holistic scoring often assumes the existence of a similar set of writing traits, but the emphasis is on making a reliable but quick assessment of a written composition to permit a summative evaluation of student achievement at the course, department, or institutional level. Assessment types differ in form because each is designed to achieve a different set of goals (Harlen & James, 1997).

The term *primary-trait scoring* may be new to media writing instructors, but the method should be very familiar. Primary-trait assessment puts particular emphasis on the "rhetorical situation created by the purpose, audience, and writing assignment" (Huot, 1990, p. 238). Media writing textbooks are replete with primary traits for each writing assignment. Student writers are admonished, for example, to write news stories that are informative yet effortless to read, radio commercials that motivate the listener to buy the product, or sitcom dialogue that generates a laugh every 30 seconds.

Although primary traits are often the focal point of classroom discussion and instructor feedback, they bear all the hallmarks of what might be called the craft perspective on teaching media writing. Instructors— often having worked as media professionals themselves—evaluate student copy or scripts according to a combination of editorial rules and subjective standards they learned on the job (Wiist, 1997). In the realm of composition instruction, however, teachers can rarely claim authority based on their experience as professional writers. Further, critics complain that primary-trait scoring, because it focuses on just a few high-level concerns of professional writers, often fails to reveal to students the nexus of writing qualities that undergird all effective writing. It assumes that students arrive in media writing courses with a mastery of the written word that few have achieved. As instructors we have to recognize that no matter how much we may want our courses to reflect a professional environment, students are not mature writers and primary-trait scoring is more appropriate in the newsroom or during a story conference than in the classroom. Thus, analytical scoring, with its diagnostic approach, appears to be the natural starting point for the assessment of student writing for media.

IMPLEMENTING ANALYTICAL ASSESSMENT IN THE CLASSROOM

It is one thing to say that analytical scoring procedures can provide students the diagnostic evaluations of their written assignments that they need to improve; however, developing an analytical scoring instrument broad enough to evaluate the variety of written assignments in an introductory media writing course is a daunting task for which media writing instructors will find few precedents. As accreditation organizations have expanded their requirements for educational assessment, however, communication departments have created committees and task forces to respond to these demands. The results, though, have not been widely publicized and seldom published. The one notable exception has been the analytical scoring procedures developed at Alverno College as part of a curriculum overhaul in the early 1970s (Ewens, 1979). Alverno adopted a competence-based curriculum, which mandated a system for instructor and student self-assessment. Finn (1997) has previously described Alverno's analytical scoring procedures in connection with a sophomore-level professional writing course. Much of that material has now been incorporated into Alverno's proprietary Diagnostic Digital Portfolio system (see http://ddp.alverno.edu).

Nevertheless, we fully believe it possible for all instructors to boot-strap their own analytical scoring systems. The only prerequisite is a cadre of committed instructors. In the case of already existing media writing courses, we believe that the most efficient approach is to de-velop an analytical assessment system based on one of the many cur-rent models that experts in composition studies have devised. When developing new media writing courses or substantially revising an old one, we recommend that such an endeavor, if possible, be undertaken by a team of instructors in which case assessment criteria are a natural outcome of faculty developing and sharing thoughts about major course assignments.

New or Revised Courses

The team-teaching scenario for new or revised courses is based on a personal experience for one of us at the University of North Carolina at Chapel Hill. The chair of the Department of Radio, Television, and Mo-tion Pictures asked three faculty members, one with an expertise in ad-vertising and public relations, a second with expertise in film drama, and a third with expertise in broadcast journalism, to develop a uniform syllabus for the department's introductory media writing course. Instead of teaching small sections individually, these three faculty members took responsibility, according to areas of expertise, for lecturing com-bined sessions of the class and developing accompanying scriptwriting assignments. In this manner, they created a joint syllabus. Between the lectures in which they explained to the students the media writing skills they were to develop and their own private meetings in which they justi-fied their choices for assignments and explained the criteria by which they should be evaluated, each was able to generalize from an in-depth knowledge of a single area of media writing to all the other types of-fered in the course.

Although the charge to devise a uniform curriculum for the introduc-tory course did not include the development of a complementary as-sessment system, they began informally articulating criteria for assessment at their weekly meetings. The key here seemed to be that the need to identify characteristics of good media writing naturally accompanied the decision to let each expert devise what he or she believed to be pedagogically sound and realistic scriptwriting assignments for all—without regard to the gaps in fellow instructors' personal experiences. Colleagues, thus, had to look for similarities between assignments and the criteria used in assessment rather than emphasizing differences. Otherwise, they would feel as if they lacked the competence to evaluate their students' work. No doubt, there was some anxiety as well as resistance. But the experience suggests that agreement on assessment criteria for diverse types of writing may be greatly facilitated by team teaching efforts where the justification for specific curricular innovations must be carefully developed and fully explained to team members.

There is, of course, the possibility that an instructional team comprised of former professionals would devise a disjointed list of primary traits. In this regard, a generic rubric can be used to guarantee that an analytical scoring system is sufficiently comprehensive. Typical of many generic rubrics is the framework adopted by the Vermont State Board of Education almost a decade ago. It includes five general categories for writing assessment: (a) purpose, (b) organization, (c) development of ideas, (d) voice or tone, and (e) command of English conventions (Vermont's Framework, 2000). Once individual team members generate their list of characteristics of good media writing, the items can be sorted under these headings and reviewed to assure that no obvious gaps exist. The Vermont State Board of Education used these categories to subsequently develop criteria for conducting performance assessments of written assignments, including reports, procedures, persuasive essays, reflective essays, and poetry, demonstrating that a thoughtful generic rubric can be broadly applied (Grade Expectations, 2004).

Existing Courses

In the case of a course that is already offered, or as a default when a new course must be developed by a single faculty member, the field of composition studies offers numerous highly elaborated models on which to build. This strategy should be especially appealing to faculty trained as social scientists. In their research, they recognize the value of building on a measurement system that has already been put into practice and tested in the field. There is no sense in reinventing the wheel when one can benefit from someone else's experience. In this regard, Spandel and Stiggins's (1990, 1997) venerable list of six essential traits of good writing—ideas and content, voice, organization, sentence fluency, word choice, and conventions—provides one of many starting points for the thoughtful media instructor to articulate how the dimensions of written composition are reflected in the popular formats of audio, video, and print media (including online postings).

Tables 11.1 through 11.3 summarize the results of such an intellectual enterprise. The three tables identify those qualities or techniques that provide evidence of writing skill in completing three print journalism (Table 11.1), three radio (Table 11.2), and three television (Table 11.3) scriptwriting assignments typical of an introductory media writing course. Spandel and Stiggins's (1990, 1997) six traits remain fundamentally the same, except for the accommodations that must be made for a multimedia environment. First the concept of voice is expanded to voices, because most extended media writing scripts present multiple voices within a single "composition." Second, the notion of word choice must give way to the concept of symbol choice because the media writing student is learning how to manipulate not only text, but full-screen video, graphics, and sound. That means many of the references listed under other traits will also signify visual and aural as well as verbal concepts.

Some caveats are in order, however. First, these qualitative matrices are meant to be suggestive rather than comprehensive. They reflect the professional experience and teaching philosophy of their author. Another instructor may wish to emphasize other aspects of any one of these assignments, and as alluded to earlier, the experience of teaching an assignment will lead to refinements in denoting the facets of its various traits. Second, these matrices are just the foundation for developing appropriate rubrics for analytical assessment. The traits that are sought in a scriptwriting assignment must be evaluated in terms of levels of achievement. Figure 11.2 reproduces a radio news story analytical scoring sheet used in a media writing course at Robert Morris University. Six traits for a radio news story and their facets from Table 11.2 are listed in the left-most column whereas six levels of achievement—from skillful (5) to severe problem (0)—are arrayed across the top. As expected, however, experience teaching the assignment led to refinements in thinking about the traits as originally conceived.

For example, the voice trait was divided into anchor's voice and attribution to highlight this duality in objective news reporting. Originally "attribution" had simply been designated as a facet of sentence fluency (see Table 11.2), but understanding the nuances of attribution turned out to be a more profound problem in the course than mastering its formal expression as implied by its inclusion with sentence fluency. Similarly, the conventions trait was divided into two categories to distinguish between those format concerns that were specific to the medium of radio and those that were inherent in the syntax of written language. The division also indicated new conventions they were learning as part of

TABLE 11.1

Elements to Be Evaluated in an Assessment of Print Journalism Assignments
Based on a Taxonomy of Writing Traits Developed by Spandel and Stiggins (1990)

Assignment	Ideas and Content	Voices	Organization	Sentence Fluency	Symbol Choice	Conventions
Speech Story	• participants • issues/themes • circumstances • background • so-what factor	• speaker • audience • supporters • opponents • authorities	• inverted pyramid • multiple elements • list of minor topics	• clarity • appropriate pace • transitional devices	• precise • unbiased • unobtrusive • "said"	• direct quotes for unique or important statements • rules of attribution
Crime Story	• who • what • where • when • why • how	• law officers • victims • witnesses • suspects	• summary lead • chronology of events • sidebars	• short active sentences • metaphorical narrative description	• accurate • unprejudiced • non-inflammatory	• verifying charges • attributing opinions • libelous expressions
Developing Business Story for Web Site	• high impact • objective information • records • reports • interviews • audio and video links	• company officials • analysts • government agencies • pressure groups	• summary lead or nut graph • heads and subheads • timelines • hypertext • interactivity	• vigorous • concise • clear • bullet lists • skimmable information	• omit needless words • jargon-free • conversational "you" • multimedia • graphs and charts	• 24/7 postings • fairness and fact-checking • hyperlinks • navigation • e-mail to reporters

TABLE 11.2

Elements to Be Evaluated in an Assessment of Radio Scriptwriting Assignments Based on a Taxonomy of Writing Traits Developed by Spandel and Stiggins (1990)

Assignment	Ideas and Content	Voices	Organization	Sentence Fluency	Symbol Choice	Conventions
Radio Public Service Announcement	• useful • salient • imaginable	• authoritative • persuasive	• problem/solution • fantasy/fulfillment	• active • concise • conversation-like	• precise • familiar • readable • speakable	• radio drama format • announcer • dialogue • testimonial • vignette
Radio Interview Feature	• informative • revealing • insightful • entertaining	• probing • engaged • friendly • unique • candid • thoughtful	• thematic • chronological • general to specific • abstract to concrete	• continuity • paraphrasing • soundbites • set-ups	• colorful • active • defining • clarifying	• radio drama format • timing • editing • pacing
Radio News	• accuracy • impact • surprise • timeliness • proximity	• informed • credible • impartial • aggressive	• effects then causes • recent to past • update then background	• leads • attributions • verb tenses	• objective • unbiased • concrete • non-inflammatory	• radio news format • names • titles • numbers • punctuation

TABLE 11.3

Elements to Be Evaluated in an Assessment of Television Scriptwriting Assignments Based on a Taxonomy of Writing Traits Developed by Spandel and Stiggins (1990)

Assignment	Ideas and Content	Voices	Organization	Sentence Fluency	Symbol Choice	Conventions
Political Ad With Storyboard— See also Radio PSAs (Table 11.2)	• name recognition • policies • social vision • opponent negatives	• diverse • approachable • genuine • recognizable	• master shots • visual logic	• repetition • slogans	• logos • political symbols • candidate poses	• live-TV format • shot types • storyboard symbols
TV News—See also Radio News (Table 11.2)	• video events • aftermath • interviews • still pictures • graphics	• anchors • reporters • officials • witnesses • victims	• establishing shots to key details • continuous chronologies • interrupted chronologies	• anchor lead-ins and tags • fluent non-redundant narration	• matching words to elements in frame	• TV news format • voiceover • sound on tape • character generator
Sit-Com Dialogue	• conflict • character • setting	• distinctive • attractive • irritating • irrepressible • empathetic	• conversation • discussion • argument • activity	• set-ups • punchlines • rejoinders • comebacks • one-liners	• odd words • ambiguities • slapstick • mishaps	• three-camera format • scene setting • directions

Radio News Script
Assignment 3 Analytical Scoring

Name: _____   Submitted: _____

Scoring Criteria	three stories	+5 skillful	+4 good	+3 adequate	some +2 flaws	many +1 flaws	severe 0 problem
Ideas and Content accurate, logical, timely relevant, cohesive							
Anchor's Voice: informed, authoritative, impartial, incisive							
Attributions: sources of information and opinions identified							
Organization: results then causes, update then background, impact then details							
Sentence Fluency: focused leads, active voice, coherent facts							
Word Choice: objective, unbiased, concrete, non-inflammatory							
Conventions: radio news format, titles, names, numbers, timing							
Reading Ease: spelling, punctuation, grammar, editing							

Additional Comments:

Grade: _____

FIG. 11.2. Radio news story analytical scoring sheet.

the assignment versus the skill set they were expected to have already mastered before they began the course. Using eight categories rather than six, in conjunction with a 5-point scale, had one additional advantage. It created an assessment rubric that added up to 40 points. Dividing the total points by 10 provided students a letter grade on a 4-point scale.

For many instructors, such quantification of writing achievement may seem excessive, and they have a point. Providing students a numerical score is not and has never been a primary goal of analytical scoring. The rubric is designed first and foremost to be a diagnostic device. Instructors are free to create any ordinal set of categories that capture their notion of achievement from "professional to beginner" to the traditional "excellent to poor." In keeping with the goal of explicitly describing assignments, rubrics should not be sprung on the student after the script has been submitted. They should be fully discussed by the time the scriptwriting assignment is made so students know what professional knowledge they are attempting to acquire. Accordingly, instructors must keep them in mind as they structure lectures, discussions, and exercises in anticipation of an assignment, because mastering the specific traits associated with the assignment is what the students are going to be held accountable for.

One final disclaimer is required in regard to the traits offered in this section. If course assessment procedures are being imposed on the communication or media arts faculty, it is highly likely that English department faculty are feeling the same pressure (or already have) in regard to its freshman composition courses. Cross-disciplinary cooperation can lead to a more coherent assessment program. If students are learning a set of writing criteria in English composition, then the list of criteria already in place should be seriously considered as a starting point for devising analytical scoring procedures for a media writing course. Not only is it valuable to integrate writing programs across the curriculum, but building on a conceptual system students already know helps them better understand the messages that their media writing instructors are trying to convey.

HOLISTIC SCORING FOR INSTITUTIONAL ASSESSMENT

Among faculty there is often much ambivalence, if not resistance, when it comes to participating in programs of institutional assessment. At Robert Morris University, we are accredited by the Middle States Commission on Higher Education (1998), which envisions a "seamless chain" from course-level assessment through program- and department-level assessments to finally the assessment of progress toward the institution's current mission and its future aims. The burden on faculty and administrators appears immense. Yet, the good news for media writing courses is that once a faculty devises an analytical scoring procedure for diagnostic assessment in the classroom, much of the difficult conceptual work for implementing institutional assessment is complete. In large part, this is true because the holistic scoring systems which are sufficient for institutional assessment can be created by neatly collapsing the intricate details of an analytical scoring system into the single global scale, which defines holistic scoring. Because media writing courses, as we noted at the beginning of this chapter, lend themselves naturally to performance assessments, nothing could be a more authentic test of useful knowledge gained. At the program or department level, however, evidence of student learning in media writing can be demonstrated through the summative assessment of a sampling of student work. Individual diagnostics are no longer required because the course, not the student, is the object of appraisal.

With more than a decade of experience, the institutional assessment system for the technical writing curriculum at the New Jersey Institute of Technology (NJIT; Coppola, 1999; Elliot, Kilduff, & Lynch, 1994) presents a very promising model for media writing courses. In 1989, the instructors for NJIT's junior-level technical writing course met collectively to design a new course that integrated the aims and goals of technical writing. Chief among their objectives was "to develop a sense of community among instructors and their students ... [and] an empirical measure of the performance of these students" (Elliot et al., 1994, p. 5). The course incorporated a variety of specific assignments that reflected real-life situations, such as writing "memoranda, letters, résumés, job posting notices, technical translations, feasibility reports, case studies, and proposals" (Elliot et al., p. 7). Student drafts would be critiqued by peers using primary trait evaluation sheets. Final copies could then be submitted to the instructor for an initial grade and feedback for subsequent revisions. Students eventually placed each assignment in their portfolios when they thought it was completed to the best of their ability and was ready for a final evaluation.

Although the portfolios were designed to provide a record of growth in students' writing ability, it soon became clear that it would not be feasible for the instructors as a group to evaluate each portfolio. Thus grading for each assignment as well as each student's course grade remained the responsibility of his or her instructor, but all students—in consultation with their instructors—were asked to submit a cover letter, résumé, and their two strongest writing samples for further evaluation. The evaluation took place at a 4-hr reading session near the end of the semester. Each student's portfolio selections—designated a *cluster* to denote a combination of writing samples—were evaluated by two instructors who headed other sections of the course. To achieve a consensus on assessment criteria and scoring levels, a scoring rubric "based on presentation of ideas, cohesion, style, usage, and overall reader response" was jointly tested and calibrated on a 4-point scale representing four levels of achievement (see Coppola, 1999, pp. 254–256, for the fully elaborated rubric). A cluster exhibiting a high level of student performance was awarded 4 points; one exhibiting a low performance received 1 point. A student cluster had to accumulate 4 points from its two readers to be accepted as a passing performance.

Elliot et al. (1994) reported their results after four semesters during which instructors evaluated clusters from a total of 308 students. On average, they achieved an interreader agreement rate of 93%, which matched the optimum rates for holistic assessments of student essays submitted to the Educational Testing Service. Furthermore, their assessments showed very stable results from semester to semester, with about 80% of their students achieving a passing performance under these circumstances. Finally, the holistic assessment scores consistently correlated with students' course grades (.65 < r < .69), providing evidence of their concurrent validity.

From the viewpoint of institutional goals, the new procedure for summative assessment permitted NJIT instructors to make two extremely useful analyses. In one case, they were able to compare holistic cluster assessments for junior-transfer students with those who had begun their course of study as freshmen at NJIT. Although both groups achieved comparable passing rates, the 4-year students achieved a statistically significant higher mean score on the assessment of their clusters. In another analysis, the instructors investigated results among Asian, Black, and Hispanic students to see if the assessment criteria favored a particular cultural or ethnic group. Interestingly, the analysis suggested that "language background, rather than race or ethnicity, explain[ed] the lower success rate of underrepresented students" (Elliot et al., 1994, p. 15). These findings, however, demanded considerable faculty time and commitment—2 years to gather the data, another year to complete the analysis, and "literally hundreds of hours were spent in designing the course, developing the scoring methodology, reading the clusters, gathering the data and drawing conclusions" (Elliot et al., 1994, p. 17).

Such an enterprise may well be beyond the scope of a small department with few sections of media writing. The NJIT results reflect data gathered over 2 years from 18 sections, each with approximately 17 students. That converts to 9 years of data collection if only one section of the course were offered each semester. But for courses with large enrollments, some of the questions that can be asked and answered are quite striking. In many media writing programs, it would be reassuring just to provide evidence that individual instructor grades correlate with departmental criteria. The NJIT instructors took the data one step further to investigate differences in performance between various segments of the student body. These results were used to help them identify areas where curricular or institutional changes were needed.

Equally intriguing is the opportunity their baseline data provided to monitor diverse aspects of their technical writing course. If some types of assignments were disproportionately underrepresented among those selected for evaluation, then the instructors would have an initial indication that students were not able to master specific types of assignments and corresponding skills. In addition, if the portfolios of the lowest 20% were submitted to analytical (diagnostic) as opposed to holistic (summative) scoring, regular patterns of low scores on one or more individual traits could identify precise skills that the poorest performing students lack (and might be required to bolster before registering for the course). With such knowledge in hand, instructors can then experiment with new strategies and examine the results. Thus, the assessment process, which in this case began with the design of a new course, evolved into a process of continual course development

DOES SYSTEMATIC ASSESSMENT ADD UP?

This chapter began with the observation that assessment procedures in media writing classes are in one sense very much on target because of the natural inclination of instructors to adopt the methods of performance assessment, that is, measure student achievement by assigning and evaluating real-life journalistic and scriptwriting tasks. This has been the norm if not the rule in media writing courses since the inception of journalism studies on college campuses, and in this regard media writing courses may stand up to external evaluation better than other communication offerings.

Furthermore, few external evaluators have cause to criticize the dedication of media writing instructors who not only constantly revise and update realistic writing assignments but devote countless hours to providing students verbal feedback on their articles and scripts. It is often solitary, exhausting work, for which there seem to be few available shortcuts. Nevertheless, in this chapter, some initial steps that can make assessments more effective have been outlined. Among these strategies are orienting students to the invisible public that constitutes their real audience, making concrete for them the differences between academic and media writing, investing time in writing the course syllabus to make explicit the objectives and goals of assignments, and employing communication models to help students construct a framework for judging their own writing.

However, the bulk of this chapter has been devoted to a much more revolutionary concept—the implementation of programs of systematic assessment. The pressure for such programs is being felt from administrators who know nothing about the teaching of media writing but are responding to political forces who want "scientific" evidence of student learning and successful academic programs. Not only is this bound to create added work, but the assessment system that suits administrators may fail to connect in any meaningful way with the impressionistic and individualist approach many media writing instructors employ in the classroom. Worse yet, many may find themselves "teaching to a test" that distorts their teaching philosophy (see White, 1994, pp. 171–173, on the negative consequences of artificial criteria).

The alternative is to "bite the bullet" and devise an analytical scoring system for student writing that neatly collapses into a holistic scoring system for institutional review. As previously suggested, this may occasion a complete revamping of media writing courses as faculty sort out exactly what competencies they want students to strive for and at what levels they think students should perform. At a minimum, faculty will have to deconstruct current media writing courses to see how component parts of typical assignments correspond to general traits that are embodied in all forms of written expression. Such a task promises much trial and error, but by articulating exactly what they are seeking in student writing, faculty may come to better understand what they are trying to teach. For a list of recommended reading, see the Appendix.

REFERENCES

Adams, K. H. (1993). *A history of professional writing instruction in American colleges: Years of acceptance, growth, and doubt.* Dallas, TX: Southern Methodist University Press.

Coppola, N. W. (1999). Setting the discourse community: Tasks and assessment for the new technical communication service course. *Technical Communication Quarterly, 8,* 249–267.

Diederich, P. B. (1974). *Measuring growth in English.* Urbana, IL: National Council of Teachers of English.

Elliot, N., Kilduff, M., & Lynch, R. (1994). The assessment of technical writing: A case study. *Journal of Technical Writing and Communication, 24,* 19–36.

Ewens, T. (1979). Transforming a liberal arts curriculum: Alverno College. In G. Grant, P. Elben, T. Ewens, Z. Gamson, W. Kohli, W. Newman, V. Olesen, & D. Riesmans (Eds.),

On competence: A critical analysis of competence-based reforms in higher education (pp. 259–298). San Francisco: Jossey-Bass.

Faigley, L., Cherry, R. D., Jolliffe, D. A., & Skinner, A. M. (1985). *Assessing writers' knowledge and processes of composing.* Norwood, NJ: Ablex.

Finn, S. (1991). *Broadcast writing as a liberal art.* Englewood Cliffs, NJ: Prentice Hall.

Finn, S. (1997). Media writing. In W. G. Christ (Ed.), *Media education assessment handbook* (pp. 165–188). Mahwah, NJ: Lawrence Erlbaum Associates, Inc.

Fry, D. (1988). *Writing coaching: A primer.* St. Petersburg, FL: Poynter Institute for Media Studies.

Gipps, C. V. (1994). *Beyond testing: Towards a theory of educational assessment.* London: Falmer.

Grade expectations for Vermont's framework of standards and learning opportunities. (2004). Retrieved March 8, 2005, from http://www.state.vt.us/educ/new/pdfdoc/pubs/grade_expectations/math_reading_writing.pdf

Hake, R. L., & Williams, J. M. (1981). Style and its consequences: Do as I do, not as I say. *College English, 43,* 433–451.

Harlen, W., & James, M. (1997). Assessment and learning: Differences and relationships between formative and summative assessment. *Assessment in Education, 4,* 365–379.

Huot, B. (1990). The literature of direct writing measurement: Major concerns and prevailing trends. *Review of Educational Research, 60,* 237–263.

Huot, B. (2002). *(Re)articulating writing assessment for teaching and learning.* Logan: Utah State University Press.

Middle States Commission on Higher Education. (1998). *Outcomes assessment plans: Guidelines for developing outcomes assessment plans at colleges and universities.* Philadelphia: Author.

Shannon, C. E. (1949). The mathematical theory of communication. In C. E. Shannon & W. Weaver (Eds.), *The mathematical theory of communication* (pp. 29–125). Urbana: University of Illinois Press.

Shuman, E. L. (1903). *Practical journalism: A complete manual of the best newspaper methods.* New York: D. Appleton and Company.

Spandel, V., & Stiggins, R. J. (1990). *Creating writers: Linking assessment and writing instruction.* New York: Longman.

Spandel, V., & Stiggins, R. J. (1997). *Creating writers: Linking assessment and writing instruction* (2nd ed.). New York: Longman.

Tucker, D. E. (1994). Course evaluation. In W. G. Christ (Ed.), *Assessing communication education: A handbook for media, speech, and theatre educators* (pp. 113–130). Hillsdale, NJ: Lawrence Erlbaum Associates, Inc.

Vermont's framework of standards and learning opportunities. (2000). Retrieved March 8, 2005, from http://www.state.vt.us/educ/new/pdfdoc/pubs/framework.pdf

White, E. M. (1985). *Teaching and assessing writing.* San Francisco: Jossey-Bass.

White, E. M. (1994). *Teaching and assessing writing: Recent advances in understanding, evaluating, and improving student performance* (2nd ed.). San Francisco: Jossey-Bass.

Wiist, W. M. (1997). Seeking a coaching style of teaching news writing. *Journalism & Mass Communication Educator, 51,* 68–74.

APPENDIX: RECOMMENDED READINGS

As Edward White expressed it 20 years ago in the foreword to *Teaching and Assessing Writing,* "Teaching people to write is one of the chronic problems of American education" (White, 1985, p. ix). On most campuses, the responsibility for remedying that problem has been given to English departments, which have responded in turn by creating the specialty field of composition studies. They have not solved the problem of poor writing, but to measure student achievement they have sought to develop practical, reliable, and valid methods of assessment. For media writing instructors, who must now integrate assessment procedures in their courses, there is no richer literature to consult, but no neat strand to follow. A trip to the English department on campus to consult with fellow faculty members may be a useful exercise. Instructors who want to understand the development of systematic procedures for writing assessment from its inception can immerse themselves in Diederich's (1974) *Measuring Growth in English,* a classic that set the groundwork for analytical scoring. A shorter route would be to begin with White's (1994) *Teaching and Assessing Writing: Recent Advances in Understanding, Evaluating, and Improving Student Performance.* This is the second edition of the 1985 classic cited earlier. It provides a truly remarkable compendium of experience and insight on how to design writing assessment programs. Among a second generation of scholars, Huot (2002) has summarized his thoughts and laid out challenges for the future most broadly in *(Re)Articulating Writing Assessment for Teaching and Learning.*

The discussion of analytical assessment and teaching in this chapter draws heavily on Spandel and Stiggins's (1990) *Creating Writers: Linking Assessment to Writing Instruction.* The efficacy of their six-trait approach has been validated in a second edition (Spandel & Stiggins, 1997) as well as on various Web sites (see e.g., http://www.nwrel.org/assessment/department.asp?d=1), devoted to the development of six-trait writing assessment programs. Finally, Elliot et al.'s (1994) article is strongly recommended as an example illustrating how holistic assessment can be used to evaluate course effectiveness. Their work has been updated by Coppola (1999), who has included a complete reproduction of the portfolio scoring forms employed by her and her colleagues.

12

Reporting and Editing

Thomas Dickson
Department of Media, Journalism, and Film
Missouri State University

A decade ago, the Educational Commission of the States (1994) called for improvement in assessment through assessment related to student outcomes. In its report, the commission stated the following: "Neither individuals nor the broader society can afford to be indifferent to concerns about the quality of our higher education institutions. . . . Nor can they allow quality to be defined solely in terms of academic studies that are isolated from the rapidly changing world in which knowledge and skills must be applied" (p. 1).

Such calls for the assessment of outcomes have resulted in a number of colleges and universities attempting to document what their students have learned during their college experience and how their programs might be changed to increase student learning. The president of the Association for American Colleges and Universities recently suggested, however, that the use of assessment remained inadequate. He stated the following: "As a community, and on most campuses, we remain unable to provide useful information on students' development of outcomes that are widely considered important, not just within the academy but for proactive participation in the economy . . ." (Schneider, 2002, p. 4). Moreover, a recent study found that, although all institutions of higher education likely do some sort of assessment, fewer than 40% of them study the link between what students experience and student outcomes (Chun, 2002).

Outcomes assessment long has been associated with media-related education. The Project on the Future of Journalism and Mass Communication Education, for example, proposed in 1984, in what was to be called the "Oregon Report," that each skills-oriented course have specific goals and expected outcomes for students. However, it stated in an updated edition of the report that "(f)ew if any faculties have carefully defined their goals with regard to the specific skills and knowledge a competent graduate should have" and that "fewer still have related such 'desired educational outcomes' to particular courses" (Project, 1987, p. 50). It also called for testing media students in their senior year to determine whether they had synthesized their coursework and reached a satisfactory level of understanding and competence.

Other evidence also suggests that media educators at the time largely ignored the Oregon Report's call for assessment. For example, Farrar (1988) noted that "remarkably few specific statements of objectives appear to exist" in media education (p. 2). In addition, in her study of the 276 institutions belonging to the Broadcast Education Association, Eastman (1993) found that only 14 (6%) of the 226 units responding used an exit test for media majors. Moreover, 10 of the 14 gave written examinations that students did not have to pass and sometimes did not have to take. Also, Ervin (1988) found that outcomes assessment was not well-understood by media educators. Although 39% of 181 media units responding to a survey stated that they were using outcomes assessment, Ervin reported that most respondents who reported that their unit had assessment measures were referring to course tests, writing assignments, or student evaluations of faculty or course content instead of tested instruments for outcomes assessment.

In addition to the lack of assessment taking place and the misunderstanding of assessment that apparently existed among media educators in the late 1980s and early 1990s, studies showed that many of the instruments used are thought to be inadequate by educators using them. Among units that apparently had put in place true outcomes assessment, Ervin (1988), for example, found that administrators often noted that the instrument was not adequate and did not measure such important skills as writing or critical thinking (p. 6). Caudill, Ashdown, and Caudill (1990, p. 14) stated that most locally developed assessment tests are seen as "either too vocational or too academically arcane."

Ervin (1988) noted that the existing standardized assessment instruments were not designed for media education and were not adequate to meet media educators' needs. He also called for educators to create standardized instruments that would meet their needs. Critics of standardized tests, however, charged that such tests didn't measure important outcomes—such as analytical ability and creativity, which defy quantitative analysis (Eastman, 1987; Nielsen & Polishook, 1990). Critics also charged that quantitative tests used as exit exams often were a compilation of questions from several program areas and did not appear to be driven by outcome objectives (Caudill et al., 1990). Eshelman (1991) suggested that such tests were basically meaningless, that they stifled creativity, that they led to test buying and cheating by students, that faculty tended to "teach to the test," and that they were easy to manipulate by units wanting to raise average scores to please administrators and state higher education coordinating boards. In addition, critics of such assessment practices charged that quantitative assessment tests tended to confuse rather than inform.

Benjamin (1990) warned that a discipline's place in the liberal arts could be jeopardized by the use of quantitative tests for assessment because they "would encourage students' tendency toward excessive specialization and vocationalism and diminish the opportunity the major provides for independent and analytical inquiry" (p. B1). Eastman (1993) also noted that development of specialty tests in media tracks would result in an emphasis on entry-level job skills training and devalue the liberal arts aspects of the field (p. 89).

The use of quantitative tests as assessment instruments remains a concern for many educators. For example, the Greater Expectations National Panel of the American Association of Colleges and Universities (AACU) looked at the use of quantitative measurements in its report on student learning needed for the 21st century. As the president (2002–2003) of the AACU stated about the report, "The Panel does not believe that students' ability to find the right answers on multiple-choice tests provides evidence that they are ready to undertake the kinds of complex analysis and learning they should do in college and will further face in their lives, societies, and work" (Schneider, 2002, p. 5).

The assessment plan outlined in this chapter is based on a direct measurement—student outcomes. Results can be quantified without the dangers of using results from quantitative tests. The plan can be used for value-added assessment, which measures the amount of change in the student during a given period of time (Benjamin & Chun, 2003), or for formative and summative assessment not tied to a preliminary assessment. The plan is performance assessment in that it is tied to how well students meet specific goals and objectives. Palomba and Banta (1999) defined performance assessment as "the process of using student activities or products, as opposed to tests or surveys, to evaluate students' knowledge, skills, and development" (p. 115). They stated that performance assessment is particularly useful for academic programs that develop "complex, integrated skills" because "it asks students to display their skills in a way that is more direct and thorough than that provided by traditional paper and pencil tests" (p. 115). Linn and Baker (1996) noted that performance-based assessments are useful for the instructor because they "are expected to be indistinguishable from the goals of instruction" (p. 86).

The performance-based plan outlined in this chapter allows a unit to assess students (and, thus, courses and programs) while avoiding the problems of quantitative tests. The plan can be used for evaluating individual units within a course, entire reporting or editing courses, a block of courses within a particular program, or the program itself. Also, effective overall assessment of a media unit (program, department, college, or school) requires that evaluation of program components be integrated into the unit's overall review. The plan is presented with the hope that it will be useful both to faculty members who are new to assessment and those who are more experienced in assessment but who would like additional perspectives. This chapter outlines an assessment plan that can be enacted without a heavy burden of time or resources and that stresses objectives that are neither too vocational nor arcane. Such a plan should be helpful for educators who want to fine-tune courses to enable students to meet the desired curricular objectives.

THE "WHY" OF ASSESSING REPORTING AND EDITING

Menkowski (1998) defined assessment as "a set of processes designed to improve, demonstrate, and inquire about student learning outcomes" (p. 1). Similarly, the "why" of assessment is "to refine course objectives, modify course content, and improve course instruction for the purpose of increasing students' retention of course information and improving student learning."

Results from the assessment of editing and reporting courses can be used in a variety of ways: to increase student achievement of course objectives; to improve course design and instruction; to assist in evaluating a particular program, such as a news-editorial or magazine program; or to augment the evaluation of an entire media unit. Beyond that, educators have a responsibility to improve higher education, and that starts at the level of student outcomes in individual courses.

The importance of assessing reporting and editing in a media unit can hardly be overstated. The courses included among the reporting-editing component of the curriculum are the "nuts and bolts" courses for news-editorial students and often are required for other majors as well. Yet journalism education has been under attack for years by editors and news directors for producing graduates who do not measure up to their expectations. The importance of assessing reporting and editing was addressed by Beasley (1990, p. B2), who wrote the following: "(I)t is imperative that even those students not at all interested in newspapers should have a good grounding in basic writing and news-gathering skills so that they will have the tools to succeed in whatever field they pursue. Otherwise, what value is there in a journalism degree?"

THE "WHERE" AND "WHO" OF ASSESSING REPORTING AND EDITING

The "where" and "who" of assessing reporting and writing involve where assessment should take place and who does the assessing as well as who is assessed. Assessment activities take place in faculty and administrative offices, in the classroom, and at the offices of media-related enterprises. Faculty and administrators must plan for assessment, and faculty members normally implement assessment and use feedback from it to improve their courses. However, graduates and media employers also have a role in assessment. Current students are the basic "target" of assessment, but graduates also should be surveyed. When students are assessed concerning their progress in accomplishing competencies established by the media unit, their progress is the basis for much of the assessment of individual courses and course components.

Haley and Jackson (1995, p. 27) proposed a hierarchy of assessment for mass communication programs that involves both the "who" and the "where" of assessment. They put individual program components at the first level and perception and performance of graduating students at the second level. The third level is evaluations of key constituents. Assessment at that level includes input from persons outside the environment of specific program components: other faculty, administrators, and potential employers. Haley and Jackson's fourth level is comprehensive overall program evaluation, which involves analysis of the inputs from the previous three levels. Their assessment program, thus, differentiates course assessment from student assessment. It reserves student assessment for seniors (summative assessment) and determines outcomes through senior essays, departmental comprehensive tests for seniors, and portfolio assessment for some majors.

Another way of visualizing the "where" and "who" of assessment is as a series of concentric circles. The innermost ring is course assessment. It comprises curriculum or learning units designed to impart particular competencies to students, both individually and collectively. The second ring represents a block of courses or a particular program, such as a degree or degree option: for example, news-editorial, visual communication, advertising, public relations, media studies, and so forth. The basic organizational unit (e.g., department or school) comprises the third ring. The fourth ring is the broader organizational unit (school or college), and the fifth ring is the academic institution itself. This chapter deals mainly with assessment activities involving the first ring (course assessment), although results from that assessment are important to assessment at the second and third rings, as well.

A variety of inputs are received at all five rings of this concentric model of assessment, and outputs can be measured at all levels. They comprise the "who" in assessment. Inputs are received from internal constituencies (students, faculty, and administrators) and external constituencies (graduates and potential employers). Internal inputs come from faculty members and administrators as they adjust course content in response to assessment results. External inputs come both from graduates and their opinions of the utility of their education after they have had some experience in the work world and from employers' opinions of the competencies of their new hires. Outputs consist of student competencies, curricular adjustments, and changes in teaching methods. They will be discussed in the sections dealing with the "when" and "how" of assessment.

THE "WHEN" AND "HOW" OF ASSESSING REPORTING AND EDITING

When assessment is done depends on how the results are to be used. Ideally, assessment is always taking place, either informally or formally. Informal assessment is taking place when the instructor obtains feedback from students orally, through surveys or through graded assignments and then makes adjustments to the course content or organization. During formal assessment, some evaluation would take place at the end of individual curriculum units (formative evaluation) and some at the end of the semester (summative). The media unit's assessment of program components should be based not only on course assessment, but also on a formal program assessment activity before graduation (such as an exit interview or a capstone course), as well as on surveys of students and employers in the workforce.

How assessment is done should be tied closely to when it is done as well as where it is done. The overall approach to assessment used in the chapter ties assessment to curriculum development because, as Heywood (1989) noted, "the processes of curriculum, lecture design and assessment are the same" (p. 23). Likewise, Palomba and Banta (1999) stated the following: "An important consideration when planning an assessment program is to link the results of assessment to other educational processes, such as curriculum review and planning and budgeting" (p. 9).

The plan set forth in this chapter is grounded in the systems approach to curriculum design developed by Banathy (1968). The systems approach to curriculum design has six steps: (a) formulate specific learning objectives; (b) develop a means to determine learner attainment of objectives; (c) analyze the learning tasks; (d) consider alternatives and design the system based on the learning content, learning experiences, curriculum components, and resources needed to achieve the stated objectives; (e) implement the system, collect information on performance, and evaluate the system; and (f) change the system and improve learning through a feedback mechanism. The first four steps can be called the *planning* process, the fifth step is the *implementation* process, and the sixth step is the system evaluation or *feedback* process.

Thus, assessment requires planning, implementation, and feedback and must be tied to curriculum design throughout the process. That means (a) developing course and program goals and objectives through a planning process that includes devising learning experiences to meet those objectives, (b) implementing methods for measuring how well course material is being learned to determine how well course and program goals and objectives are being met, and (c) using the results of assessment for modifying both courses and programs and improving instruction. What binds the three aspects of assessment together is the need to devise course content that best helps to achieve student learning. In any successful assessment plan, as Heywood (1989) wrote, the evaluator must design an appropriate method of testing for each objective and must devise specific learning strategies for students to meet the course objectives.

THE "WHAT" OF ASSESSING REPORTING AND EDITING

The "what" of assessment is the competencies that are the basis for devising course goals and desired instructional outcomes. The plan in this chapter draws from the competency-based, goal-centered approach to curriculum proposed by Tyler (1950) and the approach to developing instructional objectives suggested by Mager (1962). Outcome measures are based on student competencies that are expected to be achieved in the course or courses being assessed. Objectives must be written to show what the student learner should be able to do and not what the instructor should do to further student progress. A number of journalistic skills are needed for reporting and editing. They include such things as being able to write concisely and precisely; to use correct grammar, punctuation and spelling; to conduct interviews; to edit copy; to write captions and headlines; to use cameras, software programs, and computers and other equipment; and to design a publication page or web page or to prepare stories for a newscast. Even such skills-based competencies, however, require higher-level abilities that are associated with the liberal arts and sciences, such as critical thinking and reasoning.

Farmer (1988) devised a list of eight "transferrable skills of liberal learning," the top three of which were critical thinking, creative thinking and problem-solving strategies, and effective writing, and Brookfield (1989) suggested ways to develop critical-thinking skills. Media educators such as Blanchard (1988), Blanchard and Christ (1988, 1993), and Parsigian (1992) also have suggested that media educators should do more to improve students' higher-order cognitive skills. Grow (1989) noted that the newspaper editors he studied saw higher-order skills as being of considerably more importance than did media educators. Moreover, the Associated Press Managing Editors put critical thinking at the top of their "Agenda for Journalism Education" (Ceppos, 1994). The Association for Education in Journalism and Mass Communication (AEJMC) Curriculum Task Force (1996) called for higher-level skills to be integrated into the media curriculum at all levels.

Educators such as Krathwohl, Bloom, and Masia (1964); Chickering (1969); Tyler (1973); Anderson (1981); and Gable (1986), have noted the importance of changing students' affective as well as cognitive abilities. Anderson (1981) stated that affective measures of desired student characteristics should include intensity and direction of feeling as well as target (an object, behavior, or idea). More recently, Grow (1991) noted educators' lack of emphasis in their courses not only on critical-thinking skills but also on affective competencies. Other educators also have called for more emphasis on the affective side, particularly in developing values. Lambeth (1986) and Bugeja (1996), for example, stressed the need for developing professional values. Other educators have emphasized the need for professional judgment, which includes both domains. Hausman (1990), for example, noted the need for young journalists to understand journalistic decision-making processes, and the AEJMC Curriculum Task Force (1996) called on media educators to put more emphasis not only on what professional practices are but also on what they should be.

Putting desired competencies into categories or taxonomies for assessment purposes allows educators to determine the extent to which courses or course components include various cognitive and affective competencies. Cognitive categories traditionally have been devised hierarchically, although the idea that competencies are hierarchical has been questioned in recent years (see Shulman, 2002). The best known taxonomy was developed by Bloom (1956). Bloom's taxonomy has six cognitive "domains": knowledge, comprehension, application, analysis, synthesis, and evaluation. Krathwohl et al. (1964) added five affective domains: receiving, responding, valuing, organizing, and internalizing. Heywood (1989) criticized Bloom's taxonomies for separating the cognitive and affective domains and for paying too little attention to values (p. 106) as well as for developing categories that were not mutually exclusive and for not having a category for originality and creativity (p. 114). Erwin and Wise (2002) noted, however, that "(i)n many ways education has not moved beyond Bloom's Taxonomy of Cognitive Skills" (p. 68).

Educators have developed many other taxonomies. Chickering (1969) proposed seven affective competencies or "vectors": competence, emotions, autonomy, interpersonal relationships, purpose, identity, and integrity. Zais (1976) stated that the effective curriculum consists of knowledge, skills, processes, and values. Similarly, the Carnegie Foundation (1979) proposed the categories of knowledge, skills, principles, and values. Gable (1986) named four affective characteristics: attitudes, self-concept, interest, and values. Heywood (1989) identified three types of instructional objectives: knowledge, learning skills, and values. Christ and McCall (1994) discussed skills; attitudes, affect, and values; and knowledge. The National Postsecondary Education Cooperative (1997) devised a "taxonomy of student outcomes potentially affected by college" (p. A-1) that had 12 categories, including such things as civic development and quality of life. Shulman (2002) suggested six elements of a "table of learning," which he called a taxonomy of liberal and professional learning. It consisted of engagement and motivation, knowledge and understanding, performance and action, reflection and critique, judgment and design, and commitment and identity. He stressed that the order is immaterial.

In this chapter, four categories of instructional objectives are used: informational, procedural, conceptual, and attitudinal. Informational competencies relate to knowledge recall and comprehension, and procedural competencies involve application of information. Both are basically cognitive. Conceptual competencies have to do with creativity and with analysis, synthesis and evaluation of material, and attitudinal competencies relate to values, principles, and self-direction. Conceptual and attitudinal competencies involve both the cognitive and the affective domains. The order in which competencies are achieved (and the extent that they are accomplished) depends on the individual learner and educational situation.

Different verbs are used in constructing instructional objectives in each of the four categories. The following is a list of verbs that could be used in writing objectives in each of the categories:

- Informational—To define, to recognize, to name, to translate, to re-state, to explain, to understand, to comprehend.
- Procedural—To apply, to relate, to organize, to perform, to present, to write, to create, to conduct, to identify, to correct, to improve, to make, to find, to gather, to accomplish, to devise, to design, to undertake, to construct, to choose (a course of action), to select, to determine.
- Conceptual—To analyze, to distinguish, to synthesize, to evaluate, to rate, to challenge (the accuracy of).
- Attitudinal—To value, to appreciate, to prefer, to accept, to reject, to question (a position), to challenge (an attitude or value position).

After categories of instructional objectives have been devised and appropriate verbs selected, instructional objectives can be written. Heywood (1989) noted that the big advantage of the movement toward use of instructional objectives has been that "it has forced teachers in higher education to define what they mean when they speak of concepts as 'problem-solving', 'creativity', and 'critical thinking' " (p. 124). As Mager (1962) noted early in the objectives movement, objectives must be measurable. Erwin (1991) noted that instructional objectives should be "comprehensive and specific and should state expected changes if possible" (p. 45). For a balanced curriculum, objectives should be devised to measure student achievement in each of the four categories. Whereas upper-level courses might put more emphasis on concepts and attitudes and lower-level courses on information and procedures, higher-level skills should be integrated into courses at all levels of the curriculum. Objectives must relate to overall course goals.

Sources of objectives are faculty themselves as well as the curriculum resources used in the course, such as texts, lectures, workbooks, and assigned readings, or a useful activity or assignment. Other sources of objectives for a course are outside experts and accrediting agencies. In reporting and editing, possible sources should include media professionals. Input from "people" sources can be obtained through interviews or surveys. The major objectives become an essential ingredient in the course syllabus and should be listed there for students to read. To determine broad competencies required of reporters and editors as the basis for writing instructional objectives, this author referred to numerous reporting and editing texts as well as several major studies by educators and media organizations and accreditation standards. Lists of competencies for writing, reporting, and editing also have been devised by Jones (1978); Mills, Harvey, and Warnick (1980); Hudson (1981); Thayer (1990); and Olson and Dickson (1995), among others.

DEVELOPING AN ASSESSMENT PLAN FOR REPORTING AND EDITING

The development of an assessment plan for reporting and editing involves the three stages of assessment mentioned earlier: planning, implementation, and feedback. The following section outlines how such an assessment plan could be devised.

The Planning Stage

This stage has four steps taken from Banathy's (1968) systems approach: (a) formulating learning goals and instructional objectives, (b) developing assessment criteria to determine if the objectives have been met, (c) determining what course content is needed to achieve the desired objectives, and (d) preparing the appropriate discussion topics and learning activities.

Step 1: Formulating Learning Goals and Instructional Objectives. The first step in the planning stage is to state the overall mission or purpose of the course or group of courses. Whether planning for assessment takes place before or after the course is instituted, activities at the planning stage must involve designing appropriate goals and objectives. Planning requires collaboration among faculty members and input from a variety of outside sources. The faculty also should determine goals in relation to the course's stated purpose and the purpose of the program or overall administrative unit. Goals are broad aims or outcomes for a particular major, department, or larger academic unit, as well as for a course or a particular subunit of the course. They must be concrete, however. Mager (1962) noted that if goals are not clear and focused on by both the evaluator and the person being evaluated, then tests are misleading at best and "irrelevant, unfair, or useless at worst" (p. 4). Each goal is related to at least one course objective. The learner must be provided a copy of the expected outcomes at the start of the course, most likely in the syllabus.

An example of a mission statement that might be devised for reporting and editing is as follows: "The purpose of the program's reporting and editing components is to provide the student with interviewing and reporting abilities, news writing skills, editing ability, design and layout skills, and an understanding of the legal and professional responsibilities of journalists." A unit goal for a copy-editing unit might be as follows: "At the end of the unit, the student should be able to demonstrate an ability to make necessary revisions and improvements to a story so that it would be acceptable for publication (or broadcast)." Similar goals would be developed for each of the course components identified.

Next, actual instructional objectives students are expected to reach at the end of the course or program are devised. A well-written objective must state the expected outcome, and the verb used in the objective must relate to an observable and measurable behavior. It is important that instructional objectives be prepared before assessment criteria are devised. As Erwin (1991) noted, "The program objectives must drive the assessment methods and instruments, not the other way around" (p. 37). An example of an objective to go with the unit goal discussed earlier is as follows: "By the end of the unit, the student should be able to analyze the content of stories; to identify problems with content, clarity, mechanics, and style rule; and to make necessary changes."

Tucker (1994) noted the importance of dividing courses into units "with conceptually consistent content" (p. 116). After such units are devised, the goals and objectives can be grouped into the appropriate learning units. Reporting and editing texts provide a number of suggestions for learning units. Four broad unit themes that seem to encompass the competencies needed in reporting and editing are as follows: (a) identifying what is newsworthy, (b) gathering the necessary information, (c) preparing stories for dissemination, and (d) upholding professional standards.

Step 2: Developing Assessment Criteria to Determine if the Objectives Have Been Met.

According to Mager (1962), assessment criteria include any conditions under which the behavior will occur and a level of acceptable performance. The conditions state what will be provided or denied in carrying out the objective. The level of acceptable performance might be a time limit for a competency to be exhibited, a minimum number of correct responses, a certain percentage of correct responses, a range of accuracy, or some other standard. Criteria for the objective discussed earlier might be as follows: "The objective will be met when the student, within the hour, (a) identifies problem areas with a story or areas needing changes, and (b) makes changes to the story so that it is ready for publication or broadcast to the satisfaction of the evaluator."

Multiple assessment measures are needed to provide a more accurate picture of how well the course or courses are meeting their overall goals. The need is met by having multiple objectives and a variety of criteria rather than a pretest and posttest on one or two aspects of the course. (An example of various objectives and assessment criteria is given in Appendix A.) Assessment criteria for individual courses and multicourse units are of two types: formative (conducted during a learning experience) and summative (following a learning experience or course or shortly before graduation). Both can be used in evaluating performance of individual students or the success of individual courses in meeting objectives. Formative evaluation is being used whenever the instructor seeks to find out whether the course is accomplishing what it is designed to accomplish, whether assessment takes place following a lecture or following a unit (or module). Summative evaluation is being used when the instructor or evaluator is seeking the same information at the end of the course or at the end of a particular program or degree (Tucker, 1994). Erwin (1991) explained the purpose of formative evaluation as measuring improvement and the purpose of summative evaluation as measuring accountability.

Step 3: Determining What Course Content Is Needed to Achieve the Desired Objectives. After learning units and objectives have been devised, it is relatively easy for the instructor to assemble the necessary course material. Course content must be determined by the goals and objectives of the course and program. The purpose of assessment is to determine if the course content selected is adequate in assisting students in achieving the course objectives. If not, the content and instructional methods must be modified. The content of individual courses and components is largely determined by the text or texts used; therefore, the selection of texts is a major factor in what students will learn. It also is important that the content of various courses in a particular program is coordinated and that appropriate prerequisites are required so that students can work toward overall program objectives in an orderly and efficient fashion.

Step 4: Preparing the Appropriate Discussion Topics and Learning Activities. Course discussion and activities are the instructor's main tools to ensure that students achieve the competencies they are expected to acquire. The syllabus is vital in making students aware of what is expected of them. Heywood (1989) stated that "the syllabus is the sum of the activities designed to meet the objectives thought to be essential" (p. 21).

Possible discussion topics for the learning unit under discussion in this section are as follows: the story revision process; newsroom procedure and copy flow; responsibilities of an editor; copy editing and proofreading procedures; editing for meaning; mechanics of style, grammar, spelling, and punctuation; editing for accuracy, brevity, and completeness; writing headlines and captions; sizing photographs; designing pages; and editing sound and image. A possible learning activity for the unit being discussed is as follows: Students will analyze stories for accuracy, brevity, and clarity, and make improvements as necessary.

The following is a sample assessment plan for one concept:

Unit 1: Conceptualizing and Gathering the News

Unit Content:

This unit focuses on how the reporter defines and identifies news and obtains information for presentation.

Unit Instructional Goals and Objectives:

Unit Concept No. 1: Journalists must be able to generate story ideas by determining what is newsworthy.

Unit Goal No. 1: At the end of the unit, the student should be able to demonstrate an ability to answer the question "What is news?"

Objectives: When presented with story ideas with varying news value, the student will be able (1) *to explain* (*informational*) the purpose of news; (2) *to identify* (*procedural*) the possible news values in the stories; (3) *to evaluate* (*conceptual*) the stories based upon their newsworthiness for a specific audience; (4) *to prefer* (*attitudinal*) stories that would be most appropriate for the stated audience; and (5) *to select* (*procedural*) stories ideas that have the most potential.

Criterion: The objectives are achieved when the student selects story ideas that the evaluator finds to be sufficiently newsworthy for a particular audience.

Learning Plan:

Discussion Topics: Criteria of news value and writing for an audience.

Activity: Students will look for news values present in a variety of articles and analyze the articles' newsworthiness for different audiences.

The Implementation Stage

The second stage of the assessment is implementation of the assessment plan just devised. It involves using the assessment criteria and instruments selected in the planning stage to determine if the course content and instructional methods led to a satisfactory number of students achieving course or program objectives. Assessment should be continual, and changes to both curriculum and instruction should be implemented as needed. It isn't necessary to have a formal assessment of each course unit every semester or year. A 3-year assessment plan might be devised, for example, in which one third of the units in a course or program are assessed each year.

Students' assistance in assessment is vital to its implementation. Erwin (1991) listed several ways of obtaining students' cooperation for assessment. He suggested, for example, that faculty (a) not surprise students with assessment, (b) explain the purpose and expectations of assessment, (c) include students on assessment planning committees, (d) use existing student groups for publicity about the process, and (e) explain to them how it will benefit them (pp. 29–31).

The implementation stage of the plan consists of the actual activities of instruction and assessment using the concepts incorporated in the assessment plan. Evaluators determine what percentage of students have learned what they were supposed to learn and if that is an acceptable level of achievement. As Erwin (1991, p. 128) noted, the basis for a "program-centered" approach to assessment is that the same people involved in planning are involved in the entire process. And they should be the people most involved in the program—the course faculty.

Oetting and Cole (1978) listed 10 questions to ask at this stage of assessment: (a) "Is the educational program doing what was planned?" (b) "Is the educational program under study achieving its objectives effectively?" (c) "Are program parts equally effective?" (d) "Does the educational program maintain its effectiveness?" (e) "Are students responding as planned?" (f) "Are some students reached more effectively than others?" (g) "Is the program meeting goals other than those expected?" (h) "Is the assessment plan being followed?" (i) "Is anything happening that might distort the data?" (j) "What are the real costs of the educational program?" (quoted in Erwin, 1991, pp. 129–130). Erwin's (1991) three essentials for reporting and using assessment data are (a) accuracy, (b) quality, and (c) confidentiality (p. 150).

The System Evaluation Stage

The third stage of the process of course or program assessment is system evaluation or feedback, which involves making changes to the instructional objectives, assessment criteria, and course content based on course assessment. It should be ongoing and result in continual change in course content. It involves ensuring that the selected procedures, content, and teaching methods used in courses indeed are appropriate in helping students learn the important course material as set forth in the course objectives.

The system evaluation stage might be called a *feedback loop* (Tucker, 1994, p. 115). The process of system evaluation involves ensuring (a) that the content of the course relates directly to the objectives established during the planning process, (b) that the methods needed to ensure that the material necessary for students to achieve the objectives was presented using appropriate teaching and learning methods, and (c) that the assessment measures themselves were the best measures for evaluating student learning.

The activities of the planning and feedback stages are quite similar. In fact, after the initial assessment plan is devised, planning and feedback are merged, and the process begins again. In evaluating the course or program assessment plan, faculty would analyze the curriculum (based on unit goals and objectives), instruction (based on the learning plan as implemented by individual faculty), and assessment instruments (based on the assessment criteria in the plan) in relation to the mission statement and the assessment statement.

Faculty would determine whether the content of the course actually does relate directly to the goals and objectives established during the planning process. They would ask several questions at this stage: (a) Do the units devised adequately cover the breadth of information desired for the course or program? (That is, is any essential content omitted?) (b) Do the units devised cover material not desired? (That is, is extraneous material included?) (c) Do individual units have goals that are not appropriate to that unit? (That is, can better unit concepts be devised?) (d) Are course and program objectives appropriate and measurable?

An important ingredient at the feedback stage of assessment is information gleaned from multiple assessment measures. As noted earlier, assessment involves more than faculty members evaluating student classroom performance. Input is needed from other faculty, administrators, media employers, current students, and recent graduates. Several of the studies noted earlier provide types of questions that might be used for an assessment survey. Such assessment should be tied to the goals and objectives of the program. However, graduates' and employers' feedback can be useful in modifying those goals and objectives, as well. Surveys might consist of Likert-type scales, as used by the American Society of Newspaper Editors (ASNE, 1990) and Olson and Dickson (1995); a semantic differential, as employed by Thayer (1990); rankings, as done by the Associated Press Managing Editors (Ceppos, 1994); or ratings, as used by the Association for Education in Journalism and Mass Communication Curriculum Task Force (1996).

Some of the competencies that might be included in the survey are as follows: (a) problem-solving ability; (b) information-gathering ability; (c) ability to write concisely, precisely, and clearly; (d) understanding of media law; (e) ability to use standard grammar and correct spelling; (f) ability to punctuate correctly; (g) ability to use computers, software, cameras, and other media technology; (h) ability to identify news; (i) ability to research stories; (j) accuracy of stories; (k) fairness and balance of stories; (l) ability to do layout and design or video and audio editing; (m) interviewing skill; (n) ability to cover a beat; (o) professional ethics and standards; (p) judgment; (q) understanding of professional practices; (r) sensitivity to multiethnic, multiracial issues; (s) sensitivity to bias based on age, race, gender, or disability; and (t) adaptability.

SUMMARY

Key questions about the assessment of program components are listed in Appendix B. Assessing students for their conceptual and attitudinal competencies as well as for the information they have retained and their procedural skills helps assure that media education is not on the periphery of higher education but central to producing educated graduates. An assessment plan as outlined in this chapter should overcome the objections to assessment by critics who argue that quantitative assessment tests stifle creativity and are easy for students and faculty to manipulate. The process outlined here provides qualitative as well as quantitative means for evaluating students. Thus, it provides results that are useful for media faculty and administrators who need quantitative data to please college or university administrators and also provides results that are useful for faculty in improving their courses. Assessment of student competence as outlined here is based on abilities acquired instead of memorization of facts. It also allows faculty to report the percentage of students who have achieved course objectives and also the ratings obtained from graduates and media professionals who have hired recent graduates. And, because improvement of curriculum and instruction is built into assessment, student achievement should continue to improve without faculty having to "teach to the test."

Performance assessment based on student outcomes means that assessment is never divorced from what it is that educators are doing continuously: devising and improving curriculum. Moreover, assessment that is done not because it is mandated from above but because it is essential to what educators do allows assessment to be more than an academic exercise. It becomes something that is done as a matter of course and that is implemented by those who have most at stake in students' performance: the faculty members themselves. Results of assessment of components like reporting and editing, moreover, become inputs into the larger system of program review and can lead to broader improvements to curriculum and student outcomes. Assessment, then, becomes not just something that educators are expected or required to do. It becomes something they want to do.

REFERENCES

American Society of Newspaper Editors. (1990). *Journalism education: Facing up to the challenge of change.* Washington, DC: American Society of Newspaper Editors Foundation.

Anderson, L. W. (1981). *Assessing affective characteristics in the schools.* Boston: Allyn & Bacon.

Association for Education in Journalism and Mass Communication Curriculum Task Force. (1996). Responding to the challenge of change. *Journalism and Mass Communication Educator, 50,* 101–119.

Banathy, B. H. (1968). *Instructional systems.* Belmont, CA: Fearon.

Beasley, M. (1990, May 23). Journalism schools are not preparing their students for economic reality. *Chronicle of Higher Education,* pp. B1–B2.

Benjamin, E. (1990, July 5). The movement to assess students' learning will institutionalize mediocrity in colleges. *Chronicle of Higher Education,* pp. B1–B2.

Benjamin, R., & Chun, M. (2003, Summer). A new field of dreams: The collegiate learning assessment project. *peerReview, 5*(4), 26–29.

Blanchard, R. O. (1988). Our emerging role in liberal and media studies. *Journalism Educator, 43*(3), 28–31.

Blanchard, R. O., & Christ, W. G. (1988, August). *Beyond the generic curriculum; the enriched major for journalism and mass communication.* Paper presented at the annual convention of the Association for Education in Journalism and Mass Communication, Portland, OR.

Blanchard, R. O., & Christ, W. G. (1993). *Media education & the liberal arts: A blueprint for the new professionalism.* Hillsdale, NJ: Lawrence Erlbaum Associates, Inc.

Bloom, B. S. (Eds.). (1956). *Taxonomy of educational objectives (Vol. 1): Cognitive domain.* New York: McKay.

Brookfield, S. D. (1989). *Developing critical thinkers: Challenging adults to explore alternative ways of thinking and acting.* San Francisco: Jossey-Bass.

Bugeja, M. J. (1996). *Living ethics: Developing values in mass communication.* Boston: Allyn & Bacon.

Carnegie Foundation for the Advancement of Teaching. (1979). *Missions of the college curriculum: A contemporary review with suggestions.* San Francisco: Jossey-Bass.

Caudill, E., Ashdown, P., & Caudill, S. (1990). Assessing learning in news, public relations curricula. *Journalism Educator, 45*(2), 13–20.

Ceppos, J. (1994, January/February). Teach students to think analytically, APME members tell journalism educators. *APME News,* pp. 3–6.

Chickering, A. W. (1969). *Education and identity.* San Francisco: Jossey-Bass.

Christ, W. G., & McCall, J. (1994). Assessing "the what" of media education. In S. Morreale & M. Brooks (Eds.), *1994 SCA Summer Conference Proceedings and Prepared Remarks* (pp. 477–493). Annandale, VA: Speech Communication Association.

Chun, M. (2002, Winter/Spring). Looking where the light is better: A review of the literature on assessing higher education quality. *peerReview, 4*(2–3), 16–18.

Eastman, S. T. (1987). A model for telecommunications education. *Feedback, 28*(2), 21–25.

Eastman, S. T. (1993, May). *Assessment in mass communication.* Paper presented at the annual meeting of the International Communication Association, Washington, DC.

Educational Commission of the States. (1994). *Quality counts: Setting expectations for higher education . . . and making them count.* Washington, DC: Author.

Ervin, R. F. (1988, July). *Outcomes assessment: The rationale and the implementation.* Paper presented at the annual meeting of the Association for Education in Journalism and Mass Communication, Portland, OR.

Erwin, T. D. (1991). *Assessing student learning and development: A guide to the principles, goals, and methods of determining college outcomes.* San Francisco: Jossey-Bass.

Erwin, T. D., & Wise, S. L. (2002). A scholar-practitioner model for assessment. In T. Banta & Associates (Eds.), *Building a scholarship of assessment* (pp. 67–81). San Francisco: Jossey-Bass.

Eshelman, D. (1991, April). *Outcomes assessment strategies: Implications for broadcast education.* Paper presented at the meeting of the Broadcast Education Association, Las Vegas, NV.

Farmer, D. W. (1988). *Enhancing student learning: Emphasizing essential competencies in academic programs.* Wilkes-Barre, PA: King's College.

Farrar, R. T. (1988, July). *Competencies for outcomes assessment in mass communications graduate education: The South Carolina Experiment.* Paper presented at the Association of Schools of Journalism and Mass Communication Administrators Conference, Portland, OR.

Gable, R. K. (1986). *Instrumental development in the affective domain.* Boston: Kluwer-Nijhoff.

Grow, G. (1989, August). *Self-directed, lifelong education and journalism education.* Paper presented at the Association for Education in Journalism and Mass Communication convention, Washington, DC.

Grow, G. (1991). Higher-order skills for professional practice and self-direction. *Journalism Educator, 45*(4), 56–65.

Haley, E., & Jackson, D. (1995). A conceptualization of assessment for mass communication programs. *Journalism and Mass Communication Educator, 50,* 26–34.

Hausman, C. (1990). *The decision-making process in journalism.* Chicago: Nelson-Hall.

Heywood, J. (1989). *Assessment in education* (2nd ed.). New York: Wiley.

Hudson, J. C. (1981). Radio-TV news staff employers prefer broadcasting degree, strong liberal arts foundation. *Journalism Educator, 36*(2), 27–28, 46.

Jones, D. M. (1978). Editors, educators are close on what "makes" a newsman. *Journalism Educator, 33*(2), 17–18.

Krathwohl, D. R., Bloom, B. S., & Masia, B. B. (1964). *Taxonomy of educational objectives: Affective domain.* New York: McKay.

Lambeth, E. G. (1986). *Committed journalism: An ethic for the profession.* Bloomington: Indiana University Press.

Linn, R. L., & Baker, E. L. (1996). Can performance-based student assessments be psychometrically sound? In J. B. Barron & D. P. Wolf (Eds.), *Performance-based student assessment: Challenges and possibilities.* Chicago: University of Chicago Press.

Mager, R. (1962). *Preparing instructional objectives.* Belmont, CA: Fearon Publishers.

Menkowski, M. (1998, June). *Creating a culture of assessment: A look through the lens of Assessment Update.* An interactive session of the American Association for Higher Education Conference, Cincinnati, OH.

Mills, G., Harvey, K., & Warnick, L. B. (1980). Newspaper editors point to j-grad deficiencies. *Journalism Educator, 35*(2), 12–19.

National Postsecondary Education Cooperative. (1997). *Student outcomes information for policy-making: Final report of the national postsecondary education cooperative working group on student outcomes from a policy perspective.* University Park: Pennsylvania State University, Center for the Study of Higher Education.

Nielsen, R. M., & Polishook, I. H. (1990, April 11). Taking a measure of assessment. *Chronicle of Higher Education,* p. A14.

Oetting, E. R., & Cole, C. W. (1978). Method, design, and implementation in evaluation. In G. R. Hanson (Ed.), *New directions for student services, No. 1: Evaluating program effectiveness* (pp. 44–46). San Francisco: Jossey-Bass.

Olson, L. D., & Dickson, T. (1995). English composition courses as preparation for news writing. *Journalism and Mass Communication Educator, 50,* 47–54.

Palomba, C. A., & Banta, T. W. (1999). *Assessment essentials: Planning, implementing and improving assessment in higher education.* San Francisco: Jossey-Bass.

Parsigian, E. K. (1992). *Mass media writing.* Hillsdale, NJ: Lawrence Erlbaum Associates, Inc.

Project on the Future of Journalism and Mass Communication Education. (1987). *Planning for curricular change in journalism education* (2nd ed.). Eugene: University of Oregon, School of Journalism.

Schneider, C. G. (2002, Winter/Spring). Can value added assessment raise the level of student accomplishment? *peerReview, 4*(2–3), 4–6.

Shulman, L. S. (2002, November/December). Making differences: A table of learning. *Change, 34*(6), 37–44.

Thayer, F. D. (1990). Using semantic differential to evaluate courses. *Journalism Educator, 45*(2), 20–24.

Tucker, D. E. (1994). Course evaluation. In W. G. Christ (Ed.), *Assessing media education* (pp. 113–130). Hillsdale, NJ: Lawrence Erlbaum Associates, Inc.

Tyler, R. W. (1950). *Basic principles of curriculum and instruction.* Chicago: University of Chicago Press.

Tyler, R. W. (1973). Assessing educational achievement in the affective domain. *Measurement in Education, 4*, 1–8.

Zais, R. (1976). *Curriculum: Principles and foundations.* New York: Harper & Row.

APPENDIX A

Sample Assessment Plan for a Learning Unit

The following section is a portion of an assessment plan for a learning unit based on the strategy outlined in this chapter. It consists of the (a) mission statement, (b) assessment statement, (c) unit themes, (d) curricular objectives, and (e) unit evaluation procedures (assessment criteria).

Mission Statement. The purpose of the reporting and editing components is to provide the student with interviewing and reporting abilities, news writing skills, editing and design ability, and an understanding of the legal and professional responsibilities of journalists.

Assessment Statement. The purpose of the assessment procedure is to determine whether the course or courses are adequately preparing students to be able to gather information, prepare stories, and edit them for presentation for both print and broadcast media using acceptable professional practices.

Unit Themes. The competencies required for media reporting and editing are divided into four units, whose themes are as follows: (a) identifying what is newsworthy, (b) gathering the necessary information, (c) preparing stories for dissemination, and (d) upholding professional standards.

Curricular Objectives and Evaluation Procedures
for Unit 3 (Preparing the Story for Presentation)

Objective 1. At the end of the unit, the student should be able to *analyze* (*Conceptual*) the content of stories; *to identify* (*Informational*) problems with content, clarity, and mechanics; and *to make* (*Procedural*) necessary changes.

For *assessment criteria,* the objective will be met when the student (a) identifies problems with a story or changes needed, and (b) makes changes to the story so that it is ready for publication or broadcast to the satisfaction of the evaluator.

Objective 2. At the end of the unit, the student will be able *to evaluate* (*Conceptual*) visuals and sound for a story; *to select* (*Procedural*) the best visuals or sound; and *to determine* (*Procedural*) the best way to present them.

For *assessment criteria,* the objectives will be met when the student, when presented a choice of visuals or sound, makes a selection and prepares a story presentation that the evaluator finds satisfactory.

Objective 3. At the end of the unit, the student will be able *to comprehend* (*Informational*) the main idea of story and *to write* (*Procedural*) headlines or story lead-ins to the satisfaction of the evaluator.

For *assessment criterion,* the objectives will be met when the student presents headlines or lead-ins that the evaluator finds to be satisfactory for both content and length.

Objective 4. At the end of the unit, students will be able *to evaluate* (*Conceptual*) the news values of available stories, *to select* (*Procedural*) the best stories and visuals, and *to design* (*Procedural*) a newspaper page or *to organize* (*Procedural*) a newscast.

For *assessment criteria,* to meet the unit objectives, the student will be able to design a page or to prepare a newscast to the satisfaction of the evaluator.

APPENDIX B

Key Questions About Assessment of Program Components

1. Why should course and component assessment take place?

Results from the assessment can be used (a) to increase student achievement of course objectives, (b) to improve course design and instruction, (c) to evaluate a particular program, and (d) to augment the evaluation of an entire media unit.

2. Where should the assessment take place?

Aspects of assessment should take place in faculty and administrative offices, in the classroom, and at organizations that hire media graduates.

3. Who should carry out the assessment, and whom should they assess?

The assessment should be done not only by course instructors but also by other faculty members, administrators, graduates, and media employers. The media unit should gather assessment information on both current students and graduates.

4. When should the assessment take place?

Informal assessment is ongoing. It takes place when the instructor obtains feedback from students orally or through assignments and makes adjustments to the course content and structure. During formal assessment, evaluation should take place at the end of individual curriculum units and at the end of the semester. Assessment of program components should take place both while the student is taking courses to be assessed, shortly before graduation, and after students are in the workforce.

5. How should the assessment be done?

The development of a course or component assessment plan involves the three stages of assessment: planning, implementation, and feedback. All must be tied to curriculum design. Assessment is done by (a) developing course and program goals and objectives through a planning process that includes devising learning experiences to meet those objectives, (b) implementing methods for measuring how well course material is being learned to determine how well course and program goals and objectives are being met, and (c) using the results of assessment for modifying both courses and programs and improving instruction.

6. What should be assessed?

The "what" of assessment is the desired student competencies that are the basis for devising goals and instructional objectives. Four categories of instructional objectives are used in this chapter: (a) informational competencies, which relate to knowledge recall and comprehension; (b) procedural competencies, which involve application of information; (c) conceptual competencies, which concern creativity and analysis, synthesis and evaluation of information; and (d) attitudinal competencies, which relate to values, principles, and self-direction. Conceptual and attitudinal competencies involve both the cognitive and the affective domain and are both higher-level abilities.

7. What comprises the assessment plan?

The assessment plan consists of the (a) mission statement, (b) assessment statement, (c) unit themes, (d) curricular objectives, and (e) unit evaluation procedures (assessment criteria).

13

Math and Statistics

Paul S. Voakes
School of Journalism and Mass Communication
University of Colorado–Boulder

In most lists of goals or competencies in journalism and mass communication, mathematical competence seems to bring up the rear. This is the element of a communication education that seems most foreign to most communication educators. Unlike writing, information gathering, editing, ethics, law, and all the other traditional components of an education in professional communication, math has usually resided in a distant sector of the undergraduate experience.

Before the late 1990s, most communication faculty probably would allow that communication professionals should have some familiarity with basic mathematical facts and procedures, but who was responsible for math instruction? Surely not the writing, reporting, law, or ethics instructors. That attitude has changed—slowly—with the advent of assessment in communication education. Not only did faculties begin to take inventory of the learning outcomes they desired for their students, they began taking responsibility for the instruction of everything on the list. And some of those inventories included math.

The Poynter Institute for Media Studies led the way in the late 1990s when it developed and disseminated a "Pyramid of Competence" for media educators (Scanlan, 1999). The pyramid was composed of symbolic blocks, and sure enough, one block was labeled "Numbers." Deborah Potter, a former CNN and CBS correspondent who at the time was serving on the Poynter faculty, noted that most journalists exhibited an "aversion to all things numerical" that was causing "nothing but trouble in today's newsrooms" (Scanlan, 1999, p. 245).

As influential as the Poynter Institute is in media education, the Accrediting Council on Education in Journalism and Mass Communications (ACEJMC) exercises even more influence. In 2003, when the accrediting council revised the standards by which programs would be evaluated for accreditation, it included a list of competencies whose learning each accredited program must now measure, through assessment. The original, long list was narrowed down to 11 "professional values and competencies," and math survived the final cut (Accrediting Council, 2004): The accrediting council requires that all graduates of accredited programs should be able, among other competencies, to "apply basic numerical and statistical concepts" (Accrediting Council, 2004, p. 43).

Therein lies the anxiety for many journalism and mass communication educators. What do those six little words mean, exactly? How do we assess student competence in "basic numerical and statistical concepts"? The purpose of this chapter is to explain the rationale behind the inclusion of math and statistics in the core list, to explicate math and statistics in a way that might suggest rubrics for assessment, to suggest a variety of indirect and direct measures for math assessment, and finally, to suggest a few methods of integrating math and statistics instruction into the journalism and mass communication curriculum.

WHO NEEDS MATH?

Many students, and no doubt some of their professors, may think that the accrediting council has inflicted this learning goal on the media education community as an act of unrepentant academic sadism. The case for math and statistics, however, is a strong one. Mathematical competence benefits the communicator for a variety of reasons ranging from the enhancement of writing efficacy to the reinforcement of professional ethics.

"Mechanical" Consistency

Since the beginning of media education, instructors have insisted that students need reliable mechanical tools to enable them to develop as writers. Those tools might include knowledge of syntax, grammar, punctuation, spelling, usage, and diction. Is there an equivalent list for mathematical basics? It's rarely found in any media program, presumably because communication students will be unlikely to deal with numbers in their chosen fields. Anecdotally, recruiters and alumni tell educators that's simply not the case. In fact, Scott Maier conducted an analysis of 500 randomly selected newspaper stories (Maier, 2002) and found that more than half of them included mathematical or statistical procedures or concepts. (He also found that the stories with numbers consistently received better play than words-only stories.) With that frequency of math usage, it seems irresponsible to educate media students in "the mechanical basics" if those basics exclude math mechanics.

Quality of Writing

Our students tell us they should not have to learn (or even review) mathematics in a journalism and mass communication program because they have always been "word people"—destined to become professional writers. Once they get into advanced writing courses, of course, they learn the importance of precision, both in factual writing and in descriptive writing. Details make the writing livelier, their writing instructors tell them. The mathematical quantity or statistical result is the ultimate detail. Which is the stronger sentence: "The mayor has a comfortable income," or "The mayor reported an income of $297,500 last year"? In public relations, which is the more effective lead sentence for a press release: "The Community Kitchen reported a significant increase in the number of low-income children fed last year," or "The Community Kitchen reported a 39% increase in the number of low-income children fed last year"?

Credibility

One of the greatest challenges facing mass communication in the 21st century is the retention of credibility. When the Internet enables anyone to disseminate news and opinion to a global audience, what can the institutions of mass communication offer? For starters, they can offer reliable, accurate information gathered and presented by people trained to be accurate and reliable. But as long as the factual world still includes mathematical concepts and quantities, credibility will depend to some degree on mathematical accuracy. And quite often the smallest of errors can create credibility problems. When an advertisement states that a population is 73% White, 15% Black, 12% Hispanic, 8% Asian American, and 2% Native American, the loss of credibility is every bit as great as if the copywriter had written "the population are."

Technological Advances

Research capability is growing geometrically, and that means ever more information at the fingertips of journalists and other professional communicators. Among the more intriguing advances is the instant availability of data sets—from purchasing preferences of a certain demographic group to campaign contributions to a certain candidate. Spreadsheet software enables a quick summary of the most significant facts within the data—but only if the writer knows what he or she is looking for. In the 1990s, "computer-assisted reporting" was assigned to the few in the newsroom who were thought to have unusual computer skills. Advances have now ensured, however, that anyone who can operate a word-processing program should be able to manipulate a spreadsheet program without specialized computer skills.

Values and Ethics

Mathematical competence supports the core values and ethics of mass communication in a free and democratic society. As mentioned earlier, accuracy is a cornerstone of journalistic integrity. But when a reporter mistakes a $4 million debt for a $4 billion debt, readers, viewers, and sources will wonder if the mistake was made out of ignorance or out of malice.

Another core value of journalism is independence. Generations of journalists have prided themselves on their healthy skepticism and their resistance to material that is "spun" by those with political or monetary motives. Yet when a source dazzles a reporter with a cascade of numbers, those numbers are all too often repeated in the story, simply because the reporter lacks the confidence to regard the numbers independently. Likewise for journalistic balance and fairness. No matter how diligently an editor attempts to balance the reporting of a controversy, the side that has the impressive set of statistics is likely to seem stronger than the side that is represented by hyperbolic (verbal) assertions only. And when the impressive statistics get into the story unchallenged, then fairness is even more at risk.

Ethics is no less important in the fields of advertising and public relations. Baker and Martinson (2001) proposed a checklist with which an ad's creator might evaluate its ethical responsibility. The list has five elements: truthfulness, authenticity, respect, equity, and social responsibility. When an ad makes a truthful claim about a product, its accuracy is nearly always substantiated with quantitative evidence. In public relations, one of the highest ethical callings is the desire to bring deserving untold stories to the attention of the mainstream media. Without a solid factual basis, the challenge is much more difficult.

Mathematicians and statisticians base their findings on logic and evidence, a form of "objectivity" with which the scientific world has some experience. Should communication professionals and communication students be spurning that mentality? Statisticians' great gift to the rest of us is the ability to reduce vast, complex volumes of data into significant conclusions that lay people can understand. Isn't that what public communicators should also be doing?

MATH GOALS FOR THE COMMUNICATION STUDENT

As with assessment for any other competency, math and statistics assessment should consist of planning, implementation, and evaluation (the kind of evaluation that has immediate implications for instructional or curricular revision). To begin the planning process, assessors must agree on the learning goals. Communication educators know intuitively what is meant by a professionally competent writer, editor, or gatherer of information, and the learning goals follow freely. But how do we know whether someone embarking on a communication career is sufficiently competent in math and statistics?

Assessment standards for undergraduate mathematics education are of little use, because the assessment is examining a much higher order of mathematical reasoning and procedures than the communication professions normally demand. The Educational Testing Service (ETS) and Graduate Record Examinations (GRE) have joined forces to develop the "Major Field Tests," standardized tests for seniors graduating in math, history, psychology, and several other traditional disciplines (Pike, 2000). Regardless of one's view of standardizing testing as an assessment tool, the Major Field Test in math would be irrelevant for seniors graduating in a communication major. The learning goals are fundamentally different. As Maier (2002) and many others have pointed out, most professional communicators are not required to work in "higher math." What is more often required is a heavy dollop of common sense applied to procedures and facts learned in primary- or secondary-level math classes (Maier, 2002, p. 516). In the world of adult education, this is "numeracy"—the ability to understand and work comfortably with numbers. In the world of secondary education, this is "mathematical power"—"the confidence to solve mathematical problems and to reason and communicate mathematically" (Bush & Greer, 1999, p. 7). In fact, the National Assessment Governing Board, which regularly devises the United States' only uniform assessment of student competencies in Grades 4, 8, and 12 (Orrill & French, 2002), has a list of "content areas" for 8th- and 12th-grade students that is remarkably similar to the areas of math frequently encountered by journalists and other communicators. One of the most salient characteristics of both numeracy and mathematical power is that each is addressed at both an operational and interpretive level. A professional communicator may work for several months without having to pull out a calculator and compute a single sum; however, she may be constantly analyzing quantitative research tables and charts, looking for significant trends or findings. Alternatively, she may receive a data set that has not been summarized in ways that will serve the campaign at hand, so the communicator must spend a few hours doing nothing but computing averages, correlations, or whichever statistical procedure makes the most sense.

As with assessment of other areas, each program is free to set the standards at any level it sees fit. The purpose here is to suggest a starting point, from which any assessing body should feel free to vary. The author has synthesized the recommendations of Maier (2002) and Scanlan (1999), as well as those of the National Assessment Governing Board, with his own conclusions (having developed and taught an undergraduate course called "Math and Statistics for Journalism"), to arrive at a preliminary set of learning goals for the communicator-mathematician.

Arithmetic Computation

In the example shown earlier concerning a population's ethnic breakdown, the figures added up to more than 100%. In his study of the most common math problems plaguing reporters, Maier found ample evidence of figures simply not adding up. Journalists and other communicators must know how (with a calculator) to add, subtract, multiply, and divide—not in a vacuum but in the context of realistic, reportable situations. Another common example of simple math errors is in rounding off numbers, and understanding the effects of summing numbers that have been rounded. A little less obvious is the concept of adjusting for inflation. As an advocate, a public relations practitioner should know that although her client's average income has risen by 83% since 1983, that increase actually represents a decline in purchasing, once we adjust for inflation. Adjusting for inflation is a simple matter of reading a table, multiplying, then dividing. Even without having to compute, the communicator in the interpretive role should be aware of inflation's effects. A reporter reading a press release concerning change in dollars paid or received over time must always be on the lookout for whether inflation has been factored in.

Measurement

In addition to the basics of number sense, the assessment board for high school math urges that students understand measurement: how to compute and compare sizes, convert to other forms of measurement, and read scaled drawings. For example, how much larger is three square miles than 2,000 acres? Actually 2,000 is the larger area, but students need to know how to convert from one unit of measurement to another. How heavy is a man weighing 175 kilograms? Quite heavy indeed: he weighs about 385 pounds.

Mathematical Terminology

Students should be able to use mathematical terminology correctly—for example, know the difference between "an increase of 12%" and "an increase of 12 percentage points." If a candidate's support in a public opinion poll rose from 12% to 24%, a reporter would write that her support has risen "12 percentage points," or "by 100%," because 24 is 100% more than 12. Students should know common math terms used in business as well, such as the difference between simple interest and compound interest.

Ratio, Proportion, Percentage

This is a subset of arithmetic computation that deserves a category of its own, simply because of the frequency with which numerical relations and proportions are encountered. Cumming and Gal (2002), in recommending procedures for assessing adult numeracy, urge that percentage and percentage change be given top priority, simply because percentage is the most commonly encountered mathematical concept in adults' everyday lives. Maier (2002) did not find a plethora of percentage mistakes in his newspaper study, but he attributed that only to the efforts of the management of the newspaper under study, just before the study, to eradicate percentage-related mistakes.

Computing percentages involves multiplying and dividing, but students need to understand the logic behind the computation. If a university's tuition rose from $4,100 per year to $4,850, a student should be able to compute the percentage increase. Likewise, if the regents want to raise tuition by 12%, the student should be able to compute what the new tuition would be. And if we know that this year's ticket price of $12 per game represents a 20% increase over last year's price, the student should also be able to compute last year's price.

Estimation

This is an area that is less about computational procedures than about common sense. In his newspaper study, Maier (2002) saw repeated evidence of journalists' acceptance of their sources' "implausible claims" (p. 516). The simplest form of this error is the result of careless misstatement. If a public relations writer hears his boss mention a $10 million increase in the janitorial budget for next year, and the operating budget for the entire company is only $10 million, the writer should sense immediately that the janitorial figures makes no sense. The boss probably meant to say "$10,000", but at the very least that figure needs checking. A more complex, but equally common example, is as follows: When a spokeswoman for the Department of Transportation claims that one child (in a certain state) is killed every minute because he or she was not wearing a safety belt, a math-savvy reporter must be able to consider that, if the state's child population is about 2 million and there are about 10,000 minutes in a week, then in 200 weeks (about 4 years), all the kids in the state will have been killed. It was an implausible claim, but it's the kind of claim that is enticing to reporters and editors because it is so dramatic, and so easy for lay audiences to grasp.

Elementary Statistics

Students may not be called on to perform statistical procedures themselves, but because so much public information is based on statistical procedures, students should understand them. The margin of error, the concept of randomness in survey research, the importance of sample size, the difference between a sample and a population, the basic theories of probability, and the concept of correlation (and its distinction from causation), are a few of these basics. For example, when a candidate's favorability rating in a preelection poll rises from 39% to 41%, whereas his opponent's falls from 44% to 40%, can the reporter conclude that the first candidate has taken the lead? Not without knowing what the margin of error was in each poll. And when researchers report a "strong correlation" between average family income of a neighborhood and test scores for their children, it does not necessarily follow that giving each family thousands of supplemental dollars will increase their children's test scores. That is, correlation does not imply causation.

Central Tendency

This is another subset—this time a subset of statistics. The term refers to the measures of "average," either mean, median, or mode, and the dispersion of the data from the center, usually measured as the standard deviation. Computing a mean or median is a useful procedure for communicators to know, because it is society's most common means of reducing a data set to a single, meaningful value. But communicators must be careful in how each expression of an average is used. For example, the average salary of a professional basketball team could be $1 million a year. And the average salary of that same team could be $2.3 million a year. It could also be $400,000 a year. How? If the first "average" is the median, it is simply the middle salary in the list of all players' salaries: Half the team has salaries over $1 million, and half the team has salaries below $1 million. Two superstars' salaries of $8 million and $6 million are not reflected in the median. But if the "average" is the mean, that is, all the sum of all salaries divided by the number of players, then the highest salaries will certainly influence this "average"—which computes to $2.3 million a year. And if the "average" is the mode—the most frequently recorded value—then it could be $400,000, because two rookies could be making the league minimum of $400,000, and no one else on the team has identical salaries.

Communication students need not know how to compute a standard deviation, but they should at least recognize that a large deviation indicates that items in the group were distributed broadly, and a small deviation indicates that most items in the group were tightly packed near the average. For example, two towns could each have average household incomes of $80,000 a year, but if you then discover that the first town's standard deviation is $6,000 and the second town's standard deviation is $28,000, you've just learned something important. In the first town, 95% of the households—nearly everyone—earn between $68,000 and $92,000, which is an incredibly homogeneous group of families. In the second town, 95% of the households earn anywhere from $24,000 to $136,000. The second town will have low-income neighborhoods and wealthy neighborhoods, whereas the first probably will not.

Translation

This dimension of math competence has little to do directly with computations or procedures. One of the highest duties of mass communicators is to make complex information understandable to a lay audience, and even when the subject is math, that sense-making is usually done verbally. A skilled communicator must know, for example, how much numerical precision is needed in a given context for a given audience. When reporting a budget in the billions, it is not effective to write out line-item amounts numerically down to the last cent. Rounding off is more appropriate. A reporter may find a year-to-year change in dollar amounts, but translating that change to a percentage may be far more meaningful to the audience. Maier (2002) found that some reporters would overwhelm readers with needless numbers for numbers' sake; others would include interesting, important statistics, but without then explaining what the numbers meant in human terms. Another common issue of translation is that of statistical significance. If an advertising campaign team reads that its snack product has 87 parts per million of "real fruit" compared to 85 parts per million for the leading competitors, does the difference enable the team to base a campaign on a theme of "natural fruit goodness"? Probably not.

Graphics

Every mass medium has become a visual medium, and many communication programs (as well as the accrediting council) are insisting that students become skilled at combining images with words for greater effect. This is a dimension of math competence as well. Many times a statistical finding can be expressed more effectively in a graphic (a chart or a graph) than in a paragraph. Communicators must be able to interpret tables, charts, and graphs, and they should also know how to construct them. Maier (2002) found ample evidence of graphics not showing visually what the story was reporting verbally. But the most common mathematical mistake in constructing graphs, he found, was the inappropriate baseline. If the Dow Jones Industrial Average dropped from 10,300 to 10,250 in a week, for example, a graph with a baseline of 10,200 would imply visually that the market is crashing. A more appropriate baseline of zero, however, would show the incremental nature of the decline. Even if students are not constructing the graphic themselves, they should be able to suggest, for example, when a bar chart, pie chart, or line graph is most appropriate for the given data. If components are represented as percentages of a whole, some variation of a pie chart will be far more effective than a bar chart.

Again, these are suggestions. Each academic unit should evaluate its own priorities in each area of learning and set its goals accordingly. The nine goals discussed earlier merely reflect the author's synthesis of the priorities of adult education, middle school and high school, and media educators who have given considerable thought to what is basic math competence (see Appendix A).

IMPLEMENTING THE PLAN

Once the unit sets its learning goals, it must devise methods for measuring whether the students are living up to the expectations. Assessment usually takes the forms of direct measures and indirect measures.

Indirect Measures

When the topic is writing, ethics, visual literacy, or editing, indirect measures are somewhat easier to gather than when math is the topic. Awards from student competitions in photojournalism or advertising creativity, for example, are tried-and-true indirect measures of a program's success in teaching in those areas—as are job-placement results. There are, however, no student competitions in math and statistics for media students only, and few graduates are hired on to math-related jobs in the media. There are adjustments to other familiar indirect measures, however, that could give administrators and faculty a better sense of their math instruction.

Student Evaluations. If the unit has the authority to write its own items in student course evaluations, it could include an item or two addressing students' impressions of the course's effectiveness in teaching math or statistics procedures appropriate to that course.

Exit Interviews and Senior Surveys. Programs frequently ask graduating seniors a number of questions about their experience. Those surveys or conversations could be expanded to include questions about whether the student feels the program adequately prepared him or her to apply appropriate math concepts or procedures.

Internships. Most programs require on-site intern supervisors to fill out an evaluation of the student's performance at the conclusion of the internship. Because most internships with communications organizations naturally and inevitably involve some contact with math, the form sent to supervisors could include a few items about the student's ability to reason mathematically or to do the mathematical parts of his or her work proficiently.

Student Transcripts. Just as the transcript might indicate that a student has enhanced her visual communication skills by taking a number of courses in the Fine Arts department, the student's success in a number of math or statistics courses would indicate that high levels of competence may have been attained elsewhere on the campus.

Direct Measures

These are the measurements of greatest value in assessment, because they can evaluate a skill directly—rather than rely on students' self-reporting or the general report of others unfamiliar with the assessment goals.

Direct measures also can address the specific learning goals—in this case, the nine outlined earlier—in ways that indirect measures cannot.

In mathematics and statistics, the primary tool for assessment is some form of timed test. The emphasis of the testing changed significantly, however, beginning in the early 1990s with a reform movement in mathematics assessment at the primary and secondary levels (Wilcox & Lanier, 2000). The National Council of Teachers of Mathematics carried the banner for this movement, and its result was to change math assessment from a one-time summative measure of students' abilities, to an ongoing monitoring process that links student measurement to revisions to instructional technique and curriculum, sometimes on a weekly basis. The reform also resulted in a broader variety of tasks in an assessment instrument, such as reasoning toward a solution to a problem never encountered before, instead of using formulas recently memorized. Eastman (1994) has argued effectively against "exit tests" of any kind for students majoring in the mass media.

To assess math and statistics skills in a communication program, a timed test certainly could be administered. Nationally standardized math tests at any level are readily available, but it is unlikely that any standardized math test would tap into all of the learning goals outlined earlier, especially considering our interest in students' translating and interpreting numbers as well as using them. Furthermore, a stand-alone math test would seem inappropriate, and perhaps intimidating, to students whose math instruction has in all likelihood been embedded in other communication coursework.

DIRECT MEASURES: A CASE STUDY

Here is an alternative approach to the direct measure, in use at the University of Colorado School of Journalism and Mass Communication, that may be more suitable for the task at hand. Its basic structure can provide a template for four different iterations. Each involves an assignment, or combination of assignments, in a senior-level course (perhaps the capstone course, if the unit or sequence has one). A committee of three "external" reviewers is created: a faculty member who has not taught the course(s) involved, an adjunct instructor or graduate student in the unit, and a professional in the region who is willing to donate several hours to assessment for the school.

The committee is given a randomly selected sample (perhaps 33%) of the students' work on the assignment. In a briefing session, the committee learns the rubrics established for each of the learning goals. The rubrics are usually arrayed on a Likert-type scale, such as 5 representing understanding and use of the concept at a professionally proficient level and 1 representing such a severe lack of understanding that the student, if employable at all, would create problems for his or her new employer. If the nine goals (discussed earlier) are adopted, for example, the committee learns how to score each student paper for Arithmetic Computation; Measurement; Math Terminology; Ratio, Proportion, and Percentage; Estimation; Elementary Statistics; Central Tendency; Translation; and Graphics. The three reviewers' scores for each learning goal, for each student's paper, are averaged. The entire class's scores for each of the nine learning goals are then averaged. The results are analyzed by the relevant faculty committee.

What form would the exercise take? Here are four alternatives:

A Copy-Editing Exercise

Most editing instructors are familiar with the assignment in which a news story (or press release, or advertising copy) is "scrambled up," that is, infused with mistakes. Sometimes they are lapses in fairness or balance, sometimes they are Associated Press style mistakes, sometimes they are punctuation mistakes, sometimes all of the above. This time, the errors would be math mistakes, in nine categories (if the nine learning goals, discussed earlier, are adopted). The story, for example, might contain an implausible assertion that makes no sense if it is given a moment's thought; it would contain an error in percentage change; it would include a graphic that was misleading or inaccurate; it might represent the math clumsily in the writing; it would understate or overstate the importance of a statistical finding; it would misuse the concepts of margin of error; and it would miscalculate an average. The assignment would challenge the students to correct mistakes and rewrite when necessary, but it would not be identified as a "math-only" editing exercise. Before the instructor marks the students' work, a photocopy is handed to the external committee for its assessment of student skills in the nine identified areas. For each learning goal, a rating scale has been established. For the error in percentage change, for example, the assessor would give a 1 if the mistake goes unnoticed by the student editor, a 3 if the figure is questioned but not corrected, and a 5 (the top value) if the figure is correctly altered. Assessors would assign 2 or 4 as gradations between the stated rubrics.

A Story Assignment

In most advanced reporting courses, a number of different types of stories are assigned. One of these could be a story that uses math extensively. The instructions for the story would explicitly state that the story must include statistical findings, a graphic representation, use of percentages and averages, as well as basic math. Likewise, the stories are copied and handed to the external reviewers independently of the instructor's grading. For the graphics goal, for example, assessors would give a story a 5 if the graphic tells the most important mathematical finding in the story and does so accurately and neatly, a 3 would be given to a graphic that includes extraneous information but gets the main point across as well, and a 1 would go to an inaccurate or misleading graphic.

A Memorandum to "The Boss"

Here the assignment is to develop a story idea (or public relations or advertising campaign) in the form of a memo to a hypothetical supervisor. Rather than actually reporting the story in the field or performing the campaign, the student plans the work, but plans it in ways that show he or she is thinking mathematically. For example, a story being planned must attempt to verify a perceived trend by using survey data, and the memo must define what level of statistical result will verify conclusively that a trend is occurring. It must plan the accompanying graphics, and the memo itself must use appropriate mathematical and statistical language. Again, the memos would be turned over to the external reviewers for their application of the assessment rubrics. One such rubric might be for level of significance: the memo gets a 1 if there is no stated expectation of what the survey might find, a 3 if the memo includes a plan to use the survey data, and a 5 would go to the plan that would make a certain conclusion on the basis of a stated, statistically significant, finding.

The Portfolio

This is probably the most common form of direct measure in use in media education. In each of three courses, for example, the student would be assigned to include in the portfolio the piece of work that illustrates his or her best use of math in that particular course. After the three pieces are in the portfolio, the student writes a self-assessment of the development of his or her "math side" over the past several semesters. The portfolio is reviewed by the external committee, which looks for evidence of competence in each of the nine math goals.

THE FEEDBACK LOOP

Every assessment concludes with an analysis of the results that makes recommendations to instructors. A goal of assessment, after all, is to improve student learning in the classroom. If the direct measures of math competence, for example, expose weakness in estimation and interpretation, the faculty might agree to inject more exercises demanding "math common sense" into an early week in a few of the advanced courses. A colleague might even be persuaded to develop a module, or a few exercises for a few different contexts, that others could use. The feedback stage, however, suggests an ugly possibility: Who among us can teach math?

WHO AMONG US CAN TEACH MATH?

It could be that mass communication students aren't the only ones in the mass communication program who gravitated toward words at an early age because they didn't get along with numbers. Some communication faculty can be just as rusty (or phobic) as their students. But if a program's competencies for assessment do include math and statistics, then the faculty must take responsibility for that instruction.

A few universities have a stand-alone course dedicated to Math for Journalism, but most programs fold their math instruction into courses with other primary missions. Many instructors prefer to let the math dog lie sleeping and confront it only when it cannot be avoided. A more effective strategy might be to identify a few specific math-learning goals for each course in the journalism and mass communication curriculum, with each goal directly related to the program's larger goals for math competence. In this way, the instructor can make an organized, well-prepared presentation, with the expectation that students will apply that piece of math know-how in subsequent work for the rest of the course. In addition, however, there are many ways of raising the students' math consciousness more subtly, on a daily or weekly basis.

Sneaking Math into the Journalism-Communication Course

Most mass communication courses require students to digest the relevant news of the day—ad campaigns, public relations successes and failures, or news coverage online, on air, or on paper. Students can be asked to identify the numerical elements of the story or campaign and discuss how the numbers made it more or less effective. In this context, the mathematical world may seem, to the instructor as well as to the students, huge and beyond control. For that reason, the search for mathematical content in contemporary media should be focused on the math-learning goals the unit has previously identified, such as the nine goals discussed earlier. Here are a few more specific suggestions:

- At a more advanced level, students can bring "real-world" examples to class in which they challenge the mathematical logic or claim, or the graphical representation. Also at an advanced level, students can be assigned to suggest a follow-up story that would deepen the audience's understanding of the original story—but the follow-up would be numbers-based.

- Similarly, many classes criticize the local media regularly, with points awarded to students who identify bad headlines, bad leads, ads that "don't work," or poorly composed photographs. "Bad math" could also be included.

- Many instructors of skills courses keep students engaged with frequent quizzes—on current events, Associated Press style, grammar, or a current topic in the syllabus. They could easily add a "story problem" related to a math task the students have recently encountered, or a few examples of effective (or ineffective) writing with numbers.

- If students are required to keep a journal in which they reflect on the media content they are reading or viewing, they could also be asked to reflect, from time to time, on some aspect of the math or statistics they are viewing.

- When the class receives information as a group—background information for a story, Web sites, client information for a campaign—an instructor can encourage students to view the math skeptically.

One problem persists, however: Most communication instructors are not trained to teach mathematics. But as Maier (2002) pointed out, the learning goals for communication students do not approach higher math. This content is largely middle school math, with some elementary statistics along the way. Faculty members are used to getting help from colleagues with greater expertise in theoretical or methodological areas, and the dynamic should apply here as well. Most communication faculties are blessed with at least a few colleagues who did quantitative dissertations and who still do quantitative research, so the expertise should not be difficult to locate. (Still, however, there will be moments when a communication instructor with little math confidence will have no choice but to address math instruction head-on. For a few teaching and text suggestions, please see Appendixes B and C.)

CONCLUSION

As the least "familiar" of the competencies normally considered for the assessment of communication education, mathematics and statistics may present the greatest challenge. The challenge may become less daunting, however, if educators develop a set of math-learning goals that are most germane to their units' overall learning priorities. This chapter has proposed nine learning goals that, to many educators, seem basic to all the subdisciplines in communication. But each unit must decide for itself what kind of math competency to assess. For example, if a unit's media program is especially vigorous in the area of editing, page layout, and design, faculty could devise measures to assess students' ability to crop and size images (using their skills in ratio and proportion). If an advertising program devotes much of its curriculum to consumer research and marketing strategy, faculty could devise measures to focus on students' understanding of survey research. The overriding goal of assessment, after all, is to enable educators to decide what it is they want their students to learn, and then to discover whether those students are in fact learning those skills.

REFERENCES

Accrediting Council on Education in Journalism and Mass Communications. (2004). *Journalism and mass communications accreditation: 2004–2005.* Lawrence, KS: Author.
Baker, S., & Martinson, D. (2001). The TARES Test five principles of ethical persuasion. *Journal of Mass Media Ethics, 16,* 148–175.
Bush, W. W., & Greer, A. S. (1999). *Mathematics assessment: A practical handbook.* Reston, VA: National Council of Teachers of Mathematics.
Cumming, J., & Gal, I. (2002). Assessment in adult numeracy education: Issues and principles for good practice. In I. Gal (Ed.), *Adult numeracy development: Theory, research, practice* (pp. 305–333). Cresskill, NJ: Hampton.
Eastman, S. T. (1994). Exit examinations for the media major. In W. G. Christ (Ed.), *Assessing communication education* (pp. 351–382). Hillsdale, NJ: Lawrence Erlbaum Associates, Inc.
Maier, S. R. (2002). Numbers in the news: A mathematics audit of a daily newspaper. *Journalism Studies, 3,* 507–519.
Orrill, R., & French, V. (2002). *Mathematics Framework for the 2003 National Assessment of Educational Progress.* Washington, DC: U.S. Government Printing Office.
Pike, G. R. (2000). Assessment measures; the major field tests. *Assessment Update, 12,* 12.
Scanlan, C. (1999). *Reporting and writing: Basics for the 21st century.* New York: Oxford University Press.
Wilcox, S. K., & Lanier, P. E. (2000). *Using assessment to reshape mathematics teaching: A casebook for teachers and teacher educators, curriculum and staff development specialists.* Mahwah, NJ: Lawrence Erlbaum Associates, Inc.

APPENDIX A

Suggested Math and Statistics Competencies to Assess

Arithmetic Computation

- Use a calculator to add, subtract, multiply, and divide.

- Recognize appropriate mathematical procedure needed to answer relevant question.
- Round off numbers; understand consequences of computing with numbers that have been rounded off.
- Adjust for inflation.

Measurement

- Compute and compare sizes: length, area, volume, and so forth.
- Convert a measurement to other units of measurement.

Mathematical Terminology

- "Percent" versus "Percentage points."
- Simple versus compound interest.
- "Odds" versus "Probability."

Ratio, Proportion, Percentage

- Given two values, compute percentage.
- Given changes over time, compute percentage change.
- Given percentage change, compute "old" value or "new" value.

Estimation

- Estimate or roughly compare large quantities "in your head" (without calculator).
- Recognize and mathematically investigate implausible claims.

Elementary Statistics

- Understand and interpret margin of error.
- Understand randomness in survey research.
- Distinguish "sample" from "population."
- Understand relation of sample size to margin of error.
- Understand basic theories of probability.
- Understand correlation.
- Distinguish correlation from causation.

Central Tendency

- Compute mean, median, and mode.
- Understand and apply standard deviation.

Translation

- Explain mathematical relations with clarity and accuracy.
- Recognize appropriate degree of numerical precision.
- Recognize appropriate balance between verbiage and numbers.
- Recognize when changes or differences are significant (and worthy of audiences' attention).

Graphics

- Recognize when a graphic would supplement text effectively.
- Suggest or construct appropriate baseline for a graph or chart.
- Given a set of data, recognize whether pie, bar, or line graphic is most appropriate.

APPENDIX B

Tips for Teaching Math in the Nonmath Classroom

From the author's own experience (aided by team-teaching with mathematics faculty) as a journalism instructor teaching journalism students, here are a few suggestions:

- Logic trumps formula—Many of us learned math thinking there is only one correct way to solve a math problem, usually using a formula or algorithm. Today's students are resourceful in finding several different paths to a correct solution. Celebrate the diversity, and accept their logic gratefully.
- Let the students teach each other—Students have a shared math lexicon that older instructors may not have. There is usually at least one student in every class—even a class of journalism students—who cannot be stumped, mathematically. Give him or her the floor.
- Leave no student behind—If two thirds of the class seem to "get it," do not plunge ahead to the next math topic. Let the two thirds who get it work with the one third until everyone's confidence is high.

- Control the remote—If students are working in teams in a computer lab on a math or statistics exercise, especially using spreadsheet software, make sure the math-challenged students control the mouse; otherwise, the whizzes will leave the others in their virtual dust.

- Start simple—If the procedure or concept is complex, start from a simple, commonly shared mathematical base—and build from there.

APPENDIX C

Helpful Resources for Communicators Doing Math

Brooks, B. S., Kennedy, G., Moen, D., & Ranly, D. (2001). *News reporting and writing* (7th ed.). Boston: Bedford/St. Martin's Press. (see chapters 4 & 5)

Cohn, V., & Cope, L. (2001). *News & numbers; a guide to reporting statistical claims and controversies in health and other fields* (2nd ed.). Ames: Iowa State Press.

Houston, B. (1999). *Computer-assisted reporting: A practical guide* (2nd ed.). Boston: Bedford/St. Martin's Press.

Huff, D. (reissued 1993). *How to lie with statistics.* Portland, OR: New Books Inc.

Lerner, M. (1998). *Math smart: Essential math for these numeric times.* New York: Random House.

Livingston, C., & Voakes, P. (2005). *Working with numbers and statistics: A handbook for journalists.* Mahwah, NJ: Lawrence Erlbaum Associates, Inc.

Mencher, M. (2002). *News reporting and writing* (9th ed.). Boston: McGraw-Hill.

Meyer, P. (2002). *Precision journalism: A reporter's introduction to social science methods* (4th ed.). Lanham, MD: Rowman & Littlefield.

Paulos, J. A. (1996). *A mathematician reads the newspaper.* New York: Anchor.

Paulos, J. A. (1999). *Once upon a number: The hidden mathematical logic of stories.* New York: Perseus Books Group.

Paulos, J. A. (2001). *Innumeracy: Mathematical illiteracy and its consequences.* New York: Hill & Wang.

Rich, C. (2003). *Writing and reporting news: A coaching method* (4th ed.). Belmont, CA: Wadsworth. (see chapters 21 & 25)

Scanlan, C. (1999). *Reporting and writing: Basics for the 21st century.* New York: Oxford University Press.

Weaver, J. H. (1997). *Conquering statistics: Numbers without the crunch.* New York: Plenum.

Wickham, K. W. (2002). *Math tools for journalists.* Chicago: Marion Street Press.

14

Public Relations

Dean Kruckeberg
Department of Communication Studies
University of Northern Iowa

It is unlikely that Harvard had considered formal "outcomes assessment" for its first class of nine students in 1640, and nowhere is it recorded that this oldest U.S. institution of higher education ever offered a public relations curriculum. However, for many of today's nearly 4,200 degree-granting institutions in the United States—with their nearly 16 million students (Snyder, Tan, & Hoffman, 2004)—formalized "outcomes assessment" has become an overriding concern. Moreover, hundreds of educators at scores of these institutions continue to deliberate how to assess educational "outcomes" to evaluate their students who are studying public relations.

Calls for "outcomes assessment" are particularly problematic for public relations educators, who have represented an amorphous and ill-defined, quasi-professional field that was being taught in a range of university and college departments by faculty oftentimes having amazingly diverse academic and professional backgrounds as well as considerably different pedagogical and professional perspectives.

Grunig and Hunt (1984) have identified four models of public relations, which they consider evolutionary, but each of which is predominantly practiced by a portion of contemporary professionals; furthermore, any of the models may be emphasized, at least in derivative form, among the range of public relations faculty in the nation's colleges and universities.

First, the "press agentry/publicity" model that evolved from about 1850 to 1900 is promotional in its orientation and grew out of historic "public relations-like" activities. Second, "public-information" was the major model from about 1900 to the 1920s, with its practitioners likened to newspeople-in-residence; that model was followed by a third "two-way asymmetric" model—persuasive in intent and based on scientific behaviorism.

During the 1960s and 1970s emerged the fourth model, that is, "two-way symmetric" practice that stresses balanced and mutually beneficial communication between an organization and its publics. Although this last model, or its primary use in a "mixed-motive" model (Grunig & White, 1992), is considered superlative by many educators and practitioners, realistically all the models and their strategies, tactics and techniques should be taught; certainly, the "two-way symmetric" model is by no means being universally advocated today, and it is not necessarily being primarily taught by contemporary public relations educators.

Furthermore, public relations education programs still differ somewhat according to the disciplinary orientation of the academic units in which they are being housed as well as according to the scholarly backgrounds of the faculty teaching the public relations courses. Journalism schools were historically the almost exclusive bastion of public relations education, where the latter was frequently unappreciated and denigrated; however, communication departments in the 1970s and 1980s began offering public relations education programs when some units began losing their service role within their institutions and as they recognized their students' employment potential in public relations.

Although early journalism sequences were oftentimes accused of being excessively vocational, that is, in overemphasizing journalistic skills and (especially print) media production courses, the speech-oriented communication departments were frequently charged with attempting to redefine public relations and with making their curricula overly theoretical—failing to appreciate, and thereby omitting—sufficient journalistic skills training that was demanded by potential employers. (Of course, public relations coursework also has been taught in academic units other than in journalism and speech communication, for example, in business administration programs.) Still another issue being discussed, especially the past decade, has been the blending of the public relations, advertising and marketing functions into "integrated marketing communications." Indeed, several leading programs have integrated their public relations and advertising education. (A description of this movement and its rationale is in Duncan, Caywood, & Newsom, 1993.)

Compounding such complexities and vagaries about public relations education and the assessment of its students are issues that have emerged within journalism education throughout the years that can impact public relations education—as may fundamental issues being deliberated throughout the academy-at-large. Blanchard and Christ (1993) vehemently and credibly called for a "new professionalism" in media education, that is, a cross-media, liberal, integrative program consistent with broader undergraduate reform efforts. These scholars said such reform would reduce "excessive structure and overprescription of training in currently fashionable technique, ephemeral information and obsolescent technology..." (pp. 70–71). Some manifestations of this recommendation are evident today, for example, a continuing interest in "convergence" of media and the academy's attempt to prepare students accordingly.

The Curriculum Task Force of the Association for Education in Journalism and Mass Communication (AEJMC Curriculum Task Force, 1996) had recommended demotion of the association's media-specific (including public relations) divisions to the level of interest groups and called for "creativity and experimentation" in journalism and mass communication curricula. (Whether such "creativity and experimentation" have occurred may be debated, but the divisional structure of AEJMC has remained—including its thriving Public Relations Division.)

Furthermore, there was increasing dissatisfaction with—and a successful effort to revise—*The Design for Undergraduate Public Relations Education* (Commission on Undergraduate Public Relations Education, 1987), which had been prepared by the Commission on Undergraduate Public Relations Education. That Commission was established by the Public Relations Division of the AEJMC and the Public Relations Society of America (PRSA) Educators Section. Indeed, a new Commission was formed in 1997—with an expanded representation of eight scholarly and practitioner organizations: PRSA and its Educators Academy (formerly Educators Section), the Institute for Public Relations, National Communication Association, AEJMC, Association for Women in Communications, International Association of Business Communicators, International Communication Association, and the International Public Relations Association.

Its report was released in October 1999, and the Commission's recommendations have earned much global attention and acceptance. The Commission continues to be active (meeting at least three times a year, with its leadership and membership being continuously active), and its ongoing discussions and decisions have given considerable priority to public relations outcomes assessment—a topic that it has been actively researching the past several years. After its curriculum recommendations were published in October 1999, the Commission began exploring a universal "outcomes assessment" instrument, that is, an examination that students would take at the end of their college education that would be somewhat analogous to a Certified Public Accountant Examination or a Bar Examination. Several advantages and benefits became obvious to having a standardized examination based on the curriculum and body of knowledge recommendations of the Commission in its October 1999 report: (a) the universal "outcomes assessment" examination would encourage public relations education programs to teach the curriculum that was presented and the body of knowledge that was identified in the Commission report and would help to define and place parameters around contemporary public relations and its education; (b) students' successful scores on the examination could be rewarded with a pre-accredited status in such organizations as PRSA, giving graduates an immediate credential before being eligible in 5 years to take the universal accreditation examination used by PRSA and some other professional associations, for example, a "Foundations in Public Relations" (FPR) credential immediately after students' graduation would attest to their entry-level professional proficiency until the graduate was eligible to take the universal accreditation examination for their "Accredited in Public Relations" (APR) credential, which would also encourage students to join professional associations such as PRSA on graduation; and, of course, (c) such an examination would help satisfy educators' institutions' requirement for outcomes assessment while retaining "professional" control of this assessment before others outside public relations education could attempt to provide their own assessment criteria, for example, before journalism or speech communication educators or their professional associations could co-opt public relations education into their own assessment criteria.

Demonstration of tactical and technical skills proficiency was problematic in such an examination, and indeed several pools of examination questions and drafts of instruments could not achieve consensus in the Commission. Rather, the Commission plans to survey public relations educators and to otherwise continually monitor their methods of performing outcomes assessment to measure their students' knowledge and skills that were identified in the Commission report. Attempts will also be made to collect from these educators any materials that they use as a part of their students' outcomes assessment. Thus, the Commission's role in outcomes assessment will be descriptive of methods used nationwide, rather than prescriptive.

Finally, public relations is being taught in a contemporary academic environment in which scholars representing many disciplines continue to argue the relative merits of everything from postmodernism and critical theory to a host of related topics and issues that have the potential to impact all college and university curricula. Although Tierney (1993) said such topics were being debated primarily within the humanities and liberal arts and—to a lesser extent—within the social sciences, such issues by all means have impacted public relations scholarship and education just as they have other disciplines and professional specializations in the academy.

All of these factors and considerations may be enough to clinically depress the strongest of public relations educators who may wonder if they can adequately determine what to measure before they can resolve how to measure it, that is, can they define what is public relations so they can determine how to measure their success in educating students to prepare for such a career?

Although public relations education may first appear to be an academic "demilitarized zone," such perception of academic anarchy would be incorrect! Good public relations education is being provided in a large number of colleges and universities throughout this country by many highly competent public relations educators, and this excellence can be measured through valid and reliable student outcomes assessment. Furthermore, in reality, there is considerable consensus among educators and practitioners about what constitutes good public relations education.

CURRICULAR PARAMETERS

Right or wrong, good or bad, specific curricular parameters are dictated or recommended by such bodies as the Accrediting Council on Education in Journalism and Mass Communications (ACEJMC).[1] Furthermore, there is considerable consistency in the selection and adoption of textbooks by public relations educators, despite these educators' varying

[1]For an excellent reference, see the Accrediting Council on Education in Journalism and Mass Communications (ACEJMC) Online Information Center "quick links" at http://www.ku.edu/~acejmc/LINKS/LINKS.SHTML, from which a PDF file, "A Guide to Assessment of Student Learning in Journalism and Mass Communications," can be downloaded (ACEJMC, n.d.); see also the by-and-large compatible "Certified in Education for Public Relations" (CEPR) program of the Public Relations Society of America (PRSA), which certification may be attainable, not only by ACEJMC-accredited schools, but also by academic units that are not eligible for accreditation by ACEJMC and for which 16 programs have qualified (PRSA, n.d.); (For information about the CEPR program, contact the Public Relations Student Society of America [PRSSA] at PRSA headquarters, 33 Maiden Lane, 11th Floor, New York, NY 10038-5150, or go to http://www.prsa.org/_About/overview/certification_info.asp?ident=over5); and criteria also exist to charter college and university chapters of the Public Relations Student Society of America, of which there are 262 chapters (contact PRSSA at the PRSA headquarters, or download a PDF file of the PRSSA Chapter Application Form at http:/
/www.prssa.org/about/establish.asp; Public Relations Student Society of America, n.d.); and the International Association of Business Communicators (IABC; International Association of Business Communicators, n.d.); (For information about student chapters of IABC, of which there are 31 chapters, with 26 in the United States, two in Hong Kong, and one each

unit affiliation within their colleges and universities. Indeed, much progress also has been made in reconciling programmatic differences, in great part because of the report of the Commission on Public Relations Education (1999, October), as well as because of the active involvement the past three decades of a large number of public relations educators in a range of scholarly associations representing both journalism and speech communication as well as their participation in practitioner-based organizations. It is common for public relations educators to be active in most, if not all, of such organizations as the AEJMC, National Communication Association, International Communication Association, Public Relations Society of America, International Association of Business Communicators, International Public Relations Association, and various regional and interdisciplinary associations, for example, the International Association of Business Disciplines. Furthermore, in 2001 and 2002, at the international conferences of the Public Relations Society of America, there have been "Public Relations Summits" of members of the Commission on Public Relations Education and representatives of a still wider range of public relations organizations, for example, the Council of Public Relations Firms, that may help facilitate communication and policymaking related to public relations education.

Finally, as a generalization, journalism faculty have become far more accepting and appreciative of speech communication faculty's contributions to public relations education and scholarship, whereas communication faculty have been more cognizant (or at least more pragmatic) about the continued need for journalism skills courses in mass communication.

Special Considerations Determine "Outcomes"

In considering appropriate outcomes assessment measurements and methodologies, some special considerations must be made for public relations education. First, the responsibility of public relations educators is to prepare students for careers in professional public relations practice. Students wanting to use the degree as a preparation for other pro-

---

in Australia and the Caribbean and Northern Ireland, contact IABC, One Hallidie Plaza, Suite 600, San Francisco, CA 94102, or go to the student Web site at http://www.iabc.com/student/). The National Communication Association has a range of assessment resources and an article, "Assessment: Coming of Age," by Morreale and Backlund (n.d.) at http://www.natcom.org/Instruction/assessment/Assessment/article99.htm. The most definitive resource for curricular recommendations is by the Commission on Public Relations Education; a copy of the October 1999 report is available from PRSA, or it can be viewed online at sources including http://www.prsa.org/_resources/resources/pre21.asp and http://lamar.colostate.edu/~aejmcpr/commissionreport99.htm.

fessional education or occupations, ranging from law school to real-estate brokerage to retail management, or—for that matter—for careers as journalists, may have found a comprehensive major that is helpful to those pursuing such nonpublic relations career goals; however, it is not the responsibility of public relations educators to prepare students for these careers lest public relations becomes a watered-down, generic, "general studies" degree.

And, although public relations educators should applaud and strongly support contemporary efforts to enrich students' education in the liberal arts, from a professional perspective this support should be primarily because such liberal arts education ensures higher-quality public relations graduates. Public relations educators have primary responsibility for—and thus should maintain primary allegiance to—the best possible education preparing students to become public relations practitioners. These educators have a vested interest in assuring that their students are exposed to the widest and best possible liberal arts education as well as the greatest infusion of the liberal arts into the "professional" components of public relations education.

It also is important that public relations education is not seen as analogous to specialized "sequenced" education in journalism, for example, newspaper journalism, magazine journalism, photo-journalism, broadcast and electronic media journalism, or related media specializations serving specific "media" industries; there is not a public relations "industry" in the sense that there is a newspaper industry, magazine industry, broadcast industry, and so forth, which hire graduates as "line" employees. This understanding is especially important as some programs attempt "media convergence" and consider public relations to be no more than a traditional media specialization.

Importantly, public relations is an organizational "staff" function in a range of virtually all businesses and industries. Granted, public relations agencies hire graduates as "line" employees within their firms, but such agencies' personnel serve as external "staff" to other organizations that are their clients. Thus, public relations must be recognized as a staff function within a range of all types of organizations, rather than as a line function within a specific "media" industry. This distinction suggests a functional approach to public relations education, that is, practitioners should be able to know and to do many career tasks and not be prepared for only one specific job. Given this distinction, "outcomes assessment" that may be appropriate for students preparing for careers within specific media industries (or in converged media)—taught typically in the same academic units where public relations instruction is based—most often will be misapplied in public relations education. Blanchard and Christ (1993), in their book, *Media Education and the Liberal Arts: A*

Blueprint for the New Professionalism, make a telling remark about business schools: "Business schools long ago eliminated industry-specific approaches, replacing them with generic cross-industry subjects such as accounting, management, finance, and marketing" (p. 70).

Public relations education is more appropriately grouped with business schools' "generic cross-industry subjects" cited by the authors, for example, accounting, management, finance, and marketing, than according to "lines," for example, newspaper journalists, in media-specific industries. Therefore, public relations educators should applaud contemporary efforts to defocus media-centric education and should applaud such programs' education preparing journalism students for media "convergence." Those of us who had earned our print journalism-oriented baccalaureate degrees a third of a century ago or longer recall entry-level public relations responsibilities performing media relations for all types of media, including writing broadcast media releases, writing scripts for slide shows, writing speeches, and supervising film-strip production, as well as performing the print-oriented public relations tasks for which we were educated; today's graduates, of course, will be developing organizations' Web sites and producing video news releases, and must be proficient in a range of media applications that are far more extensive than traditional print journalism and require much broader knowledge and skills.

Case Study: Early Outcomes Assessment Effort

Without question, many journalism and speech communication programs in colleges and universities throughout the nation have developed excellent "outcomes assessment" procedures and methodologies, although problematic is the question whether their criteria are most appropriate for public relations education programs. The case study that follows is for a discrete public relations major, that is, not a sequence or emphasis, and is an early effort to develop "outcomes assessment" measurements for this major.

The University of Northern Iowa is a "comprehensive" university that has a "normal school" tradition. Its Department of Communication Studies has a tradition in speech communication—although it is a comprehensive department that offers baccalaureate degrees in a range of communication majors, as well as electronic media and public relations and a minor in print journalism. It also has several "model programs"—including public relations—for students earning their master of arts degrees in communication. The department is not ACEJMC-accredited, and the public relations degree program is not part of the Certified in Education for Public Relations (CEPR) program, although the latter has been under strong consideration and undoubtedly will be pursued in the future. However, the program fulfills the criteria for and has a chapter of the Public Relations Student Society of America.

The department's communication-public relations major was approved during the academic year 1977 to 1978, and the major began with 12 students in the following fall of 1978. It is by far the largest undergraduate major in the department, and the number of the program's baccalaureate degree holders now approaches 2,000 graduates. These former students work in a wide range of career positions throughout the United States and elsewhere in the world.

The public relations curriculum, although historically quite stable, has been refined throughout the years during the university's 2-year curriculum cycles. This interdisciplinary major includes business courses (economics, marketing, consumer behavior, organizational management, accounting), journalism courses (mass communication and society, reporting methodologies and sources, news writing for print media, editing and design, mass communication law and ethics), communication courses (interpersonal or business and professional oral, organizational, communication theories, communication research methods), and public relations (principles, public relations writing [that includes electronic media writing], public relations methods, integrated communications or global public relations, public relations cases and studies, internship and cooperative education or public relations management).

Alumni of the Public Relations Degree Program report that entry-level job success has often been contingent on the range of knowledge and skills they possess. For example, journalism schools and many communication departments do not require business courses in their curricula; such a foundation in business, coupled with journalism courses and an applied and theoretical background in communication, in addition to a comprehensive range of public relations courses, makes these graduates highly versatile in their preparation for many different types of public relations-related positions in a wide variety of industries.

As with all the department's majors and minors, the public relations major is under an enrollment management policy. Students are prospective majors until they complete 24 hr of university coursework with at least a 2.7 grade point average (GPA), complete college writing and oral communication courses, and complete with at least a combined 2.7 GPA in the major component courses of mass communication and society and principles of public relations. Students must achieve a C or better in each major course.

Although such admission criteria may seem elitist, failure to meet such standards that help to assure students' basic preparation and potential success before acceptance into the program can be viewed as exploitative of students who must face a rigorous curriculum to adequately prepare for the highly competitive public relations job market.

When asked to design a "student outcomes assessment" program for the communication-public relations major, faculty reacted with bemused puzzlement, followed by consternation and finally by apprehension—appreciating the truth of what Erwin (1991) has warned:

> To ignore calls for evaluation is to allow other groups to choose methods of assessment, which are sure to influence educational goals. Besides the new accrediting requirements regarding assessment, both public and private institutions should pay heed to discussions about a proposed national standardized testing program. If a nationwide program is implemented, it is unlikely that the diversities in our institutions will be retained.... (I)f professionals refrain from contributing, then nonprofessionals will go about evaluation unaided. (p. 7)

Other warnings prompted equal alarm, such as Christ and Blanchard's (1994) admonition that, if communication education programs appear to university committees to be fragmented, peripheral, or nonessential to a university's overall mission, they are more susceptible to being downsized or eliminated.

Liberal arts education is required or recommended by all bodies germane to public relations education. (For example, see the ACEJMC Standards of Accreditation, 2003, which are available at http://www.ku. edu/~acejmc/PROGRAMS/STANDARDS.SHTML. The new standards went into effect in September 2004 and will be applied in accreditation reviews beginning with the 2005–2006 academic year.) The International Public Relations Association used concentric circles to illustrate a recommended public relations curriculum; the "largest circle represents the general liberal arts and humanities background that is essential preparation for a successful professional" (International Public Relations Association, 1990, p. 2).

The report of the Commission on Public Relations Education (1999), *Public Relations for the 21st Century: A Port of Entry,* "recommends that the undergraduate public relations curriculum be grounded in a strong traditional liberal arts and social science education" (p. 4). Indeed, it "strongly encourages a minor or double major in the liberal arts, social sciences or business" (p. 4). Appendix A that follows this chapter cites necessary knowledge and skills that the commission identifies in its report.

Such overall emphasis on liberal arts education is hardly misplaced. Public relations practitioners are expected to know a wide breadth of general knowledge, have in-depth knowledge of their professional specialization and subspecializations, and be highly knowledgeable about the particular industries in which they work.

Anecdotal evidence supports a powerful correlation between successful, high-ranking public relations practitioners and their extensive knowledge that ranges from current events and history to economics and government policies.

Despite the importance of liberal arts to students' undergraduate education, faculty in the program were at a loss how to measure it for student outcomes assessment. In addition to a 47-hr general education curriculum (in 2004 renamed "Liberal Arts Core" and requiring 45 semester hours), students also may take a range of minors and second majors. Furthermore, there is a strong liberal arts component to students' required courses within the public relations curriculum. Likewise, in this multidisciplinary major, it would be difficult to determine how to overtly measure coursework in business—save for such knowledge evident from students' preparation of campaign proposals, and so forth. That is, at a rudimentary level, accounting expertise would be evident in a budget proposal, for example, as would be a basic understanding of management theory and practice. (However, certainly at the collegiate level, it was recognized that such assessment would be possible—as it is through the Graduate Record Exam, Graduate Management Admission Test, and Law School Admission Test testing, as examples.)

Also, successful students not only obtain an extensive breadth of general knowledge through their liberal arts education and general electives, but usually through their second major, minor, or area of concentration. In addition, they may use such education to learn intensive knowledge about a specific industry or other business. Such esoteric knowledge would be difficult to measure through student outcomes assessment because of its individualized nature among the students.

Thus, somewhat by default, student outcomes assessment procedures were focused primarily on the "professional" component of the public relations major. Taken into account was the spirit, if not the specific criteria, of accrediting and certifying agencies. However, as noted earlier, the program is in an academic unit that is not ACEJMC-accredited, and the public relations major is not CEPR-certified, although the program has a Public Relations Student Society of America chapter and is accountable under the "five-course" ruling to maintain such a chapter.

Particular attention was paid to the mission statements of the program, department, college, and university. And certainly, the resultant "outcomes assessments" reflected the professional biases of the faculty as well as consideration of alumni's experiences and students' perceived needs.

This has become truly a "living" document and will be subject to continual revision. The first document has identified eight outcomes (see Appendix B), each with specific "competencies" students should have achieved by their time of graduation. Also, taken into primary consideration were the missions and ongoing strategic plans at the university, department, and the communication-public relations undergraduate major levels; the latter mission is as follows: ". . . 1) to prepare students, within a liberal arts context, for positions in public relations within organizations and professional agencies; and 2) to prepare students for graduate study by providing them with foundations in mass communication theory, methodology and related skills and knowledge" (Kruckeberg, 1989, p. 2).

Operationalizing Measurements Is the Challenge

Of course, operationalizing, that is, providing measurements for these outcomes and competencies, has been the real challenge. Obviously, a longitudinal study is called for, as well as constant monitoring of students throughout their undergraduate careers. Assessment remains ongoing and on a virtual continuum, with the continuum beginning when students enter the major, proceeding throughout their undergraduate careers up to the time of graduation, and then periodically throughout their professional careers.

The student outcomes assessment plan relies heavily on students' portfolios. Students are formally counseled in the principles of public relations class about how to begin building their portfolios. Students are encouraged throughout their careers to continue to build their portfolios, with evidence of work from internships and cooperative education experiences, relevant summer and part-time employment, as well as work in the Public Relations Student Society of America and the student-run public relations firm.

Immediately preceding graduation, students in the program historically have been assessed by professional public relations practitioners in the capstone class, Public Relations: Cases and Studies.

Historically, an orally presented final case study is evaluated by professional public relations practitioners as well as by peers and instructors, and professionals and students who attend these final presentations also examine and evaluate students' resumes and portfolios. Although students keep their portfolios (and are encouraged to keep them updated throughout their professional careers), evaluation forms of their work were designed to provide an "audit trail."

Traditionally, careers of the program's graduates have been assessed during the 5-year department program review, during interim periods through surveys, and as well as informally through content analysis of graduates' correspondence and conversations with faculty.

Changes undoubtedly will occur in this student outcomes assessment program as public relations faculty become more sophisticated in the usage of student outcomes assessment and as accrediting body and university requirements change; indeed, the report of the Commission on Public Relations Education (1999) already has suggested the need for revisions and changes to the existing outcomes assessment criteria. However, our research has shown substantive agreement with the final product among all responsible parties; we have achieved overall consensus and have developed an "outcomes assessment" plan based on this consensus.

Student outcomes assessment is a mandate, but such evaluation also has proven to be an opportunity to better measure the educational accomplishments of students as well as a means for program improvement.

What "outcomes assessment" will do for public relations education is what it undoubtedly was intended to do for educational institutions and programs in general. Within a "professional" community of public relations educators and practitioners, immediate deliberation must continue to better determine what is public relations, what are appropriate definitional parameters, what knowledge and skills practitioners must have and what are suitable, that is, valid and reliable, measurements to determine whether a student is learning such knowledge and skills.

Public relations educators collectively and together with public relations practitioners must continue a dialogue about outcomes for public relations students and how to assess such outcomes. It is certainly true that, if we don't do this collectively and with solidarity, others may do it for us.

REFERENCES

Accrediting Council on Education in Journalism and Mass Communications. (n.d.). *ACEJMC accrediting standards.* Retrieved July 11, 2005, from http://www.ku.edu/~acejmc/PROGRAM/STANDARDS.SHTML

Accrediting Council on Education in Journalism and Mass Communications. (n.d.). *A guide to assessment of student learning in journalism and mass communications.* Retrieved July 11, 2005, from http://www.ku.edu/~acejmc/LINKS/LINKS.SHTML

Association for Education in Journalism and Mass Communication Curriculum Task Force. (1996). Responding to the challenge of change. *Journalism and Mass Communication Educator, 50,* 101–119.

Blanchard, R. O., & Christ, W. G. (1993). *Media education and the liberal arts: A blueprint for the new professionalism.* Hillsdale, NJ: Lawrence Erlbaum Associates, Inc.

Christ, W. G., & Blanchard, R. O. (1994). Mission statements, outcomes, and the new liberal arts. In W. G. Christ (Ed.), *Assessing communication education: A handbook for media, speech, and theatre educators* (pp. 31–55). Hillsdale, NJ: Lawrence Erlbaum Associates, Inc.

Commission on Public Relations Education. (1999). *Public relations for the 21st century: A port of entry.* New York: Public Relations Society of America.

Commission on Undergraduate Public Relations Education. (1987). *Design for undergraduate public relations education.* New York: Public Relations Society of America.

Duncan, T., Caywood, C., & Newsom, D. (1993). *Preparing advertising and public relations students for the communication industry in the 21st century: Report of the Task Force on Integrated Communications.* Columbia, SC: Association for Education in Journalism and Mass Communication.

Erwin, T. D. (1991). *Assessing student learning and development: A guide to the principles, goals, and methods of determining college outcomes.* San Francisco: Jossey-Bass.

Grunig, J. E., & Hunt, T. (1984). *Managing public relations.* New York: Holt, Rinehart & Winston.

Grunig, J. E., & White, R. (1992). The effect of worldviews on public relations theory and practice. In J. E. Grunig (Ed.), *Excellence in public relations and communication management* (pp. 31–64). Hillsdale, NJ: Lawrence Erlbaum Associates, Inc.

International Association of Business Communicators. (n.d.). *Student connection.* Retrieved July 11, 2005, from http://www.iabc.com/student

International Public Relations Association. (1990). *Public relations education—Recommendations and standards: Gold Paper No. 7.* Geneva, Switzerland: International Public Relations Association.

Kruckeberg, D. (1989). *Public relations degree program: 1988–89 annual report.* Cedar Falls, IA: University of Northern Iowa Department of Communication and Theatre Arts.

Kruckeberg, D. (Ed.). (1991). *Assessment plan—Communication/public relations.* Cedar Falls, IA: University of Northern Iowa Department of Communication and Theatre Arts.

Morreale, S. P., & Backlund, P. S. (n.d.). *Assessment: Coming of age.* Retrieved July 11, 2005, from http://www.natcom.org/Instruction/assessment/Assessment/article99.htm

Public Relations Society of America. (n.d.). *PRSA certification.* Retrieved July 11, 2005, from http://www.prsa.org/_About/overview/certification_info.asp?ident=over5

Public Relations Student Society of America. (n.d.). *Establish a new chapter.* Retrieved July 11, 2005, from http://www.prssa.org/about/establish.asp

Snyder, T. D., Tan, A. G., & Hoffman, C. M. (2004). *Digest of education statistics 2003* (NCES 2005-025) (pp. 213–214). U.S. Department of Education, National Center for Education Statistics. Washington, DC: Government Printing Office.

Tierney, W. G. (1993). *Building communities of difference: Higher education in the twenty-first century.* Westport, CT: Bergin & Garvey.

APPENDIX A

Necessary Knowledge and Skills as Identified by the Commission on Public Relations Education (1999, pp. 2–3, 19–20)

The Commission recommends that students graduating with undergraduate degrees possess both knowledge (what graduates should know and understand) and skills (areas of competence necessary to enter the profession).

Necessary knowledge includes: communication and persuasion concepts and strategies; communication and public relations theories; relationships and relationship building; societal trends; ethical issues; legal requirements and issues; marketing and finance; public relations history; uses of research and forecasting; multicultural and global issues; organizational change and development; management concepts and theories.

Necessary skills includes: research methods and analysis; management of information; mastery of language in written and oral communication; problem solving and negotiation; management of communication; strategic planning; issues management; audience segmentation; informative and persuasive writing; community relations, consumer relations, employee relations, other practice areas; technological and visual literacy; managing people, programs and resources; sensitive interpersonal communication; fluency in a foreign language; ethical decision-making; participation in the professional public relations community; message production; working with a current issue; public speaking and presentation; applying cross-cultural and cross-gender sensitivity.

APPENDIX B

Assessment Plan—Communication/Public Relations

Outcomes (Kruckeberg, 1991, pp. 1–5) and Commission on Public Relations Education (1999) criteria they satisfy or partially satisfy (pp. 1–2)

Outcome 1—Students will have a thorough understanding of: communication, including mass communication; such communication's role in society and in mass culture—both past and present, with insights into the future; and the role and uses of the mass media—both print and broadcast; as well as the uses of a range of specialized communication applications, including advertising, marketing and related areas. This understanding will include international and intercultural perspectives.

Satisfies or Partially Satisfies Commission-recommended knowledge (italicized):

- *communication and persuasion concepts and strategies*
- *communication and public relations theories*
- *relationships and relationship building*
- *societal trends*
- *ethical issues*
- *legal requirements and issues*

- *marketing and finance*
- *public relations history*
- *uses of research and forecasting*
- *multicultural and global issues*
- organizational change and development
- management concepts and theories

Satisfies or Partially Satisfies Commission-recommended skills (italicized):

- research methods and analysis
- management of information
- mastery of language in written and oral communication
- problem solving and negotiation
- management of communication
- strategic planning
- issues management
- *audience segmentation*
- informative and persuasive writing
- community relations, consumer relations, employee relations, other practice areas
- *technological and visual literacy*
- managing people, programs and resources
- *sensitive interpersonal communication*
- fluency in a foreign language
- ethical decision-making
- participation in the professional public relations community
- message production
- working with a current issue
- public speaking and presentation
- applying cross-cultural and cross-gender sensitivity

Outcome 2—Students will have a thorough understanding of: professionally accepted public relations fundamentals; the vocabulary of public relations and related areas and public relations perspectives as these perspectives impact upon society; and the role of public relations in contemporary world society.

Satisfies or Partially Satisfies Commission-recommended knowledge (italicized):

- *communication and persuasion concepts and strategies*
- *communication and public relations theories*
- *relationships and relationship building*
- *societal trends*
- *ethical issues*
- *legal requirements and issues*
- marketing and finance
- public relations history
- *uses of research and forecasting*
- *multicultural and global issues*
- *organizational change and development*
- management concepts and theories

Satisfies or Partially Satisfies Commission-recommended skills (italicized):

- *research methods and analysis*
- *management of information*
- mastery of language in written and oral communication
- problem solving and negotiation
- *management of communication*
- *strategic planning*
- *issues management*
- *audience segmentation*
- informative and persuasive writing
- *community relations, consumer relations, employee relations, other practice areas*
- technological and visual literacy
- managing people, programs and resources
- sensitive interpersonal communication
- fluency in a foreign language
- *ethical decision-making*
- participation in the professional public relations community
- message production
- *working with a current issue*

- public speaking and presentation
- applying cross-cultural and cross-gender sensitivity

Outcome 3—Students will have a thorough understanding of: communication methods used by public relations practitioners and of public opinion formation and change as viewed by contemporary public relations literature and scholarship.
Satisfies or Partially Satisfies Commission-recommended knowledge (italicized):

- *communication and persuasion concepts and strategies*
- *communication and public relations theories*
- *relationships and relationship building*
- societal trends
- *ethical issues*
- *legal requirements and issues*
- marketing and finance
- public relations history
- *uses of research and forecasting*
- multicultural and global issues
- organizational change and development
- management concepts and theories

Satisfies or Partially Satisfies Commission-recommended skills (italicized):

- *research methods and analysis*
- *management of information*
- mastery of language in written and oral communication
- *problem solving and negotiation*
- *management of communication*
- *strategic planning*
- *issues management*
- *audience segmentation*
- informative and persuasive writing
- *community relations, consumer relations, employee relations, other practice areas*
- technological and visual literacy
- managing people, programs and resources

- sensitive interpersonal communication
- fluency in a foreign language
- ethical decision-making
- participation in the professional public relations community
- *message production*
- working with a current issue
- public speaking and presentation
- applying cross-cultural and cross-gender sensitivity

Outcome 4—Students will have a thorough understanding of: professional mass communication and interpersonal communication skills.

Satisfies or Partially Satisfies Commission-recommended knowledge (italicized):

- *communication and persuasion concepts and strategies*
- *communication and public relations theories*
- *relationships and relationship building*
- societal trends
- ethical issues
- legal requirements and issues
- marketing and finance
- public relations history
- uses of research and forecasting
- multicultural and global issues
- organizational change and development
- management concepts and theories

Satisfies or Partially Satisfies Commission-recommended skills (italicized):

- research methods and analysis
- management of information
- *mastery of language in written and oral communication*
- problem solving and negotiation
- *management of communication*
- *strategic planning*
- *issues management*
- *audience segmentation*

- *informative and persuasive writing*
- community relations, consumer relations, employee relations, other practice areas
- *technological and visual literacy*
- *managing people, programs and resources*
- *sensitive interpersonal communication*
- *fluency in a foreign language*
- ethical decision-making
- participation in the professional public relations community
- *message production*
- working with a current issue
- *public speaking and presentation*
- applying cross-cultural and cross-gender sensitivity

Outcome 5—Students will have a thorough understanding of: the overall synthesis of public relations concepts; ethical considerations and the appropriate resolution of ethical dilemmas; and public relations problem resolution.

Satisfies or Partially Satisfies Commission-recommended knowledge (italicized):

- *communication and persuasion concepts and strategies*
- *communication and public relations theories*
- *relationships and relationship building*
- *societal trends*
- *ethical issues*
- *legal requirements and issues*
- marketing and finance
- public relations history
- uses of research and forecasting
- *multicultural and global issues*
- organizational change and development
- management concepts and theories

Satisfies or Partially Satisfies Commission-recommended skills (italicized):

- *research methods and analysis*

- *management of information*
- mastery of language in written and oral communication
- *problem solving and negotiation*
- *management of communication*
- *strategic planning*
- *issues management*
- *audience segmentation*
- informative and persuasive writing
- *community relations, consumer relations, employee relations, other practice areas*
- technological and visual literacy
- managing people, programs and resources
- *sensitive interpersonal communication*
- fluency in a foreign language
- *ethical decision-making*
- participation in the professional public relations community
- message production
- *working with a current issue*
- public speaking and presentation
- applying cross-cultural and cross-gender sensitivity

Outcome 6—Students will have a thorough understanding of: the various theories of mass communication and interpersonal communication and of their applications for public relations.

Satisfies or Partially Satisfies Commission-recommended knowledge (italicized):

- *communication and persuasion concepts and strategies*
- *communication and public relations theories*
- relationships and relationship building
- societal trends
- ethical issues
- legal requirements and issues
- marketing and finance
- public relations history
- uses of research and forecasting
- multicultural and global issues

- organizational change and development
- management concepts and theories

Satisfies or Partially Satisfies Commission-recommended skills (italicized):

- research methods and analysis
- management of information
- mastery of language in written and oral communication
- problem solving and negotiation
- *management of communication*
- strategic planning
- issues management
- *audience segmentation*
- informative and persuasive writing
- community relations, consumer relations, employee relations, other practice areas
- technological and visual literacy
- managing people, programs and resources
- sensitive interpersonal communication
- fluency in a foreign language
- ethical decision-making
- participation in the professional public relations community
- message production
- working with a current issue
- public speaking and presentation
- applying cross-cultural and cross-gender sensitivity

Outcome 7—Students will have a thorough understanding of: appropriate communication research principles, concepts, and procedures, particularly as they can be applied in public relations planning, but also in the broader societal context.

Satisfies or Partially Satisfies Commission-recommended knowledge (italicized):

- communication and persuasion concepts and strategies
- communication and public relations theories
- relationships and relationship building

- societal trends
- ethical issues
- legal requirements and issues
- marketing and finance
- public relations history
- *uses of research and forecasting*
- multicultural and global issues
- organizational change and development
- management concepts and theories

Satisfies or Partially Satisfies Commission-recommended skills (italicized):

- *research methods and analysis*
- management of information
- mastery of language in written and oral communication
- problem solving and negotiation
- management of communication
- strategic planning
- issues management
- *audience segmentation*
- informative and persuasive writing
- community relations, consumer relations, employee relations, other practice areas
- technological and visual literacy
- managing people, programs and resources
- sensitive interpersonal communication
- fluency in a foreign language
- ethical decision-making
- participation in the professional public relations community
- message production
- working with a current issue
- public speaking and presentation
- applying cross-cultural and cross-gender sensitivity

Outcome 8—Students will have a thorough understanding of: the exigencies of the professional public relations working environment.

Satisfies or Partially Satisfies Commission-recommended knowledge (italicized):

- communication and persuasion concepts and strategies
- communication and public relations theories
- relationships and relationship building
- *societal trends*
- *ethical issues*
- *legal requirements and issues*
- marketing and finance
- public relations history
- uses of research and forecasting
- *multicultural and global issues*
- organizational change and development
- management concepts and theories

Satisfies or Partially Satisfies Commission-recommended skills (italicized):

- research methous and analysis
- management of information
- mastery of language in written and oral communication
- *problem solving and negotiation*
- *management of communication*
- strategic planning
- *issues management*
- audience segmentation
- informative and persuasive writing
- community relations, consumer relations, employee relations, other practice areas
- technological and visual literacy
- *managing people, programs and resources*
- *sensitive interpersonal communication*
- fluency in a foreign language
- *ethical decision-making*
- *participation in the professional public relations community*
- message production
- *working with a current issue*

- public speaking and presentation
- applying cross-cultural and cross-gender sensitivity

APPENDIX C

Assessment Plan—Communication-Public Relations

Kruckeberg (1991) cites the first assessment plan's outcomes and competencies.

Outcomes and Competencies

Outcome 1. Students will have a thorough understanding of: communication, including mass communication; such communication's role in society and in mass culture—both past and present, with insights into the future; and the role and uses of the mass media—both print and broadcast; as well as the uses of a range of specialized communication applications, including advertising, marketing and related areas. This understanding will include international and intercultural perspectives.

Competency 1.1. Students will be familiar with and articulate in: the nature of communication within mass society and mass culture; the past and present of print and electronic media, advertising, marketing and related areas, and international/multi-cultural communication.

Competency 1.2. Students will be familiar with and articulate in: public relations principles; public relations' historical development; the concept and dynamics of publics and public opinion; persuasion strategies, tactics and techniques as they relate to the various models of public relations; and public relations ethics.

Competency 1.3. Students will be familiar with and articulate in: a range of appropriate historical and contemporary mass communication and public relations theoretical models.

Competency 1.4. Students will be familiar with and articulate in: the relationship between communication and public relations, particularly as this relationship is impacted by the nature, potential uses and range of communication forms used in public relations. Students will be able to critically understand the relationship between the mass media and public relations.

Outcome 2. Students will have a thorough understanding of: professionally accepted public relations fundamentals; the vocabulary of public relations and related areas and public relations perspectives as these perspectives impact upon society; and the role of public relations in contemporary world society.

Competency 2.1. Students will be familiar with and articulate in: contemporary public relations literature and scholarship; contemporary issues of public relations, particularly those impacting on the welfare of society; and projections and forecasts of public relations practice, particularly those impacting on society. All of these competencies will be based upon a thorough understanding of and appreciation for the history of public relations.

Competency 2.2. Students will be familiar with and articulate in: the nature, potential uses and range of communication forms used in public relations.

Competency 2.3. Students will be familiar with and articulate in: public relations as a communication management function through which organizations adapt to, alter or maintain their environments to achieve organizational goals.

Competency 2.4. Students will be familiar with and articulate in: how public relations is used to improve productivity for business, associations, government and not-for-profit organizations; how organizations can more effectively respond to regulatory initiatives and changing social trends; and how communication management can better assist in organizational strategic planning.

Outcome 3. Students will have a thorough understanding of: communication methods used by public relations practitioners and of public opinion formation and change as viewed by contemporary public relations literature and scholarship.

Competency 3.1. Students will be familiar with and articulate in: public relations formative and evaluative research methodologies; the rationale for research in public relations; and the ethical considerations related to public relations issues.

Competency 3.2. Students will be familiar with and articulate in: public relations programming, planning, decision-making and executing, being able to bring to bear an analysis of research findings and an understanding of public opinion formation and change to make informed public relations management decisions. Students will be skilled in appropriate public relations and related strategy formulation.

Outcome 4. Students will have a thorough understanding of: professional mass communication and interpersonal communication skills.

Competency 4.1. Students will be familiar with and articulate in: writing and oral presentation of public relations messages as appropriate for a range of media, including those in both print and broadcast. They will be able to both write and speak at a entry-level professional proficiency.

Competency 4.2. Students will be familiar with and articulate in: identifying communication channels to send messages to specific audiences and will be able to understand and appreciate the unique characteristics of the various media.

Competency 4.3. Students will be familiar with and articulate in: the ability to explore social/cultural environments impinging upon organizations, including multi-cultural perspectives.

Competency 4.4. Students will be familiar with and articulate in: the complexities of programming accountable objectives for themselves and for other organizational managers.

Competency 4.5. Students will be familiar with and articulate in: recognizing trends affecting channels of communication in society.

Competency 4.6. Students will be familiar with and articulate in: exploring the organizational as well as the professional responsibilities of public relations practitioners.

Outcome 5. Students will have a thorough understanding of: the overall synthesis of public relations concepts; ethical considerations and the appropriate resolution of ethical dilemmas; and public relations problem resolution.

Competency 5.1. Students will be familiar with and articulate in: general management theories and literature, including financial management; and will be able to communicate with and work together in managerial problem resolution with other managers within their organizations.

Competency 5.2. Students will be familiar with and articulate in: general management theories and the management literature's particular application to public relations problems and cases; working as a management team member, together with other organizational executives, to resolve public relations and other management problems; and formulating overall management strategies. Students will be prepared to be organizational management officers, fulfilling a critical staff role—that of public relations officers and executives—within their organizations.

Outcome 6. Students will have a thorough understanding of: the various theories of mass communication and interpersonal communication and of their applications for public relations.

Competency 6.1. Students will be familiar with and articulate in: flexible theoretical thinking as it relates to communication, being able to comprehend, select and convincingly argue theoretical positions.

Competency 6.2. Students will be familiar with and articulate in: their own theoretical disposition and will be able to compare/contrast the many applicable communication theories relevant to public relations.

Outcome 7. Students will have a thorough understanding of: appropriate communication research principles, concepts, and procedures, particularly as they can be applied in public relations planning, but also in the broader societal context.

Competency 7.1. Students will be familiar with and articulate in: their critical and analytical abilities in research design and data analysis.

Competency 7.2. Students will be familiar with and articulate in: their marketable knowledge for professional public relations practice and for future graduate study.

Outcome 8. Students will have a thorough understanding of: the exigencies of the professional public relations working environment.

Competency 8.1. Students will be familiar with and articulate in: professional office protocol and regimen.

Competency 8.2. Students will be familiar with and articulate in: portfolio and resume construction and evaluation.

Competency 8.3. Students will be familiar with and articulate in: professional evaluation and review techniques and self-evaluation.

15

Advertising

Beth E. Barnes
School of Journalism and Telecommunications
University of Kentucky

As discussed in earlier chapters, it's a rare educational program that is not grappling with assessment of student learning today. It's likely that many advertising educators, when faced with a directive to develop an assessment plan for their major, look at a list of desirable outcomes and say, "We teach all those things already." Then they look at one of the laundry lists of indirect and direct measures (such as that in *A Guide to Assessment of Student Learning in Journalism and Mass Communications,* 2001), and think "Most or all of our students do internships, we do the AAF competition, we've got a capstone course (campaigns, most likely), our creative kids do portfolios . . . we're all set." Well, maybe.

Although many, perhaps even most, advertising programs are already structured to produce assessable outputs from individual courses, it seems likely that the number of units regularly conducting true program assessment is much lower. Program assessment provides a means of looking at learning across the curriculum, not just within courses. Program assessment takes into account differences in professors' backgrounds and expectations, differences in teaching styles, and differences in individual students' curricula, depending on what electives they chose to take or what internship they were able to land. Faculty members who have taught the campaigns course many times may hope that success in that course is an excellent indicator of student learning and probable career success, but in fact that's not necessarily so. How often have faculty members who teach campaigns had a faculty colleague say, "Student X was part of your top campaign team? You're kidding—he/she barely made it through my media/research/creative course. Who else was in that group? Oh, well, that explains it."

That imagined exchange is not to imply that the majority of students who do well in campaigns are coasting on their group members' coattails, or that there are extenuating circumstances to explain success in any one course. Rather, faculty members generally see students in terms of how they perform in the one or two courses they take with that faculty member, and most evaluations of student learning are also conducted on the course level. Employers will see, and evaluate, those same students as employees based on the sum total of their learning and their ability to apply the skills they have been taught to the actual business of advertising. Programmatic assessment must adopt a similar perspective.

KEY ISSUES

For Accrediting Council on Education in Journalism and Mass Communication (ACEJMC)-accredited programs, development of an assessment plan should start with a review of the professional values and competencies. Programs not involved in the accrediting process can also use this as a starting point, or develop their own list of desired learning outcomes for students. What should an advertising student need to know on graduation to be successful, both in finding the first job and for progressing through a career?

Obviously, written and oral communication skills are an important starting point. Both can be assessed within courses; the former lends itself more easily to programmatic assessment than the latter, unless some form of oral exit presentation is used. Beyond basic communication ability, advertising students should also demonstrate critical thinking skills, knowledge of and facility with the terms and technologies of the industry, and an understanding of advertising's role within society as demonstrated through attention to ethical behavior and incorporation of cultural diversity considerations in work developed. In curricula that encourage students to specialize in one aspect of advertising (such as account planning, copywriting, etc.), demonstration of particular abilities linked to that specialty is also important.

Many of these areas form the basis for regular assessments within courses. Students take tests or complete projects to demonstrate their ability to apply concepts or execute skills. Students who cannot prove mastery of the subject matter may leave the major either voluntarily or under sanction. Many advertising programs provide rewards for students who excel in skill areas: placement in highly competitive internships, recommendations for national awards (such as American Advertising Federation's [AAF] Vance Stickell Award or the American Association of Advertising Agencies' Minority Advertising Internship Program), and the opportunity to participate in highly visible contests such as the National Student Advertising Competition. There is likely little question that these top-level students have acquired the skills needed for success.

However, an assessment plan cannot just measure the attainment of the very best students. Programmatic assessment requires attention to learning across the board, from the class standout to the student who just squeaks by. Although a programmatic assessment program does not have to examine every piece of work done by every student in every course in the curriculum, it should provide a means of looking at comprehensive learning by a cross-section of students. And, a useful assessment program in advertising must also include a way to evaluate both group work and individual contributions. Yes, students will most often work as part of a team when they're out in the professional world. But their value as a team member lies in the individual strength they bring to the team. A comprehensive assessment plan needs to recognize that dichotomy.

ASSESSMENT MEASURES IN ADVERTISING EDUCATION

Although there is not yet a body of work on assessment in advertising per se, attention has been given to several of the elements that might be expected to be part of an assessment of student learning in advertising. The principal indirect measure that has received attention is views on participation in the AAF's National Student Advertising Competition. Some work has also been done to gauge industry professionals' opinions on appropriate academic preparation of students for advertising careers. With regard to direct measures, emphasis has also been given to the development and review of creative portfolios and to the role of teamwork in the curriculum, generally discussed in terms of the capstone campaigns course. Each of these areas is reviewed briefly later. A brief discussion of work examining means of incorporating diversity topics into the advertising curriculum is also included. Although this does not fit neatly into either the indirect or direct measure categories, it is a crucial concern for many advertising educators and should be considered when developing a plan for programmatic assessment.

Readers new to the academy should note that the Advertising Division of the Association for Education in Journalism and Mass Communication has long taken a special interest in teaching topics, first through dedicated sessions at the annual conference and more recently through its sponsorship of the *Journal of Advertising Education* (*JAE*). Many of the articles cited later appeared in that publication, along with teaching tips and reviews of textbooks and instructional software. Those interested in assessment (and curriculum development) in advertising should include *JAE* on their regular reading list.

Indirect Measures

The AAF Competition. Numerous programs across the country participate in the National Student Advertising Competition sponsored by AAF, a special case of teamwork. Often, this campaign (or a similar campaign course) serves as the capstone experience in the advertising major. Because of its pervasiveness, the AAF competition has also attracted the attention of advertising scholars. Marra, Avery, and Grabe (1997) surveyed faculty advisors' perceptions on the value of the competition to their students and the effect their role as advisor had on their academic career. The former issue is relevant to this discussion; advisors overwhelmingly viewed the competition as a "valuable learning experience," and generally as more valuable than other courses in the curriculum. Weir (1999) studied AAF team structures and student goals through a survey of advisors and found similar positive evaluations of the competition. Because the AAF competition process involves evaluation of student work by professional judges, programs that participate in AAF may consider making performance in the competition a part of their overall assessment program.

Industry Professionals' Views of Advertising Education. This has been a particularly fertile area for study, perhaps because of the perceived disconnect between student preparation for advertising careers and what the industry says it wants entry-level employees to know. Much of the work in this area is based on either wide-spread surveys or focused individual interviews with advertising professionals. As such, these studies may not only provide some guidance for program development and program assessment measures, but also ideas on how to bring professionals into the assessment process.

The first of this group of studies focuses on the creative curriculum. Kendrick, Slayden, and Broyles (1996) surveyed creative directors at U.S. advertising agencies to determine their perceptions of student preparation and the desired role for universities in that preparation.

Among other results, this study indicated that creative directors are particularly interested in employees with critical thinking skills, underscoring one of the desired student learning outcomes identified earlier.

White, Smith, and Shen (2002) also examined the creative area. They asked advertising agency creative personnel and advertising educators to rate ads using a proven creativity scale, and then compared the results from the two groups. They found that the two groups were similar in their judgments, suggesting that faculty evaluations are representative of what students will find in the workplace.

McMillan, Sheehan, Heinemann, and Frazier (2001) conducted a content analysis of help-wanted ads to identify the key characteristics desired of advertising employees. After examining a sample of ads in the leading trade publication, *Advertising Age*, the authors were able to develop a list of desired skills as well as other job requirements (experience, education, etc.). Interestingly, one of the most important skills, "people skills," is not found in ACEJMC's professional values and competencies, and it is not something easily assessed through student work products.

Slater, Robbs, and Lloyd (2002) compared the findings from a survey of educators teaching the media planning course to answers obtained from agency media directors. Among other results, they found that media professionals emphasized the importance of math skills and numeracy more strongly than did educators. They also found that the professionals placed much greater value on critical and conceptual thinking compared to educators.

Morrison, Christy, and Haley (2003) surveyed account planners to identify the type of skills and training they believed necessary for success in this developing career field. The primary skill areas identified was research skills.

Direct Measures

Creative Portfolios. One of the few givens in advertising education is the necessity for students seeking careers as copywriters or art directors to develop a portfolio of work that demonstrates their creative problem-solving skills. The standard how-to book in this area is *How to Put Your Book Together and Get a Job In Advertising: The 21st Century Edition*, by Maxine Paetro (2002). Evaluation of creative portfolios and approaches to creative portfolio development have been the focus of several studies published in *Journalism and Mass Communication Educator* and *Journal of Advertising Education*. Cotzias (1996) recommended a classroom ap-

proach for helping beginning creative students master concept development, a necessary first step toward creation of portfolio pieces. Barnes
and Lloyd (1997) described the process of establishing a creative track
within the advertising major, including recommended coursework to
foster portfolio development. Robbs and Wells (1999) provided a review
of approaches to teaching creative courses at universities nationwide.
Griffin (2001) discussed creative students' learning styles and recommended an approach to student motivation.

All of these pieces share the view that education in the creative side
of advertising is fundamentally different than education on the account
management or media side. If the educational approaches are (or
should be) different, might that not also suggest that assessment of creative learning should also differ? Although these works do not directly
address the question of assessment, they do offer some guidance on
evaluation of creative work that can be folded into an assessment plan.

Related Issues

There are two areas that merit special attention in discussing possible
assessment areas in advertising education. The first, teamwork, is an
important factor in many advertising curricula and can present particular challenges to assessment. The second, diversity, has long been recognized as an important component of student learning in advertising
and so also requires particular focus in an assessment plan.

Teamwork. Both anecdotal evidence and published research suggest
that much of the work students do as they move through the advertising
curriculum involves teamwork. This is particularly true in the campaigns
course, which is a common capstone in many advertising curricula. Use
of teams can present a challenge both for course-based and program
assessment, as it can be difficult to tease out what degree of learning
has taken place at the level of the individual student as opposed to the
team as a unit.

Work in this area has largely examined ways of preparing students
for successful teamwork. Beard (1997) described the training process
he uses for students in the campaigns course, and provided student assessments of the training. He argued convincingly that, to the extent that
teamwork is part of the pedagogy in advertising, it is incumbent on instructors to give students the preparation they need to work effectively
in groups.

Robbs and Gronstedt (1997) conducted depth interviews with senior
staff in nine companies to ascertain their perspectives on teamwork.

Their findings identified phases in team development and again argued for the need for training in teamwork. Robbs extended this work in collaboration with Weisberg (Robbs & Weisberg, 1999) by developing a day-and-a-half-long teamwork training seminar for students.

Diversity. Finally, some attention has been given to methods for incorporating discussions of diversity into the advertising curriculum. Cooper (2002) provided tips on using the media planning course to foster attention to diversity, moving beyond cursory discussions on target marketing. Reichert (2002) offered suggestions on using representations of women in advertising to raise students' consciousness on stereotyping and encourage critical thinking.

More recently, the Fall 2003 issue of the *Journal of Advertising Education* included a special section on diversity. Articles by Frazier (2003), Chambers (2003), Rios (2003), Cooper (2003), and Golombisky (2003) provided varying approaches to highlighting diversity in a range of advertising courses. Understanding of and appreciation for diverse viewpoints is an ACEJMC-identified competency; given the advertising industry's emphasis on multicultural marketing, this sort of understanding is vital for any student seeking to make a career in this field.

How can this varied group of studies help to develop assessment methods for advertising education? First, they offer evidence of the importance of a number of student learning outcomes that should be part of an advertising assessment plan. Accredited programs, and those seeking initial accreditation, must incorporate ACEJMC's values and competencies into their assessment plans. If a program is concerned that its current curriculum is lacking in one of the competency areas, these studies may provide some guidance for curricular additions or modifications. Programs that have chosen not to seek accreditation may either develop their own list of desired learning outcomes based on the work cited earlier, or select those items from the ACEJMC list that are most germane to the goals of their own program.

Second, these studies help to identify some of the challenges to student learning, and consequently, assessment in advertising education. The continuing tension between what educators believe is important and what the professional community wants (perhaps best illustrated in Slater et al., 2002) will not only affect course content, but also assessment programs developed to include input from industry professionals. Understanding some of the key points of difference may aid in the development of assessment instruments and protocols for involving professionals. Similarly, the extent to which teamwork is a part of an advertising curriculum and the resulting difficulties must be addressed both in the classroom and in programmatic assessment.

DEVELOPING STUDENT LEARNING OUTCOMES

The following section reviews a process for developing student learning outcomes; it is followed by an example of one approach to advertising assessment. The program mission and curriculum should drive the development of student learning outcomes.

Mission

If the program mission talks in terms of preparing students for successful careers in advertising, then assessment measures must focus on those skills deemed important by the profession. A number of the studies cited in this chapter have examined just that issue, and the findings from that work (or a survey of employers who have hired program graduates) could be used to develop a laundry list of desired outcomes.

Alternatively, if the mission instead talks about lifelong learning, development of analytical skills, and the like, the desired student learning outcomes would likely be less skills-oriented and more focused on assessment of critical thinking abilities. Review of the mission statement should be the first step in identifying student learning outcomes. If the program does not have a mission statement, the time spent developing a mission that all program faculty members agree on will prevent problems down the road when it comes to determining what outcomes should be assessed. (For educators with professional advertising experience, this is analogous to setting agreed-on objectives before proceeding with developing the media plan, creative executions, etc.)

Curriculum

The list of required courses for the advertising major should suggest what student learning outcomes are valued by the program. A curriculum that includes multiple writing courses, for example, is one that obviously places great emphasis on honing students' writing abilities. If the required curriculum includes a case-based management course or strategic decision-making course, that suggests that analytical skills are considered important. Curricula that require a statistics-based research course encourage the development of both numeracy and analytical skills. If advertising faculty members are in agreement on the structure of the program curriculum, developing a list of desired student learning outcomes should be relatively easy. Hint: If developing that list is fraught with disagreement, it may be time for a comprehensive curriculum review.

Example. There are five courses that frequently appear in the core of most advertising programs. They are an introductory course; one course in each of the functional areas of research, media, and creative; and a campaigns course. Leaving aside the likelihood of electives, internships, and other additions to the core, here are some student learning outcomes suggested by the five basic courses:

- Knowledge of and appreciation for the historical and theoretical foundations of advertising practice (introductory course).
- Knowledge of and ability to apply the basic advertising campaign planning process (introductory and campaigns courses).
- Numerical and analytical skills (research and media courses).
- Creative problem-solving and graphic design skills (creative course).
- Teamwork skills (campaigns course).
- Writing skills (across the advertising core).

If a curriculum requires a diversity course (such as "Race and Gender in Advertising" or the like), that suggests that assessment of multicultural understanding and appreciation be part of the plan. Similarly, a required law and ethics course would emphasize knowledge and application of ethical business practices as a desired outcome. Evaluation of the program's mission and curriculum should serve as an effective guide to developing the list of desired student learning outcomes.

A STRATEGY FOR ADVERTISEMENT PROGRAM ASSESSMENT

The approach described later is based primarily on a program under development at the University of Kentucky. Although the persuasive communication major at Kentucky is Integrated Strategic Communications (ISC), the program structure is easily adaptable to a more traditional advertising program. All ISC students take a common core (introduction to ISC, a first-level writing course, research, ethics, and campaigns). Students choose one of four paths: account management, creative, public relations, or direct marketing. Each path includes two courses; students take four other electives within the program, one of which may be an internship. Students selecting the account management path take media planning and a case-based management course; creative path students take beginning and advanced creative.

Each course employs standard assessments. Students in the introductory course take tests to measure mastery of key concepts. Students in the writing class produce a variety of work in different forms. Upper-division courses include a number of projects that demonstrate critical thinking and concept application. Creative path students develop the standard creative portfolio; account management students produce a media plan and write case analyses. The campaigns course, offered in AAF and non-AAF sections, provides an opportunity for synthesis through the creation of a comprehensive strategic communications campaign. The work generated in each of these courses, taken on its own, indicates the student's success in mastering the expected skills, as judged by the faculty member responsible for that course.

This program is in the pilot stage of developing an assessment program that will provide a more comprehensive view of students' progress and that will involve area professionals and program faculty. The program has received seed money from the institutional assessment office at the university to develop this project. (Because of the growing interest in and attention to assessment nationally, many universities are actively encouraging units to develop comprehensive assessment programs. Programs in the early stages of planning may wish to check to see if there are university resources available. The institutional assessment office at the University of Kentucky provides funding, a comprehensive Web site with assessment resources, and links to campus experts. The planning grant for the project described here was tied to the university's regular program review process; the funding survived a round of campus-wide budget cuts, a good indicator of the importance of assessment at the university.)

Although the final details of the program are still being developed, an explanation of the general parameters and potential rubrics may be helpful to those working on assessment programs. The primary vehicle for this assessment project is the student portfolio. As discussed earlier, the portfolio is an accepted element of most advertising curricula. Creative path students in this program already produce formal portfolios; the work created by account management students as they move through the curriculum also lends itself to a portfolio. Students in this program have not been required to submit a portfolio prior to graduation in the past; however, the new requirement is not viewed as particularly burdensome because it only requires additional organizational work on the student's part and will provide them with a valuable job-seeking tool.

The assessment portfolios will be organized chronologically to demonstrate the students' development as critical thinkers and improved mastery of skills as they progress through the major. Portfolio contents will vary across students, but might include the following:

- Brand strategy plans that reflect use of research tools, critical thinking abilities, and writing skills.

- Media plans that demonstrate analytical thinking, numeracy skills, and clear writing.
- Creative work that indicates creative and critical thinking through effective problem solving, visual understanding through graphic design, and writing ability.
- Campaigns that demonstrate critical thinking through problem-solving approaches, application of research to identify targets and strategies, numeracy skills through development of measurable objectives, and writing ability.
- Work produced through internships, involvement in campus media, or participation in other campus organizations.

Although some of this work will have been done individually, some will have been developed through teamwork. For that work, students will be asked to write reflective thinking pieces describing their individual contribution to the creation of the work and discussing the value of the teamwork that resulted in the final product. This exercise should both provide context for the reviewers and help affirm the value of teamwork for the students.

The portfolio will be organized chronologically. The pieces will be labeled to indicate when the work was done, and, where applicable, for which course. The portfolio will also include a resume and a statement describing the student's career aspirations. How the instructions for portfolio development will be communicated to students has yet to be determined. Some possibilities include discussion in the capstone campaigns course; a series of mandatory, noncredit workshops; or explanation by the student's advisor during a regular advising session. Standardized handout material will be prepared to be given to students in whatever setting is selected.

Students will submit their portfolio at the end of the semester in which they are graduating. In spring semester, when the number of graduating students is at its peak, a random sample of the portfolios will be chosen for assessment. The intent is to assess all portfolios for fall and summer graduates, depending on the number of professionals that can be recruited for the process.

The portfolio assessment judges will be two to five community advertising professionals. Ideally, these judges will be people who have some familiarity with the work of students coming out of the program, either through having been internship sponsors, alumni of the program, or having hired program graduates. It should be beneficial to this group to have the opportunity to make suggestions on program improvements, which will be one of the outcomes of the assessment.

The judges will come to campus to review the student portfolios. There are two basic questions underlying the assessment:

1. How well have advertising students mastered the ACEJMC professional values and competencies as reflected in their past work?
2. Are these graduating students adequately prepared for entry-level jobs in the field?

Each portfolio will only be rated by one reviewer. Although having multiple reviewers would allow comparison of the consistency of reviews, it would likely be too burdensome to ask each professional judge to review every portfolio. Instead, the sequence director for the ISC major and the director of the school will review the rating form with the judges and provide an overview of the type of work they can expect to see in the portfolios. The two key questions will also be discussed with the judges. In this way, a common framework can be established among the judges before they begin to review the students' work. Judges will be encouraged to discuss the portfolios among themselves as they conduct their reviews. Faculty will not stay in the room with the judges, so as to avoid biasing the reviews, but will be easily available to answer any questions that arise or to provide clarification on any issues.

In examining the students' portfolios, the judges will be asked to evaluate the work based on professional expectations. The portfolios will be rated on their demonstration of key values and competencies:

- Critical thinking skills as shown through students' analysis of market situations and identification of solutions.
- Creative problem-solving skills illustrated either through advertising concepts or strategic plans.
- Professional writing ability.
- Understanding and application of research as a tool for problem identification and development of solutions.
- Application of relevant technologies such as media planning software, graphic design packages, and so forth.
- Understanding and application of persuasion theory illustrated through recommended action plans for brand promotion.
- Numeracy skills demonstrated in objective-setting, research analysis, and media planning.
- Appreciation for and understanding of diversity shown by inclusion of work that reflects cultural understanding and sensitivity through choice of symbols, language, and recommended media placement.

- Adherence to professional ethics, best demonstrated in a portfolio by what isn't there, that is, no deceptive claims, minimal or no evidence of stereotyping, appropriate use of research findings, and the like.

The outcomes listed earlier represent a blend of items from ACEJMC's professional values and competencies and items deemed important by program faculty. One way to develop such a list for a program is to look closely at the program curriculum. Given the sequence of required courses, what skill sets are students being trained to develop? What assumptions underlie the curriculum? For example, if the curriculum places emphasis on case-based courses, that is generally an indication that development of students' analytical skills is seen as an important goal. Faculty in a program that requires students to take one or more theory-focused courses likely see development of critical thinking abilities as a key emphasis. A curriculum made up primarily of skills courses could be assessed through examination of student work to judge mastery of the application of those skills. The point here is that the program's stated goals and approved curriculum should provide the framework for determining which student learning outcomes are most important. If the program faculty regards the list of outcomes suggested by the curriculum as weak or lacking in some areas, then perhaps the curriculum itself should be reexamined before moving forward with an assessment plan.

In each of these categories, the judges will rate the work as either beginning, developing, accomplished, or exemplary (sample found at http://edweb.sdsu.edu/triton/july/rubrics/Rubric_Template.html). For example, in the assessment category of creative problem-solving skills, assume the student whose portfolio is being reviewed has included a print ad developed to promote the sale of Mrs. Field's cookies in shopping malls. An ad that positions Mrs. Field's cookies against Chips Ahoy cookies would receive the "beginning" rating because the student has missed a key point in the situation, identification of appropriate competitors. If the student's ad instead identified other mall snack options as competition but used a tired cliché or inappropriate pun in the headline, that work might earn a score of "developing" due to a more reasoned solution, but one that is not eye-catching (a critical aspect of effective advertising). If the student's work focused on the mall environment and positioned Mrs. Field's cookies in an unexpected way likely to catch a potential consumer's attention and be remembered, the work might be scored as "accomplished." Finally, an ad that not only demonstrated an understanding of the competitive environment and was memorable but also took advantage of some of the creative opportunities in malls (kiosks, directional signage, etc.) might earn the top "exemplary" score. Judges would be advised that work receiving scores of either 3 (accomplished) or 4 (exemplary) should be work that could be used professionally either as is or with minimal editing or polishing.

It has not been determined whether the judges will be rating each piece in the portfolio on these criteria, as in the example cited earlier, or providing ratings for the portfolio as a whole. However, given the focus on programmatic assessment, the latter is more likely. In that case, scores for each area would be based on a range of student work. The judges will also be asked to comment on the development of the student's abilities over time. Is there evidence of improved skill mastery as the student moved through the curriculum, or does the work suggest a consistent level of ability? Once the judges have reviewed the portfolios, they will be invited to join the program faculty at a meal for an overarching discussion of the assessment results. During that discussion, the judges will be asked for their assessment of the program's strengths and weaknesses based on what they saw in the portfolios. What areas need more work? Are there important skill sets that are missing entirely based on the material reviewed? Are these students hirable? How do they compare to other aspirants for entry-level jobs? How much and what sort of additional training would these students need in their first 6 months on the job?

This discussion is a critically important part of the assessment process. Although a formal report detailing the portfolio review results will be prepared as well and shared with the program faculty, giving the professional assessors and the program faculty the opportunity to meet together and discuss the findings seems a much more powerful means to communicate the results. The give-and-take possible in this kind of setting should lead to actionable recommendations that will resonate with faculty.

The judge's assessment of their portfolio will be provided to the students as well. Although it's unlikely that a student will go back and rework a media plan, for example, based on a judge's comments, the evaluation might help the student better target his or her job search. For example, if a judge identifies a student as having particularly strong strategic abilities, that student might focus on jobs in account management.

The assessment summary observations and recommendations will also be shared with program alumni through printed publication and on the program Web site. Although the assessment of student portfolios can provide insights on how well the program is preparing graduates for their first jobs, alumni can help assess preparation for successful careers. Alumni will also be surveyed to ask whether they have been able to progress in their career as they hoped. This would include type of job(s), job location, and timing of promotions or raises. Alumni will be asked to reflect on what they needed to know or learn to be successful that was not covered in the program but could have or should have been.

As the pilot program unfolds and the portfolio assessment rubrics are refined, the program plans to post information related to the assessment project on its Web site (http://www.uky.edu/CommInfoStudies/JAT/). The planning grant requires sharing learning with the campus community; this information can also serve as a way of giving both alumni and current students a window into the program from a new perspective.

OTHER ASSESSMENT OPTIONS

Obviously, the portfolio-based assessment described here is only one option for assessing student learning in an advertising program. There are other measures, both direct and indirect, that might prove helpful as either a supplement to or replacement for portfolio review. Brief examples of a few alternatives follow.

Indirect Measures

At many universities, the advertising major is among the most popular with incoming students. Tracking retention of those students and time to graduation can provide an indication of program effectiveness and student satisfaction with the curriculum. For example, if a retention analysis indicates that many students transfer out of the major following the first writing course, that might suggest that students are not well-informed as to the writing requirements of the major prior to selecting it as their program of study. Or, it might suggest problems within the specific course. Because the portfolio review described earlier would only apply to students who complete the program, adding retention analysis to the overall assessment plan might capture information about students who never make it to the portfolio stage.

Many advertising programs either require or strongly recommend internships. Although material produced by students as part of their internships may well be included in student portfolios, evaluation of students by internship supervisors can provide assessments of professional skills that may be hard to measure through portfolio review. Among others, these could include ethical behavior and presentation skills. Similarly, employers of the program's graduates could be surveyed to assess how well graduates are performing in entry-level jobs. If employers report, for example, that graduates of the program have trouble with numerical work, the program curriculum might be reworked to put more emphasis on numeracy.

Employers' assessments of employee performance offer one means of assessing work readiness. Graduates' own evaluation of their experiences in the first job after graduation or subsequent positions can also provide important insights. This information can be obtained through periodic alumni surveys, inclusion of recent graduates on program advisory boards, alumni focus groups conducted during reunion times when former students will be on campus, and the like. Often, evaluations of particular courses or specific aspects of a program's curriculum will be different once a graduate has spent some time in the workforce than might have been the case immediately after the course was completed. Encouraging alumni to assess how well the skills they were taught during the program have served them in practice can help identify curricular strengths and weaknesses.

Direct Measures

Advertising is one of those topics where just about everyone has an opinion, informed or not. Advertising majors could be given a test on their entry into the program that measures their understanding of the concepts and theories underlying effective advertising development, knowledge of advertising history, familiarity with industry structure, and the like. The same or similar test could then be given again at the completion of the program to assess students' gains in knowledge. Such a test is not recommended as the sole component of an assessment plan because ability to apply such knowledge to develop effective advertising campaigns is more important than the knowledge itself, but a test like that described here could serve as a useful diagnostic if student portfolios are consistently found wanting or alumni and employer evaluations of the program are negative.

As noted earlier, many advertising programs include a capstone campaigns course that requires students to apply skills and knowledge gained throughout the curriculum. Tracking of the grades students attain in this course, and diagnosis of recurring problem areas, can help to identify weaknesses within the rest of the curriculum.

To reiterate the point made at the beginning of this chapter, whatever the measure or combination of measures selected for the assessment plan, the goal should be to conduct a program-wide assessment of student learning outcomes. Students need to master a variety of skills to become effective persuasive communicators; a useful assessment plan is one that examines that range of skills, not specific skills in isolation.

REFERENCES

A guide to assessment of student learning in journalism and mass communications. (2001). Lawrence, KS: Accrediting Council on Education in Journalism and Mass Communications.

Barnes, B. E., & Lloyd, C. V. (1997). Offering a creative track in the advertising major: A case history. *Journal of Advertising Education, 2,* 65–75.

Beard, F. (1997). Preparing campaigns students for group work. *Journal of Advertising Education, 2,* 54–64.

Chambers, J. (2003). Incorporating diversity into the advertising curriculum. *Journal of Advertising Education, 7,* 12–14.

Cooper, C. A. (2002). Using old tools to teach new tricks: How the media planning course can increase student awareness of diverse markets. *Journal of Advertising Education, 6,* 57–60.

Cooper, C. (2003). What's age, race and gender got to do with advertising? Everything! *Journal of Advertising Education, 7,* 17–19.

Cotzias, C. G. (1996). How to develop advertising concepts and demystify the creative process. *Journalism & Mass Communication Educator, 51,* 80–84.

Frazier, C. C. (2003). The diversity puzzle: Incorporating diversity into the advertising curriculum. *Journal of Advertising Education, 7,* 7–8.

Golombisky, K. (2003). Locating diversity within advertising excellence. *Journal of Advertising Education, 7,* 20–23.

Griffin, W. G. (2001). A call for a more informed approach: Motivating creative students to do their best work. *Journal of Advertising Education, 5,* 43–53.

Kendrick, A., Slayden, D., & Broyles, S. J. (1996). Real worlds and ivory towers: A survey of top creative directors. *Journalism & Mass Communication Educator, 51,* 63–74.

Marra, J., Avery, J., & Grabe, M. E. (1997). Student advertising competitions: Faculty advisor beliefs concerning the AAF National Student Advertising Competition. *Journal of Advertising Education, 2,* 21–33.

McMillan, S. J., Sheehan, K. B., Heinemann, B., & Frazier, C. (2001). What the real world really wants: An analysis of advertising employment ads. *Journal of Advertising Education, 5,* 9–21.

Morrison, M., Christy, T., & Haley, E. (2003). Preparing planners: Account planning and the advertising curriculum. *Journal of Advertising Education, 7,* 5–20.

Paetro, M. (2002). *How to put your book together and get a job in advertising: The 21st century edition.* Chicago: The Copy Workshop.

Reichert, T. (2002). Addressing the topic of female representation in advertising: A method for enhancing advertising literacy in the introductory course. *Journal of Advertising Education, 6,* 62–64.

Rios, D. L. (2003). Diversity in communication education: The "D" word is all about including others. *Journal of Advertising Education, 7,* 15–16.

Robbs, B., & Gronstedt, A. (1997). Incorporating team processes into the advertising curriculum. *Journal of Advertising Education, 2,* 35–45.

Robbs, B., & Weisberg, L. (1999). Identifying critical teamwork tools: One way to strike a balance between team training and course content. *Journal of Advertising Education, 3,* 19–28.

Robbs, B., & Wells, L. (1999). Teaching practices and emphases in advertising creative courses. *Journalism & Mass Communication Educator, 54,* 57–64.

Slater, J. S., Robbs, B., & Lloyd, C. V. (2002). Teaching the advertising media-planning course: Trying to serve two masters. *Journal of Advertising Education, 6,* 9–19.

Weir, T. (1999). The structure of AAF competition teams. *Journal of Advertising Education, 3,* 29–38.

White, A., Smith, B. L., & Shen, F. (2002). Rating creativity: Do advertising professionals and educators apply the same standards? *Journal of Advertising Education, 6,* 37–46.

MEASURING STUDENT
LEARNING OUTCOMES

16

Indirect Measures: Institutional Data, Surveys, Interviews, and Advisory Boards

Paul Parsons
School of Communications
Elon University

Like a mirror reflecting an image, indirect measures of assessment reflect program quality. Grades and student retention rates reflect on academic rigor. Internship supervisors assess the quality of a program through the performance of student interns. Exit interviews probe the level of satisfaction of graduating seniors, and surveys ask alumni to engage in reflective thinking about the quality of their education. An advisory board can evaluate student preparation to begin successful careers.

Together these are called indirect measures of assessment. They are "indirect" because they involve the following:

- Comparative data (grade distribution, probation and dismissal rates, student retention, graduation data).
- Outside evaluation (internships, job placement, advisory board evaluations, student performance in competitions).
- Participant reflection (student surveys, exit interviews, alumni surveys).

In contrast, "direct" measures of assessment—such as entry-level testing, departmental exams, capstone courses, and portfolio evaluation by the faculty—involve direct faculty assessment of student performance. Assessment requires the systematic digestion of meaningful data from both direct and indirect measures to improve curriculum, instruction, and student learning.

This chapter addresses the indirect measures based on institutional data, surveys, interviews, and advisory boards. The following chapter analyzes the indirect measures based on internships, competitions, and careers.

INSTITUTIONAL DATA

Colleges and universities are awash in data. In an era of constant data collection, institutions generate so many columns of numbers that it's doubtful they all can be systematically analyzed for meaning. Banta, Lund, Black, and Oblander (1996) said the assessment challenge is not collecting data, but connecting the data so they say something meaningful. They wrote the following: "Many colleges and universities are unaware of the rich sources of information that they currently possess about their students (for example, student background characteristics, enrollment data, and course-taking patterns). Data are there to be found if one searches, yet they must be organized, manipulated, and applied in meaningful ways" (pp. 43–44).

The Accrediting Council on Education in Journalism and Mass Communications (ACEJMC) offers examples of how institutional data analysis can serve as a valuable assessment tool. For example, by regularly comparing the distribution of grades at the time of entry to the major and again at graduation, a faculty could discover fluctuations in student preparation for the major, and progress in the major, that could prompt a review of curriculum and instruction. Similarly, comparing unit and university retention rates over time "can provide helpful context for evaluating the meaning and significance of the unit's retention and graduation rates" (ACEJMC, 2001, p. 4). In addition, the Accrediting Council said that the comparison over time of data regarding student probation and dismissal can show how the unit monitors standards of student performance. This analysis could reveal skills that are consistently weak or areas within the curriculum that seem to greatly challenge students.

Let's use the E. W. Scripps School of Journalism at Ohio University as an illustration. In 2002, the Scripps School publicly documented institutional data for assessment. The data showed that 73% of journalism majors graduated within four years compared to the university average of 43%, and the average time to graduate was 4.14 years compared to 4.43 for the university (Ohio University, 2002). An earlier assessment report showed that Scripps students had a higher retention rate between the freshmen and sophomore years than the university at large, and that journalism students scored better on the university outcomes test (Ohio University, 1996).

These data reflect well on the Scripps School. But what, really, does it mean? Students in the Scripps School may have a better retention rate because they have chosen a major, compared to many at the university who are uncertain. The outcomes test shows that Scripps students are above average. Is this because of school entrance requirements? The average graduation timeline of 4.14 years is exceedingly good. If the timeline were to substantially increase, then the faculty could seek out the cause and conceivably discover that seniors were having difficulty getting the classes they needed to graduate.

The purpose of assessment is not to gather data and return "results," but to illuminate ways to strengthen curriculum, instruction, and student learning. Kinnick (1985, p. 97) asserted that institutions tend to organize reports around data, not around issues. For institutional data to have meaning in assessment, faculty and administrators must first want to know the issues they want to address.

Student retention at the university (completing a degree vs. dropping out) is one example. Institutional data have found that high school grades and standardized test scores are the best input-predictors for college retention (Astin, 1993, p. 65). A communications program could use institutional data to analyze its own retention determinants, or to focus on a particular retention subset such as minority students.

Let's say that 75% of students who enter a journalism and mass communications program graduate with a JMC major. That figure alone tells us little. If students are transferring out of the major after the first course or two, and these happen to be students with strong grade point averages (GPAs), then this is a deeply troubling retention discovery that may suggest a lack of academic quality. But if students transfer out of the unit because of poor grades or academic suspension, that would be a sign of high academic standards.

To assess its academic quality, the School of Communications at Elon University (North Carolina) monitors several institutional data points. On the front end is student selection. The School of Communications is home to 20% of Elon's student body, and institutional data show that first-year students intent on majoring in journalism and communications have a higher Scholastic Aptitude Test score than the university average (Elon University, 2005). Once enrolled, students are asked in each university class how much effort they put into the course compared to other courses. Communications students ranked courses in their major at a 4.06 on a 5-point scale compared to a 3.88 across the university. Meanwhile, the school's GPA is below the university average (2.97 compared to 3.03). This type of data analysis can provide valuable insight into reputation and academic rigor.

A good first step in using institutional data for assessment is to conduct an inventory of the data already collected on campus, whether of students, alumni, or programs. An audit of institutional data may cause a communications unit to put two seemingly disparate data sets together to illuminate an issue. But now realism sets in. Although an audit of institutional data is laudable in theory, in practice it is likely to uncover a troubling truth: apart from data from the admissions and registrar's offices, a lot of campus data may be unusable, difficult to retrieve, or both (Astin, 1993).

Pros and Cons

The advantages of using institutional data for assessment relate to collection and analysis. The university already gathers the data, and, if it does so regularly, trends can be detected through longitudinal analysis. The disadvantages are that the data may be difficult to retrieve or use, and, even more importantly, may not address the unit's most significant questions for assessment (see Appendix A).

SURVEYS

Student and alumni surveys can be important indirect assessment measures. ACEJMC said the regular compilation, comparison, and analysis of student and alumni responses can help a unit assess the effectiveness of its curriculum and instruction and the quality and applicability of student learning. The goal is to discern "patterns of student and alumni judgment" about the strengths and weaknesses of a unit and the "short- and long-term usefulness or relevance" of what students learned (ACEJMC, 2001, p. 5).

A communications unit can obtain survey data in two basic ways. Universities conduct general surveys, and a unit could ask for breakout data to compare responses just from communications students or alumni. This has the advantage of no cost and no data collection and reporting; the university has already done so, and providing unit results is just a matter of typing in a variable.

The second way is for a unit to conduct its own survey of students or alumni. This offers complete control over the questions, with whatever degree of specificity a unit desires. The disadvantage is that a unit will have to write the survey, pursue an appropriate response rate, and appropriately analyze the data. A more popular option, then, may be adding questions to a university survey that only communications students or alumni would answer, providing a mechanism to merge the benefits of a large university data set for comparative purposes with the benefits of some communications specificity.

Surveys can ask low-level questions (Did you change your major while in college?) and high-level questions (Were you satisfied with the intellectual challenge of your major?). High-level questions require metacognition, the cognitive process of "thinking about thinking." Some students and alumni have the ability to deeply reflect on their learning processes and outcomes.

Student satisfaction is considered the single most important affective-psychological area for outcomes assessment (see Appendix B). This category encompasses a student's subjective college experience and perceptions of the value of that experience. Astin (1993) preferred two complementary questions, the first asking the student to express a degree of satisfaction with the overall college experience and the second posing a hypothetical question: If you could make your college choice again, would you still choose to enroll at the same institution? These two questions obviously would apply to the selection and satisfaction of the major just as easily as to the institution. Astin (1993) said that student satisfaction appears to be the only outcome measurement not heavily dependent on student input characteristics. Less-than-desired responses could lead a university or unit to host focus groups of students to try to understand the reasons for dissatisfaction.

Graduating Seniors

A senior survey typically concentrates on three concepts: student perceptions of what they learned, teaching effectiveness, and their preparation for the professions.

Regarding the first concept, the University of Central Florida (2002) asked seniors to evaluate how their education helped them, and 86% of journalism students (given the choices of very much, somewhat, and very little) said their education helped them "very much" to be a more effective writer, whereas only 38% said "very much" about helping them become a more effective speaker.

Regarding the second and third concepts, the University of Kentucky senior survey asked students to rate (on a scale of 4 = *excellent*, 3 = *good*, 2 = *fair*, and 1 = *poor*) the quality of instruction by faculty in their major (3.34) as well as their sense of preparation for their first career job (2.77; University of Kentucky, 1999). Asking seniors who have yet to enter the job market to assess their sense of preparation could reflect positives (successful internships, student media experience) or negatives (anxiety on entering a constricted job market).

Senior surveys typically ask a variety of questions about the faculty. The University of North Carolina (1998) statewide program assessment survey asks seniors to rate (excellent, good, fair, poor) how well faculty members in their major set high expectations for learning, respect diverse ways of learning, give frequent and prompt feedback, provide career advising, and care about a student's academic success and welfare.

A survey also can help a unit scan its learning environment in other ways:

- My major offered a good range of courses.
- Courses in my major were offered when needed.
- Too many classes in my major were too large.
- Professors in my major were available for help outside of class.

The questions that a university asks reflect that university's values. At private Elon University, which places foremost emphasis on teaching, students are asked how many faculty members they personally know (62% said 5 or more, and 22% said 10 or more), and 55% of the senior class said they had been invited to a professor's home at some point in their education. These questions are seldom, if ever, found on senior surveys at large state universities. Of course, gathering data is only the first step; interpreting the date must follow, and a unit would need to benchmark its progress if it desired for graduating seniors to personally know more faculty members.

Senior surveys can provide a fountain of information to a communications faculty engaged in assessment. The University of Colorado (1998) conducted senior surveys and reported the results by major. Asked about course difficulty several years ago, 30% of journalism students said courses were too easy, 7% said they were too hard, and the rest said the level of difficulty was about right. Two years previously, 17% of journalism students had said too easy and 17% had said too hard. Considering that the sample size was substantial, these findings would be an ideal prompt for faculty members to address why their courses were increasingly being judged by seniors as too easy. Such an act of analysis, and then corrective action, is exactly what assessment is meant to accomplish.

Other questions on the Colorado instrument asked about programmatic balance. For instance, 19% of respondents said courses in the major were too theoretical, 22% said they were too practical, and the majority said they were about right. Students also said the curriculum was too flexible because few courses were required (37%) compared to those who thought the curriculum to be too rigid (4%).

Beware of the startling survey result. One university's senior survey asks lifestyle questions as well, and those results are available by major. At this particular university (politely spared identification here), the survey found that 48% of the senior class reported drinking beer frequently, compared to 62% of communications majors. Although 31% of the senior class occasionally or regularly smoked, 43% of communications majors smoked. Not surprisingly, communications majors also reported greater use, and criticism, of the campus health center. Before we laugh this one away, think about whether a communications unit should ignore or respond to such findings in an era of caring about the holistic welfare of students. Or maybe this just isn't an academic issue.

Alumni

Alumni are prominently mentioned in the accrediting agency's assessment standard. Nowhere does it require a survey of alumni, but Standard 9 does expect that a unit "maintains contact with its alumni to assess their experiences in the professions and to gain feedback for improving curriculum and instruction" (ACEJMC, 2003, p. 11). If not by survey, then a unit must have other mechanisms for alumni feedback—perhaps a publication that invites response, or use of an alumni advisory board in the unit, or inviting back recent graduates to speak with faculty and students.

Alumni surveys have multiple benefits. Besides the positives of simply keeping in touch with former students, surveys can support assessment goals by determining how graduates perceive their education, by describing activities in which graduates are engaged, and by determining what graduates believe to be most useful in their education and what they wish they also had experienced (Shockley-Zalabak & Hulbert-Johnson, 1994, p. 304).

The University of Northern Colorado (2001) found that alumni rated their education higher than current seniors (3.5 compared to 3.1 on a 5-point scale). That may not be unusual. Alumni—especially those who have started successful careers—tend to forget the senior seminar professor who gave them grief and a C and instead remember college life fondly and credit much of their success to their college experience. In the Northern Colorado survey, 42% of journalism alumni reported employment in categories directly related to media or communications.

This raises an important question: What should the numbers be? We're all in need of benchmarks. We are swimming in numbers, but may not know if a 3.5 on a 5-point scale is good or bad, or whether 42% of graduates employed in the professions is strong or weak. We need comparison points provided either by other units on campus, or by other communications programs.

For example, first-year alumni at one state university spared identification here rated the adequacy of their educational preparation on a 7-point scale. Satisfaction by news-editorial graduates (5.29) was considerably higher than among advertising students (4.15). Comparative data like this should drive a unit to investigate why advertising students were considerably less positive. In open-ended comments, advertising students said they needed more skills in the classroom and more help with career planning. These were survey findings crying out for an assessment corrective.

Many universities administer an alumni survey 6 months or so after graduation, typically to assess if graduates have obtained meaningful employment and if the university's career center was effective in helping them. As a general benchmark, many communications units will be pleased if half or more of its graduates report media-related occupations, with the other half in private business, law or graduate school, nonprofit sectors, still seeking, or not seeking.

Surveys, of course, can be expensive and produce a low response rate. Orlik and Donald (1997) wrote how the broadcast department at Central Michigan University decided not to conduct alumni questionnaires for budgetary reasons: "Tracking all of these graduates, delivering a valid questionnaire to them, and then tabulating and analyzing the results were tasks far beyond the resources of an already multi-activity department served by a single secretary" (pp. 56–57). The faculty feared that results would be skewed anyway—too positive if only successful graduates took the initiative to stay in touch, or too negative if mailings went to parents' homes where alumni were once again living because they hadn't secured decent-paying positions.

Response rates are a significant issue, and that hinges on survey method and timing. The University of Massachusetts (2002) administered a one-page senior survey as students picked up caps and gowns, with a 63% completion rate. Northern Colorado (2001) reported a 74% response by graduating seniors hand-delivered a survey, and a 32% response by alumni to a mailed survey. The University of Colorado (1999) journalism school had a 30% alumni response 8 months after graduation. Online surveys hold additional promise, but all survey methods face similar problems with response-rate validity.

Northern Arizona University (2003) conducts a telephone survey of about 400 seniors each year to assess their level of educational satisfaction. As is common in survey research, women and Whites were over-represented as survey respondents. Men and minorities simply tend to respond at a lower rate. To give a sense of the discrepancy, Northern Arizona reported that 65% of survey respondents were women (compared to 59% of all graduating seniors) and 80% were White (compared to 75% of all seniors).

Although a survey is an ideal tool to measure how seniors or alumni perceive their education, it is difficult for a survey to measure program impact. This can be accomplished only by comparing an outcome measure with a pretest or a predicted outcome based on the characteristics of entering students.

Pros and Cons. Surveys provide quantitative results for comparison and can be administered to all students or alumni, or to a subset if desired. Another advantage is the growing acceptance of online surveys, whose only cost is in the initial setup. Traditional surveys have always had the disadvantage of cost—either the cost of printing and mailing, or the cost and time-intensiveness of phone surveys. Other disadvantages are the possibility of low response rates, historically true among men and minorities, and no possibility of following up on responses.

EXIT INTERVIEWS

An exit interview of graduating seniors is an "indirect" measure when it is akin to a survey, with self-assessment questions that ask students their level of satisfaction with the major and whether they feel prepared to start a career.

However, an exit interview would be a "direct" measure if the faculty used it to assess levels of awareness and application of subject content, a la the following: (a) What research steps would make a public opinion poll trustworthy? (b) describe "fair use" in copyright law, and (c) demonstrate the differences in writing for print and broadcast.

Just as portfolio assessment by faculty is a direct measure, this form of an exit interview would essentially be a "portfolio-in-the-head" assessment. Limburg (1994) said this form of exit interview also could include reviewing and critiquing student assignments in key courses, assessing the degree of improvement in a student's work from program entry to exit, and identifying strengths and weaknesses in the student's overall performance. At Ball State (2005), all seniors undergo an exit interview in which they prepare a professional employment portfolio for critical evaluation by a sequence coordinator.

This chapter assumes that an exit interview is an indirect measure similar to a survey. ACEJMC (2001, p. 5) said exit interviews, over time, can show patterns of student judgment concerning the strengths and weaknesses in curriculum, instruction, and student learning.

An exit interview is typically a sit-down conversation with the dean, department chair, faculty member, adviser, or designated local professional (see Appendix C). The interview focuses on the acquisition of cognitive, behavioral, and affective skills and knowledge, and how this acquisition relates to expected career requirements. Here are examples of appropriate questions for an exit interview:

- What was the best course you took in the major, and why?
- Do you believe you wrote enough papers, read enough books, and spoke enough in your classes?
- Have your future plans and your view of life changed since you began studying here?
- What advice would you give to an incoming freshman in your major?

Cumulative responses can be illuminating. One program learned that so many teachers and visiting professionals talked so much about the negatives of a broadcast journalism career (odd hours, low pay, deadline pressure) that some students chose another academic area. The faculty realized they needed to highlight the positives (importance to society, exciting career, access to decision makers) in an equal proportion. This is a way of using exit-interview results to improve instruction.

An exit interview is so much more personal than a survey. Students may open up a lot more in person, providing insights that never would have been made on paper or online. An interview also allows for two-way conversation, allowing a questioner to follow up on a point or to probe for an issue still under the surface. Of course, an interview is time consuming and requires extensive note taking for data collection. Some students also may be shy or intimidated, and might be more forthright in sharing information on paper than under a personal gaze.

In conducting an interview, start with an icebreaker question that requires a student to tell a story. A good one is as follows: "How did you choose your major?" Look for open-ended questions that encourage plenty of expression. It is more important to listen than to write. Take note of the ideas, but it's not essential to get exact quotes. In an interview setting of three or more, establish a policy that when weaknesses in the program are cited, no specific faculty names should be used, but note the semester and year in which the course was taken. Save the hardest questions for the latter part of the interview. A recommended final question is as follows: "If you had a magic wand, what would you change in your major?"

When initiating exit interviews in 1996, the College of Journalism at the University of South Carolina conducted two focus group sessions with about 15 graduating seniors each. Questions focused on the degree to which students felt prepared to enter the professional workforce, which academic experiences prepared them well (or not at all) for their careers, and their ability to articulate ethical and social values in communications (VanSlyke Turk, 1997).

Sometimes the exit interview is tied to a course. At the University of Missouri (2005), an assessment of advertising seniors occurs through the capstone course Strategic Communication Campaigns, where each student has a 30-min interview with a working professional. Although students may use the opportunity to practice interviewing skills or plug for a job, the university said that the interview is designed to assess the Advertising Department's program. The university instructs the professionals to differentiate between a student's likes–dislikes and the program's strengths–shortcomings. The University of Missouri Web site said the following of senior assessment: "Some students may not realize the value of some courses and activities until they have been out of the program for a year or more. Or, some students may have had different expectations than what the program actually was intended to deliver. Even in these instances, though, knowing this type of information might indicate we need to be more upfront about what our program covers" (University of Missouri, 2005). The professionals write a report based on collective student interviews. When all senior assessments have been conducted, the department chair shares the group findings with the advertising faculty, and the department identifies how to use the feedback to improve the program.

Some universities require seniors to complete a pre-interview written evaluation followed by the actual interview. Other programs tie the interview to a specific purpose. In 2002, the journalism program at the University of Wisconsin (2002) conducted exit interviews with the first students to complete its new curriculum.

Although exit interviews typically focus on the major, a few universities formalize the exit-interview process across campus. The University of Kansas (2002) selects students through a stratified random sample balanced by academic major and demographics. Students are paid to undergo a 45-min interview, and they do not know the questions in advance. Three faculty members rate each student following questions such as the following: What have you learned in your classes about the history of race relations in this country? What was the most important technology of the 20th century, and why? What do you think it means to be a good citizen, and would you describe yourself as one? The questions are designed to discern curricular weaknesses across campus and provide a university-wide comparison of schools and colleges. For example, journalism students at the university cumulatively scored above the university cohort in understanding diversity.

Pros and Cons. Interviews are a highly personal form of assessment. Open-ended questions encourage detailed answers, and two-way conversation allows for follow-up questions. On the negative side, individual interviews are time consuming and small-group interviews require a skilled facilitator. Some students may not fully participate, and collectively making sense of what students say requires extensive note taking and analysis.

ADVISORY BOARDS

A communications unit can obtain assessment feedback from advisory boards of all types. The most common is an alumni board, or a combination of alumni and working professionals. Some units involve community members as well, and there's a growing trend toward establishing student advisory boards.

The Journalism Alumni Board at Indiana University (2004) usually meets twice a year, with the fall meeting tied to Homecoming. The dean provides a school update, and alumni and professionals talk about ways to improve the school, such as having a mentoring program for recent graduates as they enter the workplace.

Ohio University invites journalism professionals to conduct mock job interviews during Communications Week. The advisory board's function is to advise the faculty on curriculum, professional needs, and industry trends. The school credited the board's conversations with students as leading to a dramatic expansion of computer lab availability, the addition of public speaking to the curriculum, the assignment of a graduate student to do daily critiques of the campus newspaper, and regular programs for students on how to find a job and succeed in the professional world (Ohio University, 1996).

Although professionals usually are gentle with individual students, they can be tough evaluators as a whole. Guiniven (1998) asked senior public relations executives to evaluate the skills of new graduates entering the field. Half gave graduates as a whole an A or B for media knowledge (understanding deadlines, the reporter's job, media's role in society), and the other half gave new graduates a C or below. Only 14% of the executives gave new graduates an A or B for business knowledge (basic economics, finance, marketing), whereas 38% gave new graduates a D or F. The writing skills of new graduates also did not overly impress public relations executives, with 43% giving new graduates an A or B, 40% a C, and 17% a D or F.

There's a lot to be said for presence. If professionals are speaking in classes, talking with students, having coffee with professors, walking the campus, looking at bulletin boards, and seeing the energy in the hallways, professionals are more likely to be enthusiastic about the education of communications students. When professionals have no connection with a college or university, it's understandable that they might form opinions based on a weaker new employee and become long-distance critics of what they do not see.

A professional advisory board adds excitement when it comes to campus. Knowing that newspaper editors, broadcast news directors, and corporate vice presidents have taken a day to come to campus heightens for students the importance of their ongoing education, especially if these professionals will be guests in their classes or conduct mock interviews of seniors.

Formally connecting a group of professionals to the communications unit can build relationships between the university and external constituencies. Christ, Orlik, and Tucker (1999) observed that an active advisory board is an indication of a unit that is "dynamic and outward-looking instead of sedentary and parochial" (p. 384). But the board will not succeed unless it has clearly focused goals. When professionals come to campus, they want to believe they make a difference. If they only hear reports and have lunches and then go home, they may not return.

An advisory board, then, needs to have an agenda. A dean or department head must think through how to use the board for programmatic good. That's why assessment roles seem ideally suited to an advisory board. Professionals or alumni can interview seniors, or do portfolio assessments, or speak in classes. If the unit can gather systematic feedback from the visitors, then the unit has created a useful assessment vehicle. Besides the ever-widening web of networking, Christ et al. (1999) said the presence of an advisory board "formalizes this feedback" (p. 384) for the purposes of assessment.

Advisory boards come in all shapes, sizes, and purposes. At the time of this writing, Bowling Green State (2005) had a 20-member Alumni

Advisory Board that examined final student projects from the department's capstone courses. The University of Georgia's Grady College (2005) had a 23-member advisory board with individual members and corporate members (such as CNN News Group, *Atlanta Journal-Constitution*, Cox Enterprises, and J. Walter Thompson). The University of Nevada at Reno (2005) journalism advisory board included 21 working professionals, 11 of them alumni. At the University of Iowa (2005), 25 of the 34 advisory board members for the School of Journalism and Mass Communications were alumni.

Although an advisory board consisting of alumni and working professionals is the most common, don't overlook the opportunity for assessment by a student advisory board that meets monthly with the dean or department head to provide systematic evaluation of the program. A student board should tilt toward juniors and seniors (and graduate students if a graduate degree is offered). A student group can be a sounding board for new ideas and for implementation procedures. Although few communications programs have community members as part of an advisory board, this could change as programs increasingly seek local service-learning opportunities for their students.

Pros and Cons

Using advisory boards for assessment connects students with working professionals, measures students against professional expectations, and builds relationships between the unit and external constituencies. Among the disadvantages, outsiders will have less knowledge of curriculum and instruction and therefore will not make the same connections that faculty would, and weak students may reflect negatively on the unit. Also, the unit must gather systematic feedback from advisory board members for meaningful analysis.

CONCLUSION

Each communications program is distinctive. Each should handpick the indirect assessment measures listed in this chapter (and the following) that best fit the mission, goals, objectives, and values of that program. Banta et al. (1996) noted that "assessment cannot and should not take place in the absence of a clear sense as to what matters most at the institution. Indeed, in order for assessment to lead to improvements, it must reflect what people are passionate about, committed to, and value" (p. 5). As Astin (1993) observed, assessment efforts should not be concerned about valuing that which can be measured, but instead measuring that which is valued.

REFERENCES

Accrediting Council on Education in Journalism and Mass Communications. (2001). *A guide to assessment of student learning.* Lawrence, KS: Author.

Accrediting Council on Education in Journalism and Mass Communications. (2003). *Standards of accreditation* (adopted September 2003). Lawrence, KS: Author.

Astin, A. W. (1993). *Assessment for excellence: The philosophy and practice of assessment and evaluation in higher education.* New York: American Council on Education/Oryx Press.

Ball State University. (2005). Personal interview with journalism department chair Marilyn Weaver, July 21, 2005.

Banta, T. W., Lund, J. P., Black, K. E., & Oblander, F. W. (1996). *Assessment in practice: Putting principles to work on college campuses.* San Francisco: Jossey-Bass.

Bowling Green State University. (2002). *Assessment report, 2001–02.* Retrieved July 21, 2005, from http://www.bgsu.edu/offices/provost/Assessment/Journalism2002.htm

Christ, W. G., Orlik, P. B., & Tucker, D. (1999). Self-studies, external reviews, and programmatic assessment. In W. G. Christ (Ed.), *Leadership in times of change: A handbook for communication and media administrators* (pp. 377–397). Mahwah, NJ: Lawrence Erlbaum Associates, Inc.

Elon University. (2005). Compiled by chapter author at his home institution.

Guiniven, J. E. (1998). Public relations executives view the curriculum: A needs assessment. *Journalism & Mass Communication Educator, 52,* 48–55.

Indiana University. (2004). *Dear alumni.* Retrieved March 8, 2005, from http://www.journalism.indiana.edu/alumni/newswire/archives/volXXVIIno1/stories/letter.html

Kinnick, M. K. (1985). Increasing the use of student outcomes information In P. T. Ewell (Ed.), *Assessing educational outcomes* (pp. 93–109). San Francisco: Jossey-Bass.

Limburg, V. E. (1994). Internships, exit interviews, and advisory boards. In W. G. Christ (Ed.), *Assessing communication education: A handbook for media, speech, and theatre educators* (pp. 181–200). Hillsdale, NJ: Lawrence Erlbaum Associates, Inc.

Northern Arizona University. (2003). *Trends in graduating senior satisfaction.* Flagstaff, AZ: Author.

Ohio University. (1996). *E. W. Scripps School assessment report.* Retrieved March 8, 2005, from http://www.ohiou.edu/instres/assessments/95_96assess/dept/jour.html

Ohio University. (2002). *Six-year graduation rates.* Retrieved March 8, 2005, from http://www.ohiou.edu/instres/student/gradratecoll97.html

Orlik, P. B., & Donald, R. (1997). Telecommunications programs. In W. G. Christ (Ed.), *Media education assessment handbook* (pp. 55–78). Mahwah, NJ: Lawrence Erlbaum Associates, Inc.

Shockley-Zalabak, P., & Hulbert-Johnson, R. (1994). Organizational communication. In W. G. Christ (Ed.), *Assessing communication education: A handbook for media, speech & theatre educators* (pp. 291–310). Hillsdale, NJ: Lawrence Erlbaum Associates, Inc.

University of Central Florida. (2002). *Graduating senior survey.* Retrieved March 8, 2005, from http://www.2oeas.ucf.edu/oeas2/SurveyProgram/journalism.htm

University of Colorado. (1998). *Senior survey.* Retrieved March 8, 2005, from http://www.colorado.edu/pba/surveys/senior/98/by_coll/jourtab.htm

University of Colorado. (1999). *School of Journalism and Mass Communication.* Retrieved March 8, 2005, from http://www.colorado.edu/pba/outcomes/units/jour.htm

University of Georgia. (2005). *Grady College advisory board.* Retrieved July 21, 2005, from http://www.grady.uga.edu/about_grady.php?all=About+Grady&al2=Advisory+Board&page=advisory_board.inc.php

University of Iowa. (2005). *Professional advisory board.* Retrieved July 21, 2005, from http://www.uiowa.edu/jmc/people/advisory.html

University of Kansas. (2002). *Report on the 2002 assessment of General Education.* Lawrence, KS: Office of Institutional Research and Planning.

University of Kentucky. (1999). *Graduating senior survey.* Lexington, KY: Office of Assessment and Institutional Data.

University of Massachusetts. (2002). *Graduating senior survey 2000–2002.* Amherst, MA: Office of Academic Planning and Assessment.

University of Missouri. (2005). *Senior assessment guidelines.* Retrieved March 5, 2005, from http://www.journalism.missouri.edu/undergrad/senior-assessment.html

University of Nevada at Reno. (2005). *RSJ advisory board.* Retrieved July 21, 2005, from http://www.unr.edu/journalism/peo.advisory.html

University of North Carolina. (1998). *UNC program assessment.* Retrieved March 8, 2005, from http://www.ga/unc.edu/UNCGA/assessment/uncsurveys/gss_across.html

University of Northern Colorado. (2001). *Annual assessment profiles.* Retrieved March 8, 2005, from http://asweb.unco.edu/Profiles/2000-2001/jmc.htm

University of Wisconsin. (2002). *New curriculum well under way and looking successful thus far* (letter from director Sharon Dunwoody). Retrieved January 1, 2004, from http://www.journalism.wisc.edu/alumni/documents/wj_spring02/director_spring02.html

VanSlyke Turk, J. (1997). Journalism and mass communication programs. In W. G. Christ (Ed.), *Media education assessment handbook* (pp. 79–98). Mahwah, NJ: Lawrence Erlbaum Associates, Inc.

APPENDIX A

Pros and Cons of Using Each Measure

Institutional Data

Pro: Data already collected
Allow for longitudinal analysis

Con: May be difficult to retrieve or use
May not apply to the unit's important questions

Surveys

Pro: Provide quantitative results for comparison
Can be administered to all students or alumni
Online surveys growing more common, at little cost

Con: Printing and mailing of surveys expensive
Low response rates, especially among men and minorities
No possibility of following up on responses

Interviews

Pro: Highly personal
Open-ended questions encourage fuller answers
Two-way conversation allows for follow-up questions

Con: Time-consuming
      Requires extensive note-taking for data collection
      Some students may be shy or intimidated

Advisory Boards

Pro: Measure students against professional expectations
      Connect students with working professionals
      Build relationships between unit and external constituencies
Con: Less knowledge of curriculum and instruction
      Weak students may reflect negatively on the unit
      Must gather systematic feedback for meaningful analysis

APPENDIX B

Questions That Can Be Answered With Each Measure

Institutional Data

- How does the rigor of the unit compare to the university, as defined by grade point average, student dismissal rates, or a university outcomes test?
- How has retention changed over time?
- How does the unit's job placement compare to the university at large?

Surveys

- What is the level of student satisfaction with the major?
- Did the unit offer a good range of courses, available when needed?
- How well did the faculty set high expectations for learning, give prompt feedback, and care about a student's academic success and welfare?
- What do alumni believe was most useful in their education?

Interviews

- What would students preserve or change in the major, and why?
- What is their sense of preparation for the first job?

- Did their career plans, or view of life, evolve since becoming a major?
- What advice would students give to incoming freshmen in the major?

Advisory Boards

- Do students impress professionals with their knowledge and skills?
- Do seniors have appropriate portfolios to enter the job market?

APPENDIX C

Steps in Using Each Measure

Institutional Data

1. Conduct an inventory of data already available on campus.
2. Determine if the data address important issues to the unit.
3. If so, identify who can help with data retrieval and analysis.
4. Suggest inclusion of specific assessment questions for future institutional research.

Surveys

1. Decide what you want to learn from students or alumni.
2. Study surveys conducted by others to help with question wording.
3. Select the survey method (mail, phone, online) that best accomplishes your goal within your limitations (budget, time, staffing).
4. Conduct a census or randomized sampling based on population size.
5. Analyze data against predetermined benchmarks.

Interviews

1. Draft faculty, administrators, or others to interview selected students.
2. Select students to reflect the demographics of the unit.
3. Decide whether to interview individually or in small groups.
4. If using small groups, select a skilled facilitator to lead discussions.
5. If individually, create some common questions for consistency.

6. Ask open-ended questions and follow up for detailed answers.
7. Report key findings in aggregate form.

Advisory Boards

1. Invite professionals or alumni to conduct mock job interviews.
2. Create common questions that allow for individual detours.
3. Gather their feedback, preferably before they leave campus.
4. Report key findings to the faculty for a programmatic discussion.

17

Indirect Measures: Internships, Careers, and Competitions

Don A. Grady
School of Communications
Elon University

The success of an academic program can be reflected in the success of students in external environments. This chapter examines the use of outside evaluations—internships, job placement, and student performance in competitions—as forms of indirect measurement. The previous chapter discussed other indirect measures: analysis of comparative data based on regular university compilations, self-assessment (student surveys, exit interviews, and alumni surveys), and advisory boards.

Indirect measures are based, in large part, on the assessment of student outcomes. It is the evaluation of what students know and how well they are able to perform. Whether outcomes are measured incrementally within courses, as separate courses within a curriculum, or at completion of a program, the key issue is the ability of the academic program to influence student learning. Thus, assessment requires that an academic program examine how well it achieves its goals and objectives. In addition, the assessment process may reveal unexpected information that may be useful in establishing new goals and objectives. Clearly, the ability of a program to demonstrate that it is successful in this regard is found in part in student learning, and hence, outcomes.

PROFESSIONAL ORIENTATION AND ASSESSMENT

Many journalism and mass communications programs recognize the centrality of the liberal arts to their mission. This centrality is emphasized by the Accrediting Council on Education in Journalism and Mass

Communications' (ACEJMC) "80/65" rule, which requires a minimum of 80 credit hours outside the unit with at least 65 of those credit hours in the liberal arts and sciences outside of the unit. However, most academic units also admit to having a clear professional orientation. Many academic programs either mention this professional orientation in their mission statement, or in one of the goals or objectives in their assessment plan. For example, the first item listed in the Texas Tech School of Communication mission statement is to "educate students in the knowledge, skills and perspectives necessary for future careers in communications industries" (Texas Tech University, p. 1). The first sentence in the assessment plan for the University of Georgia (2003) is as follows: "The Department of Journalism in the College of Journalism and Mass Communications helps student prepare for careers in magazines, newspapers, specialized publications, news services, journalism education, and other employment areas" (p. 1). The first goal in the Learning Outcomes Assessment statement of the Cronkite School at Arizona State University (2002–2003) is as follows: "The primary mission . . . is to prepare students to enter positions in media fields" (p. 1).

It must be acknowledged that not all schools claim a professional orientation. Nevertheless, the notion that a practical orientation is favored in the classroom and the workplace is supported by the findings of a study of broadcast journalism curricula. Duhe and Zukowski (1997) found that both academics and industry professionals prefer a "five-day-a-week" news laboratory experience over a liberal arts-journalism model or a classic liberal arts model.

A professional orientation also is reflected in ACEJMC Standard 2, which includes a list of "Professional Values and Competencies" for all graduates, regardless of specialization. Among these "core values and competencies" are the following specific references to the profession:

- Demonstrate an understanding of the history and role of *professionals* and institutions in shaping communications.
- Demonstrate an understanding of *professional* ethical principles and work ethically in pursuit of truth, accuracy, fairness and diversity.
- Conduct research and evaluate information by methods appropriate to the communications *professions* in which they work.
- Apply tools and technologies appropriate for communications *professions* in which they work. (ACEJMC, 2003 p. 3, emphasis added)

Clearly, a professional orientation in journalism and mass communications programs is alive and well, and many programs proudly state that one of their primary goals is to prepare graduates for entry-level positions in the field.

Many different types of assessment occur in an academic community. It may be helpful to consider indirect measures of assessment in terms of "perspective." Astin (1993) identified six perspectives for assessing outcomes: departmental, disciplinary, "state," student, professional, and employer. He noted how the relation between curriculum and outcome assessment is affected by the first two perspectives: "under the departmental perspective we tend to 'test what we teach,' whereas under the disciplinary perspective we are more inclined to 'teach to the test' " (p. 39). The "state" perspective on outcome relates to "minimal competencies" such as reading, writing, and computation skills. The "student" perspective examines the responsiveness of a program in meeting the "personal goals and aspirations" of students. Of the six perspectives, the two that seem most pertinent to this discussion of indirect measures for assessing academic programs are the "professional" and "employer" perspectives. The professional perspective, Astin wrote, "attempts to assess those outcomes that are relevant to entry to a profession or professional school" (p. 39), whereas the employer perspective is concerned with the "skills and personal qualities most valued by the employer of our graduates" (p. 40). Thus, these two perspectives are concerned with "value." The indirect measures discussed later examine how professionals and employers value and evaluate the knowledge and skills of students from their perspective outside the institution.

This chapter looks at three types of indirect measures based on a professional orientation: internships, careers, and competitions. They are all based on evaluations outside the academic unit. Indirect measures of these external experiences may be useful as "indicators" of student learning. In fact, ACEJMC Standard 9 recommends that such indirect measures be included in an academic unit's written assessment plan (ACEJMC, 2003). Although the collection and analysis of data related to these activities may seem anecdotal, ACEJMC recognizes that such information may prove useful in gauging the overall effectiveness of curriculum and instruction in preparing students to work in journalism and mass communications professions. According to the Accrediting Council, "this information does not measure the nature and amount of student learning, so much as indicate that learning has occurred" (ACEMJC, 2001, p. 3). In this way, professional-employer derived external measures reflect the strengths and weaknesses of an academic program.

INTERNSHIPS

The internship is one form of experiential education that is designed to extend the classroom beyond the walls of the university. As an indirect measure in assessment, the internship may provide valuable information about student learning. As listed in ACEJMC Standard 2, internships and professional experiences outside the classroom are "indicators" which may be used in assessment, as evidenced by records and statistics (ACEJMC, 2003, p. 3). As discussed earlier, the rationale behind this guideline seems apparent: that many journalism and communications programs, although firmly rooted in the liberal arts, have a clear professional orientation. Thus, an academic unit, accredited or not, will find the internship helpful in assessing the overall impact of the program.

An internship is an opportunity to connect theory and practice. It is an opportunity to associate what is learned in the classroom with the realities of the profession. Katula and Threnhauser (1999) suggested two general purposes for internships: "to offer students an understanding of organizational structures and protocol within a professional working environment" and, "to provide students an opportunity for professional development" (p. 247). More specifically, internships are helpful in making contacts, establishing references, building a resume, enhancing knowledge, improving writing and production skills, and providing access to professional-level equipment. Perhaps most pertinent to this discussion, internships are an opportunity for program assessment. Internships should have intentional learning objectives, require careful supervision by an academic coordinator and work-site supervisor, and have a structured evaluation process. As such, internships present themselves as readily available and valid indicators of the success or failure of an academic unit in achieving its goals and objectives.

The affiliation requirements for some professional organizations even mandate completion of an internship. For example, one of the six requirements for establishing a chapter of the Public Relations Student Society of America (PRSSA; n.d., p. 1) is a "supervised public relations experience (internship)." Many journalism and communication programs and employers believe that an internship is essential for students who are serious about working in the profession. According to a PRSSA commissioned study, 90% of public relations professionals surveyed believe that internships are "quite or very important" (Gibson, 1998, p. 2).

The perceived value of an internship is supported by research that shows a large number of institutions allow or require an internship. Many programs assist students in locating appropriate internship opportunities and grant academic credit (Basow & Byrne, 1993). As a result, a high percentage of students complete an internship before graduation. An Internet survey of Broadcast Education Association (BEA) institutions indicated that nearly all students completed an internship in the one third of schools where it is required, and about 40% completed an internship in the remaining two thirds of schools that do not require an internship (Shriver, 2004). Overall, this means about 60% of the students completed an internship at schools responding to the BEA survey.

Implementation of Internships

Although internships are encouraged by professionals and valued by students and academics, implementation practices vary widely by academic program. A number of important issues must be resolved if internships are to be used in assessment, including the following: whether to allow or require an internship, the number of academic credit hours required or permitted, the value and commitment to experiential learning in the curriculum, and factors that contribute to successful administration of internships, including academic preparedness and worksite supervision.

The decisions to allow or require internships, to grant academic credit, and the amount of credit, may be complex in the context of overall curricular requirements and ACEJMC constraints, where applicable. In encouraging supervised professional experiences outside the classroom, the ACEJMC Standard on Curriculum and Instruction is as follows:

> Schools may award academic credit for internships in fields related to journalism and mass communications, but credit should not exceed one semester course (or its equivalent) if the internship is away from the institution, and, for the most part, supervised by media professionals rather than academics.
>
> Students may take up to two semester courses (or their equivalent) at an appropriate professional organization where the unit can show ongoing and extensive dual supervision by the unit's faculty and professionals.
>
> Students may take up to three semester courses (or their equivalent) at a professional media outlet owned and operated by the institution where full-time faculty are in charge and where the primary function of the media outlet is to instruct students. (ACEJMC, 2003, p. 4)

Many academic programs either allow or require internships for academic credit. But the issue of academic credit is complicated by the fact that many, if not most, employers require that interns receive either credit or compensation (Whitlow, 2003). This restriction is based on Fair Labor Standards Act guidelines for nonpaying positions, such as trainees and volunteers. Students who are paid become employees. Because many employers refuse to pay interns and some view interns as free labor, students may find themselves paying tuition to work without pay. This awkward combination of circumstances makes it difficult for many programs to justify required internships. Although some students may want academic credit, others may not, because academic credit (particularly in summer school) usually involves additional tuition fees.

In examining the "credit versus no-credit issue" as implemented in selected internships programs, Whitlow (2003) found that some programs, such as the University of Illinois Journalism Department and the S.I. Newhouse School of Public Communication at Syracuse University, give academic credit because it is required by many employers. Although some programs require that credit be granted during the academic term of the internship experience, others, such as the one at the University of Illinois, link summer school experience to credit in a fall course so students can avoid additional tuition fees. Most programs generally allow one internship for 1 to 3 hours of credit, according to Whitlow. Also, most schools require a minimum number of work hours for each credit hour granted.

Some academic units require an internship because it communicates that these programs value experiential education. However, the decision to require internships commits programs to ensuring that well structured internship experiences are available for all majors. For example, the School of Communications at Elon University established a requirement that all majors complete either an internship for academic credit or a noncredit "professional work experience." Although there are academic requirements for both types of experiences, students receive credit for an internship and a "check-off" for a noncredit work experience. To ensure the successful implementation of the program and assist students in finding quality internship and work experience situations off campus, the School of Communications employs a full-time director of internships. One rationale for this level of commitment is that internships are an opportunity for a supervised indirect external measure for program assessment.

When administered successfully, an internship has been shown to be an effective tool in the curriculum for learning and assessment. A number of factors may contribute to a successful internship. One study of advertising and public relations students in accredited journalism and mass communications programs examined the relation between the success of the internship field experience and six predictors of internship success: academic preparedness, proactive-aggressiveness, positive attitude, quality of worksite supervision, organizational practices and policies, and compensation (Beard & Morton, 1999). Generally, these predictors were correlated with internship success, and the study found that "a large proportion of students had what they believe to be a successful internship" (Beard & Morton, 1999, p. 50). Of the six predictors, "the quality of supervision and organizational practices and policies ... proved to be the best predictor of a successful internship" (Beard & Morton, 1999, pp. 50–51). Notably, the study found that proactivity-aggressiveness and compensation were "moderately correlated" with internship success, that academic preparedness "proved considerably less important than other predictors," and that an internship did not lead to an increase in career focus (Beard & Morton, p. 51). Although these findings may challenge some assumptions made by some programs, the study affirms the importance of a well structured and supervised internship program.

Clearly, requirements and practices at the worksite contribute to the success of an internship. These include the opportunity to do meaningful work, the level of supervision, and the seriousness and quality of the supervisor evaluation. On the other hand, employer grievances tend to focus on interns' "lack of preparation, training and motivation" (Katula & Threnhauser, 1999, p. 248).

Despite the mixed messages about the importance of preparedness discussed earlier, academic programs and employers typically want students to be prepared before embarking on an internship. In his study of selected programs, Whitlow (2003) found that all programs had some type of prerequisite: "Internship prerequisites most commonly involve grade point average (GPA), the completion of specific courses, and/or the completion of a minimum number of academic credits (junior standing is a common expectation)" (p. 343). Although GPA and minimum credit hours may be useful in controlling the flow of marginal interns into the workplace, course preparation is thought to be critical and should be linked to the goals and objectives of an academic unit's curriculum.

Obviously, some internship sites have more highly structured programs than others, and the quality of supervision varies greatly. It seems clear that academic programs have an obligation to work closely with employers in establishing and maintaining guidelines to achieve learning objectives. These guidelines should focus and constrain student interns and worksite supervisors. Katula and Threnhauser (1999) noted the following:

> An internship which serves as a form of experiential education must be more than simply "work for credit." An internship program must be integrated into the curriculum by trained faculty, and it must adhere to the learning principles upon which its inherent legitimacy is based. When properly developed and instituted, an internship program can become a useful learning tool in the undergraduate curriculum. (p. 248)

Assessment of Internships

As an indirect measure for assessment, the cumulative performance of students who have completed an internship must be considered by the academic unit. At one level, assessment is concerned with evaluating the work of individual students. The end result of this evaluation is a grade in the course. At another level, data acquired from the evaluation of individual student interns may be used to establish records and to generate statistics for the purpose of making comparisons in program assessment.

As required by ACEJMC standards, internships and professional experiences must be supervised and evaluated when students are awarded academic credit. Academic work requirements for an internship might include the following:

- Daily or weekly diary, journal, or calendar of events.
- Description or discussion of formal and informal tasks completed.
- Reports on books or readings pertinent to employer or type of work.
- Portfolio of work completed during internship.
- Papers based on interviews with significant personnel in the company or organization.
- Final report or reflection paper.
- Debriefing session with academic supervisor.
- Worksite supervisor evaluation.
- Student evaluation of the worksite and internship experience.

Items on the aforementioned list are useful for outcomes assessment of the learning goals and objectives of a student internship. Completion of these and other requirements enables the academic supervisor to make a reasonable evaluation of an intern's work in the field and determine a fair grade in a for-credit internship.

To be useful in program assessment, the information acquired through this evaluation process must be linked to the goals and objectives established in the academic program assessment plan, showing that student learning has occurred. A typical intern evaluation form completed by a worksite supervisor might include questions related to dependability, creativity, initiative, appearance, self-confidence, emotional stability, communication skills, professional skills, pride in work, speed, and accuracy (Gross, 1981). Responses to these items may indicate something about the character of a student, but they also should link to the goals and objectives of an academic program. Where does the program teach the values of dependability, initiative, pride in work, and self-confidence? Does the program inform students about appearance? If these are not clearly defined objectives in the curriculum, why should an intern be evaluated on these items? Although "communication skills" and "professional skills" seem most directly pertinent to the evaluation of a journalism or communication intern, the framing of these items may be so general that they say little about what an intern has been able to contribute in a professional setting.

Broadly framed questions may reveal little about how these skills reflect the goals and objectives of a curriculum. More specific questions, such as queries about writing ability and productions skills, must be included if an evaluation instrument is to be helpful in program assessment. For example, the Cronkite School of Journalism and Mass Communication at Arizona State University asked worksite supervisors if they would hire interns if an entry-level position were available. In summarizing outcomes, the school tabulated and reported results in four separate concentrations: broadcast sales promotion, broadcast news, public relations, and news editorial (Arizona State University, 2002–2003). The report indicated that 96% of interns were evaluated as being ready for an entry-level position. This impressive finding suggests that the Cronkite School provides students with the knowledge and skills needed for entering the profession. Similarly, a daily or weekly journal of activities might say something about a student's writing ability and describe the tasks a student was allowed to perform. But a better method might be a "guided entry" approach to writing a journal or final report. For example, the internship coordinator might ask interns to discuss their major duties and responsibilities, explain which courses helped prepare them for completing duties, or describe why they would or would not recommend an internship site to another student.

For the purposes of assessment, core competencies should be addressed, such as effective writing skills, speaking and presentation skills, production skills, and knowledge of the discipline and profession. Also, academic requirements must provide for an examination of more broadly defined learning objectives, such as "basic knowledge" and "basic skills," for journalism and communication disciplines, as enumerated by Turk (1997). A unit must decide what basic knowledge and skills need to be assessed.

Two types of records derived from internships seem appropriate for analysis: objective measures (data) and subjective measures (anecdotal evidence).

Objective Measures.   Units should maintain and report objective measures, such as the following:

- Number of students completing internships.
- Types of internships completed (by discipline and within disciplines).
- Location of internships (local, national, and international).

- Level and status of internship sites.
- Worksite supervisors' evaluation forms (evaluation criteria should reflect program goals and objectives).
- Internship assignment grades (portfolio, journal or diary, etc.).
- Internship final grades.

Although these data are useful in offering a "snapshot" of an internship program in a particular year, they also may be particularly insightful in showing trends in an academic program, for better or worse. Such objective measures provide a context for program administrators and accreditation organizations. For example, knowing the types of internships as related to majors might reveal changes in industry employment patterns. Knowing how many students were able to complete internships in national or international media markets may help gauge the ability of students to access media opportunity at the highest professional level.

Subjective Measures. In addition, academic units should use subjective measures, such as the following:

- Worksite supervisor comments.
- Daily or weekly journals or diaries.
- Reports or reflection papers.
- Notes from debriefing session with academic supervisor.

These subjective measures provide valuable anecdotal evidence in assessing an academic program. Evaluations completed by worksite supervisors, might offer valuable impressions about the abilities of students in terms of writing, critical thinking, and production skills. For example, interns and employers don't always agree on the value of knowledge and skills in an academic program. Hilt and Lipschultz (1999) found that although both interns and employers agreed with the statement, "College should teach students hands-on skills," they disagreed with the statement, "Students learn adequate hands-on skills in college" (p. 16). Although interns felt they had adequate hands-on skills, employers did not agree.

A clear methodology for analysis must be established when using such subjective measures. Graham, Bourland-Davis, and Fulmer (1997), for example, conducted a content analysis of midterm student reports to identify specific work tasks of public relations interns. One specific program outcome read as follows: "To offer students a program consistent with current public relations practices" (p. 202). To analyze this outcome, each internship task was compared to course descriptions or syllabi. The authors used the results to recommend content modifications to existing courses and to recommend the creation of a new course to address specific aspects of public relations writing. Similar content analytic studies could be conducted on student journals, calendars, or portfolios.

Table 17.1 identifies key program objectives that may relate to the items on an intern evaluation instrument. These objectives are based in part on ACEJMC values and competencies. Appendix A offers an example of an Intern Evaluation Form that attempts to relate specific items to program objectives. The Student Intern Evaluation Form is intended for illustrative purposes only. As an assessment tool, an academic unit may or may not use this instrument to address all program objectives. A pro-

TABLE 17.1
Internship Evaluation and Program Objectives (An Assessment Tool)[a]

Objectives	Evaluation Question(s)
Values (ACEJMC)	
First Amendment principles and law	10
History and role of professionals and institutions in shaping communication	11
Diversity in a global society in relation to communications	12
Theories in use and presentations of images and information	13
Professional ethical principles in pursuit of truth, accuracy, fairness, and diversity	14
Competencies (ACEJMC)	
Think critically, creatively, and independently	1, 2, 3
Conduct research and evaluation information	4
Write correctly and clearly in forms and styles appropriate to communications professions	5, 6
Evaluate own and others work for accuracy and fairness, clarity, appropriate style, and grammatical correctness	7
Apply tools and technologies appropriate for communications professionals	8
Apply numerical and statistical concepts	9
Other (Departmental Objectives)	
Verbal (oral) and nonverbal presentation skills	15
Interpersonal communication skills	16
Reliability, punctuality, and attendance	17
Appearance, grooming, and appropriate attire	18

Note. ACEJMC = Accrediting Council on Education in Journalism and Mass Communications.

[a]ACEJMC values and competencies and "other" department objectives are used as examples of program objectives that may be addressed by assessment. For convenience, these ACEJMC objectives have been categorized by the writer as "values" or "competencies." ACEJMC does not make this distinction.

gram may decide, for example, that the Student Intern Evaluation Form is useful for evaluating competencies, but another instrument, such as a guided entry journal or a reflection paper, is more appropriate for evaluating values.

The internship is one form of indirect measures for program assessment. As an assessment tool, internship data and anecdotal evidence should help reveal important trends and consistent or conflicting information and opinions.

CAREERS

Employment is another indirect measure that may be useful in the assessment of an academic program. The ability of graduates to acquire entry-level positions in the field may prove useful in evaluating how well an academic unit achieves its goals and objectives. Similarly, consulting with employers can provide valuable information concerning how well a program's graduates are prepared for the workplace. Sometimes employers and graduates offer surprising opinions. As noted by Hilt and Lipschultz (1999), some employers express disappointment with the work quality of employees, their knowledge of the liberal arts, writing, and technological skills. Should an academic program receive similar responses from employers about its graduates, corrective actions (such as adjustments to course requirements or changes to specific courses) should be taken to improve curriculum and instruction.

Getting a job in the field is the ultimate goal for many students in journalism and mass communications. Some students change their minds late in their academic career, but many persist in their desire to work in the newspaper business, broadcasting, public relations, advertising, or in evolving careers, such as Web publishing. The future looks good, according to some observers of media careers and academic programs. A media career guide stated the following: "Despite economic forces increasing competition, most communication fields are growing, offering college graduates a wide variety of opportunities" (Seguin, 2002, p. 5). This optimistic view is supported by the results of a survey of BEA institutions that showed nearly 60% of students found employment in their field on graduation (Shriver, 2004).

Thus, it seems reasonable that using indirect external measures based on information received about the workplace from employers and graduates is an entirely appropriate way to assess the ability of students to successfully enter the profession. Although employment information is not necessarily a measure of student learning, it is yet another indirect "indicator" that learning has occurred.

Implementation of Career Evaluations

Typically, information concerning employment is acquired by surveying graduates, employers, or both. Many academic units conduct their own surveys, or attach questions targeted to majors in more widely circulated university surveys. Please refer to the previous chapter for a more detailed discussion of surveys as an indirect measure of assessment.

This discussion focuses on using surveys to address questions specifically related to employment. Survey questions for employers might seek to ascertain information about the writing ability and production skills of graduates in entry-level positions, and evolving skill requirements in the workplace.

One example of using a survey of employers is the Newspaper Majors Program of the Grady College of Journalism and Mass Communication at the University of Georgia. Its assessment plan stated the following: "College surveys of employers will allow the Grady College to assess the effectiveness of the educational program as perceived by employers of recent graduates" (University of Georgia, 1996, p. 3). The employer survey is conducted in the second year of a 3-year assessment plan cycle. Survey questions for graduates might ask for an overall impression of the value of the educational experience as a major, what courses in the major were the most valuable in an entry-level job, or about the knowledge or skills that should be included in the curriculum.

In addition, a survey of graduates should provide descriptive information about the employment situation. For example, a report on a survey of graduates for the School of Journalism and Mass Communication at the University of Colorado at Boulder included average salary data, a comparison of current salaries with graduates 4 years earlier, a comparison of graduate salaries with national salaries, a rating of "preparation" by the School of Journalism and Mass Communication for their careers, and self-reported data on job "happiness" or "satisfaction." The survey also found "69% of the respondents working in journalism-related jobs eight months after graduation" (University of Colorado, 1999, p. 6).

Another way to use information related to the careers of graduates in assessment is to cite indicators of excellence in the workplace. For example, the Visual Communication program at Ohio University lists the success of one of its graduates in its assessment report: "The pinnacle of a professional journalism career is to win a Pulitzer Prize. This year's

Pulitzer Prize in spot news photography was awarded to a VisCom graduate ..." (Ohio University, 2002, p. 6). Granted, this is a singular achievement; however, the magnitude of this award makes it an outstanding example or indicator of student learning.

Careers As Assessment

An academic unit can learn a lot about itself by analyzing the employment of graduates. A program could learn more about the knowledge and skills that employers seek for entry-level positions, or that its curriculum leads a number of alumni into law school or graduate school, or gain insight into a rapidly changing job market. For example, using data from the Annual Survey of Journalism and Mass Communication Graduates, Lowrey and Becker (2001) found that "skill with presentation technologies matters to the job-finding success" of graduates (p. 766). Similarly, an academic program also might learn what skills are essential to job-finding, or how its graduates compare with graduates from other academic programs.

COMPETITIONS

Student competitions are another indirect measure of assessment. According to ACEJMC (2001), "a unit's record over time of student entry and performance in contests may provide insight into student competence and into the effectiveness of curriculum, instruction and student learning" (p. 4). Competitions include contests, awards, scholarships, and fellowships, and publications and presentations of scholarly and creative works.

Competitions may be local, regional, national, or international. They may be sponsored by media companies, religious and professional organizations, universities, and foundations. Some competitions may offer cash awards, scholarships, or other tangible benefit. Others may simply acknowledge winners with a certificate. Competitions may be professional or academic. This distinction is usually reflected in the sponsoring organization.

Although not intended as a complete list, well-known professional competitions for students in journalism and mass communications include the following: the Hearst Journalism Awards Program (six writing, three photojournalism, two radio broadcast news, and two television broadcast news competitions each academic year), The Freedom Forum/NCAA Sports Journalism Scholarship Award, the Scripps Howard

Foundation "Top Ten" Student Scholarship Program, the Roy W. Howard National Reporting Competition, the Society of Professional Journalists (SPJ) Mark of Excellence (and other local and regional SPJ contests), National Broadcasting Society Student Electronic Media Competitions, Broadcast Education Association Student Competitions, Public Relations Student Society of America Awards (including the Award for Outstanding Public Relations Student, and the Bateman Case Study Competition), and the American Advertising Federation's (AAF) National Student Advertising Competition.

Academic competitions (scripts, articles, publications, productions, and presentations) also are impressive indicators for program assessment. Many journalism and mass communications programs define scholarship broadly based on the four categories of Ernest Boyer's framework (1990). As a result, numerous opportunities are available for students and graduates for research and creative activities, such as scriptwriting and screenplay competitions, video and film festivals, and submissions of academic papers to journals and conferences. Examples of these competitions include Association for Education in Journalism and Mass Communication (AEJMC) regional and national conferences, Broadcast Education Association, PRSSA, and the National Conference for Undergraduate Research. See Appendix B for a selected list of student competitions.

Implementation of Competitions Evaluation

Undergraduate research has become important at many institutions. Papers and projects that are submitted for consideration often grow out of courses. These academic works often represent a considerable collaborative effort between a professor and student. As observed by Rodrick and Dickmeyer (1995), "undergraduate research provides a unique opportunity for faculty members to work in a personal setting with students. In this setting it is possible to motivate and encourage both the strongest and most marginal students so they achieve their fullest potential" (p. 42). Clearly, successful juried competition of papers, projects, and other creative works must be considered in evaluating the ability of a program to achieve its goals and objectives.

Some academic programs take a structured approach to encouraging student participation in competitions. For example, one goal of the Strategic Plan of the School of Mass Communication at Texas Tech University is to increase participation in national student academic competitions. Assessment of this goal is accomplished by an annual review of "the number of courses used and the number of students who participate in national student competitions" (Texas Tech University, n.d., p. 9).

Similarly, the Scripps School of Journalism at Ohio University has a designated faculty member who oversees entries in competitions. The success of this approach is evident in the School's assessment report which indicated that Scripps students have placed in the Hearst Journalism Awards in writing and broadcasting, a Top Ten scholarship winner in the Scripps Howard Top Ten Scholarship, and an SPJ Mark of Excellence Award for a student-produced magazine (Ohio University, Scripps).

Another example of this proactive approach to encouraging student competition is described in the 2003 to 2004 Assessment Plan for the Communication Department at Southern Utah University. The plan calls for student participation in the Forensics program as one way of achieving its goal to promote skills in oral presentation. This goal is to be assessed by "national team and individual rankings and success at tournaments" (Southern Utah University, 2003–2004, p. 2).

Competitions as Assessment

Like internships and careers, competitions are indicators of student learning. Competitions are a valid form of assessment for three reasons: they involve some form of external review or evaluation of students or graduates, they provide a basis for peer comparison, and they connect the academic program to prestigious companies and organizations.

Both quantitative and qualitative indicators are used in assessing achievements in competitions. The School of Visual Communication at Ohio University reported the success of its students in several prestigious competitions as "indicators of excellence." Students won more awards in the College Photographer of the Year contest than any other school in the country, graduate students won awards in the Pictures of the Year professional photographer competition, and multiple awards in the Hearst Foundation Photojournalism Competition and numerous scholarships were received by students (Ohio University). Such awards and scholarships are yet another indication of recognition outside the academic unit.

CONCLUSION

Three types of indirect measures are discussed in this chapter: internships, careers, and competitions. Appendix C outlines steps for programs that are interested in using indirect measures as part of an assessment plan.

Each of these external measures offers a unique opportunity to gauge the success or failure of an academic program. Internships as an indicator in assessment connect theory and practice. As suggested by Limburg (1994), an internship "is the practical application of the concepts, principles and skills learned in the classroom. It could also be considered the final test for a sound curriculum in preparing the student for a profession" (p. 182). Careers are a primary focus of many journalism and mass communications programs. The ability of graduates to succeed in job acquisition and performance reflects directly on the knowledge and skills offered by a program. As such, data solicited from graduates and employers give an academic program insight into what is valued and needed by the professions. Competitions as indicators in assessment illustrate the ability of students and graduates to compete in external environments. Professional and academic competitions enable students to demonstrate how they compare with peers through an external review process.

This chapter began with a discussion of the relation between the professional orientation of journalism and communications programs and indirect measures of assessment. Although this orientation is useful in evaluating student learning in a context beyond the classroom, the process, as assessment, is not without problems. First, each internship, employment, or competition situation is unique. The constraints and opportunities in different external environments may vary greatly. As a result, quantitative and subjective measures may not be comparable and the compilation of such information may be misleading. Second, external evaluators may have unrealistic expectations about the abilities of interns, entry-level employees, or students who enter competitions. Different evaluators may have very different estimations of competencies. As a consequence, evaluations may be anecdotal at best. Third, because not all students may be required to complete an internship, seek employment in a communication-related field, or enter competitions, participants may be self-selected. This may result in a small and potentially skewed sample of students. A small self-selected sample of specific cases may or may not be representative of a wider population of students in a program. Finally, internships, careers, and competitions may not address the acquisition of high-level knowledge. The focus of external environments may be more on doing than knowing. A program may decide that assessment of substantive areas, such as theory, history, social impact, and policy, may be better evaluated using direct measures.

As with all forms of assessment, indirect measures are meaningful only as related to core values and competencies addressed by an academic unit's curriculum. Journalism and mass communications programs should engage the indirect measures discussed in this chapter as sources of additional information, external validation, and indicators of how well they succeed in achieving goals and objectives.

REFERENCES

Accrediting Council on Education in Journalism and Mass Communications. (2001). *A guide to assessment of student learning in journalism and mass communications.* Lawrence, KS: Author.

Accrediting Council on Education in Journalism and Mass Communications. (2003). Standards of accreditation (adopted September 2003). Lawrence, KS: Author.

Arizona State University, Cronkite School of Journalism and Mass Communication. (2002–2003). *Cronkite School: Learning outcome assessment.* Retrieved March 10, 2005, from http://129.219.216.161/assess/2003_?004/04Journalism.pdf

Astin, A. W. (1993). *Assessment for excellence: The philosophy and practice of assessment and evaluation in higher education.* New York: American Council on Education/Oryx Press.

Basow, R. R., & Byrne, M. V. (1993). Internship expectations and learning goals. *Journalism Educator, 47*(4), 48–54.

Beard, F., & Morton, L. (1999). Effects of internship predictors on successful field experience. *Journalism & Mass Communication Educator, 53,* 42–53.

Boyer, E. L. (1990). *Scholarship reconsidered: Priorities of the professoriate.* Princeton, NJ: Carnegie Foundation for the Advancement of Teaching.

Duhe, S. F., & Zukowski, L. A. (1997). Radio-TV journalism curriculum: First jobs and career preparation. *Journalism & Mass Communication Educator, 52,* 4–15.

Gibson, D. C. (1998). Public relations internship system evaluation: Criteria and a preliminary instrument. *Public Relations Review, 24*(1), 67–83.

Graham, B., Bourland-Davis, P., & Fulmer, H. (1997). Using the internship as a tool for assessment: A case study. *Journal of the Association of Communication Administration, 3,* 198–205.

Gross, L. (1981). *The internship experience.* Prospect Heights, IL: Waveland.

Hilt, M. L., & Lipschultz, J. H. (1999). Comparing views of broadcasters and student interns about career preparation. *Feedback, 40*(4), 14–19.

Katula, R., & Threnhauser, E. (1999). Experiential education in the undergraduate curriculum. *Communication Education, 48,* 238–255.

Limburg, V. E. (1994). Internships, exit interviews, and advisory boards. In W. G. Christ (Ed.), *Assessing communication education: A handbook for media, speech and theatre educators* (pp. 181–200). Hillsdale, NJ: Lawrence Erlbaum Associates, Inc.

Lowrey, W., & Becker, L. B. (2001). The impact of technological skill on job-finding success in the mass communication labor market. *Journalism & Mass Communication Quarterly, 78,* 754–770.

Ohio University, E. W. Scripps School of Journalism. (2002). *Assessment report.* Retrieved February 19, 2004, from http://www.ohioedu/provost/SLOA2001_2002/journalism2002b.doc.

Ohio University, School of Visual Communication. (1997–1998). *1997–98 VisCom assessment report*. Retrieved February 19, 2004, from http://www.ohiou.edu/instres/assessments/97_98assess/dept/viscom.htm

Public Relations Student Society of America. (n.d.). *Establish a new chapter.* Retrieved February 9, 2004, from http://www.prssa.org/about/establish.asp.

Rodrick, R., & Dickmeyer, L. (1995). Providing undergraduate research opportunities for communication students: A curricular approach. *Communication Education, 51,* 40–50.

Shriver, R. (2004). A look at current trends in media education in the U.S. *Feedback, 45*(1), 7–13.

Seguin, J. (2002). *Media career guide: Preparing for jobs in the 21st century* (3rd ed.). New York: Bedford/St. Martin's.

Southern Utah University, Communication Department. (2003–2004). *Assessment plan and report.* Retrieved March 11, 2005, from http://www.suu.edu/general/ir/0304/commplan.pdf

Texas Tech University. (n.d.). *School of Mass Communications strategic plan.* Retrieved March 11, 2005, from http://www.depts.ttu.edu/mcom/reports/mccomstrategicplan.pdf

Turk, J. V. (1997). Journalism and mass communication programs. In W. G. Christ (Ed.), *Media education assessment handbook* (pp. 79–98). Mahwah, NJ: Lawrence Erlbaum Associates, Inc.

University of Colorado at Boulder, Office of Planning, Budget, and Analysis. School of Journalism and Mass Communication. Last updated 6/15/1999. Retrieved March 11, 2005, from http://www.colorado.edu/pba/outcomes/units/jour.htm

University of Georgia, College of Journalism and Mass Communication, Newspaper Majors. (1996). *Assessment plan for the department of journalism.* Retrieved March 11, 2005, from http://www.uga.edu/ovpi/program_review/committee/reports/0203/news0203.pdf

Whitlow, S. (2003). The internship program. In M. Murray & R. Moore (Eds.), *Mass communication education* (pp. 339–357). Ames: Iowa State University Press.

APPENDIX A

Student Intern Evaluation Form

Student _____ Internship Period: From _____ To _____ Hrs. Worked
Company/Organization _____ Location_____
Supervisor _____ Title _____

Directions: Please evaluation the student intern from 1 (strongly agree) to 5 (strongly disagree) or NA (not applicable to the work environment or internship) on each of the items below. Comments are helpful.

1. Ability to work independently in completing task	1 2 3 4 5 NA
Comments: _____	

2. Shows creative potential in completing work assignments	1 2 3 4 5 NA
Comments: _____	

3. Ability to analyze, solve problems and think critically   1   2   3   4   5   NA
Comments: _____

4. Research and information seeking skills   1   2   3   4   5   NA
Comments: _____

5. Clear, correct and appropriate writing style   1   2   3   4   5   NA
Comments: _____

6. Knowledgeable of script style and formats   1   2   3   4   5   NA
Comments: _____

7. Ability to evaluate the work of self and others   1   2   3   4   5   NA
Comments: _____

8. Knowledgeable of and the ability to use computer
   applications and equipment   1   2   3   4   5   NA
Comments: _____

9. Ability to use basic numerical and statistical concepts   1   2   3   4   5   NA
Comments: _____

10. Understanding of laws, regulations and issues that
    pertain to work environment   1   2   3   4   5   NA
Comments: _____

11. Knowledge of the well known individuals, history and
    issues pertaining to the profession   1   2   3   4   5   NA
Comments: _____

12. Shows awareness of diversity in the workplace and in
    the creation of communication content   1   2   3   4   5   NA
Comments: _____

13. Understanding of theoretical concepts related to the
    presentation of images and information (such as,

composition of images, persuasive appeals, influence
of message on audience and society, etc.)   1   2   3   4   5   NA
Comments: _____

14. Appropriate ethical behavior for the professional
workplace   1   2   3   4   5   NA
Comments: _____

15. Demonstrates clear and appropriate verbal (oral)
and nonverbal presentation skills   1   2   3   4   5   NA
Comments: _____

16. Demonstrates good interpersonal communication skills
(works well to achieve group tasks)   1   2   3   4   5   NA
Comments: _____

17. Reliability, punctuality and attendance   1   2   3   4   5   NA
Comments: _____

18. Appearance, grooming and attire appropriate for the
workplace   1   2   3   4   5   NA
Comments: _____

19. Greatest strengths
_____
_____

20. Greatest weaknesses
_____
_____

21. Overall evaluation. (Please recommend a grade for
the work done by our intern.)   1   2   3   4   5   NA
Comments: _____

22. Would you recommend this intern for a permanent
position at your company or organization?
_____ Yes   _____ No

Signature _____ Title _____ Date_____

APPENDIX B

Selected Student Competitions' Web Sites

The American Advertising Federation's (AAF) National Student Advertising Competition: http://www.aaf.org/college/nsac.html

Academy of Television Arts & Sciences Foundation (ATAS): http://www.emmys.org/foundation/collegetvawards.php

Academy of Motion Picture Arts and Sciences Student Awards: http://www.oscars.org/saa

Association for Education in Journalism and Mass Communication: http://www.aejmc.org

Broadcast Education Association Student Competitions: http://www.beafestival.org/student.html

Columbia Scholastic Press Association (Gold Circle and Gold Crown Awards): http://www.columbia.edu/cu/cspa/

Hearst Journalism Awards Program: http://www.hearstfdn.org/hearst_journalism

The Freedom Forum/NCAA Sports Journalism Scholarship Award (NCAA Foundation Web site): http://www.ncaa.org/leadership_advisory_board/programs.html

National Association of Television Program Executives (NATPE) Student Production Contest: http://www.natpe.org/about/educational/student.shtml

National Broadcasting Society (NBS/AERho) Student Electronic Media Competitions (Ohio Northern University Web site): http://www.onu.edu/org/nbs/StudentProdApp.doc

National Conference for Undergraduate Research (NCUR): http://www.ncur.org

Public Relations Student Society of America: http://www.prssa.org/resources/MemberAwards.asp

Roy W. Howard National Reporting Competition: http://www.scripps.com/foundation/programs/rwhcomp/rwhcomp.html

Scripps Howard Foundation "Top Ten" Student Scholarship Program: http://www.scripps.com/foundation/programs/program.html

Society of Professional Journalists Mark of Excellence: http://www.spj.org/awards_moe.asp

APPENDIX C

Steps for Using Indirect Measures in an Assessment Plan

1. Identify key program objectives (may be linked to Accrediting Council on Education in Journalism and Mass Communications values and competencies).

2. Identify where and how key objectives are addressed in the academic program (goals or objectives of specific courses in the curriculum, required workshops and extracurricular activities, etc.).

3. Identify the specific objective and subjective measures that will be used to evaluate each program objective in Step 1:

   A. Internships (work-site supervisor evaluation; portfolio; journal and diaries, etc.).

   B. Careers (work-site supervisor or graduate surveys, numerical employment data, etc.).

   C. Competitions (numerical evidence of submissions and winners of contests, awards, scholarships, and fellowships, and publications and presentations of scholarly and creative works).

4. Establish clear methodologies for the evaluation of measures used in Step 3.

5. Establish guidelines for how a program will gauge the success or failure of findings (for example, is 60% employment in a communications-related field a year after graduation an indication of success or failure?).

6. Summarize, interpret, and report results (compare findings with objectives in Step 1 and guidelines in Step 5 to gauge success or failure).

7. Implement changes based on results.

18

Direct Measures: Examinations

David E. Tucker
Department of Communication
University of Toledo

Assessment: It is the systematic collection, review, and use of information about educational programs undertaken for the purpose of improving student learning and development (Palomba & Banta, 1999). Depending on age, departmental structure, state in which one resides, or personal belief, a faculty member's view toward the topic of assessment varies dramatically. Opinions abound. They run a continuum from "assessment is important" to "our very existence" to "it's a complete waste of time" (Barrington, 2003). But, whatever your position, it has been rendered essentially irrelevant. Faculty no longer have a choice about whether to do assessment. The regional accrediting associations now demand direct assessment of student performance. Moore (1992) said direct assessment techniques should provide the department with evidence that student learning, in the form of student outcomes, has really taken place. Outcomes may include the following: knowledge, understanding, application, thinking skills, general skills, attitudes, interests, appreciation. Assessment asks the following:

1. What should graduates of a specific program know, be able to do, and value?
2. Have these graduates acquired this learning?
3. How can student learning be improved?

Accrediting agencies also make it clear what assessment is not: it is not a faculty evaluation or a comprehensive program review. In addition, it does not have to be "high stakes" testing where students will fail to graduate if they fail whatever assessment procedure the department has chosen. It is, rather, an effort to improve teaching and learning by measuring student outcomes. According to the North Central Association, one of the regional agencies, a properly functioning assessment program will allow faculty members to ". . . routinely link their assessment findings to decision making and instructional and program improvement" (Higher Learning Commission/North Central Association, 2002, p. 21) On the surface, it appears to be a laudable goal that should be relatively simple to achieve. However, depending on a variety of factors, it may not be a "simple" process.

Objective exams, oral exams, performance assessments, surveys, and a capstone experience are all direct measures of student outcomes. This chapter will look at the exit exam as a method of direct assessment. Exit exams are most utilized at the elementary and secondary levels. This is generally "high-stakes" testing where the student is allowed to move up a grade or graduate from high school based on a score or set of scores received. Schools and school systems receive funding based on student scores. The scores are compared to other schools and school districts across the state and country. Developed at the state or national level, the tests cover specific material deemed by state or federal officials as important for students at that particular level. Such "high-stakes" testing is also utilized by some states (Tennessee and South Dakota among them) to measure how well their colleges and universities are doing. And, as with elementary and secondary education, funding and other resources are tied to the results (Rylander, 2000).

Such testing at the level of higher education may seem uncommon, but actually has been prevalent in teacher education and professional schools (pharmacy, engineering, business, and architecture) for a long time. At the entry level, high-stakes testing is often used in communication departments. Grammar tests are used by journalism programs for entry into basic news writing. Programs require students to pass the basic speech course or gain a "C or better" in basic classes before allowing them to continue with the program. Scholastic Assessment Test (SAT) and American College Testing (ACT) scores are used for entry into some majors. Masters and PhD programs give comprehensive exams that are essentially exit exams. So the idea of testing for achievement, or possible future achievement, is not new, even in mass communication. The movement toward the use of an exit exam seems to be waxing, not waning. A cursory Yahoo search using "exit exam + mass communication" rendered, in the first five pages, over 30 programs using exit exams in some form. So, for those faculty who believe assessment and testing will somehow disappear, the trend is not in their favor.

Some disciplines have an advantage in the area of exit exams. There is an agreed-on body of knowledge that can be tested. Curricula have been developed over the years that address this knowledge and it is fairly easy to test a student to see if he or she knows what he or she is supposed to know. For instance, the Graduate Record Exam will test students in eight different areas: Biochemistry, Biology, Chemistry, Computer Science, Literature in English, Mathematics, Physics, and Psychology. There is no Graduate Record Exam for Communication, Mass Communication, or Broadcasting. The National Communication Association (NCA) has no such exam and neither does the Broadcast Education Association (BEA) or the Association for Education in Journalism and Mass Communication (AEJMC). The argument is that communication programs differ to such a degree that no national, comprehensive exam is possible. Programs vary from the very specific (television production) to umbrella programs that require courses in a variety of areas (public speaking, mass communication, and communication theory). Therefore, it is probably true that creating a "one-size-fits-all" test would be difficult. However, it should be noted that NCA has been active in creating communication competencies for high school students. NCA also has a significant body of assessment material on its Web site (http://www.natcom.org/), including "Criteria for Assessment of Oral Communication" and "Expected Student Outcomes for Speaking and Listening." Therefore, it may be possible to agree on a set of learning outcomes for specific areas and hence create national exams by area. The idea is further explored later in the chapter.

GENERAL TESTING ISSUES

There are some general issues regarding the use of exit exams or testing for assessment purposes that should be addressed. First, it is necessary to ask what good exams do. Dietel, Herman, and Knuth (1991) gave the following as good characteristics of a classroom test:

1. The content of the tests should match the classroom objectives and what the teacher emphasized.
2. The test items should represent the full range of knowledge and skills that are the primary targets of instruction.
3. Expectations for student performance should be clear.
4. The assessment should be free of extraneous factors, which unnecessarily confuse or inadvertently cue student responses. (pp. 2–3)

Although they were discussing in-class testing, there is no reason to assume an exit exam is anything except a large in-class test. The content of the exam must match all the learning objectives and outcomes the department has listed. The test should match in its emphasis the curriculum taken by the individual student. This is just not easy to do, not even when students have taken the same classes. For example, there are many ways to teach Mass Communication and Society. It can be done chronologically. It can be done using issues. It can be done in segments (history, regulation, etc.). It can be done by industry (radio, print, television, film, etc.). There are 16 weeks in a semester and approximately 3 years worth of material that might be covered. Different people teach the class at most universities. Although teachers can agree on the class objectives, all may take different roads to get there. The construction of a test that adequately examines these issues becomes a challenge. It might be possible for a media unit to specify content and methodology, but that then raises the issue of academic freedom.

Experimental Design

An exit exam is essentially an experiment. The department has applied its treatment (the curriculum) to an experimental group (the students) and is now measuring (the exit exam) to determine if the treatment "worked." Campbell and Stanley (1963) noted that studies in which a single group is studied only once (in this case the single exit exam), "have such a total absence of control as to have no scientific value" (p. 6). They also noted, for those departments using a pretest, that the single group pretest–posttest design is almost as worthless. There are significant intervening variables that play havoc with the results. Among those are history, maturation, testing, instrumentation, regression, selection, mortality, and various forms of interaction among these variables. In other words, the data derived from such exams have no validity. They are not generalizable in the sense that the data only speak to one group. The data are, at the very least, worthless, and in some cases, they may be injurious to the department, leading the department in the wrong direction. Campbell and Stanley recommended a pretest–posttest design with a control group. Such a requirement would put extraordinary pressures on an academic department. Using a pretest essentially doubles the department's workload. Using a control would double it again. Using a pretest–posttest design with a control group also exacerbates some of the problems encountered when using single exit exams. Security, time, money, curriculum, faculty, and so on are all issues that are discussed later in this chapter. And, unless participation becomes mandatory, randomization and representation become major issues as well.

Citing a specific case from the Advertising Department of The University of Tennessee at Knoxville, Haley and Jackson (1995) pointed out that rapidly changing areas such as mass communication and advertising make a longitudinal test essentially worthless. They also pointed to the validity problems of testing only one group. Unless the test only covers material the student could have learned in the department, there is no way of knowing where it was learned. Campbell and Stanley (1963) would state that without a control group, even if you believe you are testing only information given in your department's classes, you will have no way of knowing that to be true.

Learning

The exit exam is designed to measure learning. Somehow the department is supposed to be able say, "this is what we taught, and this is what they learned." How simple or how complex the measurement of learning becomes depends to a great deal on how the department defines learning. If learning is treated as an accumulation of facts, then an objective exam is useful. If learning is treated as integrated knowledge, then an essay exam is possible. If, however, learning is seen as a complex interaction among a variety of variables, then an exam is not likely to render relevant data. The American Association for Higher Education, the American College Personnel Association, and the National Association of Student Personnel Administrators (1988), in their report, *Powerful Partnerships: A Shared Responsibility for Learning,* developed 10 principles about learning. Although it is not the purpose of this chapter to reiterate those 10 principles, a few comments about the report are warranted. First, the report makes clear that learning is the responsibility of three segments of higher education—faculty, staff, and students. Any exam measuring only a small portion of one of those elements is going to be painfully inadequate. Second, when reading the principles themselves, one begins to understand the myriad issues involved in learning. For example, Principle Number Four stated the following: "Learning is developmental, a cumulative process involving the whole person, relating past and present, integrating the new with the old, starting from but transcending personal concerns and interests" (p. 6). The report went on to say that any assessment of learning should encompass all aspects of the educational experience. Again, any exam claiming to measure such learning will be inadequate.

CONSIDERATIONS BEFORE CREATING THE EXIT EXAM

Given the lack of nationally normed exams in the area of mass communication, any department that decides to use an exit exam as a measure of direct assessment will have to create one. There are several issues that need to be considered before sitting down to write the exam. They include the following: the nature of the department, the number of full-time faculty, departmental requirements, curricular options, number of majors graduating each semester or year, uses to which the exam results will be put, money available for the development and administering of the exam and, the type(s) of exam(s) to be used. Several of these areas overlap, but are listed here separately because they all address the use of an exit exam in slightly different ways.

Learning Outcomes

The very first step a department must take is the creation of learning outcomes and objectives for the curriculum as a whole. The faculty must know what knowledge or skills set they claim to be testing. The faculty must be able to explain to students what students must know or be able to do as the result of having been a mass communication major. An exit exam purports to measure those learning objectives. It is at this point that the nature of the department becomes relevant. Depending on the makeup of the department, the learning outcomes and objectives may be wide-ranging or fairly short. For instance, in a department of mass communication, a learning outcome or objective might be, "The student will exhibit an understanding of mass communication regulation." In a department of interpersonal and public communication, a learning outcome or objective might be, "The student will employ language appropriate to the designated audience." But, a department containing both disciplines might easily have both learning outcomes and objectives and hence have to test for both. If your department does not have a list of learning outcomes and objectives for graduating seniors, then it must develop one before attempting to write an exit examination or carry on any assessment at all.

The departmental learning outcomes should derive from the classes. Each class syllabus should have a list of learning outcomes. Each syllabus should also have a description of how students will be evaluated to see if they have achieved these outcomes, with each assignment specifically stating which outcomes are being tested. From the learning outcomes of the various classes, the department should be able to create a list of departmental learning outcomes and hence a list of those things the faculty have agreed on as necessary for their graduates. If, for some reason, the class syllabi do not have learning objectives and outcomes listed, then the faculty will have to start with each individual class.

Curricular Issues

Although the curricular makeup of the department will determine the number of learning outcomes, it may also affect the number of exit exams. If the department has specific concentrations (electronic media, journalism, public relations, etc.), then an exam for each concentration might be necessary. If the department has a common core, then an exam covering the core classes is also a possibility. The more complicated the department's curricular requirements, the more complicated the exam(s).

Full-Time Faculty

The number of full-time faculty will also play a role in determining whether to use an exit exam or some other form of direct student outcome measurement. If you have few full-time faculty and a large number of graduates, an exit exam might be very appealing—particularly an objective one. This issue goes to faculty time and the uses to which the evaluation will be put. The amount of faculty time invested in the exam may be directly related to the stakes involved. Being quite frank here, if resources are going to be allocated based on the quality of the assessment, then faculty should spend a great deal of time with whatever procedure is chosen. If, however, the faculty are doing assessment because an accrediting agency now requires it, and it will have no bearing on resources, then the faculty will probably choose the path of least resistance. On the surface, the exit exam seems to provide such a path. Be careful. First, a high-quality exit exam will not be easy to create. Second, if the department creates an exam because it seemed easy and the exam does not measure adequately student outcomes, either the accrediting agency or future administrations may hold the faculty accountable.

Departmental Requirements

Departmental requirements also play a role in the development of an exam. As it implies, an exit exam is taken shortly before graduation. However, many departmental requirements may be taken early in the collegiate career. This is especially true of core classes that act as prerequisites to other upper-level classes. The department will find itself testing students on material taken several years earlier. If this material has been reinforced as the student has gone through the program, this will not be a problem. If, however, it has been 5 or 6 years since the student has been exposed to the material, then review sessions might be required. An even bigger issue is content in multiple section classes. To get an accurate reading on student learning, those classes have to be comparable. The learning outcomes need to be the same and the classes should have similar content.

The problem of concentrations in an umbrella department was mentioned earlier. But it is not just developing a test for each concentration, but how much variance there is within the concentration. If all students within a concentration are taking the same set of classes, then they will all be tested over similar material. If students can pick and choose within a concentration, then testing becomes significantly more difficult. Yet another issue surrounding the curriculum has to do with related or cognate areas. Some cognate areas may contribute more toward the student's ability to do well on an exit exam.

Number of Majors

The number of majors will play a role in how the department decides to measure student outcomes. If the department has 2 full-time faculty and 10 students graduating per year, there are a number of options available, including combinations of measurement techniques. Essay exit exams, public presentations of research projects, portfolios, and internships are all possibilities. If the department has 8 full-time faculty and over 100 graduates per year, then time becomes a major issue no matter the measurement form. All forms of assessment are going to require an investment in time. For example, if the department decides on a portfolio (discussed in detail in another chapter), then either the student or the department will have to keep track of all the items to be brought forth at the time the portfolio is evaluated. If the department decides to evaluate writing assignments, the same problem is present. Likewise, time will be an issue in the creation and grading of exit exams if such exams are to be useful in assessment procedures. Therefore, the choice of one method over another should not be dependent on the amount of time faculty believe will have to be invested in the project on an annual basis. Although some methods may seem to be more time consuming than other methods, this is probably not true.

Use of the Exit Exam

How the results of the exit exam will be used is another consideration. Accrediting agencies want the results to be used to improve teaching and learning. The goal is to see where your students are succeeding and where they are not. In those areas where students are not doing well, perhaps curricular or instructional changes can be made to improve student achievement. Although the agencies are, at this point, fairly benign and somewhat noble in their expectations, some states and administrations are not. Funding is tied to assessment and exit exams in Tennessee and South Dakota (Rylander, 2000) and is being considered in Texas and Florida. The very nature of an exit exam means there will be some number associated with the results. The expectation will then be that such a number rises each year. When the stakes are significant, as in funding, faculty lines, merit pay, or even the existence of the department, it requires both an ethically strong faculty and a commitment of resources to create and administer the exam.

Capstone Class

Monetary resources are also an issue when deciding to use an exit exam. There will be costs involved in the creation, administration, and grading of any exam. If it is not a "high-stakes" exam, it may be necessary to provide an incentive for students to even take it. Incentives may also be necessary to get the students to take the exam seriously. These problems can be partially avoided if the exam becomes a part of a regularly graded class, such as a capstone class. A capstone class combines the idea of an exit exam with that of a regular course and is fully discussed in another chapter. The course should, through its various assignments, require students to draw on their curricular experiences and exhibit the student outcomes listed by the faculty as necessary for graduation. The capstone instructor then places students at the level the instructor believes they have obtained on any particular outcome listed by the faculty. There are several drawbacks. Unless the class is team-taught, one faculty member is doing the assessment work for the entire department, and conclusions drawn from the class might vary dramatically depending on who is teaching the class. In addition, the assignments must truly reflect student outcomes as defined by the faculty. This essentially means the entire faculty must agree on the assignments for the capstone class. There will also be the problem of having one class evaluate anywhere from 8 to 20 student learning objectives and outcomes. Assume the department using the capstone class is an umbrella department and has as two of its learning outcomes "the student will exhibit the ability to persuade others in a public setting," and, "the student will be able to apply mass communication theory in everyday settings." The first issue is whether the faculty member teaching the class is qualified to judge both of those objectives. The second issue is curricular. Everyone in the class may not have taken the same classes, and third, the work on one assignment is now substituting for an entire semester's work in a previous class.

Other Issues

There are other items that must be considered by a department before going through the process of creating an exit exam. Security is an issue. This is not just a problem when the students are taking the exam. Care must be taken in guarding the questions, the answer sheet, and the final grades on the exam. There is also the problem of students taking the exam late. Someone will have been hospitalized or their father will have died (ask for an obituary) and the department will have to allow for that. The department will have to create a second exam. This exam will have to be similar in nature to the first. There will also be the necessity of keeping the results of the exams separate to determine if students benefited by taking the exam late. When exams are given each year or each semester, different questions have to be devised. Students who take the exam one year will talk to those who have yet to take the exam. Such student interaction will affect the test scores and hence the usefulness of the exam as an assessment tool. Changing the exam significantly from semester to semester or year to year raises questions of reliability and validity as well.

The department will have to address all of these questions and issues before deciding whether to use an exit exam or some other form of assessment. In an effort to show the process at work, let us look at a real-life example.

The Department of Communication at the University of Toledo is an umbrella department with approximately 600 majors and 10 full-time faculty. Courses are taught in communication, mass communication, public relations, and journalism. One hundred to 125 students per year graduate with a Communication Major. The curriculum was converged in 1997 and the Department of Communication no longer has concentrations. Instead, there are five core classes which include the following: Mass Communication and Society, Information Analysis and Synthesis, Public Presentations, Communication Theory, and a 1-hour Senior Portfolio. Students then evenly divide the rest of their course selections between Applied and Conceptual Communication. The maximum allowed in Communication is 43 semester hr. As of September 2003, the Department of Communication had a Mission Statement and each class had learning objectives and outcomes. It was thought that assessment was being handled by a survey given to graduating seniors that asked for their impressions of the curriculum, the department, and the faculty. The Department of Communication was informed that such a survey constituted indirect assessment and that some form of direct assessment was necessary. Because "high-stakes" testing has not yet come to Ohio's state universities, the faculty began to address options. One of those was to use an exit exam. Because the Department of Communication did not yet have learning outcomes for the entire curriculum, it was believed that an exam covering the core classes might be worth doing. The Department of Communication had the following learning outcomes for the core classes:

1. The student will exhibit competency in public communication both written and verbal.
2. The student will exhibit competency in problem solving.
3. The student will exhibit an understanding of mass communication and its relationship to both the individual and society.
4. The student will exhibit the ability to both find and differentiate among information sources.
5. The student will exhibit an understanding of the law and how it affects communication.
6. The student will exhibit the ability to apply communication theory to everyday problems.
7. The student will exhibit an understanding of social science theory. (Department of Communication, 2004a, p. 1)

The Department of Communication was hopeful that an objective exam given twice per year would suffice for assessment purposes. As we began working our way through the issues listed earlier, it became painfully obvious that an exit exam was not really an option. The creation of an exam covering adequately the aforementioned learning outcomes, particularly in an objective form, was not possible. The learning outcome listing both verbal and written competency ended that pretty quickly. Essay exams were discussed but entailed the same problem as the objective test in terms of verbal and written expression. Essay tests had added problems as well. There was the problem of creating enough high-quality questions to adequately get at the learning objectives, but the faculty believed that could be overcome. It was the grading of multiple essay questions for over 100 students a year that was going to be problematic. Blind grading of the essays would have to be used, thus creating a bookkeeping nightmare. Each essay would have to be given a number and then copied twice. Then, at least two professors would have to grade each question and there would have to be at least two questions for each core class. That turned out to be 8 essays for each student times 100 students. Just doing the math made the faculty tired. The cost in time alone was going to be significant. And, such a test was only going to cover the core classes. There was also the added problem of scheduling the test. One of the core classes is Communication Theory. Students do not generally take the class until their senior year, with some taking it the last semester of their senior year. The Department of Communication would, in a sense, be testing those students on material not yet covered while testing other students on material covered years earlier. Finally, because the test has no bearing on their graduation, the Department was going to have compliance problems. And, even if the students were required to take the exam, would they take it seriously enough to help with the Department's assessment issues? In other words, after all this work, the Department might have technically met its assessment requirement, but not have learned anything worth knowing. After lengthy discussions, the Department has opted for a modified portfolio methodology and reworked its learning outcomes.

DEVELOPING THE EXIT EXAM

Determining the Testing Method

Before determining the testing method it is suggested the department read two texts. The first was written by American Educational Research, the American Psychological Association, and the National Council on Measurement in Education (1999), and is titled, *Standards for Educational and Psychological Testing*. This text discussed test construction, evaluation, documentation, fairness, and application of national or departmental-wide evaluative tests. The second is *The Student Evaluation Standards* (Joint Commission on Standards for Educational Evaluation, 2003), which examines in-class evaluation procedures for propriety, utility, feasibility, and accuracy. Please understand, entire texts have been written on educational testing and entire classes, and in some cases, an entire series of classes, have been taught on the subject. There is a distinct possibility that few of us teaching college-level mass communication have been exposed to such classes. Use some outside expertise.

Assuming all of what has been discussed here takes place, a department must then determine what type, or types, of tests it's going to use. There are objective exams, essay exams, and combination exams. There are available national tests for writing and critical thinking from both Educational Testing Service (ETS) and ACT. If the department has learning outcomes that include written expression or problem solving, this may be an answer. The results will supply the department with nationally normed information about their students. Neither ETS nor ACT has Field Exams in Communication, Mass Communication, Electronic Communication, or Broadcasting. This means the department will have to create and grade any exam in these areas. The simplest to grade is the multiple-choice exam. It is blind grading as the computer does all or most of the work. The computer can give statistical breakouts on which questions are missed most often. The exam can be arranged by learning outcomes so that questions pertaining to particular outcomes can be easily broken out and examined. For assessment purposes, it is easy to determine which information students are learning and which information they have not retained. Haladyna (1999) claimed it is a misconception that such tests can only be used for factual recall. He believed that multiple-choice tests are best at measuring knowledge and do a fairly good job at measuring cognitive ability. Rodriguez (2002) said that multiple-choice tests can assess many skills, including the following: the ability to discriminate, understand concepts and principles, judge possible courses of action, infer, reason, complete statements, interpret data, and apply information. Koons (2000) believed that they can be structured to even measure critical thinking skills. He pointed to SAT-type tests wherein the student reads a passage and then is quizzed about the passage. On the surface, it appears to be a legitimate option for use in assessing a department's ability to teach. Some, however, believe that the objective exam does not get at real learning. Dietel, Herman, and Knuth (1991) discussed meaningful learning as

... reflective, constructive, and self-regulated. People are seen not as mere recorders of factual information but as creators of their own unique knowledge structures. To know something is not just to have received information but to have interpreted it and related it to other knowledge one already has. In addition, we now recognize the importance of knowing not just how to perform, but also when to perform and how to adapt the performance to new situations. Thus, the presence or absence of discrete bits of information—which is typically the focus of traditional multiple-choice tests—is not of primary importance in the assessment of meaningful learning. Rather, what is important is how and whether students organize, structure, and use that information in context to solve complex problems. (p. 4)

Davey and Neil (1994) claimed that the multiple-choice test does not "assess higher order thinking, problem solving abilities, creativity or initiative" (p. 2). Haladyna (1999) countered that the problem is that the definitions of critical thinking, problem solving, and creativity are often fluid and therefore difficult to test under any circumstances. He went on to point out that the test giver never really knows the process the test taker uses to answer a problem. The more expert one is in an area, the more likely rote memory can be used to solve a problem. That's because the expert has seen the problem before as opposed to the novice who may have to use critical thinking skills because he or she has never experienced the problem. Regardless of which side, pro or con, a researcher falls on, they all tend to agree that authoring a quality multiple-choice test is extremely difficult. If a department opts for an objective exam there are resources to help develop good questions (Frary, 1999; Kehoe, 1999; Osterlind, 1998).

The essay exam is a second option. The exam gives the department the ability to ask complex questions and gives students the opportunity to, in written form, show their ability to combine and draw on significant amounts of information. Depending on the number of students graduating, this might be a reasonable option. As with objective exams, there are the problems of developing questions, and then matching the questions to the classes taken and the learning outcomes that students should have obtained. The department will have to determine if grading will include grammar, punctuation, and spelling, in addition to content. A timed exam also measures the ability to recall information rapidly, so the department will have to determine how long students should have to complete it. The actual grading of the exam is problematic as well. If all the graders are doing is looking for specific words or phrases, then the essay exam is really an objective exam in disguise. With essay exams, there is also the issue of intergrader reliability. Each faculty member has to grade in a similar manner. This is why at least two faculty have to grade each essay. As was noted earlier, double blind grading will have to be instituted. In small departments, this probably will not insure anonymity for either the faculty grader or student. If only eight or nine students graduate each year, it is very likely that each professor will recognize which student has written which essay. Using essay exams in high-stakes testing also presents the problem of what constitutes passing and how that was measured. Assume the department has designated 70% as passing and one student receives 70% and passes, whereas a second student receives 69% and fails. The department will have to be able to defend its grading when the student who does not pass asks the department to explain the difference.

In the case of essay exams, the utilization of scoring rubrics is suggested (Moskal, 2002; Moskal & Leydens, 2002). A scoring rubric is a descriptive methodology used when a judgment of quality is involved. The faculty develop a predefined scheme as to what will be evaluated. So, in an exit exam setting, the faculty might set up the following categories: Failing, Barely Passing, Passing, and Passing with Honors. Under each category will be a list of statements describing the category and relating it to the specific question. It is possible to ascribe numeric weights to each statement in a category. In this way, grammar and punctuation might be considered but given less weight than content areas when evaluating the answer.

Moskal (2002) noted several steps involved in developing a scoring rubric. First, clearly identify the qualities that need to be displayed in the essay. Begin with those qualities that will exemplify the top category. Then develop criteria for the lowest category. After having decided what is, to use the aforementioned example, Passing with Honors, and what is Failing, then the intermediate categories should be fairly easy to derive. She suggested that the categories themselves be written as quantifiable. So instead of saying, "the student's understanding of broadcast regulation was good," the rubric will say, "the student made no false statements about broadcast regulation." Rubrics are available on-line for a wide variety of subjects. A web search is recommended.

As with learning outcomes, scoring rubrics should start with individual assignments. They should then be developed for each class based on the learning outcomes for the class and finally for the department. At the departmental level, the learning outcomes are listed down one side, whereas across the top are four levels of understanding. The department can title these levels anything it believes appropriate. Mansilla and Gardner (1998) labeled them as follows: Nothing, Naïve Understanding, Novice Understanding, Apprentice Understanding, and Master Understanding. Under each heading are given the abilities students must display to achieve that particular level. For instance, the Department of Communication at the University of Toledo has as one of its learning outcomes, "The student will exhibit the ability to appropriately explain or package a concept or message directed to a specified audience and/or situation" (Department of Communication, 2004b, p. 1). This outcome is listed down the left-hand side of the page along with the other departmental outcomes. Across the top of the page are listed Mansilla and Gardner's five categories (see Appendix A). Under each category are the requirements necessary for students to reach that level. Using the rubric as a guide, assessment procedures should be able to place students into one of these categories. This will be almost impossible if the department uses an objective exam. It will be possible using an essay exam that is itself graded using scoring rubrics.

THE NATIONAL EXAM

There are some who believe national testing of college seniors is a good idea. Koons (2000) thought students, at least those at state institutions in Texas, should be required to take two national achievement tests. One should be in their major field, the other in writing and critical thinking. He pointed to the growing number of nationally normed exams and said that his university, the University of Texas at Austin, should help develop exams for fields where there are none presently available. The results would then be compared to the students' high school grade point average and incoming SAT scores to determine what the student might have reasonably been expected to achieve. Each major is then evaluated by the "value added" through their instruction. Programs in which students do well are rewarded with additional funding. The exams are not "high stakes" for the students in that there are no passing grades, merely a score. They are, obviously, high stakes for the department or program. Koons is pushing such exams for a variety of reasons. Included are the following:

1. It provides employers meaningful information.
2. It levels the playing field for industrious students by allowing them to compare themselves to students from more prestigious institutions.
3. It gives prospective students a means of comparing programs.
4. It will provide a rational basis for funding programs, especially those that are successful.
5. It will identify excellence in teaching and reward those instructors.
6. It will improve the dynamics of teacher–student interaction by making the teacher primarily a tutor or coach rather than an evaluator or gatekeeper. (Koons, 2000, p. 2)

Perhaps the biggest objection to such a test is that professors would end up "teaching to the test." Koons (2000) answered that in the following way:

> It is an error to assume that multiple-choice exams are limited to testing factual knowledge. ETS regularly uses such exams in testing analytical and interpretive skills. In addition, it would be possible to require students to take nationally normed essay tests, such as the GRE Writing Assess-

ment or the ETS Tasks in Critical Thinking exams. Finally, a statewide collaboration between faculty, education consultants and the ETS will make possible the continuous improvement and refinement of the Subject Exams and Major Field Tests. For example, it should be possible for the exams to incorporate essay questions and problems in critical thinking. We must devise examinations that test for the skills and knowledge that we believe to be most important. Instead of "teaching the test" [sic], the faculty will have, over time, the responsibility of helping to create tests that effectively test whatever it is that they believe they ought to be teaching. The quality of instruction can only improve as faculty refine and articulate the objectives of their instruction. (p. 4)

Koons's initial goal is the creation of statewide tests by subject area. He believes this will help students looking for programs to be able to compare those programs across institutions. He also believes this will help determine which programs are functioning at the highest level and deserve more funding. It is not high stakes for the students, but it obviously will become very high stakes for the faculty and their programs. There are several drawbacks to the scenario outlined by Koons. First, he makes it sound simple. The meetings to determine statewide learning outcomes and how to test for those are likely to be far more complicated than Koons estimates. There will be power issues involved as well. Will the outcomes and test resemble the curriculum of Texas at Austin or Southwest Texas State? In addition, the results of statewide tests are likely to give legislators a reason to eliminate programs that do not do well.

Speaking against exit exams, Georgianna (2000) pointed to Massachusetts and the Comprehensive Assessment System. A high-stakes high school exam, it originally involved teachers and school administrators in the preparation and testing process. Very shortly, however, state agencies took over and teachers essentially lost control of their curriculum. Although the example is from high school and not higher education, the lesson seems obvious. When state agencies become involved, the local system (read as local college) eventually loses control.

A national exit exam is very likely to result in everyone teaching the same curriculum. It almost has to. If a department wants its students to do well, it will have to teach the curriculum that the test covers, whether it specifically has a hand in developing the test. There are very few circumstances that justify the use of an exit exam at all. What is happening and is justified is the development of scoring rubrics for a variety of purposes. The role of national organizations such as NCA, AEJMC, and the BEA should be in the role of facilitators, not as creators of some national test. As was stated earlier, a national test implies an agreed-on body of knowledge that can be tested across multitudes of students and situations. It forces those giving the test to teach to it. One of the great gifts of American higher education to the public is its diversity. The diversity of American curricula, particularly in the area of mass communication, leads to creativity unseen elsewhere. Not everyone who takes scriptwriting gets the same information. Thank goodness. Not everyone who takes mass communication gets the same perspective. Again, thank goodness. A national test moves to narrow the horizon, not expand it. It limits creative possibilities.

The national organizations listed earlier can do a great service by allowing their members to share ideas. Among these ideas should be the wide variety of teaching methods and assignments. Along with those assignments should come scoring rubrics. Instead of just giving a student a grade, the professor explains the grade by being able to specifically point to steps the student has not taken to reach the next level. Instead of just saying, "I got a C," the student can now say, "I got a C and in order to get a B, I need to do the following things." Many mass communication departments now teach a class in critical thinking. Facione and Facione (1994) have developed a scoring rubric for Holistic Critical Thinking. Level 4 (highest) is stated as follows:

> Consistently does all or almost all of the following: Accurately interprets evidence, statements, graphics, questions etc. Identifies the salient arguments (reasons and claims) pro and con. Thoughtfully analyzes and evaluates major alternative points of view. Draws warranted, judicious, non-fallacious conclusions. Justifies key results and procedures, explains assumptions and reasons. Fair-mindedly follows where evidence and reasons lead. (p. 1)

Level 1 (lowest) is stated as follows:

> Consistently does all or almost all of the following: Offers biased interpretations of evidence, statements, graphics, questions, information, or the points of view of others. Fails to identify or hastily dismisses strong, relevant counter-arguments. Ignores or superficially evaluates obvious alternative points of view. Argues using fallacious or irrelevant reasons, and unwarranted claims. Does not justify results or procedures, nor explain reasons. Regardless of the evidence or reasons, maintains or defends views based on self-interest or preconceptions. Exhibits close-mindedness or hostility to reason. (p. 1)

This scoring rubric gives both faculty and students real information about how the assignment was graded. The faculty member can justify to students why they received the grades they did. Scoring rubrics can be created for almost any assignment: TV production, persuasive speeches, newscasts, essays, and so on. The BEA has for years published a variety of syllabi for teachers to use. Perhaps it is now time to do the same for scoring rubrics.

CONCLUSIONS

It should be fairly obvious that this author does not recommend the use of exit exams. One of the reasons for this conclusion is philosophical. Exit exams imply that a number can be placed on learning. It is a very Western approach to problems. Chemicals can be measured and therefore so can people. There is a single truth and it can be found. Given the complexity and number of variables involved in learning, this strikes me as false pride. It also smacks of politics. The second reason is practical. High quality exams take significant time to produce. The process will then have to be repeated yearly. Unless required to do so by the state or your school's administration, utilizing an exit exam is a waste of time, energy, and resources. Any information gathered will not be predictive or generalizable and hence lack usefulness. The creation of a high-quality exam is difficult within the confines of a single course. The creation of an exam that adequately covers an entire major is almost impossible. To create a new exam each year that adequately covers the entire major is impossible. There are significantly better ways to fulfill an accrediting agency's call for direct student assessment. Several are available in other chapters.

REFERENCES

American Association for Higher Education, American College Personnel Association, National Association of Student Personnel Administrators. (1998, June). *Powerful partnerships: A shared responsibility for learning.* Retrieved December 8, 2003, from http://www.aahe.org/assessment/joint.htm

American Educational Research, American Psychological Association, National Council on Measurement in Education. (1999). *Standards for educational and psychological testing.* Washington, DC: American Educational Research Association.

Barrington, L. (2003). Less assessment, more learning. *Academe, 89,* 29–31.

Campbell, D. T., & Stanley, J. C. (1963). *Experimental and quasi-experimental designs for research.* Chicago, IL: Rand McNally.

Davey, L., & Neil, M. (1991). *The case against a national test. Practical assessment, research, & evaluation 2(10).* Retrieved November 12, 2003, from http://pareonline.net/getun.asp?v=2&n=10

Department of Communication, University of Toledo, Assessment plan (2004a). Unpublished document.

Department of Communication, University of Toledo, Student evaluation scoring rubric (2004b). Unpublished document.

Dietel, R. J., Herman, J. L., & Knuth, R. A. (1991). *What does research say about assessment?* Retrieved November 5, 2003, from http://www.rcrel.org/sdrs/areas/stw_esys/4assess. htm

Facione, P., & Facione, N. (1994). *Holistic critical thinking scoring rubric.* Retrieved January 28, 2003, from http://www.insightassessment.com/pdf_files/rubric.pdf

Frary, R. B. (2002). More multiple-choice item writing do's and don'ts. In L. M. Rudner & W. D. Schafer (Eds.), *What teachers need to know about assessment* (pp. 75–80). Washington, DC: National Education Association.

Georgiana, D. (2000). *Tests would show that politics rule.* Retrieved December 7, 2004, from http://www.aft.org/publications/on_campus/spet00/speakout.html

Haladyna, T. M. (1999). *Developing and validating multiple-choice test items* (2nd ed.). Mahwah, NJ: Lawrence Erlbaum Associates, Inc.

Haley, E., & Jackson, D. (1995). A conceptualization of assessment for mass communication programs. *Journalism Educator, 50*(1), 26–34.

Higher Learning Commission/North Central Association. (2002). *Assessment of student academic achievement: Levels of implementation. In addendum to the handbook of accreditation* (2nd ed.). Chicago: North Central Association of Colleges and Schools.

Joint Commission on Standards for Educational Evaluation. (2003). *The student evaluation standards.* Thousand Oaks, CA: Corwin Press, Inc.

Kehoe, J. (2002). Writing multiple-choice test items. In L. M. Rudner & W. D. Schafer (Eds.), *What teachers need to know about assessment* (pp. 69–74). Washington, DC: National Education Association.

Koons, R. C. (2000, March). The t.e.a.t.h. proposal: Reforming higher education through state-wide examinations. Retrieved January 21, 2004, from http://www.utexas.edu/cola/ depts/philosophy/faculty/Koons/TEATHE.html

Mansilla, V. B., & Gardner, H. (1998). What are the qualities of understanding? In M. S. Wiske (Ed.), *Teaching for understanding* (pp. 161–196). San Francisco: Jossey-Bass.

Moore, D. (1992). *Using tests for assessment, assessment workbook.* Muncie, IN: Ball State University.

Moskal, B. M. (2002). Scoring rubrics: What, when and how? In L. M. Rudner & W. D. Schafer (Eds.), *What teachers need to know about assessment* (pp. 86–94). Washington, DC: National Education Association.

Moskal, B. M., & Leydens, J. A. (2002). Scoring rubric development: Validity and reliability. In L. M. Rudner & W. D. Schafer (Eds.), *What teachers need to know about assessment* (pp. 95–106). Washington, DC: National Education Association.

Osterlind, S. J. (1998). *Constructing test items: Multiple-choice, constructed response, performance, and other formats* (2nd ed.). Boston: Kluwer Academic.

Palomba, C. A., & Banta, T. W. (1999). *Assessment essentials: Planning, implementing and improving assessment in higher education.* San Francisco: Jossey-Bass.

Rodriguez, M. C. (2002). Choosing an item format. In G. Tindal & T. M. Haladyna (Eds.), *Large-scale assessment programs for all students* (pp. 213–232). Mahwah, NJ: Lawrence Erlbaum Associates, Inc.

Rylander, C. K. (2000, December). *Examine giving public universities greater flexibility and increasing accountability. In recommendation of the Texas comptroller.* Retrieved November 19, 2003, from http://www.e-texas.org/recommend/ch06/ed04.html

Wiske, M. S. (1998). *Teaching for understanding.* San Francisco: Jossey-Bass.

APPENDIX A

Student Evaluation Portfolio Rubric

Core Objective	Nothing	Naïve	Novice	Apprentice	Master
Presentation: Student will exhibit the ability to appropriately explain or package a concept or message directed to a specified audience and/or situation.					
Theory/Ethics/History: Student will exhibit knowledge and be conversant with general laws, values principles of inherited wisdom and empirical research in the field of communication.					
Information Analysis/Critical Thinking: The student will exhibit knowledge and ability to evaluate sources and processes of information-manufacture in the modern world, including the ability to produce and defend new knowledge according to the conventions and standards demanded by modern, scientific open societies.					
Applied Knowledge: The student will exhibit the ability to apply the range of communication concepts/skills to solve current social/organizational problems.					

Scoring Rubric Definitions

Master:

1. Corresponds to ordinal level of "excellent" in demonstrated knowledge/ability in the core objective.
2. Fluent, in-depth knowledge of theory, practices, techniques, contexts, formats and conventions related to core objective.
3. Thoroughly grounded in disciplinary knowledge related to core objective and can relate knowledge to other disciplines.
4. Can construct/critique knowledge and/or understand processes of knowledge construction.
5. Ability to interpret and act on the world.
6. Can explain or demonstrate knowledge in creative way.

7. Can combine disciplines for performances/demonstrations of knowledge.
8. Excellent, powerful expression, grammar, syntax, composition abilities.

Apprentice:

1. Corresponds to ordinal level of "good" in demonstrated knowledge/ ability in the core objective.
2. Good grounding in disciplinary knowledge.
3. Can explore opportunities and consequences of knowledge.
4. Understands knowledge construction is a complex process initiated by others in the field.
5. Good expression, grammar, syntax, composition abilities.
6. Adequate knowledge of theory, practices, techniques, contexts, formats, and conventions related to core objective.

Novice:

1. Corresponds to ordinal level of "fair" in demonstrating knowledge/ ability in the core objective.
2. Knowledge limited to rituals of testing and school.
3. "Rehearsed" connection between and among ideas.
4. Understands knowledge only as a step-by-step process.
5. Validity of knowledge depends on external authority.
6. Fair expression, grammar, syntax, composition abilities.
7. Fair, but quite limited knowledge of theory, practices, techniques, contexts, formats and conventions related to core objective.

Naïve:

1. Corresponds to ordinal level of "poor" in demonstrated knowledge/ ability in the core objective.
2. Little or no connection between the classroom and the real world.
3. Little or no consideration of the purposes or uses of knowledge.
4. Poor grammar, syntax, expression, composition abilities.
5. Poor knowledge of theory, practices, techniques, contexts, formats and conventions related to core objective.

Nothing:

1. Corresponds to ordinal level of "failing" in demonstrated knowledge/ability in the core objective.
2. Incoherent or irrelevant work, or absence of any apparent meaningful knowledge relating to the core objective.
3. Lack of demonstrated knowledge of theory, practices, techniques, contexts, formats and conventions related to core objective.

This Student Evaluation Scoring Rubric was developed by the Department of Communication of the University of Toledo. It was developed with the aid of Martha Stone Wiske's book titled, *Teaching for Understanding* (1998). The category titles are from Mansilla and Gardner (1998).

19

Direct Measures: Embedded "Authentic" Assessment

Stacey O. Irwin
Department of Communication and Theatre
Millersville University

Assessment is authentic when we anchor testing in the kind of work real people do, rather than merely eliciting easy-to-score responses to simple questions. Authentic assessment is true assessment of performance because we thereby learn whether students can intelligently use what they have learned in situations that increase approximate adult situations, and whether they can innovate in new situations.

—Wiggins (1998, p. 21)

Media and Communication curricula focus on work about real people, with real experiences, and real responses. It makes sense then, that a media curriculum assessment plan would only seem valid and ethical if it were authentic and if it were embedded in the curriculum where it surrounded the day-to-day work in the classroom. It seems odd, almost, that there would be another choice. Media educators are often engaged in authentic and embedded assessment without realizing it. Formalizing the relation is finally putting the name with the face of what has been done for years. It is what we do when we teach our craft, when we grade our media projects, and when we evaluate student writing portfolios.

Authentic assessment is not about choosing quantitative or qualitative methodologies for evaluation, but about designing activities and projects in our courses that most appropriately relate the realism of the media discipline for students, allowing them to practice and experience

397

the subject, and then reflecting on the experience to accomplish greater learning and understanding within the curriculum. This chapter explores the roots of authentic and embedded assessment and paves the way for designing a more formal authentic assessment plan within media curricula.

WHAT DOES IT MEAN?

The etymological roots of the words "authentic" and "embedded" reveal the crux of this kind of assessment plan. An assessment plan is "authentic" when, honoring its etymological roots, it is real, not false or copied, genuine, and verified in its approach. The Greek word stems from *authentikos,* reminding us that authentic means original, primary, at first hand, and is rooted in the notion of doing something oneself. Authentic assessment is rooted in efforts that many communication-minded individuals strive for in their pedagogical approach and so it is a natural fit as an evaluative process.

The etymological roots of the word "embedded" suggest a kind of fixing into a surrounding mass, surrounded tightly or firmly, enveloped or enclosed in an essential way. The media educator becomes embedded in the work and the assessment becomes embedded in the curriculum. Embedded assessment becomes the real work of the teacher because it is embedded in the whole of the course content, and ideally, in the curriculum itself.

Authentic learning is the authentic root of embedded assessment and means "higher-order learning that is used in solving problems that are present in their context" (Glatthorn, 1999, p. 25). Authentic tasks are paramount in understanding and interpreting if and when authentic learning is underway. Developing authentic tasks involves the creation of a clearly defined and shared performance outcome. This is often stated through learning goals and defined through prompts and rubrics. A prompt is a highly descriptive and informative statement about the goals of the assessment task. A rubric is a scoring instrument that categorizes the finished task and places the work in specific levels of competency. The prompt and the rubric are designed to communicate greater correlation between what that student needs to do and what the instructor will be looking for the student to achieve.

Authentic tasks also focus on students' abilities to draw on knowledge learned in prerequisite courses or core classes. This holistic approach solidifies understanding. The authentic assessment task calls the student to think through important themes relevant to the content being taught. And, the task is embedded within an overarching context or real-world application (Oosterhof, 2003). One of the ambiguities in understanding the notion of real-world application is distinguishing the way the task will be completed. "[R]eal-world applications involve direct applications of knowledge that are highly relevant to situations outside the classroom" (Oosterhof, 2003, p. 158) but not necessarily a specific activity that a student might participate in at the work place. An assessment plan that strives for realism in its context through practice and performance will most appropriately achieve the goals of authentic and embedded assessment.

Learning occurs in degrees. To accomplish notions of authentic assessment at different degrees in the learning, a media educator may want to consider a high degree of realism or authenticity in a variety of different kinds of projects in different classes throughout the media major. An identification test might be appropriate when learning a new kind of software or technology or understanding an organizational structure. A performance test might be useful in a broadcast performance course. A portfolio of work samples might achieve authentic learning in a public relations campaigns class. A research project or hands-on experience might work best in a capstone course or senior-level video production course (Gronlund, 1998). A historical understanding of authentic and embedded kinds of assessment will better solidify an understanding of how a media educator might consider a formal move to this kind of assessment plan. Discussion on shaping an authentic assessment plan and examples of four different authentic assessment tasks are illustrated at the end of this chapter.

THE HISTORICAL CONTEXT

The authentic assessment movement started in the Kindergarten through 12th-grade (K–12) educational tradition, but has moved through the ranks of higher education in recent years. In the last decade of the 20th century, the emphasis moved away from multiple choice standardized forms of assessment testing in the primary and secondary classrooms and toward a more authentic approach to assessment. The notion of authentic assessment is bundled along with direct assessment and performative assessment as a new way of thinking through alternative assessment (Mabry, 1999). Grant Wiggins, often lauded as the father of the authentic assessment movement, paved the way for greater understanding of this new focus. Wiggins (1998) suggested that assessment that allows the context of the experience to show through is the most authentic kind of assessment design: "Assessment ought to be educative in the basic sense that students are entitled to direct testing that educates them about the purpose of schooling and the nature of adult work" (p. 22). Wiggins's work also provides a basic work print for understanding the authenticity of a task.

Higher education has also taken a turn in assessment efforts. Although college pedagogy was often designed around professional goals and theoretical constructs that were applicable to real-world activities, student achievement was often measured through multiple-choice tests, especially to assess outcomes in a course through a final exam. Large-scale and less relevant assessment projects and evaluations have recently moved toward "regular instructional activities . . . that closely reflect everyday campus activities" (Palomba & Banta, 1999, p. xii). This new turn has introduced the higher education curriculum to the kinds of assessment in development in the K–12 classroom. Portfolios and other kinds of formative assessments have become a popular and useful alternative to other less significant forms of evaluation.

Authentic assessments within the higher education curriculum are largely based on performative measures that closely reflect learning goals designed for a course and draw on the natural goals of a specific educational process (Palomba & Banta, 1999). Mabry (1999) suggested that "authenticity is a matter of degree, some tasks and some performances are more authentic or lifelike than others" (p. 44). For example, students in a scriptwriting class would find that a naturally assessable conclusion to their course would be the creation of a specific kind of script. Students in the visual arts would strive to create a visual work based on discipline-specific models or rating sheets from a video or film festival or contest. Persuasion students might be assessed through public debate on a relevant cultural or political topic. Media law students might write letters to the Federal Communications Commission regarding antitrust issues or ownership in the media. Students in a media history course might write a mock feature article for a magazine that cites specific historical movements and international development through the decades with a conclusion for relevance in today's media-driven society. Again, when the tasks are embedded in the curriculum and the coursework of a specific subject area, the assessment becomes a smooth movement among course goals, program goals, and assessment goals.

Suskie (2004) suggested that these kinds of authentic experiences are embedded assessments: "[P]rogram assessments that are embedded into coursework—often require far less work than add-on assessments" (p. 103). The assignments are already part of the course curriculum so the assessment becomes a natural fit when trying to understand the learning taking place in a program or major area of study. Media educators today are most likely already completing their own classroom assessment as part of the everyday process of educating. Authentic program assessment that is embedded in the curriculum becomes a natural extension of the entire assessment process for the university.

The Performance Movement

Authentic and embedded assessments nest within a larger explanatory assessment notion called performance assessment. This kind of assessment is focused on students' abilities to demonstrate their skills. If students understand what is expected of them, they become part of the assessment process because they can accurately begin to self assess. This comes back to the very core of assessment, the ability to "educate and improve student performance, not merely to audit it" (Wiggins, 1998, p. 7).

Again, this kind of assessment plan works well for media educators because students are largely graded based on their performance in projects, presentations, and writing assignments. These real-life tasks enfold the assessment process and provide one major focus for student learning. Suskie (2004) suggested that for performative assessment to be valid, students need to be prompted or told what is expected of them, and then they need a scoring guide or rubric to complete the evaluative scoring. This merging of learning and assessment provides the right message to the student and faculty and achieves an authentic goal of measuring student learning. Arter and McTighe (2001) plainly stated that performative assessment means "the students have actually done what ever it is that you want them to be able to do, as opposed to an approximation . . . the idea is to keep the assessment as close as possible to the skills, knowledge, and abilities that are of interest" (p. 46).

But how can media educators ensure authentic performance? One group of researchers suggest that construction of knowledge, disciplined inquiry, and values toward lifelong learning shape an authentic assessment plan (Wiggins, 1998). Construction of knowledge suggests that student work emphasizes high order thinking skills and students' abilities to consider the variety of alternatives in the learning process. Disciplined inquiry focuses on core content knowledge within the media discipline and written communication allows students to elaborate on the core content knowledge. Lifelong learning allows students to view the world beyond the classroom experience as it relates to the media field and involves the community and other professionals in the "real world" (Wiggins, 1998).

A BIT OF VOCABULARY

Each assessment design carries it's own nomenclature or vocabulary and authentic and embedded assessments are no different. Authentic assessment can be either formative or summative in nature. Formative assessment occurs throughout the semester, as students turn in projects, papers, and class work according to the course syllabus. Formative assessments allow the teacher to adjust teaching and learning and provide feedback throughout the learning process (Suskie, 2004). Summative assessments are more of a capstone experience that provide students with a chance to work through a project or idea that will be used in an assessment evaluation that may be reported to an external audience (Suskie, 2004). Both approaches can incorporate authentic assessment and be embedded in the curriculum.

Assessment efforts can also center on direct measures or indirect measures. Again, authentic assessment can work in each of these scenarios. Direct measures involve specific outcomes that point specifically to conclusive learning. Direct measures can involve written work or performance evaluated through a rubric specifically designed for the assessment project, portfolio evaluation, or student reflection based on stated learning goals and outcomes. In contrast, indirect measures offer probable signs that learning is occurring but the evidence is less clear (Suskie, 2004). Internship or co-op experiences, student evaluation forms, and course grades are all examples of indirect learning.

One additional key understanding to lay the groundwork for the creation of a successful authentic assessment process involves understanding the difference between objective and subjective assessment. Objective assessment is a "paint by numbers" approach that illustrates a breadth of knowledge that does not need expert evaluators. It involves objective tests with one clear answer that can be interpreted through an answer key. Authentic assessment is clearly situated in the subjective category of assessment. This kind of assessment focuses on skills not well defined through objective testing, promotes deep and lasting learning, and demonstration of a large number of learning goals (Suskie, 2004). Discipline-specific experts are needed to evaluate subjective assessments because there are nuances in the evaluative process that prevent a less meaningful generic evaluation. Appropriate and thoughtful summative assessment, like authentic assessment, can provide the kind of reportable evidence mandated by the higher education boards of many states. Although more time consuming, summative authentic assessments that are performative and embedded can illustrate to your institution that lasting learning is being achieved consistently over time.

A SHARED RESPONSIBILITY

An assessment plan designed with authenticity in mind needs to be evaluated in an authentic way by all of the players involved in the learning. Students, community leaders, teachers, and others must all come together to design a plan that meets assessment goals. Students are the most often overlooked stakeholders in this process. True authentic assessment brings students into the evaluation process in many ways. Attaching the assessment rubric to the syllabus at the beginning of the semester is one way to begin achieving this goal. Students quickly gain an understanding of the aim of their tasks and projects when the evaluation is part of the initial understanding of the course. Students who are part of the evaluative process are active learners because they think "about what counts as quality and developing personal standards of quality" (Mabry, 1999, p. 71). Inviting students to be part of the initial brainstorming about their assessment plan also allows them to play a part in the process that they will be involved in for many years. It raises the level of understanding about an assessment process early in learning and increases respect for an often-mandated process that may have far-reaching implications for their education.

Community leaders, outside reviewers, and internship coordinators who are active in the media field may provide additional support and understanding by participating in the assessment process. Campus members and administrators are also part of this process because some assessment results are reported to off-campus sources. The Middle States Commission on Higher Education, in their guide *Student Learning Assessment: Options and Resources* (2003), clearly stressed the variety of players in the assessment process and the role each needs to play in the development of an assessment program.

Most important, the teacher actively engaged in authentic assessment becomes a dynamic participant in the classroom experience. Teachers find that through authentic assessment, their understanding of learning in general and the particular learning their students are engaged in is illustrated in a more concrete way, and in a variety of ways, and allows for more depth in the feedback and evaluation process. Many students ask, "How am I doing? Authentic assessment allows the instructor to answer in a variety of different ways based on the authentic tasks the student has completed (Darling-Hammond, Ancess, & Falk, 1995). The increased depth in this conversation gives the student a more grounded direction to go toward to attain what he or she needs to be successful in his or her chosen media field. An instructor who is engaged in authentic assessment stresses the objectives "explain; organize; interpret; evaluate; synthesize" as the assessment task or classroom activity unfolds (Glatthorn, 1999, p. 30). This move toward metacognition through questioning the learning process as it unfolds helps students both deconstruct the problem and build toward understanding. A teacher that provides appropriate structure throughout the learning process and supports a positive learning environment by welcoming feedback in the assessment process most fully achieves the goals of a positive authentic assessment experience.

Timely reflection and feedback to the student are two important steps in the shared teacher–student experience of authentic assessment. An embedded assessment approach may be so well interfaced into a curriculum that students are unaware that assessment is in process. Glatthorn (1999) suggested the following features of feedback:

The feedback is timely, delivered as soon as possible after the performance.

The feedback is primarily objective, based upon clear criteria and specific evidence.

The feedback is multiple, using several sources.

The feedback is constructive, emphasizing both the strengths demonstrated and some of a learner's responsibilities to support the learning, reflect on the aspects that can be improved. (pp. 37–38)

Students who understand that learning, cooperation, and performance are being assessed are better able to articulate through writing, the way they work through the process and the learning (Glatthorn, 1999). Oftentimes students feel that their job is to sit in a room while the instructor rolls out a Power Point presentation from which they can take notes. The notion of active learning that is addressed early on in the classroom provides a context for authentic assessment efforts. Students need to understand that the instructor will expect active learning. Sometimes this facilitation and articulation may come in the form of reflective essays and other times this can be accomplished through learning contracts or action plans.

Because authentic assessment may take the form a group project, it is important to assign each learner a specific piece of the process to make learning possible for all students. A learner's ability to individually think through the learning process is important to authentic assessment because authentic learning is best served on the individual level. This individual accountability toward learning fosters a student's ability to acquire new knowledge and use it to understand the subject area or discipline (Glatthorn, 1999).

CONFIRMING AUTHENTICITY

The process of creating an authentic assessment begins with finding the appropriate ways to embed the assignments and projects within the curriculum. Some media programs might choose to start from a strategic plan to work this through, whereas others might find an assessment committee or curriculum committee the most appropriate place to discuss and discover ways to embed assessable performance tasks and activities to integrate authentic assessment into the curriculum. Still others might start from the classroom and build out from there. Angelo and Cross (1993) used a notion they call "Teaching Goals Inventory" or TGI, to begin assessment at the classroom level (p. 8).

Linking a strategic plan with an assessment plan provides a vision to guide learning goals and learning outcomes for a program (Baron & Boschee, 1995). This emphasis allows authentic assessment to gain the value it deserves in the educational process while it begins to take on more of a central curricular role and less of an emphasis as additional service-based "busy work." The instructor's role is shifted to teacher-scholar, as the assessment becomes research about teaching. Many colleges and universities have designed a strategic plan. Adapting such a plan into a media department program is a positive way to bring a departmental vision and learning emphasis in line and provides an enriching opportunity for faculty to talk through the learning goals they aim for their students to achieve.

Thinking through how the curriculum and the assessment approach link together is an important discussion. Scott (2001) noted the following: "there is no single method for formative assessment, but rather a need for varying the styles of both pedagogy and formative assessment to match the different components of a curriculum according to the differing nature of the aims that these components serve" (p. 21). Some experts note that aligning assessment goals with curriculum and instruction is the best way to ensure that the time spent on assessment is spent wisely. "[A]ssessment should provide a clear understanding of how we—as teachers and students—are doing on attaining these goals. Everything from instruction to "curriculum and assessment reaches toward the same goals" (Blum & Arter, 1996, p. IV–1:1). Workshops, faculty retreats, and grants are also an important resource to tap into while thinking through these kinds of authentic assessment issues. They are important resources in the collaborative efforts of formative authentic assessment.

Each assignment within the media curriculum must correspond, in some way, to the variety of ways media is part of the fabric of today's society. The bottom line is providing students with authentic tasks that provide provable results while training students to be effective communicators and media makers. "Using authentic tasks provide validity, in that they tell us about students' performance on important aspects of the domain that are generally neglected in multiple-choice and short answer tests . . ." (Scott, 2001, p. 166). Options for fashioning an authentic assessment include but are not limited to essays, journal writing, performances and projects, identification tests, posters, reaction papers, labs, reports, and a variety of writing samples. Essays and journal writing also differ from summative kinds of short-answer tests because they allow students to develop and work through ideas around an overarching principle or notion that is central to understanding one's discipline.

SOME ADDITIONAL CONSIDERATIONS

Oftentimes embarking on a new direction for assessment can cause concerns within the entire idea of assessment. Authentic assessment is often considered a time-consuming process or a process that creates difficulty in gaining reliable assessment results. Authentic assessment must rely on valid, concise, and clear rubrics and scoring sheets. This is also considered a time-consuming undertaking. Individuals involved in authentic assessment spend a great deal of time in the beginning of the process, working through rubrics with colleagues and others in their field of study. Fortunately, rubric designs are often available through a variety of print and online sources. Additionally, many instructors have designed parts of rubrics for their own grading in a specific course. Coming together for an initial brainstorming session can be a beginning step in creating valid instruments for assessment.

Another common early concern is ensuring that performance assessment tasks are actually authentic in nature. "All authentic assessments are performance assessments, but the inverse is not true" (Oosterhof, 2003, p. 147). A real-world application "does not necessarily refer to activities in which students will directly participate later in life. Instead, real-world applications involve direct applications of knowledge that are highly relevant to situations outside the classroom" (Oosterhof, 2003, p. 158). This focus on the knowledge itself can direct the creation of authentic tasks. Also, the tasks that involve student "constructed responses" (Mabry, 1999, p. 17) instead of making a selection from a list of possibilities move toward authentic assessment.

It is also important that the players involved in assessment evaluation and scoring understand the rubric and the curriculum or discipline under evaluation. Assessment training for evaluators and meetings designed to discuss the rubric right before the assessment begins are helpful ways of educating individuals to increase validity and reliability in the evaluation process. Because authentic assessment is often not easily correlated through comparisons of student work from other places, encouraging and fostering students to enter media festivals, script contests, and other regional or national evaluative events or aligning program rubrics to these kinds of evaluative ratings helps solidify a comparative nature to authentic assessment efforts.

SHAPING YOUR AUTHENTIC ASSESSMENT PLAN

The next step after choosing to move forward with an authentic assessment plan is to design the tasks and create a prompt and rubric for each assignment. Again, a prompt is the clear articulation of the assignment and the rubric is the scoring guide that will determine the assessable results.

The following section describes ideas for different kinds of authentic assessment projects for media classes, along with sample prompts and rubrics. Each idea can easily be expanded, pared down, or altered to describe a different task. The real focus is on the clear articulation of the authentic assessment task and the effective grading or assessment of each task so that the work being completed for the class and for the assessment reveals learning in concrete ways. Walvoord and Anderson (1998) suggested that grading needs to be the "process by which a teacher assesses student learning through classroom tests and assignments, the context in which good teachers establish that process, and the dialogue that surrounds grades and defines their meaning to various audiences" (p. 1). These three guiding principles need to be at the heart of authentic assessment evaluation embedded in a curriculum. Breaking down each of these notions provides a direction for beginning an authentic assessment plan.

Clear communication between a student and an instructor begins with a clear and well-written prompt. Students begin their authentic task with a clear vision of the work to be done when a prompt clearly illustrates the expectations of the assignment. Although an instructor's verbal instructions and syllabus often spells out course objectives, a list of assignments, and the weight of assignments along with goals and teaching philosophy, when students begin work on an assignment, they generally focus only on the information provided for a specific graded assignment. The requirements of the prompt need to reflect the learning goals as closely as possible and what the prompt actually requires students to do in the assignment. A prompt cannot be too vague or too detailed. Students need to negotiate the problem solving in a way that keeps the task authentic (Smith, Smith, & De Lisi, 2001). A restricted-response prompt can be designed to invoke a fairly narrow and similar response from each student and an extended-response prompt gives students an opportunity to move through an issue in a variety of ways (Suskie, 2004, p. 1). In either case, a prompt is designed to clearly articulate the assignment so students know the direction to go and student learning can be evaluated.

Students who receive a clearly defined and well-written prompt also need to understand the specific criteria that will be used in the evaluation process. This is called a rubric, scoring guide, or grading criteria (Suskie, 2004, p. 1). Arter and McTighe (2001) suggested that a rubric needs to be designed based on the kinds of tasks in which students will be involved. Will the rubric be generic or specific? How can an instructor ensure that it is effective in measuring learning? Most instructors have an informal rating sheet or checklist on paper or in memory. A rubric formalizes the process and spans the wide variety of options in the grading process. A rubric also allows the student to understand the thought process behind the instructor's letter grade decision. A rubric alleviates notions that the student did not understand the instructor's expectations or that the instructor did or didn't "like" the work, as if it were an arbitrary and personal artistic or aesthetic judgment.

To design a rubric, begin by loosely listing the criteria known to be important in the authentic task. Then, fine tune the list and move it into a scoring format that makes sense for anyone that might be involved in evaluation like external experts or other instructors. Also, use other kinds of scoring guides like professional models of competence or rubrics from other courses or disciplines as examples of ways to get started on a design (Arter & McTighe, 2001). This formal move toward grading articulation heightens the effectiveness of the evaluation and provides important expectations and feedback in the process. A rubric is most often designed like a checklist, rating scale, descriptive or holistic rating scale. These kinds of formats provide an instructor with the ability to clearly think through specific learning goals for the assignment, create a meaningful problem that corresponds to the goals, make the assignment worthwhile to the learning environment, and create clear and specific instructions pointed toward the desired outcome (Suskie, 2004).

The most effective rubrics articulate the key learning goals of the assignment, the characteristics that denote a "most correctly complete" assignment, and a list of all elements that are to be included in the assignment. Clearly articulating the completed goals an institution is looking for when grading the assignment gives students a good target to shoot for as they try to accomplish the assignment (Suskie, 2004). In most cases, the student can be given the rubric when the prompt and assignment are given so they fully understand the nature of the final evaluation.

For example, an instructor might want to use an identification test to serve as an authentic experience in a lower level production class, scriptwriting workshop, public relations campaign class, or media management course. This kind of task can be seen as authentic when the experience allows students to work through some definable goal that is demonstrated in a media career. Building a demonstration, work plan, program proposal, lighting grid, staging grid, flowchart, graph, chart, or an equipment diagnostic would be similar in nature to the notion of an identification test exercise.

The prompt would clearly state the goals of the identification test and the expected outcome from the work. What do you expect students to achieve at the completion of this identification test? What level of detail needs to be articulated by the student? How should the student work be formatted? Including page length specifications and suggestions on how a student might most effectively use his or her time in completing the test in or out of class time are helpful to the final learning goals and build an authentic nature to the assignment. It is also helpful for students to know if the instructor is willing to look at drafts of the work. The rubric would clearly state the goals in an evaluative scoring sheet that lists each area of competence, a list of written elements that need to be included in the task, and an evaluation using a sliding scale or scoring instrument that clearly states the level of competency achieved on the identification test (for four samples of authentic assessment tasks, see Appendixes A, B, C, and D.)

FINAL THOUGHTS ABOUT EMBEDDED, AUTHENTIC ASSESSMENT

"Authenticity is a matter of degree, some tasks and some performances are more authentic or lifelike than others. Some cognitively useful activities better lend themselves to real or realistic demonstration of skill than others" (Mabry, 1999, p. 44).

Authenticity and assessment are both about a desire to know if students are really learning the knowledge and skills that they need to learn, to be prepared for the next step in their education and career. A variety of activities are beneficial in the creation of an educated person. An assessment plan created by a group of informed and interested instructors who are thoughtful in the curricular process and committed to the need to evaluate student learning will automatically move toward an authentically designed assessment plan. And it is indeed a movement. Sometimes the process is slow, starting with one instructor and one classroom experience. Sometimes authentic assessment can move in large sweeping strokes because the notion of authenticity is captured by an entire program or university. Either way, the strategies and examples given here can either influence a movement to start, continue, or change direction on a unique trail toward something embedded in the curriculum, and within the assessment process, that is real, genuine, and verified in its approach.

REFERENCES

Angelo, T., & Cross, P. (1993). *Classroom assessment techniques: A handbook for college teachers* (2nd ed.). San Francisco: Jossey-Bass.

Arter, J., & McTighe, J. (2001). *Scoring rubrics in the classroom: Using performance criteria for assessing and improving student performance.* Thousand Oaks, CA: Corwin Press, Inc.

Baron, M., & Boschee, F. (1995). *Authentic assessment: The key to unlocking student success.* Lancaster, PA: Technomic Publishing Company, Inc.

Blum, R., & Arter, J. (1996). *A handbook for student performance assessment in an era of restructuring.* Alexandria, VA: Association for Supervision and Curriculum Development.

Darling-Hammond, L., Ancess, J., & Falk, B. (1995). *Authentic assessment in action: Studies of schools and students at work.* New York: Teachers College Press.

Glatthorn, A. (1999). *Performance standards & authentic learning.* Larchmont, NY: Eye On Education Inc.

Gronlund, N. (1998). *Assessment of student achievement* (6th ed.). Boston: Allyn & Bacon.

Mabry, L. (1999). *Portfolios plus: A critical guide to alternative assessment.* Thousand Oaks, CA: Corwin Press, Inc.

Middle States Commission on Higher Education. (2003). *Student learning assessment: Options and resources.* Philadelphia: Middle States Commission on Higher Education.

Oosterhof, A. (2003). *Developing and using classroom assessments* (3rd ed.). Upper Saddle River, NJ: Pearson Education.

Palomba, C., & Banta, T. (1999). *Assessment essentials: Planning, implementing, and improving assessment in higher education.* San Francisco: Jossey-Bass.

Scott, D. (2001). *Curriculum and assessment.* London: Ablex.

Smith, J., Smith, L., & De Lisi, R. (2001). *Natural classroom assessment: Designing seamless instruction and assessment.* Thousand Oaks, CA: Corwin Press, Inc.

Suskie, L. (2004). *Assessment of student learning: A common sense guide.* Bolton, MA: Anker Publishing.

Walvoord, B., & Anderson, V. (1998). *Effective grading; a tool for learning and assessment.* San Francisco: Wiley.

Wiggins, G. (1998). *Educative assessment: Designing assessments to inform and improve student performance.* San Francisco: Jossey-Bass.

APPENDIX A

Media and Politics

Authentic Task: During class time next week, you will be asked to create an administrative flowchart of the elected and paid politicians in the city you plan to live in after graduation.

Prompt: This assignment is designed to build and test your knowledge about the political system in the city you expect to move to once you graduate. As a member of the media community, it is vitally important that you know when you are meeting someone who holds a political office in your community. Understanding the political structure in any community where you will be required to negotiate the political landscape is a highly important and useful skill. This understanding is specifically geared to any media business, including television or radio reporting, campaigning, developing advertising strategies, or media research, that involves interfacing with the political community. You need to come to class with all of the knowledge you need to create a flowchart of key political positions. This means you need to do your research this week. The instructor will provide you with the list of positions during class time that need to be included on the flowchart. A student may use his or her own personal notes during the class time for the creation of the political flowchart. Each student must complete individual work.

The completed assignment should clearly list, in flowchart form, all of the stated political offices in hierarchical order beginning with the most important position at the top. The positions need to be color-coded based on their status: elected or appointed. The flowchart must be completed during one class period. This assignment should take 4–6 hours of pre-class research. Large pieces of paper will be provided in class for the creation of your flowcharts.

Rubric: The flowchart rubric clearly states the goals that the instructor will evaluate. Figure 1 illustrates a rating scale rubric for a flowchart identification test in a Media and Politics course.

Media and Politics Political Structure Flow Chart: An Identification Test Rating Scale Rubric

	Excellent	Competent	Incomplete
The flowchart is well-organized in a hierarchical pattern with the highest position at the top.	☐	☐	☐
The flowchart is neatly printed.	☐	☐	☐
The flowchart is complete.	☐	☐	☐
All names are spelled properly.	☐	☐	☐
The information is accurate.	☐	☐	☐
Paid and elected officials are appropriately color-coded.	☐	☐	☐
Accomplished the stated objectives.	☐	☐	☐

APPENDIX B

Advanced Television Production

Authentic Task: Produce, shoot and edit a five-minute public affairs special interest field segment on a significant issue to young people in this State.

Prompt: This assignment is designed to build on all of your knowledge about television producing and your skills in video production to create a piece of programming that will be appropriate to roll into a local PBS special about issues in this State. You must research a topic, interview three individuals who are players or stakeholders in the discussion, and shoot appropriate b-roll, cut ins, cut-aways and natural sound to accompany the story in the appropriate time allotted. Think audio, think video, think writing, and think presentation! The target demographic: young adults who live in this region.

This segment will not have a reporter or talent within the story but you may use a voice-over as needed. This assignment should take 10 hours of pre-production, 6 hours of production time, and 2–3 hours of post-production. Use the Ariel font for all lower-third titles, with appropriate consideration to readability and graphic presentation.

Rubric: The descriptive and specific rubric clearly states the technical and aesthetic learning goals the instructor will evaluate. Figure 2 illustrates a rating scale rubric for a field segment in an advanced television production course.

Advanced Television Production Field Segment Combination Rating Scale/Rubric

Please check the appropriate box for each question.

Sense of Project Grade A   B   C   D   F

5- Demonstrates excellent skill, 4- above average skill, 3-average skill, 2-below average skill, 1-poor demonstration of skill, N/A- not able to evaluate this section.

#		5	4	3	2	1	N/A
1	The quality, angle, color and intensity of light is appropriate for the time of day, apparent source of light within the set/location, character and mood of the segment.						
2	Titles show color compatibility and demonstrate readability, tonal separation, brightness range and safe title limitations and do not interfere with visual content.						
3	Titles and credits remain on screen long enough to be read.						
4	Framing in the shots demonstrates an understanding of the rules of composition.						
5	Cameras are at proper height in relation to the interview subjects and desired psychological effect.						
6	Dollying, trucking, panning, tracking and zooming are smooth and motivated and appropriate to the pace of the production.						
7	All audio is clear and distinct.						
8	Audio levels are appropriately mixed between ambient sound and main sound and are integrated and mixed well from shot to shot.						
9	A variety of sound is used appropriately as part of the storytelling: natural sound, sound bites, music, v/o.						
10	All cuts and transitions are motivated and in harmony with the pace and nature of the story.						
11	Consistent visual perspectives are maintained so as not to confuse the audience.						
12	Except for dramatic effect, the shot selection follows what the audience expects, wants, or needs to see at any given moment.						
13	Shot sequencing is used to build connections throughout the story to build a logical visual statement.						
14	Avoidance of continuity jumps and general continuity errors like jump cuts.						
15	Fluidity and smoothness of editing decisions.						
16	Complexity of shots						
17	Overall effectiveness of storytelling						
18	Overall effectiveness of written, visual and audio continuity. Does the piece hang together well as a whole.						
19	Overall creativity						
20	Overall effectively produced.						

Overall total___/100   Row totals_____

This rubric was designed by Stacey Irwin, William Horne, and John MacKerron and is used for assessment purposes in the Department of Electronic Media and Film, Towson University, Towson, MD.

APPENDIX C

History of Electronic Media or History of Film

Authentic Task: Research and write a film or electronic media history related article for your local newspaper's special feature section titled: *Does History Repeat Itself?* This task exhibits your ability to explore and synthesize important historical elements of a specific time period within film or electronic media history that you choose and was studied in the class this semester, and introduce the subject in a new or unique way for the average newspaper reader in your community.

Prompt: This assignment is designed to build on all of your knowledge plus additional research, about a specific historical topic in your area of study this semester in a way that might enlighten others who know nothing about your topic and its importance in history. The emphasis is on content and writing abilities. Research and write a paper that explores and synthesizes historical elements of a specific time period studied to a novice audience. Please provide a strong and compelling introduction, body of the paper, and conclusion to your work in an interesting way.

Clearly organize your feature article so it makes sense to the reader and proves your points based on researchable and cited evidence. Write in a way that shows your careful critical thinking on a historical subject based on examples used throughout the semester. Use appropriate grammar, spelling, and documentation in a history-writing style to show your understanding of this kind of writing. Emphasize originality in thought on your chosen topic and try to explore it as deeply as possible in 10–12 pages. This feature article will take approximately 10–15 hours of research with 10–12 sources cited, and the time to thoughtfully write your newspaper article.

Rubric: The scoring rubric clearly states the goals that the instructor will evaluate. Figure 3 illustrates a general history-writing rubric that is designed for use in multiple course sections across a media curriculum. The writing instructors wanted to clearly state each of the levels of evaluation and they also discussed what each category meant before the blind and randomly sampled papers were read. This sample shows a rubric for each level of competence and then an additional scoring sheet.

	Needs work	Competent	Well done
Organization—including Introduction, Body of Paper, Conclusion (20 pts)	Random organization	Evidence of proficiency in logical organization	Evidence of clear organization, strong intro, body, conclusion.
Content —Research —Documentation (20)	Limited content development, Limited understanding of research, documentation for content. Few references or indication of research	Fairly deep development, use of research and documentation is clearly proficient	Deep and complex content understanding, use of research and documentation clear and well used.
Critical Thinking Originality (20)	Limited awareness of critical thinking, cohesion, minimal development, originality	Focused critical thinking and originality	Careful critical thinking, connecting, and originality that indicates substantial understanding.
Mechanics—Grammar, spelling, documentation, (20)	Many errors in grammar, spelling, documentation Passive jargon Verb tense issues Use of "there" etc…	Few errors in grammar, spelling, documentation	Zero or 1 error in grammar, spelling, documentation
Appropriate response to assignment (10)	Limited response	Clear and logical response	Precise and rich response.
Appropriateness of style (10)	Errors in appropriateness	Fairly appropriate of style	Clearly appropriate in style

Using the history-writing rubric, please rate each anonymous paper

Name of paper_____

Reviewer: _____

GRADE you would give this paper (circle)   A   A-   B+   B   B-   C+   C   C-   D   F

	Needs work 10-14	Competent 15-17	Well done 18-20
Organization—including Introduction, Body of Paper, Conclusion (20 pts)			
Content ---Research ---Documentation (20)			
Critical Thinking Originality (20)			
Mechanics—Grammar, spelling, documentation, (20)			
Appropriate response to assignment (10)			
Appropriateness of style (10)			

This rubric was designed by Stacey Irwin, Peter Lev, and Daniel Mydlack and is used for assessment in the Department of Electronic Media and Film, Towson University, Towson, MD.

APPENDIX D

Filmmaking

Authentic Task: Create a narrative film that recognizes excellent skill in camera work, audio, sound, lighting, editing and overall effect of film work.

Prompt: This assignment is designed to build on your prior experience in narrative filmmaking as well as to advance you to the next level of understanding in film production. The emphasis is on excellence in camera work, audio, sound, lighting, editing and overall effect of film work. Though estimation of production times may vary greatly, this four to six minute narrative film production project will encompass at least 20–40 hours of preproduction time, 2–3 shoot dates, and 15–20 hours of postproduction editing and audio sweetening work.

Rubric: The scoring rubric clearly states the goals that the instructor and program will evaluate. The scoring categories move from excellent skill to poor skill level. Figure 4 illustrates a rubric that reflects the authentic task of creating a short narrative film. The film instructors wanted to clearly state each of the levels of evaluation. They also discussed what each category meant before the blind and randomly sampled films were viewed. This rubric was designed to span the experience from narrative filmmaker to advanced narrative filmmaker. The same rubric will be used with each successive course (Film I to Film III) to guide the skills student filmmakers will develop in the program. Prerequisite coursework was also considered when creating this rubric so that total learning within the film emphasis of the program major could be assessed. This sample shows a rubric that articulates each level of skill to instructors involved in assessment as well as possible outside reviewers engaging in the film assessment plan. The scoring sheet follows for a more exact scoring.

Narrative Film Production Rubric

This rubric is focused on five different areas: camera work, audio, sound, lighting, editing and overall effect of film work. Instructors have identified three general areas of assessment for the rubric. Each category reflects curricular values that the instructors in the program want to emphasize with student filmmakers.

Rubric	Excellent skill	Average skill	Poor Skill
Correct exposure	Correct exposure	Mostly correct exposure with some possible issues	Incorrect exposure
Image in focus	Completely in focus	In focus throughout film with one or two problem areas.	Problems with focus throughout film
Dynamic frame composition, camera angle, camera subject distance, camera movement if appropriate.	All appropriate to narrative structure and understanding of film.	Mostly appropriate to narrative structure and understanding of film.	Problems understanding narrative structure and understanding the film
Coverage is adequate	Excellent coverage	Average coverage	Clear issues in coverage
Audio mixed appropriately	Mix that is appropriate to to the film	Generally good mix	Consistent problems with sound mix
Good audio levels	Appropriate audio levels throughout film.	Mostly appropriate audio levels throughout film.	Consistent audio level problems throughout piece.
Good audio quality	Appropriate audio quality throughout film.	Mostly appropriate audio quality throughout film.	Consistent audio quality problems throughout piece.
Appropriate use of ambient sound	Appropriate use of ambient sound throughout film.	Mostly appropriate use of ambient sound throughout film.	Consistent problems with or lack of appropriate ambient sound throughout film.
Use of appropriate sound effects, music, and music composition if original	Excellent use of appropriate sound effects, music, and music composition if original	Some use of appropriate sound effects, music, and music composition if original	No use of appropriate sound effects, music, and music composition if original
Consistency of light and exposure	Excellent consistency of light and exposure	Some isolated problems with light and exposure	Inconsistent and problematic consistency of light and exposure
Appropriate lighting	Excellent lighting that contributes to the entire film	Generally appropriate lighting throughout the film	Inappropriate and problematic lighting
Seamless invisibility	Excellent use of seamless invisibility throughout narrative structure	Generally good use of seamless invisibility throughout narrative structure	Lack of understanding of this concept

Optimum vantage point.	Audience given information they need at appropriate time	Audience generally given information they need at appropriate time	Audience not given information they need at appropriate time
Consistent visual perspectives are maintained so as not to confuse the audience	Visual perspective maintained	Consistency maintained	Audience confused
Develops audience identification with character through POV, close ups, shot-reverse shot patterns	Strong audience identification	Isolated problems with visual perspective	Undeveloped and unclear audience identification
Appropriate creative, and originality in use of titles, credits	Original and creative use	Some creativity and appropriate use of titles	Lack of originality and appropriate use of titles
Production values: cohesiveness of sets, props, location, costuming	Strong production values	Generally good production values with few isolated problems.	Problematic production values
Directing and casting/acting	Good choices in directing, casting and acting	Some good choices in directing, casting and acting	Problematic Directing, casting/acting
Create a believable fictional world	Well created believable and fictional world	Mostly believable fictional world.	Does not create a believable fictional world
Clearly and effectively forwards the narrative	Excellent in this area	Somewhat forwards narrative	Narrative story is not forwarded

Rating Sheet

The rating sheet is based on the narrative film rubric, but breaks the assessment into five different scoring categories that range from excellent skill to poor demonstration of skill. This allows the evaluation to create a percentage that begins with 100% in the way that a course grade would begin at 100%.

5- demonstrates excellent skill, 4- above average skill, 3-average skill, 2-below average skill, 1-poor demonstration of skill

#		5	4	3	2	1
1	Correct exposure					
2	Image in focus					
3	Dynamic frame composition, camera angle, camera subject distance, camera movement if appropriate.					
4	Coverage is adequate					
5	Audio mixed appropriately					
6	Good audio levels					
7	Good audio quality					
8	Appropriate use of ambient sound					
9	Use of appropriate sound effects, music, and music composition if original					
10	Consistency of light and exposure					
11	Appropriate lighting					
12	Seamless invisibility					
13	Optimum vantage point. Audience given information they need at appropriate time					
14	Consistent visual perspectives are maintained so as not to confuse the audience					

15	Develops audience identification with character through POV, close ups, shot-reverse shot patterns					
16	Appropriate creative, and originality in use of titles, credits					
17	Production values: cohesiveness of sets, props, location, costuming					
18	Directing and casting/acting					
19	Create a believable fictional world					
20	Clearly and effectively forwards the narrative					

Overall total___/100   Row totals_____

Overall this project warrants a grade of. . . .   A   B   C   D   F
Semester projects are collected:_____
Semester assessment is conducted:_____

This rating sheet and rubric were designed by Tom Brandau, Greg Faller, Stacey Irwin and Paula Mozen. The rating sheet is used for assessment purposes in the Department of Electronic Media and Film, Towson University, Towson, MD.

20

Direct Measures: Portfolios

Ralph Donald
Department of Mass Communications
Southern Illinois University–Edwardsville

This chapter provides insight into an increasingly popular way to find out, as Jeremy Cohen put it, "What our curriculum and pedagogy is accomplishing," and "What we can do as professional educators to increase student success" (2004). A dozen years ago it was difficult to identify a media education program that required a student to complete a portfolio that summarized his or her undergraduate work. However, at this writing, a single Yahoo search for "portfolio + mass communication" yielded 60 undergraduate programs that required portfolios for this purpose. (This Yahoo search also discovered a number of graduate and certificate programs that required portfolios as part of the application process. Also, Lebanon Valley College's English Department, in which Media Studies is housed, requires a satisfactory student portfolio as a prerequisite to enrolling in their internship course. As well, this survey also discovered colleges and universities that required portfolio projects (scrapbooks, student reviews, and reflections on their media use) as early on as their Introduction to Mass Media courses.

DEFINING THE PORTFOLIO

What is a portfolio? In addition to the field of education, this term is used by photographers, graphic and fine artists, businesses (to display their work for marketing purposes), and of course, by traders in the stock market. In the academy, many kinds of compilations of student and faculty work are referred to as portfolios. As part of the tenure process, faculty teaching portfolios are common. Student portfolio use and description depend on certain factors, including the educational level (they are in use as early as elementary school) and the discipline (e.g., it's heavily used in English and in other subjects in which students compile a considerable amount of written material). Vavrus called the portfolio "a systematic and organized collection of evidence used by the teacher to monitor growth of the student's knowledge, skills and attitudes" (1990, p. 48). As well, Larson said that the name portfolio "should designate, at least, an ordered compilation of writing [or, in the case of a media student, other media products] ... A portfolio ideally should be a deliberate compilation, gathered according to some plan, for use by an identified reader or readers for specific needs or purposes" (1991, p. 138).

MEDIA STUDIES PORTFOLIOS

Educators employ portfolios according to their assessment objectives. Even within the disciplines of media studies, the portfolio concept varies. To further this discussion, and to begin to explain the kind of portfolio that a media student might compile at the end of his or her degree program, I offer my own syllabus definition: "The senior portfolio is a compilation of the best coursework and projects you have produced while in college. A portfolio can also include media products you've produced at other colleges before you transferred to this university, work you've produced during your internship or in recent professional media jobs."

MORE VARIATION IN MEDIA PORTFOLIOS

Although the earlier-mentioned Yahoo survey indicated that most schools use portfolios as a finishing experience, there is no single, nationwide definition of what a media student's portfolio should include or exclude. And this disparity is proper, because portfolios, to be of value as a direct assessment tool, must assess a set of educational outcomes that are unique to an institution and the academic unit.

There are also many different approaches to the evaluation of portfolios. This stems from the fact that evaluation methods must vary according to the unit's prescribed portfolio content. For example, this content might be confined to a student's work produced in upper division study or during a media internship. It may be evaluated by either faculty or a student's internship supervisor, or both. Other schools may exclude in-

TABLE 20.1
Evaluating Portfolios

Portfolio Content	Typically Evaluated By	Typical Evaluation Methods
Work done on internship only	Internship on-site supervisor	On-the job observation or media program's intern evaluation form
Internship work plus work done in upper-division courses	Internship on-site supervisor and faculty; perhaps also by local media professional visitors	Same as above plus either faculty's holistic or criterion-referenced evaluation
Internship plus work done in all college courses	Internship on-site supervisor and faculty; perhaps also by local media professional visitors	Same as above plus either faculty's holistic or criterion-referenced evaluation
Internship, work done in all college courses, plus other on- or off-campus media work	Internship on-site supervisor and faculty, perhaps also by local media professional visitors; also, (possibly) reviews and ratings from on- and off-campus media supervisors	Same as above plus either faculty's holistic or criterion-referenced evaluation and other methods used by on- and off-campus media supervisors
Work done in only college courses	Faculty and perhaps local media professional visitors	Faculty's holistic or criterion-referenced evaluation
Any combination of the above, plus papers, research projects from "theoretical" courses	Any combination of the personnel listed above	Any combination of the above

ternship work, limiting the portfolio's contents to media products the student produced during his or her on-campus coursework. Some units use only faculty juries to evaluate their students' portfolios, whereas others impanel a jury of faculty and visiting media professionals. Other schools require, in addition to media products, some evidence of student achievement in the more "theoretical" courses: law, ethics, theory, history, and so forth. Typically, the evidence found in portfolios that assesses student outcomes in these subject areas consists of academic papers or research reports (see Table 20.1).

DIFFERENT WAYS TO GRADE PORTFOLIOS

Grading methods for portfolios also vary. They include Pass–Fail, letter grades, and numerical scoring. For example, in my department's internship course, which determines the student's final grade by combining an evaluation by the internship supervisor and the student's portfolio score, a numerical score on the portfolio is determined holistically. Three faculty jury members individually score a student's portfolio from 0 to 100, with a score of 70 required to pass. The jury members' scores are averaged and the result is the student's portfolio score. The other half of the student's grade in this internship course is provided by an intern evaluation form filled out by the internship supervisor. This form is also scored from 0 to 100, and the final internship-senior portfolio course grade is determined by averaging these two scores.

Other college and university media programs require the senior portfolio as part of a capstone course. This method is especially popular in units that do not require all of their students to complete an internship.

WHY PORTFOLIOS?

Why are portfolios becoming popular in media education? Haley and Jackson (1995) called portfolio assessment "authentic," maintaining that this means of assessment ". . . replicates the challenges and standards of performance" encountered in the workplace (p. 30). Many academic units teaching media in the United States—and all that apply for accreditation by the Accrediting Council for Education in Journalism and Mass Communication (ACEJMC)—position themselves in the academic marketplace as professionally oriented. By this they mean that because the majority of undergraduates entering their programs have chosen careers in mass media or as media adjuncts (advertising, public relations, etc.), assessment for such units should determine whether student educational outcomes are sufficient and appropriate for the employment of graduates in the mass media. Evaluating portfolios of student work, especially if this work includes a number of media products, helps faculty and administrators assess such applied outcomes (Donald, 1995).

WHAT MEDIA BOSSES WANT

Media practitioners constantly remind media educators that the kind of graduates they seek for entry-level positions are those who both write well and are well-versed in the liberal arts and sciences. But media educators also know from experience that employers value graduates most if they can additionally demonstrate competence in the basic practical skills of the profession. (Stone, 1996) Some employers speak in lofty tones about the value of a liberal arts education, but when the time comes to actually hire someone for an entry-level position, the graduate who also knows how to compose a camera shot and edit video, gather the facts and write a news story or news release, or write and create an ad campaign—and has something in hand to show the employer to prove it—will get the job (Steinke, 1993). Including resume tapes, discs, and other evidence in some sort of organized, well-produced portfolio helps students obtain employment. And this one phenomenon assists your unit in another statistic on which you are evaluated: alumni satisfaction surveys.

These days, the typical credentials electronic media graduates bring to the job market are a bachelor's degree in their field plus an eclectic set of experiences collected while working on class projects, campus media, or on an internship or two. Graduates of some mass media programs may also have produced some form of resume tape, or, in more recent years, a multimedia disc, but many lack any proof of ability when they walk across the platform in cap and gown. Media graduates often send out hundreds of cover letters and resumes to potential employers announcing that they are ready, willing, and college-prepared for a job. Sadly, however, few are prepared to provide potential employers with any concrete evidence of their readiness. And employers, many of whom were not top students themselves, are not overly impressed by grades (Cappelli, 1992).

Because the ACEJMC, regional accrediting organizations, and state boards of higher education, now ask or require units to demonstrate assessment of student learning outcomes, and because the portfolio is considered a direct measure, many media educators have chosen to adopt one of the many forms and formats of the portfolio.

ACEJMC'S EDUCATIONAL OUTCOMES

In recent years, the ACEJMC has codified a list of desired learning outcomes for graduates in journalism and mass communication. The ACEJMC Web site defines them as follows:
Individual professions in journalism and mass communication may require certain specialized values and competencies. Irrespective of their particular specialization, all graduates should be aware of certain core values and competencies and be able to:

- understand and apply the principles and laws of freedom of speech and press, including the right to dissent, to monitor and criticize power, and to assemble and petition for redress of grievances;

- demonstrate an understanding of the history and role of professionals and institutions in shaping communications;
- demonstrate an understanding of the diversity of groups in a global society in relationship to communications;
- understand concepts and apply theories in the use and presentation of images and information;
- demonstrate an understanding of professional ethical principles and work ethically in pursuit of truth, accuracy, fairness and diversity;
- think critically, creatively and independently;
- conduct research and evaluate information by methods appropriate to the communications professions in which they work;
- write correctly and clearly in forms and styles appropriate for the communications professions, audiences and purposes they serve;
- critically evaluate their own work and that of others for accuracy and fairness, clarity, appropriate style and grammatical correctness;
- apply basic numerical and statistical concepts;
- apply tools and technologies appropriate for the communications professions in which they work. (ACEJMC)

Evaluations of intern performance, measured by many units via both intern evaluation instruments and portfolios, cannot always assess every one of these competencies for every intern, especially students interning in advertising, public relations, broadcast production, and other nonjournalistic occupations. But most of the ACEJMC objectives apply to all students, and with the right sort of evaluation form, important assessment data can be acquired from both the internship and the portfolio evaluation. And the use of the portfolio of a student's work produced in classes, campus media, and especially on the job as an intern, helps to holistically evaluate a student's ability to produce media products and conduct research into issues in mass media.

The first ACEJMC competency, relating to a working knowledge of the principles of freedom of speech and press, is encountered daily in journalism interns' efforts to gather and report the news. The mentor–intern relationship between intern and intern supervisor is key to student learning in this area. For example, clips of stories included in their portfolios in which interns were required to deal with government gatekeepers such as the police, the courts, and bureaucrats, might be termed *prima facie* evidence of the extent to which these competencies have been acquired. Likewise, although an understanding of the history and role of professionals and institutions in shaping communications is taught in every classroom in media studies units, the mentor–student relationship reinforces the importance and relevance of key concepts on the job in the "real world," where professionals are constantly working to refine and improve the state of mass communications in America. At least by inference, portfolio content reinforces the unit's confidence in student understanding in this area.

Especially for interns who have had a sheltered upbringing or who have attended colleges in which the student body is not diverse, (e.g., students from rural schools who have not experienced much of the wider world), a well-chosen internship can greatly improve his or her worldview, which helps satisfy the third ACEJMC competency, related to diversity. And, based on student achievement on the internship or in the production of campus student media products, portfolio content reinforces faculty confidence in student understanding of the concepts of diversity.

Assessment results discovered via the use of internship evaluations and portfolios are especially relevant for ACEJMC objective number four, which is concerned with applying theories in the use and presentation of images and information. Examination of portfolio contents produced for campus media or on the internship for utilization of aesthetic, communication, and ethical principles and theories displays a student's practical understanding.

ACEJMC objective number five, an understanding and ability to apply professional ethical principles, is practiced in both campus media and internship work, which will be displayed in the portfolio. The same is true for ACEJMC objective number six, the ability to think critically, creatively, and independently. Media products displayed in portfolios tell the discriminating reader much about the way a student's mind works, how creatively he or she can convey the information, and whether he or she derived facts and values independently or lazily relied on less-than-objective "official" sources.

Not all items included in a portfolio help to assess ACEJMC objective number six, the ability to conduct research and evaluate information by methods appropriate to the communications professions in which communications practitioners work. Certainly the student journalist, both in campus media work and on the internship, can easily demonstrate this trait in the content of his or her portfolio. But some media products, such as those developed while working in the creative services side of advertising, producing commercials, and so forth, do not lend themselves easily to display of competency in this objective.

However, the seventh ACEJMC competency, to write correctly and clearly in forms and styles appropriate for the communications professions, is very clearly shown in media products created for campus media and internships and displayed in the portfolio. This is extremely helpful in faculty assessment activities.

The eighth objective, a student's ability to critically evaluate his or her work, is one in which the portfolio is perhaps the best indicator. One of the important skills derived from the compilation of one's work in a portfolio is the ability to judge the quality of the items chosen for inclusion versus those that are inferior and should be left out. An added bonus in learning by repetition occurs when the student judges a media product he or she produced to be unsatisfactory and rewrites or reedits it to make it acceptable.

Objective number nine, applying basic numerical and statistical concepts, is mostly relevant to the journalism or public relations students who must, for example, examine and report on research content or create factoids in newspaper and magazine stories for their internships or for campus media. Advertising campaign proposals and other such items produced for class projects and internship work also make use of quantitative methods and can be included in portfolios to demonstrate competency.

It is easy to see how ACEJMC objective number 10, a student's ability to apply tools and technologies appropriate for the communications professions in which he or she works, is best gauged via the portfolio. Student campus media productions and media products produced on the internships are again prima facie evidence.

TWO UNIVERSITIES' PORTFOLIO PROGRAMS

In 1991, as chair of the Department of Communications at the University of Tennessee at Martin (UT-Martin), and again in 1998, as chair of the Department of Mass Communications at Southern Illinois University at Edwardsville (SIUE), I lead my faculty through the process of developing portfolio assessment for our units (see the Appendix). They adopted a senior portfolio as the official graded exit test requirement for all communications majors. Scores of 0 to 100 were possible, but a score of 70 was required to graduate. A student who failed to achieve a 70 could resubmit a revised portfolio after either its contents were revised or enlarged, or, in an unusual case, the student completed additional coursework or practicum experience.

At UT-Martin, the faculty hoped that because a satisfactory portfolio score would be required to pass the Senior Seminar and thus qualify for graduation, and because students would perceive the end product as worthwhile, portfolio assessment might provide more valid assessment plus significantly improved programmatic feedback. Then, portfolio-in-hand, students would leave the university with a professionally prepared, persuasive "sales brochure" to assist them in the job search. And because achievement of a satisfactory portfolio score required them to produce more quality media products while enrolled in the program, students, through additional or repeated learning experiences, would hopefully become more adept at the skills of the profession.

Likewise, in 1997, the faculty of SIUE were in search of a new capstone experience for their students. As an institution, SIUE requires each undergraduate to complete a "senior project." Each department is responsible for providing students with the requirements for the project. The faculty adopted the senior portfolio as their senior project. Unlike UT-Martin, which folded the portfolio requirement into the capstone course, SIUE's portfolio is part of the department's required internship course.

BORROWING FROM THE ARTS

Senior portfolio requirements command student notice by asking them to demonstrate a certain standard of holistic competence before they are permitted to graduate. Borrowing from the jury system used to assess the synthesis of learning and skills in the disciplines of music, art, and theatre, faculty believe that the quality of the media products that students have learned to create (e.g., radio news stories, scripts, TV commercials, public service announcements [PSAs], press releases, TV programs, multimedia presentations, etc.) holistically represent the educational objectives of the entire professionally oriented curricula better than any other single evaluative measure.

WHETHER TO USE PROFESSIONAL JUDGES

A faculty jury system for portfolios is common. But some programs also utilize local media professionals as part of the jury process. One reason many colleges and universities do not choose to use working pros in portfolio assessment is because of the structure or complexity of the department's curriculum. In the case of SIUE, the portfolio requirement is combined with an internship. Faculty know the students, know their work in their courses, and wish to judge student work—and student progress—themselves. Because SIUE's internship evaluation process involves intern supervisors separately judging the work the students have accomplished on the job, both academic and working professional review of student competencies are utilized. (See a copy of this form at the end of this chapter. It includes many questions posed by the faculty as well as the ACEJMC's educational objectives.) So, both the professional in the workplace and the professors who have taught the students for 4 years evaluate evidence of student achievement from their particular perspectives.

On many campuses, portfolio assessment has generated a positive qualitative ripple effect. But there are also problem areas. The remainder of this chapter discusses some of the advantages and disadvantages and provides a close-up of how the senior portfolio has been operationalized at SIUE over the last 6 years.

ADVANTAGES OF THE PORTFOLIO

• Faculty members actively support the portfolio requirement in all their courses, identifying in their syllabi which course projects are appropriate for students to save for their senior portfolios.

• As a result, faculty report a surprising benefit: Before they required senior portfolios, instructors would, for example, pass back a student's script assignment for a radio commercial, marked up with the usual amount of red pen. Ninety-nine times out of a hundred, after class was dismissed, that script would end up in a trash can in the hallway. But now the student, who knows that this project is a possible portfolio element, not only saves his or her work, but also reads the professor's criticism more carefully, makes corrections to the original, and, if he or she is cautious, saves it on both hard copy and disc for the portfolio. So, as an advertising practitioner might phrase it, requiring portfolios provides professors with "more bang for the buck" in each class assignment.

• Faculty can periodically review the success of the individual objectives within each course they teach in light of the competencies displayed by students in their portfolios. Then, as a committee, faculty within each sequence can assess how these objectives work together.

• Some faculty give their students extra course credit for "miniportfolios"—final compilations of student work throughout the semester in a single course. Assignments are rewritten, reshot, or reedited to reflect the improvements on the original assignments suggested by their professors. In describing the use of miniportfolios for courses, McClelland (1991) made the case that there is another implicit advantage: changing the student culture from a goal of doing work to get a grade for a course to "getting it right," focusing on "texts, readers, revision, development and potential—not on grades" (pp. 165–173).

• Because of this more mature focus, students seem to take their classes and their class projects more seriously, because they are later required to display a heightened competence by revising and improving their work for their portfolios. They must actually master the new skills assigned rather than just complete projects: Learning becomes the goal, not just collecting grades and credits.

• Students volunteer for work at campus media outlets. They "stay with it" until they master the skills. Becker, Kosicki, Engleman, and Viswanath (1993) said that success in the job market is much more likely for those with significant experience in campus media.

• Students seem more confident in their ability to compete for jobs after preparing a portfolio: They know they can do professional-quality work because they have a juried portfolio to prove it. Through this process, students also learn another valuable job skill: evaluating their own work, culling through their accomplishments, choosing and polishing their very best—also demonstrating to potential employers that they know quality work when they see it (Forrest, 1990; Hutchings, 1990).

• Because the faculty in each sequence sit on juries together to evaluate portfolios, they learn more about what their colleagues are doing in the classroom and what they're assigning. Redundancy in the curriculum is reduced through enhanced faculty communication. At all levels of education, portfolios are used—and praised—for the feedback they provide those who teach (Schilling & Schilling, 1993).

• Faculty also can more easily evaluate the results of courses that build on each other.

• Identifying uniform weaknesses among graduating seniors prompts faculty to alter course content or create new curriculum or requirements.

• These last two benefits are significant. Student course evaluation survey forms tell faculty little about what students have actually learned in a course: in this sense, they really only tell a professor what students liked or didn't like about the course units he or she taught. Correct his or her assignment, give out a grade, but what can the student really do, what has he or she been able to synthesize when finishing a course? But look at an end-of-semester miniportfolio assignment and one can readily see if the student really "got it." Evaluate that same student's portfolio as a graduating senior and faculty can more easily track a student's overall improvement, increased sophistication, and ability to judge the quality of their own work.

• And when faculty see the results of their efforts in context with the rest of a student's learning experiences and achievements, they can more easily pinpoint programmatic strengths and weaknesses. For example, if faculty members meet around a table to evaluate senior portfolios, discussion often leads to alterations in both course and curriculum content. After changes have been in place for a period of time, faculty can evaluate effectiveness in subsequent portfolios. For example, after a few years of evaluating what they considered to be the substandard writing in Television-Radio student portfolios at SIUE, the Television-Radio faculty created a new course to anchor the sequence, Advanced Broadcast Writing. In subsequent years' portfolios, Television-Radio student writing improved.

It is clear to UT-Martin and SIUE faculty how advantageous portfolios are to the success of their programs. Potential employers have been impressed as well. Many graduates have reported that the statement on their resume regarding the availability of a portfolio has prompted many employers to ask to see them. Graduates are advised to use this request as an excuse to visit the station, newspaper office, public relations firm, and so forth, and deliver the portfolio in person to get "face time"—one additional chance to make a positive impression.

DISADVANTAGES OF THE PORTFOLIO

No evaluation system is perfect, and portfolio assessment has potential pitfalls to consider:

• The most frequently cited concern with portfolios is the issue of authenticity. How can you be sure that students are turning in their own work? If students' professors evaluate the portfolios, there is little concern about that. Professors are well aware of whose work they are seeing, sometimes for the third or fourth time. This is key to the authenticity issue: The same professors who have assigned, evaluated, graded, and sometimes reevaluated the same work again in miniportfolios at the end of the semester are the persons judging these final senior portfolios. In a system such as this, there is little problem with student dishonesty. Later on in this chapter, read how SIUE's portfolio instructions deal with claiming only the portion of a group project a student actually produced.

• Rudner (1992) discussed a typology of rater effects that can skew the results of portfolio assessment. They include the following:

a. "The halo effect," in which positive or negative prior impressions about a particular student may color faculty jury evaluation of the portfolio.

b. "Stereotyping," in which faculty juries may unfairly consider entire groups of students as possessing certain characteristics. For example, the SIUE faculty have always considered print journalism students to be the best writers in the department. This may skew evaluations of writing upward for these students.

c. "Perception differences," in which the viewpoints and past experiences of an evaluator can affect how he or she interprets behavior (or student-produced media products).

d. "Leniency or stringency error"—When viewing another professor's assignment in a portfolio, a colleague may not "have enough knowledge to make an objective rating," resulting in "scores that are systematically higher or lower."

e. "Scale shrinking"—"Some judges will not use the end of any scale."

As valuable as portfolios are to assessment in a professional media program, it is important to note that it is not enough to rely completely on portfolio evaluation. As introduced earlier, if internships are required in the media program, students should also be evaluated by their professional mentors.

To provide extra assurance that solid learning is taking place on internships, students should evaluate their experiences in "internship papers," detailing their learning experiences while on internship. In addition, at SIUE, under the same internship course rubric, students also are required to evaluate their own experience in their mass communications studies via anonymous graduating senior assessment letters.

SHARED PURPOSE

It should be reemphasized that to be successful, any assessment plan must meet both the corporate evaluative needs of the sponsoring department and the self-evaluative needs of each student. As Banta (1993) put it, the preeminent task is to "build a sense of shared purpose among students, faculty, and administrators based on clearly articulated and communicated statements of mission and educational goals" (p. 3).

Helen Barrett (2000), in writing on her Web site about electronic teacher portfolios, nonetheless described a series of qualities that are particular to any exceptional portfolio. Aiming a portfolio program for these goals will ensure that over time, student learning, the ability to demonstrate learning, and overall student success, will improve if their portfolios

a. possess a high level of thought;

b. are polished;

c. demonstrate considerable effort;

d. are thorough;

e. are well-organized;

f. show a variety of products;

g. are unique;

h. demonstrate substantial application to their career goals;

i. shows the individual's personality;

j. demonstrates both breath and depth;

k. are highly imaginative. (Barrett, 2000)

SUMMARY

To sum up, one can only add that portfolio assessment of the kind described here serves the combined objectives of a holistic measure of student achievement, encourages student participation in active learning, provides a once-per-semester outcome evaluation of a department's curriculum and course content, gives the faculty another way to gauge the success of their efforts and delivers a valid, direct assessment of applied student learning. And for the students, the end result is a portfolio that they can also use to assist them in obtaining employment.

In 1992, when I first researched portfolio assessment, I was interested with the diversity of methods and uses that I encountered in elementary and secondary education. To end this chapter, I would like to suggest that readers acquaint themselves with this literature:

- http://ericec.org/osep/newsbriefs/news17.html (Alternative uses of portfolios for students with disabilities).
- http://www.teachervision.fen.com/lesson-plans/lesson-4528.html? detoured= (Pros and cons of portfolios for teachers and students. Note: You must register your e-mail address to access this site, but you may opt out of receiving any e-mail back from them).
- http://electronicportfolios.org/portfolios.html (Using technology to create and evaluate portfolios. This Web site also lists the URLs of a number of other helpful and interesting sites).
- http://www.degreeinfo.com/article23_1.html (This is an article, "Portfolio Assessment in Higher Education: Seeking Credibility on the Campus").
- http://ag.arizona.edu/fcs/cyfernet/cyfar/Portfo~3.htm (This in-depth discussion covers a considerable amount of ground, including strengths and weaknesses, practice and procedure).
- http://reading.indiana.edu/ieo/bibs/portfoli.html (An excellent bibliography on portfolios, including other Web sites).

REFERENCES

Accrediting Council for Education in Journalism and Mass Communication. (2003). *Policies of Accreditation.* Retrieved July 12, 2005, from http://www.ku.edu/~acejmc/PROGRAM/POLICIES.SHTML#elig

Accrediting Council for Education in Journalism and Mass Communication. (2003). *Principles of Accreditation.* Retrieved July 12, 2005, from http://www.ku.edu/~acejmc/PROGRAM/PRINCIPLES.SHTML

Banta, T. W. (Ed.). (1993). *Making a difference: Outcomes of a decade of assessment in higher education.* San Francisco: Jossey-Bass.

Barrett, H. C. (2000). *Electronic portfolios = multimedia development + portfolio development: The electronic portfolio development process.* Retrieved from http:electronicportfolios.org

Becker, L. B., Kosicki, T., Engleman, T., & Viswanath, K. (1993). Finding work and getting paid: Predictors of success in the mass communications job market. *Journalism Quarterly, 70,* 919–933.

Cappelli, P. (1992). College, students and the workplace: Assessing performance to improve the fit. *Change,* 54–58.

Cohen, J. (2004). Editor's note: Assessment . . . yours, mine and ours. *Journalism and Mass Communication Educator, 59,* 3–5.

Donald, R. (1995). The senior portfolio: Assessment with a ripple effect. *Feedback, 36*(2), 13–16.

Forrest, A. (1990). Time will tell: Portfolio-assisted assessment of general education. *Report of the American Association for Higher Education Assessment Forum,* 18–24.

Haley, E., & Jackson, D. (1995). A conceptualization of assessment for mass communication programs. *Journalism and Mass Communication Educator, 50,* 26–34.

Hutchings, P. (1990, April). Learning over time: Portfolio assessment. *AAHE Bulletin,* pp. 6–8.

Larson, R. L. (1991). Using portfolios in the assessment of writing in the academic disciplines. In P. Belanoff & M. Dickson (Eds.), *Portfolios: Process and product* (pp. 137–149). Portsmouth, NH: Boynton/Cook.

McClelland, K. (1991). Portfolios: Solution to a problem. In P. Belanoff & M. Dickson (Eds.), *Portfolios: Process and product* (pp. 165–173). Portsmouth, NH: Boynton/Cook.

Rudner, L. M. (1992). Reducing errors due to the use of judges. *Practical Assessment, Research and Evaluation.* Retrieved from http://pareonline.net/getvn.asp?v= 3&n=3

Schilling, K. M., & Schilling, K. L. (1993). Professors must respond to calls for accountability. *Chronicle of Higher Education, XXXIX,* A-40.

Steinke, G. (1993). Tennessee broadcasters prefer workers with college communications training. *Feedback, 34*(1), 7–9.

Stone, V. (1996). *News directors favor hands-on schools.* Retrieved from http://www.missouri.edu/~jourvs/ndprefs.html

Vavrus, L. (1990). Putting portfolios to the test. *Instructor, 100,* 48–53.

APPENDIX

Example of Portfolio Requirements

What follows is an abridged version of Southern Illinois University at Edwardsville's (SIUE) handout for students, describing the department's senior portfolio requirements. The entire text, including content requirements for each of SIUE's sequences, is available by e-mailing the author at rdonald@siue.edu:

MC 481 Senior Portfolio Instructions
For academic year 2003–2004, revised Spring, 2004
Southern Illinois University Edwardsville

The senior portfolio is a compilation of the best coursework and projects you have produced while in college. A portfolio can also include media products you've produced at other colleges before you transferred to SIUE, work you've produced during your internship or in professional media jobs while in college. Detailed further below are instructions on how to compile your senior portfolio.

Portfolio Instructions

The immediate purpose of the portfolio is to demonstrate to a jury of department faculty in your professional option what you have learned to do well during your time here, and whether or not you are ready to graduate. But portfolios also have another valuable and practical purpose for you: When you graduate, you cannot expect to be hired as a professional communicator (especially in this competitive job market) if you can't prove that you can do the work—and do it better than all those other mass communications graduates with whom you're competing. As this department's faculty has stressed throughout your time here, the well-laid-out contents of a Mass Communications Department graduate's published clips or photos, Ad/P.R. portfolio, multimedia CD or resume/audition tape plus writing samples could be that extra bit of evidence that will make a potential employer choose you over other applicants.

If for one reason or another, you may not now possess all the items you need, don't panic! There's still time to join the staff of the *Alestle* [campus newspaper] or WSIE-FM, etc., this semester—produce a lot, and save everything. To help you understand what we're talking about, here are a few examples of portfolio materials you can collect from your coursework, your work at WSIE, the *Alestle* and other campus publications (e.g., the *Mass Communicator,* [department alumni magazine]), and from your work while on internship or part-time media-related jobs. Also, faculty members should tell you in your classes what course assignments and projects you should keep (and improve upon) for inclusion in your portfolio.

Below are *examples* of some of the items you can include in your portfolio. Please note that these are not inclusive lists, just some examples. See your adviser or the internship coordinator if you have any questions.

- Radio production/news air checks and television production/news resume tapes;
- Other tapes, or excerpts from tapes of radio or television programs or program elements you produced;
- Any broadcast copy (news, continuity, commercials, documentaries—any kind of script or treatment/story outline used for broadcast or corporate communications). Regarding style, this department's web site <*www.siue.edu/MASSCOMM*> contains script format models (eg., 2-column TV commercial script, radio news script, 8½ × 11 TV storyboard, WGA film-style script, WGA Treatment/Story Outline format etc.), which are used by faculty in teaching all courses [in our curriculum]. These comprise the default department standards for each kind of script. All scripts in your portfolios must precisely conform to these formats. NOTE: If scripts you write on your internship require a different style—which is quite likely—that's OK. Put this work in a separate section in your portfolio and identify the section as, for example, "News Copy: KMOX Internship." But all copy written here at SIUE should conform to department style.
- Professionally oriented class projects and reports (ad campaign presentations, media plans, pitches, research reports, legal briefs);
- Multimedia CDs, web pages, photography, etc. (NOTE: Some web sites should be included on a disc (or on discs) in your portfolio. Others will work better for presentation if you make good 8½ × 11 color laser prints of these web pages and insert the prints into a special section in your portfolio. Ask your multimedia professor for advice on yours. But one thing is sure: you should never just refer the reader to an URL. The overriding strategy of this portfolio is to make reading it a convenient, enjoyable experience for the potential employer);
- Clippings of any of your published stories and/or photos in any print media;
- Newspaper, magazine or any publication page layouts you have designed;
- News, feature, op-ed pieces and other copy written for class assignments;
- Ad, P.R. or corporate copy, media kits and storyboards;
- Any work similar to the above that you have produced while working in the professional media and/or on your internship.

Finally, the last section of your portfolio should demonstrate for the MassComm faculty what you have accomplished in research, critical thinking, and your ability to apply theory in some form of scholarly inquiry. You have written a number of research papers to satisfy the requirements of the courses you have completed for the Mass Communications major. You can also use papers for courses outside the major that are MassComm-related. Include at least three of these papers in this section. Any research papers you may have presented at academic or professional conferences could certainly be included. Since many of these papers are of some length, it is suggested that you do not enclose each page in plastic, as you will for all of your other work. Instead, when you purchase your portfolio binder, choose one with pockets in the front and back. So, for example, you can place your resume tape in the front pocket and your term papers in the back pocket.

Note: Always remove instructor comments, grades, errors noted, etc., from anything you plan to put in your portfolio. Any copy, paper, project or assignment worthy of inclusion in your portfolio should be re-printed after you re-edit, sharpen and fix it. Now that you're ready to graduate, you should be much more experienced and knowledgeable than you were when you wrote these pieces. So rewrite them! Never show off your mistakes to potential employers or to the faculty jury that will review your portfolio: always put your best foot forward. If you don't present your best work now, when you're selling yourself as an entry-level professional to our faculty and potential employers, when will you? And if getting a job isn't enough of a practical reason, consider this: more than one faculty member penalize a student's score one point for every single instance of incorrect spelling, typographical or style error. Get the picture?

Also Note: Many kinds of class project materials require introductory explanations. Sometimes it's because the item or the project/campaign materials won't make complete sense to a potential employer unless you provide some context for them. Also, if you contributed a part of a group project, include in your portfolio only the part of the project that you produced. When you're displaying your portion of any group project, communicate! Put the whole project in context by preceding it with a tabbed section divider, plus an introductory page. In this introduction, describe the entire project, explain the different parts of the project, and then state clearly just what you personally contributed to the project. Then the pages that follow will make sense to a potential employer. Speaking of those tabbed sections, make the tabs look professional: make them printed tabs, never hand-lettered. Hand-lettering is unprofessional.

If you're having trouble deciding what to leave in and what to leave out, ask your faculty adviser or the internship coordinator for advice.

21

The Capstone Course

Robert C. Moore
Department of Communications
Elizabethtown College

In examining a basis for the existence of a capstone course, the literature in the field of Education, specifically Curriculum and Instruction, provides some direction. From a wide variety of definitions for curriculum, a definition by Hilda Taba seems particularly useful because it specifies the elements of curriculum:

> A curriculum usually contains a statement of aims and of specific objectives; it indicates some selection and organization of content; it either implies or manifests certain patterns of learning and teaching, whether because the objectives demand them or because the content organization requires them. Finally, it includes a program of evaluation of the outcomes. (Oliva, 1982, p. 7)

These elements are not mutually exclusive. Their integration should result in a positive and successful learning experience. The critical last element, evaluation, not only validates the learning, but also enables faculty to revise and refine courses or curricula to continually attain desired outcomes. Just as curriculum development is a systematic process, curriculum evaluation is a systematic process by which the students' total education is weighed.

Outcomes assessment must be systematic. Schools are called on not only by academic and political demands but also by the very ethics that underlie the profession, to develop numerous direct and indirect measures of student learning to provide both proof and accountability that

439

higher education is accomplishing those things that are specified by it as important. Volkwein (2003) suggested that a systematic plan of outcomes assessment gives appropriateness to the mission statement, utility of the institutional goals and objectives, adequacy of assessment measures, and the impact of programs on students.

In 2003, the Accrediting Council on Education in Journalism and Mass Communication (ACEJMC) adopted a revision of accreditation standards. Regardless of a school's desire to undergo accreditation, these standards provide a useful academic foundation for curriculum design and development recognized nationally. Standard 2, in particular, deals with curriculum design and stresses specific expectations that are to be included in courses of study. Standard 9 is applicable in that it sets out numerous expectations for student learning. Incorporation of several of these expectations into a curriculum also requires that they are able to be assessed.

The capstone course is an excellent method of direct assessment. By its very nature, the capstone course is a method of summative evaluation. It not only assesses previous cognitive learning in the major, but also provides a forum that allows an instructor to assesses the student's overall collegiate learning experience. Because, in addition to cognitive skills, learning can occur in two other domains (affective and psychomotor), a capstone course allows for a mix of evaluative styles that assess the broad range of the students' past experiences (Kemp & Smellie, 1989, p. 20). This approach also allows a student, who perhaps excels in one area more than another, to demonstrate the strengths of his or her learning. Achievement in the cognitive domain is usually represented by an ability to recall, understand, and apply knowledge. Evaluation of affective learning is characterized by expression of feelings, values, and attitudes (especially regarding events, issues, and topics related to, or impacting, the students' field of study). Finally, psychomotor learning is evaluated by the application and performance of skills. Ideally, a student's competence will be satisfactorily demonstrated in all three learning modalities.

In a summative evaluation of the students' experience in the university curriculum, a capstone course is an instrument used to directly assess the performance of students in the attainment of institutional and departmental curricular expectations. Additionally, it provides the opportunity to address and assess the relevant accrediting standards and those of professional bodies. It is an in-depth opportunity for the student to demonstrate accomplishment of the full spectrum of that learning. A useful model for such expectations is Bloom's (1956) *A Taxonomy of Educational Objectives*. These progressive levels of objectives are as follows: recall of knowledge, comprehension, application, analysis, synthesis, and evaluation. The last three levels are higher order intellectual activity. They are concerned more with the how and why of learning rather than the what.

Affective learning has been referred to by Bloom (1971) as the implicit curriculum (p. 14). It is made up of attitudes, interests, values, and feelings derived by the student through learning and by interaction with other learners and professors. The affective domain of learning advanced by David Krathwohl (Kemp, 1975) consists of five levels: receiving, responding, valuing, organization, and characterization of a value complex. This final level, the highest order, indicates that one's beliefs, ideas, and attitudes have been integrated into a total professional philosophy.

Psychomotor learning is an ongoing refinement process. Such learning is assessed as units and courses are completed. Often, new courses bring with them different and unusual forms of learning. For example, an oral performance course may develop voice delivery to a more refined stage whereas a course in interpretation may require a new application of that previously learned skill. A course in video production may require the development of an unfamiliar combination and synchronization of finely coordinated movements. Psychomotor learning encompasses gross bodily movements, finely coordinated movements, nonverbal communication, and speech behaviors (Kemp, 1975).

The capstone course expectations should be a display of a mastery of all three modalities of learning and the ability to apply them to new, unusual, and integrated project requirements. Table 21.1 specifies the pro-

TABLE 21.1
Learning Expectations in a Capstone Course

Learning Modality	Course Expectations
Cognitive Learning	
Recall of knowledge	Students are presented with a problem and draw on
Comprehension	their knowledge and research to weigh and select
Application	various data leading to a solution of the problem
Analysis	which is workable and intellectually defensible.
Synthesis	
Evaluation	
Affective Learning	
Receiving	The approach and decisions made reflect attitudes,
Responding	values, feelings, and beliefs characteristic of the
Valuing	discipline and the profession.
Organization	
Value complex	
Psychomotor Learning	
Gross bodily movements	The production of a project which serves as a solu-
Finely coordinated movements	tion to a problem and the oral and visual presen-
	tation of it.
Nonverbal communication	Both reflect a degree of skill and competency as a
Speech behaviors	communicator.

gressive levels of achievement in each of the learning modalities and the expectations of student performance in a capstone course.

Other learning theories have been advanced that present reinforcing views of the three domains of learning. Kemp and Smellie (1989) cited Gagné in clarifying the hierarchical structure of learning and also noted that learning is a

cumulative process. Basic information or simple skills ... contribute to the learning of more complex knowledge and skills. [Gagné] identified five categories of learning: verbal information, intellectual skills, cognitive strategies, motor skills, and attitudes ... These [also] fall into three phases of learning advanced by Bell-Gredler: preparation for learning, acquisition and performance, and retrieval and transfer [of knowledge, attitudes and skills]. (Kemp & Smellie, 1989, p. 16)

Kemp and Smellie (1989) also noted that Merrill classifies outcomes of learning in two dimensions. First, content is drawn from advancing levels of facts, concepts, procedures, and principles. The second outcome of learning is performance characterized by remembering, using, and finding a generality.

These approaches to learning provide a basis for course design and evaluation. Learning expectations of students should increase with their advancement through a curriculum. A capstone course might be designed that makes use of the increasing complexity of student learning when the end of the process of instruction is reached. The course uses cumulative learning, after all previous courses and objectives have been met, to relate to more than a single concept; the course draws on the whole of the learning experience and requires that it be applied in a meaningful way.

OUTCOMES ASSESSMENT AND THE CAPSTONE COURSE

For too long, university curricula have seemed to be too specialized and fragmented. More often than not, students plodded from one course to another and often were provided little opportunity to link the relevant content and skills across the various courses. The role of the capstone course is to draw all of that learning together and to provide a single opportunity or experience during which a student demonstrates that he or she has accomplished or achieved congruence with the university and department's educational goals as represented by the appropriate mission statements and courses taken (Volkwein, 2003).

Unfortunately, faculty often see few links between their courses and those of colleagues in other departments. The learning acquired by students in nonmajor courses is rarely applied to major courses in a meaningful manner. Curricula lacks integration of the total college academic experience. It is no wonder, then, that parents, legislators, and other publics are demanding accountability. They demand proof that the education being provided is both sound and has produced the desired learning in students.

The reality of higher education today is that students' major programs cannot exist in isolation from the rest of their education. Although knowledge and discipline-specific skills are important, more universities' educational goals are embracing those outlined by the Carnegie Report (Boyer, 1987) and by the Association of American Colleges (AAC, n.d.). Schools are recognizing that they "should be accountable not only for stating their expectations and standards, but for assessing the degree to which those ends have been met" (Kings College, 1986, p. 31). As Blanchard and Christ (1993) stated in *Media Education and the Liberal Arts*, "the outcomes method [of assessment] is the most tangible and rational measure [for defining a liberal education]" (p. 13). The Michigan Professional Preparation Network Report listing of 10 potential professional-liberal outcomes can be used as a framework to ascertain if a student has satisfactorily met the goals of his or her education. As an overall statement of the goals of learning, these outcomes provide a unifying strategy for the students' entire curriculum as well as an excellent framework for the major. The 10 outcomes listed by the Michigan report are as follows:

1. Communication competence is the ability to read, write, speak, and listen and to use these processes effectively to acquire, develop, and convey ideas and information.
2. Critical thinking is the ability to examine issues rationally, logically, and coherently.
3. Contextual competence is an understanding of the societal context or environment in which one is living and working.
4. Aesthetic sensibility is an enhanced aesthetic awareness of arts and human behavior for both personal enrichment and application in the enhancement of work.
5. Professional identity is a concern for improving the knowledge, skills, and values of the profession.
6. Professional ethics is an understanding of the ethics of a profession as standards that guide professional behavior.
7. Adaptive competence is anticipating, adapting to, and promoting changes important to a profession's societal purpose and the professional's role.

8. Leadership capacity is exhibiting the capacity to contribute as a productive member of the profession and assuming appropriate leadership roles.

9. Scholarly concern for improvement is recognizing the need to increase knowledge and to advance the profession through both theoretical and applied research.

10. Motivation of continued learning is exploring and expanding personal, civic, and professional knowledge and skills through a lifetime. (Blanchard & Christ, 1993, pp. 15–16)

The outcomes specified in the Michigan report and several of those specified in ACEJMC Standards 2 and 9, by Newton (n.d., p. 1), or those drawn from the proceedings of The Senior Year Experience and Students in Transition conference (Cuseo, 1998, p. 22), provide a blueprint for higher education—a benchmark by which institutional and departmental mission statements might be based. Table 21.2 lists many of these outcomes expectations and indicates how they can be categorized into one or more of the modalities of learning previously discussed.

MISSION STATEMENTS AND A RATIONALE FOR THE CAPSTONE COURSE

An American Association of Higher Education (AAHE, n.d.) document on assessment notes that it is most effective when it [is] multidimen-

TABLE 21.2
Integrating Expected Outcomes With the Modalities of Learning

	Cognitive Learning	Affective Learning	Psychomotor Learning
Communication Competence (written, spoken, mediated)	X		X
Critical Thinking	X	X	
Contextual Competence (concepts, theories)	X	X	
Aesthetic or Creative Competence		X	X
Professional Roles and Ethics		X	
Adaptive Competence	X	X	X
Leadership Capacity (ability to be independent)		X	
Scholarly Concern for Improvement (evaluation)	X	X	
Motivation for Continued Learning	X	X	
Research Capacity	X		

sional, integrated ... with explicitly stated purposes ... which illuminate questions that people really care about ... which lead to improvement [and] promote[s] change.

The capstone course may be the singular opportunity to determine if the student has assimilated the various goals of his or her total education. "The purpose [of the capstone course] ... should be defined in light of each institution's purposes (B. L. Smith, 1998, p. 90). It can be a self-directed, integrated, learning opportunity with goals established on several levels. The first and most global in nature are the general goals of higher education which have been represented here as those articulated by the Michigan Report, AAHE, and others. They tend to be written as societal goals for higher education. Based on these broad statements of outcomes, the university and department design their mission statements using the philosophical approach to education most congruent with that campus' culture and direction of that particular department. These statements of outcomes are the linchpins on which capstone courses are taught. They provide the focus for expectations in the capstone course (see chapter 3).

Each academic department, in successfully formulating a mission statement, makes an attempt to draw into its goals those of higher education and those of the educational institution. Yet, given the varied focuses possible in any discipline, especially communications, the institution perspective is refined in the departmental document. Articulation of goals at this level is vital. Here, the profile of the educated individual is specified. It is that profile, and the level of attainment of it, which is critical in an outcomes assessment, in particular, the capstone course.

Murphy (2003, p. 1) cited a rationale for capstone courses by Wagenaar (1993). Key objectives that should be demonstrated by the student are:

1. Integrating and synthesizing the field;
2. Extending the field;
3. Critiquing the field;
4. Applying the field;
5. Addressing issues raised in ... introductory course(s), but at a higher level;
6. Exploring key arguments in the field;
7. Making connections with general education;
8. Specific comparisons with other fields;
9. Critically thinking generally and within the field;
10. Examining values and views of life.

Kings College (1986) saw these objectives as being able to be articulated in what it referred to as "transferable skills." They are the skills a student masters throughout his or her learning and through which he or she communicates attainment of the course goal. They are "critical thinking, creative thinking and problem solving strategies, effective writing, effective oral communication, quantitative analysis, computer literacy, library competency, . . . [research methods, and skills in mediated communication]" (Kings College, 1986, p. 23). Alverno College faculty developed similar expectations as they defined an educated person (B. L. Smith, 1998).

In a study by Lockhart and Borland (2001), faculty ranked the relative importance of several of these items for inclusion in a capstone course. Ninety-one percent of the faculty surveyed rated "thinking effectively" as the most major in importance in a capstone course. Other elements that were important included "using complex knowledge in making decisions and judgment" (82%), "exercise and expand intellectual curiosity" (67%), "develop skills (as) life-long learners" (64%), "write effectively" (53%), and "think across areas of specialization and integrate ideas from a variety of . . . disciplines and applied fields" (53%) (p. 21).

At Elizabethtown College, the attainment of many institutional goals is incorporated into the course expectations as are the goals and objectives of the departmental mission statement. These documents also incorporate either directly or indirectly select ACEJMC expectations and those of several professional associations. Although not all of these outcomes may be appropriate in all communication curricula, requirements of the capstone course provide a means through which a faculty member may judge a student's performance against those outcomes. (The institutional and departmental mission statements referred to here can be found on the author's homepage under Research, Capstone Course, at: http://users.etown.edu/m/moorerc/).

The capstone course at Elizabethtown College is broader than courses with similar purposes at other institutions. Depending on the nature of those communication programs, capstone courses may be more or less specialized to provide outcomes assessment appropriate to the department's mission.

DESIGN OF THE COMMUNICATIONS CAPSTONE COURSE

Levine (1998) reported that only two-fifths of colleges and universities have employed the capstone approach. Henscheid's (2000) research has shown that most capstone courses are in the major. They often require a project and a presentation but those that require a thesis tend to be at small selective schools. The focus of the capstone should be to design an experience that integrates the discipline and the liberal arts. Further, it also creates an environment to assess a variety of skills seen as important in higher education. A student as a "compleat" communicator must be able to meet the competencies set out by the institution and the department. If skills development is a part of the curriculum, demonstration of abilities must go beyond "nuts and bolts." Faculty expectations are that students will use their knowledge and the information gathered to plan, design, and produce original projects that integrate various types of expression. Such expectations provide a basis, indeed a mandate, for a capstone course that can adequately assess such learning. Blanchard and Christ (1993) called this approach "cross-training . . . a flexible, fundamental, integrated approach to media education . . ." (p. 32).

Learning, not teaching, is at the center of capstone experiences. Redmond (1998) said that "breadth of understanding . . . [and] depth of abilities" are key aspects to evaluating summary learning (p. 74). Such courses are student-centered and seldom resemble those in traditional classrooms. Problem analysis, information sharing, creative solutions, and projects drive the capstone course. Student expression is critical to demonstrating successful achievement of capstone course objectives. The professor should be a mentor and guide, a consultant or counselor.

The capstone course, as presented here, is based on applied research. Students presented with a new problem must utilize their knowledge, experience, and abilities to plan and research various solutions to the problem and then correctly apply the chosen solution as an effective way to meet the purpose and goal of the problem. Multifaceted problems present challenges to the student that require the use of knowledge gained in divergent courses. Focusing that knowledge in a single capstone course provides the opportunity for applied research to meet varied demands. Additionally, in professionally oriented programs, when "real-world" problems are presented, then it is valuable that students work with "real-world" clients in developing solutions. This practical-experiential component allows the student to begin to develop a sense of professional identity by working with individuals already in the field and jointly developing a meaningful project (see chapter 17).

Glaser and Radliff (2000) called such a task or real problem a service learning experience and that its inclusion is critical to a communication capstone course. For students moving on to graduate school, systematic research and its application provides excellent background and experience. The course begins a transition from school to an eventual career as the students work closely with clients and actively draw on past learning. The benefits of such an evolution include the practice of adaptive competence, establishment of the beginnings of a professional identity, observation of professional ethics, and utilizing learning within the context of one's living and working environment—all key outcomes previously cited as critical to higher education.

THE CAPSTONE COURSE GOAL

The departmental and institutional mission statements, incorporating various elements and the spirit of the Carnegie report, the Michigan report, and authors Andreasen and Trede (1998), Carlson and Peterson (1993), Smith (1993), and others, provide a basis for the direction and development of curriculum at the institutional and departmental level. They also provide for a basis on which a capstone course goal might be formulated. One such goal statement for the course might be as follows: "The capstone course is a culminating experience that integrates coursework, knowledge, skills, and experiential learning to enable the student to demonstrate a broad mastery of specialized learning with that from across the curriculum for a promise of initial employability and further learning and career advancement."

THE CAPSTONE COURSE REQUIREMENTS

The Carnegie Foundation recommends three instruments for measuring outcomes in a capstone course. These include the following: a senior thesis (which draws on the historical, social, and ethical perspectives of the major), an oral presentation of the thesis with peer critique, and preparation of a portfolio (see chapter 20); ("Prologue and Major Recommendations," 1986). Volkwein (2003) concurred that outcomes assessment requires multiple measures of student learning (p. 4). The capstone course at Elizabethtown College requires four instruments to measure outcomes.

The Senior Thesis

The thesis examines the history, values, ethics, and social perspectives of the discipline related to a particular problem or issue. The research study extends the prior knowledge of the student through the conducting of a literature review. The student then proceeds to conceptualize the study, develop procedures, analyze the data, and make recommendations regarding the topic or problem.

The Senior Project

Students in professional or performance-based curricula might be required to produce a project specifically tied to the thesis. The purpose of the project is to provide an opportunity for the research work to actually be a workable solution to the problem presented. Production or performance at this level not only demonstrates applied skills and abilities but also allows for practically applied research.

The projects that are selected ". . . follow three major guidelines. First, the student should believe that there is a substantial need for the project. Second, the project must be approachable through recognized communications knowledge and techniques. Third, the project must be feasible within the time limits of the course" (Wallace, 1988, p. 36).

"Using projects as part of the content of such a course offers several advantages. First, this format provides for close contact with faculty . . . It provides practical career-related experiences . . . [and] offer[s] the student a sense of accomplishment as they serve . . . in a quasi-professional, practical capacity" (Wallace, 1988, p. 35). Specifically, as a client project, it is a collaborative effort at problem solving; it develops interpersonal skills and uses evidence as a support for plans and decisions. Additionally, the concept of deadlines, persuasive argument, and personal responsibility are developed. Certainly, the project assists in establishing better corporate or institutional relationships and possibly creates partnerships among a school's various departments.

The project demonstrates the level of achievement reached by the student in communication and production skills. It also, as an experiential project, requires the student to interact on a close, personal, and regular basis with a client. The integration of this internship-type experience is a key element in helping the student learn contextual and adaptive competence and in developing a professional identity (Moore, 1987).

The Oral Defense or Presentation

The content of this performance is based on the integration of the thesis and the project. It is a defense-presentation of the research study; it allows for a summarization of the literature review, discussion of its procedures, data, and recommendations. It also can review the project, exhibit the production or performance, and discuss its results applicable as a solution to the problem. As a public performance, oral and nonverbal expression can also be assessed.

The Portfolio

A formal collection of works, which covers the full collegiate career of the student, the portfolio provides the evidence, documentation, and best samples of various types of creative expression and skills learning. Options exist for this portfolio to be submitted as evidence of learning or as a tool to be used in an employment search. In either case, the portfolio should show that specific aims of the curriculum have been mastered (see chapter 20).

APPLIED RESEARCH

The senior thesis and accompanying project require the student to engage in intellectually productive research for a client. Typically referred to as applied communications research, the goal of the work is to solve problems and bring about change (Moore, 1988). O'Hair, Kreps, and Frey (1990) listed the various characteristics of a definition of applied research. Generally, applied research is the practical design of a workable solution for a real-world problem designed specifically for a particular client.

Using the terminology for the stages of applied research as identified by O'Hair and Kreps (1990), Table 21.3 lists and relates them to the cap-

TABLE 21.3
The Applied Research Model for the Senior Thesis and Project[a]

Research Activities	Course Application
Problem Identification	Client interviews, project selection, research question, and analysis.
Conceptualization	Literature search: informal and institutional sources, library and database sources, interviews.
Operationalization	Transform the research findings into concrete approaches to solving the problem. Selecting project strategies based on evidence, credibility, and audience.
Measurement	Preproduction strategies, data gathering, observations, interviews relevant to the production of the project.
Analysis	Project production. Analysis of techniques, approaches, results of the project.
Recommendations	Discuss the ways in which the solution solved the problem: successes, weaknesses, suggested revisions.

[a]Adapted from O'Hair and Kreps, 1990, p. 25.

TABLE 21.4
Outcomes Instruments as Related to Learning Modalities

Instrument	Cognitive Learning	Affective Learning	Psychomotor Learning
Senior Thesis	X	X	
Senior Project	X	X	X
Oral Presentation	X	X	X
Portfolio	X	X	X

stone course requirements, which incorporates the senior thesis and the accompanying senior project. The course requirements follow the systematic development of the research and literature review and integrates them with the project as a workable solution to a problem. Finally, and perhaps most importantly, it specifies as a final stage the process of evaluation of the solution.

Each of the course requirements, or learning measurement instruments, provides for individual differences in learning and permits demonstrated achievement in areas in which the student excels. In Table 21.4, each instrument is related to the specific type of learning modality applicable to it.

These course requirements enable the student to address and demonstrate achievement of the various outcomes statements, goal of the course, and skills expected of graduates of the curriculum by the institution. Table 21.5 summarizes and integrates those various aims of education within applicable learning styles and course requirements. (The course syllabus referred to here can be found on the author's homepage under Research, Capstone Course, at http://users.etown.edu/m/moorerc/).

ASSESSING STUDENT PERFORMANCE

The capstone course is a learning experience that has the ability to draw together many diverse elements of prior learning to help determine if the academic goals and objectives of the institution and the department have been achieved. As a direct measure of student accomplishment of them, the course requirements allow the faculty member to assess student learning and performance as having, at least satisfactorily, met those expected outcomes.

The capstone course at Elizabethtown College uses the "Aims" noted in Table 21.5 as a basis for evaluating student performance in each of the course requirements. They have been translated into a student grad-

TABLE 21.5
Aims Achieved by the Evaluation Instruments

	Thesis	Project	Presentation	Portfolio
Cognitive Learning	Scholarly concern for advancing the profession through research. Improve one's knowledge of the profession or discipline. Ability to acquire, develop, convey, and integrate knowledge and information. Critically examine issues. Quantitative and qualitative analysis. Evaluation of data collected and conclusions related to issues of thesis.	Advancing the professional through applied research. Adaptive competence in relating knowledge to a project. Discrimination between concepts applying relevant approaches to the problem. Creative thinking and design of solutions: organization, treatment, production. Leadership capacity to initiate, manage, and carry a project to conclusion.	Understanding of the communication process: informative, narrative persuasive, etc. Use of supporting strategies and information: nonverbal communication, imagery, visual support, ethospathos, questioning, presentation of proof or reinforcement. Strategy for organization: comparison and contrast, problem solving, etc. Understanding the audience, shaping of ideas appropriately.	Works exhibit a broad range of abilities. Shows imagination, concept development. Shows an understanding of the responsibilities and attributes of a communicator.

Affective Learning	Understand the societal context of learning. Convey professional values and ethics. Show motivation for continued learning.	Applying knowledge, skills, values of profession or discipline to a new or unique problem. Assume a professional identity and exhibit professional responsibilities. Shows aesthetic sensibility.	Assumption of a proper professional identity appropriate for delivery of the thesis or project. Display an attitude for performance that indicates mastery of verbal techniques: clarity, relevance, effectiveness. Creative planning and presentation of thesis or project. Performance Skills: nonverbal communication, oral communication skills, mediated presentation. Presentation skills and organization. Production and use of supporting materials.	Professional value and interest is evident in preparation of the work. Presentation of work represents a professional identity. Creative approach to the display of work.
Psycho-motor Learning	Competence in reading, writing, research. Computer Literacy. Library Competency.	Mastering the skills of the profession and application of them to a project. Design, writing scripting, visual representation and production.		Collection of mastered skills and abilities. Technical acumen evident in displayed work.

ing-evaluation guideline that sets levels of performance for the student to be "satisfactory" or better in his or her demonstrated performance.

This rubric is a commentary about the standards for grading. It then lays out expectations for how student performance will be evaluated in each of the course requirements. This guide is shared with students early in the semester, reviewed often, and specifically referred to when the instructor provides evaluative comments on the thesis, project, and oral defense. Additionally, the elements of Table 21.5 are referred to in comments made during evaluation. Students are expected to continually refer to this grading-evaluation guideline so that they are also able to make a self-assessment of the work prior to submission or performance. Students who are graded "satisfactory" or higher on each of the course assessment instruments are judged to have met the minimum expectations of the department mission and course goal and objectives. (The standards and expectations referred to here can be found on the author's homepage under Research, Capstone Course, at http://users. etown.edu/m/moorerc/).

ADVANTAGES OF THE CAPSTONE COURSE

The position presented in this chapter, and the examples provided, have focused on the integration of writing, speaking, and communicating through media. The chapter has also incorporated the need for a sense of aesthetics, creative expression, and experiential learning. The nature of differing curriculums in communications, especially those without a professional focus, requires the flexible application or alteration of capstone course requirements as necessary for the assessment provided by the course to be faithful to the specific mission statements of that department and institution.

The following list of advantages and characteristics of a capstone course are a summary of the educative value of such an experience for students presented in this chapter.

The capstone course . . .

- allows for the adaptation and integration of institutional mission statements, departmental or school mission statements, and course objectives to the general goals of higher education.
- can be a broad-based course drawing together disciplines across the university. This allows for unique partnerships to develop between departments resulting in a greater integration of them in the university fabric.
- allows conclusions to be drawn from student performance regarding the level of involvement in the liberal arts versus professional

training. It also enables faculty to address perceived weaknesses in a curriculum. Ongoing assessment in the capstone course allows for continual evaluation and development of the curriculum so that students are demonstrating that they are learning what faculty thinks they are teaching.

- can address and incorporate new approaches and objectives, as curricula and expectations change or expand.
- can be tailored to measure outcomes in any of the various divisions or configurations of the communications field. Research projects can be applied to a wide variety of interests, issues, or professional settings.
- places expectations on students so that they become independent learners. The course is student-centered and self-directed, allowing each student to work at a pace with which he or she is most comfortable and in a direction suitable to career aspirations.
- requires students to perform at higher level of learning by requiring them to engage in analysis, synthesis, and evaluation of past learning and apply it to new experiences. "Faculty report that . . . research . . . [is] the most effective method to teach [such] critical thinking" (Lockhart & Borland, 2001, p. 19).
- as a summative tool, provides the opportunity to evaluate students at the end of their major program of study and at the end of their collegiate career.
- is a multifaceted method of assessment. It goes beyond examinations and simple projects by integrating various assessment strategies. These, particularly, include a senior thesis, an applied project drawn from the thesis, a public oral defense-performance, and a portfolio.
- allows students to perform and excel in those learning modalities most appropriate to him or her.
- integrates skill demonstrations into objectives of an experiential nature, providing a real opportunity for business and industry alliances.

DISADVANTAGES OF THE CAPSTONE COURSE

Although one generally might not argue against the evaluation of learning or against the summative evaluation of the entire learning experience, capstone course experiences do have several limitations. As such, the departmental faculty needs to clearly be satisfied that this level and type of assessment is adequate from which to draw conclusions about student achievement and the curriculum.

The capstone course . . .

- evaluates students' knowledge, identity and skills subjectively.
- may allow less motivated and goal oriented students too much flexibility by focusing on independent and self-directed learning.
- can be too unfocused unless the faculty monitors departmental curricular expectations as they evolve and adjust the course.
- requires faculty to depart from self-serving or specialized agenda and focus on an integrated experience where the "compleat" communicator is more important than the specialist.
- places a great demand on student time, learning, and performance. Many students may not be up to the task.
- may allow a student to excel in a favored learning modality but does not easily assist students who perform in an average way, or below, in other modalities. There is typically no course of remediation for problems and failures.
- allows a student to approach the goal of curricular integration but does not always specify to what level that occurs. It does not specify how various levels of success can be quantified and translated into a summary of positive performance of attaining the curriculum's mission.

All four instruments (thesis, project, defense or presentation, and portfolio) of evaluation are strengths in the course. They draw their success from their variety of approaches and the way in which each of the course requirements integrate with each other to create a complete picture of student achievement. Yet, that variety and sheer workload are very demanding in terms of faculty and student commitment and time. Although tempting to make the course less time consuming, elimination of any one of the instruments weakens the course because each in isolation cannot be the summative tool of assessment that they are when integrated. Any one of the instruments does not allow for written, oral, and mediated expression in all three modalities of learning.

A survey of a variety of types of capstone courses was conducted by Henscheid (2000). The study reviews structure, goal, objectives, requirements, operation, and many other aspects of various capstone courses.

CONCLUSION

Communications programs have evolved greatly in the last century. Having originated from programs like English, curriculums gradually became more specialized and moved further away from the core program of the university. In the more recent past, the field became fragmented and more vocational (Rowland, 1991). Today, the debate has brought us back to our roots, to the liberal arts. The "new professionalism" positions the communications curriculum at the center of the university program. Driven by intellectual pursuit, the program espouses integration of learning, linkages between departments, and, perhaps most importantly, the elevation of the message to all-important status.

The diverse fields that make up the discipline of communication are blending. Yet, the one unchanging element in the mix is the message:

Creation of the message, regardless of the medium, always has been at the core of communication education. This is a distinction that critics of the discipline have long failed to understand: What is most central to our curriculum is not the how of communicating messages—what buttons to push or writing or speaking style to affect—but the what of message content. (Pease, 1994, p. 9)

Such is the focus and the value of the capstone course. The capstone course is the curricular embodiment of convergence. The course is the single opportunity for all of the knowledge and skills to be drawn together. The course ties knowledge and experience together, from the totality of the student educational experience requiring a critical assessment and unique application of 4 years of learning to the successful completion of course requirements. Drawn into the mix are the course expectations that university core courses, and those from any configuration of courses selected, will be drawn on to demonstrate a command of knowledge and ability. The course defines a basic education, a basic expectation; it outlines a level of academic and professional performance that fosters criticism and creativity. The capstone course draws together the expected outcomes of higher education, the institution, and the department, into one educational experience so that those who graduate have shown that they possess more than a sheepskin. They are ". . . well-informed, inquisitive, open-minded young people who are both productive and reflective, seeking answers to life's most important questions . . . who not only pursue their own personal interests but are also prepared to fulfill their social and civic obligations" ("Prologue and Major Recommendations," 1986, p. 16).

REFERENCES

Accrediting Council on Education in Journalism and Mass Communication. (2003). *Accrediting standards*. Retrieved December 18, 2003, from http://www.ukans.edu/~acejmc/BREAKING/New_standards_9-03.pdf

American Association of Higher Education. (n.d.). *9 principles of good practice for assessing student learning.* Retrieved January 2, 2004, from http://www.aahe.org/assessment/principl.htm

Andreasen, R. J., & Trede, L. D. (1998, December). *A comparison of the perceived benefits of selected activities between capstone and non-capstone courses in a college of agriculture.* Paper presented at the meeting of the American Vocational Association, New Orleans, LA.

Association of American Colleges. (n.d.). *A search for quality and coherence in baccalaureate education* (project on redefining the meaning and purpose of baccalaureate degrees). Washington, DC: Author.

Blanchard, R. O., & Christ, W. G. (1993). *Media education and the liberal arts.* Hillsdale, NJ: Lawrence Erlbaum Associates, Inc.

Bloom, B. S. (1956). *A taxonomy of educational objectives: Handbook I, the cognitive domain.* New York: Longman.

Bloom, B. S. (1971). Affective consequences of school achievement. In J. H. Block (Ed.), *Mastery learning* (pp. 13–28). New York: Holt, Rinehart & Winston.

Boyer, E. L. (1987). *College: The undergraduate experience in America.* New York: Harper & Row.

Carlson, C. D., & Peterson, R. J. (1993). Social problems and policy: A capstone course. *Teaching Sociology, 21,* 239–241.

Cuseo, J. B. (1998). Objectives and benefits of senior year programs. In J. N. Gardner & G. Van der Veer (Eds.), *The senior year experience: Facilitating integration, reflection, closure, and transition* (pp. 21–36). San Francisco: Jossey-Bass.

Glaser, H. F., & Radliff, A. J. (2000). *Integrating service learning into the communication capstone course.* Unpublished manuscript, University of Nebraska at Omaha. (ERIC Document Reproduction Service No. ED 444199)

Henscheid, J. M. (2000). *Professing the disciplines: An analysis of senior seminars and capstone courses* (The First-Year Monograph Series No. 30). Columbia, SC: The National Research Center for the Freshman Year Experience and Students in Transition. (ERIC Document Reproduction Service No. ED 446711)

Kemp, J. E. (1975). *Planning and producing audiovisual materials* (3rd ed.). New York: Crowell.

Kemp, J. E., & Smellie, D. C. (1989). *Planning, producing, and using instructional media* (6th ed.). New York: HarperCollins.

Kings College. (1986). *The growth of a model college.* Wilkes-Barre, PA: Author.

Levine, A. (1998). A president's personal and historical perspective. In J. N. Gardner & G. Van der Veer (Eds.), *The senior year experience: Facilitating integration, reflection, closure, and transition* (pp. 51–59). San Francisco: Jossey-Bass.

Lockhart, M., & Borland, Jr., K. W. (2001). Critical thinking goals, outcomes and pedagogy in senior capstone courses. *The Journal of Faculty Development, 18,* 19–26.

Moore, R. C. (1987, February). *A hierarchical program of experiential learning opportunities in communications education.* Paper presented at the meeting of the Association for Educational Communications and Technology, Atlanta, GA.

Moore, R. C. (1988, January). *The role of applied research in undergraduate communications education.* Paper presented at the meeting of the Association for Educational Communications and Technology, New Orleans, LA.

Murphy, P. D. (2003). *Capstone experience.* Retrieved January 3, 2004, from North Dakota State University Web site: http://www.ndsu.edu/ndsu/accreditation/assessment/capstone_experience.htm

Newton, J. (n.d.). *Research on capstone courses.* Retrieved January 5, 2004, from York University Web site: http://www.yorku.ca/jnewton/curriculum/capstone.htm

O'Hair, D., & Kreps, G. L. (1990). *Applied communication theory and research.* Hillsdale, NJ: Lawrence Erlbaum Associates, Inc.

O'Hair, D., Kreps, G. L., & Frey, L. R. (1990). Conceptual issues. In D. O'Hair & G. L. Kreps (Eds.), *Applied communication theory and research* (pp. 3–22). Hillsdale, NJ: Lawrence Erlbaum Associates, Inc.

Oliva, P. F. (1982). *Developing the curriculum.* Boston: Little, Brown.

Pease, E. C. (1994, Spring). Defining communication's role and identity in the 1990's: Promises and opportunities for journalism and communication studies. *Association of Schools of Journalism and Mass Communication Insights,* 13–17.

Prologue and major recommendations for Carnegie Foundations report on colleges. (1986, November 5). *The Chronicle of Higher Education, 33,* 16–22.

Redmond, M. V. (1998). Outcomes assessment and the capstone course in communication. *The Southern Communication Journal, 64,* 68–75.

Rowland, Jr., W. D. (1991, August). *The role of journalism and communications studies in the liberal arts: A place of honor.* Paper presented at the meeting of the Association for Education and Journalism in Mass Communication, Boston.

Smith, B. L. (1998). Curricular structures for cumulative learning. In J. N. Gardner & G. Van der Veer (Eds.), *The senior year experience: Facilitating integration, reflection, closure, and transition* (pp. 81–94). San Francisco: Jossey-Bass.

Smith, W. (1993). The capstone course at Loras College. *Teaching Sociology, 21,* 250–252.

Volkwein, J. F. (2003, May). *Implementing outcomes assessment on your campus. eJournal, 1,* Article 2. Retrieved January 5, 2004, from http://rpgroup.org/publications/eJournal/Volume_1/volkwein.htm

Wagenaar, T. C. (1993). The capstone course. *Teaching Sociology, 21,* 209–214.

Wallace, R. C. (1988). A capstone course in applied sociology. *Teaching Sociology, 16,* 34–40.

IV

USING ASSESSMENT: CASE STUDIES

22

University of Minnesota

Kathleen A. Hansen
School of Journalism and Mass Communication
University of Minnesota

The earlier chapters in this volume have reviewed the process of developing assessment plans, articulating appropriate outcomes in journalism and mass communication curricula, and devising student learning outcomes measures. This chapter describes the assessment process as it has been applied at the University of Minnesota School of Journalism and Mass Communication, and focuses particularly on the ways that process has been useful in examining the curriculum.

THE UNIVERSITY OF MINNESOTA UNDERGRADUATE PROGRAM

The School of Journalism and Mass Communication (SJMC) is a unit within the College of Liberal Arts (CLA) at the University of Minnesota. Hence, students take the majority of their coursework in subject areas outside the journalism and mass communication major and must meet the liberal education coursework requirements set by the CLA. Many journalism students carry a double major or a minor in areas such as Political Science, English, History, Psychology, or similar liberal arts subjects.

The SJMC administers a secondary admissions process to limit enrollment in the program. The SJMC has more than 1,300 undergraduate majors, premajors, and minors—the second-largest enrollment in the CLA. To manage demand for seats in courses and to allow students the opportunity to actually finish their requirements in 4 years, the SJMC processes student applications three times a year, admitting approximately

375 to 400 students each year in total. Enrollment in skills courses (reporting, copywriting, editing, etc.) is limited to 16 to 20 students in a section. Multiple sections of these courses are offered each semester and in the summer session to meet student demand.

The SJMC admits undergraduate students into one of three tracks—journalism, strategic communication, and mass communication. The journalism track encompasses all media "channels"—newspapers, magazines, television, online, photojournalism. The strategic communication track encompasses advertising and public relations (PR). The mass communication track is reserved for students who do not intend to work in a mass communication profession, but who want to study mass communication processes and effects in a liberal arts context.

The SJMC abolished traditional "sequences" many years ago. Students in the program take two required courses in common—an introduction to mass communication class and a class on information gathering and evaluation. After that common core of courses, students branch off into their respective track coursework, working in close consultation with their faculty advisers to choose the appropriate courses for their specialization. All students in the journalism and strategic communication tracks are required to take a combination of skills and "context" courses (history, law, social processes, etc.), but most of the specific courses beyond the core are not prescribed. Each student program is tailored to the interests and goals of the individual. Students in the journalism and strategic communication tracks are required, however, to complete at least one "capstone" course in their area as part of their skills course mix.

Mass communication track students take context courses for the bulk of their work in the SJMC. Their "capstone" experience consists of advanced courses in media history, law, social effects, new media, and so forth. They do not produce professional projects as do the students in the professional tracks. Instead, they write traditional academic papers that demonstrate their mastery of the core concepts in the mass communication field.

As mentioned, students work with SJMC faculty advisers. The faculty (21 tenured or tenure-track members, 3 teaching specialists) take their advising responsibilities seriously and meet with students individually to design their program plans. A journalism track program might consist of the two required core courses, a basic reporting and writing course, a publications editing course, several advanced reporting courses (by subject or "channel"), a journalism history course, a media law course, a media and popular culture course, and a new media economics course. A strategic communication track program might consist of the two required courses, an introduction to PR course, a PR writing and tactics course, a strategic communication research course, a media graphics course, a strategic communication cases course, a campaigns course, a media law course, a media and society course, a public opinion formation course, and an international communications course. The journalism track student's "capstone" course might be Advanced Electronic News Writing and Reporting. The strategic communication track student's capstone course would be Strategic Communication Campaigns.

The Twin Cities provide a rich media market with many adjunct instructors (30+ per year) teaching skills courses for the SJMC. The advantage of having such a wealth of adjunct instructors is that students have a chance to interact with top professionals who are practicing their craft and sharing their knowledge with the next generation of media practitioners. The disadvantage is that any plan to assess student learning must take into account the time constraints of adjunct instructors and the part-time nature of their engagement with the curriculum. Extensive coordination of and consultation with adjunct instructors is necessary for any assessment plan to succeed.

Another challenge is that despite the University of Minnesota–Twin Cities (U of M) role as the state's flagship, land grant, Carnegie 1 research university with a full complement of undergraduate, graduate, and professional schools and programs, many students treat the U of M as a "commuter" campus and attend school part time. Most majors in the SJMC work at least 25 hr a week in addition to attending classes, and most support themselves rather than rely on parents' financial resources. Unlike those at residential campuses in smaller communities, students at the U of M have a thousand and one things to do besides being full-time students. This makes it difficult to develop an assessment plan that might, for instance, require every student to undertake an unpaid internship or complete a practicum. The reality of many students' lives is that they simply don't have the time or financial ability to do so.

PROCESS OF DEVELOPING AN ASSESSMENT PLAN

Following the Accrediting Council on Education in Journalism and Mass Communications' (ACEJMC) establishment of a Fall 2003 deadline for all schools to have an assessment plan in place, the SJMC assembled a special task force of three faculty members focused on outcomes assessment. That task force met regularly during Fall 2002 to discuss the existing evaluation options, how the rest of the faculty should be consulted, and what additional conversations would be useful to engage individuals both inside and outside the U of M. Those conversations brought good and bad news: Many people in the CLA and at fellow ACEJMC-member institutions were happy to discuss these issues, but a survey of similar programs quickly revealed that little progress had been made anywhere as of that date.

In the Fall of 2002, all faculty were asked to complete an assessment matrix or grid for every course they teach (see Appendix A, which articulates the ACEJMC "Professional Values and Competencies"). Faculty were asked to indicate which of the 11 core values and competencies outlined by ACEJMC were included in their courses, and whether their coverage of those values and competencies was at the awareness, understanding, or application level. Faculty submitted these grids to the task force and all data were entered into a database. One faculty meeting in the Fall was devoted to a discussion of the findings of that analysis.

The SJMC Director also asked all faculty to develop course learning objectives for each course they teach (see Appendix B). Up until that time, faculty were not required to include course learning objectives on their syllabi. These learning objectives were collected by the Director and passed along to the task force. The task force asked all faculty to start including course learning objectives on their syllabi. In addition, the Undergraduate Committee was asked to begin a systematic review of the entire undergraduate curriculum based on the information from the assessment grids and the course learning objective projects.

Also in the Fall of 2002, the members of the task force reviewed the latest assessment literature (see Appendix D), developed an initial draft of all possible assessment options, and presented these to the faculty. Based on the feedback and discussion of all options, the members of the task force were directed to seek assistance from outside the SJMC in paring down the list of options to something manageable and feasible.

In Spring 2003, members of the task force met with a U of M evaluation expert from the Office of Educational Policy and Administration and learned that a number of important evaluation resources already existed on campus, including archived student course evaluation data, software applications for collecting student work, and a system to evaluate capstone course student work that was amenable to cohort evaluation. The task force decided to build on those existing resources to develop a revised plan that incorporated the measures and strategies that were considered most useful for our curriculum and most likely to be sustainable.

Also in the Spring of 2003, task force members consulted with Dean Trevor Brown of Indiana University, who chaired the ACEJMC Standards and Assessment Committee. Dean Brown reviewed the options under consideration for our plan and provided extensive feedback on each in light of the Committee's discussion about assessment to that point.

After review of all the information collected throughout the 2002 to 2003 academic year, the task force members wrote another draft of the assessment plan. This draft of the assessment plan was shared with the CLA Associate Dean for Academic Programs for feedback and review before presentation to the faculty. The Associate Dean suggested several additional resources that might prove helpful, and offered to provide assistance in implementing one element of the assessment plan (use of the university's "Portfolio" software system) in the form of naming the SJMC as a "pilot case" for that program. She also expressed gratitude that the SJMC was going through this process because the North Central Association of Colleges and Schools will require all accredited universities to implement an assessment program in the next review, and the Associate Dean is responsible for assisting CLA units in developing their plans. She said she would look to the SJMC as a model for developing and implementing such plans in departments and units throughout the CLA.

Aside from material resources, the SJMC also already possessed, prior to this evaluation plan development, a key intellectual resource: namely, a mission statement that provides a concrete sense of what the faculty want to accomplish with their work. That mission statement was central to our plan. The importance of a well-articulated mission statement to the assessment process is discussed elsewhere in this volume.

All of this work during the 2002 to 2003 academic year informed the development of the assessment plan. Much work remained to be completed by the time the Fall 2003 ACEJMC deadline for having a plan in place arrived. Our plan included a number of suggestions for additional information collection, development of measurement tools, and continuous work in evaluating the curriculum. The plan reflects the fact that assessment needs to be ongoing, systematic, and flexible enough to respond to changing circumstances.

The key elements of the assessment plan at the U of M include the direct measures of a capstone course project assessment process, and a process for reviewing student portfolios of work using the "Portfolio" software system. The indirect measures in the SJMC's plan include a review of course learning objectives over time, a review of student course evaluation data over time, and a special emphasis on demographics that will track students of color as they move through the program and provide help and support where necessary to ensure a high graduation rate.

BENEFITS OF THE PROCESS

Mission Statement Revision

The faculty voted to revise the SJMC's mission statement to incorporate the 11 core values and competencies articulated by ACEJMC. The mission statement had been expressed entirely in terms of "inputs"—that is, the statement articulated the SJMC's goals for the type of curriculum we were committed to delivering. By revising the mission statement to incorporate the student learning "outcomes" of the ACEJMC core values and competencies, the mission statement now brought the two sets of goals—inputs and outcomes—together for the first time.

Curriculum Review

With a revised mission statement in hand, the members of the Undergraduate Committee started reviewing the entire curriculum in light of the ACEJMC values and competencies. As discussed, each faculty member completed an assessment grid that identified whether and at what level the courses they teach address any of the 11 values and competencies. Responses from all faculty were compiled into a summary spreadsheet to see larger patterns or gaps. By analyzing these results, the Committee learned, for instance, that very few courses in the curriculum focused on the competencies necessary for students to master the application of basic numerical and statistical concepts. This analysis helped the Committee see where the journalism, strategic communication, and mass communication tracks had both strengths and weaknesses in helping students master the 11 core values and competencies.

The data from faculty responses also helped identify specific courses in the curriculum on which the Undergraduate Committee should focus. For instance, different faculty responses for separate sections of a specific course were quite divergent, depending on how a faculty member conceptualized the course and what types of teaching materials (texts, assignment books, etc.) were being used in each section. The Committee used these results to help the faculty teaching those sections to work together to better coordinate separate sections of the same course.

Course and Track Revisions

In light of these discrepancies, the Undergraduate Committee's work with the course syllabi for the entire curriculum was especially important. The Committee focused on reviewing the course objectives that all course syllabi were to incorporate. One of the Committee's goals was to bring course objectives into alignment across sections and instructors. Another goal was to determine whether the courses in a professional track, as a whole, exposed students to the 11 core values and competencies at the appropriate level. Members of the Committee met with faculty teaching in the three tracks to help them review all the courses in their area in light of the assessment grid data to look for overlap, gaps, and possible ways to revise the curriculum to be sure all 11 values and competencies were being covered at some point in a student's program.

Capstone Course Project Assessment

In addition to reviewing the assessment grid data and all course objectives, the Undergraduate Committee worked with individual faculty members teaching the "capstone" courses to start developing course project assessment methods. Most capstone courses in the journalism and strategic communication tracks have students develop a course project. These had been evaluated solely by the faculty teaching the course. Going forward, on a biannual basis, someone other than the instructor will be asked to serve as the evaluator of a sample of student projects. This may be done at the same time as the student presentations of their projects during class time.

Assessment Rubrics

In Fall 2003, all current instructors for SJMC capstone professional courses were invited to participate in sessions to produce a standard form, or "rubric," for assessment of capstone projects in their area (either strategic communication or one of several journalism specializations). Rubrics were tailored specifically to each capstone course and the types of projects students produce, and were designed to be applied by "outsiders" who were not the primary instructors (see Appendix C). Some faculty decided to share the rubrics with students at the outset as part of the instructions for successfully completing projects. Others use the rubrics as a grading feedback resource. In any case, developing the rubrics helped faculty clarify goals for student projects.

The plan at the time of this writing is to ask a pilot group of invited judges to use the rubric forms as measures of their evaluation of selected capstone projects developed in the Fall 2004 semester. If such forms generally are useful to the array of invited judges, the SJMC will adopt them as a standard form for distribution and use in any invited review of capstone projects.

Using the U's "Portfolio" Software

The other major direct measure was the use of "Portfolio" software. This software encourages students to build portfolios of their course projects and assignments as they move through the major. The software is available to all U of M students and faculty and allows students to collect 20 megabytes of material in one location. The software provides secure access to authorized users only and can store text, images, video, and other sorts of production work (it is available at http://portfolio. umn.edu).

Starting in the 2003 to 2004 academic year, all faculty were encouraged to require students to post their relevant assignments or projects in the "Portfolio" system. Instructors teaching Jour 3004, Information for Mass Communication, the required first course students take as new majors, introduce students to this system and require them to post their course major projects so all students have familiarity with the system as they proceed to their more advanced courses.

The Undergraduate Committee and members of the task force worked throughout the 2003 to 2004 academic year to develop a method to sample student portfolio entries for evaluation of student learning and to develop the measurement tools for assessment of student work. A group of SJMC faculty and outside evaluators will periodically review this sample of student work and apply measures of the course learning objectives and core values and competencies in the professional tracks and the mass communication track. For example, outside evaluators may be allowed access to materials in the portfolios of a set of beginning students, and to those of a set of students ready to graduate. The evaluators might be asked to "sort" the students' portfolios based on their perceived level of mastery of the "writing" competency. A "good" assessment outcome would, obviously, be one that placed the advanced students' work in the highest category.

Future Curriculum Discussions Framed Through Assessment Lens

Perhaps one of the most important benefits of developing the assessment plan was that the entire faculty was engaged in a discussion of the core values and competencies of our field and how our curriculum measured up. A curriculum is a constantly-evolving entity, and the latest evolution has now incorporated explicit goals and outcomes for student learning. No one on the faculty can imagine undertaking any future curriculum or course development project that doesn't include this assessment perspective as an important element to consider.

Student Awareness of Core Values and Competencies

As a result of the assessment project, all students are now aware of the core competencies and values of their intended professions and areas of study because they have been included on course syllabi in the very first courses students take in the major and on all other syllabi throughout the curriculum. Advisers working with students newly admitted into the major can use the ACEJMC competencies and values as a "road map" to explain to students the logic of their course choices. A number of faculty have expressed their delight in being able to discuss with students in their classes the important characteristics of the mass communication field and professions through reference to the ACEJMC principles.

In addition to the 11 core values and competencies any well-educated journalism and mass communication major should master, all students now know the specific course objectives for each course in the SJMC curriculum. It may be hard to imagine, but the SJMC had no requirement for faculty to include course objectives on syllabi before this assessment project started. Many faculty, of course, included objectives on their syllabi on their own initiative, and many developed specific objectives for individual assignments and projects. However, there was no uniform model for developing and articulating course objectives, and no process for comparing objectives across courses and throughout a specific track. The assessment process has exposed all faculty to the best practices for developing course and learning objectives, and has provided students with a clear outline of the materials they should expect to master by taking any given course.

New Faculty Knowledge

In addition, faculty have updated and expanded their familiarity with assessment best practices, trends in the field, and how sister institutions are innovating in the assessment arena. Middle-level and senior faculty at most institutions joined the academy at a time when there was little attention paid to developing stellar teachers. If one had the right academic credentials and brought the promise of producing important scholarship to a teaching position, that was deemed enough. That has obviously changed in many places, certainly for the better. But senior faculty have not necessarily had a chance to catch up. The assessment process has given senior faculty a way to engage with the literature of teaching and learning without feeling stigmatized or being asked, "Why don't you know this already if you've been teaching all these years?" Because everyone was declared to be in the same situation—in need of a crash course on the most recent and best thinking in the student learning assessment field—it provided a way for the entire faculty to bring their skills up to speed together.

Common Language

Faculty teaching sections of the same course and within a professional track now have a common language to discuss student learning goals, objectives, and teaching strategies. In addition, faculty can examine all the courses in the track with an eye toward developing course content to ensure that students have the most complete and comprehensive exposure to the field as possible, using the 11 core values and competencies as the guide. The Undergraduate Committee, in concert with the faculty teaching in the area, has targeted several courses in the curriculum for revision based on the "gaps" the assessment process exposed. We all know that discussions among faculty about course content, coverage, and approaches can be fraught with trouble—ego defensiveness, claims of abridgements of academic freedom, turf battles. The assessment process provides a nonthreatening way for "outsiders" (those who don't teach a specific course) to examine and influence course content without appearing to overstep boundaries.

Clarifying Goals and Reenergizing Faculty

The assessment process has also helped the faculty clarify course goals, teaching priorities, and grading criteria for their own courses. The discussions about new ways to engage students and assess student learning have reenergized many faculty and provided an impetus to try new things and revise tried-and-true things with new twists. For instance, faculty teaching the capstone magazine production and editing course discovered through the "rubric creation" process that they had not been clearly articulating several project evaluation standards to the students. They realized that was the reason students had problems meeting their expectations for that part of the course project work. Being "forced" to create explicit criteria for assigning below average, average, above average, or excellent assessments to the work helped the instructors revise the instructions to students about how to do the work in the first place. The faculty who have developed the rubrics for the capstone courses, in particular, have expressed amazement at how the exercise clarified their thinking.

Students Understand Expectations

Students have benefited from improved project or assignment assessment processes. They now have a clear set of expectations and a clear statement of how well (or how inadequately) they've met those expectations. Rather than assigning a letter grade or a set of points with a few written comments to help the students understand the score, faculty can now provide students with a concrete list of expectations and an explanation for why something did not measure up or was judged superior to others' work.

Documenting Outcomes

Faculty have also realized the need to focus on documenting their students' accomplishments. Most universities require faculty to document their research, teaching, and service activities each year. Prior to the assessment project work, faculty in the SJMC documented their teaching accomplishments by sharing course syllabi and assignments, by including student course evaluations in the file, perhaps by asking a peer to sit in on a class or two to prepare a peer teaching observation report for the file, and by other similar methods. Most of these focused on the "inputs" of teaching—"here is what I say I'm doing, here are the assignments I've developed to accomplish my goals, here are the views of my colleagues as to my teaching technique and mastery of the classroom setting." None of the evidence, save the student course evaluations (which do not assess student learning except by self-report with one question), address the outcomes of teaching. The assessment project has required the faculty to focus on how they might explicitly demonstrate student learning as a result of having been exposed to the teaching inputs. That means faculty have to look at what they are doing from a very different part of the process.

Many faculty realized as they reviewed assessment techniques and practices that they had been doing student learning assessment in their courses, but they had not been collecting or analyzing those results. For instance, a number of faculty reported that they regularly started their courses with an informal "exam" that attempted to gauge student familiarity with the central course concepts and knowledge areas. They would reexamine student knowledge (outside the context of a formal course exam) as the course progressed throughout the semester. This is a form of student learning assessment, obviously. But no one who was doing this regularly archived or analyzed those "exams" or thought they would have any value except as guidance for the faculty themselves to adjust course content based on feedback from students about their teaching. Once the faculty discussed using these types of techniques to document student learning, it was clear that many faculty would start collecting and analyzing that material with a new perspective on the value such things have for assessment.

Engaging Faculty in Total Curriculum Planning

Another benefit of the assessment project has been that the Undergraduate Committee has a way to engage the entire faculty in overall curriculum development goals rather than just dealing with specific issues
that arise in specific courses or tracks. The faculty have taken a fresh
look at the entire curriculum through the eyes of students enrolled in a
set of courses that we think forms a coherent whole, but that the students may not necessarily see that way. By placing the ACEJMC core
values and competencies grid over the entire curriculum, the Undergraduate Committee has been able to engage the entire faculty in taking
some ownership of the curriculum as a whole rather than simply focusing on a subset of courses or skill sets. If the faculty are going to be held
accountable for what students learn as they move through the entire
curriculum, then the faculty have to be concerned about that entire set
of courses and experiences in a way that they had not been in the past.
This has allowed the Undergraduate Committee to enlist the help and
advice of virtually everyone on the faculty, as well as a good number of
the adjunct instructors, who now have a "stake" in the overall enterprise.

College Leadership

Because the assessment task force sought the advice and help of the
CLA Associate Dean for Academic Programs, the SJMC is now positioned as a "leader" in the CLA in implementing larger CLA and U of M
goals for student learning assessment as part of the regional accreditation requirements. The CLA is thus enlisted as a partner, and perhaps as
a source of support and resources, in implementing the assessment
process (which, after all, does not happen without resources). The
SJMC benefits by its identity as a forward-thinking entity, by the gratitude
of the CLA for taking the first steps in the assessment direction, and by
being held up as an example to other CLA units as a way to do assessment "right." For instance, the Associate Dean offered to provide help
through the CLA Information Technology Fees Committee staff to adapt
the "Portfolio" software to allow for the sampling of student portfolios
that our assessment plan outlines.

Challenges in Developing the Assessment Plan

The process of developing a student learning assessment plan has not
been without difficulties. For a relatively small faculty charged with delivering a top-notch undergraduate, master's, and PhD-level curriculum,

the additional work and effort of reviewing the entire undergraduate curriculum through the assessment lens has proven a monumental undertaking. The Undergraduate Committee has taken the lead, but at the expense of other projects that are equally important and which have usually taken up the bulk of the Committee's efforts in other years. We have yet to feel the full effect of the plan we have proposed, because we have not yet gone through a full cycle of evaluating student work as we have pledged to do. It remains to be seen whether the full implementation of the SJMC's assessment plan is feasible and sustainable.

A much more serious challenge to programs such as the one at the U of M is emerging because of the impending review of communications PhD programs by the National Research Council (NRC). The resources needed to deliver a stellar undergraduate professional program in a liberal arts setting, incorporating all of the work the assessment process demands as a part of accreditation requirements, are substantial. The resources needed to deliver a stellar PhD program in a research university setting, incorporating all of the metrics of the NRC rankings process, also are substantial. In a time of shrinking resources for universities overall, these two sets of demands are on a collision course in programs that strive to do both things well. In the struggle between the undergraduate program accreditation process and the NRC PhD program rankings process, schools or departments housed in major research universities may have to bend to the will of university administrators and presidents who understandably value the NRC rankings much more highly. ACEJMC members need to take this into account in their continuing discussions about the undergraduate accreditation process.

Nonetheless, the process of developing an assessment plan for undergraduate student learning at the U of M has had positive outcomes for students, faculty, and CLA administrators. Students have a clear set of expectations against which they can measure their progress through the major. The faculty have had a chance to review the entire curriculum in light of a well-articulated set of goals for student learning, and have been encouraged to think carefully and creatively about their individual courses and teaching methods. CLA administrators have a model department to point toward as they move the rest of the CLA toward a student learning assessment mind-set for regional accreditation. The process has been a learning opportunity for everyone involved, and that, after all, is the purpose of higher education (for select references, see Appendix D).

APPENDIX A

Assessment Matrix or Grid Faculty Completed for Each Course Taught

Professional Values and Competencies	Level 1: Awareness (familiarity with specific information, including facts, concepts, laws and regulations, processes and effects)	Level 2: Understanding (assimilation and comprehension of information, concepts, theories and ideas)	Level 3: Application (competence in relating and applying skills, information, concepts, theories and ideas to the accomplishment of tasks)
Understand and apply the principles and laws of freedom of speech and press including the right to dissent, to monitor and criticize power, and to assemble and petition for redress of grievances			
Demonstrate an understanding of the history and role of professionals and institutions in shaping communication			
Demonstrate an understanding of the diversity of groups in a global society in relationship to communications			
Understand concepts and apply theories in the use and presentation of images and information			
Demonstrate an understanding of professional ethical principles and work ethically			
Think critically, creatively and independently			
Conduct research and evaluate information by methods appropriate to the communications profession in which they work			
Write correctly and clearly in forms and styles appropriate for the communications professions, audiences and purposes they serve			
Critically evaluate their own work and that of others for accuracy and fairness, clarity, appropriate style and grammatical correctness			
Apply basic numerical and statistical concepts			
Apply tools and technologies appropriate for the communications professions in which they work			

APPENDIX B

These are examples of two of eight course learning goals for Jour 3004, "Information for Mass Communication." They were developed by Kathleen A. Hansen, School of Journalism and Mass Communication (SJMC) faculty member. These course learning goals are printed on the syllabus and individual course assignments refer to the goal each exercise is addressing. Teaching assistants use the goal and objectives to help in grading assignments. Because this course is required for all SJMC majors, the course learning goals also help faculty teaching the later part of the curriculum to understand what they should expect all students to know as they enter their more advanced courses.

Course Goal: Develop the ability to identify appropriate contributors to an information search	
Action Verb	**Specific Learning Objectives Associated With Course Goal**
Describe	The characteristics of potential contributors to a mass communication information search (informal, institutional, journalistic, scholarly)
Distinguish	Between popular, scholarly and trade sources of information
Identify	Information subsidies and their sources
Distinguish	Between public-sector and private-sector institutions as sources of information

Course Goal: Develop the ability to construct and execute an efficient and effective search for information using print and electronic search tools	
Action Verb	**Specific Learning Objectives Associated With Course Goal**
Categorize	The appropriate tools for a particular search
Plan	An appropriate search strategy (selection of terminology, boundaries of the search, etc.) for the topic
Conduct	A search using appropriate print and electronic tools

APPENDIX C

This is an example of a capstone course project rubric. It was developed by Gayle Golden and Ken Stone, School of Journalism and Mass Communication teaching specialists.

Objectives	Below expectations	Meets expectations	Above expectations
Jour 4451 Advanced Electronic News Writing and Reporting			
Research Background Interviews Factual accuracy Context	Lacks context Inappropriate subjects Factual inaccuracies Unfair treatment or one-sidedness	Research provides context Proper camera subjects chosen Fair treatment of issue Facts accurate	*All of "meets expectations" plus:* High complexity of story Added or free points of view add nuance
Use of Video Steadiness and focus Visually interesting shots Proper cutaways Sequencing Lighting	Unsteady camera with bad focusing Poor lighting Boring visual images with little action Lack of cutaways	Camera steady and focused Proper lighting Captured action with interesting camera angle or subject Proper mix of cutaways	*All of "meets expectations" plus:* Lighting enhances story or subject matter Unexpected visuals that complement the script Creative use of cutaways
Use of Sound Capturing ambient sound Using ambient sound for story pace	Little or no ambient sound Ambient sound not integrated with the script	Ambient sound captured Sound used "under" and "up full" for pacing of script	*All of "meets expectations" plus:* Unexpected use of ambient sound that enhances subject
Writing Story structure (lede, foreshadowing, climax) Script relation to video Fairness Factual accuracy Conversational style	Poor story structure missing one element Script at odds with video Presentation of facts confusing Non-conversational style	Strong lede with all story elements Coherent story line Script that complements video Facts woven into story Clear, conversational style	*All of "meets expectations" plus:* Unexpected, effective lede or other story structure element Script that enhances video Facts presented in exceptional way "Elegant" or "poetic" writing touches
Performance (weighted less) Delivery of voice over Use of on-camera standups	False delivery (i.e. sing-song voice, "forced anchor") Stiff body language	Natural delivery Relaxed body language	*All of "meets expectations" plus:* Creative performance details that can include location, camera angle Exceptional eloquence that enhances story

APPENDIX D

Selected Assessment Resources

Angelo, T. A., & Cross, K. P. (1993). *Classroom assessment techniques: A handbook for college teachers* (2nd ed.). San Francisco: Jossey-Bass.

Banta, T. W., Lund, J. P., Black, K. E., & Oblander, F. W. (1996). *Assessment in practice: Putting principles to work on college campuses.* San Francisco: Jossey-Bass.

Gardiner, L., Anderson, C., & Cambridge, B. (1997). *Learning through assessment: A resource guide.* Washington, DC: AAHE.

Glassick, C. E., Huber, M. T., & Maeroff, G. I. (1997). *Scholarship assessed: Evaluation of the professoriate.* San Francisco: Jossey-Bass.

Nichols, J. O. (1995). *A practitioner's handbook for institutional effectiveness and student outcomes assessment implementation* (3rd ed.). New York: Agathon.

Palomba, C. A., & Banta T. W. (Eds.). (2001). *Assessing student competence in accredited disciplines: Pioneering approaches to assessment in higher education.* Herndon, VA: Stylus Publishing, LLC.

Stassen, M. L. A., Doherty, K., & Poe, M. (2001). *Program-based review and assessment: Tools and techniques for program improvement.* Amherst: University of Massachusetts Press.

Walvoord, B. E., & Anderson, V. J. (1998). *Effective grading: A tool for learning and assessment.* San Francisco: Jossey-Bass.

Weimer, M. (2002). *Learner-centered teaching: Five key changes to practice.* San Francisco: Jossey-Bass.

23

Arizona State University

Joe Foote
Gaylord College of Journalism and Mass Communication
University of Oklahoma

Assessment at the Cronkite School of Journalism and Mass Communication at Arizona State University (ASU) began in Spring 2000 when the School created and implemented an assessment plan all in one semester. Because of the severe time constraints, the plan remained very simple and straightforward. This strategy, for the most part, turned out to be a virtue. The School got its assessment vehicle up and running within 3 months and has collected 3 years of data. It is now in the process not only of trying to aggregate and analyze the data it has collected, but also considering a more sophisticated learning outcomes program that will provide more substantive direction for the future of the School.

Largely because of the time constraints for developing a plan, the School did not start with a series of specific learning objectives and then built a learning outcomes system around it. Rather, it started with the broad premises that the School's priorities were training students to compete successfully in the job market after graduation and socializing students into the field by providing them with a background in the ethics, history, societal responsibility, and legal constraints of the field. A key tenet in developing an assessment plan for the School was focusing on both the skills-based competencies and the analytical-based competencies in one plan.

The School's assessment activities are clearly a work in progress. All of the elements described here are seen as "starter measures" that will develop into more precise and comprehensive measures that over time will influence the quality and direction of the program.

The School's assessment plan consists of four basic elements:

1. A senior skills-based assessment of student work at the highest level skills course taken by a student in their chosen concentration (direct measure).
2. A skills-based assessment of individual students' internship experience and their qualifications for the job market (direct measure).
3. A non-skills-based examination covering material covered in the two major required courses (direct measure).
4. Analysis of student satisfaction through an alumni survey conducted by the university (indirect measure).

HIGHER SKILLS ASSESSMENT (DIRECT MEASURE)

A major hurdle for any program is building an effective, direct measure of journalism and mass communication skills. Doing so is a very labor intensive and complex task. Yet, building an assessment plan without one of these direct measures is suspect because so much of a program's reputation lies with its ability to prepare students to be productive members of the workforce. Furthermore, the new assessment standard instituted by the Accrediting Council for Education in Journalism and Mass Communication expects some type of direct measure relating to skills assessment to be incorporated into a quality assessment program.

The gold standard of direct measures of journalism skills assessment is the senior portfolio. Examining the work of students at the end of their university careers provides an important summative snapshot of the effectiveness of their training. The School has taken a few baby steps on its way to a full-fledged senior portfolio assessment. In spring 2000, the School began an external review of a sample of student work in most of its concentrations.

To construct a body of work to measure, the School sampled term projects from the skills classes that were the highest level required of everyone in that concentration. This was somewhat unwieldy because it meant a different assessment in each of five concentrations and the curriculum was changing in some of those concentrations. The faculty decided that an external evaluator and a member of the faculty would jointly review the projects. The evaluation goal was a simple one: Did the work demonstrate a proficiency that would allow that student to enter the workplace in a small media market? Projects were ranked as exemplary, proficient, acceptable, and unacceptable. No precise definitions for each category were provided.

The School paid a small honorarium to the outside evaluators and asked them to come to campus for part of a day to do the evaluations. The concentration heads recruited the outside evaluators from the ranks of media professionals in the state of Arizona. Some heads were particularly vigilant about including small market editors and news directors beyond the metropolitan Phoenix market.

Early on, the administration realized that it would be impractical to examine every student's work so it received permission from the university's assessment coordinator to draw a sample of projects to be examined. The School examined all projects in the smallest concentrations, but drew a sample from the largest.

The simplicity of the project assignment made it relatively easy for outside evaluators to do their work. Having been accustomed to hiring entry-level personnel, they felt confident about rendering a straightforward evaluation that basically came down to the question of "Would you hire this person if you were hiring for a small market?" Unfortunately, the four rankings were not explicitly tied to this general question. What does "proficient" mean compared to "acceptable" in terms of workforce qualifications? How good do you have to be to be judged as "exemplary?" Criteria for each of these rankings need to be created and explained. This is particularly important because the external reviewers frequently rotate through the program.

There were also no explicit directions concerning the split role of the faculty member and the outside evaluator. Were they to rate student work individually without any comparison and take an average? Were they to confer and reach a consensus on the value of the student work? In case of inconsistencies from year to year, did the faculty member have the right to inflate or deflate ratings to maintain a consistent standard?

With 3 years of experience under its belt, the School has learned that it can be difficult to generalize from the data because it can vary so much from concentration to concentration, from reviewer to reviewer, and from year to year. For example, in radio news, the external examiner in 2001 rated two projects exemplary, nine proficient, and two acceptable. A different reviewer in 2002 rated one project exemplary, four proficient, five acceptable, and six unacceptable. A third reviewer in 2003 rated four projects exemplary, six proficient, two acceptable, and none unacceptable. Was there that much change from year to year in the quality of the students' work or did the difference lie in the reviewer? Again, more specific criteria tied to learning objectives and guidance from the faculty evaluator may have mitigated the huge variance in ratings. It is clear that the School will have to make adjustments to how these portfolios are evaluated before it can draw any valid conclusions that can be used to effect program improvement.

In television news, where one news director examined student work for 2 consecutive years, the results were more consistent. In 2002, he rated 1 project exemplary, 6 proficient, 16 acceptable, and 8 unacceptable. The following year he rated none exemplary, 5 proficient, 21 acceptable, and 9 unacceptable. Although there was a different reviewer in 2001, the results were still consistent: none exemplary, two proficient, nine acceptable, and seven unacceptable.

Overall, there were some stark discrepancies across sequences. Only 5% of the projects from public relations (PR) and news editorial were judged as "unacceptable" over the 3-year period, whereas 15% of the radio news projects and 29% of the television news were judged as unacceptable. Why were TV news students failing six times more often than their PR and print counterparts? Why were 86% of the failures in the broadcast news area?

Similarly, more than one third of the news editorial rankings were in the exemplary range compared to only 1% in television, creating another conundrum for the faculty. At some point, the faculty and administration will have to come to grips with these discrepancies and ascertain whether the results are an artifact of the assessment process or a real indicator of quality in the program? And, how is an administrator to reconcile this? On the one hand, broadcast students won first place nationally in the Hearst writing competition in 2003 to 2004, whereas the print students did not finish in the top 10. Yet, the assessment results showed that far more print students were judged exemplary than broadcast students.

If some of the results are suspect, what can be gained from this type of analysis? The broad assessment of School students showed that over 3 years, 83% of its graduates were rated in the "acceptable" or higher range to assume an entry-level job in the industry. It now has a 3-year benchmark on which to build. If it can make the evaluation more consistent and better define criteria, the value of this measure will certainly improve.

A major disadvantage of this crude measure was that it offered little insight into the elements that might have produced a highly qualified graduate. Although we did learn that a high proportion of our graduates were deemed ready for the job market, we did not learn what value-added part of their university education got them there? When the School enters the next phase of its assessment experience, it is likely to refine these measures, teasing out some of the individual components of a quality journalism and mass communication education. Some of the outside evaluators explained why certain elements of the projects appealed to them and what areas were strongest, but there were no predefined parameters for this kind of feedback.

Even the implementation of the external skills assessment revealed some flaws in our execution of the curriculum. Two different professors taught broadcast management, the highest level course in the media management concentration. One professor required a reality-based group project that required considerable knowledge of the local television marketplace to complete. The other did not. The two professors were reluctant to conform their courses to a common syllabus so the skills assessment was postponed in this concentration until the differences could be reconciled. Three years later, there is still no evaluative measure.

This part of the assessment debate prompted cries of "academic freedom" from other faculty who were reluctant to conform their section of a multiple section course to a common syllabus. In my mind, this is symptomatic of a singular lack of emphasis on quality control in higher education. The notion of the independent professor going his or her own way with minimum interference has ruled since journalism has been taught at the university level. Because journalism education has historically not been a player in the general education curriculum, conflicts over multiple section consistency seldom arise. With assessment, however, quality control takes priority. Students, parents, and education stakeholders expect that an education has a significant degree of internal consistency across sections and professors. Once assessment measures become more refined and focused, the wisdom of this demand should become evident.

Although the School's summative skills evaluation was one-dimensional, it was an important and productive first step toward a deeper form of direct measurement. One of the most important outcomes of this exercise has been the routinization of the assessment process. It has put the School into a rhythm of examining the skill level of its students. There is now an expectation that student work will be evaluated beyond the classroom based on criteria that transcend course grades. The faculty anxiety that initially accompanied this activity has largely disappeared. The exercise has laid an excellent foundation for a segue into a full-blown portfolio review.

The external review has reassured the faculty that it is doing a competent job of instruction and that the great majority of students are ready to assume a productive role in the workplace. A full-fledged portfolio review will further expose students' full range of abilities within and across media, their ability to package their work persuasively, and their creativity beyond the narrowness of prescribed assignments.

I would hope that the second-generation assessment of skills would examine breadth as well as depth in the curriculum. In addition to their focused goal of preparing for a particular job in a particular medium, can students demonstrate other skills as well? Do they possess skills beyond their narrowly defined concentration? Do they have the ability to integrate different forms of media in a productive way? Do they exhibit any higher level characteristics that go beyond their ability to get a first job?

It would also be helpful to have a coordinated measure that invites comparison across concentrations. Historically, there has been a chauvinism in journalism schools that blatantly discriminates against certain areas of study, implying that they are lightweight inferiors in terms of skills and sophistication. Developing a common denominator of quality would provide a more objective assessment to compare students throughout the major. Having an externally validated measure of writing is another need for a direct measure in journalism. Projects that are evaluated on their creativity, their writing quality, and their visual quality (when appropriate) would help programs understand better the kinds of graduates they are producing.

INTERNSHIP ASSESSMENT (DIRECT MEASURE)

One of the most overlooked assessment measures is evaluation of the student internship (see chapter 17). These can be direct or indirect, depending on how the data are collected and used. Many programs already collect enough data to do a broad assessment of the program and most programs could do so with minimal effort. Some might ask, what is the difference between giving course grades for internships and using internships for evaluating learning outcomes? The data gathered may not be much different, but the ways in which the data are used are significantly different. When employers rate a student intern, they are in a position to rate directly the competence of the student and their prospects in the marketplace. Thus, the rating of individual students' professional performance in a systematic way provides a valuable, direct measure of assessment. A more general evaluation that is not tied to assessment of students as individuals would be an indirect measure.

Grades for internships reflect the individual achievement of a particular student for a given internship as rated by the instructor of record. The input of employer supervisors provides a valid external evaluation that offers a second perspective to an instructor's evaluation and can be aggregated across that supervisors' total experience with interns. Furthermore, all of the employer supervisors' collective input can be used to provide not only a measure of the internships' cumulative worth, but also the skills preparation of several generations of interns.

The internship evaluation is an excellent complement to the senior portfolio because they are both examining the skill level of students. There should be a high correlation between the external review of senior portfolios and the cumulative assessment of the skills exhibited during internships. One has to control, however, for the different population entering internships if a select group is chosen for the internship experience.

If the right questions are asked, the internship assessment can also provide an external measure of the students' work ethic, their integration into a workplace, their problem-solving ability, and their knowledge beyond journalism, including their broad-based liberal arts education. The first incarnation of the ASU internship assessment effort did not delve into these subsidiary areas, but focused instead on the central questions of "If there were an opening for an entry-level position at your company, would you hire this person?" and "Is this student ready for an entry-level job in a small market?" With the evaluation conducted in a top-20 market, students fared far better on the suitability for entry-level employment than they did on the readiness to work for a major market station. Yet, a sizable percentage was deemed ready for that higher level opportunity.

As with the skills project assessment, the internship assessment results revealed several inconsistencies. Over the 3-year period, 91% of School students were judged by their employers to be ready to enter the marketplace, a great tribute to the quality of the program. Yet, the failure rate among broadcast journalism students was far higher than with other concentrations. Ninety percent of the failures were in the broadcast area. Conversely, no PR and sales interns and only two of the news editorial interns were deemed unready for the workplace, casting doubts on the validity of the measure.

The next iteration of internship assessment provides an opportunity to make midcourse corrections to counter these inconsistencies and delve deeper into the qualities that quality interns possess. A great deal of feedback from employer supervisors relates to the students' intangible personal qualities and their ability to work with others. And, if students do have a very narrow view of the world that limits their potential, it will normally become manifest in an internship.

It would be nice if these factors could be incorporated into the assessment process. A challenge is to gather as much information as possible without creating an onerous burden for the employer supervisor. The School has wisely kept its evaluation very simple and straightforward. The best system is one that seamlessly gathers data necessary for evaluating the student in the internship and the program effectiveness overall with the same prompts. One would hope that these data could be used more creatively to use the internship as a direct measure of the skills training of the program and the liberal arts knowledge that students typically exhibit.

COMPREHENSIVE EXAM (DIRECT MEASURE)

In addition to skills assessment, the faculty wanted to learn more about the competencies the students were developing in two core courses required of each student in the major (Media and Society, and Law of Mass Communication). Because all students take these courses, the School decided to administer an exam in the law class each semester that measured some of the content covered in the courses. One of the law instructors constructed an exam of 20 objective questions using basic content from the two required courses and began administering it in all of the law sections in 2001.

The questions on the exam were very basic, mostly involving the structure of media and the rudiments of libel and privacy. The questions were not explicitly tied to particular, established learning outcomes.

Three years of data show consistent results. Students scored 77%, 75%, and 78% over the 3 years. No level was set for a satisfactory result, and results were not broken down according to percentiles. Clearly, there is proficiency in the areas tested among a majority of students based on the content of the exam. What the School has not done is tie the questions on the test to specific competencies. We know that most Cronkite students leave with a passing score on this exam, but little else. We do not have any additional knowledge about particular areas where they are weak or strong.

An opportunity now exists to expand the exam with a discreet section devoted to a particular competency. There is also an opportunity to give a pretest at the beginning of the Media and Society class that students take during their freshman or sophomore years that can be compared to the summative exam taken during their senior year in the law course.

STUDENT SATISFACTION SURVEY (INDIRECT MEASURE)

One of the easiest and most useful indirect measures of assessment has proven to be surveys of recent graduates by the university. Most universities have had considerable experience with this instrument and have refined it over the years to be a valuable tool. For the units using this measure, finding feedback to help the program has been relatively simple. Also, it is the most useful tool to feed back into the system to effect change. Most programs are able to use these data to make immediate improvements unlike some other assessment tools that take years to unfold.

Most recent graduate surveys ask about student satisfaction with such things as advising, job placement, orientation, internships, obtaining classes, and so forth. They also ask about how well the program prepared students in writing, oral presentations, and technology usage, as well as their overall level of satisfaction. Results are usually broken out across colleges and departments, gender, ethnicity, in-state–out-of-state, and age.

The recent graduate survey at Arizona State spoke clearly about strengths and weaknesses. For several years, the School's professional advising system in which a student kept the same advisor from matriculation to graduation received overwhelming validation. Students clearly understood the value of this personalized, consistent advising.

The major weakness also appeared across several groups of graduates—career placement. The School had relied on an informal system of career placement tied to its extremely well developed internship program. Job notices were posted informally with the School and advice was dispensed through faculty, sequence heads and internship coordinators. No faculty or staff member was specifically charged with coordinating career advice and services. There was little coordination between the university's career placement center and the School's efforts. Students who participated in the internship program (not required of all students) had much higher satisfaction than those who did not. Thus, students without an internship or other work experience on their resume felt cut off from any real help in the marketplace for employment.

Seeing graduates' consistent negative feedback in the alumni survey on job placement, the School began to change its strategy. First, it forged a much closer link with the university's career placement service. It stopped posting its own job notices and started funneling them directly to career placement. Advisors began steering students to career placement and encouraged career placement to be more proactive in inviting national media recruiters to campus. Internship coordinators started using career placement's facilities to hold interviews to expose students to their location and services.

The School tried to convince students that career placement's database, which provided opportunities for employers to search out students as well as students searching for employers, was a huge advantage in the marketplace. It was clear, however, that this partnership was not sufficient to give students the kind of localized career advice they required. Recently, the School's Director added a career counselor as a budget priority. This person, when hired, would serve as a liaison between career services, the internship coordinators, and the School, to improve the service students receive and would initiate a series of interviewing, resume writing, and career preparation workshops for students.

In addition to these two areas where the results were striking, there were other categories that validated conventional wisdom. As expected, students felt that they had received abundant experience in writing, had been given great opportunity for hands-on training, and had developed a close relationship with the faculty. Yet, it was surprising that these journalism students, who had been nurtured in small classes for most of their tenure in the School and had developed a relationship with the faculty, were not significantly more satisfied than students in most other units in the campus, including some that offered a far more impersonal atmosphere and experience. Particularly surprising was a positive response to the writing experience question from students in a department where minimal writing experience was offered. It seemed that students could be socialized into thinking that they were getting a significant amount of experience although it did not square with reality. It shows the relative isolation of individual majors and the inability of students to compare experiences outside of that cocoon.

One mistake that many departments make with senior and recent graduate surveys is looking at their own data exclusively and not comparing them to other units and the university as a whole. These surveys are one of the few assessment measures where upper level administrators can make comparisons across units. It is helpful for a journalism and mass communication department to build a solid case for the unit based on its consistent showing in these surveys. Likewise, a unit can gauge its own status within the university across a variety of measures. It is important to examine several years of data to get a realistic view of our graduates' perceptions. Yet, it is remarkable how consistent they are from year to year.

Before putting too much stock in an alumni survey, assessment coordinators should keep in mind that that the return rate on these surveys is usually low, lowering the probability that they are representative of the entire population. They rely on the recollections of alumni, which may or may not be distorted. Also, their recommendations may be dated if the curriculum or student services have changed since their time at the university.

Although the new graduates survey has been a productive measure for the School and has been used to make adjustments in the program, it is not officially part of the School's assessment plan. Sometimes departments don't realize that the mounds of data collected by the university can be an important part of their local assessment activities (see chapter 16). It would be wise for a departmental assessment coordinator to examine the full range of university data from university surveys to see what parts might be useful for journalism and mass communication assessment.

OTHER POTENTIAL ASSESSMENT AREAS (INDIRECT MEASURES)

One indirect measurement of quality that the School is already using on an informal basis is the regional and national recognition that students receive. The School is very active in the Hearst, Society of Professional Journalists, Broadcast Education, and Roy Howard awards, winning numerous prizes. The analysis of these honors over time would show a consistency of quality that routinely produces high achievers. Although this is not a measure of the quality of the entire student body, it demonstrates the ability to draw highly talented students to the program consistently and to help them achieve a level of competence that rates with the best in the nation.

RECOMMENDATIONS

In the first 3 years of its outcomes assessment experience, the School has shown that it can marshal the resources to sustain an ongoing assessment plan that features both direct and indirect measures. It has also demonstrated that it can attract a panel of respected external reviewers who are pleased to work with faculty to evaluate the program.

Armed with this initial experience, the School is ready to consider refinements and improvements. To that end, I would make the following recommendations. First, the School should make the graduate survey an official part of its assessment program. Doing so would establish a focused database for student feedback. Because the School is already using many of the results, the effort to include this measure officially would be minimal. Special attention should be paid to comparing results with those of other departments on campus.

Second, the School should expand the project evaluation in the highest skills class into a full-fledged senior portfolio evaluation. The multiple projects from five different classes have become unwieldy, and it is difficult to bring consistency across reviewers to the evaluation. A portfolio assessment would allow the student greater flexibility and creativity. The School would be able to have individual judges evaluate students across concentrations, mitigating the differences between broadcast journalism and the rest of the curriculum. Perfecting this measure should be the prime focus of any journalism program's assessment plan because it goes to the heart of professional education and a student's readiness to enter the workplace.

Third, better definition should be given to the grading scale for evaluating projects so that there can be better consistency across reviewers, across years, and between concentrations. This exposes the gap between constructing an assessment plan and executing one that provides meaningful feedback for change. Unless the measurement system is precise and consistent and tied to specific outcomes, the results can be a jumble of unusable information.

Fourth, competencies should be established for the summative project beyond the ability of the student to compete in the workplace. Individual measures of writing, organization, and analytical skills could be assessed. Although preparing a student for the workplace is an important dimension of a quality journalism education, it is not the only dimension. The portfolio should go farther than ascertaining the ability of a graduate to find a job.

Fifth, the criteria for the internship evaluation should be refined to give a more robust evaluation of the internship experience and to increase the reliability of evaluators over time and across concentrations. In its current state, the School is processing the minimum amount of information from internships to assess skills. A more detailed evaluation could gauge the writing and presentational skills of the students and their liberal arts knowledge over time. It would also be helpful if the project evaluation and the internship measurements could be interrelated to provide a stronger and more robust measurement of journalism and mass communication skills.

Sixth, specific learning competencies should be established for the comprehensive exam to deliver specific information about strengths and weaknesses of specific areas rather than a general score on a test and nothing else. It is of little use to know that a certain percentage of students can pass an exam. What is needed is evidence tied to individual learning competencies so the faculty can see over time where strengths and weaknesses of the program lie. This would require more comprehensive exam on law, ethics, history, and media structure, and a much more detailed analysis. Furthermore, the testing process should be expanded to include a pretest in the freshman class as well as a summative exam in the law class to provide a better baseline of the knowledge of entering students. A program needs to know not only where the students stand when they graduate, but the kinds of knowledge they brought to the program.

Seventh, the School should incorporate its analysis of regional and national awards contests in which Cronkite students compete into the assessment process. Although this indirect measure would gauge the quality of elite students only, it would be a valuable secondary measure to complement some of the direct measures. Because most schools compete in national contents, a longitudinal analysis of their performance could be valuable in gauging quality.

Eighth, the School should begin to aggregate data across years and across concentrations rather than reporting results only in a single year as is being done now. To really benefit from assessment and effect change, programs must think about data over time. It is only when one measures competencies and attitudes over several years that programs can ascertain strengths and weaknesses and move in a new direction with confidence. In fact, it is quite exciting to see trends develop and make decisions based on empirical evidence. One of the chief measures of maturation in an assessment plan is how it makes the transition from taking isolated snapshots to using an accumulation of those snapshots to get a broader and deeper picture.

COMPLETING THE LOOP

The assessment program in the School, like with most other programs, began as a process to achieve a requirement. It was not begun because the School wanted to test a particular hypothesis or answer a burning curricular question. Success was often seen as having evaluation measures that met the test of central administration and executing the evaluation on schedule. Outcomes sought seemed to be the validation of quality rather than the discovery of new information that might result in improvements. My experience has been that such a defensive position is quite natural and has to work its way through the system. Therefore, I see it as entirely functional to have a shakedown cruise in the mechanics of evaluation before getting down to the business of true discovery. Once the fear of assessment and its associated misconceptions fade, attention can turn to solving real problems.

Let me relate a few issues being debated in the School where assessment could enlighten the debate. For the past 4 years, the Cronkite faculty, like many others around the country, have been debating the value of convergence in the undergraduate curriculum. Frequently, the assertion is made that sacrificing depth for breadth could have negative consequences for students in the workplace. Are there significant differences in outcomes from curricula based on two different philosophies? Are students from a converged curriculum less able to compete in the workplace than from a single-medium curriculum? We will keep debating based on anecdotal evidence until someone can measure how capable graduates are from each type of program.

A collateral issue concerns the two writing classes required of all journalism students. They are basically two print courses, newswriting and reporting. A recurring question has been the effect that having all journalism students takes these courses will have. Print students are not getting the cross-platform experience that broadcast students are receiving. Is this hurting the print students' ability to compete? Is requiring broadcast students to take two print courses strengthening their writing skills and making them more marketable? Are they losing the opportunity to gain additional broadcast journalism skills in the process?

There is also the ongoing debate between professionals and journalism educators about whether journalism students are developing sufficient writing skills. This debate will run endlessly in circles until outcomes assessment reaches maturity where the question can be settled based on hard data.

The faculty is debating whether there should be a standalone ethics course or it should cc..itinue to integrate ethics into several courses. Are they currently doing enough ethics instruction? Is the integrated approach working? An expanded senior exam could help answer these questions by showing the ethics knowledge that students now have when they graduate. If a competency were already being achieved, there would be little need to create a new required course.

A new concentration, Media Analysis and Criticism, has become suspect. Several journalism faculty members have questioned what students actually learn in that concentration, whether students are employable, and whether it is as rigorous as the other concentrations. We will never know the answers unless we measure the specific outcomes in that concentration.

In a curricular revision 3 years ago, PR students were no longer required to take the reporting class. Several journalism faculty members contended that this would have adverse results on the PR students' readiness. It would have been nice to have a comprehensive assessment package in place so we could have actually measured the differences in skill levels before and after the change. Still, we could pay particular attention to the writing scores on senior portfolios to assess if PR students have sufficient writing training to be successful in their careers.

There is a debate currently over whether the production concentration, resurrected 3 years ago, should be retired once again. One of the contentions is that the concentration produces only "button pushers" and does not require the same creative standards as other concentrations. Direct measures of skills such as a senior portfolio could ascertain whether graduating students are expressing themselves creatively or just learning to use technology.

These are just a few issues that outcomes assessment could enlighten. True success will come when faculties and administrators sincerely seek answers to these kinds of problems. In the meantime, the School is slowly building the infrastructure that will allow this more mature phase to unfold.

APPENDIX

Cronkite School: Learning Outcome Assessment Program

Goals/Learning Outcomes

The primary mission of the Cronkite School is to prepare students to enter positions in media fields.

Graduates of the Cronkite School are expected to demonstrate skills in writing, reporting, editing and production while acquiring a basic knowledge of media businesses and operations. They also are expected to have a basic knowledge of mass communication law and ethics.

Students are expected to be prepared to assume an entry-level position in a professional media outlet upon graduation from the Cronkite School.

Learning assessment is designed to determine outcomes for the area concentrations in the Cronkite School.

Methodology

It was determined by the faculty that learning outcomes assessment should be conducted according to three strategies:

1. All students in the highest level class required of all Cronkite School majors, Mass Communication Law, will be given a set of 20 relevant questions constructed by the faculty who teach the course. The questions are designed to measure a basic level of knowledge of media law, ethics and history. The questions are objective and student responses were analyzed by computer following administration of the exam. As-

sessment criteria are the percentage of correct responses for each student and the mean score for all students.

2. A sample (50%) of student projects from the highest level courses in each concentration that every student in that concentration must take will be assessed. The sample should include projects from fall and spring semesters. The projects are then evaluated by media professionals in cooperation with a Cronkite School faculty member. The reviewers are asked to determine whether the student projects reflect a skill level necessary to obtain an entry-level position in, at least, a small market (defined as Arbitron 101-plus market size for broadcast stations or circulation 5,000 or less for newspapers). Project evaluation is quantified according to the scoring hierarchy: exemplary, proficient, acceptable and unacceptable. Each year, the news-editorial, broadcast journalism and public relations concentrations are assessed. Student projects from Reporting Public Affairs, Broadcast News Reporting, Advanced Broadcast Reporting and Public Relations Campaigns are evaluated. Students graduating from the new, converged curriculum will submit portfolios representing their work in Journalism, Media Analysis & Criticism, Media Management, Media Production or Strategic Media & Public Relations for evaluation.

3. Professional program student internships are assessed to determine preparation level for an entry-level position. Intern agency coordinators are asked if, based on their evaluation of the student intern, they would hire the student if an entry-level were available. The responses are used to determine if the student was prepared at an adequate level to assume an entry-level media position.

Walter Cronkite School of Journalism and Mass Communication. "Learning Outcome Assessment Program." Arizona State University, 2001.

TABLE 23.1
Cronkite School Assessment Summary

Competency/Outcome	Measurement Tools	Type of Measure	Feedback Outcomes
Highest-level Skills Assessment	Portfolio	Direct	Outcomes pending
Professional Readiness Measure	Employer assessment of student interns	Direct	Outcomes pending
Knowledge-based Outcome	Senior examination	Direct	Outcomes pending
Student Satisfaction	Alumni Survey	Indirect	Priority on career services for students; validation of advising system

24

Virginia Commonwealth University

Paula Otto
Jean M. Yerian
Judy VanSlyke Turk
Virginia Commonwealth University

Located on two downtown campuses in Richmond, VA, and with a campus in Doha, Qatar, Virginia Commonwealth University (VCU) is ranked nationally by the Carnegie Foundation as a top research institution. VCU enrolls more than 26,000 students in over 170 certificate, undergraduate, graduate, professional, and doctoral programs in the arts, sciences, humanities, and health professions, in 11 schools and 1 college.

Forty of the university's programs are unique in Virginia, and *U.S. News & World Report* ranked 20 of VCU's graduate and professional programs as among the best of their kind. Medical College of Virginia Campus hospitals, clinics, and the health sciences schools of VCU compose the VCU Medical Center, the fourth largest academic medical center in the country.

The School of Mass Communications (School) is one of the largest programs in VCU's College of Humanities and Sciences, with a growing enrollment of more than 900 undergraduate students and 120 students at the Adcenter, the School's graduate program in advertising. The School offers three sequences of specialized study at the undergraduate level: Advertising (with a concentration in creative or business), Journalism (with a concentration in print or broadcasting), and Public Relations.

Formed by a merger of the Medical College of Virginia and Richmond Professional Institute in 1968, VCU has a strong tradition of decentralization. Throughout most of its history, VCU has left the assessment of student learning outcomes in the hands (and files) of academic schools and departments.

A NEW VIEW ON ACCOUNTABILITY AND ASSESSMENT

However, recent changes in public emphasis on and scrutiny of quality assurance and enhancement in higher education made it clear that the university has a compelling interest in developing additional structure for assessment. In fact, the interest in accountability is now readily apparent both externally and internally: VCU has over 90 academic programs with specific disciplinary accreditations; the State Council of Higher Education for Virginia (SCHEV) requires public institutions to report on general education core competencies; and VCU's own Strategic Plan specifies a comprehensive program review process.

Another major driver for VCU's increase in assessment structure was an approaching reaffirmation-of-accreditation review by the Southern Association of Colleges and Schools (SACS). Like most regional accreditors, SACS asks its members to present proof of their "institutional effectiveness" (Commission on Colleges of the Southern Association of Colleges and Schools, 2004, p. 22): "The institution *identifies expected outcomes* for its educational programs and its administrative and educational support services; *assesses whether it achieves these outcomes*; and *provides evidence of improvement* based on analysis of those results" (italics added for emphasis).

VCU'S OWN ASSESSMENT TOOL

VCU is committed to developing its own system, which could be used by academic programs as well as administrative and educational support services to both "prove" (summative assessment) and "improve" (formative assessment) teaching and learning. The original development team members were from Institutional Research and Evaluation and Academic Technology, although development later included representatives from Academic Affairs, eventually being led by the university's new Director of Assessment.

The team adopted the name WEAVE for VCU's approach, an acronym for an assessment cycle in which all VCU units—academic programs and administrative and educational support services alike—would

- Write expected outcomes and objectives.
- Establish criteria for success.
- Assess performance against criteria.
- View assessment results.
- Effect improvements through actions.

In its first iteration, WEAVE was a fairly linear database. On something called a Quality Enhancement Reporting Form, an academic program specified its mission, then identified learning outcomes. Each student learning outcome (or other outcome or objective, depending on the mission) was tracked through the entire assessment process. First, the academic program stated the outcome; the program could also show the outcome's relation to general education requirements. Next, the program stated any assessment activities (measures) that would be used to assess the outcome and gave both criteria for success and time-tables for those measures. Later on, the program entered actual assessment findings and "use of assessment results."

WEAVE had several problems. For example, if an academic program used the same measure—such as a portfolio or a comprehensive exam—to assess several outcomes, WEAVE required separate entry of that measure under each individual outcome. Similarly, a program might decide to plan an action (use of results) after seeing problematic findings from several different measures; because an action would have to be entered separately for each measure, the linear nature of WEAVE led to duplicate work for users. As a result of what were called assessment assemblies on both Richmond campuses, the development team reached out to all faculty and staff users and then took their feedback to make dramatic changes.

WEAVEonline™ was introduced at VCU in March 2003. (The next version of *WEAVEonline*™, which also will be available as a hosted subscription service outside VCU, is scheduled for release in 2005.) It is an innovative Web-based assessment management system, which is a transformational addition to VCU's toolbox. For the first time, VCU has a way to automate the capture and analysis of information to support continuing improvement efforts in individual programs and services throughout the university. The application's easy-to-use interface organizes data by each unit's mission, objectives and outcomes, assessment measures and findings, planned actions to effect future improvements to programs and services, and reflective analyses. There are also built-in planning, reporting, tracking, and feedback features.

Currently, *WEAVEonline*™ automates university processes to

- Document assessment of student learning outcomes in academic programs.
- Document assessment of outcomes and objectives in administrative and educational support programs.
- Provide data needed for reports to state higher education bodies and to regional and other accrediting agencies.

- Support university program review—both academic and administrative or educational support programs.
- Provide status information on various university-wide initiatives and elements of the strategic plan.
- Provide information for annual reporting purposes.

This centralized pool of data on program intentions and performance allows vertical integration of quality improvement from the unit level through to school or college level and beyond and facilitates accreditation, program reviews, and annual reporting. Built into *WEAVEonline*™ is the automated cross-unit consolidation of information, for example, aggregation of data for all units supporting a specific general education requirement.

WEAVEonline™ both leads and supports the assessment process. Here are the questions an academic program must answer in developing its *WEAVEonline*™ entries:

- What is the academic program's core mission?
- What are the program's critical student learning outcomes?
- How do these student learning outcomes relate to the larger educational context, such as general educational competencies? (*WEAVEonline*™ also allows programs to make other associations, such as relation to any disciplinary accreditation standards.)
- What measures can the program use to monitor student performance on the outcomes? (There should be direct measures of student learning, e.g., rating of a student's news stories by a panel of faculty and local editors. There also can be indirect measures, e.g., graduates' ratings of their perceived skill development as a result of the program.)
- What "target level" of performance on each of those measures is acceptable to the program?
- How do actual results of the assessments compare with the target levels set?
- What strengths has the program affirmed through assessment?
- What assessed areas require future attention?
- If action is indicated to improve performance to acceptable levels, what action will the program take?

Academic and support programs can run self-audits in *WEAVEonline*™ to make sure their entries are complete, for example, findings are reported for all measures. Programs can export basic data to Microsoft Excel. Incorporated into the application is a detailed assessment report, which shows all associations in full and can be exported to Microsoft Word. There also is an assessment summary report that can be run at unit (program), division (school or college), and university levels.

WEAVEonline™ can record feedback on its assessment processes as well as responses to the feedback. Through a central system interface, the director of assessment can help academic and support programs identify who else at VCU is using a particular assessment approach, such as portfolios. This enables communities of practice to emerge and faculty-staff to enhance their practice by collaborating with local peers.

WEAVEonline™ is an application that fits VCU's culture. It establishes a template to ask a basic effectiveness question: "Are your efforts bringing forth the desired results?" (FranklinCovey Co., 2003). There is a sense of pride at the university about its excellent programs and services. Now there is a repository for the good news of how well the university is doing in most areas and a benchmarking process for discerning those areas that are candidates for further improvement.

The Higher Learning Commission (HLC), a Commission of the North Central Association of Colleges and Schools (NCA), another regional accreditor, published "An Assessment Culture Matrix" (2003) identifying a number of elements that would indicate an institution's "Maturing Stages of Continuous Improvement" in assessment of student academic achievement. The structure of *WEAVEonline*™ clearly addresses several key elements in "An Assessment Culture Matrix":

> The assessment program materials developed at the institutional level reflect the emphasis of the Mission and Purposes statements on the importance of identifying learning expectations, on determining the outcomes of assessing student learning across academic programs, and on using assessment results to improve student learning. (HLC/NCA, 2003, p. 72)

> The institution maintains a system of data collection that helps sustain an effective assessment program. (HLC/NCA, 2003, p. 77)

> Programmatic benchmarks are established against which students' learning outcomes are assessed. (HLC/NCA, 2003, p. 79)

The School of Mass Communications

As the undergraduate programs in VCU's School began to develop their outcome-based measures, the faculty had four goals:

- To fulfill the university's requirements.
- To incorporate goals outlined in the School's strategic plan.

- To incorporate findings from a 1997 survey of newsroom management regarding the skills students need to succeed in the communications industry.
- To incorporate the guidelines of the Accrediting Council on Education in Journalism and Mass Communications (ACEJMC).

At the same time that the university was requiring all of its units to participate in the WEAVE process described earlier, the School was preparing to undergo a major study of its curriculum and was entering the first stage of preparation for the ACEJMC accreditation process.

Because the School's permanent full-time faculty is relatively small (15), they worked on the project as a committee of the whole, with leadership from the School's director and assistant director. The School at that time had four possible curriculum sequences: advertising, broadcast journalism, print journalism, and public relations. After a significant curriculum revamping in the 2002 to 2003 academic year, the two journalism tracks were combined into one.

Guiding Principles in Developing the Assessment Plan

The School's Strategic Plan. The School's strategic plan outlines the following vision: It is the vision of the School of Mass Communications to develop a community of learning in which

- The curriculum is responsive to the rapidly changing fields of communication.
- Students and faculty collaborate to explore and master new media technologies, including digital and interactive.
- Students are prepared to produce and disseminate information in multiple formats, including written text, audio, video and the Web.

The strategic plan further outlines curriculum goals with several accompanying strategies.

Goal: The School of Mass Communications Will Deliver a Curriculum That Gives Students a Solid Foundation in Both the Theory and Practice of Journalism, Advertising, Public Relations, and Developing Media.

- Strategy: The School will implement the new undergraduate curriculum approved at the end of the 2002 to 2003 academic year.
- Strategy: The School will infuse students into the workplace through internships and other real-world experiences.

- Strategy: The curriculum will be under constant review to ensure that it keeps pace with and emphasizes "best practices" in the rapidly changing fields of communication, including but not limited to technological advances and philosophical shifts.

Goal: The School's Curriculum Will Foster Collaborative Learning, With Students Learning From Each Other, From Experts in the Professions, and From Faculty.

- Strategy: Faculty members will be encouraged to maintain "state of the art" expertise that is comparable to industry practices and expectations.
- Strategy: The School will implement the merger of the Electronic Media and News-Editorial programs into one Journalism sequence and will implement the courses that provide students with the opportunity for cross-platform and collaborative learning.
- Strategy: The School will encourage creation of opportunities for advertising and public relations majors to practice the integration of various communication tactics and techniques.
- Strategy: The curriculum will provide opportunities for students and faculty to collaborate to explore and master new technologies, including digital and interactive media.

Survey of News Managers

A 1997 nationwide survey of news managers conducted for the VCU School and the Associated Press Managing Editors by Ketchum Public Relations found the following:

- News managers believe writing is the most important skill for undergraduate journalism students to have.
- Reporting, ethics and interviewing skills are very important in the undergraduate curriculum.
- It is extremely important for journalists—and those who work in related fields such as advertising and public relations—to effectively incorporate creative thinking and analysis.
- Internship programs are extremely important.

ACEJMC STANDARDS OF ACCREDITATION

These reflect the newly revised standards, effective in the 2004 to 2005 academic year. The ACEJMC was in the process of revising the standards when the School was writing its strategic plan and assessment objectives. The School used early drafts of the new standards, as well as the existing standards, to develop its objectives. See the ACEJMC's (2004) *Journalism and Mass Communications Accreditation (2004–2005)* for a complete list of the final standards and the core values and competencies.

The two ACEJMC standards that faculty used in developing the School's assessment plan were Standard 2, Curriculum and Instruction and Standard 9. Assessment is expected to provide a curriculum and instruction that enables students to learn the knowledge, competencies and values the Council defines for preparing students to work in a diverse global and domestic society. The unit, based on requirements of Standard 9, regularly assesses student learning and uses results to improve curriculum and instruction.

Writing the School's Assessment Goals

Using the School's strategic plan, the newsroom management survey results, and the ACEJMC guidelines, the faculty first outlined three overarching objectives and nine core skill and competency measurement areas for all majors. This also followed the University's WEAVE matrix.

Objectives

Graduates of the School should be able to

1. Communicate clearly and effectively in forms and styles appropriate for the communications professions, audiences, and purposes they serve.
2. Understand a core of fundamental concepts, values, and skills that include strategy development, critical thinking, problem solving, and understanding the ethical and legal implications of the media and communication industries.
3. Apply tools and technologies appropriate for the communications profession in which they work.

Nine measures were identified for these objectives:

1. Entrance testing for *Writing for the Media* course (covers grammar, punctuation, and spelling proficiency).
2. Rating of numerous writing examples during the *Writing for the Media* course to demonstrate that students understand how to organize and present information in appropriate, correct news style, and that their writing is of substantial quality.

3. Communication skills assessment by faculty and professionals, done in capstone courses.

4. Internship evaluation of student on professional communication tasks, done by intern supervisors and faculty.

5. Rating of student's ability to demonstrate successful problem solving, critical thinking, and strategic planning and execution, as well ability to use channels of mass communications in a responsible and ethical manner by faculty and professionals in capstone courses.

6. Through questions on a final exam in the Mass Media Ethics course, rating student ability to think critically, analyze ethical dilemmas, and solve ethical problems.

7. Through questions on a final exam in the Mass Media Law course, rating student understanding of the role media play in society, and the importance of First Amendment rights in a democratic society.

8. Through College of Humanities and Sciences SmartForce testing, assessing students' basic computer competency in word processing, file management, and Internet use.

9. Rating of student's basic competency in the technology skills needed in each specialty—advertising, public relations, print journalism, and broadcast journalism—made by faculty using a scoring rubric or checklist.

Table 24.1 summarizes the objectives and measures. Whenever possible, the faculty did not use test results as a measure. However, in some cases, such as the senior-level law course which often has 50+ students, a final exam is the most practical measurement tool. Test questions are also used to measure objectives in the sophomore-level ethics course. Although not reflected in the formal measures, ethics continues to be tested informally as students progress through the curriculum and encounter ethical issues and dilemmas in producing stories and other communications materials.

Once the measures were developed, the next step was for faculty to develop expected performance levels to create a standard against which achievement could be measured and assessed. For the first year, the faculty determined appropriate levels of success (e.g., 55% passing level) based on their experience of past student performance. The first measurement cycle was the 2002 to 2003 academic year. Measures were generally administered by faculty, except where noted that outside professionals were used, such as in judging capstone coursework projects.

Although some may question the use of faculty assessing their own students as too similar to using course grades as a measurement, the

TABLE 24.1
Objectives and Measures

Objective	Measure	Type of Measure
To communicate clearly and effectively in forms and styles appropriate for the communications professions, audiences, and purposes they serve.	Entrance test on grammar, punctuation, and spelling for Writing for the Media course	Direct
To communicate clearly and effectively in forms and styles appropriate for the communications professions, audiences, and purposes they serve.	Rating of numerous writing examples during the Writing for the Media course to demonstrate student competency in organizing and presenting information in appropriate, correct news style.	Direct Note: A standard syllabus requiring certain types of writing to be taught and evaluated is used.
To communicate clearly and effectively in forms and styles appropriate for the communications professions, audiences, and purposes they serve.	Using a checkoff sheet, communication skills are assessed by faculty and professionals in capstone courses.	Indirect
To communicate clearly and effectively in forms and styles appropriate for the communications professions, audiences, and purposes they serve.	Evaluation of student performance on professional communication tasks at internship by intern provider using a standard rubric.	Indirect Note: Results are tabulated by the School's internship coordinator.
To understand a core of fundamental concepts, values, and skills that include strategy development, critical thinking, problem solving, and understanding the ethical and legal implications of the media and communication industries.	Rating by faculty and professionals of student's ability to demonstrate successful problem solving, critical thinking, and strategic planning and execution, as well as student ability to use channels of mass communications in a responsible and ethical manner in capstone courses.	Direct Note: Each capstone course has a standard rubric that is used for all sections.

To understand a core of fundamental concepts, values, and skills that include strategy development, critical thinking, problem solving, and understanding the ethical and legal implications of the media and communication industries.	Through questions on a final exam in the Mass Media Ethics course, rating student ability to think critically, analyze ethical dilemmas, and solve ethical problems.	Direct Note: Each Mass Media Ethics course includes similar questions for measurement on the final exam.
To understand a core of fundamental concepts, values, and skills that include strategy development, critical thinking, problem solving, and understanding the ethical and legal implications of the media and communication industries.	Through questions on a final exam in the Mass Media Law course, rating student understanding of the role media play in society and the importance of First Amendment rights in a democratic society.	Direct Note: Only one section of Mass Media Law is taught each semester, so there are no issues of standardization of exam questions.
To apply tools and technologies appropriate for the communications profession in which they work.	Through College of Humanities and Sciences SmartForce testing, assessing students' basic computer competency in word processing, file management, and Internet use.	Direct
To apply tools and technologies appropriate for the communications profession in which they work.	Rating of student's basic competency in the technology skills needed in each specialty—advertising, public relations, print journalism, and broadcast journalism—made by faculty using a scoring rubric or checklist.	Direct Note: This technology testing is done in courses in the sophomore, junior, and senior years.

School believes that the measures developed at a programmatic level—by the entire faculty—are valid direct measures of student comprehension and application of material and application of skills. Faculty agree on criteria and standards and so set a level of expected performance by which they will judge actual performance. They directly examine student performances rather than ask about them in some way. As Huba and Freed (2000) suggested, we can perform programmatic assessment by gathering data from faculty assessments embedded in courses. For a discussion of the actions taken as a result of findings for several of the measures, see the Appendix.

HOW WE MEASURED THE MEASURES

It was important for the faculty to create measures, beyond the course grades, with which to assess achievement. Check sheets, using a five-part rubric, were developed by faculty who taught the specific courses. These check sheets provide faculty with an efficient way to measure and report student achievement. The check sheets are then turned into the School's Assistant Director who compiles the information.

After going through 1 academic year cycle, it was apparent that some of the check sheets were not as closely aligned to the measures on *WEAVEonline*™ as they should be. The School's Assessment Committee edited the sheets during the 2003 to 2004 academic year and will do so annually. A sample of the measurement checkoff sheets can be found in Fig. 24.1.

CONCLUSION

The School's assessment process is constantly being revisited, as good assessment programs should. During the 2003 to 2004 academic year, the faculty closely examined both the measures and outcomes to make certain that they accurately reflect the School's new curriculum which went into effect in fall 2003, and as noted earlier, edited the measure checkoff sheets. The faculty is also examining whether the measures are appropriately difficult, because all but one were achieved. As the School prepares for its ACEJMC accreditation self-study in 2004 to 2005 and for its accreditation site visit in 2005 to 2006, it feels confident that going through the assessment process using VCU's WEAVE approach has prepared the unit for the assessment portion of accreditation as well as for ongoing evaluation of its curriculum and instruction.

News-Editorial Capstone Course Assessment

(Used for measure 5.)

	Excellent	Very Good	Adequate	Satisfactory	Not Satisfactory
	Demonstrates superior understanding and application of concepts	Demonstrates strong knowledge but application is not consistently outstanding	Minimal ability to grasp and apply concepts	Minimal ability that includes obvious deficiencies in some areas	Unable or unwilling to perform
Critical thinking, problem solving, strategic planning					
Conceptualizes stories/projects					
Handles obstacles to story/project development					
Prepares a clear and comprehensive budget, listing the proposed elements of the story or project					
Research					
Gathers, analyzes and distills information from a variety of appropriate and authoritative sources					
Obtains background information in paper and digital formats when needed					

FIG. 24.1. *(Continued)*

	Excellent	Very Good	Adequate	Satisfactory	Not Satisfactory
Obtains appropriate government records using Freedom of Information laws if necessary					
Plans and executes interviews with diverse sources; asks questions beyond the obvious; balances stories appropriately					
Writing					
Writes clearly and effectively, in a variety of styles (hard news, features, long form, infographic, etc.)					
Editing					
Has mastered AP style					
Produces copy free of spelling, grammatical and punctuation errors					
Checks facts before publication					
Ethics and law					
Understands and applies legal and ethical guidelines					
Execution					
Meets deadlines					

FIG. 24.1. *(Continued)*

Public Relations Campaigns Capstone Course Assessment

(Used for measure 5.)

	Excellent	Very Good	Adequate	Barely Adequate	Not Adequate
	Demonstrates superior understanding and application of concepts.	Demonstrates strong knowledge but application is not consistently outstanding.	Minimal ability that includes obvious deficiencies in some areas.	Minimal ability that includes obvious deficiencies in some areas.	Unable or unwilling to perform.
Problem Solving					
Generates primary and secondary research for client campaign.					
Works within a group to manage time, deadlines and results.					
Critical Thinking					
Based on research, identifies primary and secondary public relations objectives.					
Derives appropriate solutions to public relations objectives.					
Identifies persuasive arguments in support of conclusions and recommendations.					

FIG. 24.1. *(Continued)*

	Excellent	Very Good	Adequate	Barely Adequate	Not Adequate
Strategic Planning					
Creates public relations campaign using the four-step process.					
Develops a plan, timeline and budget for the campaign.					
Identifies appropriate evaluation tools					
Execution					
Makes a formal presentation of the campaign to a panel of judges.					
Develops a plan, timeline and budget for the campaign.					

FIG. 24.1. *(Continued)*

Advertising Campaigns Capstone Course Assessment

(Used for measure 5.)

	Excellent	Very Good	Adequate	Barely Adequate	Not Adequate
	Demonstrates superior understanding and application of concepts.	Demonstrates strong knowledge but application is not consistently outstanding	Minimal ability to grasp and apply concepts.	Minimal ability that includes obvious deficiencies in some areas.	Unable or unwilling to perform.
Problem Solving					
Generates primary and secondary research for assigned product, category, media and consumer information.					
Works within a group to manage time, deadlines and results.					
Critical Thinking					
Based on research, identifies primary and secondary marketing objectives.					
Derives appropriate solutions to communications objectives.					
Identifies persuasive arguments in support of conclusions.					

FIG. 24.1. *(Continued)*

	Excellent	Very Good	Adequate	Barely Adequate	Not Adequate
Strategic Planning					
Creates integrated communications program to be defended.					
Anticipates sales objections and answers them.					
Execution					
Creates an integrated campaign that includes a market overview, consumer information, strategic analysis, media recommendations and creative executions.					
Creates a "campaign book" that includes all relevant information presented in a finished style.					
Creates advertising and other communication for the campaign.					
Makes a formal presentation of the campaign to a panel of judges.					

FIG. 24.1. *(Continued)*

Broadcast Journalism Capstone Course Assessment

(Used for measure 5.)

	Excellent	Very Good	Adequate	Satisfactory	Not Satisfactory
	Demonstrates superior understanding and application of concepts	Demonstrates strong knowledge but application is not consistently outstanding	Minimal ability to grasp and apply concepts	Minimal ability that includes obvious deficiencies in some areas	Unable or unwilling to perform
Critical thinking, problem solving, strategic planning					
Conceptualizes stories/projects					
Handles obstacles to story/project development					
Prepares a clear and comprehensive outline, listing the proposed elements of the story or project					
Research					
Gathers, analyzes and distills information from a variety of appropriate and authoritative sources					

FIG. 24.1. *(Continued)*

	Excellent	Very Good	Adequate	Satisfactory	Not Satisfactory
Obtains background information in paper and digital formats when needed					
Obtains appropriate government records using Freedom of Information laws if necessary					
Plans and executes interviews with diverse sources; asks questions beyond the obvious; balances stories appropriately					
Writing					
Writes clearly and effectively					
Editing					
Has mastered linear and or non-linear video editing					

FIG. 24.1. *(Continued)*

	Excellent	Very Good	Adequate	Satisfactory	Not Satisfactory
Ethics and law					
Understands and applies legal and ethical guidelines					
Execution					
Meets deadlines					

FIG. 24.1. Examples of check off grids used to assess students in capstone courses.

REFERENCES

Accrediting Council on Education in Journalism and Mass Communications. (2004). *Journalism and Mass Communications Accreditation (2004–2005).* Lawrence, KS: Author.

Commission on Colleges of the Southern Association of Colleges and Schools. (2004). *Principles of accreditation: Foundations for quality enhancement.* Decatur, GA.

FranklinCovey Co. (2003). Quotation on September Monticello daily planning pages (*"Monthly Focus: Productivity—You reap what you sow. Are your efforts bringing forth the desired results?"*).

The Higher Learning Commission/NCA. (2003). *Assessment of student academic achievement: Assessment culture matrix.* Retrieved March 20, 2005, from http://www.ncahigherlearningcommission.org/resources/assessment/AssessMatrix03.pdf

Huba, M. E., & Freed, J. E. (2000). *Learner-centered assessment on college campuses.* Boston, MA: Allyn & Bacon.

Ketchum Public Relations. (1997) *Views of print and broadcast media executives toward journalism education.*

APPENDIX

Findings and Actions Taken for Several Measures

1. Entrance testing for *Writing for the Media* course (covers grammar, punctuation and spelling proficiency).

Criteria for Success (target levels)

Passing level is 55%. Expect 50% to pass on first try; expect 70% to pass on second try.

Findings in 02–03:

50% of students passed the test on the first try; of those taking the test for a second time, 50% passed. Those not passing on the second try often took more than four times to pass.

Action: As a result of these findings, a study was done to determine if the entrance exam was a good predictor of student success in the *Writing for the Media* course. A comparison of student scores on the entrance exam, student cumulative grade point averages and semester grades for the *Writing for the Media* course revealed that a student's GPA (grade point average) was a better predictor of success in the course. As a result, the faculty decided to no longer administer the entrance exam, using instead a 2.25 GPA requirement and the completion of English 101 and Mass Communications 101 with at least a C as the entrance requirement. This was effective in fall 2003. (Note: the School requires a cumulative GPA of 2.25 for entrance into the major as a sophomore or junior. The *Writing for the Media* course is taken as a pre-major.)

2. Rating of numerous writing examples during the *Writing for the Media* course to demonstrate that students understand how to organize and present information in appropriate, correct news style, and their writing is of substantial quality.

Criteria for Success (target levels)

Expect 10–15% to be excellent; 10–15% very good; 50% adequate; 10% barely adequate; 5–10% not adequate.

Findings in 02–03:

Writing: 13% excellent; 44% very good; 31% adequate; 13% barely adequate.

AP style: 25% excellent; 19% very good; 50% adequate; 6% barely adequate.

Action: None taken since achievement fell within expected levels.

3. Communication skills assessment by faculty and professionals, done in capstone courses.

Criteria for Success (target levels)

Assessment will measure to what degree a student's communication skills are at a level comparable to what would be expected of an entry-level employee in this field. Expect 15–20% to be excellent; 15–20% to be very good; 40–50% to be adequate; 5–15% to be barely adequate or not adequate.

Findings in 02–03:

Excellent 43%; Very Good 50%; Adequate 3%; Barely Adequate 3%.

Action: None taken since achievement exceeded expected levels.

4. Internship evaluation of students on professional communication tasks, done by intern supervisors and faculty.

Criteria for Success (target levels)

Assessment will measure to what degree are the student's communication skills at a level comparable to what would be expected of an entry-level employee in this field.

Expect: 15–20% to be excellent; 15–20% to be very good; 40–50% to be adequate; 5–15% to be barely adequate or not adequate.

Findings in 02–03: (based on a random sampling)

Excellent: 30%; Very good: 40%; Adequate: 20%; Barely or not adequate: 10%

Action: None taken since achievement exceeded expected levels.

5. Rating of student's ability to demonstrate successful problem solving, critical thinking and strategic planning and execution, as well ability to use channels of mass communications in a responsible and ethical manner by faculty and professionals in capstone courses.

Criteria for Success (target levels)

50% of students will be judged as having excellent or very good skills; 40% will be judged as having adequate or barely adequate skills; 10% will have below adequate skills. These skills are measured through various assignments and projects in capstone courses. Faculty then rank student achievement using a check sheet.

Findings in 02–03:

Excellent or Good: 80%

Adequate or Barely Adequate: 20%

Action: None taken since achievement exceeded expected levels.

6. Through questions on a final exam in the Media Ethics course, rating student ability to think critically, analyze ethical dilemmas and solve ethical problems.

Criteria for Success (target levels)

90% of students are expected to pass the comprehensive final exam; 90% of students will pass the course.

Findings in 02–03:

93% of students passed the final exam; 96% passed the course.

Action: None taken since findings exceeded objectives.

7. The Law course specifically measures student understanding of the role media play in society and the importance of First Amendment rights in a democratic society.

Criteria for Success (target levels)

Expect 90% of students to successfully answer 60% of questions designed to measure these concepts.

Findings in 02–03:

90% of the students got at least 65% of the material correct across the two exams.

Action: None taken since findings met objectives.

8. Through College of Humanities and Sciences SmartForce testing, student's basic computer competency in word processing, file management and Internet use are assessed.

Criteria for Success (target levels)

Students will be required to pass the Humanities and Sciences required SmartForce tests (*Mircosoft Office Beginning Word* and *Basic IT Concepts*) before being admitted to the School's Upper Division. Expect 50% of students will pass tests on the first try; 75% on the second try.

Findings in 02–03:

Because the test is administered by another unit, it was difficult to determine the number of times it took for students to successfully pass the tests. However, the School's student services coordinator, who oversees admission into the Newswriting course, diligently enforced the prerequisite requiring students to pass the computer competency test before admission into the course.

9. Rating of student's basic competency in the technology skills needed in each specialty—advertising, public relations, print journalism and broadcast journalism will be made by faculty using a scoring rubric/checklist.

Criteria for Success (target levels)

Expect 30% of students will be rated excellent or very good; 45% will be adequate; 25% will be barely or below adequate.

Finding in 02–03:

40% of students were rated as excellent or very good; 50% adequate; 10% barely or below adequate.

Action: Faculty teaching skills-based courses and those that are technology intensive are working toward more stringent standards and testing to ensure that students have appropriate technological skills.

25

Zayed University

Janet Hill Keefer
School of Journalism and Mass Communication
Drake University

We're flying this plane while we're building it.
—Dr. B. Dell Felder, Provost, Zayed University (1999–2003)

Dr. Felder's analogy, although terrifying, was apt for this upstart start-up university for Emirati women. Students started coming in 1998 to Zayed University (ZU), before all the faculty had been hired, before curricula were established, and before assumptions could be tested. It was a heady proposition: Educate Arab Muslim women in a university patterned on an American model where English would be the language of instruction. The mission was to create an educated cadre of women to lead this young and oil-rich country through the next phase of its development.

The United Arab Emirates (UAE) is barely 30 years old. It emerged from the former Trucial States that ring the Gulf of Arabia, its development and modernization fueled by the discovery of oil. Seven Emirates, all with considerable autonomy, make up the country. The federal capital is Abu Dhabi, which is also the Emirate with most of the oil. Dubai is the tourism and commercial epicenter. The other five Emirates are less developed than either Dubai or Abu Dhabi. The UAE Ministry of Planning estimates that the country's population at the end of 2003 was 4 million. Dr. Joseph Keefer of ZU's Institute for Socio-Economic Research estimates that the Emirati population at the end of 2003 was 750,000—19% of the total population, meaning that about 81% of the people who live in the UAE are expatriates imported to do almost all of the country's work.

The country is seeking to take more control of its own destiny by educating and developing its own citizens' skills so that they can replace the expatriates in most sectors of the country's economy. To that end, ZU was created as a public university based on a Western—primarily American—model. It was created to serve women. Emirati men are more easily able to go abroad for education, although it is probable that a campus for men will open at ZU within a decade.

WHO, WHAT, WHEN, WHERE, AND HOW

The UAE federal government established the institution by decree in 1998 and named it for the country's founding president, Sheikh Zayed bin Sultan al Nahayan. It has "separate but equal" campuses in Abu Dhabi and Dubai led by a single administration. The University graduated its first class in the spring of 2002. ZU currently enrolls approximately 2,100 National women and is a much smaller university than was envisioned at its founding. With the opening of a new campus in Dubai in 2006, enrollments there are expected to increase to 5,000 students. Plans are in development now for a new campus in Abu Dhabi, which is already operating at capacity.

According to a recent study completed by College of Communication and Media Sciences (CCMS) faculty members Tim Walters, Susan Swan, and Ron Wolfe, about three quarters of the fathers and mothers of CCMS students had completed high school or less. Fewer than one in four of the students came from families in which both parents had a high school education or more. Only 4% came from families in which both parents had college degrees (Walters, Swan, Wolfe, Whiteoak, & Barwind, 2004, p. 4). ZU students are more often than not the first women in their families to go to college.

OUTCOMES AS THE FOUNDATION

From the beginning, ZU decided that its academic program model would be based on learning outcomes. The program would focus on students rather than teachers. It would tie outcomes and technology together. ZU could begin this way. Nothing had to be grafted on to aging rootstock. The driving force behind ZU's outcomes-based academic program model was Provost Dell Felder, who recognized from the beginning that ZU's graduates had be able to perform and to think through the challenges that will face the country. They would have to stand up against cultural and family pressures to do so. It made sense, then, to embrace a strategy of education that would focus on doing as well as knowing. As Dr. Felder put it, "Knowledge alone is not enough. You have to apply it in changing circumstances. You have to be able to work in a diverse environment" (Wolfe, 2003, p. 16).

In the spring of 2000, a task force of faculty and staff was established to design an academic program that would produce graduates who could meet the needs of the UAE for leaders; that would integrate liberal and professional studies; that "would encourage pedagogy engaging students in interactive, collaborative and applied learning experiences; and encourage the use of technology to enhance teaching and learning" (Zayed University, 2002, p. 11).

The resulting program focuses on five University learning outcomes (ZULOs) and Major Learning Outcomes (MALOs). The ZULOs are as follows: Information and communication literacy, information technology, critical thinking, leadership and teamwork, and global studies.

The University has developed an elaborate system of introducing and assessing the learning outcomes. Students are required to take three courses in Learning Outcomes Assessment (LOA 101, 201, and 300), worth a total of 4 semester credit hr. In this series of courses, students must create an electronic portfolio of evidence to show their achievement of the learning outcomes. Each student must write and reflect about her own experiences in reaching the appropriate level of accomplishment in each of the outcomes. Faculty from across the University are trained in assessment techniques and are assigned to work with students in developing these portfolios, and still other members of all faculties take turns in evaluating them. The practice is to assign students faculty from their own colleges as instructors in the LOA classes, but the match might not always be possible.

The University has learned that the costs associated with this labor-intensive learning and assessment strategy are quite high, and it is currently seeking ways to maintain the effectiveness of the process while reducing the costs. It is likely that more of the University and Major learning outcomes will become embedded in courses while efforts are made to continue to work with students in the self-reflective process.

ZU revised its general education program in the fall semester of 2003. It has moved away from a typical "menu-driven" program in which students could choose courses from all the colleges that met "domain" requirements—such as arts and humanities, or creative expression—to compile sufficient credits to meet general education requirements. It has moved to a new 65-credit-hr program that is characterized by linked courses in broad, interdisciplinary, subject areas and continues through much of the student's career at ZU. This Colloquy in Integrated Learning is designed in part to increase student focus on the learning outcomes. During their freshman and sophomore years, students enroll in core courses that provide an intellectual experience they share with all ZU students and that will draw attention explicitly to one or more learning outcomes. Through a series of closely related interdisciplinary courses, students will develop their abilities in critical thinking, computer applications, information literacy, English, and Arabic. The new curriculum increases the emphasis on writing and critical thinking.

The University has established four levels of accomplishment for each of the ZULOs by which students are measured: beginning, developing, accomplished, and exemplary.

OUTCOMES AND THE COLLEGE OF COMMUNICATION AND MEDIA SCIENCES

The University's five colleges[1]—Arts and Sciences, Family Sciences, Business Sciences, Education, Information Systems and Communication and Media Sciences—determine their own learning outcomes and decide what levels of achievement students must reach in each one. This chapter focuses on the CCMS approach to assessing learning outcomes.

The CCMS's five learning outcomes (discussed later), labeled as competencies, closely parallel those of the University, as Table 25.1 illustrates.

Communication Competence

This learning outcome states that a CMS graduate will be able to write and speak clearly, effectively, and correctly in Arabic and English, appropriately and skillfully adapting the messages to the needs, knowledge, culture, and expectations of her target audience. This outcome is closely tied to the University's information and communication literacy outcome in that both address gathering and presenting information in Arabic and English. The CCMS, in the business of producing professional communicators, has understandably placed heavy emphasis on these outcomes in its courses. It requires three writing courses of all its majors offered within the CCMS—two in English and one in Arabic. Writing

---

[1]In the spring of 2004, the University underwent a reorganization in which one of its six original colleges, the College of Family Sciences, was disbanded as a separate academic entity and its programs and faculty were distributed between the colleges of Arts and Sciences and Education.

TABLE 25.1
Learning Outcomes

Zayed University Learning Outcomes	College Learning Outcomes
Information and communication literacy	Communication competence
	Information literacy and acquisition
Information technology	Technological competence
Critical thinking and reasoning	Task performance and competence
Global awareness–teamwork and leadership	Professionalism

and oral presentations are also carefully evaluated in its internship and capstone courses.

Information Literacy and Acquisition Competence

This learning outcome states that a CMS graduate will be able to identify appropriate information sources, effectively gather data, and apply critical thinking skills to effectively analyze the information obtained. This outcome goes along with Communication Competence because it really is impossible to separate the ability to find and retrieve good information from the ability to convey it effectively in speech and writing. It is formally introduced to students in the CCMS in COM 204, Information Gathering, which addresses basic primary and secondary research methods and tools, including the tools of the reporter: interviewing, observation, and web searching.

Technological Competence

This learning outcome states that a CMS graduate will be able to use a variety of technologies to produce effective communication and media-related products, layouts, and messages. The University's analogous outcome, Information Technology, is leading toward an expectation that all ZU graduates will have the computer skills associated with the International Computer Drivers License, which is highly valued in the UAE. The CCMS's outcome of Technological Competence addresses the more specialized technologies students will need to work in such careers as newspaper or magazine editing and design, video production, TV or radio news or production, or web design. Thus, the CCMS expects students to be competent in using software and hardware appropriate to the professional path they wish to follow. Requirements for all students to complete a course in information design mean that all of them should be able to use desktop publishing software, for example, but only students who have taken video production courses need to be conversant with digital video editing software. Training and measurement of success in these technological competencies are primarily handled in courses in information design, photojournalism, video production, infographics, and so forth. Additional assessment is possible during the capstone experience.

Task Performance Competence

This learning outcome states that a CMS graduate will be able to work both independently and collaboratively to execute responsibilities and tasks associated with her chosen profession competently and effectively. The CCMS views this outcome as being closely related to and dependent on a student's ability to think critically in the context of analyzing situations or problems and coming up with solutions. But it also goes to a much less nebulous notion of trying to determine whether students really can perform the tasks associated with their major. Can she write a competent news story or news release? Can she lay out a brochure? Can she shoot and edit a video project? Can she develop an integrated communication campaign? Her instructors in the courses in which the skills are introduced and taught offer the first line of assessment in this outcome, but the internship preassessment and postassessment process and the grading and evaluation process in the capstone courses also provide an opportunity to further evaluate this outcome.

Professionalism

This learning outcome states that a CMS graduate will exhibit professionalism in her chosen field, as reflected in her work ethic, behavior, and interactions. We've found that assessing this outcome is as difficult for us as it was for the U.S. Supreme Court to identify pornography: it's hard to define, but we know it when we see it. The chart in Appendix A lists some indicators of professionalism.

Some of them, such as punctuality, attendance, and meeting deadlines, are easy enough to measure. The University's stringent attendance policy, whereby students are "carded" on entering and leaving the campus every day, helps the CCMS get the message across that attendance and punctuality are important to academic and professional success. It's easy enough to determine when someone is present, whether she arrived on time, and whether she met her deadline for an assignment. All professors in all courses pay close attention to these things, and intern supervisors in the workplace also keep track of attendance, punctuality, and success in meeting deadlines. But some of the others, such as "positive attitude," tact, and ethical behavior, may not be directly measurable. Nevertheless, the CCMS believes it is important to list and emphasize such qualities to illustrate their importance in developing successful careers. Certainly the complete absence of any or all of these is quite noticeable to even the most casual observer. The CCMS sees its Professionalism outcome as related to the University's Teamwork and Leadership outcome, both of which can be assessed through the student's performance in an internship and in her capstone.

ASSESSING STUDENTS

The CCMS uses several assessment tactics, but it places heaviest reliance on two major assessment "moments." One comes just before the student goes to her internship, which usually corresponds closely to the time when her portfolio is assessed in LOA 300. The second comes with the completion of her capstone experience.

The University requires all students to complete an internship, which may be either 10 weeks of full-time work or 20 weeks of half-time work, for which she receives 6 credits. These internships are structured and monitored more carefully than is typically the case in the United States. The CCMS has a faculty member who is assigned a course equivalent for administering the internship program, which includes the semester-by-semester administration of internship assignments and location and developing new ones. Other members of the CCMS faculty act as supervisors of individual students once they are working at their internship placements. The supervisors visit the internship sites at least three times during the duration of the experience, and they assign students various tasks to complete during the course of the internship, which may include keeping a journal or submitting reports to the faculty supervisor while she is on the job.

The formal pre-internship assessment usually takes place in the semester before the internship semester. It focuses primarily on the communication competence outcome. The incoming "class" of interns is assembled and is tested on public speaking, writing, and reporting in English and Arabic. The speaking test requires a student to give short speeches on an assigned topic in English and in Arabic. Speeches are prepared in a classroom setting in a given amount of time. An "audience" of faculty evaluates each student's performance on a set of predetermined criteria, which may include grammatical correctness, assessment of the audience, eye contact, use of appropriate visual aids, use of appropriate information resources, and attribution. The topics of the speeches vary from semester to semester.

The writing test is handled in a similar way: students assemble in a computer lab or classroom, where they are given a topic to research on the World Wide Web. From their research, they are asked to write either a news story or a news release, depending on the major. The stories must be written in both Arabic and English. The stories are distributed among the appropriate faculty for evaluations. If a student turns in a story that her grader believes is borderline, then the faculty member and the internship coordinator review the work to determine the final evaluation.

The CCMS believes that—of all the outcomes identified—communication competence is the one that each student must master at an accomplished level before the internship placement. Any student who does not pass any part of the writing and speaking tests is given remedial help and retested. Only when she demonstrates that she has overcome her deficiencies can she go out for her internship. Students who are found to be ready for internship work then go through a pre-internship week of workshops and seminars.

The seminars provide an opportunity to address some of the simplest and most basic things that will be expected in the workplace, such as telephone manners, etiquette within a chain of command, expectations of confidentiality, punctuality, attendance on the job, and other such mundane but important competencies. These topics were identified through feedback from the first group of internship employers. Seminar topics have included the following:

- Making the most of the internship experience.
- Basic office skills.
- Learning objectives to accomplish while Interning.
- Core competencies to develop or improve on the job.
- Following the student Intern guidelines.
- Personal goals statement.
- Professional goals statement.
- Taking responsibility for your Internship experience.
- Shaping your experience to follow your work plan.
- Development of an internship portfolio.
- Workplace expectations.
- Striving for excellence: showing innovation, motivation, and leadership.
- Developing and demonstrating positive work habits.
- Learning to communicate effectively with your employer to get the most out of your experience.

- Communicating your professional development plans to your supervisor.

A DIFFERENT STARTING POINT IN THE WORKPLACE

ZU students have not had the summer work experience typical of American students. They may have had lots of babysitting experience with their younger brothers and sisters, the average number of which is about six. But they have not worked outside their homes flipping hamburgers, waiting on tables, or checking out groceries at the local supermarket. Research done by CMS faculty members in 2002 showed that fewer than half of the students (47%) had work experience outside the home, and that figure was about twice what it was before the students had come to ZU and was largely the result of the University's own World or Work (WOW) program, which places students in summer jobs. The number of students who take advantage of the program is small. About two thirds of the CCMS's students escape Dubai and Abu Dhabi and the summer heat by going on long vacations to Europe or the Levant (Walters et al., 2004, p. 5).

It is also unlikely that ZU students had any experience working with high school newspapers or other student media. Such activities, by and large, are unavailable in the UAE's public school system. ZU does not yet have a student newspaper, but there is an online radio station on each campus, and some students work for independent study credit on an alumnae magazine edited and produced in the CCMS. This situation will improve, however, within the next year, as the CCMS develops its Zayed Media Lab, a simulated media conglomerate that will eventually publish a magazine, offer television programming, and will devise and create public relations and advertising campaigns and associated work product for internal and external clients.

Employers are surveyed regularly, and the interns' direct supervisors in the workplace evaluate student performance and also provide valuable feedback on what the CCMS curriculum needs to address to better prepare the students for work. The CCMS initiated the practice of a regular survey of employers, but the University's Career Services office now handles the surveying to ensure that a given employer—who may host students from more than one college—is not inundated with questionnaires. The results of these surveys are shared with all colleges.

During the prep week, each student develops a work plan against which she measures her experience after her internship is over. She outlines a set of specific goals for herself, and she is encouraged to share those goals with her direct supervisor at the job site before she begins her work.

Although it is not a universal requirement, many internship supervisors assign students to keep journals while they are on the job. The journals are often useful when students prepare their reflective week presentations. The self-reflecting week is of major importance to students and faculty. The students often invite their internship employers to their presentations, which are often done in Microsoft PowerPoint® and include "Show and Tell" items that the student worked on during the internship.

It is hard to describe these presentations in a way that can do them justice. The students return from their work experience filled with confidence and with a level of self-awareness and professionalism they never would have imagined 8 weeks before when they were preparing to go out on their internships. The presentations are designed to be consistent in content. Each student is given 15 min to answer the following questions: What did you expect of your internship when you began? Did the experience meet your expectations? What do you think were your greatest strengths on your job? What were your greatest weaknesses? What was your most important or memorable experience on the job? What was your greatest disappointment? What suggestions do you have for improving the internship experience? Should the CCMS continue to send interns to this work site? Why or why not? Were you offered permanent employment at your work site? Would you accept a job there if it were offered? Why or why not? Do you expect to get a job after graduation?

The answers to these questions require the student to consider many aspects of her placement and her interest in finding employment outside the home after she completes her studies. They also help the CCMS determine where gaps exist in the students' pre-internship experience. In fact, feedback from students and from employers caused the CCMS to explore lengthening the internship from 10 weeks of full-time employment to 20 weeks of half-time employment. Almost all of the returning interns have said they didn't think the experience was long enough for them to really contribute or to get a real sense of what it would be like to work for a given company or ministry. At this writing, the CCMS is the only college offering a 20-week internship option.

Employers are asked to evaluate the intern's performance using an evaluation form, which helps the faculty supervisors to evaluate the student's work and assign a grade. Employer evaluations also give the CCMS an instrument by which to get an idea of what needs to be added to the curriculum or to individual courses to counteract a deficit. One finding was in the nature of a "roof leaks can be detected in the rain" discovery: students needed more work in writing in Arabic. We addressed the need by working with the Department of Arabic and Islamic Studies to add a 3-credit course in professional writing in Arabic. We expect the new emphasis on Arabic writing in the Colloquy program to be helpful in improving students' Arabic writing and speaking skills.

College faculty have done extensive research on our students, replicating studies of learning styles and life values done on students in the United States. These studies showed that, although great progress has been made, much remains to be done. The data showed clearly that inexperience with the workplace and workplace environment helped create and magnify difficulties. From merely commuting to work to managing relationships to workplace atmosphere, their students' collective naïveté made successful adaptation to work stressful and difficult. Students, although loath to admit it directly, were uncomfortable with such basics as men in the workplace, the distractions of multiculturalism, and the hurly-burly, high-energy directness of private companies (Walters et al., 2004).

Employers are generally extremely pleased and surprised by ZU students' performance. They tell us that our students are self-starters, that they devise projects to keep themselves busy when the employer may not have much for them to do. (This happens much more frequently in the UAE than in the United States. Employers are less experienced in working with interns than are their American counterparts.) Employers also say they find students' writing, speaking, problem-solving, and software skills more than satisfactory. They frequently comment that ZU students' work ethic is more highly developed than is typical of most entry-level Emirati employees.

The CCMS has found that feedback on individual students is also helpful in spotting strengths and weaknesses of the program. For example, several employers of students in the first and second internship placement periods mentioned—in various ways—that students had no idea how to use the telephone for business purposes. This was surprising, because ZU students often have several mobile telephones and seem to use them with carefree abandon, although the University forbids students to use mobiles on campus. Nevertheless, when we questioned returning interns and current students about how to make business calls, we found that, indeed, they had no idea of how to answer a business telephone. Instead of saying, "Good afternoon, this is the National Bank of Dubai's Public Information Office. My name is Huda. How may I help you?" more often than not, they'd simply say "Hello," if they answered the phone at all. Some said they were "afraid" to answer the telephone, so they simply ignored it at work when it rang. Thus telephone etiquette became an important element in prep week discussions.

Another assessment opportunity associated with the internship experience is the professional portfolio each student must prepare before she visits her potential internship employer for the first time. The task of helping interns create their portfolios has usually fallen to the internship coordinator. However, now that the outcomes assessment process has matured and yielded extensive electronic academic portfolios for each student, that task is likely to shift to a one-credit assessment course that will help the student develop her professional portfolio from her learning outcomes portfolio. This assessment provides an opportunity for the CCMS to see what the student has accomplished in creating her outcomes portfolio and can provide insight into the student's writing and critical thinking skills as well, although enrollment at the University now is small enough to allow faculty to get to know students as individuals very quickly. This assessment course began in the spring semester of 2004. The items the CCMS expects to be included in each student's pre-internship portfolio are listed in Appendix B.

The CCMS moved from pass–fail grading of the internship to the A–F grading scheme. The internship coordinators and faculty supervisors wanted a better way to mark different levels of student performance in internships and were satisfied that they had credible ways of discerning what those differences were, thanks to continuing close contacts between faculty supervisors and workplace supervisors and the interns themselves. An outline of the 2000-point grading scheme is illustrated in Table 25.2.

Capstone: Tying It All Together

Each senior at ZU must complete a capstone experience aimed at topping off and tying together all the threads of her college career—her coursework, her internship experience and her extracurricular activities. Capstones are supervised by faculty, but the students themselves are largely responsible for the design and implementation of their own projects. The project should require that each student address the learning outcomes identified by her college major. These projects are also supposed to call on the student to perform the specific tasks associated with her professional skills set. Capstone Festivals on each of the campuses provide an opportunity for the communities inside and outside the University to see and assess students' work.

The University's president, Sheikh Nahayan Mubarak Al Nahayan, Minister of Higher Education and Scientific Research, sets great store by the capstone concept and experience. He attends the festivals each year, and said at the first one, which was held in June of 2002, "Capstone projects are tangible outcomes of the educational model of Zayed Uni-

TABLE 25.2
Point System

Prep Week	
Attendance: 100 points per day (5 × 100)	500
Employer research	100
Portfolio submitted and approved	200
Internship	
Attendance	200
Midterm evaluation by employer	100
Final evaluation by employer	200
Biweekly reports	400
Reflective week presentation	300
Total Points Possible	
	2000

Letter grades for internships will be based on the points accumulated above:
1800–2000 = A
1600–1799 = B
1400–1599 = C

Students who earn fewer than 1,400 points must repeat the internship. Bonus points may be awarded to students who submit projects or work completed as part of the internship. These points may be awarded at the discretion of the faculty internship supervisor.

versity. They represent a good example where students and faculty are joining together in a very important learning experience" (Capstone Festival Speech, June 9, 2002, Dubai). "Students learn to focus on their academic discipline from a holistic perspective, and they learn to integrate various elements of their academic training," he added, noting that the projects also help students make the transition from college to career.

"I look to the Capstone experience to give each student a sense of accomplishment, a sense that her intellectual life has been enhanced and a sense that the university provides her with the best possible learning environment," he said. Sheikh Nayhan's attendance each year at the Capstone Festival is not merely ceremonial. He views the festival and the capstone projects themselves as a major window through which the community can see and assess ZU. He pays close attention to the students' topics, and he makes sure prominent Nationals and expatriates are invited to attend. The U.S. Ambassador has attended the festival in Abu Dhabi, and the Embassy's public affairs and education officers usually attend every year. The Sheikh also serves as president of the University of the United Arab Emirates and chancellor of the Higher Colleges of Technology. It is clear that he uses the Capstone Festivals to compare ZU's performance—through its students' accomplishments—with the other public institutions of higher learning in the country.

In the CCMS, capstones are generally group projects. Because the Integrated Communication major (public relations and advertising) is much larger than News and New Media, most of the CCMS's capstones have involved projects to develop integrated communication campaigns.

Some of the projects go beyond the mere development of the campaign, however, and often include the implementation of a major event that the students identified as a centerpiece of their campaign plans. Some of the events have been fairly spectacular, including one that focuses on the country's late president, Sheikh Zayed. Students collected a wide range of memorabilia and art associated with Sheikh Zayed, secured prime space in Heritage Village in Dubai (a recreation of an Arab town of the early 20th century), and invited dignitaries, including Sheikh Nahayan and Sheikh Abdullah bin Rashid al Maktoum, the Minister of Information and Culture, who—along with about 1.5 million other people—viewed the resulting exhibit, "Sheikh Zayed: A Modern Legend."

Another capstone, which drew about 600 to the Dubai campus, addressed the topic, "Marriage Without Debt," which is a serious concern for young Emiratis and for the government. A marriage of two Nationals easily can cost upwards of $25,000, and often costs much more than that. Young men are expected to provide a substantial dowry to the bride's family, gifts of money, jewelry, a car, a house (which is often subsidized by the government), parties, a honeymoon, and so forth. The country has a Marriage Fund that provides a subsidy of about $20,000 for the wedding. A National man could marry a foreign woman and avoid much of this expense. If a National woman marries a foreigner, she loses her Emirati citizenship and the considerable benefits that go with it. Consequently, National women saw themselves as getting shut out of the marriage market and facing a life of possible spinsterhood.

ZU students decided to address the issue head-on. They planned and implemented an event that included the director of the Marriage Fund, as well as young men from the Higher College of Technology in Dubai to debate with female students the issue of the high cost of marriage. (Bringing National men onto campus was no small achievement. Permission from the University's Vice President, Dr. Hanif Hassan al Qassimi, was required. Cultural mores and University rules strictly separate Nationals of the opposite sex. Men of other nationalities teach at ZU, always aware of strict rules of behavior of men toward female students.) Although the event perhaps generated more heat than light (we can't be sure because all the debate was in Arabic), it was a landmark moment for ZU and its students because of the elements of controversy surrounding the topic and because of the public and academic interaction between men and women.

The government recently announced that National men could no longer take foreign wives, but it is unlikely that there was a cause and effect relation between the capstone project and the subsequent government action. Nevertheless, the students felt that they had at least been able to express their concerns in a highly visible way. This, in itself, was unusual and gratifying to the University community.

Both of these capstone projects generated news coverage in both the English language media and Arabic media. Others have as well, which is what the students strive for, although many of the individual participants shy away from being photographed or even interviewed about their work. Faculty who oversee the projects are less interested in the public visibility of the students' work than in students' performance leading up to the public event itself. They must push the students to pay attention to the posters, publications, news releases, programs, and other collateral materials associated with each event. These kinds of concrete demonstrations of student skills are more important exhibits in the students' professional portfolio than a news story about the event in which the contributions of the individual student is often lost. It is difficult to get the students to see that when they are caught up in the excitement and intensity of carrying off a major event.

Capstones of this sort offer a chance to help students progress toward fulfilling the University's teamwork and leadership outcome, because in such an undertaking, students may have leadership tasks in some areas and team member tasks in others. Teamwork and leadership also tie in to the CCMS's Professionalism outcome.

It is an ongoing challenge for supervising faculty to find ways to get the students themselves to evaluate and rate the performances of their colleagues and to be realistic about their own performances. This is not unusual, of course. Western students and faculty face many of the same issues, but in a tribal society like the UAE, which is a federation of tribes, the phenomenon called *wahsta* complicates matters. Wahsta is associated with the influence attached to a tribal affiliation. Students with little wahsta tend to defer in all things to students with high wahsta. This means that relative wahsta levels influence leadership patterns as well as candor at peer evaluation time. Nevertheless, students learn quickly that their own grades can rise or fall because of underperformance by other team members. Indeed, some teams have "fired" team members who failed to complete tasks or meet deadlines. But an underperforming high-wahsta student would be more likely to be worked around by other members of the team.

Faculty who supervise the group capstone projects have developed strategies to make sure that students are held accountable for discrete elements of their projects. Students are graded on their separate assignments over the course of the semester. Some professors also give exams that are related to specific aspects of the project, and others introduce formal peer evaluation exercises into the projects. At the end, many of the projects face client evaluations and audience evaluations as well.

LESSONS LEARNED

Surveys of employers, examination of student portfolios, employers' evaluations of interns, faculty research on students' values and learning styles, and feedback from students themselves, have suggested several general and specific adjustments in the CCMS's programs. The addition of a special professional writing course in Arabic was one such change, as was the inclusion in prep week of instruction in basic office and workplace behavior. Taken together, all the feedback has indicated that ZU students need far more experience with working itself. In the Walters et al. (2004) study, "Educating Ms. Fatima" (p. 8), 80% of the students surveyed said that they believed ZU had adequately prepared them for the work they were expected to do during their internships. But an even larger percentage—86%—found work to be vastly different from academic work. Walters's study found that students' expectations of working conditions, salary, and interaction with coworkers, were by and large unrealistic.

To help students become more realistic job-seekers on graduation, the CCMS developed Zayed Media Lab (ZML) in hopes of providing a realistic simulation of the work environment while students are still in school. As mentioned earlier, ZML will function as a global media conglomerate in which students will create media products, as well as function as a corporation itself. In that way, students will be able to get necessary experience working on either a newspaper or magazine, working in radio or television, and handling marketing and promotional activities for the various products and services ZML will provide. It is an ambitious undertaking, but one that can be beneficial to students in the CCMS and to the community as well. The CCMS began experimenting with the ZML concept in the spring of 2004 by joining three basic courses (media writing, information design, and information gathering), which were team-taught by two members of the faculty. The classes met back-to-back twice a week, meaning that the students spent 12 contact hr a week working and thinking media. Indications are that the students benefited from the experience.

In the fall of 2003, the CCMS was invited to nominate students to go to the United States for internships in news media during the spring of 2004. The internships were funded by a U.S. State Department grant secured by

Dr. Leonard Teel of Georgia State University. As part of the process of selecting the interns, the CCMS held a day of competition during which students took a practice version of the Test of English as a Foreign Language (TOEFL), wrote a news story from research done online, wrote stories from fact patterns, and wrote a story from information gained during a mock news conference. The practice TOEFL turned out to be a very revealing test that seemed to predict success on the other measures fairly effectively. Both the CCMS and the University are dedicated to the notion of turning out bilingual graduates, so it seems likely that students will be given the TOEFL at some point during the junior year.[2]

CONCLUSION

One of the goals of the CCMS is to become accredited by the Accrediting Council on Education in Journalism and Mass Communication (ACEJMC). This means that the assessment process will soon have to incorporate or adapt the Council's principles of accreditation, which can be incorporated into the CCMS's current learning outcomes. (See ACEJMC Online Information Center, www.ku.edu/~acejmc/ for a listing of the principles of accreditation, core professional values, and suggestions for direct and indirect assessment of student learning.) The current assessment moments at the time of the internship and capstone project will provide opportunities to assess many of these outcomes directly, as will the ZML participation. Others will be incorporated into the course outcomes, where most are already subsumed in the CCMS's modest list of outcomes.

The processes and procedures already in operation in conjunction with the internships are working well. The capstone experience is salutary in its function of tying the threads of a student's education, but the CCMS will need to adopt ways to more carefully document the capstone effectiveness. Student presentations to clients should become more formalized, and a panel of faculty should join with clients in evaluating the students' presentations using an agreed-on checklist of criteria. The incorporation of a TOEFL during the junior year would yield valuable information in time to allow students to get remedial instruction in English if necessary before graduation. A similar test of their prowess in Arabic would also be an important indicator of competence.

The University itself is analyzing its current assessment procedures as it seeks accreditation from the Middle States Association for Higher Edu-

---

[2]Students must score at least 500 on the Test of English as a Foreign Language before entering the baccalaureate program. It is likely that they will be expected to attain a score of 550 on the second test, midway through the baccalaureate degree.

cation. Early discussions suggest that some of the highly individualized assessment that is done now through the LOA courses will shift to the colleges. In the meantime, the CCMS will continue to refine and document its own assessments of student and curricular success. The University and the CCMS are young and well-positioned to adopt the strategies and tactics suggested by ACEJMC as part of a set of routine measurements that are underway now and that will become more elaborate and formal over time.

REFERENCES

ACEJMC Online Information Center. www.ku.edu/~acejmc/
Walters, T., Swan, S., Wolfe, R., Whiteoak, J., & Barwind, J. (2005). *Educating Ms. Fatima.* Al-Raida, in press.
Wolfe, R. (2003, Spring). Farewell Dr. Dell. *Achievers, 1*(2), 14–17.
Zayed University. (2002). *Academic program model, academic year 2002–2003.* Dubai, UAE: Zayed University.

APPENDIX A

Learning Outcomes Descriptions

Communication Competence

On completion of this program, students in the College of Communication and Media Sciences will be able to write and speak clearly and effectively in both English and Arabic, appropriately and skillfully adapting their messages to the needs, knowledge, culture, and expectations of their target audiences.

Indicators	Assessment Criteria	Assessment Venues
Ability to present information clearly, accurately, and effectively through oral, written, and visual communication media	• Clarity • Accuracy • Organization • Proficiency in English and Arabic, written and spoken • Effective use of visual aids • Appropriate form and style • Delivery proficiency	Courses: Media Writing I & II, Writing for Integrated Communication, Print Media Editing, Professional Writing in Arabic, Public Speaking and Professional Presentation, Information Design, Video Production I & II, Capstone Internship Portfolio

(Continued)

Indicators	Assessment Criteria	Assessment Venues
Ability to adapt and tailor information to fit the needs, knowledge, expectations, and culture-related traits of target audiences	• Proficient audience analysis and massage adaptation	Courses: Media Writing I & II, Writing for Integrated Communication, Print Media Editing, Professional Writing in Arabic, Public Speaking and Professional Presentation, Information Design, Video Production I & II, Capstone Internship Portfolio
	• Accurate understanding of relevant cultures and skillful application of intercultural communication principles, thus reflecting an understanding of the diversity of groups in a global society	Courses: Intercultural Communication, Public Speaking and Professional Presentation, Information, Media Law and Ethics, Comparative International News, Capstone

Technological Competence

On completion of this program, graduates of the College of Communication and Media Sciences will be able to skillfully use a variety of technologies, both individually and in convergence with each other, to produce effective communication and media-centered products, layouts, and messages.

Indicators	Assessment Criteria	Assessment Venues
Ability to use a variety of technologies to convey effective visual information and achieve persuasive objectives	• Proficiency in using web, video, audio, and print hardware and software appropriate to the communication professions associated with students' majors, i.e., proficiency in using the following: MS Word MS PowerPoint® Adobe Photoshop® QuarkXpress® Adobe Illustrator® Final Cut Express or Pro Adobe GoLive® Digital still and video cameras • Proficiency in converging two or more of the above software applications or technologies.	Courses: Information Design, Print Media Editing, Video Production I and II, Infographics, Photojournalism, Public Speaking and Professional Presentation, Web Design, Internship Portfolio Capstone

Information Literacy and Acquisition Competence

On completion of this program, graduates of the College of Communication and Media Sciences will be able to identify appropriate information sources, effectively gather data, and apply critical thinking skills to analyze the information obtained.

Indicators	Assessment Criteria	Assessment Venues

Ability to identify appropriate information sources
Ability to conduct research and evaluate information by methods appropriate to the communication professions in which graduates intend to work
Ability to evaluate and edit own work and work of others
	• Use of resources and sources appropriate to given assignments
	• Proficiency in gathering information from the Internet, library, and human sources demonstrating skills in
	  ○ Library research
	  ○ Interviewing
	  ○ Survey development and administration
	  ○ Observation
	    Internet and IT research
	• Proficiency in applying basic numeric and statistical concepts
	• Critical thinking
		Courses: Information Design, Media Writing I and II, Writing for Integrated Communication, Professional Writing in Arabic, Integrated Campaign Planning, Print Media Editing I & II, Portfolio Internship

Task Performance Competence

On completion of this program, graduates of the College of Communication and Media Sciences will be able to work both independently and collaboratively to execute responsibilities and tasks associated with their chosen professions competently and effectively.

Indicators	Assessment Criteria	Assessment Venues

Ability to work independently to successfully accomplish objectives, projects, and tasks	• Demonstrated understanding and application of
	  ○ problem-solving
	  ○ decision-making
	  ○ task-planning
	  ○ task-implementation
	  ○ time-management
	  ○ self-reflection
		Courses throughout the majors will address task performance competence, but evaluation of the internship portfolio and the capstone project will be the places where this outcome will be emphasized most.

(Continued)

Indicators	Assessment Criteria	Assessment Venues
Ability to work collaboratively to successfully accomplish objectives, projects, and tasks	• Demonstrated understanding and application of 　○ consensus building 　○ appropriate task division 　○ positive communication climate skills 　○ conflict management 　○ effective group problem-solving and decision-making processes	The pre-internship assessment, performed by the internship coordinator, each student's faculty internship supervisor, her workplace supervisor, and other faculty as required for test administration and evaluation, will assess and evaluate. The instructors of record for the capstone courses will take the primary role in assessing and evaluating student performance and assigning grades. Clients will also have a role in assessing capstones, as will the larger audience of the University community, parents, and potential employers.

APPENDIX B

Internship Portfolio Guidelines

Checklist Items

- A resume (a personal photograph is optional).
- An official copy of the student's University transcript.
- A personal statement of goals, plus as many as appropriate of the other items listed later.

College of Communication and Media Sciences Major Learning Outcomes

1. Communication Competence
2. Technological Competence
3. Information Literacy and Acquisition Competence
4. Task Performance Competence
5. Professionalism

The College internship coordinator and internship faculty supervisors evaluate portfolios before students show them to potential internship employers. An approved portfolio is worth 200 points of the internship grade. Students are advised that their portfolios should reflect their very best work and should be completely free of errors.

Item to Be Included	Outcomes Items Should Illustrate	Quality Standards
Personal statement of career goals	1,5	• No mistakes in spelling, grammar, syntax • Clear understanding of positions and their function in the industry for which the portfolio is aimed
Writing samples, such as newspaper clips, press releases, personal profiles, features, broadcast scripts, etc. Include items that have been published or created for real clients, if possible. (Limit number of examples to a maximum of two each)	1,3,4,5	• No mistakes in spelling, grammar, syntax • Appropriate use of sources • Adequate attribution of quotations • Style appropriate to medium, audience, and purpose • Observation appropriate professional and ethical conventions
Samples of photos or illustrations, such as logos, advertisements, posters, or other collateral materials produced for class assignments, clients, clubs, or other extracurricular activities. (Limit number of examples to a maximum of two each)	1,2,3,4,5	• No mistakes in spelling, grammar, syntax • Appropriate use of sources • Examples should meet professional standards of composition, focus, typography, etc.
Samples of any pages designed using computer software produced for class assignments, clients, clubs, or other extracurricular activities. Pages designed for hard copy publications and web pages should be included, but no more than two examples of each. A photo essay of more than one page counts as one example	1,2,3,4,5	• No mistakes in spelling, grammar, syntax • Appropriate use of sources • Examples should meet professional standards of composition, focus, typography, etc.

(Continued)

Item to Be Included	Outcomes Items Should Illustrate	Quality Standards
A program from an event the student planned or in which she participated as part of a class project or campus organization	4,5	Standards of good writing and design should apply if the student had anything to do with the creation or publication of the program itself. Otherwise, the program serves to verify her participation and role in the event and the intended audience of the event
Samples of academic papers, such as research papers, course projects, reviews, bibliographies, essays, analyses, etc. Include no more than two examples	1,3,4	• No mistakes in spelling, grammar, syntax • Appropriate use of sources • Adequate attribution of quotations • Style appropriate to medium, audience, and purpose

- Certificates of awards, scholarships, and honors
- Certificates for special training
- Letters of commendation or thanks from previous employers, organizations, advisers, leaders of projects on which you worked, or faculty advisers.
- Summary reports of evaluations from the World of Work (WOW) or similar activities that indicate on-the-job experience

Assessment of Portfolios

Not all students will include each of the items listed. In addition to the quality standards associated with the portfolio items indicated, the portfolios themselves are assessed using the following criteria:

Overall professional appearance and consistency of look

Presence of appropriate items of acceptable quality

Organization. Examples of work should be captioned and include the circumstances under which each was created. A table of contents is essential.

Variety

Error-free throughout

POSTSCRIPT

26

Reflections on the Impact of Assessment on Accreditation: Foxes and Henhouses

Lana F. Rakow
School of Communication
University of North Dakota

If I were writing this chapter for the beginning of this volume, I would be focused on the impact of accreditation on assessment, not the impact of assessment on accreditation. The difference is not simply a semantic trick but one of attention to foreground and background. The first framing, the impact of accreditation on assessment, would lead me down a path of casting assessment in journalism and mass communication in the context of decisions made by the Accrediting Council on Education in Journalism and Mass Communications (ACEJMC) and what is expected of programs to meet the new requirements. The second framework to the subject, the impact of assessment on accreditation, leads me, instead, to reflect on how and why assessment is being used to change accreditation policies and practices of not only ACEJMC but of other accrediting agencies and of the organizations that recognize them. This framing allows me to talk about a greater context that needs our vigilance. My purpose is not, then, to stress the importance of assessment whose time has come—although it has—but rather to raise lingering questions about the appropriate emphasis on assessment by accreditors.

Let me say at the outside that my attention to these matters is not in any way intended to discount or diminish the importance of assessment of student learning or the excellent results of work by ACEJMC incorporating it into its policies and practices. I would hope by the time you have come to this point in the volume, you, too, would believe in its importance. Along with colleagues in this volume, I share an enthusiasm for the benefits of assessment. For over 15 years and in two different programs, I have been involved in the design and implementation of assessment-led curricula. Before ACEJMC adopted a set of 11 competencies and values expected of all students, the programs with which I was a part devised their own competencies and were assessing student performance against them in capstone or portfolio courses. I have been an advocate of the value to students of being explicit about our expectations and of requiring them to review, synthesize, and integrate what they learned. Thoughtfully designed and implemented assessment of student learning improves teaching and learning: it really is that simple.

My advocacy for assessment carried over into my work as a member of the Association for Education in Journalism and Mass Communication (AEJMC) Elected Committee on Teaching Standards for 6 years and as one of the committee's representatives to ACEJMC for 6 years. My terms on these bodies coincided with a significant moment in our field for the assessment movement. ACEJMC adopted a set of competencies and values, issued guidelines for assessment plans and practices, and adopted broad revisions to its standards to integrate assessment of learning into its evaluation process. We now have come to the point of implementation. Assessment plans are to be in place at accredited programs and they are to be collecting data for making improvements. The time for assessment has come, and it was a long time in coming.

Therefore, what I have to say here does not in any way detract from this significant accomplishment and its importance. What I do want to do is provide the background for the debates behind these accomplishments and to cast a shadow of caution over our satisfaction about where we are. First, I want to review some of the discussions involving and affecting ACEJMC as they unfolded around the issues of assessment. Please be advised that my account is partial and incomplete, based on the information, meetings, and discussions to which I was privy, beginning with my first ACEJMC meeting in September 1999. I have tried to make my own role in these matters explicit in the telling of the story. Others will no doubt want to correct or embellish my account. Second, I want to identify promises and pitfalls, or potentials and perils, of the effect of assessment on accreditation at this juncture. My aim is to spur us to be vigilant about the OVER use of assessment of student learning to the exclusion of considerations of other purposes and expectations to be made of universities and professional programs.

THE ASSESSMENT DEBATES

The cloud of assessment was hanging over ACEJMC for some time before it took action. The cloud was in the form of the U.S. Department of

Education (DOE), the federal agency which recognizes accrediting agencies who ask for its sanction. Although the DOE does not itself accredit institutions or programs, it is required to publish a list of nationally recognized accrediting agencies considered to be authorities on the quality of education provided by those who seek accreditation. To be recognized by the DOE, the accreditor must be reviewed for its adherence to standards for its accrediting work, similar to a review undergone by programs and institutions seeking accreditation from those agencies. Among the reasons that an accrediting agency would want, and need, DOE recognition is a connection to federal financial aid. An institution's accreditation by a DOE-recognized accrediting agency establishes the institution's eligibility to participate in Title IV programs (federal student financial aid programs such as the Pell Grant Program and Work-Study). The country's regional accrediting agencies have DOE recognition as do a number of other specialized accrediting bodies such as the American Bar Association and the American Psychological Association. Raising the level of student achievement as a measure of academic quality is a prominent feature of DOE criteria for recognition. Accrediting agency standards also must include an assessment of the program's curricula; faculty; facilities, equipment, and supplies; fiscal and administrative capacity; student support services; and recruiting and admissions practices. Recognized agencies also must meet stringent requirements about conflict of interest and "separate and independent" status, as well as ensuring that accredited programs are monitored for compliance between reviews (U.S. Department of Education, n.d.).

Withdrawal from DOE

Despite advance warnings from the DOE that it needed to attend to assessment of student learning, ACEJMC found itself in a situation of facing loss of recognition by DOE. Minutes of the May 2000 ACEJMC meeting (ACEJMC, 2000a) document the discussion leading to the decision to withdraw from DOE recognition. The minutes reported that the chair of the committee revising the ACEJMC's Principles of Accreditation as a step toward an assessment policy, "said the committee had assumed the Council would have to adopt an assessment policy but realized it couldn't be done quickly. He said ACEJMC would lose its recognition by the U.S. Department of Education if it did not have an assessment policy by December and that it would be better to drop the recognition voluntarily" (ACEJMC, 2000a, p. 12). Susanne Shaw, ACEJMC executive director, as reported in the minutes, "said it would be better to withdraw than to have recognition denied. She said many specialized accreditors were not recognized by the Department" (ACEJMC, 2000a, p. 12). The vote to withdraw from recognition by the DOE was 26 to 1, with two abstentions. I voted against the withdrawal.

ACEJMC did at that May 2000 meeting approve for distribution and discussion the draft of the revised Principles of Accreditation, including nine "Professional Values and Competencies," the first significant step in the process of incorporating assessment activity into accreditation expectations. Other members of the committee who drafted the new principles besides the chair, Will Norton, dean, College of Journalism and Mass Communication, University of Nebraska, were Mary Ann Ferguson, director, Communications Research Center, University of Florida; Steve Geimann, editor, telecom policy, Bloomberg News; Saundra Keyes, managing editor, *Contra Costa Times;* and Mary Ellen Woolley, senior vice president, educational services, American Advertising Federation. Ex-officio members were Council President Jerry Ceppos, vice president for news, Knight Ridder; and Accrediting Committee Chair Trevor Brown, dean, School of Journalism, Indiana University.

Discussion of DOE recognition did not end with the May 2000 meeting, however. At its September 2000 meeting, Shaw reported that additional conversations with the DOE led her to believe ACEJMC could meet DOE requirements, citing the steps that would need to be taken. However, according to minutes of the meeting (ACEJMC, 2000b), "Shaw said she thought it important to be reviewed by some other agency and the Council was preparing for a review by CHEA [the Council for Higher Education Accreditation]. She said there was not a strong benefit in affiliation with the Department" (p. 10). My own comments were recorded in the minutes: "Rakow said there was value in checks and balances and CHEA, made up of college presidents and provosts, was a bit like the fox guarding the hen house" (p. 10). It was argued in response that loss of recognition would not raise problems for schools. Given that regional accreditation covers Title IV eligibility for member schools and given the troublesome nature of DOE requirements on assessment and other matters over recent years (e.g., a complaint policy and interim review of accredited programs that was required of recognized agencies), ACEJMC was not swayed to reconsider its earlier motion to allow its DOE recognition to lapse. ACEJMC's newsletter report of the action in March 2001 did not mention the failure to meet DOE expectations on assessment (ACEJMC, 2001, p. 1).

Although it did not reconsider its decision to withdraw from DOE recognition at the September 2000 meeting, ACEJMC did adopt an assessment policy and common competencies in a revision to the Principles of Accreditation. One debated change approved at the meeting reduced the number of semester hours required outside the major from 90 to 80, thereby allowing programs to increase the number of credit hours taken in journalism and mass communication. My own concern that schools would allow students to "load up" on skills courses rather than theoretical and conceptual courses was allayed by the awareness that programs would need to demonstrate students were mastering the competencies set out by ACEJMC. With input that came from the AEJMC Teaching Standards Committee and endorsed by the AEJMC Executive Committee (Rakow, 2000), two additional competencies were added to the nine that had been proposed. Competencies involving history and diversity joined other "conceptual" ones on law, ethics, and theory, with other competencies addressing critical thinking, research, writing, editing, quantification, and technology.

To address implementation of ACEJMC's assessment policy, Council President Jerry Ceppos appointed a new committee, "Assessment, Standards Revisions, and Liberal Arts." On the committee were Trevor Brown, chair; Beth Barnes, associate professor, S.I. Newhouse School of Public Communications, Syracuse University; Saundra Keyes; Ham Smith, head, Department of Journalism and Mass Communications, Washington and Lee University; and this author. The principles took effect in September 2001. Schools were expected to have plans in place by September 2003. Assessment methods were left to the design of individual schools, but "A Guide to Assessment of Student Learning in Journalism and Mass Communications" produced by the new committee and issued by ACEJMC in 2001 encouraged programs to use multiple measures, both direct and indirect, in assessing learning, and to include representatives of professions in the assessment process. Importantly, programs are expected to assess students' attainment of the professional values and competencies specified by ACEJMC. Programming at AEJMC to alert programs to the new requirement and to help them design and implement assessment plans were sponsored by the AEJMC Teaching Standards Committee, ACEJMC, and the Association of Schools of Journalism and Mass Communication (ASJMC), giving assessment of student learning unprecedented attention in our field. The new committee undertook a revision of ACEJMC's 12 standards to account for the new assessment requirement. New standards were adopted at the ACEJMC's September, 2003 meeting, streamlining the standards into 9 from the previous 12, combining several standards while adding a separate standard on assessment and another on student services. (See the Appendix for the new standards.)

The Place of CHEA

While consideration of an assessment policy and changes to the standards was underway, recognition of ACEJMC's status as an accreditor was under review. With the problem of DOE recognition settled,

ACEJMC was left to meet criteria for recognition by the Council for Higher Education Accreditation (CHEA). Created in 1996, CHEA is the successor to a string of nongovernmental associations recognizing accrediting agencies, the most recent of which were the Council on Postsecondary Accreditation (COPA), which existed from 1974 to 1993, and the Commission on Recognition of Postsecondary Accreditation (CORPA), created as a stop gap until a new organization could be formed. A description of the demise of COPA provides us with an insight into a political agenda that continues to be apparent in the philosophy of CHEA. The organization's 1999 annual report noted the following:

> Tension among institutions, regional accreditors, and specialized accreditors—and the perception among some academic leaders that specialized accrediting organizations were growing in number and placing extensive demands on institutions—were factors that contributed to the demise of CHEA's predecessor organization, the Council on Postsecondary Accreditation. To address these problems, CHEA has devoted a great deal of attention to finding ways to strengthen accreditation by increasing its usefulness and improving its efficiency. (CHEA, 1999, p. 10)

An early CHEA newsletter noted that the organization would complement rather than compete with DOE recognition:

> . . . [T]he CHEA process is designed to improve the quality of accreditation through the identification of best practices, the use of research about assessment and accountability, and through dialogue with institutional leadership in a collegial process.
>
> If accreditation is a collegial process, should not the members of the accreditation community be the model for self-regulation? The self-governing system of peer review and evaluation requires accountability of all partners in the process. The accrediting community in higher education will enhance its own integrity and credibility if it supports an organization established for greater collaboration, cooperation, and consultation among the members of the accrediting community. (CHEA, 1996, pp. 1–2)

The newsletter went on to claim that "CHEA will monitor and mediate differences among the associations and universities" (CHEA, 1996, p. 3). In other words, CHEA's aim from the outset was to diminish conflicts between accrediting organizations and the institutions and programs they accredit, not surprising given the composition of its Board of Directors. The 2003 to 2004 Board was made up of 11 presidents or chancellors of higher education institutions, two vice chancellors or provosts, one dean, and three others (a foundation trustee, an attorney, and a managing director of a private management consulting firm; CHEA, n.d.a).

ACEJMC had been recognized by CORPA, CHEA's predecessor, in 1996. At that time its recognition was continued for 5 years (ACEJMC, 2001a). In January 2000, *prior* to ACEJMC's decision to withdraw from DOE recognition, Susanne Shaw was appointed to the CHEA Specialized Advisory Panel for a 3-year term (CHEA, 2000a). She was reappointed for a 3-year term in January 2003 (CHEA, 2002b). ACEJMC was deemed eligible to be considered for CHEA recognition in January 2001 (CHEA, 2001a) and was recognized in April 2002 (CHEA, 2002a).

Ironically, although ACEJMC gave up DOE recognition ostensibly over assessment of student learning, CHEA's interest in assessment of student learning clearly has exceeded that of the DOE. Significantly, assessment of student learning crowds out most other indicators of quality, especially when compared to the DOE's criteria. The reason for the emphasis on assessment of student learning is apparent: higher education administrators do not want accrediting agencies making demands of them that cost money or inhibit their own decision making. The explicit evidence is found in four documents that make CHEA's philosophy clear. The connection to ACEJMC's deliberations needs to be made apparent.

CHEA's policy and procedures for recognizing accrediting organizations, adopted in 1998, identifies five "recognition standards": the accreditor must advance academic quality, demonstrate accountability, encourage purposeful change and needed improvement, employ appropriate and fair procedures in decision making, and continually reassess accreditation practices (CHEA, 1998). Unlike DOE's, these standards seem designed as much to protect the institutions and programs under review as they do to ensure their accountability. Although the academic quality standard is said to include teaching, learning, research, and service evaluated within the framework of institutional mission, assessment of quality is said to especially involve assessment of student achievement as part of its encouragement of planning and scrutiny for improvement. "Encouragement of such planning and self-scrutiny should not be confused with a demand for additional resources," the policy stated (CHEA, 1998, II.11c), a warning which recognized that accreditors should stay out of institutions' financial matters. The reassessment of accreditation practices standard emphasizes "examination of the accreditor's impact on institutions and responsiveness to the broader accreditation community . . ." (CHEA, 1998, II.11e). Accrediting agencies are warned that CHEA may elect to review a recognized accrediting agency's standing where "There has been a pattern of documented concerns from institutions following accreditation reviews" (CHEA, 1998, IV.15.B), a threat that could well have a chilling effect on the watchdog role of an accrediting agency.

Since the adoption of the 1998 policy and procedures document, an even stronger push toward a focus on assessment of student learning took place in CHEA. In August 2000, it published an occasional paper, "The Competency Standards Project: Another Approach to Accreditation Review" (CHEA, 2000b). CHEA had asked the National Center for Higher Education Management Systems, using Western Governors University as its pilot, to develop a review protocol based solely on student learning outcomes. (Western Governors University, founded by governors of 19 states, offers competency-based, online degrees.) Judith Eaton, CHEA president, stated in the publication that

> ... the competency standards and review posit a clear and unmistakable connection between institutional quality and student achievement. These standards require demonstration and documentation of student competencies as central to determination of institutional quality. Institutional performance, in many ways, *is* student performance. [italics hers] (CHEA, 2000b, p. 2)

About the same time that CHEA was publishing this report of its competency project, it received a letter from the Association of American Universities and the National Association of State Universities and Land-Grant Colleges (AAU/NAASULGC), expressing their concerns about specialized accreditation (Shaw, 2001). CHEA, in response, developed a "Statement on Good Practices and Shared Responsibility in the Creation and Application of Specialized Accreditation Standards" (CHEA, 2001b). The statement, sent out for discussion in 2001, came to ACEJMC for discussion at its May 2001 meeting, accompanied by David Shulenburger, chair of the AAU/NAASULGC Task Force on Accreditation. Shulenburger also is provost at the University of Kansas, the headquarters of ACEJMC, where Shaw, ACEJMC executive director, is on the faculty of the School of Journalism.

At the ACEJMC meeting, Shulenburger pointed out "war stories" of demands made on schools by specialized accreditors, from new buildings, to class sizes, to salaries, to library expenditures. He objected to prescriptive improvements because, he explained, money must be shifted from somewhere and money may be better spent elsewhere to respond to the institution's interest in innovation. As ACEJMC minutes (ACEJMC, 2001b) summarized, "He [Shulenburger] said accrediting standards were valid as long as they improved the preparation of students and were not narrowly defined," implying that standards should not be explicit or strictly applied. In addition, the minutes reported, "He said the principle on organizational structure, resources and program personnel promoted a focus on outcomes and asked that accreditors not tie the hands of programs as to how they achieve outcomes." My own concerns expressed at the meeting are recorded in the minutes:

> Lana Rakow said there was a potential conflict between administrators and specialized accreditors and some tension might be inevitable. She said universities did more than produce measurable kinds of student outcomes. She said budget considerations, workloads and climate could stifle innovation also. She said perhaps universities shouldn't have programs if they couldn't afford to operate them properly. (ACEJMC, 2001b)

The Council's newsletter headline reporting Shulenburger's appearance at the meeting read "Provost: Don't fence me in—please" (ACEJMC, 2001c). His position is well-represented in the statement which was adopted by CHEA in September 2001. Its first principle states the following: "Standards should be designed to produce desired or needed educational outcomes for a profession and should refer to resources only to the extent required for graduates to emerge from programs intellectually prepared for their professional lives" (CHEA, 2001b, p. 1). Its third principle notes that "Standards will focus on educational quality while respecting an institutions' responsibility to set priorities and control how the institution is structured and operates" (CHEA, 2001b, p. 2). Its sixth principle states the following: "Standards that address issues of law or public policy must show that the issue contributes to effective student outcomes" (CHEA, 2001b, p. 2). Its Principle 9 is as follows:

> Standards and the application of standards that address structure, resources and program personnel are to enable institutions, school and programs to be creative and diverse in determining how to organize themselves structurally, how best to use their resources and what personnel and other policies and procedures are needed to achieve student learning outcomes. Such standards are appropriate only if they impact the adequate preparation of students to practice in a particular field. (CHEA, 2001b, p. 2)

Finally, CHEA's stripes are revealed in its September 2003, "Statement of Mutual Responsibilities for Student Learning Outcomes: Accreditation, Institutions, and Programs." Noting that "the salience of student learning outcomes in accreditation" is increasing (CHEA, 2003, p. 1), the statement charges accrediting organizations with the responsibility to "Ensure that using evidence of student learning outcomes plays a central role in determining the accredited status of an institution or program" (CHEA, 2003, p. 2). Institutions should provide information about student learning outcomes and "supplement this information with additional evidence about the soundness of institutional and program operations" (CHEA,

2003, p. 2). Only in the background section of the statement is a broader role for universities explained, for example, that institutional or program effectiveness "may also include good effects that go beyond students, such as research and creative activity or service to various intellectual and geographic communities" (CHEA, 2003, p. 4).

IMPLICATIONS FOR HIGHER EDUCATION

As it happened, CHEA's philosophy did not carry the day in assessment and standards considerations by ACEJMC. I want to be clear that I believe the decisions about assessment ultimately made by ACEJMC are sound and reasonable. CHEA's preoccupation with assessment as the first and foremost measure of program quality did not get carried out in any substantial way in the revised standards. The ordering of the new standards and the place of the new assessment standard among them remained under discussion until the very end. At the last moment before the vote to adopt, the assessment standard was moved from the middle of the standards to the end. Making assessment the first standard was discussed, but, as noted by the minutes, "Brown [committee chair] said the committee did think about order so as not to make assessment the sole standard. He said they were trying to alter the balance and emphasis, while retaining focus on some traditional contributions to the education process" (ACEJMC, 2003). A motion was made, instead, to move the standard to the end, "where it would wrap things up" (ACEJMC, 2003). Unfortunately, the assessment standard was switched with the Professional and Public Service standard, one that I consider to be the most critical of the standards, as I explain later, but which now holds the obscure place of number 8. (For the text and order of the new standards, see the Appendix.)

If CHEA's position on assessment did not carry the day in decisions made by ACEJMC, should we be at all concerned about ACEJMC's recognition by CHEA, or about its loss of recognition by DOE, or about the fate of accreditation in higher education? I'm going to explore here two broad considerations that might help us evaluate the implications for our field and for institutions of these assessment efforts and the role of accreditation.

Tools for Improvement

Let me first evaluate the significance of what ACEJMC has done with assessment of student learning and its revised standards. In sum, ACEJMC has required accredited programs to have an assessment plan that measures student mastery of what the program defines as its competencies, but the competencies must include the 11 provided by ACEJMC. ACEJMC does not require any particular methods of assessment except that both direct and indirect methods be used, that professionals should be involved, and that results should guide improvement in curriculum and instruction. Although assessment of student learning is accorded its due, the new standards maintain a balance of considerations for evaluating quality and effectiveness of programs worthy of accreditation, including diversity, research, facilities and budget, student services, and public service.

The significance of these steps should not be underestimated. For the first time, this field has an explicit and required core of knowledge and skills that cuts across specialties. Although it may seem that mandating these 11 competencies will restrict innovation in curricula, the competencies should open doors to experimentation. The competencies are not tied to industries but are linked to professions and their practices. Programs of study can be designed that cut across our traditional industry and career specialties (journalism, broadcasting, advertising, public relations), leading to new areas of study and new forms of curricular integration. Because they lead to mastery of the competencies rather than require a certain amount of "seat time" in a class, new curricular and cocurricular activities can be developed. Teaching and learning should improve, leading to improvements in the quality of our graduates, and, most importantly, to improvements in the quality of journalism and mass communication practices in society.

In step with the competencies, the new standards of accreditation address a broad role for professional programs that, although recognizing the educational responsibilities of our programs, do not end there. In Standard 8 on Professional and Public Service, we have room for imagining the place of journalism and mass communication programs in the larger context of journalism and mass communication practices which, ultimately, need to be measured against the criteria of service to the public good. We cannot in our professional programs limit ourselves to the role of providing entry-level employees to communications employers. We, too, have a role to play in the checks and balances of accountability to which journalism and mass communication practices should be held. We need to be leaders in the development of—as well as critique of—communications professions, not servants of business, industry, or government in a role that compromises our autonomy and public trust.

Standards of Recognition

The second significant outcome from the events of the past few years is the role and philosophy of CHEA in recognizing accrediting organizations. Most troubling because of its direct link to ACEJMC as a specialized accreditor is its "Statement on Good Practices and Shared Responsibility in the Creation and Application of Specialized Accreditation Standards" (CHEA, 2001b), which so emphatically elevates evaluation of student learning above other criteria, muzzling critique of central administrative authority and priorities. CHEA called this statement "advisory in nature" (Eaton, 2001), but as of this writing, CHEA is considering changes to its recognition policy that would incorporate sentiment and language from the statement. Of particular note are additions that, on the one hand, restrict agencies from using standards that refer to resources except as required for the intellectual preparation of graduates, whereas on the other hand, adding a sixth requirement of recognized agencies that the accrediting agencies (not the institutions or programs they accredit) have sufficient resources to carry out effective accreditation (CHEA, n.d.b). Controlled by university presidents, intent on achieving "collegiality" between institutions and accrediting agencies, and carrying the stick of review of an agency's recognition if institutions or programs complain, CHEA's recognition requirements are an exercise in conflict of interest. My concerns about the fox guarding the henhouse were not, I fear, misplaced.

How important is it that assessment of student learning has taken center stage in CHEA's mind while consideration of institutional resources has been all but removed? Very. Let's imagine for a moment that *faculty*, not administrators, were to develop criteria for evaluating excellence of an institution or program. I can imagine that the cornerstone for the criteria would be academic freedom, rather than student learning. Attention to student learning, after all, is meaningless in an institution in which faculty and students cannot engage in free inquiry and the critique and production of knowledge. Without academic freedom, universities cannot fulfill their unique role in society. In the case of our field, of course, academic freedom parallels the significance placed on free speech by our professional colleagues and must include our right to critique media institutions and practices, as well as the institutions for which we work. Similarly, amount and distribution of resources likely would be emphasized. University presidents may be willing to accept or defend inadequate budgets (answering, as they do, to boards which hire and fire them), and they may want the flexibility to allocate money internally to shape institutions as they see fit, but faculty work with the results. Faculty have the responsibility, if not now the authority, to look out for the overall academic integrity of an institution, with less reason to blow with current political winds.

CHEA justifies its attention to student learning on the grounds of accountability to the public. What does it mean to serve the public? What kind of accountability would be required?

It isn't surprising to me that the DOE sees assessment of student learning as the means for institutions to be publicly accountable for their performance. The federal government is unlikely to champion academic freedom as a criterion for determining institutional quality, yet DOE standards seem to be a better check and balance on institutions and programs than CHEA's. One would like to hope for more from a nongovernmental organization devoted to improving the quality of higher education and to serving as an advocate for accreditation, but such an organization would need more independence from the very institutions reviewed by the agencies it recognizes. Although student learning is an easy sell to public officials, parents, and students, academic freedom requires a champion. It doesn't appear to be an oversight that university presidents have ignored something as obvious as academic freedom as an indicator of quality and performance, and it takes little imagination to see why they do not want accreditors to look at how they spend their money and if they have enough to fulfill their public purposes.

Accreditation should ensure that higher education and professional and specialized programs are meeting their social responsibilities. Who is in the best position to make those determinations? CHEA makes a point of the need for public accountability, cooperation in the "accreditation community," and for the value of peer review of programs and outcomes. Presumably, faculty and the public should be involved in meaningful ways on CHEA's board and the boards of recognized agencies. On our own ACEJMC, members are referred to in the bylaws as "educators" and "industry representatives." The president appoints three representatives of the public. Reference to industry representatives is indicative of a problem of conflating communications professions with commercial enterprises. Of the educators, ASJMC has six representatives, AEJMC has four, the Broadcast Education Association has two, the American Academy of Advertising has two, the Association for Communications Administration has one, and Black College Communications Association has one. These seats typically are held by deans, directors, and chairs of accredited programs. Faculty members without administrative responsibilities for accredited programs are few and far between; they are only likely to get to the ACEJMC table through the AEJMC Teaching Standards Committee.

On reflection, my assessment of what has gone on about assessment is both complimentary and cautious. We now have strong tools to do a better job of educating students. We have the leeway to imagine programs that genuinely serve the public interest. Yet we must take care that assessment is not used by CHEA or others to hijack the accreditation process. We need vigilance and advocacy for the unique institutional role that universities play in society as knowledge institutions and for the unique role that journalism and mass communication programs play in universities, providing leadership and accountability for the practices of journalism and mass communication. We need faculty to be better represented at accrediting tables so that assessment of student learning and assessment of program and institutional quality is truly a peer review process. We need assurances against the conflicts of interest that lie unnamed at the heart of some of our practices.

My recommendation is that we address these needs by creating an independent task force to review the relations and processes underlying accreditation and recognition of accrediting agencies. Of course, creating such a task force is not without its own problems. Who will appoint it, who will it report to, who will serve on it? AEJMC would be the logical body to initiate its creation, yet given the historically close relationship among AEJMC, ACEJMC, and ASJMC, the independence of such a task force will be a challenge. If these logistical problems can be solved, a task force should be charged with these responsibilities:

1. Review advantages and disadvantages to affiliation with the DOE or CHEA. Are we at risk that another organization could step in to seek DOE recognition to accredit journalism and mass communication programs, or communication programs more generally? Does CHEA have an agenda that creates a chilly climate for review of professional programs?

2. Review representation on ACEJMC's Accrediting Committee and Accrediting Council for appropriate balance and role of professionals, program administrators, faculty, and public members. Do program administrators have too heavy a representation and faculty and public members too light a representation? Is there a pattern of service on the Accrediting Committee and Accrediting Council and on-site teams by some programs and some administrators?

3. Review the impact of ACEJMC's current affiliation with a particular campus. Do the benefits of being located on this or any other campus outweigh the lost autonomy created by central administrative oversight?

4. Position our field as a leader in raising tough questions about the appropriate balance between assessment of student learning and assessment of other indicators of institutional quality. What are the essential characteristics of colleges and universities that should be preserved and improved for them to fulfill their public purposes?

Thanks in large part to the efforts of ACEJMC, our field has made a giant step forward in institutionalizing the assessment of student learning.

But we need to be vigilant. Now we need to learn how to institutionalize the assessment of accountability that comes with accreditation.

APPENDIX

New Standards of the Accrediting Council on Education in Journalism and Mass Communications (Effective September 2004, ACEJMC, n.d.)

1. Mission, Governance and Administration. The policies and practices of the unit ensure that is has an effectively and fairly administered working and learning environment.
2. Curriculum and Instruction. The unit provides a curriculum and instruction that enable students to learn the knowledge, competences and values the Council defines for preparing students to work in a diverse global and domestic society.
3. Diversity and Inclusiveness. The unit has a diverse and inclusive program that serves and reflects society.
4. Full-Time and Part-Time Faculty. The unit hires, supports and evaluates a capable faculty with a balance of academic and professional credentials appropriate for the unit's mission.
5. Scholarship: Research, Creative and Professional Activity. With unit support, faculty members contribute to the advancement of scholarly and professional knowledge and engage in scholarship (research, creative and professional activity) that contributes to their development.
6. Student Services. The unit provides students with the support and services that promote learning and ensure timely completion of their program of study.
7. Resources, Facilities and Equipment. The unit plans for, seeks and receives adequate resources to fulfill and sustain its mission.
8. Professional and Public Service. The unit advances journalism and mass communication professions and fulfills its obligations to its community, alumni and the greater public.
9. Assessment of student learning. The unit regularly assess student learning and uses results to improve curriculum and instruction.

Note. Excerpted from: www.ku.edu/~acejmc/PROGRAM/STAND-ARDS.SHTML

REFERENCES

Accrediting Council on Education in Journalism and Mass Communications. (n.d.). *ACEJMC Accrediting Standards.* Retrieved March 10, 2005, from http://www.ku.edu/~acejmc/ PROGRAM/STANDARDS.SHTML

Accrediting Council on Education in Journalism and Mass Communications. (2000a, May). *Minutes of the meeting of the Accrediting Council.* Lawrence, KS: Author.

Accrediting Council on Education in Journalism and Mass Communications. (2000b, September). *Minutes of the meeting of the Accrediting Council.* Lawrence, KS: Author.

Accrediting Council on Education in Journalism and Mass Communications. (2001a, March). Council drops federal recognition, undergoes CHEA review. *ACEJMC Ascent, 8,* 1.

Accrediting Council on Education in Journalism and Mass Communication. (2001b, May). *Minutes of the meeting of the Accrediting Council.* Lawrence, KS: Author.

Accrediting Council on Education in Journalism and Mass Communications. (2001c, June). Provost: Don't fence me in—please. *ACEJMC Ascent, 8, 2.*

Accrediting Council on Education in Journalism and Mass Communications. (2001d, September). *Minutes of the meeting of the Accrediting Council.* Lawrence, KS: Author.

Accrediting Council on Education in Journalism and Mass Communications. (2003, September). *Minutes of the meeting of the Accrediting Council.* Lawrence, KS: Author.

Council for Higher Education Accreditation. (n.d.a). *CHEA Board of Directors.* Retrieved February 1, 2004, from http://www.chea.org/About/chea_board.cfm

Council for Higher Education Accreditation. (n.d.b). *Draft one: Recognition of accrediting organizations policy and procedures.* Retrieved June 10, 2004, from http:// www.chea.org/recognition/CHEA_RecognitionPolicyDraftOne.pdf

Council for Higher Education Accreditation. (1996, November). *The CHEA Chronicle, 1,* Article 3, Retrieved February 1, 2004, from http://www.chea.org/Chronical/vol1/no3/index.cfm

Council for Higher Education Accreditation. (1998, September 28). *Recognition of accrediting organizations: Policy and procedures.* Retrieved February 1, 2004, from http:// www.chea.org/About/Recognition.cfm

Council for Higher Education Accreditation. (1999). *1999 CHEA annual report.* Washington, DC: Author.

Council for Higher Education Accreditation. (2000a, January 24). *CHEA Board of Directors meeting.* Retrieved February 1, 2004, from http://www.chea.org/Events/Boardmeetings/ 2000January:cfm

Council for Higher Education Accreditation. (2000b, August). *The Competency Standards Project: Another approach to accreditation review* (Prepared by the National Center for Higher Education Management Systems). Washington, DC: Author.

Council for Higher Education Accreditation. (2001a, January 22). *CHEA Board of Directors meeting.* Retrieved February 1, 2004, from www.chea.org/Events/BoardMeetings/ 2001January.cfm

Council for Higher Education Accreditation. (2001b, September). *Statement on good practices and shared responsibility in the creation and application of specialized accreditation standards.* Washington, DC: Author.

Council for Higher Education Accreditation. (2002a, April 30). *CHEA Board of Directors meeting.* Retrieved February 1, 2004, from www.chea.org/Events/BoardMeetings/ 2002April.cfm

Council for Higher Education Accreditation. (2002b, September 24). *CHEA Board of Directors meeting.* Washington, DC. Retrieved February 1, 2004, from www.chea.org/Events/ BoardMeetings/2002September.cfm

Council for Higher Education Accreditation. (2003, September). *Statement of mutual responsibilities for student learning outcomes: Accreditation, institutions, and programs.* Washington, DC: Author.

Eaton, J. S. (2001, October 26). *Memorandum to member institutions and accrediting organizations.* Washington, DC: Council for Higher Education Accreditation.

Rakow, L. F. (2000, August 18). Correspondence to Susanne Shaw. Grand Forks: University of North Dakota.

Shaw, S. (2001, April 17). *To Accrediting Council members.* Lawrence, KS: Accrediting Council on Education in Journalism and Mass Communications.

U.S. Department of Education. (n.d.). *Accreditation in the United States.* Retrieved February 1, 2004, from http://www.ed.gov/adminis/finaid/accred/accreditation_p11.html

Author Index

Subject Index